Internetworking Troubleshooting Handbook

H. Kim Lew
Spank McCoy
Tim Stevenson
Kathleen Wallace
Kevin Downes

CISCO SYSTEMS

CISCO PRESS

M T P
MACMILLAN
TECHNICAL
PUBLISHING
U·S·A

Macmillan Technical Publishing
201 West 103rd Street
Indianapolis, IN 46290 USA

Internetworking Troubleshooting Handbook

H. Kim Lew, Spank McCoy, Tim Stevenson, Kathleen Wallace, Kevin Downes

Copyright© 1999 Cisco Systems, Inc.

Cisco Press logo is a trademark of Cisco Systems, Inc.

Published by:
Macmillan Technical Publishing
201 West 103rd Street
Indianapolis, IN 46290 USA

Printed in the United States of America 1 2 3 4 5 6 7 8 9 0

Library of Congress Cataloging-in-Publication Number: 98-85488

ISBN: 1-57870-024-8

Warning and Disclaimer

This book is designed to provide information about **internetworking troubleshooting**. Every effort has been made to make this book as complete and as accurate as possible, but no warranty or fitness is implied.

The information is provided on an "as is" basis. The author, Macmillan Technical Publishing, and Cisco Systems, Inc., shall have neither liability nor responsibility to any person or entity with respect to any loss or damages arising from the information contained in this book or from the use of the discs or programs that may accompany it.

The opinions expressed in this book belong to the author and are not necessarily those of Cisco Systems, Inc.

Feedback Information

At Cisco Press, our goal is to create in-depth technical books of the highest quality and value. Each book is crafted with care and precision, undergoing rigorous development that involves the unique expertise of members from the professional technical community.

Readers' feedback is a natural continuation of this process. If you have any comments regarding how we could improve the quality of this book, or otherwise alter it to better suit your needs, you can contact us at ciscopress@mcp.com. Please make sure to include the book title and ISBN in your message.

We greatly appreciate your assistance.

Associate Publisher	Jim LeValley
Executive Editors	Alicia Buckley
	Julie Fairweather
Cisco Systems Program Manager	H. Kim Lew
Managing Editor	Caroline Roop
Acquisitions Editors	Tracy Hughes
	Lynette Quinn
Development Editor	Kitty Wilson Jarrett
Project Editor	Sherri Fugit
Technical Editor	Tim Boyles
Team Coordinator	Amy Lewis
Book Designer	Louisa Klucznik
Cover Designer	Sandra Schroeder
Proofreader	Megan Wade
Layout Technicians	Christy M. Lemasters
	Trina Wurst
Indexer	Tim Wright

Trademark
Acknowledgments

About the Authors

H. Kim Lew is a program manager for Cisco Press. He has worked as a writer, course developer, marketing manager, and editorial columnist in the internetworking industry for more than a decade. Since 1990, he has worked at Cisco Systems in various program management, management, and information product development roles. He now telecommutes full-time from Redmond, Washington.

Spank McCoy has created technical documentation for all aspects of data networking technologies since 1979. His interest in computer communications began with his work on the unmanned space program at NASA Jet Propulsion Laboratories in the early 70s. Currently employed at Cisco Systems, Inc., he has worked as a consultant and staff writer for Apple Computer, Hewlett-Packard, Sony Microsystems, Ungermann-Bass, and Zilog. Mr. McCoy is a co-author of *PC LAN Primer*.

Tim Stevenson is a writer, course developer, and web technology specialist in Cisco Systems Knowledge Products organization. While at Cisco, he has developed router troubleshooting and technology-oriented material and is one of the department's key web technology experts.

Kathleen Wallace is co-founder of Wallace Technical Communications, an Internet service provider serving the small business and home office professionals in the San Francisco Bay Area. She has worked as a programmer, staff technical writer, and contract writer for a variety of computing and networking firms, including Apple Computer Inc., Cisco Systems, and National Semiconductor Corporation.

Kevin Downes is a senior network systems consultant with International Network Services (INS). His network certifications include Cisco CCIE, Bay Networks CRS, Certified Network Expert (CNX) Ethernet, Novell CNE, and Banyan Systems CBE. He has published several articles on the subjects of network infrastructure design, network operating systems, and Internet Protocol. He completed his B.S. in Computer Information Systems from Strayer University in 1993.

Acknowledgments

As with several derivative Cisco publications brought to Cisco Press, *Internetworking Troubleshooting Handbook* owes much of its content to the collaborative efforts of many Cisco employees over a number of iterations. In its original form, this book was referred to as *Troubleshooting Internetworking Systems*, which was originally developed by H. Kim Lew, later updated by Kim and Spank McCoy, and then again updated by Kathleen Wallace. Tim Stevenson built on this foundation to create the *Internetwork Troubleshooting Guide*. Both these publications live on as legacy Cisco documents. Kevin Downes updated Cisco's *Internetwork Troubleshooting Guide* to create Cisco Press's *Internetworking Troubleshooting Handbook*.

Our intent in updating this material and presenting it via Cisco Press is to deliver practical information to our customer community and the networking community at large. It is our hope that you find this material useful in your daily operations.

The authors acknowledge the many current and former Cisco employees who contributed in building the content of this publication. Key participants included Jim Young, Amir Khan, John Wright, Keith Redfield, Won Lee, Pasvorn Boonmark, Steve Cunningham, Nga Vu, Imran Qureshi, Atif Khan, Arun Sastry, John Bashinski, Dave Katz, Dino Farinacci, Larry Bowden, Praveen Akkiraju, Steve Russell, Srinivas Vegesna, Phil Remaker, Priscilla Oppenheimer, Bruce Pinsky, Joanna Gardner, Dennis Peng, Charlie Justus, Morris Ng, Sue Phelan,

Mark Allen, Ivan Chan, Dennis Wind, Rosa Elena Lorenzana, Cerafin Castillo, John Chong, Jeff Schults, Jack Nichols, and Dianne Dunlap.

The nature of this publication's development required substantial management support to coordinate the subject matter expert time spent in creating the material. The authors acknowledge Joe Pinto, Brad Wright, Doug Allred, and Charles Baugh as instrumental management sponsors who recognized the importance of this kind of material to customers and nurtured its creation during its early development stages.

Contents at a Glance

Table of Contents

Preface

No single troubleshooting resource can anticipate every possible glitch that can be encountered in internetworks. But any significant contribution that can be made toward preventing connectivity blockages is a step in the right direction. We hope that this publication contributes to the body of knowledge that makes networks more manageable.

AUDIENCE

Internetworking Troubleshooting Handbook is intended for network administrators who are responsible for troubleshooting internetworks that implement Cisco products and Cisco-supported protocols.

Administrators should have hands-on experience in configuring, administering, and troubleshooting a network, should know how to configure routers, switches and bridges, and should be familiar with the protocols and media that their hardware has been configured to support. Awareness of the basic topology of their network is also essential.

DOCUMENT ORGANIZATION

The *Internetworking Troubleshooting Handbook* provides the information necessary to troubleshoot many problems commonly encountered in internetworks using Cisco hardware and software products. This publication consists of the following six parts:

- The chapters in Part 1, "Introduction to Troubleshooting," provide an introduction to troubleshooting techniques and an overview of common troubleshooting tools.

- The chapters in Part 2, "Hardware, Booting, and Media Problems," provide information for troubleshooting hardware problems, LAN media problems, and booting (system initialization) problems.

- The chapters in Part 3, "Troubleshooting Desktop and Entreprise Routing Protocols," provide information on troubleshooting common connectivity and performance problems in TCP/IP, Novell IPX, AppleTalk, IBM, and other widely-implemented network environments.

- The chapters in Part 4, "Troubleshooting Serial Lines and WAN Connections," provide information on troubleshooting problems that commonly occur on serial lines and WAN links such as ISDN, Frame Relay, and X.25.

- The chapters in Part 5, "Troubleshooting Bridging and Switching Environments," provide information on troubleshooting problems commonly encountered in ATM switching, LAN switching, and bridging environments.

- The chapters in Part 6, "Troubleshooting Other Internetwork Problems," provide information on troubleshooting CiscoWorks installations, and on troubleshooting security implementations, including TACACS troubleshooting and password recovery.

- Appendixes provide supplemental troubleshooting information, including information on creating core dumps, memory maps for different Cisco routers, technical support information, and a list of references and recommended reading. In addition, at the end of the book are several perforated troubleshooting worksheets to assist you in gathering information when problems occur.

USING THIS PUBLICATION

This publication is designed to provide users with the information needed to troubleshoot *common* problems encountered in Cisco-based internetworks. Most chapters focus on describing symptoms, identifying their causes, and suggesting specific actions to resolve the problem. Some material describes preventative measures or tips for identifying problems by interpreting command output.

DOCUMENT CONVENTIONS

Our software and hardware documentation uses the following conventions:

- The symbol ^ represents the key labeled *Control*.

For example, *^D* means hold down the *Control* key while you press the *D* key.

- A string is defined as a nonquoted set of characters. For example, when setting up a community string for SNMP to "public," do not use quotes around the string, or the string will include the quotation marks.

Command descriptions use these conventions:

- Examples that contain system prompts denote interactive sessions, indicating that the user enters commands at the prompt. The system prompt indicates the current command mode. For example, the prompt `router(config)#` indicates global configuration mode.
- Commands and keywords are in **boldface** font.
- Arguments for which you supply values are in *italic* font.
- Elements in square brackets ([ ]) are optional.
- Alternative but required keywords are grouped in braces ({ }) and separated by vertical bars (|).

Examples use these conventions:

- Terminal sessions and information the system displays are in `screen` font.
- Information you enter is in `boldface screen` font.
- Nonprinting characters, such as passwords, are in angle brackets (< >).
- Default responses to system prompts are in square brackets ([ ]).
- Exclamation points (!) at the beginning of a line indicate a comment line.
- When part of the command output has been omitted (to conserve space), the deleted output is indicated with italicized brackets and ellipsis (*[...]*)

NOTES

This is a special paragraph that means *reader take note*. It usually refers to helpful suggestions, the writer's assumptions, or reference to materials not contained in this manual.

CAUTION

Means *reader be careful*. In this situation, you might do something that could result in equipment damage or loss of data.

PART 1

Introduction to Troubleshooting

## CHAPTER 1

Troubleshooting Overview

Internetworks come in a variety of topologies and levels of complexity—from single-protocol, point-to-point links connecting cross-town campuses, to highly meshed, large-scale wide-area networks (WANs) traversing multiple time zones and international boundaries. The industry trend is toward increasingly complex environments, involving multiple media types, multiple protocols, and often interconnection to "unknown" networks. Unknown networks may be defined as a transit network belonging to a Internet service provider (ISP) or a telco that interconnects your private networks. In these unknown networks, you do not have control of such factors as delay, media types, or vendor hardware.

More complex network environments mean that the potential for connectivity and performance problems in internetworks is high, and the source of problems is often elusive. The keys to maintaining a problem-free network environment, as well as maintaining the ability to isolate and fix a network fault quickly, are documentation, planning, and communication. This requires a framework of procedures and personnel to be in place long before any network changes take place. The goal of this book is to help you isolate and resolve the most common connectivity and performance problems in your network environment.

SYMPTOMS, PROBLEMS, AND SOLUTIONS

Failures in internetworks are characterized by certain symptoms. These symptoms might be general (such as clients being unable to access specific servers) or more specific (routes not in routing table). Each symptom can be traced to one or more problems or causes by using specific troubleshooting tools and techniques. Once identified, each problem can be remedied by implementing a solution consisting of a series of actions.

This book describes how to define symptoms, identify problems, and implement solutions in generic environments. You should always apply the specific context in which you are troubleshooting to determine how to detect symptoms and diagnose problems for your specific environment.

GENERAL PROBLEM-SOLVING MODEL

When you're troubleshooting a network environment, a systematic approach works best. Define the specific symptoms, identify all potential problems that could be causing the symptoms, and then systematically eliminate each potential problem (from most likely to least likely) until the symptoms disappear.

Figure 1–1 illustrates the process flow for the general problem-solving model. This process flow is not a rigid outline for troubleshooting an internetwork; it is a foundation from which you can build a problem-solving process to suit your particular environment.

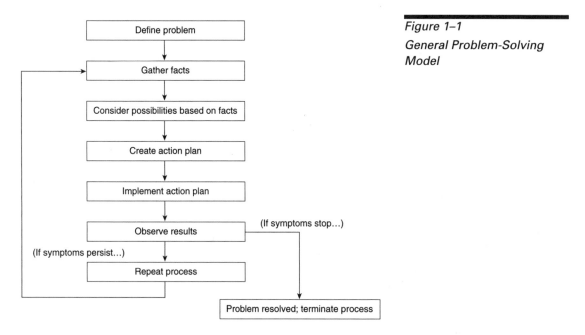

Figure 1–1

General Problem-Solving Model

The following steps detail the problem-solving process outlined in Figure 1–1:

Step 1   When analyzing a network problem, make a clear problem statement. You should define the problem in terms of a set of symptoms and potential causes.

To properly analyze the problem, identify the general symptoms and then ascertain what kinds of problems (causes) could result in these symptoms. For example, hosts might not be responding to service requests from clients (a symptom). Possible causes might include a misconfigured host, bad interface cards, or missing router configuration commands.

Step 2   Gather the facts you need to help isolate possible causes.

Ask questions of affected users, network administrators, managers, and other key people. Collect information from sources such as network management systems, protocol analyzer traces, output from router diagnostic commands, or software release notes.

Step 3   Consider possible problems based on the facts you gathered. Using the facts you gathered, you can eliminate some of the potential problems from your list.

Depending on the data, you might, for example, be able to eliminate hardware as a problem, so that you can focus on software problems. At every opportunity, try to narrow the number of potential problems so that you can create an efficient plan of action.

Step 4   Create an action plan based on the remaining potential problems. Begin with the most likely problem and devise a plan in which only *one* variable is manipulated.

Changing only one variable at a time allows you to reproduce a given solution to a specific problem. If you alter more than one variable simultaneously, you might solve the problem, but identifying the specific change that eliminated the symptom becomes far more difficult and will not help you solve the same problem if it occurs in the future.

Step 5   Implement the action plan, performing each step carefully while testing to see whether the symptom disappears.

Step 6   Whenever you change a variable, be sure to gather results. Generally, you should use the same method of gathering facts that you used in Step 2 (that is, working with the key people affected in conjunction with utilizing your diagnostic tools).

Step 7   Analyze the results to determine whether the problem has been resolved. If it has, then the process is complete.

Step 8   If the problem has not been resolved, you must create an action plan based on the next most likely problem in your list. Return to Step 4, change one variable at a time, and reiterate the process until the problem is solved.

NOTES

If you exhaust all the common causes and actions (either those outlined in this book or ones that you have identified for your environment), you should contact your Cisco technical support representative.

PREPARING FOR NETWORK FAILURE

It is always easier to recover from a network failure if you are prepared ahead of time. Possibly the most important requirement in any network environment is to have current and accurate information about that network available to the network support personnel at all times. Only with complete information can intelligent decisions be made about network change, and only with complete information can troubleshooting be done as quickly and easily as possible. During the process of troubleshooting the network that it is most critical to ensure that this documentation is kept up-to-date.

To determine whether you are prepared for a network failure, answer the following questions:

- Do you have an accurate physical and logical map of your internetwork?

  Does your organization or department have an up-to-date internetwork map that outlines the physical location of all the devices on the network and how they are connected, as well as a logical map of network addresses, network numbers, subnetworks, and so forth?

- Do you have a list of all network protocols implemented in your network?

  For each of the protocols implemented, do you have a list of the network numbers, subnetworks, zones, areas, and so on that are associated with them?

- Do you know which protocols are being routed?

  For each routed protocol, do you have correct, up-to-date router configuration?

- Do you know which protocols are being bridged?

  Are there any filters configured in any bridges, and do you have a copy of these configurations?

- Do you know all the points of contact to external networks, including any connections to the Internet?

  For each external network connection, do you know what routing protocol is being used?

- Do you have an established baseline for your network?

  Has your organization documented normal network behavior and performance at different times of the day so that you can compare the current problems with a baseline?

If you can answer yes to all questions, you will be able to recover from a failure more quickly and more easily than if you are not prepared.

## CHAPTER 2

Troubleshooting Tools

This chapter presents information about the wide variety of tools available to assist you in troubleshooting your internetwork, including information on using router diagnostic commands, using Cisco network management tools, and third-party troubleshooting tools.

USING ROUTER DIAGNOSTIC COMMANDS

Cisco routers provide numerous integrated commands to assist you in monitoring and troubleshooting your internetwork. The following sections describe the basic use of these commands:

- The **show** commands help monitor installation behavior and normal network behavior, as well as isolate problem areas.
- The **debug** commands assist in the isolation of protocol and configuration problems.
- The **ping** commands help determine connectivity between devices on your network.
- The **trace** commands provide a method of determining the route by which packets reach their destination from one device to another.

Using *show* Commands

The **show** commands are powerful monitoring and troubleshooting tools. You can use the **show** commands to perform a variety of functions:

- Monitor router behavior during initial installation
- Monitor normal network operation
- Isolate problem interfaces, nodes, media, or applications
- Determine when a network is congested
- Determine the status of servers, clients, or other neighbors

Following are some of the most commonly used **show** commands:

- **show interfaces**—Use the **show interfaces** exec command to display statistics for all interfaces configured on the router or access server. The resulting output varies, depending on the network for which an interface has been configured.

  Some of the more frequently used **show interfaces** commands include the following:

  - **show interfaces ethernet**
  - **show interfaces tokenring**
  - **show interfaces fddi**
  - **show interfaces atm**
  - **show interfaces serial**
  - **show controllers**—This command displays statistics for interface card controllers. For example, the **show controllers mci** command provides the following fields:

    ```
    MCI 0, controller type 1.1, microcode version 1.8
        128 Kbytes of main memory, 4 Kbytes cache memory
    22 system TX buffers, largest buffer size 1520
        Restarts: 0 line down, 0 hung output, 0 controller error
    Interface 0 is Ethernet0, station address 0000.0c00.d4a6
        15 total RX buffers, 11 buffer TX queue limit, buffer size 1520
        Transmitter delay is 0 microseconds
    Interface 1 is Serial0, electrical interface is V.35 DTE
        15 total RX buffers, 11 buffer TX queue limit, buffer size 1520
        Transmitter delay is 0 microseconds
        High speed synchronous serial interface
    Interface 2 is Ethernet1, station address aa00.0400.3be4
        15 total RX buffers, 11 buffer TX queue limit, buffer size 1520
        Transmitter delay is 0 microseconds
    Interface 3 is Serial1, electrical interface is V.35 DCE
        15 total RX buffers, 11 buffer TX queue limit, buffer size 1520
        Transmitter delay is 0 microseconds
        High speed synchronous serial interface
    ```

  Some of the most frequently used **show controllers** commands include the following:

  - **show controllers token**
  - **show controllers FDDI**
  - **show controllers LEX**
  - **show controllers ethernet**
  - **show controllers E1**
  - **show controllers MCI**
  - **show controllers cxbus**
  - **show controllers t1**
  - **show running-config**— Displays the router configuration currently running

○ **show startup-config**—Displays the router configuration stored in nonvolatile RAM (NVRAM)

○ **show flash**—Group of commands that display the layout and contents of flash memory

○ **show buffers**—Displays statistics for the buffer pools on the router

○ **show memory**—Shows statistics about the router's memory, including free pool statistics

○ **show processes**—Displays information about the active processes on the router

○ **show stacks**—Displays information about the stack utilization of processes and interrupt routines, as well as the reason for the last system reboot

○ **show version**—Displays the configuration of the system hardware, the software version, the names and sources of configuration files, and the boot images

There are hundreds of other **show** commands available. For details on using and interpreting the output of specific **show** commands, refer to the Cisco Internetwork Operating System (IOS) command references.

Using debug Commands

The **debug** privileged exec commands can provide a wealth of information about the traffic being seen (or *not* seen) on an interface, error messages generated by nodes on the network, protocol-specific diagnostic packets, and other useful troubleshooting data. To access and list the privileged exec commands, complete the following tasks:

Step 1   Enter the privileged exec mode:

```
Command:
Router> enable
Password: XXXXXX
Router#
```

Step 2   List privileged exec commands:

```
Router# debug ?
```

CAUTION

Exercise care when using **debug** commands. Many **debug** commands are processor intensive and can cause serious network problems (such as degraded performance or loss of connectivity) if they are enabled on an already heavily loaded router. When you finish using a **debug** command, remember to disable it with its specific **no debug** command (or use the **no debug all** command to turn off all debugging).

Use **debug** commands to isolate problems, not to monitor normal network operation. Because the high processor overhead of **debug** commands can disrupt router operation, you should use them only when you are looking for specific types of traffic or problems and have narrowed your problems to a likely subset of causes.

Output formats vary with each **debug** command. Some generate a single line of output per packet, and others generate multiple lines of output per packet. Some generate large amounts of output, and others generate only occasional output. Some generate lines of text, and others generate information in field format.

To minimize the negative impact of using **debug** commands, follow this procedure:

Step 1   Use the **no logging console** global configuration command on your router. This command disables all logging to the console terminal.

Step 2   Telnet to a router port and enter the **enable** exec command. The **enable** exec command will place the router in the **privileged exec** mode. After entering the **enable** password, you will receive a prompt that will consist of the router name with a # symbol.

Step 3   Use the **terminal monitor** command to copy **debug** command output and system error messages to your current terminal display.

By redirecting output to your current terminal display, you can view **debug** command output remotely, without being connected through the console port.

If you use **debug** commands at the console port, character-by-character processor interrupts are generated, maximizing the processor load already caused by using **debug**.

If you intend to keep the output of the **debug** command, spool the output to a file. The procedure for setting up such a **debug** output file is described in the *Debug Command Reference*.

This book refers to specific **debug** commands that are useful when troubleshooting specific problems. Complete details regarding the function and output of **debug** commands are provided in the *Debug Command Reference*.

In many situations, using third-party diagnostic tools can be more useful and less intrusive than using **debug** commands. For more information, see the section "Third-Party Troubleshooting Tools" later in this chapter.

Using the *ping* Command

To check host reachability and network connectivity, use the **ping** exec (user) or privileged exec command. After you log in to the router or access server, you are automatically in user exec command mode. The exec commands available at the user level are a subset of those available at the privileged level. In general, the user exec commands allow you to connect to remote devices, change terminal settings on a temporary basis, perform basic tests, and list system information. The **ping** command can be used to confirm basic network connectivity on AppleTalk, ISO Conectionless Network Service (CLNS), IP, Novell, Apollo, VINES, DECnet, or XNS networks.

For IP, the **ping** command sends Internet Control Message Protocol (ICMP) Echo messages. ICMP is the Internet protocol that reports errors and provides information relevant to IP packet addressing. If a station receives an ICMP Echo message, it sends an ICMP Echo Reply message back to the source.

The extended command mode of the **ping** command permits you to specify the supported IP header options. This allows the router to perform a more extensive range of test options. To enter **ping** extended command mode, enter **yes** at the extended commands prompt of the **ping** command.

It is a good idea to use the **ping** command when the network is functioning properly to see how the command works under normal conditions and so you have something to compare against when troubleshooting.

For detailed information on using the **ping** and extended **ping** commands, refer to the *Cisco IOS Configuration Fundamentals Command Reference*.

Using the trace Command

The **trace user** exec command discovers the routes that a router's packets follow when traveling to their destinations. The **trace** privileged exec command permits the supported IP header options to be specified, allowing the router to perform a more extensive range of test options.

The **trace** command works by using the error message generated by routers when a datagram exceeds its time-to-live (TTL) value. First, probe datagrams are sent with a TTL value of 1. This causes the first router to discard the probe datagrams and send back "time exceeded" error messages. The **trace** command then sends several probes and displays the round-trip time for each. After every third probe, the TTL is increased by one.

Each outgoing packet can result in one of two error messages. A "time exceeded" error message indicates that an intermediate router has seen and discarded the probe. A "port unreachable" error message indicates that the destination node has received the probe and discarded it because it could not deliver the packet to an application. If the timer goes off before a response comes in, **trace** prints an asterisk (*).

The **trace** command terminates when the destination responds, when the maximum TTL is exceeded, or when the user interrupts the trace with the escape sequence.

As with **ping**, it is a good idea to use the **trace** command when the network is functioning properly to see how the command works under normal conditions and so you have something to compare against when troubleshooting.

For detailed information on using the **trace** and extended **trace** commands, refer to the *Cisco IOS Configuration Fundamentals Command Reference*.

USING CISCO NETWORK MANAGEMENT TOOLS

Cisco offers several network management products that provide design, monitoring, and troubleshooting tools to help you manage your internetwork.

The following three internetwork management tools are useful for troubleshooting internetwork problems:

- CiscoWorks internetwork management software, a set of Simple Network Management Protocol (SNMP)–based tools.

- The TrafficDirector RMON application, a remote monitoring tool that enables you to gather data, monitor activity on your network, and find potential problems.

- The VlanDirector switch management application, a management tool that provides an accurate picture of your VLANs.

CiscoWorks Internetwork Management Software

CiscoWorks is a series of SNMP-based internetwork management software applications. CiscoWorks applications are integrated on several popular network management platforms and build on industry-standard platforms to provide applications for monitoring device status, maintaining configurations, and troubleshooting problems.

Following are some of the applications included in the CiscoWorks product that are useful for troubleshooting your internetwork:

- Device Monitor—Allows the network manager to specify which network devices to monitor for information about environmental and interface statistics. The configuration includes settings to specify how often CiscoWorks should check this information and whether to log it in to the Log Manager application.

- Health Monitor—Displays information about the status of a device, including buffers, CPU load, memory available, and protocols and interfaces being used.

- Show Commands—Enable you to view data similar to output from router **show** exec commands.

- Path Tool—Displays and analyzes the path between two devices to collect utilization and error data.

- Device Polling—Probes and extracts data about the condition of network devices.

- CiscoView—Provides dynamic monitoring and troubleshooting functions, including a graphical display of Cisco devices, statistics, and comprehensive configuration information.

- Offline Network Analysis—Collects historical network data for offline analysis of performance trends and traffic patterns.

- CiscoConnect—Allows you to provide Cisco with debugging information, configurations, and topology information to speed resolution of network problems.

CiscoWorks implements numerous other applications that are useful for administering, designing, and monitoring your internetwork. Refer to the *Cisco Systems Product Catalog* for more information.

The TrafficDirector RMON Application

The TrafficDirector advanced packet filters let users monitor all seven layers of network traffic. Using Cisco IOS embedded RMON agents and SwitchProbe standalone probes, managers can view enterprise-wide network traffic from the link, network, transport, or application layers. The TrafficDirector multilayer traffic summary provides a quick, high-level assessment of network loading and protocol distributions. Network managers then "zoom in" on a specific segment, ring, switch port, or trunk link and apply real-time analysis and diagnostic tools to view hosts, conversations, and packet captures.

TrafficDirector threshold monitoring enables users to implement a proactive management environment. First, thresholds for critical Management Information Base (MIB) variables are set within the RMON agent. When these thresholds are exceeded, traps are sent to the appropriate management station to notify the network administrator of an impending problem.

The VlanDirector Switch Management Application

The VlanDirector switch management application simplifies VLAN port assignment and offers other management capabilities for VLANs. VlanDirector offers the following features for network administrators:

- Accurate representation of the physical network for VLAN design and configuration verification
- Capability to obtain VLAN configuration information on a specific device or link interface
- Discrepancy reports on conflicting configurations
- Ability to troubleshoot and identify individual device configurations that are in error with system-level VLANs
- Quick detection of changes in VLAN status of switch ports
- User authentication and write protection security

THIRD-PARTY TROUBLESHOOTING TOOLS

In many situations, third-party diagnostic tools can be more useful than commands that are integrated into the router. For example, enabling a processor-intensive **debug** command can be disastrous in an environment experiencing excessively high traffic levels. However, attaching a network analyzer to the suspect network is less intrusive and is more likely to yield useful information without interrupting the operation of the router. The following are some typical third-party troubleshooting tools used for troubleshooting internetworks:

- Volt-Ohm meters, digital multimeters, and cable testers are useful in testing the physical connectivity of your cable plant.
- Time domain reflectors (TDRs) and optical time domain reflectors (OTDRs) are devices that assist in the location of cable breaks, impedence mismatches, and other physical cable plant problems.

- Breakout boxes and fox boxes are useful for troubleshooting problems in peripheral interfaces.

- Network analyzers such the Network General Sniffer decode problems at all seven OSI layers and can be identified automatically in real-time, providing a clear view of network activity and categorizing problems by criticality.

Volt-Ohm Meters, Digital Multimeters, and Cable Testers

Volt-ohm meters and digital multimeters are at the lower end of the spectrum of cable testing tools. These devices measure parameters such as AC and DC voltage, current, resistance, capacitance, and cable continuity. They are used to check physical connectivity.

Cable testers (scanners) also enable you to check physical connectivity. Cable testers are available for shielded twisted pair (STP), unshielded twisted pair (UTP), 10BaseT, and coaxial and twinax cables. A given cable tester might be able to perform any of the following functions:

- Test and report on cable conditions, including near-end crosstalk (NEXT), attenuation, and noise

- Perform TDR, traffic monitoring, and wire map functions

- Display Media Access Control (MAC) layer information about LAN traffic, provide statistics such as network utilization and packet error rates, and perform limited protocol testing (for example, TCP/IP tests such as **ping**)

Similar testing equipment is available for fiber-optic cable. Due to the relatively high cost of this cable and its installation, fiber-optic cable should be tested both before installation (on-the-reel testing) and after installation. Continuity testing of the fiber requires either a visible light source or a reflectometer. Light sources capable of providing light at the three predominant wavelengths, 850 nanometers (nm), 1300 nm, and 1550 nm, are used with power meters that can measure the same wavelengths and test attenuation and return loss in the fiber.

TDRs and OTDRs

At the top end of the cable testing spectrum are TDRs. These devices can quickly locate open and short circuits, crimps, kinks, sharp bends, impedance mismatches, and other defects in metallic cables.

A TDR works by "bouncing" a signal off the end of the cable. Opens, shorts, and other problems reflect the signal back at different amplitudes, depending on the problem. A TDR measures how much time it takes for the signal to reflect and calculates the distance to a fault in the cable. TDRs can also be used to measure the length of a cable. Some TDRs can also calculate the propagation rate based on a configured cable length.

Fiber-optic measurement is performed by an OTDR. OTDRs can accurately measure the length of the fiber, locate cable breaks, measure the fiber attenuation, and measure splice or connector losses. An OTDR can be used to take the "signature" of a particular installation, noting attenuation and splice losses. This baseline measurement can then be compared with future signatures when a problem in the system is suspected.

Breakout Boxes, Fox Boxes, and BERTs/BLERTs

Breakout boxes, fox boxes, and bit/block error rate testers (BERTs/BLERTs) are digital interface testing tools used to measure the digital signals present at PCs, printers, modems, the channel service unit/digital service unit (CSU/DSU), and other peripheral interfaces. These devices can monitor data line conditions, analyze and trap data, and diagnose problems common to data communication systems. Traffic from data terminal equipment (DTE) through data communications equipment (DCE) can be examined to help isolate problems, identify bit patterns, and ensure that the proper cabling has been installed. These devices cannot test media signals such as Ethernet, Token Ring, or FDDI.

Network Monitors

Network monitors continuously track packets crossing a network, providing an accurate picture of network activity at any moment, or a historical record of network activity over a period of time. They do not decode the contents of frames. Monitors are useful for baselining, in which the activity on a network is sampled over a period of time to establish a normal performance profile, or baseline.

Monitors collect information such as packet sizes, the number of packets, error packets, overall usage of a connection, the number of hosts and their MAC addresses, and details about communications between hosts and other devices. This data can be used to create profiles of LAN traffic as well as to assist in locating traffic overloads, planning for network expansion, detecting intruders, establishing baseline performance, and distributing traffic more efficiently.

Network Analyzers

A *network analyzer* (also called a *protocol analyzer*) decodes the various protocol layers in a recorded frame and presents them as readable abbreviations or summaries, detailing which layer is involved (physical, data link, and so forth) and what function each byte or byte content serves.

Most network analyzers can perform many of the following functions:

- Filter traffic that meets certain criteria so that, for example, all traffic to and from a particular device can be captured
- Time stamp captured data
- Present protocol layers in an easily readable form
- Generate frames and transmit them onto the network
- Incorporate an "expert" system in which the analyzer uses a set of rules, combined with information about the network configuration and operation, to diagnose and solve, or offer potential solutions to, network problems

PART 2

Hardware, Booting, and Media Problems

## CHAPTER 3

Troubleshooting Hardware and Booting Problems

This chapter provides procedures for troubleshooting hardware and booting problems. Although it provides specific procedures for some Cisco products, always refer to your hardware installation and maintenance publication for more detailed information about your specific platform, including descriptions of specific LEDs, configuration information, and additional troubleshooting information.

This chapter begins with the following sections on hardware problems:

- Cisco 7500 Series Startup—Describes hardware and boot process troubleshooting for Cisco 7500 series routers

- Cisco 7000 Series Startup—Describes hardware and boot process troubleshooting for Cisco 7000 series routers

- Cisco 4000 and Cisco 3000 Series Startup—Describes hardware and boot process troubleshooting for Cisco 4000 and Cisco 3000 series routers

- Cisco 2500 Series Startup—Describes hardware and boot process troubleshooting for Cisco 2500 series routers

- Cisco 2000 Series Startup—Describes hardware and boot process troubleshooting for Cisco 2000 series routers

- Catalyst 5000 Series Startup—Describes hardware and boot process troubleshooting for Catalyst 5000 series LAN switches

- Catalyst 3000 Series Startup—Describes hardware and boot process troubleshooting for Catalyst 3000 series LAN switches

- Catalyst 2900 Series Startup—Describes hardware and boot process troubleshooting for Catalyst 2900 series LAN switches

- Catalyst 1600 Token Ring Switch Startup—Describes hardware and boot process troubleshooting for Catalyst 1600 Token Ring LAN switches

- LightStream 2020 Startup—Describes hardware and boot process troubleshooting for LightStream 2020 ATM switches
- Testing and Verifying Replacement Parts—Provides suggested actions when swapping router hardware

The remaining sections describe symptoms, problems, and solutions for Flash boot, netboot, ROM boot, and other bootup problems:

- Booting: Router Fails to Boot from Flash Memory
- Booting: Vector Error Occurs When Booting from Flash Memory
- Booting: Router Partially Boots from Flash and Displays Boot Prompt
- Booting: Router Cannot Netboot from TFTP Server
- Booting: Router Cannot Netboot from Another Router
- Booting: Timeouts and Out-of-Order Packets Prevent Netbooting
- Booting: Invalid Routes Prevent Netbooting
- Booting: Client ARP Requests Timeout during Netboot
- Booting: Undefined Load Module Error When Netbooting
- Booting: Router Hangs After ROM Monitor Initializes
- Booting: Router Is Stuck in ROM Monitor Mode
- Booting: Scrambled Output When Booting from ROM
- Booting: Local Timeouts Occur When Booting from ROM
- Booting: Unresponsive Terminal Connection to Unconfigured Access Server

BOOTING THE ROUTER

Cisco routers can initialize the system (boot) in four ways:

- Netboot—Routers can boot from a server using the Trivial File Transfer Protocol (TFTP), the DEC Maintenance Operation Protocol (MOP), or the Remote Copy Protocol (RCP) across any of the supported media types (such as Ethernet, Token Ring, Fiber Distributed Data Interface [FDDI], High-Speed Serial Interface [HSSI], and serial lines).
- Flash memory—Routers can boot from Flash memory, a nonvolatile storage medium that can be electrically erased and reprogrammed.
- ROM—Routers can boot a system from built-in read-only memory (ROM).
- PC Flash memory card—Routers can boot from a removable Flash memory card.

This section provides general information about router booting.

Netbooting Tips

During netbooting sessions, routers behave like hosts. They route via proxy Address Resolution Protocol (ARP), Serial Line Address Resolution Protocol (SLARP) information, Internet Control Message Protocol (ICMP) redirects, or a default gateway. When netbooting, routers ignore dynamic routing information, static IP routes, and bridging information. As a result, intermediate routers are responsible for handling ARP and User Datagram Protocol (UDP) requests correctly. For serial and HSSI media, ARP is not used.

Before netbooting from a server, you should **ping** the server from the ROM software. If you cannot **ping** the server, follow the procedures described in the section "Booting: Router Cannot Netboot from TFTP Server" later in this chapter. If you still cannot **ping** the server, there is probably a server configuration or hardware problem. Refer to your TFTP server documentation or contact your technical support representative for assistance.

Fault-Tolerant Boot Strategies

Although netbooting is useful, network or server failures can make netbooting impossible. After you have installed and configured the router's Flash memory, configure the boot sequence for the router to reduce the impact of a server or network failure. The following order is recommended:

1. Boot an image from Flash memory.
2. Boot an image using a netboot.
3. Boot from a ROM image.

Following is an example of how to configure a router with a fault-tolerant boot sequence.

```
goriot# configure terminal
Enter configuration commands, one per line.  End with CNTL/Z.
goriot(config)# boot system flash gsxx
goriot(config)# boot system gsxx 131.108.1.101
goriot(config)# boot system rom
goriot(config)# ^Z
goriot#
%SYS-5-CONFIG_I: Configured from console by console
goriot# copy running-config startup-config
[ok]
goriot#
```

Using this strategy, a router has three sources from which to boot: Flash memory, netboot, and ROM. Providing alternative sources can help to mitigate any failure of the TFTP server or the network.

NOTES

The configuration register must be set to allow ROM image booting after failed netbooting attempts. For more information, refer to the hardware configuration manual for your platform.

Timeouts and Out-of-Order Packets

When netbooting, a client might need to retransmit requests before receiving a response to an ARP request. These retransmissions can result in timeouts and out-of-order packets.

Timeouts (shown as periods in a netbooting display) and out-of-order packets (shown as uppercase Os) do not necessarily prevent a successful netboot. It is acceptable to have either or both timeouts or out-of-order packets occur during the netboot process.

The following examples show console output from netbooting sessions that were successful even though timeouts and out-of-order packets occurred (exclamation points represent successfully received packets):

```
Booting gs3-bfx from 131.108.1.123: !.!!!!!!!!!!!!!!!!!!!!!!
```

```
Booting gs3-bfx from 131.108.1.123: !O.O!!!!!!!!!!!!!!!!!!!!!!!!!!
```

If a netboot generates excessive out-of-order packets and timeouts, problems might result. These problems are discussed later in this chapter, in the section "Booting: Timeouts and Out-of-Order Packets Prevent Netbooting."

Information for Technical Support

If you cannot resolve your booting problem using the procedures outlined in this chapter, collect the following information for your technical support representative:

- ROM images. (Use the **show version** exec command.)
- Programmable ROM labels. (This information is printed on the physical chip, and an example is shown in Figure 3–1.)

Figure 3–1

An Example of a Boot ROM Label—Boot ROM Version 11.1(2)

```
U30 v11 1(2)
RS P2-ROMMON
O17-2111-04
Cisco Systems
```

- NVRAM configurations for client and adjacent routers.
- Debugging output from adjacent routers using the following privileged exec commands:
  - **debug ip packet**
  - **debug arp**
  - **debug ip udp**
  - **debug tftp**

For more information about these **debug** commands, refer to the *Debug Command Reference*.

TROUBLESHOOTING HARDWARE

This section discusses procedures for connectivity problems related to booting. It describes specific booting symptoms, the problems that are likely to cause each symptom, and the solutions to those problems.

Cisco 7500 Series Startup

When you start up a Cisco 7500 series router, the following should occur:

- The AC (or DC) OK LED should go on immediately and should remain on as long as the system is receiving power.

- The blower should be operating.

- The Route Switch Processor (RSP) and front-panel Normal LEDs should go on (to indicate normal system operation) and should remain on during system operation; the CPU Halt LED should remain off.

- The Enabled LED on each interface processor should go on (to indicate that the RSP has completed initialization of the interface processor).

When the 7500 series system has initialized successfully, the system banner should be displayed on the console screen. If it is not displayed, make sure that the console terminal is properly connected to the RSP console port and that the terminal is set correctly. The system banner should look similar to the following:

```
System Bootstrap, Version 4.6(5), SOFTWARE
Copyright (c) 1986-1995 by cisco Systems
RSP2 processor with 16384 Kbytes of memory
### [...] ###
F3: 2012356+47852+194864 at 0x1000
            Restricted Rights Legend
Use, duplication, or disclosure by the Government is
subject to restrictions as set forth in subparagraph
(c) of the Commercial Computer Software - Restricted
Rights clause at FAR sec. 52.227-19 and subparagraph
(c) (1) (ii) of the Rights in Technical Data and Computer
Software clause at DFARS sec. 252.227-7013.
            cisco Systems, Inc.
            170 Tasman Drive
            San Jose, CA 95134
GS Software (RSP-K), Version 10.3(571) [fc3], RELEASE SOFTWARE
Copyright (c) 1986-1995 by cisco Systems, Inc.
[...]
Press RETURN to get started!
```

If a problem occurs, try to isolate the problem to a specific subsystem. The Cisco 7500 series routers have the following subsystems:

- Power subsystem—Power supplies, external power cable, and backplane
- Cooling subsystem—Depending on your system, includes the following:
  - Cisco 7505: Fan tray, fan tray spare with six individual fans, and fan control board
  - Cisco 7507: Chassis blower
  - Cisco 7513: Blower module, including blower, blower-speed control board, front-panel LEDs, and the module itself
- Processor subsystem—Depending on your system, includes all interface processors and either the RSP1 or the RSP2

Table 3–1 outlines the areas where Cisco 7500 series startup problems may occur and describes solutions to those problems.

Table 3–1   *Hardware: Cisco 7500 Series Startup Problems and Solutions*

Possible Problem Area	Solution	
Power subsystem	Step 1	Check to see whether the blower is operating and LEDs on the processor modules are on. If the blower and LEDs are on but the Power Supply LED is off, there is probably a faulty Power Supply LED.
	Step 2	Make sure the power switch is set correctly to the on position.
	Step 3	Make sure the power source, power cable, and power supply are functioning correctly. Swap parts to see whether one of the components is faulty.
	Step 4	Ensure that the blower module is seated properly. Make sure that the blower control board edge connector is inserted fully in the backplane socket.

Table 3–1 *Hardware: Cisco 7500 Series Startup Problems and Solutions, Continued*

Possible Problem Area	Solution

Cooling subsystem	**Step 1** Check to see whether the blower is operating when you start up the system. If the blower is not operating, there might be a problem with the blower or the +24 V DC power:
	
	 • If the Output Fail LED is on, there might be a problem with the +24V DC supply to the blower or fan tray at either the power supply or the blower control board.
	
	 • If the blower is not operating and the Output Fail LED is off, ensure that the blower module is seated properly. Ensure that the blower control board edge connector is inserted fully in the backplane socket.
	
	 Step 2 If the system and blower start up but shut down after about two minutes, one or more fans might have failed or might be operating out of tolerance. You will probably see an error message similar to the following:
	
	 `%ENVM-2-FAN: Fan has failed, shutdown in 2 minutes`
	
	 If the blower or the blower control board fails, you must replace the blower module.
	
	 Step 3 If you see the following message at startup, the system has detected an overtemperature condition or out-of-tolerance power inside the chassis:
	
	 `Queued messages:`
	 `%ENVM-1-SHUTDOWN: Environmental Monitor initiated`
	 `shutdown`
	
	 If an environmental shutdown results from an out-of-tolerance power condition, the Output Fail LED goes on before the system shuts down.
	
	 This shutdown message might also indicate a faulty component or temperature sensor. Before the system shuts down, use the **show environment** or **show environment table** commands to display the internal chassis environment.
	
	 Step 4 Ensure that heated exhaust air from other equipment is not entering the inlet vents, and that there is sufficient clearance around the chassis to allow cooling air to flow.

Table 3–1   *Hardware: Cisco 7500 Series Startup Problems and Solutions, Continued*

Possible Problem Area	Solution
Processor subsystem	**Step 1** Check the RSP[1] LEDs. If no LEDs come on, ensure that the power supplies and blower are functioning properly.
	Step 2 Check the seating of the RSP. If the RSP is not seated properly, it will hang the system.
	Step 3 If the RSP CPU Halt LED is on, the system has detected a processor hardware failure. Contact a technical support representative for instructions.
	Step 4 Check to see whether the RSP Normal LED is on, indicating that the system software has initialized successfully and the system is operational.
	Step 5 Check the Enabled LED on each interface processor. This LED should go on when the RSP has initialized the interface processor.
	Step 6 If the Enabled LED on an individual interface processor is off, the interface processor might have pulled away from the backplane. If the interface processors are not seated properly, they will hang the system.

[1] RSP = Route Switch Processor

Cisco 7000 Series Startup

When you start up a Cisco 7000 series router, the following should occur:

- The DC OK LED should go on and should remain on as long as the system is receiving source power.
- The fans should be operating.
- The Route Processor (RP) Normal LED should go on and stay on to indicate normal system operation; the Halt CPU LED should remain off.
- The Enabled LED on the Switch Processor (SP) or Silicon Switch Processor (SSP) and each interface processor should go on when the RP has completed initialization of the interface processor or SP (or SSP) for operation.

When the system has initialized successfully, the system banner should be displayed on the console screen. If it is not displayed, make sure that the console terminal is properly connected to the RP console port and that the terminal is set correctly. The system banner should look similar to the following:

```
System Bootstrap, Version 4.6(5), SOFTWARE
Copyright (c) 1986-1995 by cisco Systems
RP1 processor with 16384 Kbytes of memory
```

```
### [...] ###
F3: 2012356+47852+194864 at 0x1000


                Restricted Rights Legend

Use, duplication, or disclosure by the Government is
subject to restrictions as set forth in subparagraph
(c) of the Commercial Computer Software - Restricted
Rights clause at FAR sec. 52.227-19 and subparagraph
(c) (1) (ii) of the Rights in Technical Data and Computer
Software clause at DFARS sec. 252.227-7013.

                cisco Systems, Inc.
                170 West Tasman Drive
                San Jose, California 95134-1706

GS Software (GS7), Version 10.3(1) [fc3], RELEASE SOFTWARE
Copyright (c) 1986-1995 by cisco Systems, Inc.

RP1 (68040) processor with 16384K bytes of memory.
[...]

Press RETURN to get started!
```

If problems occur, try to isolate the problem to a specific subsystem. The Cisco 7000 series routers have the following subsystems:

- Power subsystem—Includes power supplies, fans, external power cable, and internal power harness that connects to the backplane

- Cooling subsystem—Depending on your system, the cooling subsystem includes the following:

  ○ Cisco 7000: Chassis blower

  ○ Cisco 7010: Fan tray assembly, including six individual fans, the fan control board, and the tray itself

- Processor subsystem—Includes the RP, SP (or SSP), and all interface processors

Table 3–2 outlines the areas where Cisco 7000 series startup problems may occur and describes solutions to those problems.

Table 3–2   *Hardware: Cisco 7000 Series Startup Problems and Solutions*

Possible Problem Area	Solution
Power subsystem	**Step 1** Check to see whether the DC OK LED is on.
	Step 2 If the LED is not on but the fans are operating and LEDs on the processor modules are on, the Power Supply LED might be faulty.
	Step 3 If the LED is not on and there is no other activity, make sure the power switch is fully in the on position.
	Step 4 Make sure the power source, power cable, and power supply are functioning correctly. Swap parts to see whether one of the components is faulty.
	Step 5 Ensure that the fan tray is seated properly. Make sure the fan control board edge connector is inserted fully in the backplane socket.

Table 3–2   *Hardware: Cisco 7000 Series Startup Problems and Solutions, Continued*

Possible Problem Area	Solution

Cooling subsystem	**Step 1** Check to see whether the fans are operating.
	
	Step 2 If the fans are not operating and the DC OK LED is off, there might be a problem with the +24V DC power.
	
	Step 3 Ensure that the fan tray is seated properly. Make sure that the fan control board edge connector is inserted fully in the backplane socket.
	
	Step 4 If the system and the fans start up but shut down after about two minutes, one or more fans has failed or is operating out of tolerance. You will see an error message similar to the following:
	
	`%ENVM-2-FAN: Fan array has failed, shutdown in 2 minutes`
	
	If one or more fans or the fan control board fails, you must replace the fan tray.
	
	Step 5 If you see the following error message, the system has detected an overtemperature condition or out-of-tolerance power inside the chassis:
	
	`Queued messages:`
	`%ENVM-1-SHUTDOWN: Environmental Monitor initiated`
	`shutdown`
	
	If an environmental shutdown results from an out-of-tolerance power condition, the DC OK LED will go off before the system shuts down.
	
	This shutdown message could also indicate a faulty component or temperature sensor. Use the **show environment** or **show environment table** command to display the internal chassis environment.
	
	Step 6 Make sure that heated exhaust air from other equipment is not entering the inlet vents, and that there is sufficient clearance around the chassis to allow cooling air to flow.

Table 3–2 *Hardware: Cisco 7000 Series Startup Problems and Solutions, Continued*

Possible Problem Area	Solution
Processor subsystem	**Step 1** Check to see whether the RP[1] LEDs come on when system power is turned on.
	Step 2 If none of the RP LEDs come on, make sure that both the fan and power supply are functioning properly.
	Step 3 If the power supply and fans appear operational but none of the RP LEDs are on, an improperly connected RP, SP[2] (or SSP[3]), or interface processor might have hung the bus.
	Step 4 If the SP (or SSP) Enabled LED is off but any of the RP LEDs are on, make sure the SP (or SSP) is seated in its slot properly.
	Step 5 Check to see whether the Boot Error LED is on. If the LED is on, the system software is unable to start up. If you have a spare RP with the system software ROMs installed, replace the installed RP with the spare to see whether the system will boot.
	Step 6 Check to see whether the RP CPU Halt LED is on. If it is, the system has detected a processor hardware failure. Contact a technical support representative for more information.
	Step 7 Check to see whether all interface processor Enabled LEDs are on.
	Step 8 If the Enabled LED on an individual interface processor is off, make sure that the interface processor has not pulled away from the backplane.

[1] RP = Route Processor
[2] SP = Switch Processor
[3] SSP = Silicon Switch Processor

Cisco 4000 and Cisco 3000 Series Startup

When you start up a Cisco 4000 or a Cisco 3000 series router, the following should occur:

- The System OK LED should come on and stay on as long as power is supplied.
- The fans should be operating.

When the system has initialized successfully, the system banner should be displayed on the console screen. The system banner should look similar to the following:

```
System Bootstrap, Version 4.14(9), SOFTWARE
Copyright (c) 1986-1994 by cisco Systems
4000 processor with 16384 Kbytes of main memory
```

```
Loading xx-j-mz.112-0.15 at 0x4A790, size = 3496424 bytes [OK]
F3: 8988+3487404+165008 at 0x12000
Self decompressing the image : ###[...]#### [OK]

                    Restricted Rights Legend

Use, duplication, or disclosure by the Government is
subject to restrictions as set forth in subparagraph
(c) of the Commercial Computer Software - Restricted
Rights clause at FAR sec. 52.227-19 and subparagraph
(c) (1) (ii) of the Rights in Technical Data and Computer
Software clause at DFARS sec. 252.227-7013.

              cisco Systems, Inc.
              170 West Tasman Drive
              San Jose, California 95134-1706


Cisco Internetwork Operating System Software
IOS (tm) 4000 Software (XX-J-M), Version 11.2(0.15), BETA TEST SOFTWARE
Copyright (c) 1986-1996 by cisco Systems, Inc.
Compiled Wed 03-Jul-96 01:21 by susingh
Image text-base: 0x00012000, data-base: 0x006F6494


cisco 4000 (68030) processor (revision 0xA0) with 16384K/4096K bytes of memory.
Processor board ID 5007155
G.703/E1 software, Version 1.0.
Bridging software.
SuperLAT software copyright 1990 by Meridian Technology Corp).
X.25 software, Version 2.0, NET2, BFE and GOSIP compliant.
TN3270 Emulation software (copyright 1994 by TGV Inc).
Basic Rate ISDN software, Version 1.0.
2 Ethernet/IEEE 802.3 interfaces.
4 Serial network interfaces.
8 ISDN Basic Rate interfaces.
128K bytes of non-volatile configuration memory.
4096K bytes of processor board System flash (Read/Write)


Press RETURN to get started!
```

If problems occur, try to isolate the problem to a specific subsystem. The Cisco 4000 and Cisco 3000 series routers have the following subsystems:

- Power subsystem—This subsystem includes the power supply and the wiring.

- Cooling subsystem—This subsystem includes the blower assembly, which should come on when power is applied.

- Network processor modules (NPMs)—This subsystem includes all NPMs installed in the router chassis.

- System cables—This subsystem includes all the external cables that connect the router to the network.

Table 3–3 outlines the areas where Cisco 4000 and Cisco 3000 series startup problems may occur and describes solutions to those problems.

Table 3–3 *Hardware: Cisco 4000 and Cisco 3000 Series Startup Problems and Solutions*

Possible Problem Area	Solution	
Power and cooling subsystems	Step 1	Check to see whether the blower is operating. If it is not, check the AC power input, AC power source, router circuit breaker, and power supply cable.
	Step 2	If the system shuts down after being on a short time, check the power supply. If the power supply appears operational, the router might have shut down due to overheating. Check the console for error messages similar to the following:
		`%SYS-1-OVERTEMP: System detected OVERTEMPERATURE condition. Please resolve cooling problem immediately!`
		Make sure that the fans are working and that there is no air blockage to cooling vents.
	Step 3	If the system partially boots but LEDs do not light, contact your technical support representative.
NPMs[1] and cables	Step 1	Make sure that NPMs are properly connected to the motherboard connector.
	Step 2	Check the external cables.
	Step 3	Check the processor or software for proper configuration.
	Step 4	Check the external console connection and verify that the console baud rate is correct.

[1] NPM = network processor module

Cisco 2500 Series Startup

When you start up a Cisco 2500 series router, the following should occur:

- The System OK LED should come on and stay on as long as power is supplied.
- The fans should be operating.

When the system has initialized successfully, the system banner should be displayed on the console screen. The system banner should look similar to the following:

```
System Bootstrap, Version (3.3), SOFTWARE
Copyright (c) 1986-1993 by cisco Systems
2500 processor with 16384 Kbytes of main memory

Unknown or ambiguous service arg - udp-small-servers
Unknown or ambiguous service arg - tcp-small-servers
Booting igs-in-l.110-9 from Flash address space
F3: 3844616+90320+228904 at 0x3000060

                Restricted Rights Legend

Use, duplication, or disclosure by the Government is
subject to restrictions as set forth in subparagraph
(c) of the Commercial Computer Software - Restricted
Rights clause at FAR sec. 52.227-19 and subparagraph
(c) (1) (ii) of the Rights in Technical Data and Computer
Software clause at DFARS sec. 252.227-7013.

            cisco Systems, Inc.
            170 West Tasman Drive
            San Jose, California 95134-1706



Cisco Internetwork Operating System Software
IOS (tm) 3000 Software (IGS-IN-L), Version 11.0(9), RELEASE SOFTWARE (fc1)
Copyright (c) 1986-1996 by cisco Systems, Inc.
Compiled Tue 11-Jun-96 01:15 by loreilly
Image text-base: 0x03020F8C, data-base: 0x00001000

cisco 2500 (68030) processor (revision A) with 16384K/2048K bytes of memory.
Processor board ID 01062462, with hardware revision 00000000
Bridging software.
X.25 software, Version 2.0, NET2, BFE and GOSIP compliant.
Basic Rate ISDN software, Version 1.0.
1 Ethernet/IEEE 802.3 interface.
2 Serial network interfaces.
1 ISDN Basic Rate interface.
32K bytes of non-volatile configuration memory.
4096K bytes of processor board System flash (Read ONLY)



    Press RETURN to get started!
```

If problems occur, try to isolate the problem to a specific subsystem. The Cisco 2500 series routers have the following subsystems:

- Power subsystem—This subsystem includes the power supply and the wiring.

- Cooling subsystem—This subsystem includes the fan, which should go on when power is applied.

- Network interfaces—This subsystem includes all network interfaces, such as Ethernet, Token Ring, serial, or ISDN Basic Rate Interface (BRI).
- System cables—This subsystem includes all the external cables that connect the router to the network.

Table 3–4 outlines the areas where Cisco 2500 series startup problems may occur and describes solutions to those problems.

Table 3–4   *Hardware: Cisco 2500 Series Startup Problems and Solutions*

Possible Problem Area	Solution
Power and cooling subsystems	**Step 1** If the Power LED is off, make sure the power supply is plugged in to the wall receptacle and that the cable from the power supply to the router is connected.
	Step 2 If the system shuts down after being on a short time, there might have been a thermal-induced shutdown caused by a faulty fan, or the power to the system might have been lost. Ensure that the system is receiving power and that the chassis intake and exhaust vents are clear.
	Step 3 If the system does not boot up but LEDs are on, check the 12V power supply.
	Step 4 If the system partially boots but LEDs are not on, check the 5V power supply.
Network interfaces and cables	**Step 1** If a network interface is not recognized by the system, check the interface cable connection and the LED on the network interface.
	Step 2 If a network interface is recognized but will not initialize, check the interface cable connection.
	Step 3 If the system will not boot properly or constantly or intermittently reboots, there might be a processor or software problem. Make sure that DRAM SIMM modules are seated properly.
	Step 4 If the system boots but the console screen is frozen, check the external console connection and verify that the console baud rate is correct.
	Step 5 If the system powers on and boots with a particular interface disconnected, check the network interface connection.

Cisco 2000 Series Startup

When you start up a Cisco 2000 series router, the following should occur:

- The OK LED should come on and stay on as long as power is supplied.
- The fans should be operating.

When the system has initialized successfully, the system banner should be displayed on the console screen.

Table 3–5 outlines the possible Cisco 2000 series startup problem and describes solutions to that problem.

Table 3–5 *Hardware: Cisco 2000 Series Startup Problem and Solutions*

Possible Problem	Solution	
Bootup problem	**Step 1**	Check to see whether the fan is operating. If it is not, check the fan or the 12V power supply.
	Step 2	If the system shuts down after being on for a short time, check the power supply.
	Step 3	If the power supply appears operational, the router might have shut down due to overheating. Ensure that the chassis intake and exhaust vents are clear.
	Step 4	If the system does not boot up but the System OK LED is on, check the 12V power supply to make sure it is not faulty.
	Step 5	If the system partially boots but the System OK LED is not on, check the 5V power supply to make sure it is not faulty.

Catalyst 5000 Series Startup

When you start up a Catalyst 5000 series LAN switch, the following should occur:

- The PS1 and PS2 LEDs on the supervisor engine module faceplate should be green.
- The system fan assembly should be operating and the Fan LED on the supervisor engine module should come on.
- The Status LED on the supervisor engine module and all interfaces should be orange until the boot is complete.

When the system boot is complete, the supervisor engine module should initialize the switching modules. The status LED on each switching module goes on when initialization has been completed, and the console screen displays a script and system banner similar to the following:

```
        ATE0
ATS0=1
Catalyst 5000 Power Up Diagnostics
Init NVRAM Log
```

```
LED Test
ROM CHKSUM
DUAL PORT RAM r/w
RAM r/w
RAM address test
Byte/Word Enable test
RAM r/w 55aa
RAM r/w aa55
EARL test
BOOTROM Version 1.4, Dated Dec  5 1995 16:49:40
BOOT date: 00/00/00 BOOT time: 03:18:57
SIMM RAM address test
SIMM Ram r/w 55aa
SIMM Ram r/w aa55
Start to Uncompress Image ...
IP address for Catalyst not configured
BOOTP will commence after the ports are online
Ports are coming online ...
Cisco Systems Console
```

If problems occur, try to isolate the problem to a specific subsystem. The Catalyst 5000 series LAN switches have the following subsystems:

- Power subsystem—This subsystem includes the power supplies and power supply fans.

- Cooling subsystem—This subsystem includes the chassis fan assembly, which should be operating when the system power is on.

- Processor and interface subsystem—This subsystem includes the supervisor engine module (which contains the system operating software), the network interfaces, and all associated cabling.

Table 3–6 outlines the areas where Catalyst 5000 series startup problems may occur and describes solutions to those problems.

Table 3–6 *Hardware: Catalyst 5000 Series Startup Problems and Solutions*

Possible Problem Area	Solution	
Power subsystem	Step 1	Check to see whether the PS1 LED is on. If it is not, ensure that the power supply is connected properly and is flush with the back of the chassis. Make sure that captive installation screws are tight.
	Step 2	Check the AC source and the power cable. Connect the power cord to another power source if one is available and turn the power back on. If the LED fails to go on after you connect the power supply to a new power source, replace the power cord.
	Step 3	If the LED fails to go on when the switch is connected to a different power source with a new power cord, the power supply is probably faulty. If a second power supply is available, install it in the second power supply bay and contact a customer service representative for further instructions.
	Step 4	Repeat these steps for the second power supply if present.
Cooling subsystem	Step 1	Check to see whether the Fan LED on the supervisor engine module is green. If it is not, check the power subsystem to see whether it is operational.
	Step 2	If the Fan LED is red, the fan assembly might not be seated properly in the backplane.
		To ensure that the fan assembly is seated properly, loosen the captive installation screws, remove the fan assembly, and reinstall it. Tighten all captive installation screws and restart the system.
	Step 3	If the Fan LED is still red, the system has probably detected a fan assembly failure. Contact a technical support representative for assistance.

Table 3–6 *Hardware: Catalyst 5000 Series Startup Problems and Solutions, Continued*

Possible Problem Area	Solution
Processor and interface subsystem	**Step 1** Check the supervisor engine module Status and Link LEDs. These should both be green if all diagnostic and self-tests were successful and ports are operational. For more information about interpreting the supervisor engine module LEDs, refer to the user guide for your switch. **Step 2** Check the LEDs on individual interface modules. In most cases these should be green (or should flicker green, in the case of Transmit and Receive LEDs) if the interface is functioning correctly. For detailed information on interpreting interface module LEDs, refer to the user guide for your switch. **Step 3** Check all cabling and connections. Replace any faulty cabling.

Catalyst 3000 Series Startup

When you start up a Catalyst 3000 series LAN switch, the following should occur:

- The Power LED should come on.

- The fan should begin operating and should stay on while power is applied to the system.

- On some models, the DIAG LED should come on, stay on for the duration of the system's self-test diagnostics, and then turn off.

While booting, the console screen displays a script and system banner, which should be similar to the following:

```
Cisco Catalyst Boot Firmware P/N 57-1327-02, Copyright 1995
- Initiating bootstrapping sequence.
- Boot image integrity check...Passed.
- Control transferred to boot process.
- Relocating main image to DRAM.......Done.
- Main image integrity check...succeeded.
- Control transferred to main process.
Cisco Catalyst 3000 System Software Version 1.1.1-B7, Copyright 1994,
1995.
System started on Fri. November 17, 1995  13:02:46
4 Megabytes System memory
2 Megabytes Network memory
- Initialization started
- File system initialized
- System temperature is within safe operating levels
- Warmboot initialization started
- Checking file system integrity
```

```
- LAN ports detected:
  - 10Base-T  : 1 2 3 4 5 6 7 8 9 10 11 12 13 14 15 16
  - StkPort   : 25
- Initializing Ports: 1 2 3 4 5 6 7 8 9 10 11 12 13 14 15 16 25
- Initializing system address table
- No existing diagnostic information, forcing diagnostic mode
- Starting Power Up Diagnostics test
  - UART loopback test on diagnostic port...Passed
  - UART loopback test on console port...Passed
  - RTC memory test...Passed
  - Real Time Clock test...Passed
  - CPU loopback test.............Passed
  - Ethernet Port loopback test..................Passed
  - Ethernet Port fast transmit loopback test.................Passed
  - Ethernet Port fast receive loopback test.................Passed
  - Ethernet Port cross port loopback test.................Passed
  - Ethernet Port broadcast test.................Passed

  - Catalyst Stack Port loopback test...Passed
  - Catalyst Stack Port cross port loopback test...Passed
  - Catalyst Stack Port broadcast test...Passed
  - CPU broadcast test...Passed
- Completed Power Up Diagnostics test
- System entering stand-alone mode
- Catalyst  initiating bootp requests on one or more VLANs
- System initialization complete
- Enabling port: 1 2 3 4 5 6 7 8 9 10 11 12 13 14 15 16 25
Press RETURN key to activate console...
```

If problems occur, try to isolate the problem to a specific subsystem. The Catalyst 3000 series LAN switches have the following subsystems:

- Power subsystem—This subsystem includes the input power, AC power cable, and power supply.

- Cooling subsystem—This subsystem includes the fans, which should be operating when the system power is on.

- Network interfaces and system cables subsystem—This subsystem includes all the network interfaces and the cables that connect the equipment to the network.

Table 3–7 outlines the areas where Catalyst 3000 series startup problems may occur and describes solutions to those problems.

Table 3–7   *Hardware: Catalyst 3000 Series Startup Problems and Solutions*

Possible Problem Area	Solution
Power and cooling subsystems	**Step 1** Check to see whether the Power LED is on. If it is not on and the fans are not running, check the AC power cord and the AC receptacle the cord is plugged in to. Make sure the cord is intact and properly attached. Swap the cord with another cord to see whether the cord is faulty. Make sure the receptacle is receiving power. **Step 2** If the Fault LED comes on after power up or after the unit has been running for a period of time, cycle the power to the unit. **Step 3** Check to see whether the fans are running and that the chassis intake vents and exhaust ports are clear. **Step 4** View the console to check whether a temperature error has been reported. If you continue to experience power problems, or if temperature errors are being reported to the console and you cannot isolate a specific cause and correct it, contact the Cisco TAC.[1]
Network interfaces and system cables subsystem	**Step 1** If a network interface is not recognized by the system, check the interface cable and connection and the LED that corresponds to the network interface. **Step 2** If a network interface is recognized but will not communicate properly, check the interface cable and connections. **Step 3** If the system will not boot properly or intermittently reboots, the processor may be faulty or the hardware or software setup may be incorrect. **Step 4** If the system boots but the console is frozen, check the external console connection and verify the console setup.

[1] TAC = Technical Assistance Center

Catalyst 2900 Series Startup

When you start up a Catalyst 2900 series LAN switch, the following should occur:

- The PS LED on the supervisor engine module faceplate should come on and stay green while power is applied to the system.

- The system fan assembly and Fan LED should come on and stay on while power is applied to the system.

- The Status LED on the supervisor engine module and on each interface should be orange until the boot is complete.

When the system boot is complete, the supervisor engine module initializes the switching modules. The status LED on each switching module goes on when initialization has been completed, and the console screen displays a script and system banner similar to the following:

```
BOOTROM Version 2.1, Dated May 22 1996 15:17:09

Boot date: 05/22/96 BOOT time: 15:17:09

Executing from RAM


Cisco Systems Console


Sending RARP request with address 00:40:0b:a0:05:b8

Sending bootp request with address 00:40:0b:a0:05:b8

Sending RARP request with address 00:40:0b:a0:05:b8

Sending bootp request with address 00:40:0b:a0:05:b8

No bootp or rarp response received

Enter password:
```

If problems occur, try to isolate the problem to a specific subsystem. The Catalyst 2900 series LAN switches have the following subsystems:

- Power subsystem—This subsystem includes the power supplies and power supply fans.

- Cooling subsystem—This subsystem includes the chassis fan assembly, which should be operating when the system power is on.

- Processor and interface subsystem—This subsystem includes the supervisor engine module (which contains the system operating software), the network interfaces, and all associated cabling.

Table 3–8 outlines the areas where Catalyst 2900 series startup problems may occur and describes solutions to those problems.

Table 3–8   *Hardware: Catalyst 2900 Series Startup Problems and Solutions*

Possible Problem Area	Solution	
Power subsystem	**Step 1**	Check the Power LED. If it is off, ensure that the power supply cord is not damaged and that it is properly attached to the power supply and to an AC receptacle.
	Step 2	If the LED is red, the power supply has detected an anomaly or voltage outage and needs to be serviced. Contact your technical support representative for instructions.
Cooling subsystem	**Step 1**	Check to see whether the Fan LED on the supervisor engine module is green. If it is not, check the power subsystem to see whether it is operational.
	Step 2	If the Fan LED is red, contact a technical support representative for assistance.
Series processor and interface subsystem	**Step 1**	Check the supervisor engine module Status and Link LEDs. These should both be green if all diagnostic and self-tests were successful and ports are operational. For more information about interpreting the supervisor engine module LEDs, refer to the user guide for your switch.
	Step 2	Check the LEDs on individual interface modules. In most cases these should be green (or should flicker green, in the case of transmit and receive LEDs) if the interface is functioning correctly. For detailed information on interpreting interface module LEDs, refer to the user guide for your switch.
	Step 3	Check all cabling and connections. Replace any faulty cabling.

Catalyst 1600 Token Ring Switch Startup

When you start up a Catalyst 1600 Token Ring switch, the self-test program automatically checks to see whether the switch is operating correctly. The self-test begins by testing low-level hardware functions and then conducts high-level self-tests. During the high-level self-test, the LCD panel displays the following:

- The version number of the boot software, and the date and time that the software was released
- The number of each stage in the self-test (these are usually displayed too quickly for the numbers to be visible)
- A "System Self Test PASSED" message indicating that the self-test is complete and the Catalyst 1600 has passed the test

Table 3–9 outlines possible Catalyst 1600 Token Ring switch startup problems and describes symptoms to those problems.

Table 3–9   *Hardware: Catalyst 1600 Token Ring Switch Startup Problems and Symptoms*

Possible Problem	Symptom
Low-level test failure	The startup process is halted.
High-level test failure	The self-test program restarts and the number of the failed test is displayed. High-level tests are repeated until the self-test is completed successfully.
Hardware error	Contact your technical support representative. Be sure to note the number of the failed test and the version number of the software containing the self-test program.

LightStream 2020 Startup

When you start up a LightStream 2020 ATM switch, the blowers start running and the test and control system (TCS) applies power to the cards and initiates a series of diagnostics known as the power-on self-test (POST). POST diagnostics run automatically on each card whenever the system or the slot is powered up or when the card is reset. If a card passes POST, the green RDY LED turns on. If a card fails POST, its yellow FLT LED turns on.

Table 3–10 outlines the possible LightStream 2020 problems and describes solutions to those problems.

Table 3–10   *Hardware: LightStream 2020 Startup Problems and Solutions*

Possible Problem	Solution
System initialization problem	**Step 1** Make sure power cords and data cables are firmly connected at both ends. **Step 2** Make sure all cards (front and back of the chassis) are firmly seated in the midplane and screwed securely to the chassis. **Step 3** Make sure power supplies, blowers, and disk drives are properly connected and screwed securely to the chassis.
Blower problem	If you are experiencing any of the following symptoms, you might need to replace the blower: • The temperature on one or more cards is out of the recommended range. • The system is powered on, but the blower is not turning, is making noise, or is exhausting air. • Two minutes after the system is powered on, the blower fails to reduce its speed in a room temperature environment. • The system is powered on, but the blower's green LED is off. The LED indicates that the blower is turning at a rate of at least 1500 rotations per minute.
Bulk power tray problems	In a system with one power tray, no power will be present if the power tray is faulty. There might be a problem with the power tray if cycling the system's power has no effect. A system with two power trays can operate normally when only one is working. If you suspect a problem, use the CLI[1] command **show chassis powersupply**. If a status line for an occupied slot says anything other than Good, check the faulty power tray to see that it is properly connected. Replace the power tray if necessary.

Table 3–10 *Hardware: LightStream 2020 Startup Problems and Solutions, Continued*

Possible Problem	Solution
Switch card problems	If you are experiencing any of the following symptoms, you might need to replace the switch card:
	• POST[2] fails (the FLT[3] LED stays lit and POST results indicate a problem).
	• The Switch card fails even when moved to the other slot. (If the card fails in one slot but operates properly in another, suspect a problem with the midplane.)
	• Diagnostics that loop data through the switch card fail on two or more function cards.
	• The Switch card fails to come up or to select a TCS[4] hub.
	• Traffic is not passing through the system, but the line cards and NPs[5] are operational.
	• The system has data transmission problems that do not go away when you replace the card that appears to be failing or that occur in several cards simultaneously. (Problems of this type may also indicate a faulty midplane.)
	• The switch card cannot be fully inserted into its slot. This probably indicates damage to the connectors on either the card or the midplane. Inspect all the connectors and replace the card or the midplane if you find damage.

Table 3–10 *Hardware: LightStream 2020 Startup Problems and Solutions, Continued*

Possible Problem	Solution
Network processor problems	If the NP fails to power up, check its access card at the back of the chassis. An NP requires an NPAC[6]; it cannot operate with any other kind of access card.
	If the system fails to boot, it could indicate either a problem with the NP, a problem with the NP's hard disk drive, or a problem with the software on the hard drive.
	If you are experiencing any of the following symptoms, you might need to replace the NP card:
	• POST fails (the FLT LED stays lit and the POST results indicate a problem).
	• The NP fails even when moved to the other slot. (If the card fails in one slot but operates properly in the other, suspect a problem with the midplane.)
	• Hardware diagnostics fail.
	• You cannot get to the CLI to run the diagnostics.
	• The card fails to load.
	• The NP or its access card cannot be fully inserted into its slot. This probably indicates damage to the connectors on either the card or the midplane. Inspect all the connectors and replace the card or the midplane if you find damage.

Table 3-10   *Hardware: LightStream 2020 Startup Problems and Solutions, Continued*

Possible Problem	Solution

Interface module problems	The following tips will help you distinguish between problems in a line card and problems in an access card:
	
	• Run the manufacturing diagnostics and check the information provided for the access card.
	
	• Swap another line card of the same type. If the second card has the same problem as the first one, the access card is probably at fault. If the second card works properly, the first line card is likely to be the source of the problem.
	
	• Faults in the line card are more common than faults in the access card. If you cannot determine which card is causing a problem, try replacing the line card.
	
	• Use the looping tests described in the *LightStream 2020 Network Operations Guide*.
	
	If you are having trouble bringing up an interface module, check the following:
	
	• Make sure the access card behind the line card is compatible with the line card.
	
	The low-speed line card (LSC) is compatible with the following access card:
	
	  ○ Low-speed access card (LSAC)
	
	The medium-speed line card (MSC) is compatible with the following access cards:
	
	  ○ T3 medium speed access card (T3 MSAC)
	
	  ○ E3 G.804 medium speed access card (E3 G.804 MSAC)
	
	  ○ E3 PLCP medium speed access card (E3 PLCP MSAC)
	
	The cell line card (CLC) is compatible with the following access cards:
	
	  ○ OC-3c single mode access card (OC3AC SM)—1 or 2 ports
	
	  ○ OC-3c multimode access card (OC3AC MM)—1 or 2 ports
	
	  ○ T3 access card (T3AC)—4 or 8 ports
	
	  ○ E3 access card (E3AC)—4 or 8 ports

Table 3–10   *Hardware: LightStream 2020 Startup Problems and Solutions, Continued*

Possible Problem	Solution
Interface module problems (*Continued*)	The packet line card is compatible with the following access cards: ○ FDDI access card ○ Ethernet access card ○ Fiber Ethernet access card ○ T1 circuit emulation access card ○ E1 circuit emulation access card The NP is compatible with the following access card: ○ NPAC • If an FDDI[7] module does not pass traffic, make sure the FDDI cables for each port are attached to the proper connectors. • If you are bringing up a low-speed module, make sure the interface jumpers on the access card are set to match the physical interfaces marked on the fantails (V.35, X.21 or RS-449). • If you are bringing up an E1 circuit emulation module, make sure the interface jumpers on the access card are set properly. If you are having signal quality problems with a physical interface on an access card, check the following: • Make sure that cables are within the specifications of your media type. • Make sure that connectors are not damaged. Check optical connectors for dirt or scratches on the optical surface. For electrical connectors, check that pins are not bent, broken, or loose.

Table 3–10 *Hardware: LightStream 2020 Startup Problems and Solutions, Continued*

Possible Problem	Solution
Interface module problems (*Continued*)	If you are experiencing any of the following symptoms, you might need to replace the line card or its access card: • POST fails (the FLT LED stays lit and the POST indicates a problem). • A card fails even when moved to another slot. (When you move a line card, be sure to pair it with an appropriate access card. When you move an access card, pair it with an appropriate line card.) • Hardware diagnostics fail. • The line card fails to load. • The line card hangs repeatedly. • The line card or access card cannot be fully inserted into its slot. This probably indicates damage to the connectors on either the card or the midplane. Inspect all the connectors and replace the card or the midplane if you find damage. • Two or more ports are passing no traffic, dropping many cells, or flapping. If only one port has symptoms, there is probably a problem with the line, the external DSU/CSU if one is present, the access card, or the remote device. Use the looping tests described in the *LightStream 2020 Network Operations Guide* to help isolate the problem.

Table 3–10 *Hardware: LightStream 2020 Startup Problems and Solutions, Continued*

Possible Problem	Solution
Disk assembly problems	Disk assembly problems are indicated by the following symptoms: • The node fails to boot. • Files become corrupted. • In a system with two NPs, the primary NP appears to fail and the backup takes over. The failed NP might pass diagnostics. • The system fails to read or write floppy disks. In the case of a write failure, check the write protect switch on the disk. If a disk problem is indicated, check the disk assembly connector for bent or broken pins. If any pins are bent or damaged, they are the likely source of the problem. Replace the disk assembly connector. If the connector is in good condition, the problem may be in the disk assembly itself, or in the software on the disk. If you suspect a problem with the software, you should be able to correct it by reinstalling the software as described in the *LightStream 2020 Network Operations Guide.*
Midplane problems	Midplane problems are indicated by the following symptoms: • A card fails in one slot but operates normally in other slots. • Data transmission problems do not go away when you replace the FRU[8] that appears to be failing, or problems occur in several FRUs simultaneously. (Problems of this type might also indicate a faulty switch card.) • Failure of a card to fully insert into its slot. This probably indicates damage to the connectors on either the card or the midplane. Inspect all the connectors and replace the card or the midplane if you find damage. • Electrical failure or electrical problems that do not go away when you replace the FRU that appears to be failing, or that occur in several FRUs simultaneously. Electrical problems include out-of-range voltages.

[1] CLI = command-line interface
[2] POST = power-on self-test
[3] FLT = fault
[4] TCS = test and control system
[5] NP = network processor
[6] NPAC = network processor access card
[7] FDDI = Fiber Distributed Data Interface
[8] FRU = field-replaceable unit

Testing and Verifying Replacement Parts

If you are replacing a part or card to remedy a suspected problem, make only one change at a time.

To test a system, start with a simple hardware configuration and add one card at a time until a failed interface appears or is isolated. Use a simple software configuration and test connectivity using a **ping** test.

If you determine that a part or card replacement is required, contact your sales or technical support representative. Specific instructions concerning part or card installation are outlined in the configuration note provided with the replacement.

For modular routers, make sure that you seat all cards correctly. Check the seating of cards if the system is not booting properly. Use the ejector levers to reseat all processor modules, and then reboot.

CAUTION

Before accessing the chassis interior and removing any cards, turn off power to the chassis. Use extreme caution around the chassis. Potentially harmful voltages are present.

CAUTION

To prevent damage to components that are sensitive to electrostatic discharge (ESD), attach ESD protection before opening a chassis. Make certain that the power cord is connected but that power is off. ESD damage prevention guidelines are provided in the hardware installation and maintenance publication for your router.

If a part replacement appears to solve a problem, reinstall the suspect part to verify the failure. *Always* double-check a repair.

TROUBLESHOOTING BOOTING PROBLEMS

This section discusses troubleshooting procedures for connectivity problems related to booting. It describes specific booting symptoms, the problems that are likely to cause each symptom, and the solutions to those problems.

Booting: Router Fails to Boot from Flash Memory

Symptom: When a user is booting a router from Flash memory, the boot process appears to complete, but the router does not route traffic or communicate with neighbors. exec commands might or might not appear to function.

Table 3–11 outlines the problems that might cause this symptom and describes solutions to those problems.

Table 3–11   *Booting: Router Fails to Boot from Flash Memory*

Possible Problem	Solution
Incorrect or corrupted image (exec does not function)	**Step 1** Check the configuration register using the **show version** exec command. Set the register to boot from Flash memory. For information about configuration register settings, refer to your hardware installation and maintenance documentation.
	Step 2 Power cycle the router.
	Step 3 Within the first 60 seconds of booting, press the Break key to access the ROM monitor.
	Step 4 At the ROM monitor prompt (>), enter **o/r 0x1** to set the configuration register to boot from ROM.
	Step 5 Enter **i** to reinitialize the router, which causes the router to enter setup mode.
	Step 6 Obtain the correct system image. If necessary, contact your technical support representative to determine which image is correct.
	Step 7 After the correct image is identified, use the **copy tftp flash** privileged exec command at the router to retrieve the image.
	Step 8 Check the configuration register using the **show version** exec command. Set the register to boot from Flash memory.
	Step 9 Use the **show running-config** privileged exec command to see whether the router configuration contains the **boot system flash** global configuration command.
	Note: Issuing the **copy running-config startup-config** command at this point on a Cisco 2500, Cisco 3000, Cisco 4000, or Cisco 7000 series will overwrite the configuration. Make sure you have a backup of your configuration file.

Table 3–11 *Booting: Router Fails to Boot from Flash Memory, Continued*

Possible Problem	Solution

Incorrect or corrupted image (exec does not function) (*Continued*)	**Step 10** Include the **boot system flash** command if it is not in the configuration. Be sure to use the **copy running-config startup-config** command after this change.
	
	Step 11 Enter the **reload** privileged exec command to restart the router.
	
	Syntax:
	
	The following is the syntax for the **reload** command:
	
	reload [text] | [in [hh:]mm [text]] | [at hh:mm [month day | day month] [text]] | [cancel]
	
	Examples:
	
	The following example illustrates how to use the **reload** command to immediately reload the software on the router:
	
	`Router# reload`
	
	The following example illustrates how to use the **reload** command to reload the software on the router in 10 minutes:
	
	`Router# reload in 10`
	`Router# Reload scheduled for 11:57:08 PDT Fri Apr 21 1996 (in 10 minutes)`
	`Proceed with reload? [confirm]`
	`Router#`

Table 3–11   *Booting: Router Fails to Boot from Flash Memory, Continued*

Possible Problem	Solution
Incorrect or corrupted image (exec functions)	**Step 1** Obtain the correct system image. If necessary, contact your technical support representative to determine which image is appropriate.
	Step 2 Use the **copy tftp flash** privileged exec command to retrieve the image.
	Step 3 Check the configuration register using the **show version** exec command. Set the register to boot from Flash memory. For information about configuration register settings, refer to your hardware installation and maintenance documentation.
	Step 4 Use the **show running-config** privileged exec command to determine whether the active configuration contains the **boot system flash** global configuration command. Use the **show startup-config** privileged exec command to determine whether the **boot system flash** command is included in the configuration stored in NVRAM.[1]
	Step 5 Include the **boot system flash** command if it is not in the configuration. Be sure to use the **copy running-config startup-config** privileged exec command to save your modification after this change.
	Step 6 Enter the **reload** privileged exec command to restart the router.
	Syntax:
	The following is the syntax for the **reload** command:
	reload [text] I [in [hh:]mm [text]] I [at hh:mm [month day I day month] [text]] I [cancel]
	Examples:
	The following example illustrates how to use the **reload** command to immediately reload the software on the router:
| | ```
Router# reload
``` |
```

Table 3–11 *Booting: Router Fails to Boot from Flash Memory, Continued*

Possible Problem	Solution

Incorrect or corrupted image (exec functions) (*Continued*)	The following example illustrates how to use the **reload** command to reload the software on the router in 10 minutes:
	
	`Router# reload in 10`
	`Router# Reload scheduled for 11:57:08 PDT Fri Apr`
	`21 1996 (in 10 minutes)`
	`Proceed with reload? [confirm]`
	`Router#`

[1] NVRAM = nonvolatile random-access memory

Booting: Vector Error Occurs When Booting from Flash Memory

Symptom: Vector errors occur when a user is booting a router from Flash memory.

Table 3–12 outlines the problems that might cause this symptom and describes solutions to those problems.

Table 3–12 *Booting: Vector Error Occurs When Booting from Flash Memory*

Possible Problem	Solution	
Compressed system image	**Step 1**	Power-cycle the router.
	Step 2	Within the first 60 seconds of booting, press the Break key to access the ROM monitor.
	Step 3	At the ROM monitor prompt (>), enter **o/r** to set the configuration register to boot from ROM.
	Step 4	Enter **b** to boot the router. The router enters setup mode.
	Step 5	Press **Ctrl-C** to bypass the setup.
	Step 6	Enter the **configure memory** privileged exec command.
	Step 7	Obtain an uncompressed system image. From the router prompt, use the privileged exec command **copy flash tftp** to send the compressed image back to the TFTP[1] server. Decompress the image at the TFTP server. This cannot be done at the router.
	Step 8	Use the **copy tftp flash** privileged exec command at the router to retrieve the uncompressed image. The following is an example of the use of the **copy tftp flash** command: **router# copy flash tftp** *filename*

Table 3–12   *Booting: Vector Error Occurs When Booting from Flash Memory, Continued*

Possible Problem	Solution

Compressed system image (*Continued*)	The router asks you for the IP address of the TFTP server and the name of the image file you are copying to the server. A sample of the output for this command using IP address *131.108.10.6* and filename *ic92130n* follows:
	
	```IP address of remote host [255.255.255.255]? 131.108.10.6```
	```Name of file to copy []? ic92130n```
	```writing ic92130n !!!```
	```router#```

	Step 9 Check the configuration register using the **show version** exec command. Set the router to boot from Flash memory.
	Step 10 Use the **show running-config** privileged exec command to determine whether the router configuration includes the **boot system flash** global configuration command in the correct order with respect to the other **boot system** commands. **Note:** The **boot system** global configuration commands are saved in the order in which they were entered. The most recent entry goes to the bottom of the list. For the recommended ordering, refer to the section "Fault-Tolerant Boot Strategies" earlier in this chapter.
	Step 11 Configure the **boot system flash** command if it is missing. Confirm that the order of **boot system** commands is correct. Use the **copy running-config startup-config** command to save this change. The required syntax is as follows: **copy running-config** {**rcp** | **startup-config** | **tftp** | *file-id*} (Cisco 7000, Cisco 7200, and Cisco 7500 series only) **Syntax Description:** • **rcp**—Specifies a copy operation to a network server using RCP. • **startup-config**—Specifies the configuration used for initialization as the destination of the copy operation. The Cisco 4500 series cannot use this keyword. • **tftp**—Specifies a TFTP server as the destination of the copy operation. • *file-id*—Specifies *device:filename* as the destination of the copy operation. The device argument is optional, but when it is used, the colon (:) is required.
	Step 12 Enter the **reload** privileged exec command to restart the router.

Table 3–12 *Booting: Vector Error Occurs When Booting from Flash Memory, Continued*

Possible Problem	Solution
Router hardware problem	Troubleshoot router hardware as discussed earlier in this chapter.

[1] TFTP = Trivial File Transfer Protocol

Booting: Router Partially Boots from Flash and Displays Boot Prompt

Symptom: When a user is booting a Cisco 2000, Cisco 2500, Cisco 3000, or Cisco 4000 series router from Flash memory, the boot process halts and the console displays the boot prompt [**router(boot)>**]. In addition, the router does not route, although exec commands might appear to be operational.

Table 3–13 outlines the problems that might cause this symptom and describes solutions to those problems.

Table 3–13 *Booting: Router Partially Boots from Flash and Displays Boot Prompt*

Possible Problem	Solution

No system image in Flash memory	**Step 1** Use the **show flash** exec command to determine whether an image exists in Flash memory.
	
	Step 2 If no image exists, use the **copy tftp flash** privileged exec command to copy the system image from your TFTP[1] server to the router's Flash memory.The following is an example of the use of the **copy tftp flash** command:
	
	router# copy flash tftp *filename*
	
	The router asks you for the IP address of the TFTP server and the name of the image file you are copying to the server. A sample of the output for this command using IP address *131.108.10.6* and filename *ic92130n* follows:
	
	`IP address of remote host [255.255.255.255]? 131.108.10.6`
	`Name of file to copy []? ic92130n`
	`writing ic92130n !!!!!!!!!!!!!!!!!!!!!!!!!!!!!!!!!!!!!!!!!!!!!!`
	`router#`

Table 3–13   *Booting: Router Partially Boots from Flash and Displays Boot Prompt, Continued*

Possible Problem	Solution

No system image in Flash memory (*Continued*)	**Step 3** Enter the **reload** privileged exec command to reboot the router.
	
	Syntax:
	
	The following is the syntax for the **reload** command:
	
	**reload [text]
		[in [hh:]mm [text]]	[at hh:mm [month day	day month] [text]]	[cancel]**
					
					Examples:
					
					The following example illustrates how to use the **reload** command to immediately reload the software on the router:
					
					`Router# `**`reload`**
					
					The following example illustrates how to use the **reload** command to reload the software on the router in 10 minutes:
					
					`Router# `**`reload in 10`**
					`Router# `**`Reload scheduled for 11:57:08 PDT Fri Apr 21 1996`**
					`(in 10 minutes)`
					`Proceed with reload? [confirm]`
					`Router#`

Table 3–13 *Booting: Router Partially Boots from Flash and Displays Boot Prompt, Continued*

Possible Problem	Solution
Missing **boot system flash** global configuration command	**Step 1** Use the **show running-config** privileged exec command to determine whether the configuration includes a **boot system flash** global configuration command entry. Use the **show startup-config** privileged exec command to determine whether the **boot system flash** command is included in the configuration stored in NVRAM[2].
	Step 2 Check the order of the **boot system** commands. For the recommended ordering, refer to the section "Fault-Tolerant Boot Strategies" earlier in this chapter.
	Step 3 Add the **boot system flash** command or reorder the **boot system** commands if necessary.
	Step 4 Save the configuration change to NVRAM using the **copy running-config startup-config** privileged exec command. The required syntax is as follows: **copy running-config** {**rcp** | **startup-config** | **tftp** | *file-id*} (Cisco 7000, Cisco 7200, and Cisco 7500 series only) **Syntax Description:** • **rcp**—Specifies a copy operation to a network server using RCP. • **startup-config**—Specifies the configuration used for initialization as the destination of the copy operation. The Cisco 4500 series cannot use this keyword. • **tftp**—Specifies a TFTP server as the destination of the copy operation. • *file-id*—Specifies a *device:filename* as the destination of the copy operation. The device argument is optional; but when it is used, the colon (:) is required.
Misconfigured configuration register	Use the **show version** exec command to check the configuration register setting. Make sure it is set to boot from Flash memory. Refer to your hardware installation and maintenance publication for details regarding configuration register settings.

[1] TFTP = Trivial File Transfer Protocol
[2] NVRAM = nonvolatile random-access memory

Booting: Router Cannot Netboot from TFTP Server

Symptom: Router cannot boot from a TFTP server. The router tries to obtain its system image over the network but fails.

The following output is an example of a failed netboot session:

```
Booting gs3-bfx..........[failed]
```

Table 3–14 outlines the problems that might cause this symptom and describes solutions to those problems.

NOTES

More specific symptoms related to TFTP servers and netbooting are described later in this chapter.

Table 3–14   *Booting: Router Cannot Netboot from TFTP Server*

Possible Problem	Solution
Network is disconnected or isolated	**Step 1** Boot the router from ROM or Flash memory if possible.
	Step 2 Use the **ping** exec command to send a message to the broadcast address (*255.255.255.255*).
	Step 3 If there is no response from the server, use the **show arp** exec command to look for an entry in the ARP table that is associated with the server.
	Step 4 Use the **show ip route** exec command to view the IP routing table. Look for an entry in the table for the network or subnet of the server.
	Sample Display:
	The following is sample output from the **show ip route** command when entered without an address:

	<pre>Router# **show ip route**
	Codes: I - IGRP derived, R - RIP derived, O - OSPF derived
	       C - connected, S - static, E - EGP derived, B - BGP derived
	       * - candidate default route, IA - OSPF inter area route
	       E1 - OSPF external type 1 route, E2 - OSPF external type 2 route
	Gateway of last resort is 131.119.254.240 to network 129.140.0.0
	O E2 150.150.0.0 [160/5] via 131.119.254.6, 0:01:00, Ethernet2
	E 192.67.131.0 [200/128] via 131.119.254.244, 0:02:22, Ethernet2
	O E2 192.68.132.0 [160/5] via 131.119.254.6, 0:00:59, Ethernet2
	O E2 130.130.0.0 [160/5] via 131.119.254.6, 0:00:59, Ethernet2
	E 128.128.0.0 [200/128] via 131.119.254.244, 0:02:22, Ethernet2
	E 129.129.0.0 [200/129] via 131.119.254.240, 0:02:22, Ethernet2
	E 192.65.129.0 [200/128] via 131.119.254.244, 0:02:22, Ethernet2</pre>

	If a path to a boot server exists, a disconnected network is not the problem. If no path exists, make sure that a path is available before again attempting to netboot.

Table 3–14 *Booting: Router Cannot Netboot from TFTP Server, Continued*

Possible Problem	Solution	
TFTP server is down	**Step 1**	Check the TFTP server to determine whether it is up and running. You can do this by attempting to make a TFTP connection from the boot server to itself. The connection will be successful if the TFTP server is running.
	Step 2	If the TFTP server is not running, initialize it. The initialization process will vary depending on the type of boot server.
		For a BSD UNIX server, check the */etc/inetd.conf* file. If the TFTP server is not included in this file, add the appropriate line and cause inetd to reload its configuration.
Router image in wrong directory	**Step 1**	Look at the server configuration file to see whether it points to the directory in which the router image is located.
	Step 2	Move the router image to the correct directory if necessary.
	Step 3	Make sure the */tftpboot* directory is reachable over the network.
Router system image file permissions are incorrect	**Step 1**	Check the permissions of the system image file.
	Step 2	If necessary, change the permissions for the file. On a UNIX boot server, set the permissions for the file to owner read/write, group read, and global read (the UNIX command for setting these permissions is **chmod 644** *filename*).
Bad protocol address	**Step 1**	Check the server configuration file to make sure the IP address of the host is correct.
	Step 2	Change the configuration if it is incorrect.

Table 3–14   *Booting: Router Cannot Netboot from TFTP Server, Continued*

Possible Problem	Solution	
Missing or misconfigured default gateway specification	Step 1	Use the **show running-config** privileged exec command to view the router configuration. Check for the **ip default-gateway** global configuration command, which defines a default gateway.
		Syntax:
		ip default-gateway *ip-address*
		Syntax Description:
		• *ip-address*—IP address of the router.
	Step 2	If the command is missing, add it to the configuration. If the command is present, make sure it specifies the correct IP address.
Misconfigured **boot system** command	Step 1	Use the **show running-config** privileged exec command to view the router configuration. Check the boot server address (IP address of a TFTP server or MAC[1] address of a MOP[2] server) that is configured on the router.
	Step 2	If the address is specified incorrectly, specify the correct boot server address using the **boot system** global configuration command.
Wrong filename is specified	Step 1	Use the **show running-config** privileged exec command to view the router configuration. Check the boot filename that is configured on the router.
	Step 2	Make sure the filename is specified correctly. Change the filename if necessary. Check the host documentation for details about setting the name of the system image on the TFTP server.
	Step 3	Some versions of the ROM are case sensitive. Try changing the case of the filename. Contact your technical support representative for more information.

Table 3–14   *Booting: Router Cannot Netboot from TFTP Server, Continued*

Possible Problem	Solution
Incorrect configuratio n register setting	To netboot from a server, you must set the configuration register properly. The specific configuration for netbooting depends on the platform that is being booted. **Step 1** Check the configuration register setting for your system. **Step 2** Determine whether you want to manually or automatically netboot from a TFTP server. To manually netboot, the configuration register must be set to **0x0**; otherwise, you will be netbooting using the default system image name or the image specified by the **boot system** global configuration command. Refer to the Cisco IOS configuration guides and command references and your hardware installation and maintenance publications for more details about setting the configuration register.

[1] MAC = Media Access Control
[2] MOP = Maintenance Operation Protocol

Booting: Router Cannot Netboot from Another Router

Symptom: A router cannot boot properly when a user is booting from another router that is acting as a TFTP server.

NOTES

This symptom can be caused by any of the problems outlined in the sections on netbooting in this chapter. This section focuses on problems with the router that is acting as a TFTP server.

Table 3–15 outlines the problems that might cause this symptom and describes solutions to those problems.

Table 3–15   *Booting: Router Cannot Netboot from Another Router*

Possible Problem	Solution
Missing or incorrect **tftp-server** global configuration command	**Step 1** Use the **show running-config** privileged exec command to determine whether the **tftp-server system** global configuration command is missing or incorrectly specified. **Step 2** Add or modify the **tftp-server system** global configuration command as necessary on the router acting as the TFTP server. Specify the name of a file in Flash memory.
| Incomplete image in Flash memory | Use the **show flash** exec command to determine whether the image is incomplete. This display might show that the image is deleted and indicate the reason. <br><br> Following is an example of **show flash** output indicating that the image is deleted: <br><br> ```
babar# show flash
2048K bytes of flash memory sized on embedded flash.
File  name/status
0  xx-k.914-0.16
 1  xx3-confg
 2  xx-k.91-4.2 [deleted] [invalid cksum]
[0/2097152 bytes free/total]
``` |
```

Table 3–15 *Booting: Router Cannot Netboot from Another Router, Continued*

Possible Problem	Solution	

Incorrect image in Flash memory	**Step 1**	A "wrong system software" message is displayed when a router attempts to boot an incorrect image. In this case, the router is being booted from the ROM monitor.
		
		Following is an example of the ROM monitor output after an attempt to boot an incorrect image:
		
		`> b gs3-klingon 131.108.9.40`
		
		`Booting gs3-klingon from 131.108.9.40:!!!!!!!!!!!!!!!!!!!!!!!!`
		`!!!!!!!!!!!!!!!!!!!!!!!!!!!!!!!!!!!!!!!!!!!!!!!!O!!!!!!!!!!!!!!`
		`!!!!!!!!!!!!!!!!!!!!!!!!!!!!!!!!!!!!!!!!!!!!!!!!!!!!!!!!!!!!!!!`
		`!!!!!!!!!!!!!!!!!!!!!!!!!!!!!!!!!!!!!!!!!!!!!!!!!!!!!!!!!!!!!!!`
		`!!!!!!!!!!!!!!!!!!!!!!!!!!!!!!!!!!!!!!!!!.!!!!!!!!!!!!!!!!!!!!!`
		`!!!!!!!!!!!!!!!!!!!!!!!!!!!!!!!!!!!!!!!!!!!!!!!!!!!!!!!!!!!!!!!`
		`!!!!!!!!!!!!!!!!!!!!!!!!!!!!!!!!!!!!!!!!!!!!!!!!!!!!!!!!!!!!!!!`
		`!!!!!!!!!!!!!!!!!!!!!!!!!![OK - 2056792/3394950 bytes]`
		`F3: 2011628+45132+192972 at 0x1000`
		
		`Wrong system software for this hardware`

	Step 2	Obtain the correct image. If necessary, contact your technical support representative to determine which image is correct.
	Step 3	When you identify the correct image, use the **copy tftp flash** privileged exec command to retrieve the image.

Booting: Timeouts and Out-of-Order Packets Prevent Netbooting

Symptom: Timeouts or out-of-order packets prevent successful netbooting. The number of timeouts and out-of-order packets indicated on the router's console display might vary.

The following example shows a netbooting session that contains excessive timeouts and out-of-order packets:

```
Booting gs3-bfx from 131.108.1.123: !O.O!.O..O!!!OOO.O!!.O.O.....
```

The client router might boot in this situation. However, when excessive timeouts and out-of-order packets occur, there is probably a network problem, and netbooting (as well as network service availability) might be inconsistent.

Table 3–16 outlines the problems that might cause this symptom and describes solutions to those problems.

Table 3–16 *Booting: Timeouts and Out-of-Order Packets Prevent Netbooting*

Possible Problem	Solution	
Link is saturated	**Step 1**	Boot the router from ROM and **ping** the TFTP server. Determine whether timeouts and out-of-order packets appear.
	Step 2	Check local network concentrators for excessive collisions on the same network. If there are excessive collisions, reorganizing your network topology might help reduce collisions.
	Step 3	Use the **show interfaces** exec command on routers in the path or place a network analyzer between the router and server. Look for dropped packets and output errors.
	Step 4	If approximately 15% or more of the traffic is being dropped, or if any output errors occur, congestion might be the problem.
	Step 5	Wait until the traffic subsides before attempting to netboot the router. If the problem is chronic, increase bandwidth or move the server closer to the router being booted.
Link is down	**Step 1**	Check the continuity of the path from the booting router to the boot server using **ping** or **trace** exec commands.
	Step 2	If a break is found, restore the link and attempt to netboot again.

Booting: Invalid Routes Prevent Netbooting

Symptom: Invalid routes prevent successful netbooting. If the router is sending packets over an invalid path, a message similar to one of the following is displayed on the console:

```
Booting gs3-bfx!0000.........[timed out]

Booting gs3-bfx!.0.0.0.0.........[timed out]

Booting gs3-bfx!!!!!!!!!!!0000000000.........[timed out]
```

In some cases, there might be an initial response from a server but the netboot sequence still fails. The boot message would be similar to the following:

```
Booting gs3-bfx!.........[failed]
```

Table 3–17 outlines the problems that might cause this symptom and describes solutions to those problems.

Table 3–17   *Booting: Invalid Routes Prevent Netbooting*

Possible Problem	Solution	
Bad routing paths on neighbor routers	**Step 1**	Verify that neighbor routers can **ping** the server.
	Step 2	Use the **trace** exec command to determine the path to the server.
	Step 3	Use the **show arp** privileged exec command to examine the ARP[1] tables or the **show ip route** privileged exec command to view the IP routing table. Verify that the server is listed and that the routing table entries are appropriate.
	Step 4	Use the **clear arp-cache** and **clear ip-route** privileged exec commands to force the router to repopulate its ARP and routing tables.
	Step 5	Try to netboot the router again.
Problems caused by multiple paths	**Step 1**	Shut down all extra interfaces except the one over which you intend to netboot the router.
	Step 2	Use the **no ip proxy-arp** interface configuration command on all neighboring routers to disable their ability to provide proxy ARP responses. Make this change with care because it can cause problems for other network traffic. If you do not want to disable proxy ARP, boot the router from ROM and configure the **ip default-gateway** global configuration command.
	Step 3	Try to netboot the router again.

[1] ARP = Address Resolution Protocol

Booting: Client ARP Requests Timeout During Netboot

Symptom: Client ARP requests timeout during a netboot. If the router does not receive an ARP response, a message similar to the following is displayed on the console:

```
Booting gs3-bfx..........[timed out]
```

Table 3–18 outlines the problems that might cause this symptom and describes solutions to those problems.

Table 3–18 *Booting: Client ARP Requests Timeout During Netboot*

Possible Problem	Solution	
Intermediate routers have ARP filtering enabled	**Step 1**	Boot the router from ROM.
	Step 2	Make sure you can **ping** the server from the router.
	Step 3	Use the **copy running-config tftp** privileged exec command to test TFTP connectivity to the server.
	Step 4	If the preceding steps are successful, check the configuration at the intermediate router using the **show arp** exec command.
	Step 5	Enable the **debug arp** privileged exec command to determine whether neighbor proxy ARP responses are being generated.
		Caution: Because debugging output is assigned high priority in the CPU process, it can render the system unusable. For this reason, use **debug** commands only to troubleshoot specific problems or during troubleshooting sessions with Cisco technical support staff. Moreover, it is best to use **debug** commands during periods of lower network traffic and fewer users. Debugging during these periods decreases the likelihood that increased **debug** command processing overhead will affect system use.
	Step 6	If the neighbor is not sending proxy ARP responses and its configuration contains the **no ip proxy-arp** interface configuration command, disable ARP filtering by removing the entry.
		Note that proxy ARP is enabled by default.
	Step 7	If you need to have a **no ip proxy-arp** entry in the neighbor router configurations, use the **ip default-gateway** global configuration command on the router to specify a default gateway.

Table 3–18 *Booting: Client ARP Requests Timeout During Netboot, Continued*

Possible Problem	Solution
Missing or misconfigured IP helper address on intermediate router	**Step 1** Check the configurations of all routers in the path. Make sure that all intermediate routers have an IP helper address specified that points to the TFTP server. **Syntax:** **ip helper-address** *address* **Syntax Description:** • *address*—Destination broadcast or host address to be used when forwarding UDP[1] broadcasts. You can have more than one helper address per interface. **Step 2** Include helper addresses as required using the **ip helper-address** interface configuration command. If you are unicasting to your server, you do not need to use the IP helper address, but if you are broadcasting to 255.255.255.255 (by omitting the IP address of the server), add the **ip helper-address** command on the *neighboring* router interface used in the netbooting broadcast.

[1] UDP = User Datagram Protocol

Booting: Undefined Load Module Error When Netbooting

Symptom: An undefined load module error occurs during a netboot. The console display indicates an "undefined load module" error, and the router is unable to boot.

Table 3–19 outlines the problem that might cause this symptom and describes solutions to that problem.

Table 3–19   *Booting: Undefined Load Module Error When Netbooting*

Possible Problem	Solution	
Filename mismatch	**Step 1**	If you are booting manually, refer to the user guide for your router to see the proper command-line format.
	Step 2	Check the router configuration file. Compare the filename specified in the **boot system** *filename* [*address*] global configuration command entry with the actual router image filename. Make sure they match.
	Step 3	If the filenames differ, change the name in the configuration file.
		Remember to use the router image filename in the **boot system** global configuration command specification and the configuration filename with the **boot host** and **boot network** global configuration commands.

Booting: Router Hangs After ROM Monitor Initializes

Symptom: When a user is booting a Cisco 7000 series, AGS+, AGS, ASM-CS, MGS, IGS, or CGS router from ROM, the system hangs after the ROM monitor initializes.

Table 3–20 outlines the problems that might cause this symptom and describes solutions to those problems.

Table 3–20   *Booting: Router Hangs After ROM Monitor Initializes*

Possible Problem	Solution	
Incorrect EPROM[1] size setting	**Step 1**	Power down the system.
	Step 2	Inspect EPROM size jumpers. Refer to the hardware installation and maintenance publication for your router to determine the proper setting.
	Step 3	Move jumpers as required.

Table 3–20 *Booting: Router Hangs After ROM Monitor Initializes, Continued*

Possible Problem	Solution
Configuration register is not set correctly	**Step 1** Check your configuration settings (boot ROM jumpers and software configuration). If no jumper is set at bit 0, and no other boot field is defined, you must reconfigure your system so that it can boot properly.
	Step 2 To enable your router to boot properly, do one of the following:
	• Configure the software configuration register of the router using the **config-register** *value* global configuration command. (This applies to the IGS, Cisco 2500, Cisco 3000, and Cisco 7000 platforms running Cisco IOS Release 10.0 or later in the EPROM.)
	• Set the boot ROM jumper to permit booting.
	• Include the correct **boot system** global configuration commands to boot the system.
	• Set bit 0 to a value of 1 to force booting from ROM.
	Refer to the Cisco IOS configuration guides and command references, as well as your hardware installation and maintenance publications, for more information about configuring your router for the various booting options.

[1] EPROM = erasable programmable read-only memory

Booting: Router Is Stuck in ROM Monitor Mode

Symptom: Router is stuck in ROM monitor mode. When a user is booting a router from ROM, the system boots into ROM monitor mode but does not boot the complete system image.

Table 3–21 outlines the problems that might cause this symptom and describes solutions to those problems.

Table 3–21   *Booting: Router Is Stuck in ROM Monitor Mode*

Possible Problem	Solution	
Incorrect configuration register setting	**Step 1**	At the ROM monitor prompt (>), enter **b** to boot the system.
	Step 2	If a configuration exists in NVRAM, the system displays the vacant message. Press the Enter key to continue.
		If a configuration does not exist in NVRAM, the setup menu appears. Skip the setup process.
	Step 3	Use the **show version** exec command to determine the configuration register setting.
	Step 4	Look for an invalid configuration register setting. The default is **0x101**, which disables the Break key and forces the router to boot from ROM. A typical "bad" setting has a 0 in the least significant bit (for example **0x100**).
		For details about setting the configuration register, refer to your hardware installation and maintenance publication.
Break key pressed during boot process	At the ROM monitor prompt, enter **c** to allow the router to continue booting.	
Console cable inserted or removed during boot process, or console power-cycled during boot process	**Step 1**	Press the Enter key and wait for the ROM monitor prompt (>).
	Step 2	If the ROM monitor prompt appears, enter **c** at the prompt to continue the booting process.

Booting: Scrambled Output When Booting from ROM

Symptom: When a user is booting from ROM, the router displays indecipherable text output on the console.

Table 3–22 outlines the problems that might cause this symptom and describes solutions to those problems.

Table 3–22 *Booting: Scrambled Output When Booting from ROM*

Possible Problem	Solution	
Wrong terminal speed setting	**Step 1**	Use the monitor setup menu to check the terminal line speed setting for the monitor.
	Step 2	Check the terminal speed configured on the router as specified in the configuration register setting (default is 9600 baud, 8 databits, 2 stop bits, and no parity).
	Step 3	If the terminal speed of the monitor and the router do not match, modify as necessary.
		Refer to your hardware installation and maintenance documentation for details about setting up the monitor.
Router hardware problem	Check all hardware for damage, including cabling (broken wire), adapters (loose pin), router ports, and so forth. For more information, refer to the hardware troubleshooting information discussed earlier in this chapter.	

Booting: Local Timeouts Occur When Booting from ROM

Symptom: "Local timeout" error messages are generated when a user is booting from ROM. The router is unable to complete its boot process and will not start the ROM monitor.

Table 3–23 outlines the problem that might cause this symptom and describes solutions to that problem.

Table 3–23 *Booting: Local Timeouts Occur When Booting from ROM*

Possible Problem	Solution	
EPROM problem	Generally, this problem occurs only if you have just replaced your system EPROMs.	
	Step 1	Power down the system.
	Step 2	Inspect each EPROM. Make sure each EPROM is correctly positioned in the socket (with notches properly aligned) in the correct socket.
	Step 3	If a pin is bent, straighten it carefully. Reinstall the EPROM and power up the system. If a pin breaks off, the EPROM must be replaced.
	Step 4	If an EPROM has been installed backward and power has been applied to it, the EPROM has been damaged and must be replaced.
	Step 5	If local timeouts persist, contact your technical support representative.

Booting: Unresponsive Terminal Connection to Unconfigured Access Server

Symptom: A terminal connected to an unconfigured access server is unresponsive. The terminal, attached to the console port of an unconfigured Cisco access server, displays bootup banners and begins the Setup routine, but the user cannot input commands from the terminal keyboard.

Table 3–24 outlines the problems that might cause this symptom and describes solutions to those problems.

Table 3–24   *Booting: Unresponsive Terminal Connection to Unconfigured Access Server*

Possible Problem	Solution
Flow control configured on the terminal conflicts with the EIA/TIA-232 control signals supported by the access server console port (RJ-45 to DB-25)	**Step 1** Check whether flow control is configured on your terminal. **Step 2** Disable all flow control on the terminal. With flow control enabled, the terminal will wait indefinitely for a CTS[1] signal because the RJ-45 console port on the access server does not assert CTS. For information on how to check for and disable flow control on your specific terminal, consult the documentation provided by your terminal manufacturer. **Step 3** Alternatively, you can "strap," or short, CTS high by providing the proper voltage on the CTS signal lead to make the signal active. Find an unused signal that is known to be active and strap CTS to it. The terminal sees CTS being asserted (indicating that the access server is ready to receive data) and allows input to be entered. **Step 4** On an already configured access server, another solution is to connect your terminal to the auxiliary port of the access server. The auxiliary port, unlike the console port, asserts CTS, and the terminal will therefore allow input. However, on a new access server with no configuration, this is *not* an alternative because the bootup banners and Setup routine are seen only on the console port.
Hardware problem	**Step 1** Check all hardware—including cabling (broken wires), adapters (loose pins), access server ports, and the terminal itself—for damage. **Step 2** Replace any hardware that is damaged or excessively worn. For more information, refer to the hardware troubleshooting information earlier in this chapter.

[1] CTS = clear-to-send

## CHAPTER 4.

Troubleshooting Ethernet

Ethernet was developed by Xerox Corporation's Palo Alto Research Center (PARC) in the 1970s. Ethernet was the technological basis for the IEEE 802.3 specification, which was initially released in 1980. Shortly thereafter, Digital Equipment Corporation, Intel Corporation, and Xerox Corporation jointly developed and released an Ethernet specification (Version 2.0) that is substantially compatible with IEEE 802.3. Together, Ethernet and IEEE 802.3 currently maintain the greatest market share of any local-area network (LAN) protocol. Today, the term *Ethernet* is often used to refer to all carrier sense multiple access collision detect (CSMA/CD) LANs that generally conform to Ethernet specifications, including IEEE 802.3.

When it was developed, Ethernet was designed to fill the middle ground between long-distance, low-speed networks and specialized, computer-room networks carrying data at high speeds for very limited distances. Ethernet is well suited to applications where a local communication medium must carry sporadic, occasionally heavy traffic at high peak data rates.

ETHERNET AND IEEE 802.3

Ethernet and IEEE 802.3 specify similar technologies. Both are CSMA/CD LANs. Stations on a CSMA/CD LAN can access the network at any time. Before sending data, CSMA/CD stations "listen" to the network to see if it is already in use. If it is, the station wishing to transmit waits. If the network is not in use, the station transmits. A collision occurs when two stations listen for network traffic, "hear" none, and transmit simultaneously. In this case, both transmissions are damaged, and the stations must retransmit at some later time. Backoff algorithms determine when the colliding stations retransmit. CSMA/CD stations can detect collisions, so they know when they must retransmit.

Both Ethernet and IEEE 802.3 LANs are broadcast networks. In other words, all stations see all frames, regardless of whether they represent an intended destination. Each station must examine received frames to determine whether the station is a destination. If it is a destination, the frame is passed to a higher protocol layer for appropriate processing.

75

Differences between Ethernet and IEEE 802.3 LANs are subtle. Ethernet provides services corresponding to Layers 1 and 2 of the OSI reference model, whereas IEEE 802.3 specifies the physical layer (Layer 1) and the channel-access portion of the link layer (Layer 2), but does not define a logical link control protocol. Both Ethernet and IEEE 802.3 are implemented in hardware. Typically, the physical manifestation of these protocols is either an interface card in a host computer or circuitry on a primary circuit board within a host computer.

Physical Connections

IEEE 802.3 specifies several different physical layers, whereas Ethernet defines only one. Each IEEE 802.3 physical layer protocol has a name that summarizes its characteristics. The coded components of an IEEE 802.3 physical-layer name are shown in Figure 4–1.

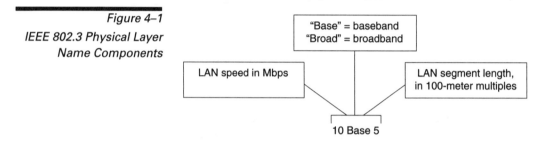

Figure 4–1

IEEE 802.3 Physical Layer Name Components

A summary of Ethernet Version 2 and IEEE 802.3 characteristics appears in Table 4–1.

Table 4–1   *Ethernet Version 2 and IEEE 802.3 Physical Characteristics*

Characteristic	Ethernet Value	IEEE 802.3 Values				
		10Base5	10Base2	1Base5	10BaseT	10Broad36
Data rate (Mbps)	10	10	10	1	10	10
Signaling method	Baseband	Baseband	Baseband	Baseband	Baseband	Broadband
Maximum segment length (m)	500	500	185	250	100	1800
Media	50-ohm coax (thick)	50-ohm coax (thick)	50-ohm coax (thin)	Unshielded twisted-pair wire	Unshielded twisted-pair wire	75-ohm coax
Topology	Bus	Bus	Bus	Star	Star	Bus

Ethernet is most similar to IEEE 802.3 10Base5. Both of these protocols specify a bus topology network with a connecting cable between the end stations and the actual network medium. In the case of Ethernet, that cable is called a transceiver cable. The *transceiver cable* connects to a transceiver device attached to the physical network medium. The IEEE 802.3 configuration is much the same, except that the connecting cable is referred to as an *attachment unit interface* (AUI), and the transceiver is called a *media attachment unit* (MAU). In both cases, the connecting cable attaches to an interface board (or interface circuitry) within the end station.

Frame Formats

Ethernet and IEEE 802.3 frame formats are shown in Figure 4–2.

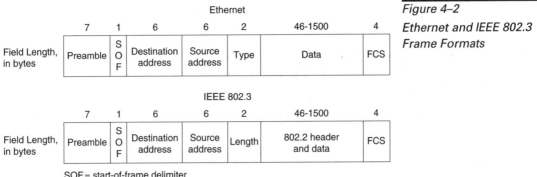

Figure 4–2

Ethernet and IEEE 802.3 Frame Formats

Both Ethernet and IEEE 802.3 frames begin with an alternating pattern of ones and zeros called a *preamble*. The preamble tells receiving stations that a frame is coming.

The byte before the destination address in both an Ethernet and an IEEE 802.3 frame is a start-of-frame (SOF) delimiter. This byte ends with two consecutive one bits, which serve to synchronize the frame reception portions of all stations on the LAN.

Immediately following the preamble in both Ethernet and IEEE 802.3 LANs are the destination and source address fields. Both Ethernet and IEEE 802.3 addresses are 6 bytes long. Addresses are contained in hardware on the Ethernet and IEEE 802.3 interface cards. The first three bytes of the addresses are specified by the IEEE on a vendor-dependent basis, and the last three bytes are specified by the Ethernet or IEEE 802.3 vendor. The source address is always a unicast (single node) address, whereas the destination address may be unicast, multicast (group), or broadcast (all nodes).

In Ethernet frames, the 2-byte field following the source address is a type field. This field specifies the upper-layer protocol to receive the data after Ethernet processing is complete.

In IEEE 802.3 frames, the 2-byte field following the source address is a length field, which indicates the number of bytes of data that follow this field and precede the frame check sequence (FCS) field.

Following the type/length field is the actual data contained in the frame. After physical-layer and link-layer processing are complete, this data will eventually be sent to an upper-layer protocol. In the case of Ethernet, the upper-layer protocol is identified in the type field. In the case of IEEE 802.3, the upper-layer protocol must be defined within the data portion of the frame, if at all. If data in the frame is insufficient to fill the frame to its minimum 64-byte size, padding bytes are inserted to ensure at least a 64-byte frame.

After the data field is a 4-byte FCS field containing a cyclic redundancy check (CRC) value. The CRC is created by the sending device and recalculated by the receiving device to check for damage that might have occurred to the frame in transit.

TROUBLESHOOTING ETHERNET

Table 4–2 provides troubleshooting procedures for common Ethernet media problems.

Table 4–2   *Troubleshooting Procedures for Common Ethernet Media Problems*

Media Problem	Suggested Actions	
Excessive noise	**Step 1**	Use the **show interfaces ethernet** exec command to determine the status of the router's Ethernet interfaces. The presence of many CRC errors but not many collisions is an indication of excessive noise.
	Step 2	Check cables to determine whether any are damaged.
	Step 3	Look for badly spaced taps causing reflections.
	Step 4	If you are using 100BaseTX, make sure you are using Category 5 cabling and not another type, such as Category 3.
Excessive collisions	**Step 1**	Use the **show interfaces ethernet** command to check the rate of collisions. The total number of collisions with respect to the total number of output packets should be around 0.1 percent or less.
	Step 2	Use a TDR to find any unterminated Ethernet cables.
	Step 3	Look for a jabbering transceiver attached to a host. (This might require host-by-host inspection or the use of a protocol analyzer.)

Table 4–2 *Troubleshooting Procedures for Common Ethernet Media Problems, Continued*

Media Problem	Suggested Actions
Excessive runt frames	In a shared Ethernet environment, runt frames are almost always caused by collisions. If the collision rate is high, refer to the problem "Excessive collisions" earlier in this table.
	If runt frames occur when collisions are not high or in a switched Ethernet environment, then they are the result of underruns or bad software on a network interface card.
	Use a protocol analyzer to try to determine the source address of the runt frames.
Late collisions[1]	**Step 1** Use a protocol analyzer to check for late collisions. Late collisions should never occur in a properly designed Ethernet network. They usually occur when Ethernet cables are too long or when there are too many repeaters in the network.
	Step 2 Check the diameter of the network and make sure it is within specification.
No link integrity on 10BaseT, 100BaseT4, or 100BaseTX	**Step 1** Make sure you are not using 100BaseT4 when only two pairs of wire are available. 100BaseT4 requires four pairs.
	Step 2 Check for 10BaseT, 100BaseT4, or 100BaseTX mismatch (for example, a card different from the port on a hub).
	Step 3 Determine whether there is cross-connect (for example, be sure straight-through cables are not being used between a station and the hub).
	Step 4 Check for excessive noise (see the problem "Excessive noise" earlier in this table).

[1] A late collision is a collision that occurs beyond the first 64 bytes of an Ethernet frame.

When you're troubleshooting Ethernet media in a Cisco router environment, the **show interfaces ethernet** command provides several key fields of information that can assist with isolating problems. The following section provides a detailed description of the **show interfaces ethernet** command and the information it provides.

show interfaces ethernet

Use the **show interfaces ethernet privileged** exec command to display information about an Ethernet interface on the router:

> show interfaces ethernet unit [accounting]
> show interfaces ethernet [*slot | port*] [accounting] (for the Cisco 7200 series and Cisco 7500)
> show interfaces ethernet [*type slot | port-adapter | port*] (for ports on VIP cards in the Cisco 7500 series routers)

Syntax Description

- *unit*—Must match a port number on the selected interface.

- **accounting**—(Optional) Displays the number of packets of each protocol type that have been sent through the interface.

- *slot*—Refer to the appropriate hardware manual for slot and port information.

- *port*—Refer to the appropriate hardware manual for slot and port information.

- *port-adapter*—Refer to the appropriate hardware manual for information about port adapter compatibility.

Command Mode

Privileged exec

Usage Guidelines

This command first appeared in Cisco IOS Release 10.0. If you do not provide values for the argument *unit* (or *slot* and *port* on the Cisco 7200 series or *slot* and *port-adapter* on the Cisco 7500 series), the command will display statistics for all network interfaces. The optional keyword **accounting** displays the number of packets of each protocol type that have been sent through the interface.

Sample Display

The following is sample output from the **show interfaces** command for the Ethernet 0 interface:

```
Router# show interfaces ethernet 0
Ethernet 0 is up, line protocol is up
    Hardware is MCI Ethernet, address is aa00.0400.0134 (via 0000.0c00.4369)
        Internet address is 131.108.1.1, subnet mask is 255.255.255.0
        MTU 1500 bytes, BW 10000 Kbit, DLY 1000 usec, rely 255/255, load 1/255
        Encapsulation ARPA, loopback not set, keepalive set (10 sec)
            ARP type: ARPA, PROBE, ARP Timeout 4:00:00
        Last input 0:00:00, output 0:00:00, output hang never
        Output queue 0/40, 0 drops; input queue 0/75, 2 drops
        Five minute input rate 61000 bits/sec, 4 packets/sec
        Five minute output rate 1000 bits/sec, 2 packets/sec
    2295197 packets input, 305539992 bytes, 0 no buffer
```

```
Received 1925500 broadcasts, 0 runts, 0 giants
3 input errors, 3 CRC, 0 frame, 0 overrun, 0 ignored, 0 abort
    0 input packets with dribble condition detected
3594664 packets output, 436549843 bytes, 0 underruns
8 output errors, 1790 collisions, 10 interface resets, 0 restarts
```

show interfaces ethernet *Field Descriptions*

Field	Description
Ethernet...is up...is administratively down	Indicates whether the interface hardware is currently active and whether it has been taken down by an administrator. "Disabled" indicates that the router has received more than 5,000 errors in a keepalive interval, which is 10 seconds by default.
line protocol is {up | down | administratively down}	Indicates whether the software processes that handle the line protocol believe the interface is usable (that is, whether keepalives are successful) or if it has been taken down by an administrator.
Hardware	Hardware type (for example, MCI Ethernet, SCI, cBus Ethernet) and address.
Internet address	Internet address followed by subnet mask.
MTU	Maximum transmission unit of the interface.
BW	Bandwidth of the interface in kilobits per second.
DLY	Delay of the interface in microseconds.
rely	Reliability of the interface as a fraction of 255 (255/255 is 100 percent reliability), calculated as an exponential average over five minutes.
load	Load on the interface as a fraction of 255 (255/255 is completely saturated), calculated as an exponential average over five minutes.
Encapsulation	Encapsulation method assigned to interface.
ARP type:	Type of Address Resolution Protocol assigned.
loopback	Indicates whether loopback is set.
keepalive	Indicates whether keepalives are set.
Last input	Number of hours, minutes, and seconds since the last packet was successfully received by an interface. Useful for knowing when a dead interface failed.
Last output	Number of hours, minutes, and seconds since the last packet was successfully transmitted by an interface.

Field	Description
output	Number of hours, minutes, and seconds since the last packet was successfully transmitted by the interface. Useful for knowing when a dead interface failed.
output hang	Number of hours, minutes, and seconds (or never) since the interface was last reset because of a transmission that took too long. When the number of hours in any of the "last" fields exceeds 24 hours, the number of days and hours is printed. If that field overflows, asterisks are printed.
Last clearing	Time at which the counters that measure cumulative statistics (such as number of bytes transmitted and received) shown in this report were last reset to zero. Note that variables that might affect routing (for example, load and reliability) are not cleared when the counters are cleared. *** indicates that the elapsed time is too large to be displayed. 0:00:00 indicates that the counters were cleared more than 231ms (and less than 232ms) ago.
Output queue, input queue, drops	Number of packets in output and input queues. Each number is followed by a slash, the maximum size of the queue, and the number of packets dropped due to a full queue.
Five minute input rate, Five minute output rate	Average number of bits and packets transmitted per second in the past five minutes. If the interface is not in promiscuous mode, it senses network traffic it sends and receives (rather than all network traffic). The five-minute input and output rates should be used only as an approximation of traffic per second during a given five-minute period. These rates are exponentially weighted averages with a time constant of five minutes. A period of four time constants must pass before the average will be within 2 percent of the instantaneous rate of a uniform stream of traffic over that period.
packets input	Total number of error-free packets received by the system.
bytes input	Total number of bytes, including data and MAC encapsulation, in the error-free packets received by the system.
no buffers	Number of received packets discarded because there was no buffer space in the main system. Compare with ignored count. Broadcast storms on Ethernet networks and bursts of noise on serial lines are often responsible for no input buffer events.
Received...broadcasts	Total number of broadcast or multicast packets received by the interface.

Field	Description
runts	Number of packets that are discarded because they are smaller than the medium's minimum packet size. For instance, any Ethernet packet that is less than 64 bytes is considered a runt.
giants	Number of packets that are discarded because they exceed the medium's maximum packet size. For example, any Ethernet packet that is greater than 1,518 bytes is considered a giant.
input error	Includes runts, giants, no buffer, CRC, frame, overrun, and ignored counts. Other input-related errors can also cause the input error count to be increased, and some datagrams may have more than one error; therefore, this sum may not balance with the sum of enumerated input error counts.
CRC	Cyclic redundancy checksum generated by the originating LAN station or far-end device does not match the checksum calculated from the data received. On a LAN, this usually indicates noise or transmission problems on the LAN interface or the LAN bus itself. A high number of CRCs is usually the result of collisions or a station transmitting bad data.
frame	Number of packets received incorrectly having a CRC error and a noninteger number of octets. On a LAN, this is usually the result of collisions or a malfunctioning Ethernet device.
overrun	Number of times the receiver hardware was unable to hand received data to a hardware buffer because the input rate exceeded the receiver's ability to handle the data.
ignored	Number of received packets ignored by the interface because the interface hardware ran low on internal buffers. These buffers are different from the system buffers mentioned previously in the buffer description. Broadcast storms and bursts of noise can cause the ignored count to be increased.
input packets with dribble condition detected	Dribble bit error indicates that a frame is slightly too long. This frame error counter is incremented just for informational purposes; the router accepts the frame.
packets output	Total number of messages transmitted by the system.
bytes	Total number of bytes, including data and MAC encapsulation, transmitted by the system.
underruns	Number of times the transmitter has been running faster than the router can handle. This may never be reported on some interfaces.

Field	Description
output errors	Sum of all errors that prevented the final transmission of datagrams out of the interface being examined. Note that this may not balance with the sum of the enumerated output errors, as some datagrams may have more than one error and others may have errors that do not fall into any of the specifically tabulated categories.
collisions	Number of messages retransmitted due to an Ethernet collision. This is usually the result of an overextended LAN (Ethernet or transceiver cable too long, more than two repeaters between stations, or too many cascaded multiport transceivers). A packet that collides is counted only once in output packets.
interface resets	Number of times an interface has been completely reset. This can happen if packets queued for transmission were not sent within several seconds. On a serial line, this can be caused by a malfunctioning modem that is not supplying the transmit clock signal, or by a cable problem. If the system notices that the carrier detect line of a serial interface is up, but the line protocol is down, it periodically resets the interface in an effort to restart it. Interface resets can also occur when an interface is looped back or shut down.
restarts	Number of times a Type 2 Ethernet controller was restarted because of errors.

CHAPTER 5

Troubleshooting Fiber Distributed Data Interface

The Fiber Distributed Data Interface (FDDI) standard was produced by the ANSI X3T9.5 standards committee in the mid-1980s. During this period, high-speed engineering workstations were beginning to tax the capabilities of existing local-area networks (LANs)—primarily Ethernet and Token Ring. A new LAN was needed that could easily support these workstations and their new distributed applications. At the same time, network reliability was becoming an increasingly important issue as system managers began to migrate mission-critical applications from large computers to networks. FDDI was developed to fill these needs.

After completing the FDDI specification, ANSI submitted FDDI to the International Organization for Standardization (ISO). ISO has created an international version of FDDI that is completely compatible with the ANSI standard version.

Although FDDI implementations are not as common as Ethernet or Token Ring, FDDI has gained a substantial following that continues to increase as the cost of FDDI interfaces diminishes. FDDI is frequently used as a backbone technology as well as a means to connect high-speed computers in a local area.

FDDI TECHNOLOGY BASICS

FDDI specifies a 100-Mbps, token-passing, dual-ring LAN using a fiber-optic transmission medium. It defines the physical layer and media-access portion of the link layer, and is roughly analogous to IEEE 802.3 and IEEE 802.5 in its relationship to the Open System Interconnection (OSI) reference model.

Although it operates at faster speeds, FDDI is similar in many ways to Token Ring. The two types of networks share many features, including topology (ring), media-access technique (token passing), and reliability features (redundant rings, for example). For more information on Token Ring and related technologies, refer to Chapter 6, "Troubleshooting Token Ring."

One of the most important characteristics of FDDI is its use of optical fiber as a transmission medium. Optical fiber offers several advantages over traditional copper wiring, including security (fiber does not emit electrical signals that can be tapped), reliability (fiber is immune to electrical interference), and speed (optical fiber has much higher throughput potential than copper cable).

FDDI defines use of two types of fiber: single mode (sometimes called monomode) and multimode. Modes can be thought of as bundles of light rays entering the fiber at a particular angle. *Single-mode fiber* allows only one mode of light to propagate through the fiber, whereas *multimode fiber* allows multiple modes of light to propagate through the fiber. Because multiple modes of light propagating through the fiber may travel different distances (depending on the entry angles), causing them to arrive at the destination at different times (a phenomenon called *modal dispersion*), single-mode fiber is capable of higher bandwidth and greater cable run distances than multimode fiber. Because of these characteristics, single-mode fiber is often used for interbuilding connectivity, and multimode fiber is often used for intrabuilding connectivity. Multimode fiber uses light-emitting diodes (LEDs) as the light-generating devices, whereas single-mode fiber generally uses lasers.

FDDI Specifications

FDDI is defined by four separate specifications (see Figure 5–1):

- Media Access Control (MAC)—Defines how the medium is accessed, including frame format, token handling, addressing, an algorithm for calculating a cyclic redundancy check value, and error recovery mechanisms.

- Physical Layer Protocol (PHY)—Defines data encoding/decoding procedures, clocking requirements, framing, and other functions.

- Physical Layer Medium (PMD)—Defines the characteristics of the transmission medium, including the fiber-optic link, power levels, bit error rates, optical components, and connectors.

- Station Management (SMT)—Defines the FDDI station configuration, ring configuration, and ring control features, including station insertion and removal, initialization, fault isolation and recovery, scheduling, and collection of statistics.

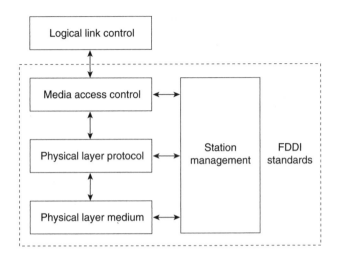

Figure 5–1
FDDI Standards

Physical Connections

FDDI specifies the use of dual rings. Traffic on these rings travels in opposite directions. Physically, the rings consist of two or more point-to-point connections between adjacent stations. One of the two FDDI rings is called the *primary ring*; the other is called the *secondary ring*. The primary ring is used for data transmission, and the secondary ring is generally used as a backup.

Class B or single-attachment stations (SASs) attach to one ring; Class A or dual-attachment stations (DASs) attach to both rings. SASs are attached to the primary ring through a concentrator, which provides connections for multiple SASs. The concentrator ensures that failure or power down of any given SAS does not interrupt the ring. This is particularly useful when PCs, or similar devices that frequently power on and off, connect to the ring.

A typical FDDI configuration with both DASs and SASs is shown in Figure 5–2.

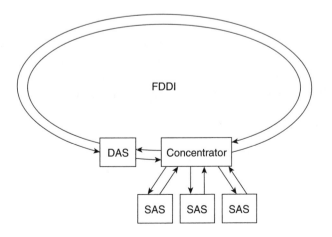

Figure 5–2
FDDI Nodes: DAS, SASs, and Concentrator

Each FDDI DAS has two ports, designated A and B. These ports connect the station to the dual FDDI ring. Therefore, each port provides a connection for both the primary and the secondary ring, as shown in Figure 5–3.

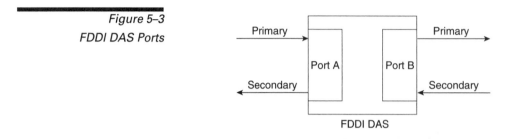

Figure 5–3
FDDI DAS Ports

Traffic Types

FDDI supports real-time allocation of network bandwidth, making it ideal for a variety of different application types. FDDI provides this support by defining two types of traffic: synchronous and asynchronous. Synchronous traffic can consume a portion of the 100-Mbps total bandwidth of an FDDI network, and asynchronous traffic can consume the rest. Synchronous bandwidth is allocated to those stations requiring continuous transmission capability. Such capability is useful for transmitting voice and video information, for example. Other stations use the remaining bandwidth asynchronously. The FDDI SMT specification defines a distributed bidding scheme to allocate FDDI bandwidth.

Asynchronous bandwidth is allocated using an eight-level priority scheme. Each station is assigned an asynchronous priority level. FDDI also permits extended dialogues, where stations may temporarily use all asynchronous bandwidth. The FDDI priority mechanism can essentially lock out stations that cannot use synchronous bandwidth and have too low an asynchronous priority.

Fault-Tolerant Features

FDDI provides a number of fault-tolerant features, the most important of which is the *dual ring*. If a station on the dual ring fails or is powered down or if the cable is damaged, the dual ring is automatically "wrapped" (doubled back onto itself) into a single ring, as shown in Figure 5–4. In this figure, when Station 3 fails, the dual ring is automatically wrapped in Stations 2 and 4, forming a single ring. Although Station 3 is no longer on the ring, network operation continues for the remaining stations.

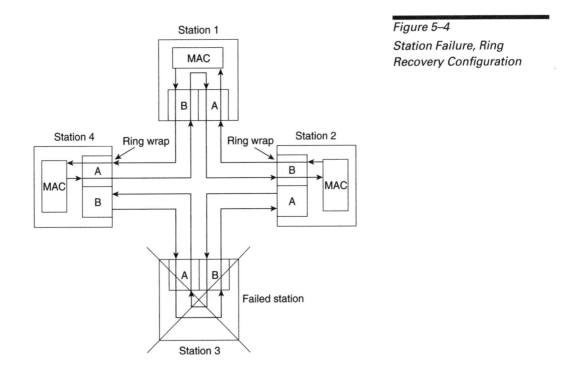

Figure 5–4

Station Failure, Ring Recovery Configuration

Figure 5–5 shows how FDDI compensates for a wiring failure. Stations 3 and 4 wrap the ring within themselves when wiring between them fails.

As FDDI networks grow, the possibility of multiple ring failures grows. When two ring failures occur, the ring is wrapped in both cases, effectively segmenting the ring into two separate rings that cannot communicate with each other. Subsequent failures cause additional ring segmentation.

Optical bypass switches can be used to prevent ring segmentation by eliminating failed stations from the ring. This is shown in Figure 5–6.

Critical devices such as routers or mainframe hosts can use another fault-tolerant technique called *dual homing* to provide additional redundancy and help guarantee operation. In dual-homing situations, the critical device is attached to two concentrators. One pair of concentrator links is declared the active link; the other pair is declared passive. The passive link stays in backup mode until the primary link (or the concentrator to which it is attached) is determined to have failed. When this occurs, the passive link is automatically activated.

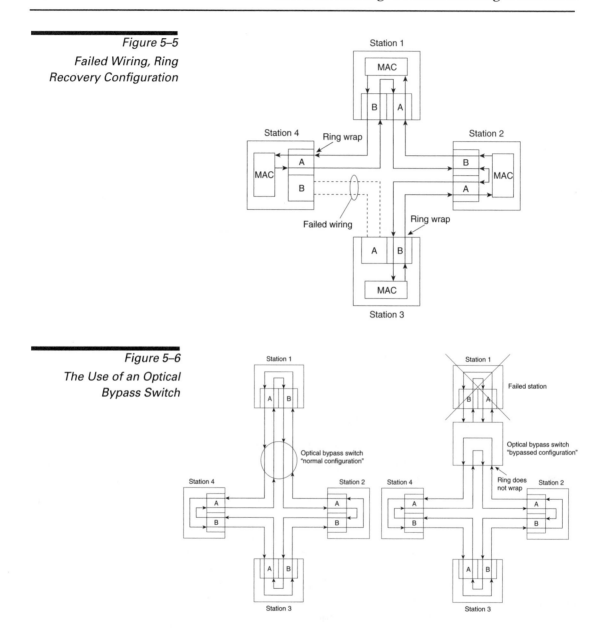

Figure 5–5

Failed Wiring, Ring Recovery Configuration

Figure 5–6

The Use of an Optical Bypass Switch

Frame Format

FDDI frame formats (shown in Figure 5–7) are similar to those of Token Ring.

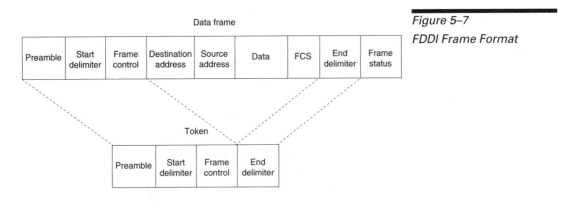

Figure 5–7

FDDI Frame Format

The fields of an FDDI frame are as follows:

- Preamble—Prepares each station for the upcoming frame.

- Start delimiter—Indicates the beginning of the frame. It consists of signaling patterns that differentiate it from the rest of the frame.

- Frame control—Indicates the size of the address fields, whether the frame contains asynchronous or synchronous data, and other control information.

- Destination address—Contains a unicast (singular), multicast (group), or broadcast (every station) address. As with Ethernet and Token Ring, FDDI destination addresses are 6 bytes.

- Source address—Identifies the single station that sent the frame. As with Ethernet and Token Ring, FDDI source addresses are 6 bytes.

- Data—Contains either information destined for an upper-layer protocol or control information.

- Frame check sequence (FCS)—Filled by the source station with a calculated cyclic redundancy check (CRC) value dependent on the frame contents (as with Token Ring and Ethernet). The destination station recalculates the value to determine whether the frame may have been damaged in transit. If it has been damaged, the frame is discarded.

- End delimiter—Contains nondata symbols that indicate the end of the frame.

- Frame status—Allows the source station to determine whether an error occurred and whether the frame was recognized and copied by a receiving station.

CDDI

The high cost of fiber-optic cable has been a major impediment to the widespread deployment of FDDI to desktop computers. At the same time, shielded twisted-pair (STP) and unshielded twisted-pair (UTP) copper wire is relatively inexpensive and has been widely deployed. The implementation of FDDI over copper wire is known as Copper Distributed Data Interface (CDDI).

Before FDDI could be implemented over copper wire, a problem had to be solved. When signals strong enough to be reliably interpreted as data are transmitted over twisted-pair wire, the wire radiates electromagnetic interference (EMI). Any attempt to implement FDDI over twisted-pair wire had to ensure that the resulting energy radiation did not exceed the specifications set in the United States by the Federal Communications Commission (FCC) and in Europe by the European Economic Council (EEC). Three technologies reduce energy radiation:

- Scrambling—When no data is being sent, FDDI transmits an idle pattern that consists of a string of binary ones. When this signal is sent over twisted-pair wire, the EMI is concentrated at the fundamental frequency spectrum of the idle pattern, resulting in a peak in the frequency spectrum of the radiated interference. By scrambling FDDI data with a pseudo-random sequence prior to transmission, repetitive patterns are eliminated. The elimination of repetitive patterns results in a spectral peak that is distributed more evenly over the spectrum of the transmitted signal.

- Encoding—Signal strength is stronger, and EMI is lower when transmission occurs over twisted-pair wire at lower frequencies. MLT3 is an encoding scheme that reduces the frequency of the transmitted signal. MLT3 switches between three output voltage levels so that peak power is shifted to less than 20 MHz.

- Equalization—Equalization boosts the higher frequency signals for transmission over UTP. Equalization can be done on the transmitter (predistortion), at the receiver (postcompensation), or both. One advantage of equalization at the receiver is the ability to adjust compensation as a function of cable length.

TROUBLESHOOTING FDDI

This section provides troubleshooting procedures for common FDDI media problems.

Table 5–1 outlines problems commonly encountered on FDDI networks and offers general guidelines for solving those problems.

Table 5–1 *Media Problems: FDDI*

Media Problem	Suggested Actions
Nonfunctional FDDI ring	**Step 1** Use the **show interfaces fddi** exec command to determine the status of the router's FDDI interfaces.
	Step 2 If the **show interfaces fddi** command indicates that the interface and line protocol are up, use the **ping** command between routers to test connectivity.
	Step 3 If the interface and line protocol are up, make sure the MAC addresses of upstream and downstream neighbors are as expected.
	Step 4 If all zeros appear in either of the address fields for these neighbors, there is probably a physical connection problem.
	In this case (or if the status line does *not* indicate that the interface and line protocol are up), check patch-panel connections or use an OTDR[1] or light meter to check connectivity between neighbors. Ensure that signal strength is within specifications.
Upstream neighbor has failed and bypass switch is installed	Bypass switches can cause signal degradation because they do not repeat signals as a normal transceiver does.
	Step 1 Check upstream neighbor to determine whether it is operational.
	Step 2 If the node is down and a bypass switch is in place, resolve any problems found in the upstream neighbor.

[1] OTDR = optical time-domain reflectometer

When you're troubleshooting FDDI media in a Cisco router environment, the **show interfaces fddi** command provides several key fields of information that can assist in isolating problems. The following section provides a detailed description of the **show interfaces fddi** command and the information it provides.

show interfaces fddi

To display information about the FDDI interface, use the **show interfaces fddi** exec command:

> **show interfaces fddi** *number* [**accounting**]
> **show interfaces fddi** [*slot* | *port*] [**accounting**] (Cisco 7000 series and Cisco 7200 series)
> **show interfaces fddi** [*slot* | *port-adapter* | *port*] [**accounting**] (Cisco 7500 series routers)

Syntax Description

- *number*—Port number on the selected interface.

- **accounting**—(Optional) Displays the number of packets of each protocol type that have been sent through the interface.

- *slot*—Refers to the appropriate hardware manual for slot and port information.

- *port*—Refers to the appropriate hardware manual for slot and port information.

- *port-adapter*—Refers to the appropriate hardware manual for information about port adapter compatibility.

Command Mode

exec

Usage Guidelines

This command first appeared in Cisco IOS Release 10.0.

This information was modified in Cisco IOS Release 11.3 to include sample output for FDDI full-duplex, single-mode, and multimode port adapters (PA-F/FD-SM and PA-F/FD-MM).

Sample Displays

The following is a sample partial display of FDDI-specific data from the **show interfaces fddi** command on a Cisco 7500 series router:

```
Router> show interfaces fddi 3/0
Fddi3/0 is up, line protocol is up
  Hardware is cxBus Fddi, address is 0000.0c02.adf1 (bia 0000.0c02.adf1)
  Internet address is 131.108.33.14, subnet mask is 255.255.255.0
  MTU 4470 bytes, BW 100000 Kbit, DLY 100 usec, rely 255/255, load 1/255
  Encapsulation SNAP, loopback not set, keepalive not set
  ARP type: SNAP, ARP Timeout 4:00:00
  Phy-A state is  active, neighbor is  B, cmt signal bits 008/20C, status ILS
  Phy-B state is  active, neighbor is  A, cmt signal bits 20C/008, status ILS
```

```
ECM is in, CFM is thru, — is ring_op
Token rotation 5000 usec, ring operational 21:32:34
Upstream neighbor 0000.0c02.ba83, downstream neighbor 0000.0c02.ba83
Last input 0:00:05, output 0:00:00, output hang never
Last clearing of "show interface" counters 0:59:10
Output queue 0/40, 0 drops; input queue 0/75, 0 drops
Five minute input rate 69000 bits/sec, 44 packets/sec
Five minute output rate 0 bits/sec, 1 packets/sec
    113157 packets input, 21622582 bytes, 0 no buffer
    Received 276 broadcasts, 0 runts, 0 giants
    0 input errors, 0 CRC, 0 frame, 0 overrun, 0 ignored, 0 abort
    4740 packets output, 487346 bytes, 0 underruns
    0 output errors, 0 collisions, 0 interface resets, 0 restarts
    0 transitions, 2 traces, 3 claims, 2 beacons
```

The following is a sample display of the **show interfaces fddi** command for the full-duplex FDDI port adapter on a Cisco 7500 series router:

```
Router# show interfaces fddi 0/1/0
Fddi0/1/0 is up, line protocol is up
  Hardware is cxBus FDDI, address is 0060.3e33.3608 (bia 0060.3e33.3608)
  Internet address is 2.1.1.1/24
  MTU 4470 bytes, BW 100000 Kbit, DLY 100 usec, rely 255/255, load 1/255
  Encapsulation SNAP, loopback not set, keepalive not set
  ARP type: SNAP, ARP Timeout 04:00:00
  FDX supported, FDX enabled, FDX state is operation
  Phy-A state is maintenance, neighbor is Unknown, status HLS
  Phy-B state is active, neighbor is A, status SILS
  ECM is in, CFM is c_wrap_b, — is ring_op,
  Requested token rotation 5000 usec, negotiated 4997 usec
  Configured tvx is 2500 usec
  LER for PortA = 0A, LER for PortB = 0A ring operational 00:02:45
  Upstream neighbor 0060.3e73.4600, downstream neighbor 0060.3e73.4600
  Last input 00:00:12, output 00:00:13, output hang never
  Last clearing of "show interface" counters never
  Queueing strategy: fifo
  Output queue 0/40, 0 drops; input queue 0/75, 0 drops
  5 minute input rate 0 bits/sec, 0 packets/sec
  5 minute output rate 0 bits/sec, 0 packets/sec
      62 packets input, 6024 bytes, 0 no buffer
      Received 18 broadcasts, 0 runts, 0 giants
      0 input errors, 0 CRC, 0 frame, 0 overrun, 0 ignored, 0 abort
      71 packets output, 4961 bytes, 0 underruns
      0 output errors, 0 collisions, 0 interface resets
      0 output buffer failures, 0 output buffers swapped out
      3 transitions, 0 traces,  100 claims, 0 beacon
```

Table 5–2 describes the **show interfaces fddi** display fields.

Table 5-2 `show interfaces` `fddi` *Field Descriptions*

Field	Description
Fddi is {*up*	*down*	*administratively down*}	Gives the interface processor unit number and tells whether the interface hardware is currently active and can transmit and receive or whether it has been taken down by an administrator.
line protocol is {*up*	*down*}	Indicates whether the software processes that handle the line protocol consider the interface usable.
Hardware	Provides the hardware type, followed by the hardware address.
Internet address	IP address, followed by subnet mask.
MTU	Maximum transmission unit of the interface.
BW	Bandwidth of the interface in kilobits per second.
DLY	Delay of the interface in microseconds.
rely	Reliability of the interface as a fraction of 255 (255/255 is 100 percent reliability), calculated as an exponential average of over five minutes.
load	Load on the interface as a fraction of 255 (255/255 is completely saturated), calculated as an exponential average of over five minutes.
Encapsulation	Encapsulation method assigned to interface.
loopback	Indicates whether loopback is set.
keepalive	Indicates whether keepalives are set.
ARP type	Type of Address Resolution Protocol assigned.
FDX	Displays full-duplex information. Values are **not supported** and **supported**. When the value is **supported**, the display indicates whether full-duplex is enabled or disabled. When enabled, the state of the FDX negotiation process is displayed. The negotiation states only relate to the full-duplex negotiation process. You must also ensure that the interface is up and working by looking at other fields in the **show interfaces fddi** command such as line protocol and —. Negotiation states are • **idle**—Interface is working but not in full-duplex mode yet. If persistent, it could mean that the interface did not meet all negotiation conditions (for example, there are more than two stations in the ring). • **request**—Interface is working but not in full-duplex mode yet. If persistent, it could mean that the remote interface does not support full-duplex or full-duplex is not enabled on the interface. • **confirm**—Transient state. • **operation**—Negotiations completed successfully, and both stations are operating in full-duplex mode.

Table 5–2 `show interfaces` `fddi` *Field Descriptions, Continued*

Field	Description
**Phy-{A	B}**	Lists the state the Physical A or Physical B connection is in; one of the following: **off, active, trace, connect, next, signal, join, verify,** or **break**.
neighbor	State of the neighbor: • **A**—Indicates that the CMT[1] process has established a connection with its neighbor. The bits received during the CMT signaling process indicate that the neighbor is a Physical A type DAS[2] or concentrator that attaches to the primary ring IN and the secondary ring OUT when attaching to the dual ring. • **S**—Indicates that the CMT process has established a connection with its neighbor and that the bits received during the CMT signaling process indicate that the neighbor is one Physical type in a single-attachment station SAS[3]. • **B**—Indicates that the CMT process has established a connection with its neighbor and that the bits received during the CMT signaling process indicate that the neighbor is a Physical B dual attachment station or concentrator that attaches to the secondary ring IN and the primary ring OUT when attaching to the dual ring. • **M**—Indicates that the CMT process has established a connection with its neighbor and that the bits received during the CMT signaling process indicate that the router's neighbor is a Physical M-type concentrator serving as a master to a connected station or concentrator. • **unk**—Indicates that the network server has not completed the CMT process and, as a result, does not know about its neighbor.
cmt signal bits	Shows the transmitted/received CMT bits. The transmitted bits are **0x008** for a Physical A type and **0x20C** for Physical B type. The number after the slash (**/**) is the received signal bits. If the connection is not active, the received bits are zero (**0**); see the line beginning **Phy-B** in the display. This applies to FDDI processor FIP[4] interfaces only.

[1]CMT = connection management
[2]DAS = dual-attachment station
[3]SAS = single-attachment station
[4]FIP = FDDI processor

Table 5–2 `show interfaces` `fddi` *Field Descriptions, Continued*

Field	Description
status	Status value displayed is the actual status on the fiber. The FDDI standard defines the following values: • **LSU**—Line state unknown, the criteria for entering or remaining in any other line state have not been met. • **NLS**—Noise line state, entered upon the occurrence of 16 potential noise events without satisfying the criteria for entry into another line state. • **MLS**—Master line state, entered upon the receipt of eight or nine consecutive **HQ** or **QH** symbol pairs. • **ILS**—Idle line state, entered upon receipt of four or five idle symbols. • **HLS**—Halt line state, entered upon the receipt of 16 or 17 consecutive H symbols. • **QLS**—Quiet line state, entered upon the receipt of 16 or 17 consecutive Q symbols or when carrier detect goes low. • **ALS**—Active line state, entered upon receipt of a **JK** symbol pair when carrier detect is high. • **OVUF**—Elasticity buffer overflow/underflow. The normal states for a connected Physical type are **ILS** or **ALS**. If the report displays the **QLS** status, this indicates that the fiber is disconnected from Physical B, or that it is not connected to another Physical type, or that the other station is not running.
ECM is...	ECM is the SMT entity coordination management, which overlooks the operation of CFM and PCM. The ECM state can be one of the following: • **out**—Router is isolated from the network. • **in**—Router is actively connected to the network. This is the normal state for a connected router. • **trace**—Router is trying to localize a stuck beacon condition. • **leave**—Router is allowing time for all the connections to break before leaving the network. • **path_test**—Router is testing its internal paths. • **insert**—Router is allowing time for the optical bypass to insert. • **check**—Router is making sure optical bypasses switched correctly. • **deinsert**—Router is allowing time for the optical bypass to deinsert.

Table 5–2 `show interfaces` `fddi` *Field Descriptions, Continued*

Field	Description
CFM is...	Contains information about the current state of the MAC connection. The configuration management state can be one of the following: • **isolated**—MAC is not attached to any Physical type. • **wrap_a**—MAC is attached to Physical A. Data is received on Physical A and transmitted on Physical A. • **wrap_b**—MAC is attached to Physical B. Data is received on Physical B and transmitted on Physical B. • **wrap_s**—MAC is attached to Physical S. Data is received on Physical S and transmitted on Physical S. This is the normal mode for a SAS.
— is...	— (ring management) is the SMT MAC-related state machine. The — state can be one of the following: • **isolated**—MAC is not trying to participate in the ring. This is the initial state. • **non_op**—MAC is participating in ring recovery, and ring is not operational. • **ring_op**—MAC is participating in an operational ring. This is the normal state while the MAC is connected to the ring. • **detect**—Ring has been nonoperational for longer than normal. Duplicate address conditions are being checked. • **non_op_dup**—Indications have been received that the address of the MAC is a duplicate of another MAC on the ring. Ring is not operational. • **ring_op_dup**—Indications have been received that the address of the MAC is a duplicate of another MAC on the ring. Ring is operational in this state. • **directed**—MAC is sending beacon frames notifying the ring of the stuck condition. • **trace**—Trace has been initiated by this MAC, and the — state machine is waiting for its completion before starting an internal path test.
token rotation	Token rotation value is the default or configured rotation value as determined by the **fddi token-rotation-time** command. This value is used by all stations on the ring. The default is 5,000 microseconds. For FDDI full-duplex, this indicates the value in use prior to entering full-duplex operation.

Table 5–2 `show interfaces` `fddi` *Field Descriptions, Continued*

Field	Description
negotiated	Actual (negotiated) target token rotation time.
ring operational	When the ring is operational, the displayed value will be the negotiated token rotation time of all stations on the ring. Operational times are displayed by the number of hours/minutes/seconds the ring has been up. If the ring is not operational, the message "ring not operational" is displayed.
Configured tvx	Transmission timer.
LER	Link error rate.
Upstream | downstream neighbor	Displays the canonical MAC address of outgoing upstream and downstream neighbors. If the address is unknown, the value will be the FDDI unknown address (0x00 00 f8 00 00 00).
Last input	Number of hours, minutes, and seconds since the last packet was successfully received by an interface. Useful for knowing when a dead interface failed.
output	Number of hours, minutes, and seconds since the last packet was successfully transmitted by an interface.
output hang	Number of hours, minutes, and seconds (or never) since the interface was last reset because of a transmission that took too long. When the number of hours in any of the "last" fields exceeds 24 hours, the number of days and hours is printed. If that field overflows, asterisks are printed.
Last clearing	Time at which the counters that measure cumulative statistics (such as number of bytes transmitted and received) shown in this report were last reset to zero. Note that variables that might affect routing (for example, load and reliability) are not cleared when the counters are cleared. *** indicates the elapsed time is too large to be displayed. 0:00:00 indicates the counters were cleared more than 231 ms (and less than 232 ms) ago.
Queueing strategy	First-in, first-out queuing strategy (other queuing strategies you might see are priority-list, custom-list, and weighted fair).
Output queue, input queue, drops	Number of packets in output and input queues. Each number is followed by a slash, the maximum size of the queue, and the number of packets dropped due to a full queue.

Table 5-2 `show interfaces` `fddi` *Field Descriptions, Continued*

Field	Description
5 minute input rate, 5 minute output rate	Average number of bits and packets transmitted per second in the past five minutes.
	The five-minute input and output rates should be used only as an approximation of traffic per second during a given five-minute period. These rates are exponentially weighted averages with a time constant of five minutes. A period of four time constants must pass before the average will be within 2 percent of the instantaneous rate of a uniform stream of traffic over that period.
packets input	Total number of error-free packets received by the system.
bytes	Total number of bytes, including data and MAC encapsulation, in the error-free packets received by the system.
no buffer	Number of received packets discarded because there was no buffer space in the main system. Compare with ignored count. Broadcast storms on Ethernet networks and bursts of noise on serial lines are often responsible for no input buffer events.
broadcasts	Total number of broadcast or multicast packets received by the interface.
runts	Number of packets that are discarded because they are smaller than the medium's minimum packet size.
giants	Number of packets that are discarded because they exceed the medium's maximum packet size.
CRC	Cyclic redundancy checksum generated by the originating LAN station or far-end device does not match the checksum calculated from the data received. On a LAN, this usually indicates noise or transmission problems on the LAN interface or the LAN bus itself. A high number of CRCs is usually the result of collisions or a station transmitting bad data.
frame	Number of packets received incorrectly that have a CRC error and a noninteger number of octets. On a LAN, this is usually the result of collisions or a malfunctioning Ethernet device. On an FDDI LAN, this also can be the result of a failing fiber (cracks) or a hardware malfunction.
overrun	Number of times the serial receiver hardware was unable to hand received data to a hardware buffer because the input rate exceeded the receiver's ability to handle the data.

Table 5–2 `show interfaces` `fddi` *Field Descriptions, Continued*

Field	Description
ignored	Number of received packets ignored by the interface because the interface hardware ran low on internal buffers. These buffers are different from the system buffers mentioned previously in the **buffer** description. Broadcast storms and bursts of noise can cause the ignored count to be increased.
packets output	Total number of messages transmitted by the system.
bytes	Total number of bytes, including data and MAC encapsulation, transmitted by the system.
underruns	Number of transmit aborts (when the router cannot feed the transmitter fast enough).
output errors	Sum of all errors that prevented the final transmission of datagrams out of the interface being examined. Note that this might not balance with the sum of the enumerated output errors because some datagrams can have more than one error and others can have errors that do not fall into any of the specifically tabulated categories.
collisions	Because an FDDI ring cannot have collisions, this statistic is always zero.
interface resets	Number of times an interface has been reset. The interface may be reset by the administrator or automatically when an internal error occurs.
restarts	Should always be zero for FDDI interfaces.
output buffer failures	Number of no-resource errors received on the output.
output buffers swapped out	Number of packets swapped to DRAM.
transitions	Number of times the ring made a transition from ring operational to ring nonoperational, or vice versa. A large number of transitions indicates a problem with the ring or the interface.
traces	Indicates the number of times this interface started a trace. Trace count applies to both the FCI, FCIT, and FIP.
claims	Pertains to FCIT and FIP only. Indicates the number of times this interface has been in claim state.
beacons	Pertains to FCIT and FIP only. Indicates the number of times the interface has been in beacon state.

CHAPTER 6

Troubleshooting Token Ring

The Token Ring network was originally developed by IBM in the 1970s. It is still IBM's primary local-area network (LAN) technology, and is second only to Ethernet/IEEE 802.3 in general LAN popularity. The IEEE 802.5 specification is almost identical to, and completely compatible with, IBM's Token Ring network. In fact, the IEEE 802.5 specification was modeled after IBM Token Ring, and continues to shadow IBM's Token Ring development. The term *Token Ring* is generally used to refer to both IBM's Token Ring network and IEEE 802.5 networks.

TOKEN RING/IEEE 802.5 COMPARISON

Token Ring and IEEE 802.5 networks are basically quite compatible, but the specifications differ in relatively minor ways. IBM's Token Ring network specifies a star, with all end stations attached to a device called a *multistation access unit* (MAU), whereas IEEE 802.5 does not specify a topology (although virtually all IEEE 802.5 implementations also are based on a star). Other differences exist, including media type (IEEE 802.5 does not specify a media type, whereas IBM Token Ring networks use twisted-pair wire) and routing information field size. Figure 6–1 summarizes IBM Token Ring network and IEEE 802.5 specifications.

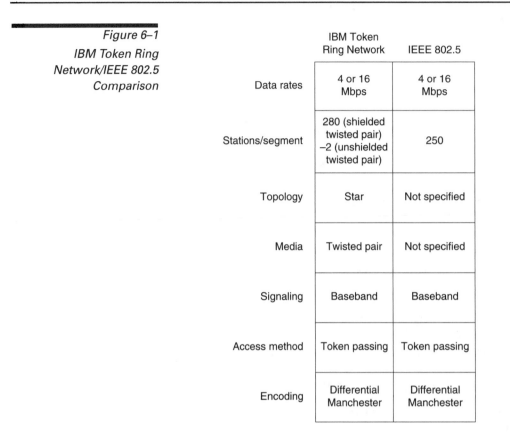

Figure 6–1

IBM Token Ring Network/IEEE 802.5 Comparison

	IBM Token Ring Network	IEEE 802.5
Data rates	4 or 16 Mbps	4 or 16 Mbps
Stations/segment	280 (shielded twisted pair) –2 (unshielded twisted pair)	250
Topology	Star	Not specified
Media	Twisted pair	Not specified
Signaling	Baseband	Baseband
Access method	Token passing	Token passing
Encoding	Differential Manchester	Differential Manchester

TOKEN PASSING

Token Ring and IEEE 802.5 are the primary examples of token-passing networks. Token-passing networks move a small frame, called a *token*, around the network. Possession of the token grants the right to transmit. If a node receiving the token has no information to send, it simply passes the token to the next end station. Each station can hold the token for a maximum period of time.

If a station possessing the token does have information to transmit, it seizes the token, alters 1 bit of the token (which turns the token into a start-of-frame sequence), appends the information it wishes to transmit, and finally sends this information to the next station on the ring. While the information frame is circling the ring, there is no token on the network (unless the ring supports early token release), so other stations wishing to transmit must wait. Therefore, collisions cannot occur in Token Ring networks. If early token release is supported, a new token can be released when frame transmission is complete.

The information frame circulates the ring until it reaches the intended destination station, which copies the information for further processing. The information frame continues to circle the ring and is finally removed when it reaches the sending station. The sending station can check the returning frame to see whether the frame was seen and subsequently copied by the destination.

Unlike carrier sense multiple access collision detect (CSMA/CD) networks—such as Ethernet—token-passing networks are deterministic. In other words, it is possible to calculate the maximum time that will pass before any end station will be able to transmit. This feature and several reliability features, which are discussed in the section "Fault Management Mechanisms" later in this chapter, make Token Ring networks ideal for applications where delay must be predictable and robust network operation is important. Factory automation environments are examples of such applications.

PHYSICAL CONNECTIONS

IBM Token Ring network stations are directly connected to MAUs, which can be wired together to form one large ring (as shown in Figure 6–2). Patch cables connect MAUs to adjacent MAUs. Lobe cables connect MAUs to stations. MAUs include bypass relays for removing stations from the ring.

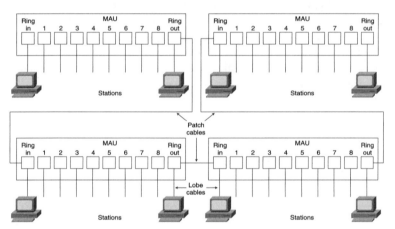

Figure 6–2

IBM Token Ring Network Physical Connections

THE PRIORITY SYSTEM

Token Ring networks use a sophisticated priority system that permits certain user-designated, high-priority stations to use the network more frequently. Token Ring frames have two fields that control priority: the *priority field* and the *reservation field*.

Only stations with a priority equal to or higher than the priority value contained in a token can seize that token. Once the token is seized and changed to an information frame, only stations with a priority value higher than that of the transmitting station can reserve the token for the next pass around the network. When the next token is generated, it includes the higher priority of the reserving station. Stations that raise a token's priority level must reinstate the previous priority after their transmission is complete.

FAULT MANAGEMENT MECHANISMS

Token Ring networks employ several mechanisms for detecting and compensating for network faults. For example, one station in the Token Ring network is selected to be the active monitor. This station, which can potentially be any station on the network, acts as a centralized source of timing information for other ring stations and performs a variety of ring maintenance functions. One of these functions is the removal of continuously circulating frames from the ring. When a sending device fails, its frame may continue to circle the ring. This can prevent other stations from transmitting their own frames and essentially lock up the network. The active monitor can detect such frames, remove them from the ring, and generate a new token.

The IBM Token Ring network's star topology also contributes to overall network reliability. Because all information in a Token Ring network is seen by active MAUs, these devices can be programmed to check for problems and selectively remove stations from the ring if necessary.

A Token Ring algorithm called *beaconing* detects and tries to repair certain network faults. Whenever a station detects a serious problem with the network (such as a cable break), it sends a beacon frame. The beacon frame defines a failure domain, which includes the station reporting the failure, its nearest active upstream neighbor (NAUN), and everything in between. Beaconing initiates a process called *autoreconfiguration*, where nodes within the failure domain automatically perform diagnostics in an attempt to reconfigure the network around the failed areas. Physically, the MAU can accomplish this through electrical reconfiguration.

FRAME FORMATS

Token Ring networks define two frame types: tokens and data/command frames. Both formats are shown in Figure 6–3.

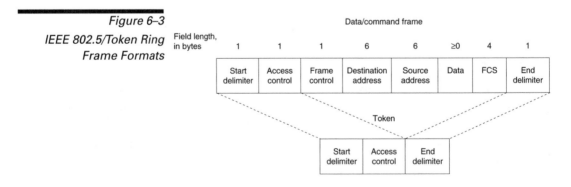

Figure 6–3
IEEE 802.5/Token Ring
Frame Formats

Tokens

Each token is 3 bytes in length and consists of a start delimiter, an access control byte, and an end delimiter.

The start delimiter serves to alert each station to the arrival of a token (or data/command frame). This field includes signals that distinguish the byte from the rest of the frame by violating the encoding scheme used elsewhere in the frame.

The access control byte contains the priority and reservation fields, as well as a token bit (used to differentiate a token from a data/command frame) and a monitor bit (used by the active monitor to determine whether a frame is circling the ring endlessly).

Finally, the end delimiter signals the end of the token or data/command frame. It also contains bits to indicate a damaged frame and a frame that is the last in a logical sequence.

Data/Command Frames

Data/command frames vary in size, depending on the size of the information field. Data frames carry information for upper-layer protocols; command frames contain control information and have no data for upper-layer protocols.

In data/command frames, a frame control byte follows the access control byte. The frame control byte indicates whether the frame contains data or control information. In control frames, this byte specifies the type of control information.

Following the frame control byte are the two address fields, which identify the destination and source stations. As with IEEE 802.3, addresses are 6 bytes in length.

The data field follows the address fields. The length of this field is limited by the ring token holding time, which defines the maximum time a station may hold the token.

Following the data field is the frame check sequence (FCS) field. This field is filled by the source station with a calculated value dependent on the frame contents. The destination station recalculates the value to determine whether the frame may have been damaged in transit. If damage did occur, the frame is discarded.

As with the token, the end delimiter completes the data/command frame.

TROUBLESHOOTING TOKEN RING

This section provides troubleshooting procedures for common Token Ring media problems. It describes a specific Token Ring symptom, the problems that are likely to cause this symptom, and the solutions to those problems.

Media Problems: Token Ring

Table 6–1 outlines problems commonly encountered on Token Ring networks and offers general guidelines for solving those problems.

Table 6-1   *Media Problems: Token Ring*

Media Problem	Suggested Actions
Nonfunctional Token Ring	**Step 1** Use the **show interfaces token** command to determine the status of the router's Token Ring interfaces.
	Step 2 If the status line indicates that the interface and line protocol are not up, check the cable from the router to the MAU.[1] Make sure that the cable is in good condition. If it is not, replace it.
	Step 3 If you are performing a new installation, make sure that the MAU has been properly initialized. For information on initializing your MAU, refer to the manufacturer's documentation.
Ring speed mismatch	**Step 1** Check the ring speed specification on all nodes attached to the Token Ring backbone. The ring speed configured for all stations must be the same (either 4 Mbps or 16 Mbps). Use the **show running-config** privileged exec command to determine which speed is specified on the router.
	Step 2 If necessary, modify ring speed specifications for clients, servers, and routers. On routers, use the **ring-speed** interface configuration command to change the ring speed.
	Change jumpers as needed for modular router platforms that do not support software speed configuration. For more information about ring speed specifications, refer to the hardware installation and maintenance manual for your system.
Relay open in MAU	**Step 1** If an "open lobe fault" message appears on the console at system power up, check the cable connection to the MAU.
	Step 2 Use the **clear interface** privileged exec command to reset the Token Ring interface and reinsert the router into the ring.
	For all Token Ring cards except the CTR and access routers, you must use the **clear interface** command to reinitialize the Token Ring interface if the interface is down.
	Step 3 Use the **show interfaces token** exec command to verify that the interface and line protocol are up.
	Step 4 If the interface is operational, but the "open lobe fault" message persists and the router still cannot connect to the ring, connect the router to a different MAU port.
	Step 5 If the message continues to appear, disconnect all devices from the MAU and reset the MAU's relay with the tool provided by the MAU vendor.

Table 6-1 *Media Problems: Token Ring, Continued*

Media Problem	Suggested Actions
Relay open in MAU *(Continued)*	**Step 6** Reattach the router and determine whether it can connect to the ring. If resetting the relay does not solve the problem, try replacing the MAU with one that is known to be operational.
	Step 7 If the router still cannot connect to the ring, check internal cable connections of the router Token Ring cards. Ensure that cables associated with the respective port numbers are correctly wired and that they are not swapped.
	Step 8 If the router still cannot connect to the ring, replace the cables that connect the router to the MAU with working cables.
	Step 9 Use the **clear interface** command to reset the interface and reinsert the router into the ring. Use the **show interfaces token** command to verify that the interface and line protocol are up.
	Step 10 Alternatively, you can connect the router to a spare MAU to which no stations are connected. If the router can attach to the ring, replace the original MAU.
Duplicate MAC[2] address	This problem can arise when routers are using locally administered MAC addresses.
	Step 1 Use a network analyzer to check the Duplicate Address test frames from a booting station. If the station gets a response, then there is another station already configured with the MAC address of the booting station.
	Step 2 If there are two stations with the same MAC addresses, change the MAC address of one of the stations and reinitialize the node.
Congested ring	**Step 1** Insert the router during an off-peak period.
	Step 2 If insertion is successful during off-peak periods, but unsuccessful during peak load, segment your internetwork to distribute traffic.
RPS[3] conflict	**Step 1** Use the **no lnm rps** interface configuration command to disable the RPS function on the router that you are trying to insert into the ring.
	Step 2 Try to insert the router into the ring.
	Step 3 If you can insert the router with RPS disabled, there is a conflict between RPS implementations. Contact your technical support representative for more information.

[1] MAU = multistation access unit
[2] MAC = Media Access Control
[3] RPS = Ring Parameter Server

show interfaces tokenring

When troubleshooting Token Ring media in a Cisco router environment, you can use the **show interfaces tokenring** command to provide several key fields of information that can assist in isolating problems. This section provides a detailed description of the **show interfaces tokenring** command and the information it provides in Table 6–2.

Use the **show interfaces tokenring** privileged exec command to display information about the Token Ring interface and the state of source route bridging:

> **show interfaces tokenring** *unit* [**accounting**]
> **show interfaces tokenring** *slot* | *port* [*accounting*] (for the Cisco 7500 series and Cisco 7200 series)
> **show interfaces tokenring** [*slot* | *port-adapter* | *port*] (for ports on VIP cards in the Cisco 7500 series routers)

Syntax Description

- *unit*—Must match the interface port line number.

- **accounting**—(Optional) Displays the number of packets of each protocol type that have been sent through the interface.

- *slot*—Refers to the appropriate hardware manual for slot and port information.

- *port*—Refers to the appropriate hardware manual for slot and port information.

- *port-adapter*—Refers to the appropriate hardware manual for information about port adapter compatibility.

Command Mode

Privileged exec

Usage Guidelines

This command first appeared in Cisco IOS Release 10.0.

The command description was modified in Cisco IOS Release 11.3 to account for support on new full-duplex Token Ring port adapters.

If you do not provide values for the parameters *slot* and *port*, the command will display statistics for all the network interfaces. The optional keyword **accounting** displays the number of packets of each protocol type that have been sent through the interface.

Sample Display

The following is sample output from the **show interfaces tokenring** command:

```
Router# show interfaces tokenring
TokenRing 0 is up, line protocol is up
Hardware is 16/4 Token Ring, address is 5500.2000.dc27 (bia 0000.3000.072b)
```

```
     Internet address is 150.136.230.203, subnet mask is 255.255.255.0
  MTU 8136 bytes, BW 16000 Kbit, DLY 630 usec, rely 255/255, load 1/255
     Encapsulation SNAP, loopback not set, keepalive set (10 sec)
     ARP type: SNAP, ARP Timeout 4:00:00
     Ring speed: 16 Mbps
     Single ring node, Source Route Bridge capable
  Group Address: 0x00000000, Functional Address: 0x60840000
     Last input 0:00:01, output 0:00:01, output hang never
     Output queue 0/40, 0 drops; input queue 0/75, 0 drops
     Five minute input rate 0 bits/sec, 0 packets/sec
     Five minute output rate 0 bits/sec, 0 packets/sec
     16339 packets input, 1496515 bytes, 0 no buffer
  Received 9895 broadcasts, 0 runts, 0 giants
  0 input errors, 0 CRC, 0 frame, 0 overrun, 0 ignored, 0 abort
        32648 packets output, 9738303 bytes, 0 underruns
        0 output errors, 0 collisions, 2 interface resets, 0 restarts
        5 transitions
```

Table 6–2 describes the **show interfaces token ring** display field.

Table 6–2 `show interfaces tokenring` *Field Descriptions*

Field	Description
Token Ring is { *up*	*down* }	Interface is either currently active and inserted into ring (up) or inactive and not inserted (down). On the Cisco 7500 series, gives the interface processor type, slot number, and port number.
Token Ring is Reset	Hardware error has occurred.
Token Ring is Initializing	Hardware is up, in the process of inserting the ring.
Token Ring is Administratively Down	Hardware has been taken down by an administrator.
line protocol is {up	down	administratively down}	Indicates whether the software processes that handle the line protocol believe the interface is usable (that is, whether keepalives are successful).
Hardware	Hardware type. **Hardware is Token Ring** indicates that the board is a CSC-R board. **Hardware is 16/4 Token Ring** indicates that the board is a CSC-R16 board. Also shows the address of the interface.
Internet address	Lists the Internet address followed by subnet mask.
MTU	Maximum transmission unit of the interface.
BW	Bandwidth of the interface in kilobits per second.
DLY	Delay of the interface in microseconds.

Table 6–2 `show interfaces tokenring` *Field Descriptions, Continued*

Field	Description
rely	Reliability of the interface as a fraction of 255 (255/255 is 100 percent reliability), calculated as an exponential average over five minutes.
load	Load on the interface as a fraction of 255 (255/255 is completely saturated), calculated as an exponential average over five minutes.
Encapsulation	Encapsulation method assigned to interface.
loopback	Indicates whether loopback is set.
keepalive	Indicates whether keepalives are set.
ARP type:	Type of Address Resolution Protocol assigned.
Ring speed:	Speed of Token Ring—4 or 16 Mbps.
{*Single ring* | *multiring node*}	Indicates whether a node is enabled to collect and use source routing information (RIF) for routable Token Ring protocols.
Group Address:	Interface's group address, if any. The group address is a multicast address; any number of interfaces on the ring may share the same group address. Each interface may have at most one group address.
Last input	Number of hours, minutes, and seconds since the last packet was successfully received by an interface. Useful for knowing when a dead interface failed.
Last output	Number of hours, minutes, and seconds since the last packet was successfully transmitted by an interface.
output hang	Number of hours, minutes, and seconds (or never) since the interface was last reset because of a transmission that took too long. When the number of hours in any of the "last" fields exceeds 24 hours, the number of days and hours is printed. If that field overflows, asterisks are printed.
Last clearing	Time at which the counters that measure cumulative statistics (such as number of bytes transmitted and received) shown in this report were last reset to zero. Note that variables that might affect routing (for example, load and reliability) are not cleared when the counters are cleared. *** indicates the elapsed time is too large to be displayed. 0:00:00 indicates the counters were cleared more than 231 ms (and less than 232 ms) ago.

Table 6–2 `show interfaces tokenring` *Field Descriptions, Continued*

Field	Description
Output queue, drops **Input queue, drops**	Number of packets in output and input queues. Each number is followed by a slash, the maximum size of the queue, and the number of packets dropped due to a full queue.
Five minute input rate, **Five minute output rate**	Average number of bits and packets transmitted per second in the past five minutes. The five-minute input and output rates should be used only as an approximation of traffic per second during a given five-minute period. These rates are exponentially weighted averages with a time constant of five minutes. A period of four time constants must pass before the average will be within 2 percent of the instantaneous rate of a uniform stream of traffic over that period.
packets input	Total number of error-free packets received by the system.
bytes input	Total number of bytes, including data and MAC encapsulation, in the error-free packets received by the system.
no buffer	Number of received packets discarded because there was no buffer space in the main system. Compare with *ignored* count. Broadcast storms on Ethernet networks and bursts of noise on serial lines are often responsible for no input buffer events.
broadcasts	Total number of broadcast or multicast packets received by the interface.
runts	Number of packets that are discarded because they are smaller than the medium's minimum packet size.
giants	Number of packets that are discarded because they exceed the medium's maximum packet size.
CRC	The cyclic redundancy checksum generated by the originating LAN station or far-end device does not match the checksum calculated from the data received. On a LAN, this usually indicates noise or transmission problems on the LAN interface or the LAN bus itself. A high number of CRCs is usually the result of a station transmitting bad data.
frame	Number of packets received incorrectly having a CRC error and a noninteger number of octets.

Table 6–2 `show interfaces tokenring` *Field Descriptions, Continued*

Field	Description
overrun	Number of times the serial receiver hardware was unable to hand receive data to a hardware buffer because the input rate exceeded the receiver's ability to handle the data.
ignored	Number of received packets ignored by the interface because the interface hardware ran low on internal buffers. These buffers are different than the system buffers mentioned previously in the buffer description. Broadcast storms and bursts of noise can cause the ignored count to be increased.
packets output	Total number of messages transmitted by the system.
bytes output	Total number of bytes, including data and MAC encapsulation, transmitted by the system.
underruns	Number of times that the far-end transmitter has been running faster than the near-end router's receiver can handle. This may never be reported on some interfaces.
output errors	Sum of all errors that prevented the final transmission of datagrams out of the interface being examined. Note that this may not balance with the sum of the enumerated output errors, as some datagrams may have more than one error and others may have errors that do not fall into any of the specifically tabulated categories.
collisions	Because a Token Ring cannot have collisions, this statistic is nonzero only if an unusual event occurred when frames were being queued or taken out of the queue by the system software.
interface resets	The number of times an interface has been reset. The interface may be reset by the administrator or automatically when an internal error occurs.
restarts	Should always be zero for Token Ring interfaces.
transitions	Number of times the ring made a transition from up to down, or vice versa. A large number of transitions indicates a problem with the ring or the interface.

PART 3

Troubleshooting Desktop and Enterprise Routing Protocols

## CHAPTER 7

Troubleshooting TCP/IP

In the mid-1970s, the Defense Advanced Research Projects Agency (DARPA) became interested in establishing a packet-switched network to provide communications between research institutions in the United States. DARPA and other government organizations understood the potential of packet-switched technology and were just beginning to face the problem virtually all companies with networks now have—communication between dissimilar computer systems.

With the goal of heterogeneous connectivity in mind, DARPA funded research by Stanford University and Bolt, Beranek, and Newman (BBN) to create a series of communication protocols. The result of this development effort, completed in the late 1970s, was the Internet Protocol suite, of which the Transmission Control Protocol (TCP) and the Internet Protocol (IP) are the two best known protocols.

INTERNET PROTOCOLS

Internet protocols can be used to communicate across any set of interconnected networks. They are equally well suited for local-area network (LAN) and wide-area network (WAN) communications. The Internet suite includes not only lower-layer specifications (such as TCP and IP), but also specifications for such common applications as mail, terminal emulation, and file transfer. Figure 7–1 shows some of the most important Internet protocols and their relationships to the OSI reference model.

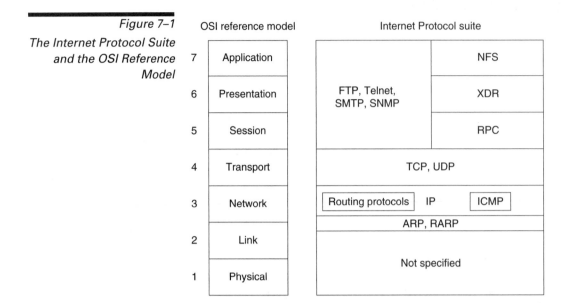

Figure 7–1

The Internet Protocol Suite and the OSI Reference Model

Creation and documentation of the Internet Protocol suite closely resemble an academic research project. The protocols are specified in documents called Requests for Comments (RFCs). RFCs are published and then reviewed and analyzed by the Internet community. Protocol refinements are published in new RFCs. Taken together, the RFCs provide a colorful history of the people, companies, and trends that have shaped the development of what is today the world's most popular open-system protocol suite.

THE NETWORK LAYER

IP is the primary Layer 3 protocol in the Internet protocol suite. In addition to internetwork routing, IP provides fragmentation and reassembly of datagrams and error reporting. Along with TCP, IP represents the heart of the Internet Protocol suite. The IP packet format is shown in Figure 7–2.

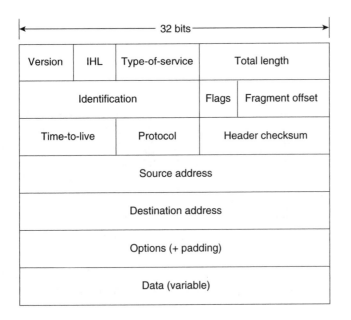

Figure 7–2
The IP Packet Format

The fields of the IP packet are as follows:

- Version—Indicates the version of IP currently used.

- IP header length (IHL)—Indicates the datagram header length in 32-bit words.

- Type-of-service—Specifies how a particular upper-layer protocol would like the current datagram to be handled. Datagrams can be assigned various levels of importance through this field.

- Total length—Specifies the length of the entire IP packet, including data and header, in bytes.

- Identification—Contains an integer that identifies the current datagram. This field is used to help piece together datagram fragments.

- Flags—A 3-bit field of which the low-order 2 bits control fragmentation. One bit specifies whether the packet can be fragmented; the second bit specifies whether the packet is the last fragment in a series of fragmented packets.

- Time-to-live—Maintains a counter that gradually decrements down to zero, at which point the datagram is discarded. This keeps packets from looping endlessly.

- Protocol—Indicates which upper-layer protocol receives incoming packets after IP processing is complete.

- Header checksum—Helps ensure IP header integrity.

- Source address—Specifies the sending node.

- Destination address—Specifies the receiving node.
- Options—Allows IP to support various options, such as security.
- Data—Contains upper-layer information.

Addressing

As with all network-layer protocols, the addressing scheme is integral to the process of routing IP datagrams through an internetwork. An IP address is 32 bits in length, divided into either two or three parts. The first part designates the network address; the second part (if present) designates the subnet address; and the final part designates the host address. Subnet addresses are present only if the network administrator has decided that the network should be divided into subnetworks. The lengths of the network, subnet, and host fields are all variable.

IP addressing supports five different network classes, and the far left bits indicate the network class:

- Class A networks are intended mainly for use with a few very large networks because they provide only 7 bits for the network address field.
- Class B networks allocate 14 bits for the network address field and 16 bits for the host address field. This address class offers a good compromise between network and host address space.
- Class C networks allocate 22 bits for the network address field. Class C networks provide only 8 bits for the host field, however, so the number of hosts per network may be a limiting factor.
- Class D addresses are reserved for multicast groups, as described formally in RFC 1112. In Class D addresses, the 4 highest-order bits are set to 1, 1, 1, and 0.
- Class E addresses are also defined by IP but are reserved for future use. In Class E addresses, the 4 highest-order bits are all set to 1.

IP addresses are written in dotted decimal format (for example, 34.10.2.1). Figure 7–3 shows the address formats for Class A, B, and C IP networks.

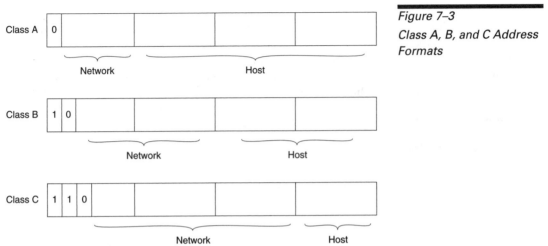

Figure 7–3
Class A, B, and C Address Formats

IP networks can also be divided into smaller units, called *subnets*. Subnets provide extra flexibility for network administrators. For example, assume that a network has been assigned a Class B address, and all the nodes on the network currently conform to a Class B address format. Then assume that the dotted decimal representation of this network's address is 128.10.0.0 (all zeros in the host field of an address specifies the entire network). Rather than change all the addresses to some other basic network number, the administrator can subdivide the network using subnetting. This is done by borrowing bits from the host portion of the address and using them as a subnet field, as shown in Figure 7–4.

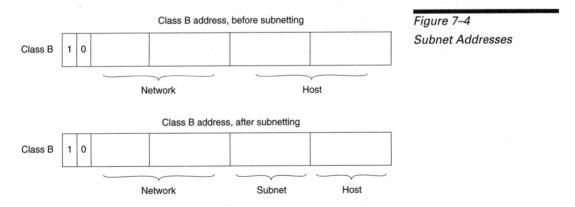

Figure 7–4
Subnet Addresses

If a network administrator has chosen to use 8 bits of subnetting, the third octet of a Class B IP address provides the subnet number. For example, address 128.10.1.0 refers to network 128.10, subnet 1; address 128.10.2.0 refers to network 128.10, subnet 2; and so on.

The number of bits borrowed for the subnet address is variable. To specify how many bits are used, IP provides the subnet mask. Subnet masks use the same format and representation technique as IP addresses. Subnet masks have ones in all bits except those bits that specify the host field. For example, the subnet mask that specifies 8 bits of subnetting for Class A address 34.0.0.0 is 255.255.0.0. The subnet mask that specifies 16 bits of subnetting for Class A address 34.0.0.0 is 255.255.255.0. Both of these subnet masks are shown in Figure 7–5.

Figure 7–5

A Sample Subnet Mask

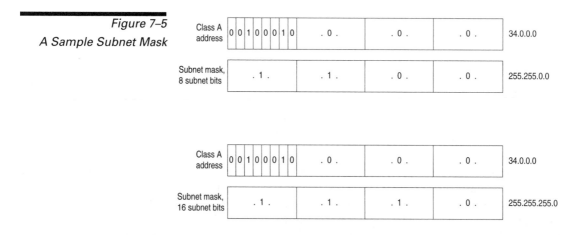

On some media (such as IEEE 802 LANs), media addresses and IP addresses are dynamically discovered through the use of two other members of the Internet Protocol suite: the Address Resolution Protocol (ARP) and the Reverse Address Resolution Protocol (RARP). ARP uses broadcast messages to determine the hardware Media Access Control (MAC)–layer address corresponding to a particular internetwork address. ARP is sufficiently generic to allow use of IP with virtually any type of underlying media-access mechanism. RARP uses broadcast messages to determine the Internet address associated with a particular hardware address. RARP is particularly important to diskless nodes, which may not know their internetwork address when they boot.

Internet Routing

Routing devices in the Internet have traditionally been called gateways—an unfortunate term because elsewhere in the industry, the term *gateway* applies to a device with somewhat different functionality. Gateways (which we will call *routers* from this point on) within the Internet are organized hierarchically. Some routers are used to move information through one particular group of networks under the same administrative authority and control (such an entity is called an *autonomous system*). Routers used for information exchange within autonomous systems are called *interior routers*, and they use a variety of interior gateway protocols (IGPs) to accomplish this purpose. Routers that move information between autonomous systems are called *exterior routers*, and they use an exterior gateway protocol for this purpose. The Internet architecture is shown in Figure 7–6.

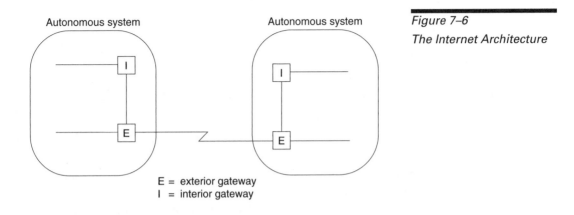

Figure 7–6

The Internet Architecture

E = exterior gateway
I = interior gateway

IP routing protocols are dynamic. Dynamic routing calls for routes to be calculated at regular intervals by software in the routing devices. This contrasts with static routing, where routes are established by the network administrator and do not change until the network administrator changes them. An IP routing table consists of destination address/next hop pairs. A sample entry, shown in Figure 7–7, is interpreted as meaning "to get to network 34.1.0.0 (subnet 1 on network 34), the next stop is the node at address 54.34.23.12."

Destination address	Next hop
34.1.0.0	54.34.23.12
78.2.0.0	54.34.23.12
147.9.5.0	
17.12.0.0	54.32.12.10
	54.32.12.10

Figure 7–7

An Example of an IP Routing Table

IP routing specifies that IP datagrams travel through internetworks one hop at a time. The entire route is not known at the outset of the journey. Instead, at each stop, the next destination is calculated by matching the destination address within the datagram with an entry in the current node's routing table. Each node's involvement in the routing process consists only of forwarding packets based on internal information, regardless of whether the packets get to their final destination. In other words, IP does not provide for error reporting back to the source when routing anomalies occur. This task is left to another Internet protocol, the Internet Control Message Protocol (ICMP).

ICMP

ICMP performs a number of tasks within an IP internetwork. The principal reason it was created was for reporting routing failures back to the source. In addition, ICMP provides helpful messages such as the following:

- Echo and reply messages to test node reachability across an internetwork

- Redirect messages to stimulate more efficient routing

- Time exceeded messages to inform sources that a datagram has exceeded its allocated time to exist within the internetwork

- Router advertisement and router solicitation messages to determine the addresses of routers on directly attached subnetworks

A more recent addition to ICMP provides a way for new nodes to discover the subnet mask currently used in an internetwork. All in all, ICMP is an integral part of all IP implementations, particularly those that run in routers.

IRDP

The ICMP Router Discovery Protocol (IRDP) uses router advertisement and router solicitation messages to discover addresses of routers on directly attached subnets.

The way IRDP works is that each router periodically multicasts router advertisement messages from each of its interfaces. Hosts discover the addresses of routers on the directly attached subnet by listening for these messages. Hosts can use router solicitation messages to request immediate advertisements, rather than wait for unsolicited messages.

IRDP offers several advantages over other methods of discovering addresses of neighboring routers. Primarily, it does not require hosts to recognize routing protocols, nor does it require manual configuration by an administrator.

Router advertisement messages allow hosts to discover the existence of neighboring routers, but not which router is best to reach a particular destination. If a host uses a poor first-hop router to reach a particular destination, it receives a redirect message identifying a better choice.

THE TRANSPORT LAYER

The Internet transport layer is implemented by TCP and the User Datagram Protocol (UDP). TCP provides connection-oriented data transport, whereas UDP operation is connectionless.

TCP

TCP provides full-duplex, acknowledged, and flow-controlled service to upper-layer protocols. It moves data in a continuous, unstructured byte stream where bytes are identified by sequence numbers. TCP can also support numerous simultaneous upper-layer conversations. The TCP packet format is shown in Figure 7–8.

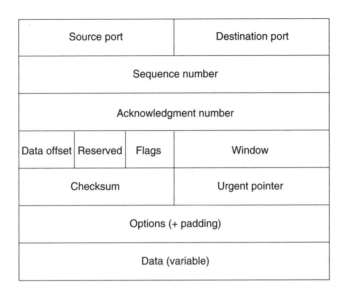

Figure 7–8
The TCP Packet Format

The fields of the TCP packet are as follows:

- Source port and destination port—Identify the points at which upper-layer source and destination processes receive TCP services.

- Sequence number—Usually specifies the number assigned to the first byte of data in the current message. Under certain circumstances, it can also be used to identify an initial sequence number to be used in the upcoming transmission.

- Acknowledgment number—Contains the sequence number of the next byte of data the sender of the packet expects to receive.

- Data offset—Indicates the number of 32-bit words in the TCP header.

- Reserved—Reserved for future use.

- Flags—Carries a variety of control information.

- Window—Specifies the size of the sender's receive window (that is, buffer space available for incoming data).

- Checksum—Indicates whether the header was damaged in transit.

- Urgent pointer—Points to the first urgent data byte in the packet.

- Options—Specifies various TCP options.

- Data—Contains upper-layer information.

UDP

UDP is a much simpler protocol than TCP and is useful in situations where the reliability mechanisms of TCP are not necessary. The UDP header has only four fields: source port, destination port, length, and UDP checksum. The source and destination port fields serve the same functions as they do in the TCP header. The length field specifies the length of the UDP header and data, and the checksum field allows packet integrity checking. The UDP checksum is optional.

UPPER-LAYER PROTOCOLS

The Internet Protocol suite includes many upper-layer protocols, representing a wide variety of applications, including network management, file transfer, distributed file services, terminal emulation, and electronic mail. Table 7–1 maps the best-known Internet upper-layer protocols to the applications they support.

Table 7–1 *Internet Protocol/Application Mapping*

Application	Protocols
File transfer	FTP
Terminal emulation	Telnet
Electronic mail	SMTP
Network management	SNMP
Distributed file services	NFS, XDR, RPC, X Window

File Transfer Protocol (FTP) provides a way to move files between computer systems. Telnet allows virtual terminal emulation. The Simple Network Management Protocol (SNMP) is a network management protocol used for reporting anomalous network conditions and setting network threshold values. X Window is a popular protocol that permits intelligent terminals to communicate with remote computers as if they were directly attached. Network file system (NFS), external data representation (XDR), and remote-procedure call (RPC) combine to allow transparent access to remote network resources. The Simple Mail Transfer Protocol (SMTP) provides an electronic mail transport mechanism. These and other network applications use the services of TCP/IP and other lower-layer Internet protocols to provide users with basic network services.

IP MULTICAST

The Internet Protocol suite was designed for communications between two computers using unicast addresses (that is, an address specifying a single network device). To send a message to all devices connected to the network, a single network device uses a broadcast address. These two forms of addressing have until now been sufficient for transferring traditional data (such as files and virtual terminal connections).

Now that application developers are trying to deliver the same data (such as the audio and video required for conferencing) to some, but not all, devices connected to the network, another form of addressing is required. The new form of addressing is called *multicast addresses*, and it involves the transmission of a single IP datagram to multiple hosts. This section describes the following techniques for supporting IP multicast addresses:

- UDP flooding
- Subnet broadcast
- Internet Group Membership Protocol

Because IP networks tend to have complex topologies with alternate paths built in for redundancy, each technique is evaluated for its ability to deliver data without burdening the network with duplicate packets.

UDP Flooding

UDP flooding depends on the spanning tree algorithm to place interfaces in the forwarding and blocking states. By placing certain interfaces in the blocking state, the spanning tree algorithm prevents the propagation of duplicate packets. The router sends specific packets (typically UDP packets) out the interfaces that are in the forwarding state. This technique saves bandwidth by controlling packet flow in topologies that feature redundant routers and alternate paths to the same destination. Figure 7–9 illustrates packet flow.

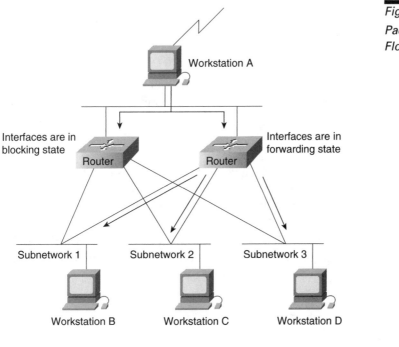

Figure 7–9
Packet Flow in UDP Flooding

Interfaces are in blocking state

Interfaces are in forwarding state

Workstation A

Router

Router

Subnetwork 1

Subnetwork 2

Subnetwork 3

Workstation B

Workstation C

Workstation D

⟶ UDP packets

Subnet Broadcast

Subnet broadcast (defined in RFC 922) supports the sending of packets to all the subnets of a particular network number. Packet duplication occurs when there are alternative paths in a network. In Figure 7–10, when Workstation A uses subnet broadcasting to send a packet to each workstation on Subnetwork 2, a duplicate packet also arrives.

Figure 7–10
Subnet Broadcast

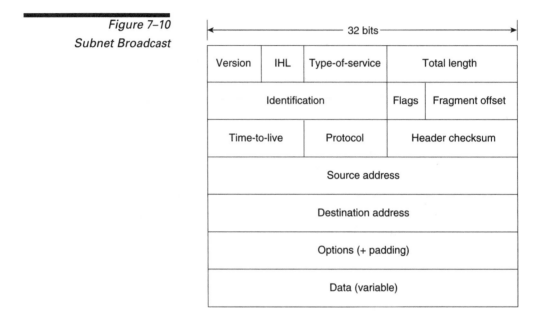

Whenever there is a duplicate path in the network, a duplicate packet is delivered. Because many multicast applications are data intense, packet duplication is a significant disadvantage of subnet broadcast.

Internet Group Membership Protocol

Internet Group Membership Protocol (IGMP), defined in RFC 1112, relies on Class D IP addresses for the creation of multicast groups. By using a specific Class D address, an individual host dynamically registers itself in a multicast group. Hosts identify their group memberships by sending IGMP messages. Traffic is then sent to all members of that multicast group.

Routers listen to IGMP messages and periodically send out queries to discover which groups are active on which LANs. To build multicast routes for each group, routers communicate with each other using one or more of the following routing protocols:

- Distance Vector Multicast Routing Protocol
- Multicast Open Shortest Path First
- Protocol Independent Multicast

These routing protocols are discussed in the following sections.

Distance Vector Multicast Routing Protocol

Distance Vector Multicast Routing Protocol (DVMRP), defined in RFC 1075, uses a technique called *reverse path flooding*. With reverse path flooding, on receipt of a packet, the router floods the packet out all paths except the path that leads back to the source of the packet, which ensures that a data stream reaches all LANs. If the router is attached to a LAN that does not want to receive a particular multicast group, the router sends a "prune" message back to the source to stop the data stream. When running DVMRP, routers periodically reflood the network to reach new hosts, using an algorithm that takes into account the frequency of flooding and the time required for a new multicast group member to receive the data stream.

To determine which interface leads back to the source of a data stream, DVMRP implements its own unicast routing protocol. The DVMRP unicast routing protocol is similar to RIP and is based on hop counts only. The path that multicast traffic follows may not be the same as the path that unicast traffic follows.

The need to reflood prevents DVMRP (especially early versions that do not implement pruning) from scaling well. Despite its limitations, DVMRP is widely deployed in the IP research community. It has been used to build the multicast backbone (MBONE) across the Internet.

The MBONE is used, for example, to transmit conference proceedings and deliver desktop video conferencing. Networks that wish to participate in the MBONE dedicate special hosts to the MBONE. The hosts establish tunnels to each other over the IP Internet and run DVMRP over the tunnels. The MBONE is a very high consumer of bandwidth both because of the nature of the traffic (audio and video) and because it is implemented with host-based tunnels. Host-based tunnels tend to result in packet duplication, which the backbone networks transmit unnecessarily.

In addition, the MBONE relies on extremely knowledgeable administrators for support. Despite their efforts, the MBONE has caused significant disruption to the Internet when popular events or multiple events are active.

Multicast Open Shortest Path First

Multicast Open Shortest Path First (MOSPF) is an extension to OSPF, which is a unicast routing protocol that requires each router in a network to be aware of all available links in the network. Each OSPF router calculates routes from itself to all possible destinations. MOSPF works by including multicast information in OSPF link states. MOSPF calculates the routes for each source/multicast group pair when the router receives traffic for that pair. These routes are cached until a topology change occurs, which requires MOSPF to recalculate the topology.

MOSPF works only in internetworks that are using OSPF and is best suited for environments in which relatively few source/group pairs are active at any one time. MOSPF performance degrades in environments that have many active source/group pairs and in environments in which links are unstable.

Protocol Independent Multicast

Multicast traffic tends to fall into one of two categories: traffic that is intended for almost all LANs (known as *dense*) and traffic that is intended for relatively few LANs (known as *sparse*). Protocol Independent Multicast (PIM) is an Internet draft (under discussion by the IETF Multicast Routing Working Group) that has two modes of behavior for the two traffic types: dense mode (DM) and sparse mode (SM). A router that is running PIM can use dense mode from some multicast groups and sparse mode for other multicast groups:

- *Dense mode*—In dense mode, PIM uses reverse path flooding and is similar to DVMRP. One significant difference between PIM and DVMRP is that PIM does not require a particular unicast protocol to determine which interface leads back to the source of a data stream. Instead, PIM uses whatever unicast protocol the internetwork is using.

- *Sparse mode*—In sparse mode, PIM is optimized for environments in which there are many data streams but each data stream goes to a relatively small number of the LANs in the internetwork. For this type of traffic, reverse path flooding wastes bandwidth.

PIM-SM works by defining a rendezvous point. When a sender wants to send data, it first sends to the rendezvous point. When a host wants to receive data, it registers with the rendezvous point. Once the data stream begins to flow from the sender, to the rendezvous point, and to the receiver, the routers in the path optimize the path automatically to remove any unnecessary hops, including the rendezvous point.

Comparison of Multicast Routing Protocols

Table 7–2 compares the characteristics of the routing protocols when handling multicast traffic.

Table 7–2   *Comparison of Multicast Routing Protocols*

Protocol	Unicast Protocol Requirements	Flooding Algorithm	Environment
DVMRP	RIP	Reverse path flooding	Small
MOSPF	OSPF	SPF	Few senders, stable links
PIM-DM	Any	RPF	Dense distribution pattern
PIM-SM	Any	None	Sparse distribution pattern

TROUBLESHOOTING TCP/IP

This section presents protocol-related troubleshooting information for Transmission Control Protocol/Internet Protocol (TCP/IP) connectivity and performance problems.

This chapter focuses on general TCP/IP problems and on routing problems related to RIP, the Interior Gateway Routing Protocol (IGRP), Enhanced IGRP, OSPF, the Border Gateway Protocol (BGP), and the Hot Standby Router Protocol (HSRP). Each of the following sections describes a specific symptom, the problems that are likely to cause each symptom, and the solutions to those problems.

This section covers the most common network issues in IP networks:

- TCP/IP: Local Host Cannot Access Remote Host
- TCP/IP: Routes Learned from the Wrong Interface or Protocol
- TCP/IP: Routing Not Functioning Properly on New Interface
- TCP/IP: Host Connections Fail Using Certain Applications
- TCP/IP: Problems Forwarding BOOTP and Other UDP Broadcasts
- TCP/IP: Poor Performance
- RIP/IGRP: Routes Missing from Routing Table
- OSPF: Routers Not Establishing Neighbors
- OSPF: Routes Missing from Routing Table
- IP Enhanced IGRP: Routers Not Establishing Neighbors
- IP Enhanced IGRP: Routes Missing from Routing Table
- IP Enhanced IGRP: Router Stuck in Active Mode
- BGP: Routes Missing from Routing Table
- BGP: Routers Not Advertising Routes
- HSRP: Hosts Cannot Reach Remote Networks

The symptoms described in the following sections are generic in nature and pertain to general TCP/IP internetwork problems. However, when host configuration problems are discussed, they are addressed assuming the use of UNIX end systems. Similar types of actions might be applicable for non-UNIX hosts, but the discussion does not specifically address non-UNIX end-station problems.

TCP/IP: Local Host Cannot Access Remote Host

Symptom: Hosts on one network cannot communicate with hosts on a remote network. The networks are separated by one or more routers and might include WAN or other links. One or more routing protocols are running on the routers.

Table 7–3 outlines the problems that might cause this symptom and describes solutions to those problems.

Table 7–3   *TCP/IP: Local Host Cannot Access Remote Host*

Possible Problem	Solution
Default gateway is not specified or is misconfigured on local or remote host	If hosts are not running *routed*, a default gateway should be configured.

<table>
<tr><td></td><td>**Step 1**</td><td>Determine whether the local and remote hosts have a default gateway specification. Use the following UNIX command:

`unix-host% `**`netstat -rn`**

Check the output of this command for a default gateway specification.</td></tr>
<tr><td></td><td>**Step 2**</td><td>If the default gateway specification is incorrect, or if it is not present at all, you can change or add a default gateway using the following UNIX command at the local host:

`unix-host% `**`route add default`** `address `**`1`**

where *address* is the IP address of the default gateway (the router local to the host). The value 1 indicates that the specified gateway is one hop away.

You might need to reboot the host for this change to take effect.</td></tr>
<tr><td></td><td>**Step 3**</td><td>It is recommended that you specify a default gateway as part of the boot process. Specify the IP address of the gateway in the */etc/defaultrouter* UNIX host file. This filename might be different on your UNIX system.

If you are working with a PC or a Macintosh, consult the corresponding documentation to determine how to set the default gateway.</td></tr>
<tr><td>Misconfigured or missing *routed* default routes</td><td>**Step 1**</td><td>If the host is running *routed*, use the **netstat -rn** UNIX command to view the host's routing table. The entry with Destination "default" denotes the default route.</td></tr>
<tr><td></td><td>**Step 2**</td><td>The default route entry should point to the router that has the route to the remote host. If there is no default route entry, use the **route** UNIX command to manually configure the default gateway:

`unix-host% `**`route add default`** `address `**`1`**</td></tr>
</table>

Table 7–3 *TCP/IP: Local Host Cannot Access Remote Host, Continued*

Possible Problem	Solution
DNS[1] host table is incomplete	If the DNS receives a lookup request for a host name that is not in its cache, it cannot reply to the request, and the client cannot establish a connection.
	Step 1 At the UNIX prompt, enter the following command:
	`unix-host% host address`
	where *address* is the IP address of a server, router, or other network node.
	Step 2 If the result of this host command is **Host not found**, but you can open the connection using the host's IP address rather than its name, try connecting to other hosts using their names. If connections to other hosts can be opened using their names, then the host table might be incomplete.
	Add hostname-to-address mappings to the DNS cache for every host on the network.
	Step 3 If you cannot open any connections using host names, the DNS might not be up and running. For troubleshooting information, see the following problem, "DNS is not up and running."
DNS is not up and running	If issuing the **host** command at the UNIX prompt returns a **Host not found** message, but you are able to open a connection using the host's IP address, the DNS might not be up and running.
	Consult the DNS software documentation or your system administrator for information on configuring and enabling the DNS.

Table 7–3   *TCP/IP: Local Host Cannot Access Remote Host, Continued*

Possible Problem	Solution
Routing is not enabled on one or more routers	**Step 1** Use the **trace** exec command to isolate the problem router (or routers).
	Syntax:
	trace [*protocol*] [*destination*]
	Syntax Description:
	• *protocol*—(Optional) Protocols that can be used are AppleTalk, CLNS[2], IP, and VINES.
	• *destination* —(Optional) Destination address or host name on the command line. The default parameters for the appropriate protocol are assumed and the tracing action begins.
	The following are the characters that can appear in **trace** output:
	• **nn/msec**—For each node, the round-trip time in milliseconds for the specified number of probes.
	• *—The probe timed out
	• ?—Unknown packet type
	• Q—Source quench
	• P—Protocol unreachable
	• N—Network unreachable
	• U—Port unreachable
	• H—Host unreachable
	Step 2 When you find a suspect router, determine whether routing is enabled on the router. Enter the **show ip route** privileged exec command to view the routing table. Examine the output to see whether the routing table is populated with routing information.
	Step 3 If routing information is not being exchanged (that is, if the output of the **show ip route** command shows no entries that were learned from a routing protocol), use the **show running-config** privileged exec command on the router.

Table 7–3 *TCP/IP: Local Host Cannot Access Remote Host, Continued*

Possible Problem	Solution

Routing is not enabled on one or more routers (*Continued*)	**Step 4** Look for a **router** global configuration command for the routing protocol that should be enabled.
	
	For example, if the router should be running IGRP, look for an entry such as the following:
	
	`router igrp 109`
	`  network 192.168.52.0`
	`  network 192.168.48.0`
	
	Step 5 If routing is not enabled on the router (or routers), enable the proper routing protocol using the **router** global configuration command.
	
	Step 6 In router configuration mode, enter the appropriate **network** commands to associate networks with the routing process, as applicable.
	
	For example, to enable IGRP routing for networks 193.166.66.0 and 193.168.25.0, enter the following configuration commands:
	
	`Router(config)# router igrp 109`
	`Router(config-router)# network 193.166.66.0`
	`Router(config-router)# network 193.168.25.0`
	
	For complete information on configuring specific IP routing protocols, see the *Cisco IOS Network Protocols Configuration Guide, Part 1* and *Network Protocols Command Reference, Part 1*.

Routing is misconfigured on one or more routers	Narrow down the specific symptoms and troubleshoot the problem using the procedures outlined later in this chapter. For example, check the routing tables on various routers using the **show ip route** privileged exec command. If you are running IGRP and there are routes missing from the routing table (that is, you see no routes to certain networks that you know are connected), refer to the section "RIP/IGRP: Routes Missing from Routing Table" later in this chapter.

[1] DNS = Domain Name System
[2] CLNS = Connectionless Network Service

TCP/IP: Routes Learned from the Wrong Interface or Protocol

Symptom: Routes in the routing table were learned from the wrong interface or protocol. For example, networks that should be reached through one interface are shown in the routing table to be reachable through another interface instead. This problem occurs only in a multiprotocol environment (see the section "Split Horizon Example," later in this chapter).

Table 7–4 outlines the problems that might cause this symptom and describes solutions to those problems.

Table 7–4 *TCP/IP: Routes Learned from the Wrong Interface or Protocol*

Possible Problem	Solution
Split horizon is disabled	**Step 1** Use the **show ip interface** privileged exec command on the remote router to see the router configuration.
	Step 2 Make sure that split horizon is enabled. Check the output of the **show ip interface** command for the following: `Split horizon is enabled`

	Step 3 If split horizon is not enabled, enter the **ip split-horizon** interface configuration command on the remote router interface.
	
	 For example, to enable split horizon on serial interface 0, enter the following commands:
	 `C4500(config)#interface s0`
	 `C4500(config-if)#ip split-horizon`

	Note: The default split-horizon setting for all LAN interfaces is **enabled**. However, for WAN multipoint interfaces configured with X.25, Frame Relay, or SMDS[1] encapsulation, the default split-horizon setting is disabled.

[1] SMDS = Switched Multimegabit Data Service

Split Horizon Example

Sometimes in a multipoint WAN environment it is desirable to leave split horizon disabled. However, steps should be taken to prevent routing information from being learned from the wrong interface or protocol. For example, in the environment shown in Figure 7–11, Router 2 might incorrectly receive information about RIP networks from Router 3 if the routers are not configured correctly.

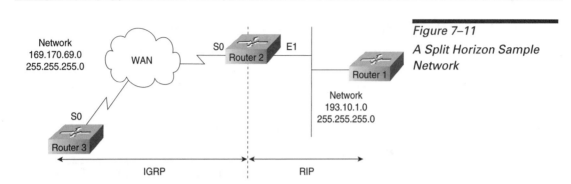

Figure 7–11

A Split Horizon Sample Network

RIP routing information learned by Router 2 from Router 1 is redistributed into the IGRP domain. IGRP routing updates are sent to Router 3 from Router 2. If split horizon is disabled on Router 3, Router 3's updates to Router 2 will include information about network 193.10.1.0 (which was originally learned from RIP updates sent from Router 1 to Router 2).

Because IGRP routes by default are given a lower (better) administrative distance than RIP routes, Router 2 will route traffic to network 193.10.1.0 out serial interface 0 (toward Router 3) rather than out Ethernet interface 1 (toward Router 1).

Enabling split horizon on Router 3's serial interface prevents the router from advertising any of the RIP routes it has learned. However, in some cases, enabling split horizon is not desirable (for example, in a hub-and-spoke environment). In such a situation, route filtering using an input distribution list can be configured on Router 2's serial interface 0, as the following example shows:

```
Router_2(config)#router igrp 100
Router_2(config-router)#distribute-list 5 in
Router_2(config)#access-list 5 deny 193.10.1.0 255.255.255.0
Router_2(config)#access-list 5 permit 168.170.69.0 255.255.255.0
```

The syntax for the **distribute-list** command is as follows:

distribute-list {*access-list-number* | *name*} **in** [*type number*]

- *access-list-number* | *name*—Standard IP access list number or name. The list defines which networks are to be received and which are to be suppressed in routing updates.

- **in**—Applies the access list to incoming routing updates.

- *type*—(Optional) Interface type.

- *number*—(Optional) Interface number on which the access list should be applied to incoming updates. If no interface is specified, the access list will be applied to all incoming updates.

This distribution list specifically denies routing updates from Router 3 that advertise network 193.10.1.0, thus preventing Router 2 from learning information about this network from the wrong protocol and the wrong interface. Be sure to configure explicit **permit** statements for any traffic that you do want Router 2 to accept.

TCP/IP: Routing Not Functioning Properly on New Interface

Symptom: A new interface is added to a router, but when routing is configured, it does not function properly on the new interface.

Table 7–5 outlines the problems that might cause this symptom and describes solutions to those problems.

Table 7–5 *TCP/IP: Routing Not Functioning Properly on New Interface*

Possible Problem	Solution	
Interface or LAN protocol is down	**Step 1**	Use the **show interfaces** privileged exec command to see whether the interface is "administratively down":
| | | ```
Router#show interface serial 0
Serial0 is administratively down, line protocol is down
  Hardware is HD64570
  Internet address is 10.1.1.5 255.255.255.252
  [...]
``` |
| | **Step 2** | If the interface is "administratively down," bring up the interface using the **no shutdown** interface configuration command. The following is an example of performing the **no shutdown** command: |
| | | ```
Router(config)#int serial0
Router(config-if)# no shutdown
Router(config-if)#
``` |
| | **Step 3** | Use the **show interfaces** command again to see whether the interface is now up. |
| | **Step 4** | If the interface is still down, there might be a hardware or media problem. See the procedures outlined in the chapter that covers your media type. |

Table 7–5 *TCP/IP: Routing Not Functioning Properly on New Interface, Continued*

Possible Problem	Solution
Misconfigured or missing **network** router configuration command	**Step 1** Use the **show running-config** privileged exec command to view the router configuration.
	Step 2 Make sure that there is a **network** router configuration command specified for the network to which the interface belongs.
	For example, if you assign the new interface IP address 192.168.52.42, enter the following commands to enable RIP[1] on the interface:
	``` c4500(config)#router rip c4500(config-router)#network 192.168.52.0 ```
	Make sure that process IDs, addresses, and other variables are properly specified for the routing protocol you are using. For more information, refer to the Cisco IOS configuration guides and command references.
No active interfaces are configured with an IP address (OSPF[2] only)	OSPF uses an IP address on the router as its router ID. Therefore, to configure the OSPF protocol on a router, you need at least one active interface configured with an IP address. If there is no active interface with an IP address, the router will return the following error:
	``` 2509(config)#router ospf 100 2509(config)# OSPF: Could not allocate router id ```
	Step 1 Use the **show ip interfaces** privileged exec command on the router to make sure there is a router interface that is up and configured with an IP address.
	Step 2 If there is no active interface with an IP address, configure an interface with the **ip address** interface configuration command. If necessary, use the **no shutdown** interface configuration command to bring an interface up. The following example shows the steps to enter configuration mode, assign an IP address to serial 0, and perform a no shutdown command on the interface:
	``` Router#conf t Enter configuration commands, one per line. End with CNTL/Z. Router(config)#interface serial 0 Router(config-if)#ip address 10.1.1.5 255.255.255.252 Router(config-if)#no shutdown Router(config-if)# ```

[1] RIP = Routing Information Protocol
[2] OSPF = Open Shortest Path First

TCP/IP: Host Connections Fail Using Certain Applications

Symptom: Connection attempts using some applications are successful, but attempts using other applications fail. For instance, you might be able to **ping** a host successfully, but Telnet connections fail.

Table 7–6 outlines the problems that might cause this symptom and describes solutions to those problems.

Table 7–6   *TCP/IP: Host Connections Fail Using Certain Applications*

Possible Problem	Solution
Misconfigured access lists or other filters	**Step 1** Use the **show running-config** command to check each router in the path. See if there are IP access lists configured on the router.
	Step 2 If there are IP access lists enabled on the router, disable them using the appropriate commands. An access list may be filtering traffic from a TCP or UDP[1] port. For example, to disable input access list 80, enter the following command: `C4000(config-if)#no ip access-group 80 in`
	Step 3 After disabling all the access lists on the router, determine whether the application in question operates normally.
	Step 4 If the application operates normally, an access list is probably blocking traffic.
	Step 5 To isolate the problem list, enable access lists one at a time until the application no longer functions. Check the problem access list to determine whether it is filtering traffic from any TCP or UDP ports.

	Step 6 If the access list denies specific TCP or UDP ports, make sure that it does not deny the port used by the application in question (such as TCP port 23 for Telnet).
	
	Enter explicit **permit** statements for those ports used by applications you want to have functional. The following commands allow DNS and NTP[2] requests and replies:
	
	`access-list 101 permit udp 0.0.0.0 255.255.255.255 0.0.0.0`
	`255.255.255.255 eq 53`
	`access-list 101 permit udp 0.0.0.0 255.255.255.255 0.0.0.0`
	`255.255.255.255 eq 123`

Table 7–6 *TCP/IP: Host Connections Fail Using Certain Applications, Continued*

Possible Problem	Solution
Misconfigured access lists or other filters (*Continued*)	**Step 7** If you altered an access list, enable the list to see whether the application can still operate normally.
	Step 8 If the application operates normally, perform the preceding steps to isolate any other problem access lists until the application operates correctly with all access lists enabled.
	For more information about misconfigured access lists, see the section "Misconfigured Access List Example" later in this chapter. For more information on configuring access lists, see the Cisco IOS configuration guides and command references.

[1] UDP = User Datagram Protocol
[2] NTP = Network Time Protocol

Misconfigured Access List Example

Misconfigured access lists can cause connectivity and performance problems. In the environment shown in Figure 7–12, the network administrator can successfully reach Router Z from Router X using the **telnet** and **ping** commands. However, when attempts are made to trace the route using the **trace** command, the connection fails.

Figure 7–12

A Misconfigured Access List Sample Network

When examining the configuration of Router Y, the network administrator finds the following extended access list configured on the router:

```
C4500#show ip access-lists
Extended IP access list 101
    permit tcp any any eq telnet
    permit icmp any any
C4500#show running-config
[...]
interface Serial0
 ip address 192.168.54.92 255.255.255.0
 ip access-group 101 out
[...]
```

The access list permits only ICMP (used by the **ping** application) and TCP (used by the Telnet application) traffic to pass serial interface 0. Any traffic destined for UDP ports, including the default ports used by the trace application (UDP ports 33434 and above), is implicitly denied.

To allow trace traffic to pass through Router Y, the network administrator makes the following change to the access list:

```
C4500#configure terminal
C4500(config)#access-list 101 permit udp any any gt 33433
C4500(config)#^Z
C4500#
%SYS-5-CONFIG_I: Configured from console by console
C4500#show ip access-lists
Extended IP access list 101
    permit tcp any any eq telnet
    permit icmp any any
    permit udp any any gt 33433
C4500#
```

TCP/IP: Problems Forwarding BOOTP and Other UDP Broadcasts

Symptom: Problems occur when forwarding BOOTP or other UDP broadcast packets. UDP broadcasts sent from network hosts are not forwarded by routers. Diskless workstations cannot boot.

Table 7–7 outlines the problems that might cause this symptom and describes solutions to those problems.

TCP/IP: Poor Performance

Symptom: Performance for one or more network hosts is slow. Connections to servers take an excessive amount of time to establish.

Table 7–7 *TCP/IP: Problems Forwarding BOOTP and Other UDP Broadcasts*

Possible Problem	Solution	
Missing or misconfigured **ip helper-address** specification	**Step 1**	Use the **debug ip udp** privileged exec command on the router that should be receiving packets from the host. Check the output of the command to see whether packets are being received from the host.
		Caution: This **debug** command can use considerable CPU cycles on the router. Do not enable it if your network is heavily congested. You can attach a protocol analyzer to see whether UDP broadcasts are being received from the host if your network is congested.
	Step 2	If the router receives packets from the host, there is a problem with the host or the application. Consult the documentation for the host or application.
		If the router does receive packets from the host, use the **show running-config** privileged exec command to check the configuration of the router interface that first receives the packet from the host.
	Step 3	Look for an **ip helper-address** *address* interface configuration command entry for that interface. Make sure that the specified address is correct (it should be the IP address of a server application such as a BOOTP server). If there is no command entry, then no helper address is configured.
	Step 4	If there is no IP helper address configured, or if the wrong address is specified, add or change the helper address using the **ip helper-address** *address* interface configuration command.
		For example, to configure the IP address 192.168.192.6 as the helper address on router Ethernet interface 0, enter the following commands:

```
C4500(config)#interface e0
C4500(config-if)#ip helper-address 192.168.192.6
```

Table 7–7   *TCP/IP: Problems Forwarding BOOTP and Other UDP Broadcasts, Continued*

Possible Problem	Solution

UDP broadcasts being forwarded out nondefault ports	Specifying an IP helper address ensures that broadcasts from only a certain default set of UDP ports are forwarded. UDP broadcasts forwarded out other ports require further configuration.
	
	Enter an **ip forward-protocol udp** *port* global configuration command on the router for each applicable port. For example, to forward UDP broadcasts from port 200, enter the following command:
	
	`C4500(config)#ip forward-protocol udp 200`
	
	To allow forwarding of all UDP broadcasts, enter the following command:
	
	`C4500(config)#ip forward-protocol udp`

UDP broadcast forwarding is disabled on specific UDP ports	**Step 1** Use the **show running-config** privileged exec command on the router and look for any **no ip forward-protocol udp** global configuration command entries. Such entries disable the forwarding of UDP traffic out specific ports.
	
	For example, entering the **no ip forward-protocol udp 53** global configuration command disables the forwarding of all UDP traffic out port 53, which is the default port for DNS broadcasts. The following entry is shown in the configuration:
	
	`no ip forward-protocol udp domain`
	
	Step 2 If UDP broadcasts are disabled at specific UDP ports, enter the **ip forward-protocol udp** *port* global configuration command (you can also specify a keyword, such as **domain**, rather than the port number).
	
	For example, to reenable DNS broadcasts, enter the following command:
	
	`C4500(config)#ip forward-protocol udp domain`
	
	To allow forwarding of BOOTP broadcasts, enter the following command:
	
	`C4500(config)#ip forward-protocol udp bootp`
	
	To allow forwarding of all UDP broadcasts, enter the following command:
	
	`C4500(config)#ip forward-protocol udp`

Table 7–7 *TCP/IP: Problems Forwarding BOOTP and Other UDP Broadcasts, Continued*

Possible Problem	Solution
Access list or other filters are misconfigured	**Step 1** Use the **show running-config** command to check the configuration of each router in the path. See if there are access lists configured on the router.
	Step 2 If there are access lists enabled on the router, disable them using the appropriate commands. For example, to disable input access list 10, enter the following command: `C4000(config-if)#no ip access-group 10 in`
	Step 3 After disabling all access lists, determine whether the BOOTP or other UDP broadcasts are forwarded normally. If broadcasts are forwarded normally, an access list is probably blocking traffic.
	Step 4 To isolate the problem access list, enable access lists one at a time until broadcasts are no longer forwarded.
	Step 5 Check the problem access list to see whether it is filtering traffic from any UDP ports. If an access list denies specific UDP ports, make sure that it does not deny ports used to forward the broadcast traffic in question (such as UDP port 67 for BOOTP or port 68 for BOOTP replies). Enter explicit **permit** statements for those ports used to forward broadcasts that you want to have forwarded. The following is an example of using a **permit** statement in an access list: `Router(config)#access-list 101 permit udp any any eq` `Router(config)#access-list 101 permit udp any any eq`
	Step 6 If you altered an access list, enable the list to see whether broadcasts are still forwarded normally.
	Step 7 If problems persist, perform the preceding steps on routers in the path until broadcast traffic is forwarded correctly.
	For more information about misconfigured access lists, see Table 7–4 and the section "Misconfigured Access List Example" earlier in this chapter. For more information on configuring access lists, see the Cisco IOS configuration guides and command references.

Table 7–8 outlines the problems that might cause this symptom and describes solutions to those problems.

Table 7–8   *TCP/IP: Poor Performance*

Possible Problem	Solution
Misconfigured *resolv.conf* file on DNS client	Check the */etc/resolv.conf* file on DNS clients. If the file is misconfigured, the client might wait until a query to one server times out before trying a second server, an NIS[1], or its host tables. This can cause excessive delays.
DNS is not set up for reverse lookups	If the DNS server is not configured to perform reverse lookups, reverse lookup attempts by end systems will time out. This can cause excessive delays for hosts attempting to establish connections. Consult your DNS software documentation for information on how to properly configure the DNS for reverse lookups.
DNS host table is incomplete	If the DNS host table is incomplete, reverse lookups will be unsuccessful, causing timeouts and therefore delays. **Step 1** At the UNIX prompt, enter the following command: `unix-host% `**`host`**` ip-address` where *ip-address* is the IP address of a server, router, or other network node. **Step 2** If the result of this command is **Host not found**, but you can open the connection using the host's IP address rather than its name, then the host table might be incomplete. Add address-to-hostname mappings to the DNS host table for every host on the network.

[1] NIS = Network Information Service

RIP/IGRP: Routes Missing from Routing Table

Symptom: Routes are missing from the routing table. Hosts on one network cannot access hosts on a different network. Error messages stating "host or destination unreachable" are generated.

The problem might be occurring in an internetwork running only RIP or IGRP, or a combination of the two.

Table 7–9 outlines the problems that might cause this symptom and describes solutions to those problems.

Table 7–9 *RIP/IGRP: Routes Missing from Routing Table*

Possible Problem	Solution

Misconfigured or missing **network** router configuration command	**Step 1** Use the **show running-config** privileged exec command to view the router configuration.
	
	Step 2 Make sure that a **network** router configuration command is specified for every network to which a router interface belongs.
	
	For example, if the IP address of one interface is 192.168.52.42, and the IP address of another interface is 108.168.54.10, enter the following commands to enable RIP on the interfaces:
	
	`c4500(config)#router rip`
	`c4500(config-router)#network 192.168.52.0`
	`c4500(config-router)#network 108.168.0.0`
	
	Make sure the correct process IDs, addresses, and other variables are properly specified for the routing protocol you are using. For more information, consult the Cisco IOS configuration guides and command references.

Misconfigured route filtering	**Step 1** Use the **show running-config** command to check suspect routers. **Step 2** See if any **distribute-list in** or **distribute-list out** router configuration commands are configured on the router. The **distribute-list in** command filters specific information in routing updates received by a router. The **distribute-list out** command prevents a router from including specific information in routing updates that it transmits. The information that is filtered is specified with an access list.

Table 7–9   *RIP/IGRP: Routes Missing from Routing Table, Continued*

Possible Problem	Solution
Misconfigured route filtering (*Continued*)	**Step 3** If **distribute-list** commands are configured on the router, disable them using the **no** version of the command. For example, to disable an incoming filter that references access list 10, enter the following command: `C7500(config)#`**`no distribute-list 10 in`** **Step 4** After disabling all distribution lists on the router, use the **clear ip route** privileged exec command to clear the routing table. **Step 5** Determine whether the routes appear in the routing table by using the **show ip route** privileged exec command. **Step 6** If routes appear properly in the routing table, the access list referenced by the **distribute-list** command is probably configured to deny certain updates. **Step 7** To isolate the problem list, enable distribution lists until routes stop appearing in the routing table. (You might have to use the **clear ip route** command after enabling each list.) **Step 8** Use the **show running-config** command and make sure that the problem list does not deny updates inappropriately. If the access list denies updates from specific addresses, make sure that it does not deny the address of a router from which routing updates should be received. Change the access list to allow the router to receive updates from the proper addresses. At the end of every access list is an implied "deny all traffic" criteria statement. Therefore, if a packet does not match any of your criteria statements, the packet will be blocked. Configure explicit **permit** statements for those addresses from which the router should receive updates. **Step 9** If you altered an access list, enable the distribution list using the **distribute-list** command. Use the **clear ip route** command and check whether the missing routing information appears in the routing table.

Table 7–9 *RIP/IGRP: Routes Missing from Routing Table, Continued*

Possible Problem	Solution
Misconfigured route filtering (*Continued*)	In the following example, the Enhanced IGRP routing process accepts only two networks—network 0.0.0.0 and network 131.108.0.0:
	```\naccess-list 1 permit 0.0.0.0\naccess-list 1 permit 131.108.0.0\naccess-list 1 deny 0.0.0.0 255.255.255.255\nrouter eigrp\n network 131.108.0.0\n distribute-list 1 in\n```
	Step 10 If the routes appear, perform the preceding steps on all routers in the path until the routing information appears properly, with all distribution lists enabled.
	For more information on configuring access lists, see the Cisco IOS configuration guides and command references.
Subnet mask mismatch	Problems occur when two or more interfaces on the same major network have different subnet masks configured.
	Step 1 Use the **show running-config** privileged exec command to view the configuration of each router in the major network.
	Step 2 Use the **show ip interface** privileged exec command. Check the subnet mask specified for each interface. There is a subnet mask mismatch if two or more interfaces on the same major network have different subnet masks.
	Step 3 If two interfaces on the same network have different subnet masks, you must change the subnet mask specification for one of the interfaces using the **ip address** *ip-address mask* interface configuration command (or use a classless routing protocol such as OSPF or Enhanced IGRP).
	For example, to configure Ethernet interface 1 with the IP address 192.168.52.46 using a subnet mask of 255.255.255.0, enter the following commands:
	```\nC4000(config)#interface e1\nc4000(config-if)#ip address 192.168.52.46 255.255.255.0\n```
	For more information about subnet masks, see the section "Host and Router Subnet Mask Mismatch Example" later in this chapter.

Table 7–9   *RIP/IGRP: Routes Missing from Routing Table, Continued*

Possible Problem	Solution
Missing **default-metric** command	This problem is restricted to environments in which route redistribution is being performed between autonomous systems or between multiple routing protocols.

<table>
<tr><td>Step 1</td><td>Use the show running-config privileged exec command on suspect routers. Look for default-metric router configuration command entries. This command assigns default metric values to redistributed routes.</td></tr>
<tr><td>Step 2</td><td>IGRP requires a default-metric parameter to redistribute routes. If you are running IGRP, define the default metrics for redistributed routes using the default-metric router configuration command.

The following example shows a configuration that redistributes RIP routes and assigns them IGRP metrics with values as follows: bandwidth = 1000, delay = 100, reliability = 250, loading = 100, and mtu = 1500:</td></tr>
</table>

```
router igrp 109
network 131.108.0.0
redistribute rip
default-metric 1000 100 250 100 1500
```

<table>
<tr><td>Step 3</td><td>If you are running RIP, you do not have to configure a default metric in order to redistribute routes. By default, the metric assigned to all routes redistributed into RIP is 1. However, this value can be changed using the default-metric command.

If a default-metric statement that is applied to RIP appears in the configuration, make sure that the metric value it assigns will not adversely affect network performance. If you are unsure, restore the default value for the routing metric using the no default-metric router configuration command.</td></tr>
</table>

For more information on the **default-metric** router configuration command, see the Cisco IOS configuration guides and command references.

Table 7–9 *RIP/IGRP: Routes Missing from Routing Table, Continued*

Possible Problem	Solution
Routes are not being redistributed properly between autonomous systems or between routing protocols	This problem is restricted to environments in which route redistribution is being performed between autonomous systems or between multiple routing protocols.

Step 1 Use the **show running-config** privileged exec command on routers that border multiple networks running different routing protocols.

Step 2 Examine the **router** global configuration command entries for the enabled routing protocols.

Step 3 If the router is running IGRP only, check whether the autonomous system designated for all connected networks is the same.

Routes are not automatically redistributed between different autonomous systems. If the **router igrp** commands indicate different autonomous systems, route redistribution must be manually configured using the **redistribute** router configuration command.

For example, to redistribute routes between IGRP autonomous system 71 (network 15.0.0.0) and IGRP autonomous system 109 (network 192.31.7.0), enter the following commands:

```
C7010(config)#router igrp 71
C7010(config-router)#redistribute igrp 109
C7010(config-router)#distribute-list 3 out igrp 109
C7010(config-router)#access-list 3 permit 192.31.7.0
C7010(config)#router igrp 109
C7010(config-router)#redistribute igrp 71
C7010(config-router)#distribute-list 5 out igrp 71
C7010(config-router)#access-list 5 permit 15.0.0.0
```

Step 4 If the router is running multiple routing protocols, look for a **redistribute** router configuration command entry. Make sure that routing information is being properly exchanged between protocols.

For example, to redistribute routes between RIP (running in network 15.0.0.0) and IGRP autonomous system 109 (network 128.1.0.0), enter the following commands:

```
C7010(config)#router igrp 109
C7010(config-router)#network 128.1.0.0
C7010(config-router)#redistribute rip
C7010(config-router)#default-metric 10000 100 255 1 1500
C7010(config-router)#distribute-list 10 out rip
C7010(config-router)#access-list 10 permit 15.0.0.0
```

Table 7–9   *RIP/IGRP: Routes Missing from Routing Table, Continued*

Possible Problem	Solution
Routes are not being redistributed properly between autonomous systems or between routing protocols (*Continued*)	**Step 5** If you want static routes to be redistributed between autonomous systems or between two different routing protocols, use the **redistribute static** router configuration command. For example, to redistribute static routes in IGRP autonomous systems, add the following command to the configuration: `C7010(config-router)#`**`redistribute static`** For more information on using the **redistribute** router configuration command, see the Cisco IOS configuration guides and command references.

Host and Router Subnet Mask Mismatch Example

In classful IP networks, every router and host in the same major network should share a common subnet mask. If there are disagreements on the length of the subnet mask, packets are not routed correctly.

Table 7–10 shows how a UNIX host and a router will interpret an IP address differently if they have different subnet masks specified for the same major network.

Table 7–10   *Host and Router Subnet Mask Mismatch Example*

Routing Information	Host Value	Router Value
Destination IP address	192.31.7.49	192.31.7.49
Subnet mask	255.255.255.240	255.255.255.224
Interpreted address	Subnet address 48, host 1	Subnet address 32, host 17

The host interprets the IP address 192.31.7.49 as being Host 1 on the third subnet (subnet address 48). However, because it is using a different subnet mask, the router interprets the address as being Host 17 on the first subnet (subnet address 32). Depending on the network topology and the router configuration, packets destined for IP address 192.31.7.49 might be sent to the wrong destination host, sent from the wrong interface, or dropped altogether.

OSPF: Routers Not Establishing Neighbors

Symptom: OSPF routers are not establishing neighbor relationships properly. The result is that routing information is not exchanged between routers.

Table 7–11 outlines the problems that might cause this symptom and describes solutions to those problems.

Table 7–11   *OSPF: Routers Not Establishing Neighbors*

Possible Problem	Solution
Misconfigured or missing **network** router configuration command	**Step 1** Use the **show ip ospf interfaces** exec command to determine which interfaces have OSPF[1] enabled.
	Step 2 If the output indicates that an interface that should be running OSPF is not doing so, use the **show running-config** privileged exec command to view the router configuration.
	Step 3 Make sure that **network** router configuration commands are specified for each interface on which OSPF should run.
	For example, if the IP address of Ethernet interface 0 is 192.168.52.42 with a subnet mask of 255.255.255.0, enter the following commands to enable OSPF on the interface:
	`c4500(config)#router ospf 100` `c4500(config-router)#network 192.168.52.0 0.0.0.255 area 0`
	Make sure the proper process IDs, addresses, wildcard masks, and other variables are properly specified. To configure an OSPF routing process, use the **router ospf** global configuration command:
	router ospf *process-id*
	Syntax Description:
	• *process-id*—Internally used identification parameter for an OSPF routing process. It is locally assigned and can be any positive integer. A unique value is assigned for each OSPF routing process.
	Note: There is no correlation between OSPF wildcard masks (used in OSPF **network** commands) and the subnet mask configured as part of an interface IP address.
	Step 4 Check other OSPF routers on the network using the preceding steps. Make sure that OSPF is configured properly on all neighboring routers so that neighbor relationships can be established.

Table 7–11   *OSPF: Routers Not Establishing Neighbors, Continued*

Possible Problem	Solution
Mismatched Hello or dead timers, E-bits (set for stub areas), area IDs, authentication types, or network masks	The values set for the Hello timer and dead timer intervals, E-bits (this bit is set if the router is configured in a stub area), area IDs, authentication types, and network masks should all be the same throughout an OSPF area and in some cases the entire OSPF network.

Step 1 Use the **show ip ospf neighbor** privileged exec command to identify the OSPF neighbors of each router.

Step 2 If the output does not list an expected neighbor, use the **show ip ospf interface** privileged exec command on the router and its expected neighbor. Examine the Hello and dead timer interval values configured on OSPF interfaces.

The following is an example of the **show ip ospf interface** command:

```
C7010#show ip ospf interface
[...]
Timer intervals configured, Hello 12, Dead 48, Wait 40,
Retransmit 5
```

Step 3 Compare the values configured for the timers on each router. If there is a mismatch, reconfigure the timer values so that they are the same on the router and its neighbor.

For example, to change the Hello timer interval to 10 on Ethernet interface 0/1, enter the following commands:

```
C7010(config)#interface e0/1
C7010(config-if)#ip ospf hello-interval 10
```

The following is an overview of the **ip ospf hello-interval** command:

ip ospf hello-interval *seconds*

Syntax Description:

• *seconds*—Unsigned integer that specifies the interval in seconds. The value must be the same for all nodes on a specific network. The default is 10 seconds.

Table 7–11 *OSPF: Routers Not Establishing Neighbors, Continued*

Possible Problem	Solution

Mismatched Hello or dead timers, E-bits (set for stub areas), area IDs, authentication types, or network masks (*Continued*)	**Step 4** Use the **debug ip ospf adj** privileged exec command. Check the output for mismatched values.
	
	In the following example, there is a network mask mismatch. The mask received from router 141.108.10.3 is 255.255.255.0, and the mask configured on the router C4500 is 255.255.255.252:
	
	```C4500#debug ip ospf adj```
	```OSPF: Mismatched hello parameters from 141.108.10.3```
	```Dead R 40 C 40, Hello R 10 C 10 Mask R 255.255.255.0 C```
	```255.255.255.252```
	
	Step 5 If mismatches are indicated in the debug output, try to resolve the mismatch. For detailed information about configuring OSPF, see the Cisco IOS *Network Protocols Configuration Guide, Part 1.*
	
	Step 6 Perform the same steps for all these parameters. Ensure that all routers in an area have the same area ID, check whether all routers in the area are configured as stub routers, check whether the same authentication type is configured for all routers, and so forth. For information on configuring these parameters, consult the Cisco IOS *Network Protocols Configuration Guide, Part 1.*
	
	Note: Timer values are extremely important when Cisco routers interoperate with routers from other vendors.

Table 7–11   *OSPF: Routers Not Establishing Neighbors, Continued*

Possible Problem	Solution
Access list is misconfigured	**Step 1** Use the **show access-list** privileged exec command on suspect routers to see whether there are IP access lists configured on the router.
	Step 2 If there are IP access lists enabled on the router, disable them using the appropriate commands. For example, to disable input access list 10, use the following command: `C4000(config-if)#no ip access-group 10 in`
	Step 3 After disabling all access lists on the router, determine whether the router is able to establish neighbor relationships normally. Use the **show ip ospf neighbor** privileged exec command. If the proper neighbor relationships have been established, an access list is probably filtering OSPF hello packets.
	Step 4 To isolate the problem access list, enable access lists one at a time until the router cannot establish neighbors (use the **clear ip ospf neighbors** privileged exec command to force the router to clear the neighbor table).
	Step 5 Check the access list to see whether it is filtering traffic from port 89, the port used by OSPF. At the end of every access list is an implied "deny all traffic" criteria statement. Therefore, if a packet does not match any of your criteria statements, the packet will be blocked. If an access list denies OSPF traffic, enter an explicit **permit** statement for port 89 to ensure that neighbor relationships can be established properly. (You can also use the **ospf** keyword when configuring the access list.) For example, to configure input access list 101 to allow OSPF traffic to pass, enter the following on the router: `C4500(config)#access-list 101 permit ospf any any`
	Step 6 If you altered an access list, enable the list and enter the **clear ip ospf neighbors** privileged exec command. Then enter the **show ip ospf neighbor** command to see whether neighbor relationships are established normally.
	Step 7 If the router is establishing neighbors, perform the preceding steps for other routers in the path until all access lists are enabled and the router can still establish neighbors normally.
	For more information on configuring access lists, see the Cisco IOS configuration guides.

Table 7–11 *OSPF: Routers Not Establishing Neighbors, Continued*

Possible Problem	Solution	
| Virtual link and stub area configuration mismatch | **Step 1** | A virtual link cannot be configured across a stub area. Check router configurations for routers configured both as part of a stub area and as an ABR[2] that is part of a virtual link. Use the **show running-config** privileged exec command and look for command entries that are similar to the following:<br><br>```
area 2 stub
area 2 virtual-link 192.169.100.10
``` |
| | **Step 2** | If both of these commands are present, there is a misconfiguration. Remove one of the commands (using the **no** form of the command) to resolve the misconfiguration. |

[1] OSPF = Open Shortest Path First
[2] ABR = area border router

OSPF: Routes Missing from Routing Table

Symptom: OSPF routes and networks are not being advertised to other routers. Routers in one area are not receiving routing information for other areas. Some hosts cannot communicate with hosts in other areas, and routing table information is incomplete.

Table 7–12 outlines the problems that might cause this symptom and describes solutions to those problems.

Table 7–12 *OSPF: Routes Missing from Routing Table*

Possible Problem	Solution	
OSPF routers not establishing neighbors	Follow the procedures outlined in the section "OSPF: Routers Not Establishing Neighbors" earlier in this chapter.	
Routing information from IGRP or RIP is not redistributed correctly into OSPF	**Step 1**	Check the router configuration using the **show running-config** privileged exec command.
	Step 2	Look for a **redistribute** router configuration command entry. Make sure that redistribution is configured and that the **subnets** keyword is used with the command. The **subnets** keyword must be included when IGRP or RIP is redistributed into OSPF; otherwise, only major routes (not subnet routes) are redistributed.
| | **Step 3** | If the **redistribute** command is not present, or if the **subnets** keyword is not specified, add or change the configuration using the following commands:<br><br>```
C7000(config)#router ospf 100
C7000(config)#redistribute ospf subnets
``` |

Table 7–12   *OSPF: Routes Missing from Routing Table, Continued*

Possible Problem	Solution

No ABR is configured in an area, isolating that area from the OSPF backbone	**Step 1** Use the **show running-config** privileged exec command on OSPF routers to verify that at least one ABR exists for the area. ABRs must belong to area 0, the OSPF backbone, as well as to another area. Look for **network** statements which indicate that the router is part of area 0.
	
	 To define the interfaces on which OSPF runs and to define the area ID for those interfaces, use the **network area** router configuration command:
	
	 network *address wildcard-mask* **area** *area-id*
	
	 Syntax Description:
	
	 • *address*—IP address.
	
	 • *wildcard-mask*—IP-address-type mask that includes "don't care" bits.
	
	 • *area-id*—Area that is to be associated with the OSPF address range. It can be specified as either a decimal value or as an IP address. If you intend to associate areas with IP subnets, you can specify a subnet address as the *area-id*.
	
	 Step 2 If no ABR exists in an area, configure one where appropriate. Use the **network** router configuration command.
	
	 For example, to configure OSPF process 100 to participate in the OSPF backbone area, enter the following commands:
	
	 `C4500(config)#router ospf 100`
	 `C4500(config-router)#network 192.21.3.7 0.0.0.255 area 0`

Table 7–12   *OSPF: Routes Missing from Routing Table, Continued*

Possible Problem	Solution
Interface network type mismatch on Frame Relay WAN	In an OSPF Frame Relay environment, if one end of the link is a multipoint interface and the other end is a point-to-point interface, by default the multipoint interface will advertise the link as a non-broadcast network and the point-to-point interface will advertise the link as a point-to-point network. This creates a conflict in the link-state database and can prevent routing information from being learned properly.

Step 1 Check each router interface on each side of the link to see whether the network types are mismatched. Use the **show ip ospf interface** privileged exec command to check the network type configured for the interface.

Following is an example of the output from the **show ip ospf interface** command:

```
Ethernet0 is up, line protocol is up
Internet Address 192.168.52.14 255.255.255.0, Area 0
Process ID 1, Router ID 192.168.52.14,
Network Type BROADCAST, Cost: 10
[...]
```

In this example, the network type is broadcast.

Step 2 Change the point-to-point interface to a multipoint interface by configuring subinterfaces, or change the network type of the point-to-point interface to broadcast using the **ip ospf network broadcast** interface configuration command.

The following example sets your OSPF network as a broadcast network:

```
interface serial 0
  ip address 160.89.77.17 255.255.255.0
  ip ospf network broadcast
  encapsulation frame-relay
```

For information on configuring subinterfaces, see the Cisco IOS configuration guides.

Table 7–12   *OSPF: Routes Missing from Routing Table, Continued*

Possible Problem	Solution
Area is configured as a stub area	Route redistribution is not possible in OSPF stub areas. No external routes are advertised into a stub area, and if the **area** *area-id* **stub no-summary** router configuration command is used, no summary routes (inter-area routes) will be advertised into the stub area.
	Step 1 If you want summary routes to be advertised into the stub area, but you do not see them in the routing table, use the **show running-config** privileged exec command to view the router configuration.

	Step 2 Look for an **area** *area-id* **stub no-summary** command entry. If this command is present, disable it by entering the following commands:
	
	`C4500(config)#router ospf 100`
	`C4500(config-router)#no area 1 stub no-summary`
	
	This disables the **no-summary** keyword and keeps the router configured as a stub.

	Step 3 To advertise external routes into the area, you must configure the area as a non-stub. Make certain that all routers in the area are reconfigured as non-stub routers.
Misconfigured route filtering	**Step 1** Use the **show running-config** command to check suspect routers.
	Step 2 See if there are any **distribute-list in** or **distribute-list out** router configuration commands configured on the router.
	The **distribute-list in** command prevents specific information learned in LSAs[1] from being included in the OSPF routing table. The **distribute-list out** command prevents a router from including specific information in routing updates that it transmits. However, in OSPF, **distribute-list out** can be configured *only* on an ASBR[2] to filter external routes.
	Note: Although **distribute-list** commands prevent specific information from being included in the OSPF routing table, information about those networks is contained in the link-state database and is flooded through the network in LSAs. This means that downstream routers will include that information in their routing tables unless they, too, filter those routes from the routing table.

Table 7–12 *OSPF: Routes Missing from Routing Table, Continued*

Possible Problem	Solution
Misconfigured route filtering (*Continued*)	**Step 3** If **distribute-list** commands are configured on the router, disable them using the **no** version of the command. For example, to disable an incoming filter that references access list 10, enter the following command: `C7500(config)#no distribute-list 10 in` **Step 4** After disabling all distribution lists, use the **clear ip route** privileged exec command to clear the routing table. **Step 5** Determine whether the routes appear in the routing table by using the **show ip route** privileged exec command. If routes appear properly in the routing table, the access list referenced by the **distribute-list** command is probably configured to deny certain updates. **Step 6** To isolate the problem list, enable distribution lists one at a time until the routes no longer appear in the table. **Step 7** Use the **show running-config** command and check the access list to make sure it does not deny updates inappropriately. If the access list denies updates from specific addresses, make sure that it does not deny the address of a router from which routing updates should be received. Change the access list to allow the router to receive updates from the proper addresses. At the end of every access list is an implied "deny all traffic" criteria statement. Therefore, if a packet does not match any of your criteria statements, the packet is blocked. Configure explicit **permit** statements for those addresses from which the router should receive updates. **Step 8** If you altered an access list, enable the distribution list using the **distribute-list** command. Use the **clear ip route** command and check whether the missing routing information appears in the routing table. **Step 9** If the routes appear in the routing table, perform the preceding steps on every router in the path until all distribution lists are enabled and routing information appears properly in the routing table. For more information on configuring access lists, see the Cisco IOS configuration guides.

Table 7–12 *OSPF: Routes Missing from Routing Table, Continued*

Possible Problem	Solution

Virtual link is misconfigured	**Step 1** Check the configuration of the routers at each end of the virtual link using the **show running-config** privileged exec command.
	
	Look for **area** *area-id* **virtual-link** *router-id* router configuration command entries. These commands are used to configure the virtual link.
	
	Step 2 Use the **show ip ospf** exec command to find the router ID (IP address) of the routers.
	
	Step 3 Add the **area** *area-id* **virtual-link** *router-id* command if it is missing, or modify it if it is incorrect. Make sure that the proper area ID and router ID (IP address) are specified. The routers at each end of the virtual link must point to one another across the transit area.
	
	For example, in the network shown in Figure 7–13, a virtual link from Router B to Router A is created across the transit area, Area 1.
	
	The following commands are entered on Router A:
	
	```\nC4500(config)#router ospf 250\nC4500(config-router)#network 121.10.0.0 0.0.255.255\narea 0\nC4500(config-router)#network 169.192.56.0 0.0.0.255\narea 0\nC4500(config-router)#area 1 virtual-link 121.10.100.46\n```
	
	On Router B, the following commands are used:
	
	```\nC4000(config)#router ospf 250\nC4000(config-router)#network 121.10.0.0 0.0.255.255\narea 0\nC4000(config-router)#network 108.31.0.0 0.0.255.255 area 2\nC4000(config-router)#area 1 virtual-link 121.10.1.1\n```

[1] LSA = link state advertisement
[2] ASBR = autonomous system border router

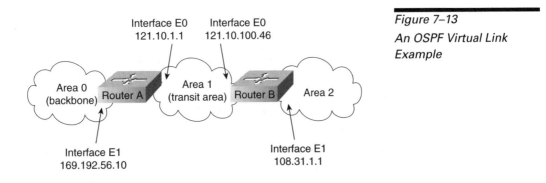

Figure 7–13
An OSPF Virtual Link
Example

IP Enhanced IGRP: Routers Not Establishing Neighbors

Symptom: Enhanced IGRP routers are not establishing neighbor relationships properly. Routing information is not distributed to routers.

Table 7–13 outlines the problems that might cause this symptom and describes solutions to those problems.

Table 7–13 *IP Enhanced IGRP: Routers Not Establishing Neighbors*

Possible Problem	Solution	
Misconfigured or missing **network** router configuration command	**Step 1**	Use the **show ip eigrp neighbors** exec command on an Enhanced IGRP router. Make sure that all directly connected Enhanced IGRP routers appear in the output.
	Step 2	If some connected routers are not shown in the output, use the **show running-config** privileged exec command to view the configuration of the suspect routers.
	Step 3	Make sure that a **network** router configuration command is specified for every network to which a router interface belongs.
		For example, if the IP address of Ethernet interface 0 is 192.168.52.42, enter the following commands to enable Enhanced IGRP on the interface:
		`c4500(config)#`**`router eigrp 100`** `c4500(config-router)#`**`network 192.168.52.0`**

Table 7–13   *IP Enhanced IGRP: Routers Not Establishing Neighbors, Continued*

Possible Problem	Solution
Mismatched autonomous system number specification	**Step 1** View the router configuration using the **show running-config** privileged exec command on each router in the autonomous system. **Step 2** Check the **router eigrp** global configuration commands to make sure that all routers that should be communicating are in the same autonomous system. Only Enhanced IGRP routers in the same autonomous system will form neighbor relationships and thus exchange routing information.
Access list is misconfigured	**Step 1** Execute the **debug ip packet** and **debug eigrp packets** privileged exec commands. The former command indicates whether IP packets are being sent and received and whether there are encapsulation problems. The latter command indicates whether Enhanced IGRP hello packets are being sent and received properly. **Caution:** These **debug** commands can use considerable CPU cycles on the router. Do not enable them if your network is already heavily congested. **Step 2** If a router appears to be sending IP and Enhanced IGRP packets correctly, but a connected router does not receive them, check the configuration of the connected router for access lists that might be filtering out packets. **Step 3** Disable all access lists enabled on the router using the **no ip access-group** *access-list-number* **in** interface configuration command. **Step 4** Monitor the output from the **debug ip packet** and **debug eigrp packets** commands. Determine whether packets are now being received normally. **Step 5** If packets are received normally, an access list is probably filtering packets. To isolate the problem list, enable access lists one at a time until packets are no longer forwarded. **Step 6** Check the access list to see whether it is filtering traffic from the source router. If it is, alter the access list to allow the traffic to pass. Enter explicit **permit** statements for traffic that you want the router to forward normally. **Step 7** Enable the altered access list with the **ip access-group** command to see whether packets continue to pass normally. **Step 8** If packets pass normally, perform the preceding steps on any other routers in the path until all access lists are enabled and packets are forwarded properly.

IP Enhanced IGRP: Routes Missing from Routing Table

Symptom: Routes are missing from the routing table of routers running Enhanced IGRP. Hosts on one network cannot access hosts on a different network. Hosts on the same network might or might not be able to communicate. The problem might occur in internetworks running only Enhanced IGRP or in an internetwork running Enhanced IGRP and another routing protocol.

Table 7–14 outlines the problems that might cause this symptom and describes solutions to those problems.

Table 7–14   *IP Enhanced IGRP: Routes Missing from Routing Table*

Possible Problem	Solution
Routers not establishing neighbors	For information on troubleshooting this problem, see the section "IP Enhanced IGRP: Routers Not Establishing Neighbors," earlier in this chapter.
Routes are not redistributed between different autonomous systems	Routes are not automatically redistributed between different Enhanced IGRP autonomous systems.
	Step 1 Use the **show running-config** privileged exec command on routers bordering multiple autonomous systems.
	Step 2 If multiple autonomous systems are configured on the router (indicated by multiple **router eigrp** global configuration command entries), make sure that route redistribution is manually configured using the **redistribute** router configuration command.
	For example, if the router belongs to autonomous system 100 and autonomous system 200, enter the following commands to redistribute Enhanced IGRP routes between the two autonomous systems:

	<pre>C2509(config)#router eigrp 100
	C2509(config-router)#redistribute eigrp 200
	C2509(config-router)#exit
	C2509(config)#router eigrp 200
	C2509(config-router)#redistribute eigrp 100</pre>

	Step 3 If you want static routes to be redistributed, you must use the **redistribute static** router configuration command.
	For more information on using the **redistribute** router configuration command, see the Cisco IOS configuration guides and command references.

Table 7–14   *IP Enhanced IGRP: Routes Missing from Routing Table, Continued*

Possible Problem	Solution

Routes are not being redistributed between different routing protocols	**Step 1** Use the **show running-config** privileged exec command on routers that border networks running different routing protocols.
	
	Step 2 Look for a **redistribute** router configuration command entry. Make sure that routing information is being properly exchanged between protocols.
	
	For example, to redistribute routes between IGRP autonomous system 500 and Enhanced IGRP autonomous system 200, enter the following commands:
	
	`C2509(config)#router igrp 500`
	`C2509(config-router)#redistribute eigrp 200`
	`C2509(config-router)#exit`
	`C2509(config)#router eigrp 200`
	`C2509(config-router)#redistribute igrp 500`
	
	Step 3 To redistribute static routes, you must use the **redistribute static** router configuration command.
	
	For more information on using the **redistribute** router configuration command, see the Cisco IOS configuration guides and command references.

Hello interval or hold-time value mismatch	**Step 1** Use the **show running-config** privileged exec command on all routers in the network. **Step 2** Look for **ip hello-interval eigrp** and **ip hold-time eigrp** interface configuration command entries. The values configured by these commands should be the same for all IP routers on the network. At minimum, backbone routers should be configured with the same hello interval and hold-time values. **Step 3** If there are routers with mismatched hello interval or hold-time values, reconfigure them to bring them into conformance with the rest of the routers on the network. You can return these timer values to their defaults by using the **no ip hello-interval eigrp** and the **no ip hold-time interval eigrp** interface configuration commands.

Table 7–14 *IP Enhanced IGRP: Routes Missing from Routing Table, Continued*

Possible Problem	Solution
Default routing metrics are incorrectly configured	**Step 1** Use the **show running-config** privileged exec command on suspect routers. Look for **default-metric** router configuration command entries. This command changes the default metric values assigned to redistributed routes. **Step 2** If a **default-metric** statement appears in the configuration, examine the values that it defines. Be certain that these values will reliably and accurately translate routing metrics between the routing protocols implemented on your network. To restore the default values for the routing metrics, use the **no default-metric** router configuration command for the appropriate routing protocol. For more information on the IP Enhanced IGRP **default-metric** router configuration command, see the Cisco IOS configuration guides.

IP Enhanced IGRP: Router Stuck in Active Mode

Symptom: An IP Enhanced IGRP router is stuck in Active mode. Multiple "Stuck-in-Active" messages are sent to the console:

```
%DUAL-3-SIA: Route 198.169.52.51 Stuck-in-Active
```

For a more detailed explanation of Enhanced IGRP Active mode, see the section "Enhanced IGRP and Active/Passive Modes" later in this chapter.

NOTES

Occasional messages of this type are *not* a cause for concern. This is how an Enhanced IGRP router recovers if it does not receive replies to its queries from all its neighbors. However, if these error messages occur frequently, you should investigate the problem.

Table 7–15 outlines the problems that might cause this symptom and describes solutions to those problems.

Table 7-15 *IP Enhanced IGRP: Router Stuck in Active Mode*

Possible Problem	Solution
Active timer value is misconfigured	**Step 1** Check the configuration of each Enhanced IGRP router by using the **show running-config** privileged exec command.
	Step 2 Look for the **timers active-time** router configuration command entry associated with the **router eigrp** global configuration command entry.
	The active timer determines the maximum period of time that an Enhanced IGRP router will wait for replies to its queries. If the active timer value is set too low, there might not be enough time for all the neighboring routers to send their replies to the active router.
	Step 3 Make sure that the value set by the **timers active-time** command is consistent among routers in the same autonomous system.
	A value of 3 (three minutes, which is the default value) is recommended in order to allow all Enhanced IGRP neighbors to reply to queries.
Interface or other hardware problem	**Step 1** Use the **show ip eigrp neighbors** exec command and examine the Uptime and Q Cnt (queue count) fields in the output.
	If the uptime counter is continually resetting or if the queue count is consistently high, there might be a hardware problem.
	Step 2 Determine where the problem is occurring by looking at the output of the "Stuck-in-Active" error message, which indicates the direction in which the problem node is located.
	Step 3 Make sure the suspect router still works. Check the interfaces on the suspect router. Use the **show interfaces** exec command to display statistics for all interfaces configured on the router.
	For more information, see Chapter 3, "Troubleshooting Hardware and Booting Problems."
Flapping route	**Step 1** If there is a flapping serial route (caused by heavy traffic load), queries and replies might not be forwarded reliably. Route flapping caused by heavy traffic on a serial link can cause queries and replies to be lost, resulting in the active timer timing out.
	Step 2 Increase the bandwidth of the link. For more information, see Chapter 15, "Troubleshooting Serial Line Problems."

Enhanced IGRP and Active/Passive Modes

An Enhanced IGRP router can be in either Passive or Active mode. A router is said to be passive for a network when it has an established path to that network in its routing table.

If the Enhanced IGRP router loses the connection to a network (for example, Network A), it becomes active for that network. The router sends out queries to all its neighbors in order to find a new route to Network A. The router remains in active mode until it has either received replies from *all* its neighbors or until the active timer, which determines the maximum period of time a router will stay active, expires.

If the router receives a reply from each of its neighbors, it computes the new next hop to Network A and becomes passive for that network. However, if the active timer expires before all its neighbors reply, the router removes from its neighbor table any neighbors that did not reply, again enters active mode, and sends a "Stuck-in-Active" message to the console.

BGP: Routes Missing from Routing Table

Symptom: BGP routers and networks are not advertised to other routers. Routers do not receive routing information from other routers. Some hosts cannot communicate with hosts in other areas, and routing table information is incomplete.

Table 7–16 outlines the problems that might cause this symptom and describes solutions to those problems.

Table 7–16 *BGP: Routes Missing from Routing Table*

Possible Problem	Solution
BGP routers not advertising routes	If BGP routers are not advertising routes properly, routing information might not appear in the routing table. For information on troubleshooting this problem, see the section "BGP: Routers Not Advertising Routes," later in this chapter.
Missing **neighbor remote-as** command	The **neighbor remote-as** router configuration command is used to add entries to the BGP neighbor table.
	Step 1 Check local and remote routers and make sure the specified autonomous system numbers and neighbors are correct.
	The following example specifies that a router at the address 131.108.1.2 is a neighbor in autonomous system number 109:
	``` router bgp 110 network 131.108.0.0 neighbor 131.108.1.2 remote-as 109 ```
	Step 2 Make sure any route filters that are enabled are not misconfigured.

Table 7–16   *BGP: Routes Missing from Routing Table, Continued*

Possible Problem	Solution

Access list is misconfigured	**Step 1** Use the **show access-list** privileged exec command on suspect routers to see whether there are access lists configured on the router.
	
	Step 2 If there are access lists enabled on the router, disable them using the appropriate commands. For example, to disable input access list 10, use the following command:
	
	`C4000(config)#no ip access-group 10 in`
	
	Step 3 After disabling all access lists on the router, determine whether the missing routing information is now appearing in routing tables.
	
	Step 4 If the information is now appearing, it is likely that an access list is filtering traffic. To isolate the problem access list, enable access lists one at a time until the routing information is no longer appearing in the routing table.
	
	Step 5 Check the access list to see whether it is filtering traffic from specific TCP ports. If an access list denies specific TCP ports, make sure that it does not deny TCP port 179, the port used by BGP.
	
	Enter an explicit **permit** statement for port 179 to ensure that BGP traffic is forwarded normally.
	
	Example:
	
	`access-list 101 permit tcp 0.0.0.0 255.255.255.255`
	`0.0.0.0 255.255.255.255 eq 179`
	
	Step 6 If you altered an access list, enable the list to see whether routing information can still pass normally.
	
	Step 7 If routing information is no longer missing, perform the preceding steps on any other routers in the path until all access lists are enabled and routing information appears in the appropriate routing tables.
	
	For more information on configuring access lists, see the Cisco IOS configuration guides.

BGP: Routers Not Advertising Routes

Symptom: BGP routers are not advertising routes. Routing updates from a BGP router do not contain information about certain network destinations that should be advertised.

Table 7–17 outlines the problems that might cause this symptom and describes solutions to those problems.

Table 7–17 *BGP: Routers Not Advertising Routes*

Possible Problem	Solution	
Missing **network** router configuration command	**Step 1**	Use the **show running-config** privileged exec command to view the router configuration.
	Step 2	Make sure that a **network** router configuration command is specified for every network that the BGP router should advertise (these networks need not be directly connected).
		For example, if you want the BGP router to advertise networks 192.168.52.0 and 108.168.0.0, enter the following commands to have the router include those networks in its routing updates:
		``c4500(config)#router bgp 100
c4500(config-router)#network 192.168.52.0
c4500(config-router)#network 108.168.0.0```
Interior gateway protocol (such as RIP, IGRP, OSPF, and so on) routing problem	**Step 1**	Check for other routing protocol problems to be sure that BGP is getting routing information from any interior gateway protocols running in the internetwork.
		For example, if there is a problem with RIP routing, it might affect the operation of BGP. BGP routers might not have any information about certain networks, making it impossible to advertise routing information about certain networks configured in BGP.
	Step 2	Isolate and troubleshoot interior gateway protocol problems before troubleshooting BGP. See the appropriate sections in this chapter for information specific to the protocols you are running. As a workaround, you can configure static BGP routes, but routing is not dynamic in this case.

Table 7-17   *BGP: Routers Not Advertising Routes, Continued*

Possible Problem	Solution
Misconfigured **aggregate-address** command	The **aggregate-address** router configuration command allows BGP to specify a summary address for one or more specific network addresses. For example, to summarize the addresses 195.10.20.0 and 195.10.130.0, use the aggregate address 195.10.0.0. Problems can occur under the following circumstances: • The aggregate address summarizes addresses that are not in the router's BGP routing table. In this case, a router is advertising networks to which it does not have a BGP route. For example, a router is configured with the aggregate address 195.10.0.0 summarizing networks 195.10.20.0 and 195.10.130.0. However, network 195.10.192.0 is in another autonomous system that is inaccessible through the router. Traffic destined for network 195.10.192.0 will be forwarded to the router, because it is incorrectly advertising a route to that network (via the aggregate address). • There are no individual networks configured (using the **network** router configuration command) or routes in the BGP routing table to which the aggregate address refers. **Step 1** Use the **show running-config** privileged exec command to view the router configuration. Look for an **aggregate-address** command entry associated with the **router bgp** global configuration command. **Step 2** Use the **show ip bgp** privileged exec command to view the addresses in the BGP routing table. **Step 3** Make sure that the addresses summarized by the **aggregate-address** command are all present in the BGP routing table.

HSRP: Hosts Cannot Reach Remote Networks

Symptom: Hosts cannot reach hosts on remote networks. Routers in the network are running HSRP.

Table 7-18 outlines the problems that might cause this symptom and describes solutions to those problems.

Table 7–18 *HSRP: Hosts Cannot Reach Remote Networks*

Possible Problem	Solution	
Default gateway is not specified or is incorrectly specified on local or remote hosts	Step 1	Determine whether local and remote hosts have a default gateway specification. Use the following UNIX command: `host% netstat -rn` Check the output of this command for a default gateway specification.
	Step 2	In a network running HSRP, hosts must use the hot standby IP address as their default gateway specification. Use the **show standby** privileged exec command to check the current hot standby IP address.
	Step 3	You can change or add a default gateway using the following UNIX command at the host: `host% route add default address 1` where *address* is the IP address of the default gateway (the router local to the host). The value 1 indicates that the specified gateway is one hop away. You might need to reboot the host for this change to take effect.
	Step 4	It is recommended that you specify a default gateway as part of the boot process. Specify the IP address of the gateway in the UNIX host file */etc/defaultrouter*. This filename might be different on your UNIX system. If you are working with a PC or a Macintosh, consult the accompanying documentation to determine how to set the default gateway.

Table 7–18   *HSRP: Hosts Cannot Reach Remote Networks, Continued*

Possible Problem	Solution
HSRP is not configured or is misconfigured	**Step 1** Try to **ping** the hot standby IP address. If the **ping** is unsuccessful, proceed to Step 2. If the **ping** is successful, proceed to Step 4.
	Step 2 Use the **show standby** privileged exec command to see information about the HSRP configuration. If the command does not return any output, HSRP is not configured on the router interface.
	Step 3 If HSRP is not configured, configure it on the routers that you want to belong to the hot standby group.
	For example, to configure a router as the active hot standby router with hot standby address 192.192.192.3, enter the following commands:
	``` C4500(config)#interface e0 C4500(config-if)#standby ip 192.192.192.3 C4500(config-if)#standby priority 110 C4500(config-if)#standby preempt ```
	The **standby priority** interface configuration command sets the router's HSRP priority; the default priority is 100.
	To configure a router as the backup hot standby router, enter the following commands:
	``` C4500(config)#interface e0 C4500(config-if)#standby ip 192.192.192.3 ```
	Step 4 If the backup hot standby router is misconfigured and the active router fails, the backup router might not go active.
	One potential misconfiguration is a missing hot standby address in the backup router. You can successfully configure a router as a hot standby router simply by entering the following commands:
	``` C4500(config)#interface e0 C4500(config-if)#standby ip ```
	That is, you do not have to include the hot standby IP address in the **standby ip** command. As long as one hot standby router has the hot standby IP address in its configuration, every other hot standby router will learn the address from that router. However, if only one router has the hot standby address configured, and that router fails, other hot standby routers will not know the hot standby address and HSRP will not work.
	Be sure that at least two hot standby routers have the hot standby address in their configuration.

Table 7–18 *HSRP: Hosts Cannot Reach Remote Networks, Continued*

Possible Problem	Solution
No routes in active hot standby router	If HSRP appears to be configured correctly, but connectivity fails, make sure that your other routing protocols are working correctly. If your other routing protocols are not advertising routes correctly, hot standby routers will have incomplete or empty routing tables, and traffic will not be forwarded correctly.

Follow the troubleshooting procedures outlined in this chapter to ensure that your other routing protocols work correctly. |

Troubleshooting Novell IPX

NetWare is a network operating system (NOS) and related support services environment created by Novell, Inc., and introduced to the market in the early 1980s. Then, networks were small and predominantly homogeneous; local-area network (LAN) workgroup communication was new; and the idea of a personal computer (PC) was just becoming popular.

Much of NetWare's networking technology was derived from Xerox Network Systems (XNS), a networking system created by Xerox Corporation in the late 1970s.

By the early 1990s, NetWare's NOS market share had risen to between 50 percent and 75 percent. With more than 500,000 NetWare networks installed worldwide and an accelerating movement to connect networks to other networks, NetWare and its supporting protocols often coexist on the same physical channel with many other popular protocols, including TCP/IP, DECnet, and Apple-Talk.

NOVELL TECHNOLOGY BASICS

As an NOS environment, NetWare specifies the upper five layers of the OSI reference model. It provides file and printer sharing, support for various applications, such as electronic mail transfer and database access, and other services. Like other NOSs, such as the Network File System (NFS) from Sun Microsystems, Inc., and LAN Manager from Microsoft Corporation, NetWare is based on a client/server architecture. In such architectures, clients (sometimes called workstations) request certain services, such as file and printer access from servers.

Originally, NetWare clients were small PCs, whereas servers were slightly more powerful PCs. As NetWare became more popular, it was ported to other computing platforms. Currently, NetWare clients and servers can be represented by virtually any kind of computer system, from PCs to main-frames.

A primary characteristic of the client/server system is that remote access is transparent to the user. This is accomplished through remote procedure calls, a process by which a local computer program running on a client sends a procedure call to a remote server. The server executes the remote procedure call and returns the requested information to the local computer client.

Figure 8–1 illustrates a simplified view of NetWare's best-known protocols and their relationship to the OSI reference model. With appropriate drivers, NetWare can run on any media-access protocol. The figure lists those media-access protocols currently supported with NetWare drivers.

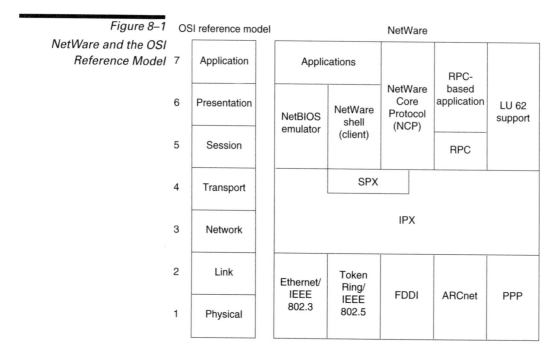

Figure 8–1 NetWare and the OSI Reference Model

MEDIA ACCESS

NetWare runs on Ethernet/IEEE 802.3, Token Ring/IEEE 802.5, Fiber Distributed Data Interface (FDDI), and ARCnet. NetWare also works over synchronous wide-area network (WAN) links using the Point-to-Point Protocol (PPP).

Attached Resource Computer Network (ARCnet) is a simple network system that supports all three primary cable types (twisted-pair, coaxial, and fiber-optic) and two topologies (bus and star). It was developed by Datapoint Corporation and introduced in 1977. Although ARCnet has not attained the popularity enjoyed by Ethernet and Token Ring, its low cost and flexibility have resulted in many loyal supporters.

THE NETWORK LAYER

Internetwork Packet Exchange (IPX) is Novell's original network-layer protocol. When a device to be communicated with is located on a different network, IPX routes the information to the destination through any intermediate networks. Figure 8–2 shows the IPX packet format.

Checksum
Packet length
Transport control / Packet type
Destination network
Destination node
Destination socket
Source network
Source node
Source socket
Upper-layer data

Figure 8–2

IPX Packet Format

The fields of the IPX packet are as follows:

- Checksum—A 16-bit field that is set to ones.

- Packet length—A 16-bit field that specifies the length, in bytes, of the complete IPX datagram. IPX packets can be any length up to the media maximum transmission unit (MTU) size. There is no packet fragmentation.

- Transport control—An 8-bit field that indicates the number of routers the packet has passed through. When the value of this field reaches 15, the packet is discarded under the assumption that a routing loop might be occurring.

- Packet type—An 8-bit field that specifies the upper-layer protocol to receive the packet's information. Two common values for this field are 5, which specifies Sequenced Packet Exchange (SPX), and 17, which specifies the NetWare Core Protocol (NCP).

- Destination network, destination node, and destination socket—Specify destination information.

- Source network, source node, and source socket—Specify source information.

- Upper-layer data—Contains information for upper-layer processes.

Although IPX was derived from XNS, it has several unique features. From the standpoint of routing, the encapsulation mechanisms of these two protocols are the most important difference. Encapsulation is the process of packaging upper-layer protocol information and data into a frame.

For Ethernet, XNS uses standard Ethernet encapsulation, whereas IPX packets are encapsulated in Ethernet Version 2.0 or IEEE 802.3 without the IEEE 802.2 information that typically accompanies these frames. Figure 8–3 illustrates Ethernet, standard IEEE 802.3, and IPX encapsulation.

NOTES

NetWare 4.0 supports encapsulation of IPX packets in standard IEEE 802.3 frames. It also supports Subnetwork Access Protocol (SNAP) encapsulation, which extends the IEEE 802.2 headers by providing a type code similar to that defined in the Ethernet specification.

Figure 8–3

Ethernet, IEEE 802.3, and IPX Encapsulation Formats

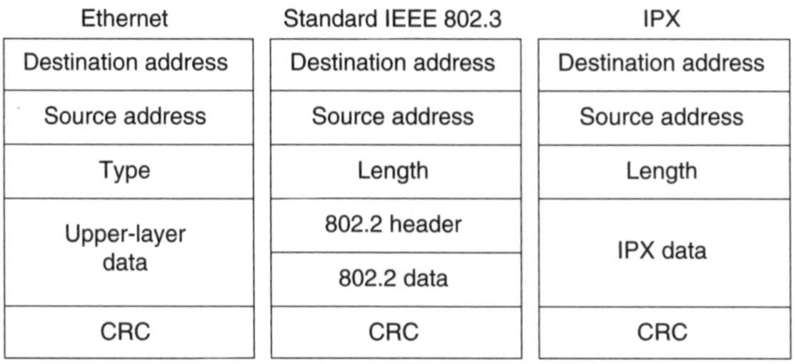

Ethernet	Standard IEEE 802.3	IPX
Destination address	Destination address	Destination address
Source address	Source address	Source address
Type	Length	Length
Upper-layer data	802.2 header	IPX data
	802.2 data	
CRC	CRC	CRC

To route packets in an internetwork, IPX uses a dynamic routing protocol called the Routing Information Protocol (RIP). Like XNS, RIP derived from work done at Xerox for the XNS protocol family.

In addition to the difference in encapsulation mechanisms, Novell also added a protocol called the Service Advertising Protocol (SAP) to its IPX protocol family. SAP allows nodes that provide services (such as file servers and print servers) to advertise their addresses and the services they provide.

Novell also supports IBM logical unit (LU) 6.2 network addressable units (NAUs). LU 6.2 allows peer-to-peer connectivity across IBM communication environments. Using NetWare's LU 6.2 capability, NetWare nodes can exchange information across an IBM network. NetWare packets are encapsulated within LU 6.2 packets for transit across the IBM network.

THE TRANSPORT LAYER

Sequenced Packet Exchange (SPX) is the most commonly used NetWare transport protocol. Novell derived this protocol from the XNS Sequenced Packet Protocol (SPP). As with the Transmission Control Protocol (TCP) and many other transport protocols, SPX is a reliable, connection-oriented protocol that supplements the datagram service provided by Layer 3 protocols.

Novell also offers Internet Protocol (IP) support in the form of User Datagram Protocol (UDP)/IP encapsulation of other Novell packets, such as SPX/IPX packets. IPX datagrams are encapsulated inside UDP/IP headers for transport across an IP-based internetwork.

UPPER-LAYER PROTOCOLS

NetWare supports a wide variety of upper-layer protocols, but several are somewhat more popular than others. The NetWare shell runs in clients (often called *workstations* in the NetWare community) and intercepts application I/O calls to determine whether they require network access for satisfaction. If they do, the NetWare shell packages the requests and sends them to lower-layer software for processing and network transmission. If they do not, they are simply passed to local I/O resources. Client applications are unaware of any network access required for completion of application calls. NetWare remote-procedure call (NetWare RPC) is another more general redirection mechanism supported by Novell.

NCP is a series of server routines designed to satisfy application requests coming from, for example, the NetWare shell. Services provided by NCP include file access, printer access, name management, accounting, security, and file synchronization.

NetWare also supports the Network Basic Input/Output System (NetBIOS) session-layer interface specification from IBM and Microsoft. NetWare's NetBIOS emulation software allows programs written to the industry-standard NetBIOS interface to run within the NetWare system.

NetWare application-layer services include NetWare Message Handling Service (NetWare MHS), Btrieve, NetWare loadable modules (NLMs), and various IBM connectivity features. NetWare MHS is a message delivery system that provides electronic mail transport. Btrieve is Novell's implementation of the binary tree (btree) database access mechanism. NLMs are implemented as add-on modules that attach into the NetWare system. NLMs for alternate protocol stacks, communication services, database services, and many other services are currently available from Novell and third parties.

TROUBLESHOOTING NOVELL IPX

This section presents protocol-related troubleshooting information for Novell IPX connectivity and performance problems. It describes specific Novell IPX symptoms, the problems that are likely to cause each symptom, and the solutions to those problems.

The following sections outline the most common issues in Novell IPX networks:

- Novell IPX: Client Cannot Connect to Server on Same LAN
- Novell IPX: Client Cannot Connect to Server on Remote LAN
- Novell IPX: Clients Cannot Connect to Server over PSN
- Novell IPX: Client Cannot Connect to Server over ISDN
- Novell NetBIOS: Applications Cannot Connect to Server over Router
- IPX RIP: No Connectivity over IPX RIP Router

- IPX RIP: SAP Updates Not Propagated by Router
- IPX Enhanced IGRP: No Connectivity over IPX Enhanced IGRP Router
- IPX Enhanced IGRP: Routers Not Establishing Neighbors
- IPX Enhanced IGRP: SAP Updates Not Propagated by Router
- IPX Enhanced IGRP: Router Stuck in Active Mode
- Novell IPX: Intermittent Connectivity
- Novell IPX: Slow Performance

Novell IPX: Client Cannot Connect to Server on Same LAN

Symptom: Clients cannot make connections to servers located on the same LAN. Also, clients cannot connect to servers on remote networks.

Table 8–1 outlines the problems that might cause this symptom and describes solutions to those problems.

Table 8–1   *Novell IPX: Client Cannot Connect to Server on Same LAN*

Possible Problem	Solution	
Misconfigured client or server	**Step 1**	Make sure the software on both clients and servers is the current version, is configured correctly, and has loaded correctly. On clients, check the network drivers and the configuration specified in the *net.cfg* file.
	Step 2	On servers, make certain that SAPs[1] are being generated properly and that any NLMs[2] are loaded properly. Use the **track on** command to monitor routing and SAP activity.
	Step 3	Check the encapsulation on clients and servers to make sure they are not mismatched.
	For specific information on configuring your client or server, refer to the documentation provided with the device.	
Not enough user licenses	Make sure there is a sufficient number of NetWare user licenses available. Use the Monitor utility screen on a NetWare server to see the total number of connections available and the number of connections in use.	

Table 8–1 *Novell IPX: Client Cannot Connect to Server on Same LAN, Continued*

Possible Problem	Solution
Mismatched network numbers	All servers attached to the same cable must bind to the same external network number. If there are mismatched network numbers, packets will not be forwarded properly.
	Step 1 Watch for error messages on the system console similar to the following:
	`Router configuration error detected`
	`Node address claims network x` `should be y`
	These error messages indicate that a server on the LAN has a conflicting network number. *Node address* is the node address of the network card from which the incorrect address came. *x* is the network number specified in packets received from the node. *y* is the network number configured on the server generating the error.
	Step 2 All servers on the same LAN must have the same external network number (if they use the same frame type). If the network numbers do not match, reconfigure the conflicting server with the correct external network number.
Client, server, or other hardware problem	Check all NIC[3], transceivers, hub ports, switches, and other hardware. Check all appropriate LEDs to see whether there are error indications. Replace any faulty or malfunctioning hardware.
	For information on troubleshooting a client, server, or other hardware problem not related to Cisco routers, refer to the documentation provided with the hardware.

Table 8–1   *Novell IPX: Client Cannot Connect to Server on Same LAN, Continued*

Possible Problem	Solution
Media problem	**Step 1** Check all cabling and connections. Make sure cables are not damaged and that all connections are correct and make proper contact. **Step 2** Use the **show interfaces** exec command to check for input or output errors or other indications of problems on the media. **Step 3** If the command output shows excessive errors, use the **clear interface counter** privileged exec command to clear the interface counters. **Step 4** Check the output of the **show interfaces** command again. If the errors are incrementing rapidly, there is probably a problem with the media. For more detailed information on troubleshooting media problems, refer to the troubleshooting chapter that covers the media type used in your network.

[1] SAP = Service Advertising Protocol
[2] NLM = NetWare loadable module
[3] NIC = Network interface card

Novell IPX: Client Cannot Connect to Server on Remote LAN

Symptom: Clients cannot make connections to servers on another network over one or more routers interconnected by LAN networks. Clients can connect to servers on their local network. Table 8–2 outlines the problems that might cause this symptom and describes solutions to those problems.

NOTES

If clients cannot connect to servers on their local network, refer to the section "Novell IPX: Client Cannot Connect to Server on Same LAN" earlier in this chapter. If there is a WAN network between the local and remote LANs, WAN problems must be considered a source of problems as well. Refer to the IPX-specific WAN problems outlined later in this chapter, or to the general WAN problems outlined in other chapters in this book.

Table 8–2   *Novell IPX: Client Cannot Connect to Server on Remote LAN*

Possible Problem	Solution	
Router interface is down	**Step 1**	Use the **show interfaces** exec command on the router to check the status of the router interfaces. Verify that the interface and line protocol are up.
	Step 2	If the interface is administratively down, use the **no shutdown** interface configuration command to bring the interface back up.
	Step 3	If the interface or line protocol is down, refer to the troubleshooting chapter that covers the media type used in your network.
Mismatched Ethernet encapsulation methods	**Step 1**	Use the **show ipx interface** privileged exec command to check the encapsulation type specified in the router configuration. By default, Cisco routers use Novell's Frame Type Ethernet 802.3 encapsulation. (Cisco refers to this as *novell-ether* encapsulation.)
	Step 2	Compare the encapsulation type configured on router interfaces with the encapsulation type that is being used by clients and servers.
	Step 3	If the router uses one encapsulation type but the clients and servers use a different type, then there is a mismatch.
		Change the encapsulation type used on either the clients and servers or the router, as appropriate, so that all devices use the same encapsulation method. On routers, specify the encapsulation type with the **ipx network** *network* **encapsulation** *encapsulation-type* interface configuration command. For information on changing the encapsulation type on clients and servers, consult the vendor documentation.

Table 8–2   *Novell IPX: Client Cannot Connect to Server on Remote LAN, Continued*

Possible Problem	Solution
LIPX[1] problem	If you are using NetWare 3.12 or above and you have LIPX enabled, a client and server could conceivably negotiate a packet size larger than a router could support. This can cause intermediate routers to drop packets. Without LIPX, the server checks the network number for the buffer size request packet from the client, and if the network number is different from the server's (which means the packet is from another network over a router), it orders clients to use 512 bytes (hard coded) instead.

For information on configuring LIPX, refer to the vendor documentation. |
| Ring speed specification mismatch | In a Token Ring environment, all devices must agree on the configured ring speed (4 or 16 Mbps), or connectivity will fail.

Step 1   Use the **show interfaces token** exec command on the router. Look for the ring speed value in the output. Compare this value with the ring speed specification on Novell servers.

Step 2   If the ring speeds do not match, change the server or router configuration, as appropriate, so that all stations agree on the ring speed. On routers, use the **ring-speed** interface configuration command to change the ring speed. For information about configuring the ring speed on Novell servers, consult the vendor documentation. |
| Duplicate node numbers on routers | **Step 1**   Use the **show running-config** privileged exec command to examine the current configuration of each router in the path.

Step 2   Check the node number specified in the **ipx routing** *node* global configuration command. The node number is either a user-specified node number or the MAC address of the first Ethernet, Token Ring, or FDDI[2] in the router.

Step 3   The node number configured on each router must be unique. If the number is the same on multiple routers, enter the **no ipx routing** global configuration command to disable IPX routing on the router.

Step 4   Reinitialize IPX routing by entering the **ipx routing** command (do not specify a node number). Use the **show running-config** command to verify that the rest of the IPX configuration is still correct. |

Table 8–2 *Novell IPX: Client Cannot Connect to Server on Remote LAN, Continued*

Possible Problem	Solution
Duplicate network numbers	Every network number must be unique throughout the entire Novell IPX internetwork. A duplicate network number will prevent packets from being forwarded properly.
	Step 1 Use the **show ipx servers** and the **show ipx route** privileged exec commands. Check the output of these commands for server addresses that have been learned from the wrong interface.
	For example, if you know that you have a server on the local network with network number 3c.0000.0c01.2345 and the **show** command output shows that this server is located on a remote network, there is probably a server on the remote network that's using the same network number.
	Step 2 If you suspect a duplicate network number, use a process of elimination to identify the misconfigured server. This can be difficult, particularly if you do not have access to every network device in the Novell IPX internetwork. When you have identified the misconfigured server, modify the server configuration to eliminate the duplicate network number.
Router hardware problem	Check all router ports, interface processors, and other router hardware. Make sure cards are seated properly and that no hardware is damaged. Replace faulty or malfunctioning hardware.
	For detailed information on troubleshooting router hardware problems, refer to Chapter 3, "Troubleshooting Hardware and Booting Problems."

Table 8–2   *Novell IPX: Client Cannot Connect to Server on Remote LAN, Continued*

Possible Problem	Solution
Backdoor bridge between segments	**Step 1** Use the **show ipx traffic** exec command on intermediate routers. Determine whether the bad hop count field is incrementing.
	Step 2 If the bad hop count counter is incrementing, use a network analyzer to look for packet loops on suspect segments. Look for RIP[3] and SAP updates as well. If a backdoor bridge exists, you are likely to see hop counts that increment to 16, at which time the route disappears and reappears unpredictably.
	Step 3 Look for packets from known *remote* network numbers that appear on the *local* network. Look for packets whose source address is the MAC[4] address of the remote node instead of the MAC address of the router.
	Step 4 Examine packets on each segment. A back door is present on the segment if packets appear whose source address is the MAC address of a remote node instead of that of the router.
	Step 5 Remove the backdoor bridge to close the loop.
Routing protocol problem	Misconfigurations and other routing protocol issues can cause connectivity and performance problems. For information on troubleshooting specific IPX routing protocols, see the appropriate section later in this chapter.

[1] LIPX = Large Internet Packet Exchange
[2] FDDI = Fiber Distributed Data Interface
[3] RIP = Routing Information Protocol
[4] MAC = Media Access Control

Novell IPX: Clients Cannot Connect to Server over PSN

Symptom: Clients cannot connect to servers over a packet-switched network (PSN), such as Frame Relay, X.25, or SMDS. Clients can connect to local servers.

___ **NOTES** _____

Procedures for troubleshooting connectivity problems not specific to PSN environments are described in the section "Novell IPX: Client Cannot Connect to Server on Remote LAN" earlier in this chapter.

Table 8–3 outlines the problems that might cause this symptom and describes solutions to those problems.

Table 8–3 *Novell IPX: Client Cannot Connect to Server over PSN*

Possible Problem	Solution
Address mapping error	**Step 1** Use the **show running-config** privileged exec command to view the configuration of the router.
	Step 2 Depending on your PSN environment, look for any **x25 map ipx**, **frame-relay map ipx**[1], or **smds static-map ipx** interface configuration command entries in the router configuration.
	Make sure the address mapping specified by these commands is correct:
	• For X.25, address mapping maps host protocol addresses to the host's X.121 address.
	• For Frame Relay, address mapping maps a next hop protocol address and the DLCI[2] used to connect to the address.
	• For SMDS[3], address mapping defines static entries for SMDS remote peer routers.
	For more information about configuring address maps, refer to the *Cisco IOS Wide-Area Networking Configuration Guide* and *Wide Area Networking Command Reference*.

Table 8–3   *Novell IPX: Client Cannot Connect to Server over PSN, Continued*

Possible Problem	Solution	

Encapsulation mismatch	Step 1	Use the **show interfaces** privileged exec command to determine the encapsulation type being used (such as X.25, Frame Relay, or SMDS encapsulation). Look for output similar to the following:
		
		``
		Serial0 is up, line protocol is up
		  Hardware is MCI Serial
		    Internet address is 192.168.54.92 255.255.255.0
		    MTU 1500 bytes, BW 1544 Kbit, DLY 20000 usec, rely
		255/255, load 1/255
		    Encapsulation FRAME-RELAY, loopback not set, keepalive
		set (10 sec)
		``

	Step 2	If an **encapsulation** command is not present, the default is HDLC[4] encapsulation. For PSN interconnection, you must explicitly specify the proper encapsulation type (such as **encapsulation x25** for an X.25 connection). Configure the proper encapsulation type and use the **show interfaces** command to verify that the encapsulation type is correct.
Misconfigured DLCI assignments (Frame Relay only)	Step 1	Use the **show frame-relay map** exec command on the hub router to see the Frame Relay map assignments currently configured.
	Step 2	Check each Frame Relay map statement to ensure that the DLCI assignments are correctly configured. Make sure you use the DLCIs obtained from your Frame Relay provider. Remember that DLCI values are locally significant.
Misconfigured LMI[5] type (Frame Relay only)	Step 1	Use the **debug frame-relay lmi** privileged exec command to see the LMI type being used by the Frame Relay switch.
	Step 2	The LMI type is determined by your Frame Relay provider. Make sure you use the LMI type specified by the provider.

Table 8–3 *Novell IPX: Client Cannot Connect to Server over PSN, Continued*

Possible Problem	Solution
Frame Relay broadcast queue full (Frame Relay only)	This problem is most likely to occur on the hub router in a Frame Relay hub-and-spoke topology. **Step 1** Use the **show interfaces** privileged exec command to check for dropped Frame Relay broadcast frames. **Step 2** If the number of drops on the broadcast queue is excessively high, increase the size of the queue using the **frame-relay broadcast-queue** *size byte-rate packet-rate* interface configuration command. **Command Syntax:** **frame-relay broadcast-queue** *size byte-rate packet-rate* **Command Syntax:** • *size*—Number of packets to be held in the broadcast queue. The default is 64 packets. • *byte-rate*—Maximum number of bytes to be transmitted per second. The default is 256000 bytes per second. • *packet-rate*—Maximum number of packets to be transmitted per second. The default is 36 packets per second.
Hub router not forwarding SAPs (Frame Relay only)	In a Frame Relay hub-and-spoke topology, SAPs received on one of the hub router's interfaces will not be forwarded back out the same interface because of the split horizon rule, which states that an incoming packet cannot be placed on the same network interface from which it originated, preventing an infinite routing loop if a link fails. To allow SAPs to be forwarded appropriately, you must configure subinterfaces on the Frame Relay interface of the hub router. Assign a subinterface to each spoke site. The hub router will treat each subinterface as a physical interface, allowing it to advertise SAPs without violating the split horizon rule. For specific information on configuring subinterfaces, see the *Wide-Area Networking Configuration Guide*. **Note:** Other problems can prevent a router from forwarding SAP packets. For more information, see the section "IPX RIP: SAP Updates Not Propagated by Router" later in this chapter.

Table 8–3 *Novell IPX: Client Cannot Connect to Server over PSN, Continued*

Possible Problem	Solution
Missing or misconfigured multicast address (SMDS only)	**Step 1** Use the **show running-config** privileged exec command to view the router configuration. Check for an **smds multicast ipx** interface configuration command entry. **Step 2** If the command is not present, add it to the configuration. If the command is present, confirm that the multicast address configured is correct. The SMDS multicast address is specified by your SMDS provider.

[1] You can eliminate the need for Frame Relay address maps by using Inverse ARP instead. Use the **frame-relay interface-dlci** *dlci* **broadcast** interface configuration command to configure an interface to use Inverse ARP. For more information about the use of this command, refer to the Cisco IOS *Wide-Area Networking Configuration Guide* and *Wide Area Networking Command Reference*.
[2] DLCI = data-link connection identifier
[3] SMDS = Switched Multimegabit Data Service
[4] HDLC = High-Level Data Link Control
[5] LMI = Local Management Interface

Novell IPX: Client Cannot Connect to Server over ISDN

Symptom: Clients cannot connect to servers over an ISDN link. Clients can connect to local servers.

— **NOTES** ——————————————————————————————

Procedures for troubleshooting connectivity problems not specific to ISDN environments are described in the section "Novell IPX: Client Cannot Connect to Server on Remote LAN" earlier in this chapter. Procedures for troubleshooting ISDN connectivity problems not specific to IPX environments are described in Chapter 17, "Troubleshooting ISDN Connections."

Table 8–4 outlines the problems that might cause this symptom and describes solutions to those problems.

Table 8–4 *Novell IPX: Client Cannot Connect to Server over ISDN*

Possible Problem	Solution	
Static RIP and SAP statements missing or misconfigured	Step 1	Use the **show running-config** privileged exec command to view the router configuration. Check for **ipx route** and **ipx sap** global configuration command entries. Both commands, which specify static routes and static SAP entries, respectively, are required in an ISDN environment so that clients and servers on the local network are aware of clients and servers on the remote network.
	Step 2	If you do not have static routes and static SAP entries configured, configure them using the **ipx route** and **ipx sap** commands. For detailed information on configuring static routes and SAP entries, refer to the *Cisco IOS Network Protocols Configuration Guide, Part 1* and *Network Protocols Command Reference, Part 1*.
Access lists specified in dialer lists misconfigured	Step 1	Use the **show running-config** privileged exec command to view the router configuration. Check the access lists configured for use by dialer lists.
	Step 2	Make sure the access lists deny only RIP routing updates, SAP advertisements, and Novell serialization packets. If other packets are denied, connectivity problems can occur.
	Step 3	Make sure access lists end with an **access-list** *access-list-number* **permit -1** statement, which permits all other IPX traffic to trigger the dialer.

Novell NetBIOS: Applications Cannot Connect to Server over Router

Symptom: Applications that use Novell NetBIOS (such as Windows 95) cannot connect to servers over a router. Clients cannot connect to servers on the same LAN.

Table 8–5 outlines the problems that might cause this symptom and describes solutions to those problems.

Table 8–5   *Novell NetBIOS: Applications Cannot Connect to Server over Router*

Possible Problem	Solution
Missing **ipx type-20-propagation** commands	**Step 1** Use the **debug ipx packet** privileged exec command or a network analyzer to look for Novell packets with a specification of type 20. **Caution:** Exercise caution when using the **debug ipx packet** command. Because debugging output is assigned high priority in the CPU process, it can render the system unusable. For this reason, use **debug** commands only to troubleshoot specific problems or during troubleshooting sessions with Cisco technical support staff. Moreover, it is best to use **debug** commands during periods of lower network traffic and fewer users. Debugging during these periods decreases the likelihood that increased **debug** command processing overhead will affect system use. **Step 2** Use the **show running-config** privileged exec command to check for **ipx type-20-propagation** interface configuration command entries on routers in the path from client to server. **Step 3** If the **ipx type-20-propagation** command is not present, add it to the interface configuration for every router interface in the path from client to server.

Table 8–5 *Novell NetBIOS: Applications Cannot Connect to Server over Router, Continued*

Possible Problem	Solution	
Missing **ipx helper-address** command	**Step 1**	Use the **debug ipx packet** privileged exec command or a network analyzer to look for Novell packets with a specification other than type 20 (such as type 0 or type 4). Sometimes applications do not conform to the Novell standard and use packet types other than type 20.
		Caution: Exercise caution when using the **debug ipx packet** command. Because debugging output is assigned high priority in the CPU process, it can render the system unusable. For this reason, use **debug** commands only to troubleshoot specific problems or during troubleshooting sessions with Cisco technical support staff. Moreover, it is best to use **debug** commands during periods of lower network traffic and fewer users. Debugging during these periods decreases the likelihood that increased **debug** command processing overhead will affect system use.
	Step 2	If you see packets other than type 20, use the **show running-config** privileged exec command to view the router configuration. Check to see whether the **ipx helper-address** interface configuration command is configured on the interface to which the client is attached.
	Step 3	If the **ipx helper-address** command is not present, configure it on the router interfaces. Make sure the helper address is the IPX protocol address of the NetBIOS server that the client needs to reach. The following is the syntax for the **ipx helper-address** command:
		ipx helper-address *network.node*
		Syntax Description:
		• *network*—Network on which the target IPX server resides. This is an eight-digit hexadecimal number that uniquely identifies a network cable segment. It can be a number in the range 1 to FFFFFFFE. A network number of –1 indicates all-nets flooding. You do not need to specify leading zeros in the network number. For example, for the network number 000000AA you can enter just AA.
		• *node*—Node number of the target Novell server. This is a 48-bit value represented by a dotted triplet of four-digit hexadecimal numbers (xxxx.xxxx.xxxx). A node number of FFFF.FFFF.FFFF matches all servers.

Table 8–5   *Novell NetBIOS: Applications Cannot Connect to Server over Router, Continued*

Possible Problem	Solution
Workstation not running NetBIOS over IPX	Make sure your workstation is running NetBIOS over IPX and not NetBIOS over another protocol, such as NetBEUI. For information about what protocols your workstation is running, refer to the vendor documentation.

IPX RIP: No Connectivity over IPX RIP Router

Symptom: IPX RIP routers are blocking connections. Clients cannot connect to servers over one or more routers running IPX RIP.

NOTES

Procedures for troubleshooting connectivity problems not specific to IPX RIP routing are described in the section "Novell IPX: Client Cannot Connect to Server on Remote LAN" earlier in this chapter.

Table 8–6 outlines the problems that might cause this symptom and describes solutions to those problems.

Table 8–6   *IPX RIP: No Connectivity over IPX RIP Router*

Possible Problem	Solution	
IPX RIP routing not configured or misconfigured on the router	**Step 1**	Use the **show running-config** privileged exec command to view the router configuration.
	Step 2	Check the configuration to make sure there is an **ipx routing** global configuration command entry. If there is not, enter the **ipx routing** command to enable IPX routing. Issuing the **ipx routing** command on a router automatically enables IPX RIP routing on all interfaces that have a network number assigned to them.
Missing **ipx network** commands on interface	**Step 1**	Use the **show ipx interface** privileged exec command to view the state of all IPX interfaces.
	Step 2	If the output indicates that there are no interfaces running IPX, or if an interface that should be running IPX is not, you must configure the appropriate interfaces with an IPX address. The Novell server administrator can provide the IPX network number for the segment to which your router is attached.

Table 8–6   *IPX RIP: No Connectivity over IPX RIP Router, Continued*

Possible Problem	Solution

Missing **ipx network** commands on interface (*Continued*)	To enable IPX protocol processing on an interface, enter the **ipx network** *number* interface configuration command:
	
	ipx network *network* [**encapsulation** *encapsulation-type* [**secondary**]]
	
	Syntax Description:
	
	• *network*—Network number. This is an eight-digit hexadecimal number that uniquely identifies a network cable segment. It can be a number in the range 1 to FFFFFFFE. You do not need to specify leading zeros in the network number. For example, for the network number 000000AA you can enter just AA.
	
	• **encapsulation** *encapsulation-type*—(Optional) Type of encapsulation. It can be one of the following values:
	
	  o **arpa** (for Ethernet interfaces only)—Use Novell's Ethernet II encapsulation. This encapsulation is recommended for networks that handle both TCP/IP and IPX traffic.
	
	  o **hdlc** (for serial interfaces only)—Use HDLC encapsulation.
	
	  o **novell-ether** (for Ethernet interfaces only)—Use Novell's Ethernet 802.3 encapsulation. This encapsulation consists of a standard 802.3 MAC header followed directly by the IPX header with a checksum of FFFF. It is the default encapsulation used by NetWare Version 3.11.
	
	  o **sap** (for Ethernet interfaces)—Use Novell's Ethernet 802.2 encapsulation. This encapsulation consists of a standard 802.3 MAC header followed by an 802.2 LLC header. This is the default encapsulation used by NetWare Version 4.0. (for Token Ring interfaces)—This encapsulation consists of a standard 802.5 MAC header followed by an 802.2 LLC header. (for FDDI interfaces)—This encapsulation consists of a standard FDDI MAC header followed by an 802.2 LLC header.

Table 8–6   *IPX RIP: No Connectivity over IPX RIP Router, Continued*

Possible Problem	Solution
Missing **ipx network** commands on interface (*Continued*)	○ **snap** (for Ethernet interfaces)—Use Novell Ethernet Snap encapsulation. This encapsulation consists of a standard 802.3 MAC header followed by an 802.2 SNAP LLC header. (for Token Ring and FDDI interfaces)—This encapsulation consists of a standard 802.5 or FDDI MAC header followed by an 802.2 SNAP LLC header.
	• **secondary**—(Optional) Indicates an additional network configured after the first (primary) network.
RIP timer mismatch	You can change RIP timer values changed on servers running NetWare 4.x or later. Mismatches between routers and servers can cause connectivity problems.
	Step 1 Use the **show ipx interfaces** privileged exec command on the router to view the state of IPX interfaces. Look for output similar to the following:
	``` C4500#show ipx interface [...] Updates each 60 seconds, aging multiples RIP: 3 SAP: 3 [...] ```
	Compare the timer value configured on the router with that configured on Novell servers.
	Step 2 The timer values configured on servers and routers should be the same across the whole IPX network.
	Reconfigure the router or the servers to bring the timer values into conformance. On the router, use the **ipx update-time** interface configuration command to change the RIP timer interval.
	For information on changing the timer value configured on Novell servers, consult your server documentation.

Table 8–6 *IPX RIP: No Connectivity over IPX RIP Router, Continued*

Possible Problem	Solution	
Router not propagating RIP updates	Step 1	Use the **debug ipx routing** activity privileged exec command on the router. Look for routing updates sent by the router out each interface.
	Step 2	If you do not see RIP updates being sent out the interfaces, try disabling RIP routing using the **no ipx routing** global configuration command and then reenabling it using the **ipx routing** command. Use the **show running-config** command to verify that the rest of the IPX configuration is still correct.
	Step 3	If disabling and reenabling IPX does not work, try restarting the router.
Misconfigured network filters	Step 1	Use the **show access-lists** privileged exec command on suspect routers to see whether there are Novell IPX access lists configured.
	Step 2	Use the **show running-config** privileged exec command to view the router configuration. You can see whether access lists are specified in an **ipx input-network-filter** or **ipx output-network-filter** interface configuration command. **Examples:** In the following example, access list 876 controls which networks are added to the routing table when IPX routing updates are received on Ethernet Interface 1:

```
access-list 876 permit 1b
interface ethernet 1
ipx input-network-filter 876
```

Routing updates for Network 1b will be accepted. Routing updates for all other networks are implicitly denied and are not added to the routing table.

The following example is a variation of the preceding that explicitly denies Network 1a and explicitly allows updates for all other networks:

```
access-list 876 deny 1a
access-list 876 permit -1
```

Table 8–6   *IPX RIP: No Connectivity over IPX RIP Router, Continued*

Possible Problem	Solution
Misconfigured network filters (*Continued*)	**Step 3** If access lists are used by one of these commands, disable the filters by using the **no ipx input-network-filter** or **no ipx output-network-filter** command.
	Step 4 Check whether the client can access the server normally. If the connection is successful, one access list or more needs modification.
	Step 5 To isolate the problem access list, apply one IPX filter at a time until you can no longer create connections.
	Step 6 When the problem access list is isolated, examine each **access-list** statement to see whether it blocks traffic from desired networks. If it does, configure explicit **permit** statements for networks that you want to be advertised normally in updates.
	Step 7 After altering the access list, re-enable the filter to make sure connections between the client and the server still work. Continue testing access lists until all your filters are enabled and the client can still connect to the server.
Routes not redistributed correctly	**Step 1** Use the **show ipx route** privileged exec command to see the IPX routing table.
	Step 2 Examine the routing table and make sure routes have been learned by the expected protocol and from the expected interface.
	Step 3 Use the **show running-config** privileged exec command to view the router configuration. Check each **ipx router** global configuration command entry and the associated **redistribute** commands, if any.

Table 8–6 *IPX RIP: No Connectivity over IPX RIP Router, Continued*

Possible Problem	Solution
Routes not redistributed correctly (*Continued*)	**Step 4** Make certain redistribution is configured between IPX RIP and the desired protocols. Make sure all the desired networks are specified for redistribution. **Note:** Route redistribution is enabled automatically between IPX RIP and Enhanced IGRP[1] and between IPX RIP and NLSP.[2] For detailed information on configuring route redistribution, see the *Network Protocols Configuration Guide, Part 1.*
Router not propagating SAPs	For information on troubleshooting this problem, refer to the following section "IPX RIP: SAP Updates Not Propagated by Router."

[1] Enhanced IGRP = Enhanced Interior Gateway Routing Protocol
[2] NLSP = NetWare Link Services Protocol

IPX RIP: SAP Updates Not Propagated by Router

Symptom: Novell SAP packets are not forwarded through a router running IPX RIP. Clients might be unable to connect to servers over one or more routers, or they might intermittently be able to connect.

— **NOTES** —————————————————————————

Procedures for troubleshooting IPX RIP problems not specific to SAPs are described in the section "IPX RIP: No Connectivity over IPX RIP Router" earlier in this chapter. Additional problems relating to intermittent connectivity problems are described in the section "Novell IPX: Intermittent Connectivity" later in this chapter.

Table 8–7 outlines the problems that might cause this symptom and describes solutions to those problems.

Table 8–7 *IPX RIP: SAP Updates Not Propagated by Router*

Possible Problem	Solution	
SAP timer mismatch	**Step 1**	Use the **show running-config** privileged exec command to view the router configuration. Look for **ipx sap-interval** interface configuration command entries.
		Example:
		In the following example, SAP updates are sent (and expected) on serial interface 0 every five minutes:
| | | ```
interface serial 0
ipx sap-interval 5
``` |
	Step 2	On LAN interfaces, it is recommended that you use the default SAP interval of one minute because the interval on servers cannot be changed. To restore the default value, use the **no ipx sap-interval** command. The following is the syntax for the **ipx sap-interval** command:
		ipx sap-interval *minutes*
		no ipx sap-interval
		Syntax Description:
		• *minutes*—Interval, in minutes, between SAP updates sent by the communication server. The default value is one minute. If minutes is 0, periodic updates are never sent.
		On serial interfaces, make sure whatever interval you configure is the same on both sides of the serial link. Use the **ipx sap-interval** interface configuration command to change the SAP interval.
```

Table 8–7   *IPX RIP: SAP Updates Not Propagated by Router, Continued*

Possible Problem	Solution
Misconfigured SAP filters	**Step 1** Use the **show access-lists** privileged exec command on suspect routers to see whether there are Novell IPX access lists configured. Use the **show running-config** privileged exec command to see whether there are SAP filters that use any of the configured access lists. At the end of this chapter is a list of Novell SAPs that includes the SAP description and hex and decimal values.
	Step 2 If SAP filters are configured, disable them by removing **ipx input-sap-filter** and **ipx output-sap-filter** interface configuration commands as appropriate (using the **no** version of the command).
	Step 3 Use the **debug ipx sap activity** privileged exec command to see whether SAP traffic is forwarded normally. The **debug** command output shows the server name, network number, and MAC address of SAP packets.
	Caution: Because debugging output is assigned high priority in the CPU process, it can render the system unusable. For this reason, use **debug** commands only to troubleshoot specific problems or during troubleshooting sessions with Cisco technical support staff. Moreover, it is best to use **debug** commands during periods of lower network traffic and fewer users. Debugging during these periods decreases the likelihood that increased **debug** command processing overhead will affect system use.
	Step 4 If SAP information is forwarded properly by the router, a SAP filter is causing SAP updates to be dropped by the router.
	Step 5 To isolate the problem SAP filter, reenable filters one at a time until SAP packets are no longer forwarded by the router.
	Step 6 Change the referenced access list to allow the SAP traffic you want to be forwarded to pass through the router. Make sure all necessary ports are configured with an explicit **permit** statement.
	Step 7 Continue enabling filters one at a time and checking to see that SAP traffic is still being forwarded properly until you have verified that all filters are configured properly.

Table 8–7   *IPX RIP: SAP Updates Not Propagated by Router, Continued*

Possible Problem	Solution	
Novell server not sending SAP updates	**Step 1**	Use the **debug ipx sap activity** privileged exec command or a protocol analyzer to look for SAP updates from servers.
		Caution: Because debugging output is assigned high priority in the CPU process, it can render the system unusable. For this reason, use **debug** commands only to troubleshoot specific problems or during troubleshooting sessions with Cisco technical support staff. Moreover, it is best to use **debug** commands during periods of lower network traffic and fewer users. Debugging during these periods decreases the likelihood that increased **debug** command processing overhead will affect system use.
	Step 2	If a server is not sending SAP updates, make sure the server is attached to the network and is up and running.
	Step 3	Make sure the server is properly configured to send SAPs. For information on configuring your server software properly, refer to your vendor documentation.
Novell servers not processing SAP updates as quickly as router is generating them	**Step 1**	Use the **show interfaces** privileged exec command to check for output drops.
	Step 2	If there are excessive drops, use the **show ipx servers** exec command on the router. Compare the output of this command with the output of the **display servers** system console command on Novell servers.
	Step 3	If the **display servers** output for a Novell server shows only a partial listing of the SAP entries shown by the router, the Novell servers might not be able to process SAP updates as quickly as the router is generating them.
	Step 4	Use the **ipx output-sap-delay** interface configuration command to configure the delay between packets in a multipacket SAP update. Novell specifies a delay of 55 ms.
		Syntax:
		The following is the syntax for the **ipx output-sap-delay** command:
		ipx output-sap-delay *delay*
		Syntax Description:
		• *delay*—Delay, in milliseconds, between packets in a multiple-packet SAP update.

IPX Enhanced IGRP: No Connectivity over IPX Enhanced IGRP Router

Symptom: IPX Enhanced IGRP routers are blocking connections. Clients cannot connect to servers over one or more routers running IPX Enhanced IGRP.

NOTES

Procedures for troubleshooting connectivity problems not specific to IPX Enhanced IGRP routing are described in the section "Novell IPX: Client Cannot Connect to Server on Remote LAN" earlier in this chapter.

Table 8–8 outlines the problems that might cause this symptom and describes solutions to those problems.

Table 8–8   *IPX Enhanced IGRP: No Connectivity over IPX Enhanced IGRP Router*

Possible Problem	Solution
IPX Enhanced IGRP is not configured or is misconfigured on the router	Unlike IPX RIP, IPX Enhanced IGRP is *not* enabled by default on all interfaces when the **ipx routing** global configuration command is issued.
	Step 1 Use the **show running-config** privileged exec command to view the router configuration.
	Step 2 Check the configuration to make sure there is an **ipx routing** global configuration command entry. This command enables IPX routing globally.
	Step 3 If the command is not present, use the **ipx routing** global configuration command to enable IPX routing. The following is the syntax for the **ipx routing** command:
	ipx routing [*node*]
	Syntax Description:
	• *node*—(Optional) Node number of the router. This is a 48-bit value represented by a dotted triplet of four-digit hexadecimal numbers (xxxx.xxxx.xxxx). It must not be a multicast address.
	If you omit *node*, the router uses the hardware MAC address currently assigned to it as its node address. This is the MAC address of the first Ethernet, Token Ring, or FDDI interface card. If no satisfactory interfaces are present in the router (for example, there are only serial interfaces), you must specify *node*.

Table 8–8   *IPX Enhanced IGRP: No Connectivity over IPX Enhanced IGRP Router, Continued*

Possible Problem	Solution
IPX Enhanced IGRP not configured or is misconfigured on the router (*Continued*)	**Step 4** Check the router configuration for an **ipx router eigrp** *autonomous-system-number* global configuration command and associated **ipx network** interface configuration commands.
	Step 5 If these commands are not present, configure the Enhanced IGRP process and then assign it to the appropriate interfaces with the **ipx network** commands.
	The following example enables RIP on networks 1 and 2 and Enhanced IGRP on network 1:
	``` ipx routing ! interface ethernet 0 ipx network 1 ! interface ethernet 1 ipx network 2 ! ipx router eigrp 100 network 1 ```
Missing **ipx network** command on interface	**Step 1** Use the **show ipx interface** privileged exec command to view the state of all IPX interfaces.
	Step 2 If the output indicates that there are no interfaces running IPX, or if an interface that should be running IPX is not, you must configure the appropriate interfaces with an IPX address.
	To enable IPX protocol processing on an interface, enter the **ipx network** *number* interface configuration command.
IPX RIP not enabled on network with connected Novell servers	Novell servers do not understand IPX Enhanced IGRP. You must ensure that IPX RIP is enabled on interfaces connected to LAN segments with attached Novell servers.
	Use the **show running-config** privileged exec command on suspect routers to view the router configuration. Make sure that any interfaces connected to a LAN segment with attached Novell servers have IPX RIP enabled.
	It is not necessary to disable the other routing protocol, but running IPX Enhanced IGRP and IPX RIP on the same interface can sometimes create performance problems.

Table 8-8 *IPX Enhanced IGRP: No Connectivity over IPX Enhanced IGRP Router, Continued*

Possible Problem	Solution
Misconfigured filters	**Step 1** Use the **show access-lists** privileged exec command on suspect routers to see whether there are Novell IPX access lists configured.
	Step 2 Use the **show running-config** privileged exec command to view the router configuration. See whether access lists are specified in an **ipx input-network-filter** or **ipx output-network-filter** interface configuration command.
	Step 3 If access lists are used by one of these commands, disable the filters using the **no ipx input-network-filter** or **no ipx output-network-filter** command.
	Step 4 Check whether the client can access the server normally. If the connection is successful, one access list or more needs modification.
	Step 5 To isolate the problem access list, apply one IPX filter at a time until you can no longer create connections.
	Step 6 When the problem access list is isolated, examine each **access-list** statement to see whether it is blocking traffic from desired networks. If it is, configure explicit **permit** statements for networks that you want to be advertised normally in updates.
	Step 7 After altering the access list, reenable the filter to make sure connections between the client and the server still work. Continue testing access lists until all your filters are enabled and the client can still connect to the server.

Table 8–8   *IPX Enhanced IGRP: No Connectivity over IPX Enhanced IGRP Router, Continued*

Possible Problem	Solution
Routes not redistributed properly	Route redistribution between IPX Enhanced IGRP autonomous systems and between Enhanced IGRP and other routing protocols is not enabled by default. You must manually configure redistribution between different autonomous systems or routing protocols. **Step 1** Use the **show running-config** privileged exec command on any routers that border two Enhanced IGRP autonomous systems. Look for **redistribute** *protocol* IPX router configuration command entries. **Step 2** If the command is not present, you must enter the appropriate **redistribute** *protocol* command to allow route redistribution between different autonomous systems or routing protocols. For detailed information on configuring route redistribution, see the *Network Protocols Configuration Guide, Part 1.*
Routers not establishing neighbors properly	For information on troubleshooting this problem, see the section "IPX Enhanced IGRP: Routers Not Establishing Neighbors" later in this chapter.
Router not propagating SAPs	For information on troubleshooting this problem, refer to the section "IPX Enhanced IGRP: SAP Updates Not Propagated by Router" later in this chapter.

IPX Enhanced IGRP: Routers Not Establishing Neighbors

Symptom: IPX Enhanced IGRP routers do not establish neighbors properly. Routers that are known to be connected do not appear in the neighbor table.

NOTES

Procedures for troubleshooting IPX Enhanced IGRP problems not specific to establishing neighbors are described in the section "IPX Enhanced IGRP: No Connectivity over IPX Enhanced IGRP Router" earlier in this chapter.

Table 8–9 outlines the problems that might cause this symptom and describes solutions to those problems.

Table 8–9 *IPX Enhanced IGRP: Routers Not Establishing Neighbors*

Possible Problem	Solution	
Routers are in different autonomous systems	Step 1	Neighbor relationships will not be established between routers in different autonomous systems. Make sure the routers you want to be neighbors are in the same autonomous system.
	Step 2	Use the **show running-config** privileged exec command to view the router configuration. Check the **ipx router eigrp** command entries to see which autonomous systems the router belongs to.
Hello or hold-time timer mismatch	Step 1	Use the **show running-config** privileged exec command on each router in the network. Look for **ipx hello-interval eigrp** and **ipx hold-time eigrp** interface configuration command entries. The values configured by these commands should be the same for all IPX routers in the network.
	Step 2	If any router has a conflicting hello interval or hold-time value, reconfigure it to conform with the rest of the routers on the network. You can return these values to their defaults with the **no ipx hello-interval eigrp** and **no ipx hold-time interval eigrp** interface configuration commands.

Table 8–9   *IPX Enhanced IGRP: Routers Not Establishing Neighbors, Continued*

Possible Problem	Solution
Link problem	**Step 1** Use the **show interfaces** privileged exec command to check whether the interface is up and functioning correctly. The following is sample output from the **show interfaces** command: ```Router#show interfaces fastethernet1/0 FastEthernet1/0 is up, line protocol is up Hardware is cyBus FastEthernet Interface, address is 0010.5498.d020 (bia 0010. 5498.d020) Internet address is 210.84.3.33/24 MTU 1500 bytes, BW 100000 Kbit, DLY 100 usec, rely 230/255, load 1/255 Encapsulation ARPA, loopback not set, keepalive set (10 sec), hdx, 100BaseTX/FX``` **Step 2** Use the **show ipx eigrp neighbors** privileged exec command to make sure all Enhanced IGRP neighbors are shown in the neighbor table. **Step 3** If not all neighbors are in the neighbor table, there might be a link problem. Refer to other chapters in this book for information on troubleshooting specific link types.

IPX Enhanced IGRP: SAP Updates Not Propagated by Router

Symptom: Novell SAP packets are not forwarded through a router running IPX Enhanced IGRP. Clients might be unable to connect to servers over one or more routers, or they might connect only intermittently.

NOTES

Procedures for troubleshooting IPX Enhanced IGRP problems not specific to SAPs are described in the section "IPX Enhanced IGRP: No Connectivity over IPX Enhanced IGRP Router" earlier in this chapter.

Table 8–10 outlines the problems that might cause this symptom and describes solutions to those problems.

Table 8–10 *IPX Enhanced IGRP: SAP Updates Not Propagated by Router*

Possible Problem	Solution
Misconfigured SAP filters	**Step 1** Use the **show access-lists** privileged exec command on suspect routers to see whether there are Novell IPX access lists configured. Use the **show running-config** privileged exec command to see whether there are SAP filters that use any of the configured access lists. At the end of this chapter is a list of Novell SAPs that includes the SAP description and hex and decimal values.
	Step 2 If SAP filters are configured, disable them by removing the **ipx input-sap-filter** and **ipx output-sap-filter** interface configuration commands as appropriate (using the **no** version of the command).
	Step 3 Use the **debug ipx sap activity** privileged exec command to see whether SAP traffic is being forwarded normally. The **debug** command output shows the server name, network number, and MAC address of SAP packets.
	Caution: Because debugging output is assigned high priority in the CPU process, it can render the system unusable. For this reason, use **debug** commands only to troubleshoot specific problems or during troubleshooting sessions with Cisco technical support staff. Moreover, it is best to use **debug** commands during periods of lower network traffic and fewer users. Debugging during these periods decreases the likelihood that increased **debug** command processing overhead will affect system use.
	Step 4 If SAP information is being forwarded properly by the router, a SAP filter is causing SAP updates to be dropped by the router.
	Step 5 To isolate the problem SAP filter, reenable filters one at a time until SAP packets are no longer forwarded by the router.
	Step 6 Change the referenced access list to allow the SAP traffic you want to be forwarded to pass through the router. Make sure all necessary ports are configured with an explicit **permit** statement.
	Step 7 Continue enabling filters one at a time and checking to see that SAP traffic is being forwarded properly until you have verified that all filters are configured properly.

Table 8–10 *IPX Enhanced IGRP: SAP Updates Not Propagated by Router, Continued*

Possible Problem	Solution
SAP updates are being sent incrementally rather than periodically	Connectivity problems can occur when LAN interfaces are configured to send incremental (not periodic) SAP updates on segments that have attached Novell clients or servers. Incremental SAP updates are sent only when there is a change in the SAP table.
	Step 1 Use the **show running-config** privileged exec command to view the router configuration. Look for **ipx sap-incremental eigrp** interface configuration command entries on interfaces with attached Novell clients or servers.
	Step 2 If the command is present and the interface in question has attached Novell clients or servers, you must disable the **ipx sap-incremental eigrp** command. This command should be configured on an interface only if all the nodes attached to that interface are Enhanced IGRP peers.
Link problem	**Step 1** Use the **show interfaces** privileged exec command and look for drops and interface resets.
	The following is sample output from the **show interfaces** command:
| | ```
Router#show interfaces fastethernet 1/0
FastEthernet1/0 is up, line protocol is up
Hardware is cyBus FastEthernet Interface, address is
0010.5498.d020 (bia 0010. 5498.d020)
  Internet address is 208.84.3.33/24
  MTU 1500 bytes, BW 100000 Kbit, DLY 100 usec, rely
255/255, load 1/255
  Encapsulation ARPA, loopback not set, keepalive set (10
sec), hdx, 100BaseTX/FX
  ARP type: ARPA, ARP Timeout 04:00:00
  Last input 00:00:07, output 00:00:07, output hang never
  Last clearing of "show interface" counters never
  Queueing strategy: fifo
  Output queue 0/40, 0 drops; input queue 0/75, 0 drops
``` |
```

Table 8–10 *IPX Enhanced IGRP: SAP Updates Not Propagated by Router, Continued*

Possible Problem	Solution
Link problem (*Continued*)	**Step 2** If you see many drops or interface resets, use the **debug ipx sap activity** privileged exec command and then the **clear ipx eigrp neighbor** privileged exec command.
	Caution: Because debugging output is assigned high priority in the CPU process, it can render the system unusable. For this reason, use **debug** commands only to troubleshoot specific problems or during troubleshooting sessions with Cisco technical support staff. Moreover, it is best to use **debug** commands during periods of lower network traffic and fewer users. Debugging during these periods decreases the likelihood that increased **debug** command processing overhead will affect system use.
	If there is a link problem, the **debug ipx sap activity** command will not produce any output.
	Step 3 Refer to the appropriate chapter elsewhere in this book for information on troubleshooting the particular link type. For example, for serial links, refer to Chapter 15, "Troubleshooting Serial Line Problems."

IPX Enhanced IGRP: Router Stuck in Active Mode

Symptom: An IPX Enhanced IGRP router is stuck in Active mode. The router repeatedly sends error messages similar to the following:

```
%DUAL-3-SIA: Route 3c.0800.0c00.4321 Stuck-in-Active
```

NOTES

Occasional messages of this type are *not* a cause for concern. This is how an Enhanced IGRP router recovers if it does not receive replies to its queries from all its neighbors. However, if these error messages occur frequently, you should investigate the problem.

For a more detailed explanation of Enhanced IGRP Active mode, see the section "Enhanced IGRP and Active/Passive Modes" later in this chapter.

Table 8–11 outlines the problems that might cause this symptom and describes solutions to those problems.

Table 8–11 *IPX Enhanced IGRP: Router Stuck in Active Mode*

Possible Problem	Solution	
Active timer value is misconfigured	Step 1	The active timer specifies the maximum period of time that an Enhanced IGRP router will wait for replies to its queries. If the active timer value is set too low, there might not be enough time for all the neighboring routers to send their replies to the active router. A value of 3 (3 minutes, which is the default value) is strongly recommended to allow all Enhanced IGRP neighbors to reply to queries.
	Step 2	Check the configuration of each Enhanced IGRP router using the **show running-config** privileged exec command. Look for a **timers active-time** router configuration command entry.
	Step 3	The value set by the **timers active-time** command should be consistent among routers in the same autonomous system. A value of 3 (3 minutes, which is the default value) is strongly recommended to allow all Enhanced IGRP neighbors to reply to queries.
Interface or other hardware problem	Step 1	Use the **show ipx eigrp neighbors** exec command and examine the Uptime and Q Cnt (queue count) fields in the output. The following is sample output from the **show ipx eigrp neighbors** command:

```
Router# show ipx eigrp neighbors
IPX EIGRP Neighbors for process 200
H  Address            Interface       Hold   Uptime   Q    Seq   SRTT  RTO
                                      (secs) (h:m:s)  Cnt  Num   (ms)  (ms)
6  90.0000.0c02.096e  Tunnel44444     13     0:30:57  0    21    9     20
5  80.0000.0c02.34f2  Fddi0           12     0:31:17  0    62    14    28
4  83.5500.2000.a83c  TokenRing2      13     0:32:36  0    626   16    32
3  98.0000.3040.a6b0  TokenRing1      12     0:32:37  0    43    9     20
2  80.0000.0c08.cbf9  Fddi0           12     0:32:37  0    624   19    38
1  85.aa00.0400.153c  Ethernet2       12     0:32:37  0    627   15    30
0  82.0000.0c03.4d4b  Hssi0           12     0:32:38  0    629   12    24
```

		If the uptime counter is continually resetting or if the queue count is consistently high, there might be a hardware problem.
	Step 2	Check the output of the "Stuck-in-Active" error message. The output indicates the general direction of the problem node, but if there are multiple nodes in that direction, the problem could be in any one of them.
	Step 3	Make sure the suspect router still works. Check the interfaces on the suspect router. Make sure the interface and line protocol are up and determine whether the interface is dropping packets. For more information on troubleshooting hardware, see Chapter 3, "Troubleshooting Hardware and Booting Problems."

Table 8–11 *IPX Enhanced IGRP: Router Stuck in Active Mode, Continued*

Possible Problem	Solution
Flapping route	**Step 1** Check for a flapping serial route (caused by heavy traffic load) by using the **show interfaces** privileged exec command. Flapping is a routing problem where an advertised route between two nodes alternates (flaps) back and forth between two paths due to a network problem that causes intermittent interface failures. You might have a flapping route if there are large numbers of resets and carrier transitions.
	Step 2 If there is a flapping route, queries and replies might not be forwarded reliably. Route flapping caused by heavy traffic on a serial link can cause queries and replies to be lost, resulting in the active timer timing out.
	Take steps to reduce traffic on the link or to increase the bandwidth of the link.
	For more information about troubleshooting serial lines, refer to Chapter 3, "Troubleshooting Serial Line Problems."

Enhanced IGRP and Active/Passive Modes

An Enhanced IGRP router can be in either Passive or Active mode. A router is said to be passive for a network when it has an established path to the network in its routing table. The route is in Active state when a router is undergoing a route recomputation. If there are always feasible successors, a route never has to go into Active state and avoids a route recomputation.

If the Enhanced IGRP router loses the connection to a network, it becomes active for that network. The router sends out queries to all its neighbors in order to find a new route. The router remains in Active mode until it has either received replies from *all* its neighbors or until the active timer, which determines the maximum period of time a router will stay active, has expired.

If the router receives a reply from each of its neighbors, it computes the new next hop to the network and becomes passive for that network. However, if the active timer expires, the router removes any neighbors that did not reply from its neighbor table, again enters Active mode, and issues a "Stuck-in-Active" message to the console.

Novell IPX: Intermittent Connectivity

Symptom: Connectivity between clients and servers is intermittent. Clients might be able to connect some of the time, but at other times no connectivity to certain servers or networks is possible.

Table 8–12 outlines the problems that might cause this symptom and describes solutions to those problems.

Table 8–12   *Novell IPX: Intermittent Connectivity*

Possible Problem	Solution
SAP timer mismatch	**Step 1** Use the **show running-config** privileged exec command to view the router configuration. Look for **ipx sap-interval** interface configuration command entries.
	Step 2 On LAN interfaces, it is recommended that you use the default SAP interval of 1 minute because the interval on servers cannot be changed. To restore the default value, you can use the **no ipx sap-interval** command.
	On serial interfaces, make sure that whatever interval you configure is the same on both sides of the serial link. Use the **ipx sap-interval** interface configuration command to change the SAP interval.
RIP timer mismatch	You can change RIP timer values on servers running NetWare 4.x or later. Mismatches between routers and servers can cause connectivity problems.

	Step 1 Use the **show ipx interfaces** privileged exec command on the router to view the state of IPX interfaces. Look for output similar to the following:
	
	`C4500#show ipx interface`
	`[...]`
	`Updates each 60 seconds, aging multiples RIP: 3 SAP: 3`
	`[...]`
	
	Compare the timer value configured on the router with that configured on Novell servers.

	Step 2 The timer values configured on servers and routers should be the same across the entire IPX network.
	Reconfigure the router or the servers to bring the timer values into conformance. On the router, use the **ipx update-time** interface configuration command to change the RIP timer interval.
	For information on changing the timer value configured on Novell servers, consult your server documentation.

Table 8–12 *Novell IPX: Intermittent Connectivity, Continued*

Possible Problem	Solution
SAP updates are sent incrementally rather than periodically	In IPX Enhanced IGRP environments, problems can occur when interfaces are configured to send incremental (not periodic) SAP updates on segments that have attached Novell servers. (Incremental SAP updates are sent only when there is a change in the SAP table.)
	Step 1 Use the **show running-config** privileged exec command to view the router configuration. Check to see whether there are **ipx sap-incremental eigrp** interface configuration command entries enabled on interfaces with attached Novell clients or servers.
	Step 2 If the **incremental** command is present and the interface in question has attached Novell clients or servers, you must disable the **ipx sap-incremental eigrp** command by using the **no** version of the command. This command should be configured on an interface only if all the nodes attached to that interface are Enhanced IGRP peers.
Novell servers not processing SAP updates as quickly as router is generating them	**Step 1** Use the **show interfaces** privileged exec command to check for output drops.
	Step 2 If there are excessive drops, use the **show ipx servers** exec command on the router. Compare the output of this command with the output of the **display servers** system console command on Novell servers.
	Step 3 If the **display servers** output for a Novell server shows only a partial listing of the SAP entries shown by the router, the Novell servers might be unable to process SAP updates as quickly as the router is generating them.
	Step 4 Use the **ipx output-sap-delay** interface configuration command to configure the delay between packets in a multipacket SAP update. Novell specifies a delay of 55 ms.

Table 8–12   *Novell IPX: Intermittent Connectivity, Continued*

Possible Problem	Solution
SAP updates dropped from hub router's output queue	Slow serial lines can cause the router to drop SAP packets before they are transmitted.
	Step 1 Use the **show interfaces serial** exec command and examine the output queue drops field. A large number of dropped packets might indicate that SAP updates are being dropped before they can be transmitted across the serial link.
	Step 2 Use the **show ipx servers** exec command on the router. Compare the output of this command with the output of the **display servers** system console command on Novell servers.
	Step 3 If the **display servers** output for a Novell server shows only a partial listing of the SAP entries shown by the router, the router might be dropping SAP packets from the output queue.
	Step 4 Eliminate the forwarding of any SAP updates that are not absolutely necessary. Configure filters using the **ipx input-sap-filter, ipx output-sap-filter,** and **ipx router-sap-filter** interface configuration commands, as appropriate.
	Step 5 Increasing the output hold queue on the serial interface might also improve performance. Use the **hold-queue** *length* **out** interface configuration command to increase the output hold queue length. The default output **hold-queue** limit is 100 packets. The general rule when using the **hold-queue** command is for slow links, use a small output **hold-queue** limit. This approach prevents storing packets at a rate that exceeds the transmission capability of the link. For fast links, use a large output **hold-queue** limit. A fast link may be busy for a short time (and thus require the hold queue), but can empty the output hold queue quickly when capacity returns.
	Step 6 If SAP filters and increased queue lengths do not solve the problem, increase the available bandwidth if possible. Add a second serial line or obtain a single link with more available bandwidth.[1]

Table 8–12   *Novell IPX: Intermittent Connectivity, Continued*

Possible Problem	Solution
Router is stuck in active mode (EIGRP only)	If you consistently receive "Stuck-in-Active" messages about a particular network, you probably have a flapping route (typically caused by heavy traffic load). Route flapping can cause routes to come and go in the routing table, resulting in intermittent connectivity to some networks.
	Take steps to reduce traffic on the link or to increase the bandwidth of the link.
	For more information about troubleshooting serial lines, refer to Chapter 15, "Troubleshooting Serial Line Problems."

[1] If increasing the bandwidth is not possible, buffer management might help alleviate the problem. Contact the Cisco Technical Assistance Center for assistance in tuning buffers.

Novell IPX: Slow Performance

Symptom: Slow network performance is experienced in a Novell IPX network.

Table 8–13 outlines the problems that might cause this symptom and describes solutions to those problems.

Table 8–13   *Novell IPX: Slow Performance*

Possible Problem	Solution	
Novell servers not processing SAP updates as quickly as router is generating them	Step 1	Use the **show interfaces** privileged exec command to check for output drops.
	Step 2	If there are excessive drops, use the **show ipx servers** exec command on the router. Compare the output of this command with the output of the **display servers** system console command on Novell servers.
	Step 3	If the **display servers** output for a Novell server shows only a partial listing of the SAP entries shown by the router, the Novell servers might be unable to process SAP updates as quickly as the router is generating them.
	Step 4	Use the **ipx output-sap-delay** interface configuration command to configure the delay between packets in a multipacket SAP update. Novell specifies a delay of 55 ms.

Table 8–13   *Novell IPX: Slow Performance, Continued*

Possible Problem	Solution
Periodic SAP updates are using excessive bandwidth	In a non-IPX RIP environment (such as on a serial link running Enhanced IGRP), you can reduce SAP traffic by configuring routers to send incremental rather than periodic SAP updates. Incremental SAP updates are sent only when there is a change to the SAP table.
	You should have incremental SAP updates enabled only on interfaces that have *no* Novell clients or servers attached. Novell clients and servers require periodic SAP updates.
	Use the **ipx sap-incremental eigrp** interface configuration command to enable incremental SAP updates.
IPX RIP and IPX Enhanced IGRP are enabled on the same interface	Running both IPX Enhanced IGRP and IPX RIP on the same interface is sometimes desired or required in an IPX network. However, doing so can cause performance problems in some cases by creating excess traffic and processor overhead.
	Step 1 Use the **show running-config** privileged exec command to view the router configuration. Check the **network** router configuration commands associated with **ipx router rip** and the **ipx router eigrp** global configuration commands to see whether both routing protocols are enabled on the same interface.
	Step 2 If both protocols are enabled, determine whether one or the other can be disabled without affecting the proper operation of the network. If there is no need for both protocols to be running on the same interface, remove the superfluous configuration commands as appropriate.
Router is stuck in active mode (Enhanced IGRP only)	If you consistently receive "Stuck-in-Active" messages about a particular network, you probably have a flapping route (typically caused by heavy traffic load). Route flapping can force routers to use a less preferred route, resulting in slower performance.
	Take steps to reduce traffic on the link or increase the bandwidth of the link.
	For more information about troubleshooting serial lines, refer to Chapter 15, "Troubleshooting Serial Line Problems."

NOVELL SAPS

The list of Novell SAPs in Table 8–14 is unverified information contributed from various sources. Novell, in an official capacity, does not and has not provided any of this information.

Table 8–14 *Novell SAPs, Their Descriptions, and Their Decimal and Hex Values*

Decimal	Hex	SAP Description
0	0000	Unknown
1	0001	User
2	0002	User Group
3	0003	Print Queue or Print Group
4	0004	File Server (SLIST source)
5	0005	Job Server
6	0006	Gateway
7	0007	Print Server or Silent Print Server
8	0008	Archive Queue
9	0009	Archive Server
10	000a	Job Queue
11	000b	Administration
15	000F	Novell TI-RPC
23	0017	Diagnostics
32	0020	NetBIOS
33	0021	NAS SNA Gateway
35	0023	NACS Async Gateway or Asynchronous Gateway
36	0024	Remote Bridge or Routing Service
38	0026	Bridge Server or Asynchronous Bridge Server
39	0027	TCP/IP Gateway Server
40	0028	Point to Point (Eicon) X.25 Bridge Server
41	0029	Eicon 3270 Gateway
42	002a	CHI Corp
44	002c	PC Chalkboard

Table 8–14 *Novell SAPs, Their Descriptions, and Their Decimal and Hex Values, Continued*

Decimal	Hex	SAP Description
45	002d	Time Synchronization Server or Asynchronous Timer
46	002e	ARCserve 5.0 / Palindrome Backup Director 4.x (PDB4)
69	0045	DI3270 Gateway
71	0047	Advertising Print Server
74	004a	NetBlazer Modems
75	004b	Btrieve VAP/NLM 5.0
76	004c	Netware SQL VAP/NLM Server
77	004d	Xtree Network Version Netware XTree
80	0050	Btrieve VAP 4.11
82	0052	QuickLink (Cubix)
83	0053	Print Queue User
88	0058	Multipoint X.25 Eicon Router
96	0060	STLB/NLM
100	0064	ARCserve
102	0066	ARCserve 3.0
114	0072	WAN Copy Utility
122	007a	TES-Netware for VMS
146	0092	WATCOM Debugger or Emerald Tape Backup Server
149	0095	DDA OBGYN
152	0098	Netware Access Server (Asynchronous gateway)
154	009a	Netware for VMS II or Named Pipe Server
155	009b	Netware Access Server
158	009e	Portable Netware Server or SunLink NVT
161	00a1	Powerchute APC UPS NLM
170	00aa	LAWserve
172	00ac	Compaq IDA Status Monitor
256	0100	PIPE STAIL

Table 8–14 *Novell SAPs, Their Descriptions, and Their Decimal and Hex Values, Continued*

Decimal	Hex	SAP Description
258	0102	LAN Protect Bindery
259	0103	Oracle DataBase Server
263	0107	Netware 386 or RSPX Remote Console
271	010f	Novell SNA Gateway
273	0111	Test Server
274	0112	Print Server (HP)
276	0114	CSA MUX (f/Communications Executive)
277	0115	CSA LCA (f/Communications Executive)
278	0116	CSA CM (f/Communications Executive)
279	0117	CSA SMA (f/Communications Executive)
280	0118	CSA DBA (f/Communications Executive)
281	0119	CSA NMA (f/Communications Executive)
282	011a	CSA SSA (f/Communications Executive)
283	011b	CSA STATUS (f/Communications Executive)
286	011e	CSA APPC (f/Communications Executive)
294	0126	SNA TEST SSA Profile
298	012a	CSA TRACE (f/Communications Executive)
299	012b	Netware for SAA
301	012e	IKARUS virus scan utility
304	0130	Communications Executive
307	0133	NNS Domain Server or Netware Naming Services Domain
309	0135	Netware Naming Services Profile
311	0137	Netware 386 Print Queue or NNS Print Queue
321	0141	LAN Spool Server (Vap, Intel)
338	0152	IRMALAN Gateway
340	0154	Named Pipe Server
358	0166	NetWare Management

Table 8–14   *Novell SAPs, Their Descriptions, and Their Decimal and Hex Values, Continued*

Decimal	Hex	SAP Description
360	0168	Intel PICKIT Comm Server or Intel CAS Talk Server
369	0171	UNKNOWN
371	0173	Compaq
372	0174	Compaq SNMP Agent
373	0175	Compaq
384	0180	XTree Server or XTree Tools
394	018A	UNKNOWN Running on a Novell Server
432	01b0	GARP Gateway (net research)
433	01b1	Binfview (Lan Support Group)
447	01bf	Intel LanDesk Manager
458	01ca	AXTEC
459	01cb	Shiva NetModem/E
460	01cc	Shiva LanRover/E
461	01cd	Shiva LanRover/T
472	01d8	Castelle FAXPress Server
474	01da	Castelle LANPress Print Server
476	01dc	Castille FAX/Xerox 7033 Fax Server/Excel Lan Fax
496	01f0	LEGATO
501	01f5	LEGATO
563	0233	NMS Agent or Netware Management Agent
567	0237	NMS IPX Discovery or LANtern Read/Write Channel
568	0238	NMS IP Discovery or LANtern Trap/Alarm Channel
570	023a	LABtern
572	023c	MAVERICK
574	023e	UNKNOWN Running on a Novell Server

Table 8-14 *Novell SAPs, Their Descriptions, and Their Decimal and Hex Values, Continued*

Decimal	Hex	SAP Description
575	023f	Used by 11 various Novell Servers / Novell SMDR
590	024e	Netware Connect
618	026a	Network Management Service (NMS) Console
619	026b	Time Synchronization Server (Netware 4.x)
632	0278	Directory Server (Netware 4.x)
989	03dd	Banyan ENS for Netware Client NLM
772	0304	Novell SAA Gateway
776	0308	COM or VERMED 1
778	030a	Galacticomm's Worldgroup Server
780	030c	Intel Netport 2 or HP JetDirect or HP Quicksilver
800	0320	Attachmate Gateway
807	0327	Microsoft Diagnostiocs
808	0328	WATCOM SQL server
821	0335	MultiTech Systems Multisynch Comm Server
835	2101	Performance Technology Instant Internet
853	0355	Arcada Backup Exec
858	0358	MSLCD1
865	0361	NETINELO
894	037e	Twelve Novell file servers in the PC3M family
895	037f	ViruSafe Notify
902	0386	HP Bridge
903	0387	HP Hub
916	0394	NetWare SAA Gateway
923	039b	Lotus Notes
951	03b7	Certus Anti Virus NLM
964	03c4	ARCserve 4.0 (Cheyenne)
967	03c7	LANspool 3.5 (Intel)

Table 8–14 *Novell SAPs, Their Descriptions, and Their Decimal and Hex Values, Continued*

Decimal	Hex	SAP Description
983	03d7	Lexmark printer server (type 4033-011)
984	03d8	Lexmark XLE printer server (type 4033-301)
990	03de	Gupta Sequel Base Server or NetWare SQL
993	03e1	Univel Unixware
996	03e4	Univel Unixware
1020	03fc	Intel Netport
1021	03fd	Print Server Queue
1196	04ac	On-Time Scheduler NLM
1034	040A	ipnServer Running on a Novell Server
1035	040B	UNKNOWN
1037	040D	LVERRMAN Running on a Novell Server
1038	040E	LVLIC Running on a Novell Server
1040	0410	UNKNOWN Running on a Novell Server
1044	0414	Kyocera
1065	0429	Site Lock Virus (Brightworks)
1074	0432	UFHELP R
1075	0433	Synoptics 281x Advanced SNMP Agent
1092	0444	Microsoft NT SNA Server
1096	0448	Oracle
1100	044c	ARCserve 5.01
1111	0457	Canon GP55 Running on a Canon GP55 network printer
1114	045a	QMS Printers
1115	045b	Dell SCSI Array (DSA) Monitor

Table 8–14 *Novell SAPs, Their Descriptions, and Their Decimal and Hex Values, Continued*

Decimal	Hex	SAP Description
1169	0491	NetBlazer Modems
1200	04b0	CD-Net (Meridian)
1217	04C1	UNKNOWN
1299	0513	Emulux NQA Something from Emulex
1312	0520	Site Lock Checks
1321	0529	Site Lock Checks (Brightworks)
1325	052d	Citrix OS/2 App Server
1343	0535	Tektronix
1344	0536	Milan
1387	056b	IBM 8235 modem server
1388	056c	Shiva LanRover/E PLUS
1389	056d	Shiva LanRover/T PLUS
1408	0580	McAfee's NetShield anti-virus
1466	05BA	Compatible Systems Routers
1569	0621	IBM AntiVirus NLM
1571	0623	UNKNOWN Running on a Novell Server
1900	076C	Xerox
1947	079b	Shiva LanRover/E 115
1958	079c	Shiva LanRover/T 115
2154	086a	ISSC collector NLMs
2175	087f	ISSC DAS agent for AIX
2857	0b29	Site Lock
3113	0c29	Site Lock Applications
3116	0c2c	Licensing Server
9088	2380	LAI Site Lock

Table 8–14 *Novell SAPs, Their Descriptions, and Their Decimal and Hex Values, Continued*

Decimal	Hex	SAP Description
9100	238c	Meeting Maker
18440	4808	Site Lock Server or Site Lock Metering VAP/NLM
21845	5555	Site Lock User
25362	6312	Tapeware
28416	6f00	Rabbit Gateway (3270)
30467	7703	MODEM
32770	8002	NetPort Printers (Intel) or LANport
32776	8008	WordPerfect Network Version
34238	85BE	Cisco Enhanced Interior Routing Protocol (EIGRP)
34952	8888	WordPerfect Network Version or Quick Network Management
36864	9000	McAfee's NetShield anti-virus
38404	9604	CSA-NT_MON
46760	b6a8	Ocean Isle Reachout Remote Control
61727	f11f	Site Lock Metering VAP/NLM
61951	f1ff	Site Lock
62723	F503	SCA-NT
64507	fbfb	TopCall III fax server
65535	ffff	Any Service or Wildcard
0	0000	Unknown

CHAPTER 9

Troubleshooting AppleTalk

In the early 1980s, as Apple Computer, Inc., was preparing to introduce the Macintosh computer, Apple engineers knew that networks would become a critical need. They wanted to ensure that a Macintosh-based network was a seamless extension of the revolutionary Macintosh user interface. With these two goals in mind, Apple decided to build a network interface into every Macintosh and to integrate that interface into the desktop environment. Apple's new network architecture was called AppleTalk.

Although AppleTalk is a proprietary network, Apple has published AppleTalk specifications in an attempt to encourage third-party development. Today, many companies—including Novell, Inc., and Microsoft Corporation—are successfully marketing AppleTalk-based products.

The original implementation of AppleTalk, which was designed for local workgroups, is now commonly referred to as AppleTalk Phase 1. With the installation of more than 1.5 million Macintosh computers in the first five years of the product's life, however, Apple found that some large corporations were exceeding the built-in limits of AppleTalk Phase 1, so they enhanced the protocol. The enhanced protocol, known as AppleTalk Phase 2, improved the routing capabilities of AppleTalk and allowed AppleTalk to run successfully in larger networks.

APPLETALK TECHNOLOGY BASICS

AppleTalk was designed as a client/server distributed network system. In other words, users share network resources (such as files and printers) with other users. Computers supplying these network resources are called *servers*; computers using a server's network resources are called *clients*. Interaction with servers is essentially transparent to the user because the computer itself determines the location of the requested material and accesses it without further information from the user. In addition to their ease of use, distributed systems also enjoy an economic advantage over peer-to-peer systems because important materials can be located in a few, rather than many, locations.

229

In Figure 9–1, AppleTalk protocols are shown adjacent to the OSI reference model layers to which they map.

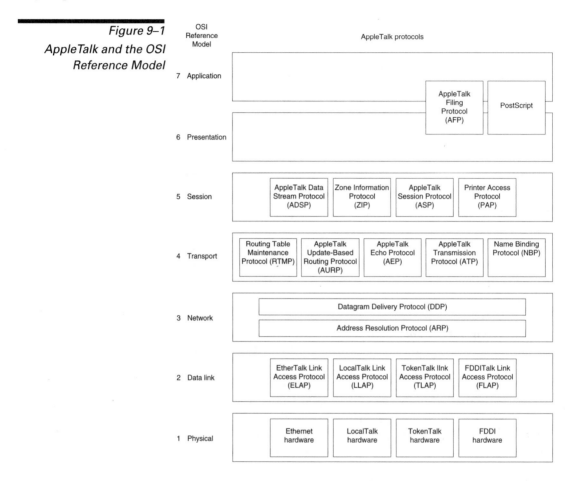

Figure 9–1
AppleTalk and the OSI
Reference Model

Media Access

Apple designed AppleTalk to be link-layer independent. In other words, it can theoretically run on top of any link-layer implementation. Apple supports a variety of link-layer implementations, including Ethernet, Token Ring, Fiber Distributed Data Interface (FDDI), and LocalTalk. Apple refers to AppleTalk over Ethernet as EtherTalk, to AppleTalk over Token Ring as TokenTalk, and to AppleTalk over FDDI as FDDITalk. The link-layer protocols that support AppleTalk over these media are EtherTalk Link Access Protocol (ELAP), LocalTalk Link Access Protocol (LLAP), TokenTalk Link Access Protocol (TLAP), and FDDITalk Link Access Protocol (FLAP). LocalTalk is Apple's proprietary media-access system. It is based on contention access, bus topology, and base-band signaling, and runs on shielded twisted-pair media at 230.4 kbps. The physical interface is EIA/TIA-422 (formerly RS-422), a balanced electrical interface supported by EIA/TIA-449 (formerly RS-449). LocalTalk segments can span up to 300 meters and support a maximum of 32 nodes.

THE NETWORK LAYER

This section describes AppleTalk network-layer concepts and protocols. It includes discussion of protocol address assignment, network entities, and AppleTalk protocols that provide OSI reference model Layer 3 functionality.

Protocol Address Assignment

To ensure minimal network administrator overhead, AppleTalk node addresses are assigned dynamically. When a Macintosh running AppleTalk starts up, it chooses a protocol (network-layer) address and checks whether that address is currently in use. If it is not, the new node has successfully assigned itself an address. If the address is currently in use, the node with the conflicting address sends a message indicating a problem, and the new node chooses another address and repeats the process. Figure 9–2 shows the AppleTalk address selection process.

The mechanics of AppleTalk address selection are media dependent. The AppleTalk Address Resolution Protocol (AARP) is used to associate AppleTalk addresses with particular media addresses. AARP also associates other protocol addresses with hardware addresses. When either AppleTalk or any other protocol stack must send a packet to another network node, the protocol address is passed to AARP. AARP first checks an address cache to see whether the relationship between the protocol and the hardware address is already known. If it is, that relationship is passed up to the inquiring protocol stack. If it is not, AARP initiates a broadcast or multicast message inquiring about the hardware address for the protocol address in question. If the broadcast reaches a node with the specified protocol address, that node replies with its hardware address. This information is passed up to the inquiring protocol stack, which uses the hardware address in communications with that node.

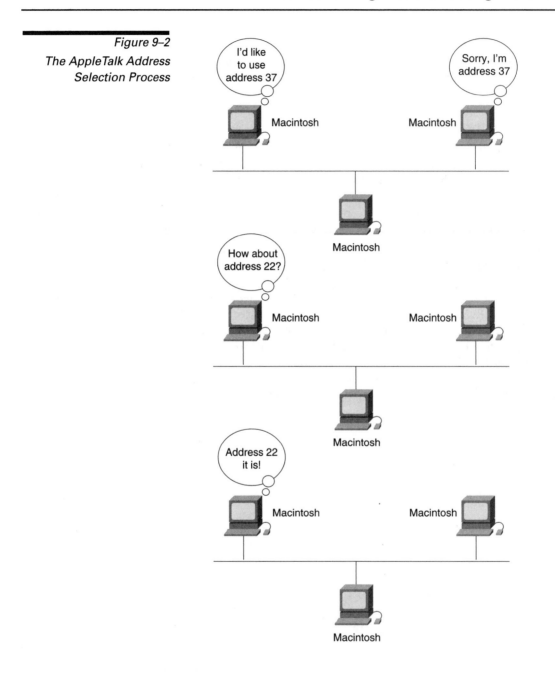

Figure 9–2
The AppleTalk Address
Selection Process

Network Entities

AppleTalk identifies several network entities. The most elemental is a node, which is simply any device connected to an AppleTalk network. The most common nodes are Macintosh computers and laser printers, but many other types of computers are also capable of AppleTalk communication, including IBM PCs, Digital Equipment Corporation VAX computers, and a variety of workstations. The next entity defined by AppleTalk is the network. An AppleTalk network is simply a single logical cable. Although the logical cable is frequently a single physical cable, some sites use bridges to interconnect several physical cables. Finally, an AppleTalk zone is a logical group of (possibly non-contiguous) networks. These AppleTalk entities are shown in Figure 9–3.

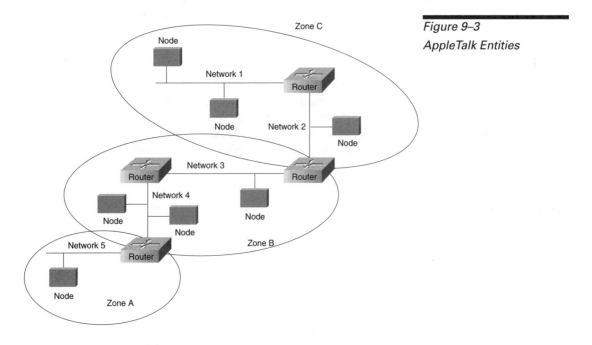

Figure 9–3
AppleTalk Entities

Datagram Delivery Protocol

AppleTalk's primary network-layer protocol is the Datagram Delivery Protocol (DDP). DDP provides connectionless service between network sockets. Sockets can be assigned either statically or dynamically.

AppleTalk addresses, which are administered by the DDP, consist of two components: a 16-bit network number and an 8-bit node number. The two components are usually written as decimal numbers, separated by a period (for example, 10.1 means network 10, node 1). When an 8-bit socket identifying a particular process is added to the network number and node number, a unique process on a network is specified.

AppleTalk Phase 2 distinguishes between nonextended and extended networks. In a nonextended network such as LocalTalk, each AppleTalk node number is unique. Nonextended networks were the sole network type defined in AppleTalk Phase 1. In an extended network such as EtherTalk and TokenTalk, each network number/node number combination is unique.

Zones are defined by the AppleTalk network manager during the router configuration process. Each node in an AppleTalk network belongs to a single specific zone. Extended networks can have multiple zones associated with them. Nodes on extended networks can belong to any single zone associated with the extended network.

THE TRANSPORT LAYER

AppleTalk's transport layer is implemented by several protocols: Routing Table Maintenance Protocol (RTMP), AppleTalk Update Routing Protocol (AURP), AppleTalk Echo Protocol (AEP), AppleTalk Transaction Protocol (ATP), and Name Binding Protocol (NBP).

RTMP

The protocol that establishes and maintains AppleTalk routing tables is RTMP. RTMP routing tables contain an entry for each network that a datagram can reach. Each entry includes the router port that leads to the destination network, the node ID of the next router to receive the packet, the distance in hops to the destination network, and the current state of the entry (good, suspect, or bad). Periodic exchange of routing tables allows the routers in an internetwork to ensure that they supply current and consistent information. Figure 9–4 shows a sample RTMP table and the corresponding network architecture.

Figure 9–4
A Sample AppleTalk Routing Table

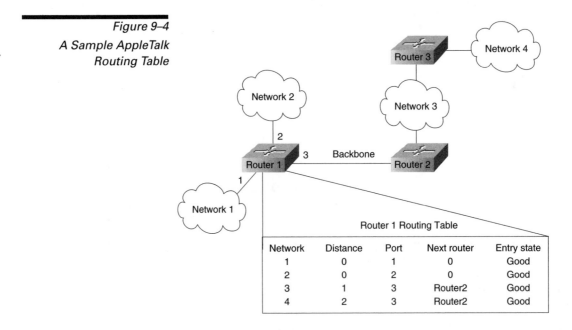

Router 1 Routing Table

Network	Distance	Port	Next router	Entry state
1	0	1	0	Good
2	0	2	0	Good
3	1	3	Router2	Good
4	2	3	Router2	Good

AppleTalk's NBP associates AppleTalk names (expressed as network-visible entities, or NVEs) with addresses. An NVE is an AppleTalk network-addressable service, such as a socket. NVEs are associated with one or more entity names and attribute lists. Entity names are character strings such as printer@net1, whereas attribute lists specify NVE characteristics.

Named NVEs are associated with network addresses through the process of name binding. Name binding can be done when the user node is first started up, or dynamically, immediately before first use. NBP orchestrates the name binding process, which includes name registration, name confirmation, name deletion, and name lookup.

Zones allow name lookup in a group of logically related nodes. To look up names within a zone, an NBP lookup request is sent to a local router, which sends a broadcast request to all networks that have nodes belonging to the target zone. The Zone Information Protocol (ZIP) coordinates this effort.

ZIP maintains network number–to–zone name mappings in zone information tables (ZITs). ZITs are stored in routers, which are the primary users of ZIP, but end nodes use ZIP during the startup process to choose their zone and to acquire internetwork zone information. ZIP uses RTMP routing tables to keep up with network topology changes. When ZIP finds a routing table entry that is not in the ZIT, it creates a new ZIT entry. Figure 9–5 shows a sample ZIT.

Network number	Zone
1	My
2	Your
3	Marketing
4	Documentation
5-5	Sales

Figure 9–5

A Sample AppleTalk ZIT

AURP

AURP allows a network administrator to connect two or more AppleTalk internetworks through a foreign network (such as Transmission Control Protocol/Internet Protocol [TCP/IP]) to form an AppleTalk wide-area network (WAN). The connection is called a tunnel, which functions as a single, virtual data link between the AppleTalk internetworks, as shown in Figure 9–6.

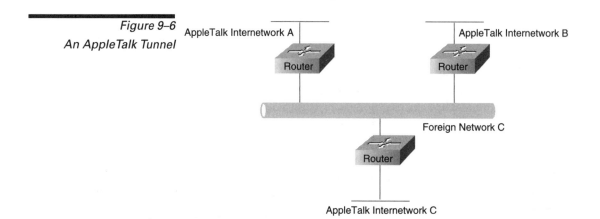

Figure 9–6
An AppleTalk Tunnel

A router that connects an AppleTalk internetwork to a tunnel (that is, a router that runs AURP) is called an *exterior router*. The exterior router sends AppleTalk data packets and routing information through the foreign network by encapsulating the packets with the header information required by the foreign network system. The receiving exterior router removes the foreign header information and sends the packets out the appropriate interface. Packets are encapsulated in User Datagram Protocol (UDP) headers in the initial implementation of AURP.

When only two exterior routers are connected to a tunnel, that tunnel is called a *point-to-point tunnel*. When more than two exterior routers are connected to the tunnel, that tunnel is called a *multipoint tunnel*. If all exterior routers connected to a multipoint tunnel can send packets to each other, the tunnel is said to be *fully connected*. If one or more exterior routers are not aware of other exterior routers, the tunnel is said to be *partially connected*. Each exterior router functions both as an AppleTalk router within its local internetwork and as an end node in the foreign network that connects the AppleTalk internetworks.

The main function of AURP is to maintain accurate routing tables for the entire AppleTalk WAN by the exchange of routing information between exterior routers. In addition, AURP encapsulates AppleTalk data packets with the headers required by the foreign network.

AURP uses the principle of split horizons (which states that it is never useful to send information about a route back in the direction from which the information came) to limit the propagation of routing updates. For that reason, an exterior router sends routing information about only the networks that comprise its local internetwork to other exterior routers connected to the tunnel.

When an exterior router becomes aware of another exterior router on the tunnel, the two exterior routers exchange their lists of network numbers and associated zone information. Thereafter, an exterior router sends routing information only when the following events occur:

- A network is added to the routing table.
- A change in the path to a network causes the exterior router to access that network through its local internetwork rather than through the tunnel or to access that network through the tunnel rather than through the local internetwork.

- A network is removed from the routing table.
- The distance to a network is changed.

When an exterior router receives AppleTalk data packets or routing information that needs to be forwarded over the tunnel, the AURP module converts that information to AURP packets. The AURP packets are encapsulated in the header information required by the foreign network and sent over the tunnel to the destination exterior router, as shown in Figure 9–7.

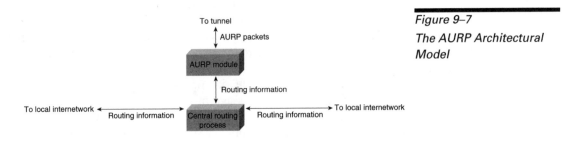

Figure 9–7

The AURP Architectural Model

At the destination exterior router, the AURP module removes the headers required by the foreign system from the AURP packets and sends AppleTalk data packets to their final destination. The exterior router uses the AURP packets that contain routing information to update its routing information tables but does not propagate that information to any other exterior router.

NOTES

As defined by Apple Computer, AURP converts RTMP and ZIP packets into AURP packets and vice versa. As implemented by Cisco, AURP converts Enhanced IGRP packets as well as RTMP and ZIP packets.

AEP

AEP is an extremely simple protocol which generates packets that can be used to test the reachability of various network nodes.

ATP

ATP is suitable for transaction-based applications such as those found in banks or retail stores. ATP transactions consist of requests (from clients) and replies (from servers). Each request/reply pair has a particular transaction ID. Transactions occur between two socket clients. ATP uses exactly once (XO) and at-least-once (ALO) transactions. XO transactions are used in situations where performing the transaction more than once would be unacceptable. Banking transactions are examples of transactions that, if performed more than once, result in invalid data.

ATP is capable of most important transport-layer functions, including data acknowledgment and retransmission, packet sequencing, and fragmentation and reassembly. ATP limits message segmentation to eight packets, and ATP packets cannot contain more than 578 data bytes.

UPPER-LAYER PROTOCOLS

AppleTalk supports several upper-layer protocols:

- AppleTalk Data Stream Protocol (ADSP) establishes and maintains full-duplex data streams between two sockets in an AppleTalk internetwork. ADSP is a reliable protocol in that it guarantees that data bytes are delivered in the same order as sent and that they are not duplicated. ADSP numbers each data byte to keep track of the individual elements of the data stream. ADSP also specifies a flow-control mechanism. The destination can essentially slow source transmissions by reducing the size of its advertised receive window. ADSP also provides an out-of-band control message mechanism. Attention packets are used as the vehicle for moving out-of-band control messages between two AppleTalk entities. These packets use a separate sequence number stream to differentiate them from normal ADSP data packets.

- The AppleTalk Session Protocol (ASP) establishes and maintains sessions (logical conversations) between an AppleTalk client and a server.

- AppleTalk's Printer Access Protocol (PAP) is a connection-oriented protocol that establishes and maintains connections between clients and servers. (Use of the term *printer* in this protocol's title is purely historical.)

- The AppleTalk Filing Protocol (AFP) helps clients share server files across a network.

TROUBLESHOOTING APPLETALK

This section presents protocol-related troubleshooting information for AppleTalk connectivity and performance problems. In addition to general AppleTalk problems, this chapter also covers AppleTalk Enhanced IGRP, AppleTalk Remote Access (ARA), AURP, and FDDITalk problems.

The section "AppleTalk Configuration and Troubleshooting Tips" discusses preventive measures and tips to help you configure and troubleshoot your AppleTalk internetwork. The remaining sections describe specific AppleTalk symptoms, the problems that are likely to cause each symptom, and the solutions to those problems.

The following sections cover the most common network issues in AppleTalk environments:

- AppleTalk: Users Cannot Access Zones or Services
- AppleTalk: Zones Missing from Chooser
- AppleTalk: No Devices in Chooser
- AppleTalk: Network Services Intermittently Unavailable
- AppleTalk: Old Zone Names Appear in Chooser (Phantom Zones)

- AppleTalk: Connections to Services Drop
- AppleTalk: Interface Fails to Initialize AppleTalk
- AppleTalk: Port Stuck in Restarting or Acquiring Mode
- AppleTalk Enhanced IGRP: Clients Cannot Connect to Servers
- AppleTalk Enhanced IGRP: Routers Not Establishing Neighbors
- AppleTalk Enhanced IGRP: Routes Missing from Routing Table
- AppleTalk Enhanced IGRP: Poor Performance
- AppleTalk Enhanced IGRP: Router Stuck in Active Mode
- AURP: Routes Not Propagated Through AURP Tunnel
- FDDITalk: No Zone Associated with Routes
- ARA: ARA Client Unable to Connect to ARA Server
- ARA: Connection Hangs After "Communicating At..." Message
- ARA: Cannot Send or Receive Data over ARA Dialin Connection
- ARA: Slow Performance from Dialin Connection

AppleTalk Configuration and Troubleshooting Tips

This section offers configuration and troubleshooting tips that can help you prevent or more easily repair problems in AppleTalk internetworks.

It consists of information on preventing AppleTalk problems, preventing internetwork reconfiguration problems, changing zone names, using AppleTalk Discovery Mode, and forcing an interface up to allow a router to start functioning if the network is misconfigured.

Preventing AppleTalk Problems

Table 9–1 lists suggestions to help you avoid problems when configuring a router for AppleTalk.

Table 9–1 *AppleTalk Problem-Prevention Techniques*

Preventive Action	Description
Every router connected to a network must agree on the configuration of that network	Every router on an AppleTalk network (that is, on a single cable segment) must agree on the configuration of the network. Therefore, network numbers, cable ranges, timer values, zone names, and other parameters should be the same for every router on the segment.
Every network number in an internetwork must be unique	Network numbers must be unique throughout the entire AppleTalk network. Duplicate network numbers can cause connectivity- and performance-related problems.

Table 9–1   *AppleTalk Problem-Prevention Techniques, Continued*

Preventive Action	Description
Upgrade to AppleTalk Phase 2 wherever possible	To minimize interoperability problems, upgrade all router Ethernet interfaces to Phase 2. Phase 1/Phase 2 networks can be problematic, as can nonextended AppleTalk networks.
When you change a router or interface configuration, enable the **debug apple error** privileged exec command to log errors	The **debug apple error** privileged exec command tracks the progress and status of changes in the internetwork and alerts you to any errors. You can also run this command periodically when you suspect network problems. In a stable network, this command returns no output. You can establish a syslog server at your site and add the configuration command **appletalk event-logging** to the router. This keeps a running log, with timestamps, of significant events on your network. Disable this command with the **no debug apple error** command when you have completed diagnostic activities.
Design your network with attention to the direction in which traffic will flow and minimize the number of different zones in the internetwork	Careful zone mapping can minimize unnecessary NBP[1] traffic. Planning is particularly important in WANs where traffic traversing WAN links (such as X.25) can be quite expensive. In System 6, if a user opens the Chooser, the Macintosh continually sends NBP BrReq packets. In System 7, a logarithmic backoff minimizes the amount of traffic generated. Give all the backbone/WAN connections the same zone name rather than put them in a zone with a LAN. In most internetworks, it is not desirable to have the zone names for all backbone or WAN connections appear in the Chooser list. If you make the zone name of all the WAN links the same (for example, ZZSerial), only that entry appears in the Chooser menu.
Set AppleTalk timers to the default values throughout the internetwork	A stable network almost *never* has nondefault timer values configured. Timers should be consistently set to the *same value* throughout the internetwork, or at a minimum, throughout the backbone of the internetwork. Check with a qualified technical support representative before changing AppleTalk default timer values.

[1] NBP = Name Binding Protocol

Using the test appletalk and ping appletalk Commands

In Cisco IOS Release 11.1 and later, use the **test appletalk** privileged exec command to help identify problem nodes. Use the **nbp** (Name Binding Protocol) options of the command to perform informational lookups of NBP-registered entities. The information returned when using the **nbp** options is useful when AppleTalk zones are listed in the Chooser but services in those zones are unavailable.

When running the **test appletalk** facility, use the confirm option to check that a name of a specified type is registered on a device. For example, **nbp confirm 24279.173 my-mac:AFPServer@engineering** confirms that the name my-mac is registered on the device 24279.173 in the engineering zone. The object type is AFPServer. The syntax for the **nbp confirm** command is as follows:

> **nbp confirm** *appletalk-address* [:skt] *object:type@zone*

The syntax description is as follows:

- *appletalk-address*—AppleTalk network address in the form **network.node**. The argument **network** is the 16-bit network number in the range 1 to 65279. The argument node is the 8-bit node number in the range 0 to 254. Both numbers are decimal.
- :skt—(Optional) Name of socket.
- *object:type*—Name of device and the type of service. The colon (:) between object and type is required.
- @*zone*—Name of the AppleTalk zone where the entity *object:type* resides.

In software releases prior to Cisco IOS Release 11.0, the **ping appletalk** exec command serves a similar function. Use this command to verify that a node is reachable from the router (for example, **ping appletalk 2.24** pings AppleTalk node 2.24).

The following display shows input to and output from the user **ping** command:

```
Router> ping appletalk 2.24
Type escape sequence to abort.
Sending 5, 100-byte AppleTalk Echoes to 2.24, timeout is 2 seconds:
!!!!!
Success rate is 100 percent, round-trip min/avg/max = 4/4/8 ms
```

The **ping** privileged exec command also supports several AppleTalk parameters that provide additional troubleshooting capabilities. In particular, use the NBP option when AppleTalk zones are listed in the Chooser but services are not available. If a configuration contains the **appletalk name-lookup-interval** global configuration command, the NBP option of the AppleTalk **ping** function displays nodes by their NBP registration names.

Preventing Internetwork Reconfiguration Problems

Configuration conflicts can occur when zone names or cable range numbers are changed. In particular, problems arise when routing devices about which you are not administratively aware exist on the internetwork.

Many devices can act as routers (for example, Novell servers, Pathworks servers, or UNIX workstations running CAP to do print and file sharing). In general, if you are changing zone names or cable range numbers in your internetwork, shut down all routers so that a Cisco router does not see a conflict and prevent AppleTalk from initializing on the interface.

Before changing the configuration, use the **show appletalk neighbors** exec command to determine on which routers you should disable AppleTalk routing. You should disable AppleTalk on all routers that are on the same network segment and that have sent RTMP updates in the past 10 seconds. Disable AppleTalk routing on all of the appropriate interfaces, wait approximately 10 minutes, and then bring up the seed router.

Changing Zone Names

When changing a zone name on an existing network, perform the following actions:

Step 1   Disable AppleTalk on all router interfaces on the cable for approximately 10 minutes. This allows all routers in the internetwork to age out the network number from their routing tables.

Step 2   Configure the new zone list.

Step 3   Re-enable AppleTalk on all interfaces.

These actions are required because AppleTalk makes no provisions for informing neighbors in the internetwork about a changed zone list. Routers make ZIP queries only when a new (or previously aged-out) network appears on the internetwork.

Adding a new zone to an extended cable configuration prevents the router from bringing up an AppleTalk interface after the interface has been reset. This is because its configuration no longer matches that of its neighbors (that is, it detects a configuration mismatch error).

AppleTalk Discovery Mode

When bringing up an interface on an existing cable where a long zone list is defined, using Apple-Talk discovery mode helps you save effort and avoid mistakes.

The following steps outline bringing up an interface in discovery mode:

Step 1   Bring up the interface in discovery mode (using the **appletalk cable-range 0-0** interface configuration command). When a router is in discovery mode, the router changes its configuration to match the advertised cable range if the advertised cable range is different from that configured on the router. The **debug apple events** privileged exec command lets you know when the discovery process is complete by displaying an "operational" message.

Step 2   After discovery is complete, and while in interface configuration mode, enter the **no appletalk discovery** interface configuration command for the specific AppleTalk interface being initialized. This saves the acquired information and forces the configuration to be validated at port startup.

The router should not be in discovery mode for normal operation (it is recommended that discovery mode be used only when initially configuring networks). After the initial configuration, configure all routers for seed, or nondiscovery, mode. If you enable AppleTalk discovery and the interface is restarted, you must have another operational communication server or router on the directly connected network or the interface will not start up. It is not advisable to have all communication servers and routers on a network configured with discovery mode enabled. If all communication servers were to restart simultaneously (for instance, after a power failure), the network would become inaccessible until at least one communication server or router were restarted with discovery mode disabled.

Step 3   Use the **copy running-config startup-config** privileged exec command to save the acquired information to nonvolatile RAM (NVRAM).

Step 4   Verify the configuration with the **show running-config** privileged exec command.

Forcing an Interface Up

In certain situations, you might need to force an interface to come up even though its zone list conflicts with that of another router on the network. You can do this by using the **appletalk ignore-verify-errors** global configuration command. Usually the other router is one over which you have no administrative control but which you know has an incorrect zone list.

The **appletalk ignore-verify-errors** command allows you to bypass the default behavior of an Apple-Talk interface. By default, the AppleTalk interface does not come up if its zone list conflicts with that of its neighbors. However, you should use this command with *extreme* caution; bringing up an interface with a zone list that conflicts with that of other routers can cause serious network problems. In addition, the other router *must* be reconfigured at some point so that all the routers in the internetwork agree on the zone list.

After all the AppleTalk routers on the network segment have conforming zone lists, disable the **appletalk ignore-verify-errors** command using the **no** form of the command. For complete information on the **appletalk ignore-verify-errors** global configuration command, see the Cisco IOS *Network Protocols Command Reference, Part 1.*

AppleTalk: Users Cannot Access Zones or Services

Symptom: Users cannot access zones or services that appear in the Chooser. Users might or might not be able to access services on their own network.

Table 9–2 outlines the problems that might cause this symptom and describes solutions to those problems.

Table 9–2   *AppleTalk: Users Cannot Access Zones or Services*

Possible Problems	Solution	
Configuration mismatch	**Step 1**	Use the **show appletalk interface** exec command. Check the output for a "port configuration mismatch" message.
		If the command output contains a "mismatch" message, the router configuration disagrees with that of the listed neighbor.
		If the command output does not include the "mismatch" message, use the **clear apple interface** privileged exec command on the interface in question. If the interface becomes operational after clearing, a configuration mismatch does not exist.
	Step 2	Enter the **show appletalk interface** exec command again. If its output still contains a "port configuration mismatch" message, check whether all router configurations agree on the network number or cable range and the zone or zone list.
	Step 3	If router configurations disagree on these parameters, alter router configurations to bring all routers into alignment.
	Step 4	If problems persist, put the problem router in discovery mode by specifying the interface configuration command **appletalk address 0.0** on a nonextended network or the **appletalk cable-range** 0-0 command on an extended network. This causes the router to get its configuration information from the network.
		For more information about configuration mismatches, see the section "AppleTalk Configuration Mismatches" later in this chapter.

Table 9–2 *AppleTalk: Users Cannot Access Zones or Services, Continued*

Possible Problems	Solution
Duplicate network numbers or overlapping cable-range	In AppleTalk, network numbers must be unique within an internetwork. If duplicate network numbers exist, packets might not be routed to their intended destinations.
	If AppleTalk services do not appear in the Chooser for particular networks, those networks probably have duplicate network numbers.
	Step 1 Change the network number or cable-range of the suspect network to a unique value using the **appletalk cable-range** interface configuration command.
	Step 2 Use the **show appletalk route** privileged exec command to view the routing table. If the network number or cable-range continues to appear in routing tables, you have found the duplicate (because the other network using that number will continue to send routing updates).
	If the network number or cable-range disappears from the internetwork after 40 seconds, you have not found the duplicate. Change the network number or cable-range specification back to its previous value and try again to isolate the duplicate network number.
	Step 3 If you changed the network number or cable-range on the interface, remember to reenter the zone name and any other interface configurations for AppleTalk on that interface.

Table 9–2   *AppleTalk: Users Cannot Access Zones or Services, Continued*

Possible Problems	Solution
Phase 1 and Phase 2 rule violations	**Step 1** Use the **show appletalk globals** exec command to determine whether the internetwork is in compatibility mode. **Step 2** Enable the **appletalk name-lookup-interval** global configuration command and use the **show appletalk neighbors** exec command to determine which specific neighbor (by NBP[1] name) is in compatibility mode. **Step 3** To resolve the problem, you can perform one of the following actions: • Upgrade AppleTalk Phase 1 routers to AppleTalk Phase 2 and reconfigure the internetwork • Ensure that all routers are in compliance with the two Phase 1 and Phase 2 rules For more information on Phase 1 and Phase 2 rule violations, see the section "Phase 1 and Phase 2 Rule Violations" later in this chapter.
Misconfigured access lists or other filters	**Step 1** Use the **show appletalk access-list** exec command on routers in the path from source to destination. **Step 2** Disable any access lists (or just those on a particularly suspect router) using the **no appletalk access-group** interface configuration command. If there are distribution lists or other filters configured, disable them. **Step 3** After disabling access lists, check whether remote zones and services become accessible. **Step 4** If zones and services are now available, a misconfigured access list is the likely problem. To isolate the problem access list, enable lists one at a time until connectivity fails. **Step 5** Check the access lists and associated configuration commands for errors. Configure explicit **permit** statements for traffic that you want to pass through the router normally. **Step 6** If problems persist, there might be more than one misconfigured access list. Continue enabling access lists one at a time and fixing misconfigured access lists until the problem is solved.

[1] NBP = Name Binding Protocol

AppleTalk Configuration Mismatches

A configuration mismatch occurs if all the AppleTalk routers on a given cable do not agree on the configuration of that cable. This means that all routers must have matching network numbers, a matching default zone, and a matching zone list.

To protect against configuration errors that violate this rule, Cisco AppleTalk routers block activation of any port on which a violation of this rule exists. At interface initialization, if other routers on the network do not agree with the way a router is configured, the router does not allow Apple-Talk to become operational on that interface. Cisco routers attempt to restart such an interface every two minutes to avoid outages that result from transient conditions.

However, if the router is already operational and another router whose configuration does not match becomes active, the router continues to operate on that interface until the interface is reset. At that point, the interface fails to become active. When the **show appletalk interface** exec command is issued, the router indicates a port configuration mismatch.

The following is sample output from the **show appletalk interface** command when a configuration mismatch exists:

```
Ethernet 0 is up, line protocol is up
AppleTalk routing disabled, Port configuration mismatch
AppleTalk cable range is 4-5
AppleTalk address is 4.252, Valid
AppleTalk zone is "Maison Vauquer"
AppleTalk port configuration conflicts with 4.156
AppleTalk discarded 8 packets due to input errors
AppleTalk discarded 2 packets due to output errors
AppleTalk route cache is disabled, port initializing
```

Line 2 of the command output shows that routing has been disabled due to a port configuration mismatch. Line 6 indicates the AppleTalk address of the conflicting router.

You can also display the NBP registered name of the conflicting router, which can simplify resolution of a port mismatch problem. To see registered NBP names, enable the **appletalk name-lookup-interval** global configuration command. This causes the **show appletalk interface** exec command output to display nodes by NBP registration name.

Phase 1 and Phase 2 Rule Violations

When Phase 1 and Phase 2 routers are connected to the same internetwork, the internetwork specifications must conform to two rules:

- There can be no "wide" cable range specifications in the Phase 2 extended portion of the internetwork. That is, no cable ranges can span more than a single (unary) network number. For example, the cable ranges 2–2, 9–9, and 20–20 are all acceptable. The cable ranges 10–12 and 100–104 are not acceptable.

- Multiple zones cannot be assigned to unary cable ranges.

If these rules are not followed, connectivity between the nonextended and extended portions of an internetwork becomes degraded and might be lost. In particular, services located on nonextended networks using Phase 1 routers will not be visible on the other side of the Phase 1 router.

NOTES

On Cisco routers, Phase 1 refers to the router Ethernet interfaces being configured with a single network address and Ethernet I encapsulation, instead of with a cable-range and Ethernet SNAP encapsulation. A Cisco router running Software Release 8.2 or later is a Phase 2–compliant router regardless of how the interfaces are configured.

Another Phase 1 and Phase 2 issue is the handling of NBP packets. Phase 1 AppleTalk has three types of NBP packets, and Phase 2 AppleTalk has four types of NBP packets. This difference can lead to communication problems between Phase 1 and Phase 2 routers. Table 9–3 lists the NBP packet types for AppleTalk Phase 1 and Phase 2.

Table 9–3   *Comparison of Phase 1 and Phase 2 NBP Packet Types*

Phase 1 NBP Packet	Phase 2 NBP Packet
BrRq (Broadcast Request)	BrRq (Broadcast Request)
—	FwdReq (Forward Request)
LkUp (Lookup)	LkUp (Lookup)
LkUp-Reply (Lookup Reply)	LkUp-Reply (Lookup Reply)

As shown in Table 9–3, Forward Request packets do not exist in Phase 1. Only Phase 2 routers know what to do with them. Phase 1 routers that receive Forward Request packets simply drop them.

AppleTalk: Zones Missing from Chooser

Symptom: Certain zones do not appear in the Chooser. The zones are not visible from multiple networks. In some cases, when the Chooser is opened, the zone list changes.

Table 9–4 outlines the problems that might cause this symptom and describes solutions to those problems.

Table 9–4   *AppleTalk: Zones Missing from Chooser*

Possible Problems	Solution	
Configuration mismatch	**Step 1**	Use the **show appletalk interface** exec command. Check the output for a "port configuration mismatch" message.
		If the command output contains a "mismatch" message, the router configuration disagrees with that of the listed neighbor.
		If the command output does not include the "mismatch" message, use the **clear apple interface** privileged exec command on the interface in question. If the interface becomes operational after clearing, a configuration mismatch does not exist.
	Step 2	Enter the **show appletalk interface** exec command again. If its output still contains a "port configuration mismatch" message, check whether all router configurations agree on the network number or cable range and the zone or zone list.
	Step 3	If router configurations disagree on these parameters, alter router configurations to bring all routers into alignment.
	Step 4	If problems persist, put the problem router in discovery mode by specifying the interface configuration command **appletalk address 0.0** on a nonextended network or the **appletalk cable-range 0-0** command on an extended network. This causes the router to get its configuration information from the network.
		For more information about configuration mismatches, see the section "AppleTalk Configuration Mismatches" earlier in this chapter.

Table 9–4   *AppleTalk: Zones Missing from Chooser, Continued*

Possible Problems	Solution
Misconfigured access lists or other filters	**Step 1** Use the **show appletalk access-list** exec command on routers in the path from source to destination.
	Step 2 Disable any access lists (or just those on a particularly suspect router) using the **no appletalk access-group** interface configuration command. If there are distribution lists or other filters configured, disable them.
	Step 3 After disabling access lists, check whether remote zones and services become accessible.
	Step 4 If zones and services are now available, a misconfigured access list is the likely problem. To isolate the problem access list, enable lists one at a time until connectivity fails.
	Step 5 Check the access lists and associated configuration commands for errors. Configure explicit **permit** statements for traffic that you want to pass through the router normally.
	Step 6 If problems persist, there might be more than one misconfigured access list. Continue enabling access lists one at a time and fixing misconfigured access lists until the problem is solved.
Route flapping (unstable route)	Excessive traffic load on internetworks with many routers can prevent some routers from sending RTMP[1] updates every 10 seconds as they should. Because routers begin to age out routes after missing two consecutive RTMP updates, the inconsistent arrival of RTMP updates can result in constant route changes.
	Step 1 Use the **show interfaces** exec command to check the traffic load. Check the load for each interface.
	The following example is output from the **show interfaces** command:
| | ```
Ethernet0 is up, line protocol is up
  Hardware is Lance, address is 0000.0c32.49b1 (bia
0000.0c32.49b1)
  Internet address is 192.168.52.26/24
 MTU 1500 bytes, BW 10000 Kbit, DLY 1000 usec, rely 255/255,
load 1/255
  [...]
``` |
```

Table 9–4 *AppleTalk: Zones Missing from Chooser, Continued*

Possible Problems	Solution
Route flapping (unstable route) (*Continued*)	The load field displayed in the **show interfaces** command is the load on the interface as a fraction of 255 (255/255 is completely saturated), calculated as an exponential average over five minutes.
	Step 2 If the load is less than 50%, reconfiguring timer values might solve the problem by allowing RTMP updates more time to propagate through the network.
	If the load is more than 50%, you might need to segment the network to reduce the number of routers (and therefore the amount of traffic) on each network segment.
| | **Step 3** Use the **debug apple events** privileged exec command to determine whether routes are being aged incorrectly. The output should resemble the following:<br><br>```
Router#debug apple events
AppleTalk Events debugging is on
Router#
%AT-6-PATHNOTIFY: Ethernet0: AppleTalk RTMP path to
250-250 down; reported bad by 200.41
```<br><br>**Caution:** Because debugging output is assigned high priority in the CPU process, it can render the system unusable. For this reason, use **debug** commands only to troubleshoot specific problems or during troubleshooting sessions with Cisco technical support staff. Moreover, it is best to use **debug** commands during periods of lower network traffic and fewer users. Debugging during these periods decreases the likelihood that increased **debug** command processing overhead will affect system use. |
	Step 4 If routes are being aged incorrectly, use the **appletalk timers** global configuration command to correct the problem. Suggested timer values are 10, 30, and 90 to start, but do not exceed 10, 40, and 120. The first number must always be 10, and the third value should be three times the second.
	You can return the timers to their defaults (10, 20, 60) by using the **no appletalk timers** global configuration command.
	Timers should be consistently set to the same value throughout the internetwork, or at a minimum, throughout the backbone of the internetwork.
```

Table 9–4 *AppleTalk: Zones Missing from Chooser, Continued*

Possible Problems	Solution
ZIP storm	A ZIP storm occurs when a router propagates a route for which it currently has no corresponding zone name; the route is then propagated by downstream routers.

Note: Cisco routers provide a firewall against ZIP storms in the internetwork. If a Cisco router receives a routing update from a neighbor, it does not propagate that new route until it receives the accompanying zone name.

Step 1 Use the **show appletalk traffic** command and check the field showing the number of ZIP requests.

The following example is output from the **show appletalk traffic** command:

```
Router#sh apple traffic
[...]
ZIP:   44 received, 35 sent, 6 netinfo
[...]
Router#
```

Compare this output with the output shown by the command 30 seconds later.

Step 2 If the traffic counters for ZIP requests are incrementing very rapidly (by more than 10 every 30 seconds), a ZIP storm is probably occurring.

Use the **debug apple zip** privileged exec command to identify the network for which the zone is being requested by neighboring routers. You can also use the **show apple private** exec command to check the number of pending ZIP requests.

Step 3 Identify the router that injected the network number into the internetwork (and that is causing the excessive ZIP traffic). The **show appletalk traffic** and **show appletalk route** exec commands provide information that can help you find the suspect router.

Table 9-4 *AppleTalk: Zones Missing from Chooser, Continued*

Possible Problems	Solution	
ZIP storm (*Continued*)		For example, you can use the **show appletalk route** exec command to view the AppleTalk routing table. Check whether a network shows up in the routing table, even though the display indicates that no zone is set.
		If you find a network for which no zone is set, a node on that network is probably not responding to ZIP requests, resulting in the ZIP storm.
	Step 4	Determine why the node is not responding to ZIP requests. Access lists or other filters might be the cause. ZIP storms can also result from a defect in the software running on the node. Contact the vendor to determine whether there is a known problem.
Too many zones in internetwork	The Chooser in System 6 can display only a limited number of zones, which presents problems in large internetworks that have many zones.	
	If the Macintosh is running a version of System 6, upgrade it to System 7 or System 7.5.	

[1] RTMP = Routing Table Maintenance Protocol

AppleTalk: No Devices in Chooser

Symptom: Zones appear in the Chooser, but when a service (such as AppleShare) and a zone are selected, no devices appear in the device list.

Table 9–5 outlines the problem that might cause this symptom and describes solutions to that problem.

Table 9–5 *AppleTalk: No Devices in Choose*

Possible Problems	Solution	
Misconfigured access lists	**Step 1**	Use the **show appletalk access-list** exec command on routers in the path from source to destination.
	Step 2	Disable any access lists (or just those on a particularly suspect router) using the **no appletalk access-group** interface configuration command.
	Step 3	After disabling access lists, check whether devices appear in the Chooser.
	Step 4	If devices now appear in the Chooser, a misconfigured access list is probably filtering NBP traffic. To isolate the problem access list, enable lists one at a time until devices no longer appear.
	Step 5	Check the access lists and associated configuration commands for errors. Configure explicit **permit** statements for traffic that you want to pass through the router normally.
	Step 6	If problems persist, there might be more than one misconfigured access list. Continue enabling access lists one at a time and fixing misconfigured access lists until the problem is solved.
	For detailed information about filtering NBP traffic using access lists, refer to the Cisco IOS *Network Protocols Configuration Guide, Part 1.*	

AppleTalk: Network Services Intermittently Unavailable

Symptom: Network services are intermittently unavailable. Services come and go without warning.

Table 9–6 outlines the problems that might cause this symptom and describes solutions to those problems.

Table 9–6 *AppleTalk: Network Services Intermittently Unavailable*

Possible Problems	Solution
Duplicate network numbers or overlapping cable-range	In AppleTalk, network numbers must be unique within an internetwork. If duplicate network numbers exist, packets might not be routed to their intended destinations.
	If AppleTalk services do not appear in the Chooser for particular networks, those networks probably have duplicate network numbers.
	Step 1 Change the network number or cable-range of the suspect network to a unique value using the **appletalk cable-range** interface configuration command.
	Step 2 Use the **show appletalk route** privileged exec command to view the routing table. If the network number or cable-range continues to appear in routing tables, you have found the duplicate (because the other network using that number will continue to send routing updates).
	If the network number or cable-range disappears from the internetwork after 40 seconds, you have not found the duplicate. Change the network number or cable-range specification back to its previous value and try again to isolate the duplicate network number.
	Step 3 If you changed the network number or cable-range on the interface, remember to reenter the zone name and any other interface configurations for AppleTalk on that interface.

Table 9–6 *AppleTalk: Network Services Intermittently Unavailable, Continued*

Possible Problems	Solution
Route flapping (unstable route)	Excessive traffic load on internetworks with many routers can prevent some routers from sending RTMP updates every 10 seconds as they should. Because routers begin to age out routes after missing two consecutive RTMP updates, the inconsistent arrival of RTMP updates can result in constant route changes.
	Step 1 Use the **show interfaces** exec command to check the traffic load. Check the load for each interface.
	The following example is output from the **show interfaces** command:
	``` Ethernet0 is up, line protocol is up Hardware is Lance, address is 0000.0c32.49b1 (bia 0000.0c32.49b1) Internet address is 192.168.52.26/24 MTU 1500 bytes, BW 10000 Kbit, DLY 1000 usec, rely 255/255, load 1/255 [...] ```
	The load field displayed in the **show interfaces** command is the load on the interface as a fraction of 255 (255/255 is completely saturated), calculated as an exponential average over five minutes.
	Step 2 If the load is less than 50%, reconfiguring timer values might solve the problem by allowing RTMP updates more time to propagate through the network.
	If the load is more than 50%, you might need to segment the network to reduce the number of routers (and therefore the amount of traffic) on each network segment.
	Step 3 Use the **debug apple events** privileged exec command to determine whether routes are being aged incorrectly. The output should resemble the following:
	``` Router#debug apple events AppleTalk Events debugging is on Router# %AT-6-PATHNOTIFY: Ethernet0: AppleTalk RTMP path to 250-250 down; reported bad by 200.41 ```
	The **debug apple events** command is useful for solving AppleTalk network problems because it provides an overall picture of the stability of the network. In a stable network, the **debug apple events** command does not return any information. If, however, the command generates numerous messages, the messages can indicate where the problems might lie.

Table 9–6 *AppleTalk: Network Services Intermittently Unavailable, Continued*

Possible Problems	Solution
Route flapping (unstable route) (*Continued*)	Turning on debug apple events will not cause **apple event-logging** to be maintained in nonvolatile memory. Only turning on **apple event-logging** explicitly will store it in nonvolatile memory. Furthermore, if **apple event-logging** is already enabled, turning on or off debug apple events will not affect **apple event-logging**.
	Caution: Because debugging output is assigned high priority in the CPU process, it can render the system unusable. For this reason, use **debug** commands only to troubleshoot specific problems or during troubleshooting sessions with Cisco technical support staff. Moreover, it is best to use **debug** commands during periods of lower network traffic and fewer users. Debugging during these periods decreases the likelihood that increased **debug** command processing overhead will affect system use.
	Step 4 If routes are being aged incorrectly, use the **appletalk timers** global configuration command to correct the problem. Suggested timer values are 10, 30, and 90 to start, but do not exceed 10, 40, and 120. The first number must always be 10, and the third value should be three times the second.
	You can return the timers to their defaults (10, 20, 60) by using the **no appletalk timers** global configuration command.
	Timers should be consistently set to the same value throughout the internetwork, or at a minimum, throughout the backbone of the internetwork.
ZIP storm	A ZIP storm occurs when a router propagates a route for which it currently has no corresponding zone name; the route is then propagated by downstream routers.
	Note: Cisco routers provide a firewall against ZIP storms in the internetwork. If a Cisco router receives a routing update from a neighbor, it does not propagate that new route until it receives the accompanying zone name.

Table 9–6 *AppleTalk: Network Services Intermittently Unavailable, Continued*

Possible Problems	Solution

ZIP storm (*Continued*)	**Step 1** Use the **show appletalk traffic** command to check the field showing the number of ZIP requests:
	
	```Router#sh apple traffic```
	```[...]```
	```ZIP: 44 received, 35 sent, 6 netinfo```
	```[...]```
	```Router#```
	
	Compare this output with the output shown by the command 30 seconds later.
	
	Step 2 If the traffic counters for ZIP requests are incrementing very rapidly (by more than 10 every 30 seconds) a ZIP storm is probably occurring.
	
	Use the **debug apple zip** privileged exec command to identify the network for which the zone is being requested by neighboring routers. You can also use the **show apple private** exec command to check the number of pending ZIP requests.
	
	Step 3 Identify the router that injected the network number into the internetwork (and that is causing the excessive ZIP traffic). The **show appletalk traffic** and **show appletalk route** exec commands provide information that can help you find the suspect router.
	
	For example, you can use the **show appletalk route** exec command to view the AppleTalk routing table. Check whether a network shows up in the routing table, even though the display indicates that no zone is set.
	
	If you find a network for which no zone is set, a node on that network is probably not responding to ZIP requests, resulting in the ZIP storm.
	
	Step 4 Determine why the node is not responding to ZIP requests. Access lists or other filters might be the cause.
	
	ZIP storms can also result from a defect in the software running on the node. Contact the vendor to determine whether there is a known problem.

AppleTalk: Old Zone Names Appear in Chooser (Phantom Zones)

Symptom: Old AppleTalk zone names continue to appear in the Chooser. Even after zone names are removed from the configuration, "phantom" zones continue to appear in the Chooser.

Table 9–7 outlines the problems that might cause this symptom and describes solutions to those problems.

Table 9–7 *AppleTalk: Old Zone Names Appear in Chooser (Phantom Zones)*

Possible Problems	Solution	
Configuration mismatch	**Step 1**	Use the **show appletalk interface** exec command. Check the output for a "port configuration mismatch" message.
		If the command output contains a "mismatch" message, the router configuration disagrees with that of the listed neighbor.
		If the command output does not include the "mismatch" message, use the **clear apple interface** privileged exec command on the interface in question. If the interface becomes operational after clearing, a configuration mismatch does not exist.
	Step 2	Enter the **show appletalk interface** exec command again. If its output still contains a "port configuration mismatch" message, check whether all router configurations agree on network number or cable range and the zone or zone list.
	Step 3	If router configurations disagree on these parameters, alter router configurations to bring all routers into alignment.
	Step 4	If problems persist, put the problem router in discovery mode by specifying the interface configuration command **appletalk address 0.0** on a nonextended network or the **appletalk cable-range 0-0** command on an extended network. This causes the router to get its configuration information from the network.
	For more information about configuration mismatches, see the section "AppleTalk Configuration Mismatches" earlier in this chapter.	

Table 9–7 *AppleTalk: Old Zone Names Appear in Chooser (Phantom Zones), Continued*

Possible Problems	Solution
Invalid zone names in routing table	AppleTalk does not provide a way to update ZIP tables when changing the mapping of zone names to networks or cable ranges.
	For example, if the zone name for network number 200 is Twilight Zone, but you decide to change the zone to No Parking Zone, the zone name on the interface can be changed, and the new zone name takes effect locally.
	However, unless you keep network 200 off the internetwork long enough for it to be completely aged out of the routing tables, some routers will continue to use the old zone name (this is called a *phantom zone*). Alternatively, if you cannot keep the network off the internetwork that long, change the underlying network number when you change the zone name of a cable.
	Step 1 Use the **show running-config** privileged exec command to view the router configuration. Check the network numbers configured for each AppleTalk interface.
	Step 2 Make sure that there are no network numbers configured that were previously assigned to a zone that has been deleted. Change the cable-range using the **appletalk cable-range** interface configuration command or disable the network until it is aged out of routing tables.
	Step 3 Use the **show appletalk zones** command to verify that the zone no longer appears in the zone list.

AppleTalk: Connections to Services Drop

Symptom: Users complain that their AppleTalk sessions suddenly drop for no apparent reason.

Table 9–8 outlines the problem that might cause this symptom and describes solutions to that problem.

Table 9–8   *AppleTalk: Connections to Services Drop*

Possible Problems	Solution
Route flapping (unstable route)	Excessive traffic load on internetworks with many routers can prevent some routers from sending RTMP updates every 10 seconds as they should. Because routers begin to age out routes after missing two consecutive RTMP updates, the inconsistent arrival of RTMP updates can result in constant route changes.
	Step 1 Use the **show interfaces** exec command to check the traffic load. Check the load for each interface.
	The following example is output from the **show interfaces** command:
	``` Ethernet0 is up, line protocol is up Hardware is Lance, address is 0000.0c32.49b1 (bia 0000.0c32.49b1) Internet address is 192.168.52.26/24 MTU 1500 bytes, BW 10000 Kbit, DLY 1000 usec, rely 255/255, load 1/255 [...] ```
	The load field displayed in the **show interfaces** command is the load on the interface as a fraction of 255 (255/255 is completely saturated), calculated as an exponential average over five minutes.
	Step 2 If the load is less than 50%, reconfiguring timer values might solve the problem by allowing RTMP updates more time to propagate through the network.
	If the load is more than 50%, you might need to segment the network to reduce the number of routers (and therefore the amount of traffic) on each network segment.
	Step 3 Use the **debug apple events** privileged exec command to determine whether routes are being aged incorrectly. The output should resemble the following:
	``` Router#debug apple events AppleTalk Events debugging is on Router# %AT-6-PATHNOTIFY: Ethernet0: AppleTalk RTMP path to 250-250 down; reported bad by 200.41 ```

Table 9–8 *AppleTalk: Connections to Services Drop, Continued*

Possible Problems	Solution
Route flapping (unstable route) (*Continued*)	**Caution:** Because debugging output is assigned high priority in the CPU process, it can render the system unusable. For this reason, use **debug** commands only to troubleshoot specific problems or during troubleshooting sessions with Cisco technical support staff. Moreover, it is best to use **debug** commands during periods of lower network traffic and fewer users. Debugging during these periods decreases the likelihood that increased **debug** command processing overhead will affect system use.
	Step 4 If routes are being aged incorrectly, use the **appletalk timers** global configuration command to correct the problem. Suggested timer values are 10, 30, and 90 to start, but do not exceed 10, 40, and 120. The first number must always be 10, and the third value should be three times the second.
	You can return the timers to their defaults (10, 20, 60) by using the **no appletalk timers** global configuration command.
	Timers should be consistently set to the same value throughout the internetwork, or at a minimum, throughout the backbone of the internetwork.

AppleTalk: Interface Fails to Initialize AppleTalk

Symptom: Router interface connected to a network will not initialize AppleTalk.

Table 9–9 outlines the problems that might cause this symptom and describes solutions to those problems.

Table 9–9 *AppleTalk: Interface Fails to Initialize AppleTalk*

Possible Problems	Solution
Configuration mismatch	**Step 1** Use the **show appletalk interface** exec command. Check the output for a "port configuration mismatch" message. If the command output contains a "mismatch message," the router configuration disagrees with that of the listed neighbor. If the command output does not include the "mismatch" message, use the **clear apple interface** privileged exec command on the interface in question. If the interface becomes operational after clearing, a configuration mismatch does not exist. **Step 2** Enter the **show appletalk interface** exec command again. If its output still contains a "port configuration mismatch" message, check to see whether all router configurations agree on network number or cable range and the zone or zone list. **Step 3** If router configurations disagree on these parameters, alter router configurations to bring all routers into alignment. **Step 4** If problems persist, put the problem router in discovery mode by specifying the interface configuration command **appletalk address 0.0** on a nonextended network or the **appletalk cable-range 0-0** command on an extended network. This causes the router to get its configuration information from the network. For more information about configuration mismatches, see the section "AppleTalk Configuration Mismatches" earlier in this chapter.

Table 9–9   *AppleTalk: Interface Fails to Initialize AppleTalk, Continued*

Possible Problems	Solution
Phase 1 and Phase 2 rule violations	**Step 1** Use the **show appletalk globals** exec command to determine whether the internetwork is in compatibility mode. **Step 2** Enable the **appletalk name-lookup-interval** global configuration command and use the **show appletalk neighbors** exec command to determine which specific neighbor (by NBP name) is in compatibility mode. **Step 3** To resolve the problem, you can perform one of the following actions: • Upgrade AppleTalk Phase 1 routers to AppleTalk Phase 2 and reconfigure the internetwork • Ensure that all routers are in compliance with the two Phase 1 and Phase 2 rules For more information on Phase 1 and Phase 2 rule violations, see the section "Phase 1 and Phase 2 Rule Violations" earlier in this chapter.

AppleTalk: Port Stuck in Restarting or Acquiring Mode

Symptom: A router port is stuck in restarting or acquiring mode (as shown in the output of the **show apple interface** privileged exec command). The router cannot discover routes or poll neighbors on an attached cable.

Table 9–10 outlines the problems that might cause this symptom and describes solutions to those problems.

Table 9–10   *AppleTalk: Port Stuck in Restarting or Acquiring Mode*

Possible Problems	Solution
Router is in discovery mode, and no seed router exists on the network	**Step 1** Put the router in nondiscovery mode by assigning a network number or cable range to the problem interface using the **appletalk address** or **appletalk cable-range** interface configuration command. **Step 2** If the problem persists, consult your technical support representative for more assistance.

Table 9-10 *AppleTalk: Port Stuck in Restarting or Acquiring Mode, Continued*

Possible Problems	Solution
Crossed serial circuits with multiple lines between two routers	**Step 1** Check the physical attachment of serial lines to ensure that they are correctly wired. **Step 2** If necessary, rewire the lines and check the output of the **show interfaces** and **show appletalk interface** commands to confirm that the interface and line protocol are up. **Step 3** If the router still cannot find routes, consult your technical support representative for more assistance.
Software problem	If the router issues a message that says "restart port pending," upgrade to the latest system software maintenance release or contact your technical support representative.

AppleTalk Enhanced IGRP: Clients Cannot Connect to Servers

Symptom: Macintosh clients cannot connect to servers in an AppleTalk Enhanced IGRP network environment.

Table 9–11 outlines the problems that might cause this symptom and describes solutions to those problems.

Table 9–11 *AppleTalk Enhanced IGRP: Clients Cannot Connect to Servers*

Possible Problem	Solution
Routers not establishing neighbors properly	For information on troubleshooting this problem, see the section "AppleTalk Enhanced IGRP: Routers Not Establishing Neighbors" later in this chapter.
Routes missing from routing table	For information on troubleshooting this problem, see the section "AppleTalk Enhanced IGRP: Routes Missing from Routing Table" later in this chapter.
Appletalk Enhanced IGRP enabled on network with connected Macintosh computers	Macintosh computers do not understand AppleTalk Enhanced IGRP. RTMP must be enabled on interfaces with Macintosh computers on the connected LAN segment. By default, AppleTalk RTMP routes are automatically redistributed into enhanced IGRP, and AppleTalk enhanced IGRP routes are automatically redistributed into RTMP.
	Step 1 Use the **show running-config** privileged exec command on routers to make sure that RTMP is enabled on interfaces connected to LAN segments with connected Macintosh computers.
	Step 2 If RTMP is not enabled, enable it using the **appletalk protocol rtmp** interface configuration command.
	Step 3 If desired, disable AppleTalk Enhanced IGRP on the interface using the **no appletalk protocol eigrp** interface configuration command.

AppleTalk Enhanced IGRP: Routers Not Establishing Neighbors

Symptom: AppleTalk Enhanced IGRP routers do not establish neighbors properly. Routers that are connected do not appear in the neighbor table.

Table 9–12 outlines the problems that might cause this symptom and describes solutions to those problems.

Table 9–12 *AppleTalk Enhanced IGRP: Routers Not Establishing Neighbors*

Possible Problem	Solution
AppleTalk Enhanced IGRP is not globally configured on the appropriate routers	**Step 1** Use the **show running-config** privileged exec command to check the configuration of routers that should be running Enhanced IGRP. Look for **appletalk routing eigrp** global configuration command entries. This command enables AppleTalk Enhanced IGRP routing on the router.
	Step 2 If AppleTalk Enhanced IGRP routing is not enabled on the router, use the **appletalk routing eigrp** *router-id* global configuration command to enable it. Make sure that the router ID is unique throughout the network.
	Step 3 Perform the same actions on other routers that should be running AppleTalk Enhanced IGRP. The router ID must be different for each router.
AppleTalk Enhanced IGRP is not enabled on interfaces	Use the **show running-config** privileged exec command on routers that are running Enhanced IGRP. Check the interface configurations for **appletalk protocol eigrp** interface configuration command entries. This command must be present in order for an interface to generate AppleTalk Enhanced IGRP hello messages and routing updates.

Table 9–12   *AppleTalk Enhanced IGRP: Routers Not Establishing Neighbors, Continued*

Possible Problem	Solution
Timer values are mismatched	**Step 1** Use the **show appletalk eigrp neighbors** exec command. Make sure that all directly connected AppleTalk Enhanced IGRP routers appear in the output.
	Step 2 Examine the uptime field in the **show appletalk eigrp neighbors** output. A continuously resetting uptime counter indicates that hello packets from the neighboring router are arriving sporadically. This might be caused by a timer value mismatch or by hardware problems.
	Step 3 Use the **show interface** exec command to determine whether the interface and line protocol are up. Look for high numbers in the queue fields and excessive drop counts. The queue fields displays the maximum size of the queue and the number of packets dropped due to a full queue.
	If there are many drops, if the queue count is high, or if the interface or line protocol is down, there is probably something wrong with the interface or other hardware. For more information on troubleshooting hardware, see Chapter 3, "Troubleshooting Hardware and Booting Problems," and Chapter 15, "Troubleshooting Serial Line Problems."
	Step 4 Use the **show running-config** privileged exec command on all AppleTalk Enhanced IGRP routers in the network. Look for **appletalk eigrp-timers** interface configuration command entries. The values configured by this command must be the same for all AppleTalk Enhanced IGRP routers on the network.
	Step 5 If any routers have conflicting timer values, reconfigure them to conform with the rest of the routers on the network. These values can be returned to their defaults with the **no appletalk eigrp-timers** interface configuration command.
Older version of the Cisco IOS software	If problems persist, upgrade to the latest release of the Cisco IOS software.

AppleTalk Enhanced IGRP: Routes Missing from Routing Table

Symptom: Routes are missing from the routing table of routers running AppleTalk Enhanced IGRP. Clients (Macintosh computers) on one network cannot access servers on a different network. Clients might or might not be able to connect to servers on the same network. The problem might occur in internetworks running only Enhanced IGRP or in an internetwork running Enhanced IGRP and RTMP.

Table 9–13 outlines the problems that might cause this symptom and describes solutions to those problems.

Table 9–13 *AppleTalk Enhanced IGRP: Routes Missing from Routing Table*

Possible Problem	Solution
Routers not establishing neighbors properly	For information on troubleshooting this problem, see the section "AppleTalk Enhanced IGRP: Routers Not Establishing Neighbors" earlier in this chapter.
AppleTalk Enhanced IGRP is not enabled on interfaces	Use the **show running-config** privileged exec command on routers that are running Enhanced IGRP. Check the interface configurations for **appletalk protocol eigrp** interface configuration command entries.
	This command must be present in order for an interface to generate AppleTalk Enhanced IGRP hello messages and routing updates.
Older version of the Cisco IOS software	If problems persist, upgrade to the latest release of the Cisco IOS software.

AppleTalk Enhanced IGRP: Poor Performance

Symptom: Network performance in an AppleTalk Enhanced IGRP environment is poor. Connections between clients and servers are slow or unreliable.

Table 9–14 outlines the problems that might cause this symptom and describes solutions to those problems.

Table 9–14 *AppleTalk Enhanced IGRP: Poor Performance*

Possible Problem	Solution
AppleTalk Enhanced IGRP and RTMP are running simultaneously on the same interface	Use the **show running-config** privileged exec command on network routers. Check the interface configurations to determine whether AppleTalk Enhanced IGRP and RTMP are both enabled on the same interface. Running both AppleTalk Enhanced IGRP and RTMP on the same interface increases bandwidth and processor overhead. Determine whether both routing protocols need to be running on the interface and disable one or the other if necessary or desired.
Older version of the Cisco IOS software	If problems persist, upgrade to the latest release of the Cisco IOS software.

AppleTalk Enhanced IGRP: Router Stuck in Active Mode

Symptom: An AppleTalk Enhanced IGRP router is stuck in Active mode. The router repeatedly sends error messages similar to the following to the console:

```
%DUAL-3-SIA: Route 2.24 Stuck-in-Active
```

> **NOTES**
>
> Occasional messages of this type are *not* a cause for concern. This is how an Enhanced IGRP router recovers if it does not receive replies to its queries from all its neighbors. However, if these error messages occur frequently, you should investigate the problem.

For a more detailed explanation of Enhanced IGRP Active mode, see the section "Enhanced IGRP Active/Passive Modes" later in this chapter.

Table 9–15 outlines the problems that might cause this symptom and describes solutions to those problems.

Table 9–15 *AppleTalk Enhanced IGRP: Router Stuck in Active Mode*

Possible Problems	Solution
Active timer value is misconfigured	The active timer determines the maximum period of time that an Enhanced IGRP router will wait for replies to its queries. If the active timer value is set too low, there might not be enough time for all the neighboring routers to send their replies to the Active router.
	Step 1 Check the configuration of each Enhanced IGRP router using the **show running-config** privileged exec command. Look for the **timers active-time** router configuration command entry associated with the **appletalk routing eigrp** global configuration command entry.
	Step 2 The value set by the **timers active-time** command should be consistent among routers in the same autonomous system. A value of 3 (3 minutes, the default value) is strongly recommended to allow all Enhanced IGRP neighbors to reply to queries.

Table 9–15 *AppleTalk Enhanced IGRP: Router Stuck in Active Mode, Continued*

Possible Problems	Solution

Interface or other hardware problem	**Step 1** If queries and replies are not sent and received properly, the active timer times out and causes the router to issue an error message. Use the **show appletalk eigrp neighbors** exec command and examine the uptime and Q Cnt (queue count) fields in the output.
	
	The following example is output from the **show appletalk eigrp neighbor** command:
	
	``
	Router#show appletalk eigrp neighbor
	AT/EIGRP Neighbors for process 1, router id 1
	  H Address Interface Hold Uptime SRTT RTO Q Seq
	                                     (sec) (ms) Cnt Num
	  0. 200.41 Et0 10 0:00:37 0 3000 0 2
	``
	
	If the uptime counter is continually resetting or if the queue count is consistently high, there might be a hardware problem. The uptime counter is the elapsed time, in hours, minutes, and seconds, since the local router first heard from this neighbor.
	
	Step 2 Determine where the problem is by looking at the output of the "Stuck-in-Active" error message, which indicates the AppleTalk address of the problematic node.
	
	Step 3 Make sure the suspect router is still functional. Check the interfaces on the suspect router. Make sure the interface and line protocol are up and determine whether the interface is dropping packets.
	
	For more information on troubleshooting hardware, see Chapter 3, "Troubleshooting Hardware and Booting Problems."

Flapping route	If there is a flapping serial route (caused by heavy traffic load), queries and replies might not be forwarded reliably. Route flapping caused by heavy traffic on a serial link can cause queries and replies to be lost, resulting in the active timer timing out. Take steps to reduce traffic on the link, or increase the bandwidth of the link.
Older version of the Cisco IOS software	If problems persist, upgrade to the latest release of the Cisco IOS software.

Enhanced IGRP Active/Passive Modes

An Enhanced IGRP router can be in either Passive or Active mode. A router is said to be passive for a network when it has an established path to that network in its routing table. The route is in Active state when a router is undergoing a route recomputation. If there are always feasible successors, a route never has to go into Active state and avoids a route recomputation.

If the Enhanced IGRP router loses the connection to a network, it becomes active for that network. The router sends out queries to all its neighbors in order to find a new route to the network. The router remains in Active mode until it has either received replies from *all* its neighbors or until the active timer, which determines the maximum period of time a router will stay active, has expired.

If the router receives a reply from each of its neighbors, it computes the new next hop to the network and becomes passive for that network. However, if the active timer expires, the router removes from its neighbor table any neighbors that did not reply, again enters Active mode, and issues a "Stuck-in-Active" message to the console.

AURP: Routes Not Propagated Through AURP Tunnel

Symptom: AppleTalk routes are not propagated through an AURP tunnel. Routes that are known to exist on one side of the tunnel do not appear in the routing tables of the exterior router on the other side of the tunnel. Changes on the remote network (such as a route going down) are not learned by the exterior router on the other side of the tunnel.

Table 9–16 outlines the problems that might cause this symptom and describes solutions to those problems.

Table 9–16 *AURP: Routes Not Propagated Through AURP Tunnel*

Possible Problems	Solution
Misconfigured AURP tunnel	**Step 1** Use the **show appletalk interfaces** exec command to make sure the tunnel interface is up.
	Step 2 Use the **show running-config** privileged exec command to view the router configuration. Check the **tunnel source** and **tunnel destination** interface configuration command entries.
	Step 3 Exterior routers must have their tunnel interface configured with a **tunnel source** and a **tunnel destination** command. Make sure that the **tunnel destination** command on each router points to the IP address of the remote exterior router's tunnel interface.

Table 9–16 *AURP: Routes Not Propagated Through AURP Tunnel, Continued*

Possible Problems	Solution
Missing **appletalk route-redistribution** command	**Step 1** If changes on the remote network are not learned through the tunnel, use the **show running-config** privileged exec command to view the router configuration. Check for an **appletalk route-redistribution** global configuration command entry. **Step 2** If the command is not present, add it to the configuration.
Problem with underlying IP network	If there are routing problems in the transit network (the IP network through which the AURP tunnel passes), then AppleTalk traffic might have difficulty traversing the tunnel. To troubleshoot your TCP/IP network, follow the procedures outlined in Chapter 7, "Troubleshooting TCP/IP."

FDDITalk: No Zone Associated with Routes

Symptom: Routers on an FDDI ring have routes to networks across the ring, but no zones are associated with the routes. The output of the **show appletalk route** command indicates "no zone set" for those routes.

NOTES

On other media, routes with no zone set are the result of other problems, such as ZIP storms. See the sections "AppleTalk: Zones Missing from Chooser" and "AppleTalk: Network Services Intermittently Unavailable" in this chapter for more information.

Table 9–17 outlines the problem that might cause this symptom and describes solutions to that problem.

Table 9–17 *FDDITalk: No Zone Associated with Routes*

Possible Problems	Solution
FDDITalk version mismatch	If any routers in the internetwork are using software releases prior to Cisco IOS Release 10.0, there is a possibility of a FDDITalk version mismatch. Make sure that all routers on the ring are using either pre-FDDITalk or FDDITalk and not be a combination of the two.
	Following are the FDDITalk implementations for each software release:
	• In software releases prior to 9.0(2), routers can use only pre-FDDITalk.
	• In software releases prior to Cisco IOS Release 10.0, routers use the Apple implementation of FDDITalk by default.
	However, if a pre-FDDITalk router exists on the FDDI network, routers fall back to pre-FDDITalk. A router can be forced to use FDDITalk with the **no appletalk pre-fdditalk** interface configuration command.
	• In Cisco IOS Release 10.0 and later, the default is to use the Apple implementation of FDDITalk.
	However, you can force a router to use pre-FDDITalk with the **appletalk pre-fdditalk** interface configuration command.

ARA: ARA Client Unable to Connect to ARA Server

Symptom: An ARA client (such as a Macintosh) attempts to connect to an ARA server (such as a Cisco access server) and cannot initiate a remote session. The user might be able to connect briefly, but the connection is immediately terminated.

Table 9–18 outlines the problems that might cause this symptom and describes solutions to those problems.

Table 9–18   *ARA: ARA Client Unable to Connect to ARA Server*

Possible Problems	Solution	
Missing **arap network** command entry	Step 1	Use the **show running-config** privileged exec command to view the router configuration. If you are running Cisco IOS Release 10.2 or later, look for an **arap network** global configuration command entry.
	Step 2	Configure the **arap network** global configuration command to enable ARA on the router or access server. The syntax for the *arap network* command is as follows: **arap network** [*network-number*] [*zone-name*] **Syntax Description:** • *network-number*—(Optional) The AppleTalk network number. The network number must be unique on your AppleTalk network. This network is where all ARAP[1] users appear when they dial in to the network. • *zone-name*—(Optional) The AppleTalk zone name.
AppleTalk routing is not enabled on the appropriate interfaces	Step 1	Use the **show apple interfaces** exec command to determine whether interfaces are operational and whether AppleTalk routing is enabled on the correct interfaces.
	Step 2	If AppleTalk routing is not enabled on the proper interfaces, enable it where appropriate. Refer to the Cisco IOS *Network Protocols Configuration Guide, Part 1* for detailed information on configuring an interface for AppleTalk routing.
Modem, serial line, or hardware problems	For serial line troubleshooting information, see Chapter 15, "Troubleshooting Serial Line Problems." For modem troubleshooting information, see Chapter 16, "Troubleshooting Dialin Connections." For hardware troubleshooting information, see Chapter 3, "Troubleshooting Hardware and Booting Problems."	

[1] ARAP = AppleTalk Remote Access Protocol

ARA: Connection Hangs After "Communicating At..." Message

Symptom: An ARA client (for example, a Macintosh) tries to connect to an ARA server (such as a Cisco access server) over client and server modems. The client receives a connect message such as "Communicating at 14.4 Kbps" but then hangs for 10–30 seconds and finally shows a "connection failed" message.

Table 9–19 outlines the problem that might cause this symptom and describes solutions to that problem.

Table 9–19 *ARA: Connection Hangs After "Communicating At..." Message*

Possible Problems	Solution	
MNP4 Link Request packets sent by client ARA stack are responded to by the serving modem instead of the ARA server	**Step 1**	Check the version numbers of the ARA software on the client and the Cisco IOS software on the access server.
		If you are using ARA version 1.0 or Cisco IOS software prior to Release 10.2, it is advisable to upgrade to ARA 2.0 and Cisco IOS Release 10.2 or later. ARA 2.0 modifies the framing of MNP4 Link Request packets, allowing them to be passed to the access server rather than responded to by the serving modem.
	Step 2	If you cannot upgrade your software, try modifying the behavior of the modem to use a LAPM-to-No Error Correction fallback instead of a LAPM-to-MNP4-to-No Error Correction fallback. The modem no longer listens for and respond to MNP4 messages, allowing MNP4 packets to reach the access server.
		Note: Many modems cannot be configured in this manner.
	Step 3	If your modem does not use LAPM error correction, it might be possible to modify *all* ARA client scripts to extend the 500 ms pause before exiting. Configure an additional delay that takes into account the behavior of the *serving* modem.

ARA: Cannot Send or Receive Data over ARA Dialin Connection

Symptom: ARA connections are established, but users cannot send or receive ARA data over the link.

Table 9–20 outlines the problems that might cause this symptom and describes solutions to those problems.

Table 9–20 *ARA: Cannot Send or Receive Data over ARA Dialin Connection*

Possible Causes	Suggested Actions
Missing **arap network** command entry	**Step 1** Use the **show running-config** privileged exec command to view the router configuration. If you are running Cisco IOS Release 10.2 or later, look for an **arap network** global configuration command entry.
	Step 2 Configure the **arap network** global configuration command to enable ARA on the router or access server. The syntax for the **arap network** command is as follows:
	arap network [*network-number*] [*zone-name*]
	Syntax Description:
	• *network-number*—(Optional) The AppleTalk network number. The network number must be unique on your AppleTalk network. This network is where all ARAP users appear when they dial in to the network.
	• *zone-name*—(Optional) The AppleTalk zone name.
Missing **autoselect** command	**Step 1** Use the **show running-config** privileged exec command to view the router configuration. Check to see whether the **autoselect arap** line configuration command is configured on the router.
	Step 2 If the command is not present, add it to the configuration.
MNP5 enabled on answering modem	**Step 1** Check to see whether the answering modem has MNP5 error correction enabled.
	Step 2 If MNP5 is enabled on the answering modem, disable it. For information on checking or changing the modem configuration, refer to the modem documentation.
Zone list is empty	**Step 1** Use the **show appletalk route** and **show appletalk zones** privileged exec commands to determine whether the router can see its ARA routes and zones.
	Step 2 Use the show **appletalk interface ethernet** exec command and make sure that the output matches your Apple network parameters.
	Step 3 Change the interface configuration as required.
TACACS[1] problem	For information on troubleshooting TACACS problems, refer to Chapter 24, "Troubleshooting Security Implementations."

[1] TACACS = Terminal Access Controller Access Control System

ARA: Slow Performance from Dialin Connection

Symptom: Performance on remote dialin ARA sessions is slow.

Table 9–21 outlines the problem that might cause this symptom and describes solutions to that problem.

Table 9–21   *ARA: Slow Performance from Dialin Connection*

Possible Problems	Solution

Flow control is not enabled, is enabled only on one device (either DTE or DCE), or is misconfigured	**Step 1** Configure hardware flow control on the line using the **flowcontrol hardware** line configuration command. Hardware flow control is recommended for access server-to-modem connections.
	
	For example, to configure hardware flow control on line 2 of an access server, enter the following commands:
	
	```C2500(config)#line 2```
	```C2500(config-line)#flowcontrol hardware```
	
	Note: If you cannot use flow control, limit the line speed to 9600 bps. Faster speeds can result in lost data.
	
	Step 2 After enabling hardware flow control on the access server or router line, initiate a reverse Telnet session to the modem via that line.
	
	For instructions on initiating a reverse Telnet session, see the section "Establishing a Reverse Telnet Session to a Modem" in Chapter 16, "Troubleshooting Dialin Connections."
	
	Step 3 Use a modem command string that includes the RTS/CTS flow command for your modem. This command ensures that the modem is using the same method of flow control (that is, hardware flow control) as the Cisco access server or router. See your modem documentation for exact configuration command syntax.
	
	For more information about troubleshooting access server-to-modem connections, see Chapter 16, "Troubleshooting Dialin Connections." For information on troubleshooting hardware problems, see Chapter 3, "Troubleshooting Hardware and Booting Problems."

Troubleshooting IBM

This chapter focuses on connectivity and performance problems associated with bridging and routing in IBM-based networks. When troubleshooting IBM-based networks, it is important to have a knowledge of Synchronous Data Link Control (SDLC) and source-route bridging (SRB). The following sections provide an overview of SDLC and SRB.

SDLC

IBM developed the SDLC protocol in the mid-1970s for use in Systems Network Architecture (SNA) environments. SDLC was the first of an important new breed of link-layer protocols based on synchronous, bit-oriented operation. Compared to synchronous character-oriented (for example, Bisync from IBM) and synchronous byte-count–oriented protocols (for example, Digital Data Communications Message Protocol [DDCMP] from Digital Equipment Corporation), bit-oriented synchronous protocols are more efficient, more flexible, and often faster.

After developing SDLC, IBM submitted it to various standards committees. The International Organization for Standardization (ISO) modified SDLC to create the High-Level Data Link Control (HDLC) protocol. The International Telecommunication Union Telecommunication Standardization Sector (ITU-T, formerly CCITT) subsequently modified HDLC to create Link Access Procedure (LAP), and then Link Access Procedure, Balanced (LAPB). The Institute of Electrical and Electronic Engineers (IEEE) modified HDLC to create IEEE 802.2. Each of these protocols has become important in its own domain. SDLC remains the SNA primary link-layer protocol for wide-area network (WAN) links.

Technology Basics

SDLC supports a variety of link types and topologies. It can be used with point-to-point and multipoint links, bounded and unbounded media, half-duplex and full-duplex transmission facilities, and circuit-switched and packet-switched networks.

SDLC identifies two types of network nodes:

- Primary—Controls the operation of other stations (called secondaries). The primary polls the secondaries in a predetermined order. Secondaries can then transmit if they have outgoing data. The primary also sets up and tears down links and manages the link while it is operational.

- Secondary—Controlled by a primary. Secondaries can send information only to the primary, but cannot do this unless the primary gives permission.

SDLC primaries and secondaries can be connected in four basic configurations:

- Point-to-point—Involves only two nodes, one primary and one secondary.

- Multipoint—Involves one primary and multiple secondaries.

- Loop—Involves a loop topology, with the primary connected to the first and last secondaries. Intermediate secondaries pass messages through one another as they respond to the requests of the primary.

- Hub go-ahead—Involves an inbound and an outbound channel. The primary uses the outbound channel to communicate with the secondaries. The secondaries use the inbound channel to communicate with the primary. The inbound channel is daisy-chained back to the primary through each secondary.

Frame Format

The SDLC frame format is shown in Figure 10–1.

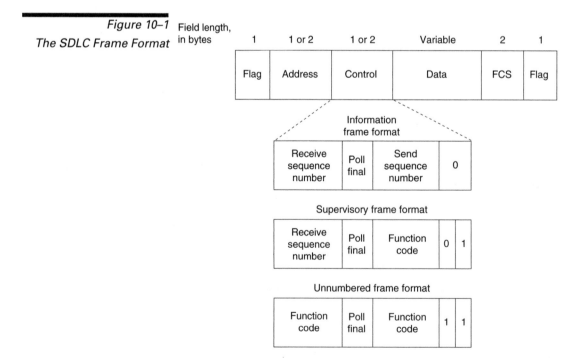

Figure 10–1
The SDLC Frame Format

As Figure 10–1 shows, SDLC frames are bounded by a unique flag pattern. The address field always contains the address of the secondary involved in the current communication. Because the primary is either the communication source or destination, there is no need to include the address of the primary—it is already known by all secondaries.

The control field uses three different formats, depending on the type of SDLC frame used. The three SDLC frames are described as follows:

- Information (I) frames—These frames carry upper-layer information and some control information. Send and receive sequence numbers and the poll final (P/F) bit perform flow and error control. The send sequence number refers to the number of the frame to be sent next. The receive sequence number provides the number of the frame to be received next. Both the sender and the receiver maintain send and receive sequence numbers. The primary uses the P/F bit to tell the secondary whether it requires an immediate response. The secondary uses this bit to tell the primary whether the current frame is the last in its current response.

- Supervisory (S) frames—These frames provide control information. They request and suspend transmission, report on status, and acknowledge the receipt of I frames. They do not have an information field.

- Unnumbered (U) frames—These frames, as the name suggests, are not sequenced. They are used for control purposes. For example, they are used to initialize secondaries. Depending on the function of the unnumbered frame, its control field is 1 or 2 bytes. Some unnumbered frames have an information field.

The frame check sequence (FCS) precedes the ending flag delimiter. The FCS is usually a cyclic redundancy check (CRC) calculation remainder. The CRC calculation is redone in the receiver. If the result differs from the value in the sender's frame, an error is assumed.

A typical SDLC-based network configuration appears in Figure 10–2. As illustrated, an IBM establishment controller (formerly called a cluster controller) in a remote site connects to dumb terminals and to a Token Ring network. In a local site, an IBM host connects (via channel-attached techniques) to an IBM front-end processor (FEP), which can also have links to local Token Ring local-area networks (LANs) and an SNA backbone. The two sites are connected through an SDLC-based 56-kbps leased line.

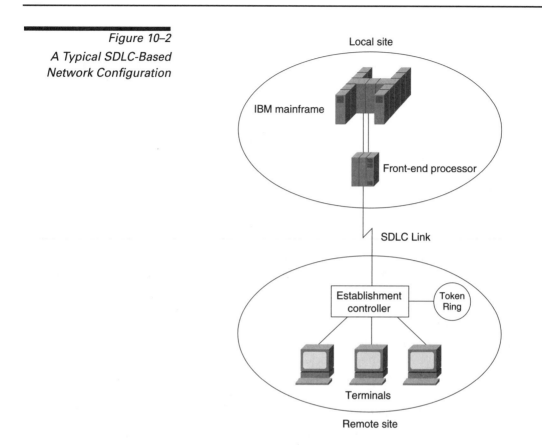

Figure 10–2
A Typical SDLC-Based
Network Configuration

SRB

The SRB algorithm was developed by IBM and proposed to the IEEE 802.5 committee as the means to bridge between all LANs. The IEEE 802.5 committee subsequently adopted SRB into the IEEE 802.5 Token Ring LAN specification.

Since its initial proposal, IBM has offered a new bridging standard to the IEEE 802 committee: the source-route transparent (SRT) bridging solution. SRT bridging eliminates pure SRBs entirely, proposing that the two types of LAN bridges be transparent bridges and SRT bridges. Although SRT bridging has support, SRBs are still widely deployed.

SRB Algorithm

SRBs are so named because they assume that the complete source-to-destination route is placed in all inter-LAN frames sent by the source. SRBs store and forward the frames as indicated by the route appearing in the appropriate frame field. Figure 10–3 illustrates a sample SRB network.

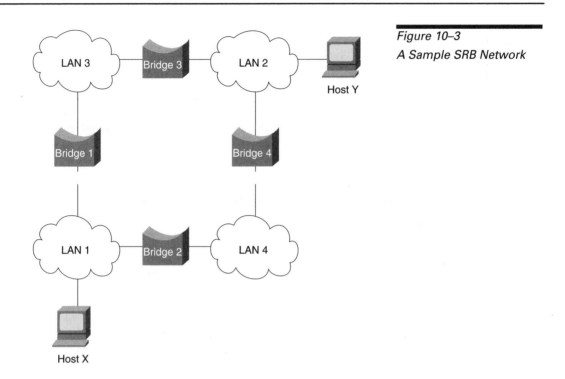

Figure 10–3
A Sample SRB Network

Referring to Figure 10–3, assume that Host X wishes to send a frame to Host Y. Initially, Host X does not know whether Host Y resides on the same or a different LAN. To determine this, Host X sends out a test frame. If that frame returns to Host X without a positive indication that Host Y has seen it, Host X must assume that Host Y is on a remote segment.

To determine the exact remote location of Host Y, Host X sends an explorer frame. Each bridge receiving the explorer frame (Bridges 1 and 2 in this example) copies the frame onto all outbound ports. Route information is added to the explorer frames as they travel through the internetwork. When Host X's explorer frames reach Host Y, Host Y replies to each individually using the accumulated route information. Upon receipt of all response frames, Host X chooses a path based on some predetermined criteria.

In the example in Figure 10–3, this process will yield two routes:

- LAN 1 to Bridge 1 to LAN 3 to Bridge 3 to LAN 2
- LAN 1 to Bridge 2 to LAN 4 to Bridge 4 to LAN 2

Host X must select one of these two routes. The IEEE 802.5 specification does not mandate the criteria Host X should use in choosing a route, but it does make several suggestions, including the following:

- First frame received
- Response with the minimum number of hops

- Response with the largest allowed frame size
- Various combinations of the above criteria

In most cases, the path contained in the first frame received will be used.

After a route is selected, it is inserted into frames destined for Host Y in the form of a routing information field (RIF). A RIF is included only in those frames destined for other LANs. The presence of routing information within the frame is indicated by the setting of the most significant bit within the source address field, called the routing information indicator (RII) bit.

Frame Format

The IEEE 802.5 RIF is structured as shown in Figure 10–4.

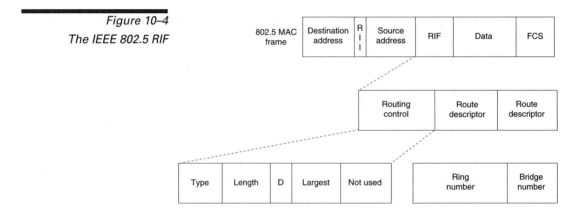

Figure 10–4

The IEEE 802.5 RIF

The fields of the RIF are as follows:

- The routing control field, which consists of the following subfields:
  - The type subfield in the RIF indicates whether the frame should be routed to a single node, a group of nodes that make up a spanning tree of the internetwork, or all nodes. The first type is called a specifically routed frame; the second type is called a spanning-tree explorer; and the third type is called an all-paths explorer. The spanning-tree explorer can be used as a transit mechanism for multicast frames. It can also be used as a replacement for the all-paths explorer in outbound route queries. In this case, the destination responds with an all-paths explorer.
  - The length subfield indicates the total length (in bytes) of the RIF.
  - The D bit indicates the direction of the frame (forward or reverse).
  - The largest field indicates the largest frame that can be handled along this route.
- The route descriptor field, of which there can be more than one. Each route descriptor field carries a ring number/bridge number pair that specifies a portion of a route. Routes, then, are simply alternating sequences of LAN and bridge numbers that start and end with LAN numbers.

TROUBLESHOOTING IBM

This section focuses on connectivity and performance problems associated with bridging and routing in IBM-based networks. This section covers specific IBM-related symptoms, the problems that are likely to cause each symptom, and the solutions to those problems.

This section covers the most common network issues in IBM networks:

- Local SRB: Host Cannot Connect to Server
- Local RSRB: Routing Does Not Function
- RSRB: Host Cannot Connect to Server (Peers Not Open)
- RSRB: Host Cannot Connect to Server (Peers Open)
- RSRB: Periodic Communication Failures
- RSRB: NetBIOS Client Cannot Connect to Server
- Translational Bridging: Client Cannot Connect to Server
- SRT Bridging: Client Cannot Connect to Server
- SDLC: Router Cannot Communicate with SDLC Device
- SDLC: Intermittent Connectivity
- SDLC: Client Cannot Connect to Host over Router Running SDLLC
- SDLC: Sessions Fail over Router Running STUN
- CIP: CLAW Connection Does Not Come Up
- CIP: No Enabled LED On
- CIP: CIP Will Not Come Online to Host
- CIP: Router Cannot ping Host or Host Cannot ping Router
- CIP: Host Cannot Reach Remote Networks
- CIP: Host Running Routed Has No Routes

Local SRB: Host Cannot Connect to Server

Symptom: Connections fail over a router configured as an SRB connecting two or more Token Rings.

Table 10–1 outlines the problems that might cause this symptom and describes solutions to those problems.

Table 10–1 *Local SRB: Host Cannot Connect to Server*

Possible Problem	Solution
Ring number mismatch	A router interface configured for bridging fails to insert into a ring when it detects a ring number mismatch, and posts an error message to the console.
	Step 1 Get the ring number (specified in hexadecimal) from IBM SRBs (either by examining the configuration of other SRBs or from the system administrator).
	Step 2 Use the **show running-config** privileged exec command to view the configuration of routers configured as SRBs. Look for **source-bridge** interface configuration command entries that assign ring numbers (displayed in decimal) to the rings that are connected to the router's interfaces.[1]
	For example, the following configuration entry shows the entry for local ring 10, bridge number 500, and remote ring 20:
	`source-bridge 10 500 20`
	Note: Parallel bridges situated between the same two rings must have different bridge numbers.
	Step 3 Convert IBM SRB ring numbers to decimal and verify that the ring numbers configured on all internetworking nodes agree.
	Step 4 If the ring numbers do not agree, reconfigure the router interface or IBM SRBs so that the ring numbers match. Use the **source-bridge** command to make configuration changes; the syntax is as follows:
	source-bridge *source-ring-number bridge-number target-ring-number* [*conserve-ring*]
	Syntax Description:
	• *source-ring-number*—Ring number for the interface's Token Ring or FDDI[2] ring. It must be a decimal number in the range 1 to 4095 that uniquely identifies a network segment or ring within the bridged Token Ring or FDDI network

Table 10–1 *Local SRB: Host Cannot Connect to Server, Continued*

Possible Problem	Solution

Ring number mismatch (*Continued*)	• *bridge-number*—Number that uniquely identifies the bridge connecting the source and target rings. It must be a decimal number in the range 1 to 15.
	
	 • *target-ring-number*—Ring number of the destination ring on this router. It must be unique within the bridged Token Ring or FDDI network. The target ring can also be a ring group. Must be a decimal number.
	
	 • *conserve-ring*—(Optional) Keyword to enable SRB over Frame Relay. When this option is configured, the SRB software does not add the ring number associated with the Frame Relay PVC[3], the partner's virtual ring) to outbound explorer frames. This option is permitted for Frame Relay subinterfaces only.
	
	 Example:
	
	 In the following example, Token Rings 129 and 130 are connected via a router:
	
	 `interface tokenring 0`
	 `  source-bridge 129 1 130`
	 `!`
	 `interface tokenring 1`
	 `  source-bridge active 130 1 129`

End system does not support RIF[4]	**Step 1** Place a network analyzer on the same ring to which the end system is connected. **Step 2** Look for RIF frames sent from the end system (RIF frames have the high-order bit of the source MAC[5] address set to 1). **Step 3** If no RIF frames are found, the end system does not support RIF and cannot participate in source routing. If the protocol is routable, you can route the protocol or configure transparent bridging. If you use transparent bridging, be careful not to create loops between the SRB and the transparent bridging domains. **Step 4** If your environment requires SRB, contact your workstation or server vendor for SRB drivers or for information about setting up your workstation or server to support SRB.

Table 10-1 *Local SRB: Host Cannot Connect to Server, Continued*

Possible Problem	Solution
Hop count exceeded	Use the **show** *protocol* **route** command to check the hop count values on routers and bridges in the path. Packets that exceed the hop count are dropped.
	Alternatively, you can enable the **debug source event** privileged exec command to see whether packets are being dropped because the hop count has been exceeded.
	Caution: Because debugging output is assigned high priority in the CPU process, it can render the system unusable. For this reason, use **debug** commands only to troubleshoot specific problems or during troubleshooting sessions with Cisco technical support staff. Moreover, it is best to use **debug** commands during periods of lower network traffic and fewer users. Debugging during these periods decreases the likelihood that increased **debug** command processing overhead will affect system use.
	Increase the hop count if it is less than the default value, 7. Otherwise, the network must be redesigned so that no destination is more than 7 hops away.

Table 10–1 *Local SRB: Host Cannot Connect to Server, Continued*

Possible Problem	Solution
Router is not configured to forward spanning explorers	Spanning explorer packets are equivalent to a single-route broadcast. Routers must therefore be configured to route them.

Step 1 Use the **show source-bridge** exec command to determine whether the spanning explorer count is incrementing.

Step 2 If the spanning explorer count is not incrementing, use the **show running-config** privileged exec command on routers to see whether the **source-bridge spanning** interface configuration command is configured. This command configures the router to forward spanning explorers.

Step 3 If the command entry is not present in the configuration, add it to any router that is required to pass spanning explorers. The command syntax is as follows:

source-bridge spanning *bridge-group* [**path-cost** *path-cost*]

Syntax Description:

- *bridge-group*—Number in the range 1 to 9 that you choose to refer to a particular group of bridged interfaces.

- **path-cost**—(Optional) Path cost for a specified interface.

- *path-cost*—(Optional) Path cost for the interface. The valid range is 0 to 65535.

Example:

The following example adds Token Ring 0 to bridge group 1 and assigns a path cost of 12 to Token Ring 0:

```
interface tokenring 0
 source-bridge spanning 1 path-cost 12
```

Step 4 Use the **show source-bridge** exec command to determine whether explorers are being sent.

Step 5 If explorers are not being sent, place a network analyzer on the same ring to which the end system is connected.

Step 6 If you find spanning all-ring frames, use the **show running-config** privileged exec command to make sure the router is properly configured. If sessions still cannot be established over the SRB, contact your technical support representative for more assistance.

[1] Although you can enter the ring number in hexadecimal or decimal, it always appears in the configuration as a decimal number.
[2] FDDI = Fiber Distributed Data Interface
[3] PVC= permanent virtual circuit
[4] RIF = routing information field
[5] MAC = Media Access Control

Local SRB: Routing Does Not Function

Symptom: Routed protocols are not forwarded properly by routers in a local SRB environment. SRBs bridge traffic normally.

Table 10–2 outlines the problems that might cause this symptom and describes solutions to those problems.

Table 10–2   *Local SRB: Routing Does Not Function*

Possible Problem	Solution
Routing problem	For detailed information on troubleshooting routing problems, refer to the chapters in this book that cover the routing protocols in question. For example, if you are running Novell IPX, see Chapter 8, "Troubleshooting Novell IPX."
Missing **multiring** command	**Step 1** Use the **show running-config** privileged exec command on the router. Look for a **multiring** interface configuration command entry. This command enables the collection and use of RIF information on router interfaces.
	Step 2 If the **multiring** command is not present, add the command to the configuration using the following command: `C4000(config-if)#multiring all`
Incomplete ARP[1] table	**Step 1** Determine whether you can **ping** hosts.
	Step 2 If the host does not respond, use the **show arp** exec command to determine whether an entry for the host exists in the ARP table.
	Step 3 If an entry exists, there is probably a routing problem. Determine whether you have a source-route path to the destination hardware (MAC) address. Use the **show rif** exec command to match the RIF with the hardware address of the host.
	Step 4 If no entry exists, use a network analyzer to see whether ARP requests are getting through to the remote ring and to see whether replies come back.

[1] ARP = Address Resolution Protocol

RSRB: Host Cannot Connect to Server (Peers Not Open)

Symptom: Hosts cannot make connections to servers across a router configured as a remote source-routing bridge (RSRB). The output of the **show source-bridge** privileged exec command shows that SRB peers are not open.

NOTES

If you succeed in getting peers to open but hosts are still unable to communicate with servers, refer to the section "RSRB: Host Cannot Connect to Server (Peers Open)" later in this chapter.

Table 10–3 outlines the problems that might cause this symptom and describes solutions to those problems.

Table 10–3 *RSRB: Host Cannot Connect to Server (Peers Not Open)*

Possible Problem	Solution
Missing or misconfigured **source-bridge remote-peer** command on the router	**Step 1** Use the **show source-bridge** exec command to check for remote peers. If the output shows that peers are open, refer to the section "RSRB: Host Cannot Connect to Server (Peers Open)" later in this chapter. **Step 2** If the output shows that peers are not open, use the **show running-config** privileged exec command to view the router configuration. Verify that there are two **source-bridge remote-peer** global configuration command entries present—one should point to the IP address of the local router and the other should point to the IP address of the remote router. **Step 3** If either or both of the commands are missing or point to the wrong address, add or modify the commands as required. For detailed information about configuring routers for RSRB, see the Cisco IOS *Bridging and IBM Networking Configuration Guide* and *Bridging and IBM Networking Command Reference*.

Table 10–3 *RSRB: Host Cannot Connect to Server (Peers Not Open), Continued*

Possible Problem	Solution
No route to the remote peer	If you are using TCP[1] or FST[2] encapsulation between the local and remote SRB, follow these steps: **Step 1** Test IP connectivity using the extended **ping privileged** exec command. Use the local peer ID as the source address and the remote peer ID as the destination address. **Step 2** If the ping fails, use the **show ip route** exec command to view the IP routing table. **Step 3** If the **show ip route** output does not show a route to the intended remote peer, there is probably an IP routing problem or a problem with the hardware or cabling in the path from the local to the remote SRB. For information on troubleshooting IP routing, refer to Chapter 7, "Troubleshooting TCP/IP." For information about troubleshooting hardware problems, see Chapter 3, "Troubleshooting Hardware and Booting Problems."
Serial link problem	If there is a direct connection between the local and remote SRB (that is, you are not using FST or TCP encapsulation), follow these steps: **Step 1** Check to make sure that the next hop router is directly adjacent. **Step 2** If the router is adjacent, perform other tests to ensure that the link is functioning properly. For more information, refer to Chapter 15, "Troubleshooting Serial Line Problems." **Step 3** If the next hop is not directly adjacent, redesign your network so that it is.

Table 10–3   *RSRB: Host Cannot Connect to Server (Peers Not Open), Continued*

Possible Problem	Solution
End system not generating explorer traffic	**Step 1** Use the **show source-bridge** privileged exec command to see whether the explorer count is incrementing.
	Step 2 If the explorer count is not incrementing, use the **show running-config** privileged exec command to view the router configuration. Check for a **source-bridge spanning** interface configuration command on the local and remote routers.
	Step 3 If the **source-bridge spanning** command is not configured on the routers, configure it on the interfaces connecting the local and remote SRBs. This command is required if the end system is using single-route explorers. The command syntax is as follows:
	source-bridge spanning *bridge-group* [**path-cost** *path-cost*]
	Syntax Description:
	• *bridge-group*—Number in the range 1 to 9 that you choose to refer to a particular group of bridged interfaces.
	• **path-cost**—(Optional) Path cost for a specified interface.
	• *path-cost*—(Optional) Path cost for the interface. The valid range is 0 to 65535.
	Example:
	The following example adds Token Ring 0 to bridge group 1 and assigns a path cost of 12 to Token Ring 0:
| | ```
interface tokenring 0
 source-bridge spanning 1 path-cost 12
``` |
```

Table 10–3 *RSRB: Host Cannot Connect to Server (Peers Not Open), Continued*

Possible Problem	Solution	
Encapsulation mismatch	**Step 1**	Use the **show interfaces** exec command to verify that the interface and line protocol are up. If the status line indicates any other state, refer to Chapter 15, "Troubleshooting Serial Line Problems."
	Step 2	Verify that the configured encapsulation type matches the requirements of the network to which the serial interface is attached.
		For example, if the serial interface is attached to a leased line but the configured encapsulation type is Frame Relay, there is an encapsulation mismatch.
	Step 3	To resolve the mismatch, change the encapsulation type on the serial interface to the type appropriate for the attached network.
Hop count exceeded	**Step 1**	Use the **show** *protocol* **route** command to check the hop count values on routers and bridges in the path. Packets that exceed the hop count are dropped.
		Alternatively, you can enable the **debug source event** privileged exec command to see whether packets are being dropped because the hop count has been exceeded.
		Caution: Because debugging output is assigned high priority in the CPU process, it can render the system unusable. For this reason, use **debug** commands only to troubleshoot specific problems or during troubleshooting sessions with Cisco technical support staff. Moreover, it is best to use **debug** commands during periods of lower network traffic and fewer users. Debugging during these periods decreases the likelihood that increased **debug** command processing overhead will affect system use.
	Step 2	Increase the hop count if it is less than the default value, 7. Otherwise, the network must be redesigned so that no destination is greater than 7 hops away.

[1] TCP = Transmission Control Protocol
[2] FST = Fast Sequenced Transport

RSRB: Host Cannot Connect to Server (Peers Open)

Symptom: Hosts cannot make connections to servers across a router configured as an RSRB. The output of the **show source-bridge** privileged exec command shows that SRB peers are open.

The following is an example of output from the **show source-bridge** command:

```
ionesco#show source-bridge
[...]
Peers:                    state  lv  pkts_rx  pkts_tx  expl_gn   drops TCP
    TCP 150.136.92.92       -      2     0        0         0       0  0
    TCP 150.136.93.93     open    2*    18       18         3       0  0
[...]
```

Table 10–4 outlines the problems that might cause this symptom and describes solutions to those problems.

Table 10–4 *RSRB: Host Cannot Connect to Server (Peers Open)*

Possible Problem	Solution
End system misconfiguration	**Step 1** If the end system is on the ring local to the router, use the **show lnm station** privileged exec command on the local router. This command lists the stations on the local ring.
	The following is an example of the **show lnm station** command:
	show lnm station [*address*]
	Syntax Description:
	• *address*—(Optional) Address of a specific LNM[1] station.
	Sample Display:
	The following is sample output from the **show lnm station** command when a particular address (in this case, **1000.5abc15**) has been specified:
	``` Router# show lnm station 1000.5a6f.bc15 isolating error counts station int ring loc. weight line inter burst ac abort 1000.5a6f.bc15 T1 0001 0000 00 - N 00000 00000 00000 00000 00000 Unique ID: 0000.0000.0000 NAUN: 0000.3000.abc4 Functional: C000.0000.0000 Group: C000.0000.0000 Physical Location: 00000 Enabled Classes: 0000 Allowed Priority: 00000 Address Modifier: 0000 Product ID: 00000000.00000000.00000000.00000000.0000 Ucode Level: 00000000.00000000.0000 Station Status: 00000000.0000 Last transmit status: 00 ```

Table 10–4   *RSRB: Host Cannot Connect to Server (Peers Open), Continued*

Possible Problem	Solution	
End system misconfiguration (*Continued*)	Step 2	Check the command output for the MAC address of the workstation or server. If the MAC address is not present in the output, check the configuration of the end system.
	Step 3	If the problem persists, use a network analyzer to check network traffic generated by the end system. If you do not have a network analyzer, use the **debug token-ring** and the **debug source-bridge** commands.
		Caution: Using the **debug token-ring** and the **debug source-bridge** commands on a heavily loaded router is not advised. These commands can cause further network degradation or complete network failure if not used judiciously.
	Step 4	Check the output of the **debug** commands to see whether the end system is sending traffic to the correct MAC addresses or destination names (in the case of NetBIOS).
End system does not support RIF	Step 1	Place a network analyzer on the same ring to which the end system is connected.
	Step 2	Look for RIF frames sent from the end system (RIF frames have the high-order bit of the source MAC address set to 1).
	Step 3	If no RIF frames are seen, the end system does not support RIF and cannot participate in source routing.
		If the protocol is routable, you can route the protocol or configure transparent bridging. If you use transparent bridging, be careful not to create loops between the SRB and the transparent bridging domains.
	Step 4	If your environment requires SRB, contact your workstation or server vendor for SRB drivers or for information about setting up your workstation or server to support SRB.

Table 10–4 *RSRB: Host Cannot Connect to Server (Peers Open), Continued*

Possible Problem	Solution
Explorer traffic not reaching remote ring	**Step 1** Using a network analyzer or the **debug source-bridge** command, watch network traffic to see whether explorers from the end system reach the remote ring.
	Step 2 If traffic reaches the remote ring successfully, check the configuration of the destination end system (for example, a server) to see why that station does not reply to the explorer traffic from the source.
	If traffic does not reach the remote ring, use the **show source-bridge** command to check ring lists. If information about the ring has not been learned, check router configurations.
	Step 3 If you are using NetBIOS, use the **show netbios name-cache** exec command to see whether traffic is passing through the network properly. If it is not, check router configurations.
	For detailed information about configuring routers for RSRB, refer to the Cisco IOS *Bridging and IBM Networking Configuration Guide* and *Bridging and IBM Networking Command Reference*.

[1] LNM = LAN Network Manager

RSRB: Periodic Communication Failures

Symptom: Communication failures occur periodically over a router configured as an RSRB.

Table 10–5 outlines the problems that might cause this symptom and describes solutions to those problems.

Table 10–5   *RSRB: Periodic Communication Failures*

Possible Problem	Solution
Misconfigured T1 timers	If you are not using local acknowledgment, misconfigured T1 timers can cause periodic timeouts. **Step 1** Use a network analyzer to see how long it takes for packets to travel from one end of the network to the other. **Step 2** Use a **ping** test to the remote router and note the round-trip delay. Compare this value with the configured T1 timer values on end systems. **Step 3** If the round-trip delay is close to or exceeds the T1 timer value, acknowledgments are probably being delayed or dropped by the WAN. For delays, increase the T1 configuration on end systems. For drops, check buffers and interface queues. **Step 4** Enable local acknowledgment to see whether that solves the problem.
WAN link problem	For information on troubleshooting serial line problems, refer to Chapter 15, "Troubleshooting Serial Line Problems." For information on troubleshooting different WAN environments, refer to the appropriate chapter elsewhere in this book.

RSRB: NetBIOS Client Cannot Connect to Server

Symptom: NetBIOS clients cannot connect to NetBIOS servers over a router configured as an RSRB.

Table 10–6 outlines the problems that might cause this symptom and describes solutions to those problems.

Table 10–6 *RSRB: NetBIOS Client Cannot Connect to Server*

Possible Problem	Solution
| Incorrect mapping of NetBIOS name cache server-to-client mapping | **Step 1** For each router on which NetBIOS name caching is enabled, use the **show rif** exec command to determine whether the RIF entry shows the correct path from the router to *both* the client and the server.<br><br>The following is an example of the **show rif** exec command:<br><br>```
cantatrice#show rif
Codes: * interface, - static, + remote
Hardware Addr  How   Idle (min)  Routing Information Field
5C02.0001.4322 rg5              -  0630.0053.00B0
5A00.0000.2333 TR0             3  08B0.0101.2201.0FF0
5B01.0000.4444 -               -  -
0000.1403.4800 TR1             0  -
0000.2805.4C00 TR0             *  -
0000.2807.4C00 TR1             *  -
0000.28A8.4800 TR0             0  -
0077.2201.0001 rg5            10  0830.0052.2201.0FF0
```<br><br>In this display, entries marked with an asterisk (\*) are the router's interface addresses. Entries marked with a dash (-) are static entries. Entries with a number denote cached entries. If the RIF timeout is set to something other than the default, 15 minutes, the timeout is displayed at the top of the display.<br><br>**Step 2** Use the **show running-config** privileged exec command to view the router configuration. Make sure that the **source-bridge proxy-explorer** interface configuration command is included in the Token Ring configuration. Proxy explorers must be enabled on any interface that uses NetBIOS name caching.<br><br>**Step 3** Use the **show netbios-cache** exec command to see whether the NetBIOS cache entry shows the correct mappings of server and client names to MAC addresses. |
```

Table 10–6   *RSRB: NetBIOS Client Cannot Connect to Server, Continued*

Possible Problem	Solution
Incorrect mapping of NetBIOS name cache server-to-client mapping (*Continued*)	The following is an example of the **show netbios-cache** exec command:

```
cantatrice#show netbios-cache
  HW Addr          Name              How        Idle       NetBIOS Packet
                                                           Savings
  1000.5a89.449a   IC6W06_B          TR1        6          0
  1000.5a8b.14e5   IC_9Q07A          TR1        2          0
  1000.5a25.1b12   IC9Q19_A          TR1        7          0
  1000.5a25.1b12   IC9Q19_A          TR1        10         0
  1000.5a8c.7bb1   BKELSA1           TR1        4          0
  1000.5a8b.6c7c   ICELSB1           TR1        -          0
  1000.5a31.df39   ICASC_01          TR1        -          0
  1000.5ada.47af   BKELSA2           TR1        10         0
  1000.5a8f.018a   ICELSC1           TR1        1          0
```

The following are the fields reported by the **show netbios-cache** command:

- **show netbios**—Cache field descriptions
- **HW Addr**—MAC address mapped to the NetBIOS name in this entry.
- **Name**—NetBIOS name mapped to the MAC address in this entry.
- **How**—Interface through which this information was learned.
- **Idle**—Period of time (in seconds) since this entry was last accessed. A hyphen in this column indicates that it is a static entry in the NetBIOS name cache.
- **NetBIOS Packet Savings**—Number of packets to which local replies were made (thus preventing transmission of these packets over the network).

Step 4   Use the **show running-config** privileged exec command at each router to examine the mapping of addresses specified in **netbios name-cache** global configuration command entries.

The following example shows a configuration in which the NetBIOS server is accessed remotely:

```
source-bridge ring-group 2
rif 0110.2222.3333 0630.021.0030 ring group 2
netbios name-cache 0110.2222.3333 DEF ring-group 2
```

Table 10–6 *RSRB: NetBIOS Client Cannot Connect to Server, Continued*

Possible Problem	Solution

Misconfigured source-bridge command	**Step 1** For each router on which NetBIOS name caching is enabled, use the **show source-bridge** command to obtain the version of the remote connection. The value specified should be 2 or 3. If the value is 1, connections will not get through, and you must modify your configuration.
	
	Example:
	
	The following is sample output from the **show source-bridge** command:
	
	<pre>Router# show source-bridge
	Local Interfaces: receive transmit
	          srn bn trn r p s n max hops cnt cnt drops
	TR0 5 1 10 * * 7 39:1002 23:62923
	Ring Group 10:
	  This peer: TCP 150.136.92.92
	  Maximum output TCP queue length, per peer: 100
	  Peers: state lv pkts_rx pkts_tx expl_gn drops TCP
	    TCP 150.136.92.92 - 2 0 0 0 0 0
	    TCP 150.136.93.93 open 2* 18 18 3 0 0
	Rings:
	    bn: 1 rn: 5 local ma: 4000.3080.844b TokenRing0 fwd: 18
	    bn: 1 rn: 2 remote ma: 4000.3080.8473 TCP 150.136.93.93 fwd: 36
	Explorers: ------- input ------- ------- output -------
	          spanning all-rings total spanning all-rings total
	    TR0 0 3 3 3 5 8
	Router#</pre>
	Step 2 If the router is running a software release prior to Cisco IOS Release 10.0, specify either **version 2** or **version 3** in the **source-bridge remote-peer** interface configuration command. The syntax is as follows:
	
	source-bridge remote-peer *ring-group tcp ip-address* [*lf size*] [*local-ack*] [*priority*] [*version number*]
	
	If the router is running Cisco IOS Release 10.0 or later, the specification of a version is ignored.
	
	For more information, refer to the Cisco IOS *Bridging and IBM Networking Configuration Guide* and *Bridging and IBM Networking Command Reference*.

Translational Bridging: Client Cannot Connect to Server

Symptom: Clients cannot communicate over a router configured as a translational bridge.

> **CAUTION**
>
> ---
>
> In certain situations, replacing existing translational bridges with Cisco translational bridges can cause interoperability problems. Some translational bridge implementations map functional addresses between media (such as local-area transport [LAT] functional address 0900.2B00.00FA on Ethernet) to a broadcast address on the Token Ring side (such as C000.FFFF.FFFF). Cisco does not support this functionality. Furthermore, you cannot use translational bridging with any protocol that embeds the MAC address of a station inside the Information field of the MAC frames (examples include IP ARP and Novell IPX).

Table 10–7 outlines the problems that might cause this symptom and describes solutions to those problems.

Table 10–7   *Translational Bridging: Client Cannot Connect to Server*

Possible Problem	Solution
Media problem	Verify the line using the **show interfaces** exec command. If the interface or line protocol is down, troubleshoot the media. For LAN media, refer to the chapter that covers your media type.
Ethernet–to–Token Ring address mapping is misconfigured	**Step 1** Use the **show bridge** exec command to verify the existence of the Ethernet station. Ethernet and Token Ring addresses use opposite bit ordering schemes. The Token Ring address 0110.2222.3333 is equivalent to the Ethernet address 8008.4444.cccc.

Table 10-7   *Translational Bridging: Client Cannot Connect to Server, Continued*

Possible Problem	Solution
Ethernet–to–Token Ring address mapping is misconfigured (*Continued*)	**Step 2** Use the **show spanning** exec command to determine whether the Ethernet port is in forwarding mode. **Example:** The following is sample output from the **show span** command:

```
RouterA> show span
Bridge Group 1 is executing the IBM compatible spanning tree
protocol
  Bridge Identifier has priority 32768, address 0000.0c0c.f68b
  Configured hello time 2, max age 6, forward delay 4
  Current root has priority 32768, address 0000.0c0c.f573
  Root port is 001A (TokenRing0/0), cost of root path is 16
  Topology change flag not set, detected flag not set
  Times:   hold 1, topology change 30, notification 30
           hello 2, max age 6, forward delay 4, aging 300
  Timers: hello 0, topology change 0, notification 0
Port 001A (TokenRing0/0) of bridge group 1 is forwarding. Path
cost 16
  Designated root has priority 32768, address 0000.0c0c.f573
  Designated bridge has priority 32768, address 0000.0c0c.f573
  Designated port is 001B, path cost 0, peer 0
  Timers: message age 1, forward delay 0, hold 0
Port 002A (TokenRing0/1) of bridge group 1 is blocking. Path cost
16
  Designated root has priority 32768, address 0000.0c0c.f573
  Designated bridge has priority 32768, address 0000.0c0c.f573
  Designated port is 002B, path cost 0, peer 0
  Timers: message age 0, forward delay 0, hold 0
Port 064A (spanRSRB) of bridge group 1 is disabled. Path cost 250
  Designated root has priority 32768, address 0000.0c0c.f573
  Designated bridge has priority 32768, address 0000.0c0c.f68b
  Designated port is 064A, path cost 16, peer 0
  Timers: message age 0, forward delay 0, hold 0
```

A port (spanRSRB) is created with each virtual ring group. The port is disabled until one or more peers go into open state in the ring group.

Table 10–7 *Translational Bridging: Client Cannot Connect to Server, Continued*

Possible Problem	Solution

Ethernet–to–Token Ring address mapping is misconfigured (*Continued*)	**Step 3** Use the **show rif** exec command to determine whether the target Token Ring station is visible on the internetwork.
	
	When configured for translational bridging, the router extracts the RIF of a packet received from the Token Ring network and saves it in a table. The router then transmits the packet on the Ethernet network. Later, the router reinserts the RIF when it receives a packet destined for the originating node on the Token Ring side.
	
	Example:
	
	The following is sample output from the **show rif** command:
	
	<pre>Router# show rif
	Codes: * interface, - static, + remote
	Hardware Addr How Idle (min) Routing Information Field
	5C02.0001.4322 rg5 - 0630.0053.00B0
	5A00.0000.2333 TR0 3 08B0.0101.2201.0FF0
	5B01.0000.4444 - - -
	0000.1403.4800 TR1 0 -
	0000.2805.4C00 TR0 * -
	0000.2807.4C00 TR1 * -
	0000.28A8.4800 TR0 0 -
	0077.2201.0001 rg5 10 0830.0052.2201.0FF0</pre>
	Step 4 If Ethernet and Token Ring end systems are visible, statically configure any relevant server MAC addresses in the client configurations so that clients can listen to the server advertisements directly.
	
	One case in which static mapping is required is when bridging DEC LAT traffic over a translational bridge. LAT services on Ethernet are advertised on a multicast address that is mapped by some translational bridges to a broadcast address on the Token Ring side. Routers do not support this mapping.

Table 10–7   *Translational Bridging: Client Cannot Connect to Server, Continued*

Possible Problem	Solution
Vendor code mismatch	Older Token Ring implementations require that the vendor code (OUI[1] field) of the SNAP[2] header be 000000. Cisco routers modify this field to be 0000F8 to specify that the frame was translated from Ethernet Version 2 to Token Ring. This can cause problems on older Token Ring networks.
	Specify the **ethernet-transit-oui** interface configuration command to force the router to make the vendor code field 000000. This change is frequently required when there are IBM 8209s (IBM Token Ring-to-Ethernet translating bridges) in the network.
	The following is an example of the **ethernet-transit-oui** command:
	ethernet-transit-oui [*90-compatible* | *standard* | *cisco*]
	Syntax Description:
	• *90-compatible*—OUI used 0000F8 by default, when talking to other Cisco routers. Provides the most flexibility.
	• *standard*—OUI used 000000 when talking to IBM 8209 bridges and other vendor equipment. Does not provide for as much flexibility as the other two choices.
	• *cisco*—OUI used 00000C, provided for compatibility with future equipment.
	Example:
	The following example specifies Cisco's OUI form:
	```\ninterface tokenring 0\n ethernet-transit-oui cisco\n```
Cisco and non-Cisco translational bridges in parallel	**Step 1** Check for translational bridges in parallel with the Cisco translational bridge. If there are any parallel non-Cisco translational bridges, loops will probably be created.
	Step 2 Because implementing translational bridging defeats the spanning-tree mechanism of both transparent bridging and SRB environments, you must eliminate all loops caused by inserting the translational bridge. A transparent spanning tree and a source-bridge spanning tree cannot communicate with one another.

Table 10–7 *Translational Bridging: Client Cannot Connect to Server, Continued*

Possible Problem	Solution
Trying to bridge protocols that embed MAC addresses in the Information field of the MAC frame (such as IP ARP[3], Novell IPX, or AARP[4])	If MAC addresses are embedded in the Information field of the MAC frame, bridges will be unable to read the address. Bridges will therefore be unable to forward the traffic. **Step 1** If you are attempting to bridge this type of protocol, route the protocol instead. **Step 2** If you still cannot communicate over the router, contact your technical support representative.

[1] OUI = organizational unique identifier
[2] SNAP = Subnetwork Access Protocol
[3] ARP = Address Resolution Protocol
[4] AARP = AppleTalk Address Resolution Protocol

SRT Bridging: Client Cannot Connect to Server

Symptom: Clients cannot communicate over a router configured to perform SRT bridging. Packets are not forwarded by the SRT bridge.

> **NOTES**
>
> SRT bridging allows you to implement transparent bridging in Token Ring environments. It is *not* a means of translating between SRB on a Token Ring and transparent bridging on Ethernet (or other) media.

Table 10–8 outlines the problems that might cause this symptom and describes solutions to those problems.

Table 10–8 *SRT Bridging: Client Cannot Connect to Server*

Possible Problem	Solution
Trying to bridge frames containing RIF from Token Ring network to Ethernet network over an SRT bridge	Use translational bridging instead of SRT bridging to allow SRB-to-transparent bridging translation. Because SRT bridging works only between Ethernet and Token Ring, any packet containing a RIF is dropped when SRT bridging is used.
Attempting to transfer large frame sizes	Problems will occur if Token Ring devices transmit frames exceeding the Ethernet MTU[1] of 1500 bytes. Configure hosts on the Token Ring to generate frame sizes less than or equal to the Ethernet MTU.

Table 10–8 *SRT Bridging: Client Cannot Connect to Server, Continued*

Possible Problem	Solution
Trying to bridge protocols that embed the MAC address in the Information field of the MAC frame (such as IP ARP, Novell IPX, or AARP)	If MAC addresses are embedded in the Information field of the MAC frame, bridges will be unable to read the address. Bridges will therefore be unable to forward the traffic. **Step 1** If you are attempting to bridge this type of protocol, route the protocol instead. **Step 2** If you still cannot communicate over the router, contact your technical support representative.
Media problem	Verify the line using the **show interfaces** exec command. If the interface or line protocol is down, troubleshoot the media. For LAN media, refer to the chapter that covers your media type.

[1] MTU = maximum transmission unit

SDLC: Router Cannot Communicate with SDLC Device

Symptom: Router cannot communicate with an IBM SDLC device.

Table 10–9 outlines the problems that might cause this symptom and describes solutions to those problems.

Table 10–9 *SDLC: Router Cannot Communicate with SDLC Device*

Possible Problem	Solution
Physical layer problem	**Step 1** Use the **show interfaces** exec command to determine whether the interface and line protocol are up. **Step 2** If the interface and line protocol are both up, troubleshoot link-layer problems as described later in this table. **Step 3** If the output does not indicate up/up, make sure the device is powered on. Make sure all cabling is correct, securely connected, and undamaged. Make sure the cabling does not exceed the recommended length for the speed of the connection. **Step 4** If the interface or line protocol is still down, use a breakout box to check the signals on the line.

Table 10–9 *SDLC: Router Cannot Communicate with SDLC Device, Continued*

Possible Problem	Solution
Physical layer problem (*Continued*)	**Note:** On some Cisco platforms, such as the Cisco 7000 running a recent Cisco IOS release, the output of the **show interfaces** command will indicate the state of line signals.
	If the router is full-duplex DCE[1], check for DTR[2] and RTS[3]. If these signals are not high, proceed to Step 5. If these signals are high, the interface should be up. If it is not, contact your technical support representative.
	On a Cisco 7000, if the breakout box shows that the DTR and DTS signals are high but the **show interfaces** command shows that they are not, check the router cabling. In particular, make sure that the 60-pin high-density cable is not plugged in to the router upside-down.
	If the router is half-duplex DCE, check for DTR. If DTR is not high, proceed to Step 5. If DTR is high, the interface should be up. If it is not, contact your technical support representative.
	Note: Half-duplex is not supported on Cisco 7000 series routers.
	If the router is full- or half-duplex DTE, check for CD. If CD is not high, proceed to Step 5. If CD is high, the interface should be up. If it is not, contact your technical support representative.
	Step 5 If the router is full-duplex DCE, make sure the device is configured for permanent RTS high. If the device does not allow you to configure permanent RTS, set the signal high by strapping DTR from the device side to RTS on the router side (see Figure 10–5).
	Step 6 If the router is DCE, it is typical to be required to provide clock to the device. Make sure the **clock rate** interface configuration command is present in the router configuration. Use the **show running-config** privileged exec command on the router to view the interface configuration. The following example shows the clock rate information for interface serial 0.

Table 10–9 *SDLC: Router Cannot Communicate with SDLC Device, Continued*

Possible Problem	Solution
Physical layer problem (*Continued*)	**Example:** The following example sets the clock rate on the first serial interface to 64000 bits per second: ``` interface serial 0 clock rate 64000 ``` If the router is DTE, it should get clock from an external device. Make sure that a device is providing clock properly. Make sure that the clocking source is the same for all devices.
Link-layer problem (router is primary)	**Step 1** Use the **debug sdlc** privileged exec command[4] to see whether the router is sending SNRMs.[5] **Caution:** Because debugging output is assigned high priority in the CPU process, it can render the system unusable. For this reason, use **debug** commands only to troubleshoot specific problems or during troubleshooting sessions with Cisco technical support staff. Moreover, it is best to use **debug** commands during periods of lower network traffic and fewer users. Debugging during these periods decreases the likelihood that increased **debug** command processing overhead will affect system use. **Step 2** If the router is not sending SNRMs, check the physical layer (see the preceding problem in this table). If the router is sending SNRMs, the device should send UAs[6] in reply. **Step 3** If the device is not sending UAs, make sure the addresses of the router and device are correct. **Step 4** If you are using a V.35 connection, make sure that the SCT/SCTE[7] setting is correct on the interface. The router should use SCTE if the router is DCE, and SCT if the router is DTE. The SCT/SCTE setting might be changed with a jumper or with the software configuration command **dce-terminal-timing enable**, depending on the platform. Some platforms do not allow you to change this setting.

Table 10–9   *SDLC: Router Cannot Communicate with SDLC Device, Continued*

Possible Problem	Solution

Link-layer problem (router is primary) (*Continued*)	**Example:**
	
	The following example prevents phase shifting of the data with respect to the clock:
	
	``
	interface serial 0
	  dce-terminal-timing enable
	``
	
	Step 5 Make sure that the device and the router are using the same signal coding (NRZ[8] or NRZI[9]). NRZ is enabled by default on the router. To enable NRZI encoding, use the **nrzi-encoding** interface configuration command.
	
	Example:
	
	In the following example, serial interface 1 is configured for NRZI encoding:
	
	``
	interface serial 1
	  nrzi-encoding
	``
	
	Step 6 Try reducing the line speed to 9600 bps using the **clock rate** interface configuration command. Use the **clock rate** interface configuration command to configure the clock rate for the hardware connections on serial interfaces such as NIMs[10] and interface processors to an acceptable bit rate.
	
	Syntax:
	
	The following is the syntax of the **clock rate** command:
	
	clock rate *bps*
	
	Syntax Description:
	
	• *bps*—Desired clock rate in bits per second: 1200, 2400, 4800, 9600, 19200, 38400, 56000, 64000, 72000, 125000, 148000, 250000, 500000, 800000, 1000000, 1300000, 2000000, 4000000, or 8000000.
	
	Example:
	
	The following example sets the clock rate on the first serial interface to 64,000 bits per second:
	
	``
	interface serial 0
	  clock rate 64000
	``
	
	Step 7 Make sure that cabling is correct, securely attached, and undamaged.

Table 10–9 *SDLC: Router Cannot Communicate with SDLC Device, Continued*

Possible Problem	Solution

Link-layer problem (router is secondary)	**Step 1** Use the **debug sdlc** privileged exec command to see whether the router is receiving SNRMs.
	
	Caution: Because debugging output is assigned high priority in the CPU process, it can render the system unusable. For this reason, use **debug** commands only to troubleshoot specific problems or during troubleshooting sessions with Cisco technical support staff. Moreover, it is best to use **debug** commands during periods of lower network traffic and fewer users. Debugging during these periods decreases the likelihood that increased **debug** command processing overhead will affect system use.
	
	Step 2 If the router is not receiving SNRMs, check the primary device. Make sure the physical layer is operational (see the problem "Physical layer problem" in this table). If the router is receiving SNRMs, it should send UAs in reply.
	
	Step 3 If the router is not sending UAs, make sure the addresses of the router and device are correct.
	
	Step 4 If you are using a V.35 connection, make sure that the SCT/SCTE setting is correct on the interface. The router should use SCTE if the router is DCE and SCT if the router is DTE.
	
	The SCT/SCTE setting might be changed with a jumper or with the software configuration command **dce-terminal-timing enable**, depending on the platform. Some platforms do not allow you to change this setting.
	
	Example:
	
	The following example prevents phase shifting of the data with respect to the clock:
	
	`interface serial 0`
	`  dce-terminal-timing enable`
	
	Step 5 Use a breakout box to check for CTS high on the line.
	
	Step 6 Make sure that both the device and the router are using the same signal coding (NRZ or NRZI). NRZ is enabled by default on the router. To enable NRZI encoding, use the **nrzi-encoding** interface configuration command.

Table 10–9   *SDLC: Router Cannot Communicate with SDLC Device, Continued*

Possible Problem	Solution	
Link-layer problem (router is secondary) (*Continued*)		**Example:**
		In the following example, serial interface 1 is configured for NRZI encoding:
		``` interface serial 1 nrzi-encoding ```
	Step 7	Try reducing the line speed to 9600 bps using the **clock rate** interface configuration command. Use the **clock rate** interface configuration command to configure the clock rate for the hardware connections on serial interfaces such as NIMs and interface processors to an acceptable bit rate.
		Syntax:
		The following is the syntax of the **clock rate** command:
		clock rate *bps*
		Syntax Description:
		• *bps*—Desired clock rate in bits per second: 1200, 2400, 4800, 9600, 19200, 38400, 56000, 64000, 72000, 125000, 148000, 250000, 500000, 800000, 1000000, 1300000, 2000000, 4000000, or 8000000.
		Example:
		The following example sets the clock rate on the first serial interface to 64000 bits per second:
		``` interface serial 0 clock rate 64000 ```
	Step 8	Make sure that cabling is correct, securely attached, and undamaged.

[1] DCE = full-duplex data communications
[2] DTR = data terminal ready
[3] RTS = request to send
[4] To reduce the amount of screen output produced by the **debug sdlc** command, configure the **sdlc poll-pause-timer 1000** command to reduce the frequency at which the router sends poll frames. Remember to return this command to its original value (the default is 10 milliseconds).
[5] SNRM = send normal response mode
[6] UA = unnumbered acknowledgment
[7] SCT/SCTE = serial clock transmit/serial clock transmit external
[8] NRZ = nonreturn to zero
[9] NRZI = nonreturn to zero inverted
[10] NIM = network interface module

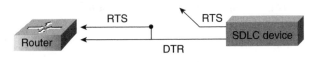

Figure 10–5
Strapping DTR to RT

SDLC: Intermittent Connectivity

Symptom: User connections to hosts time out over a router configured to perform SDLC transport.

Table 10–10 outlines the problem that might cause this symptom and describes solutions to that problem.

Table 10–10 *SDLC: Intermittent Connectivity*

Possible Problem	Solution	
SDLC timing problems	**Step 1**	Place a serial analyzer on the serial line attached to the source station and monitor packets.
	Step 2	If duplicate packets appear, check the router configuration using the **show running-config** privileged exec command. Check to see whether the **local-ack** keyword is present in the configuration.
	Step 3	If the **local-ack** keyword is missing, add it to the router configuration for SDLC interfaces.
	Step 4	Local acknowledgment parameters can be adjusted in the router, the attached device, or both. Adjust SDLC protocol parameters as appropriate. These parameters are used to customize SDLC transport over various network configurations. In particular, you might need to tune various LLC2 timer values.
		The following is a sample configuration using the **local-ack** command:

		<pre>interface Serial 1
		mtu 4400
		no ip address
		hold-queue 150 in
		encapsulation stun
		stun group 1
		stun sdlc-role primary
		sdlc line-speed 19200
		sdlc n1 35200
		sdlc address 04 echo
		stun route address 4 tcp 156.28.11.1 local-ack clockrate 19200</pre>

	For more information about configuring SDLC, refer to the Cisco IOS *Bridging and IBM Networking Configuration Guide* and *Bridging and IBM Networking Command Reference*.	

SDLC: Client Cannot Connect to Host over Router Running SDLLC

Symptom: Users cannot open connections to hosts on the other side of a router configured to support SDLC Logical Link Control (SDLLC).

Table 10–11 outlines the problems that might cause this symptom and describes solutions to those problems.

Table 10–11   *SDLC: Client Cannot Connect to Host over Router Running SDLLC*

Possible Problem	Solution
SDLC physical or data link-layer problem	**Step 1** Use the **show interface** *slot/port* exec command to check the state of the connection with the SDLC device.
	Step 2 Look for USBUSY in the output, which indicates that the router is attempting to establish an LLC connection. If the router is not USBUSY, make sure that the physical and link layers are working properly. For more information, refer to the section "SDLC: Router Cannot Communicate with SDLC Device" earlier in this chapter.
	Step 3 If the router is USBUSY, proceed to the next problem in this table.

Table 10–11   *SDLC: Client Cannot Connect to Host over Router Running SDLLC, Continued*

Possible Problem	Solution
Router not sending test frames to FEP[1]	**Step 1** With the **debug sdllc** and **debug llc2 packet** privileged exec commands enabled on the router, check whether the router is sending test frames to the FEP.

Caution: Because debugging output is assigned high priority in the CPU process, it can render the system unusable. For this reason, use **debug** commands only to troubleshoot specific problems or during troubleshooting sessions with Cisco technical support staff. Moreover, it is best to use **debug** commands during periods of lower network traffic and fewer users. Debugging during these periods decreases the likelihood that increased **debug** command processing overhead will affect system use.

Step 2 If the router is sending test frames to the FEP, proceed to the next problem in this table.

Step 3 If the router is not sending test frames to the FEP, use the **show running-config** privileged EXEC command to view the router configuration. Make sure that the **sdllc partner** interface configuration command is present.

Step 4 If the **sdlc partner** command is not present, add it to the configuration. Make sure that it points to the hardware address of the FEP on the Token Ring. The following is the syntax for the **sdlc partner** command:

sdlc partner *mac-address sdlc-address*

Syntax Description:

• *mac-address*— 48-bit MAC address of the Token Ring host.

• *sdlc-address*—SDLC address of the serial device that will communicate with the Token Ring host. The valid range is 1 to FE. |

Table 10–11   *SDLC: Client Cannot Connect to Host over Router Running SDLLC, Continued*

Possible Problem	Solution	
FEP on Token Ring not replying to test frames	Step 1	With the **debug sdllc** and **debug llc2 packet** privileged exec commands enabled on the router, check whether the FEP is replying to test frames sent by the router.
		Caution: Because debugging output is assigned high priority in the CPU process, it can render the system unusable. For this reason, use **debug** commands only to troubleshoot specific problems or during troubleshooting sessions with Cisco technical support staff. Moreover, it is best to use **debug** commands during periods of lower network traffic and fewer users. Debugging during these periods decreases the likelihood that increased **debug** command processing overhead will affect system use.
	Step 2	If the FEP is responding, proceed to the next problem in this table.
	Step 3	If the FEP is not responding, check the MAC address of the router's partner (the FEP). Make sure that the address is correctly specified in the **sdllc partner** command entry on the router. The following is the syntax of the **sdlc partner** command:
		sdlc partner *mac-address sdlc-address*
		Syntax Description:
		• *mac-address*—48-bit MAC address of the Token Ring host.
		• *sdlc-address*—SDLC address of the serial device that will communicate with the Token Ring host. The valid range is 1 to FE.
	Step 4	Check whether RSRB peers are up. If the peers are not open, refer to the section "RSRB: Host Cannot Connect to Server (Peers Not Open)" earlier in this chapter.
	Step 5	If the RSRB peers are up, attach a network analyzer to the Token Ring with the FEP attached and make sure that the router's test frames are arriving on the ring and that the FEP is replying.

Table 10–11 *SDLC: Client Cannot Connect to Host over Router Running SDLLC, Continued*

Possible Problem	Solution
XID[2] not sent by router	**Step 1** With the **debug sdllc** and **debug llc2 packet** privileged exec commands enabled on the router, check whether the router is sending XID frames to the FEP.
	Caution: Because debugging output is assigned high priority in the CPU process, it can render the system unusable. For this reason, use **debug** commands only to troubleshoot specific problems or during troubleshooting sessions with Cisco technical support staff. Moreover, it is best to use **debug** commands during periods of lower network traffic and fewer users. Debugging during these periods decreases the likelihood that increased **debug** command processing overhead will affect system use.
	Step 2 If the router is sending XID frames to the FEP, proceed to the next problem in this table.
	Step 3 If the router is not sending XID frames, use the **show running-config** privileged exec command to view the router configuration. Make sure there is an **sdllc xid** interface configuration command entry present.
	Step 4 If the **sdllc xid** command is not configured on the router, add it to the configuration. The following is the syntax for the **sdlc xid** command:
	sdlc xid *address xid*
	Syntax Description:
	• *address*—Address of the SDLC station associated with this interface.
	• *xid*—XID the Cisco IOS software will use to respond to XID requests the router receives. This value must be 4 bytes (8 digits) in length and is specified with hexadecimal digits.
	Example:
	The following example specifies an XID value of 01720002 at address C2:
| | ```
interface serial 0
  sdlc xid c2 01720002
``` |
```

Table 10–11 *SDLC: Client Cannot Connect to Host over Router Running SDLLC, Continued*

Possible Problem	Solution
FEP not replying to XID	**Step 1** With the **debug sdllc** and **debug llc2 packet** privileged exec commands enabled on the router, check to see whether the FEP is replying to XID frames from the router.
	Step 2 If the FEP is responding, proceed to the next problem in this table.

	Step 3 If the FEP is not responding, check the XID values configured by the **sdllc xid** command on the router. The values for IDBLK and IDNUM on the router must match the values in VTAM on the FEP. The following is the syntax for the **sdlc xid** command:
	
	sdlc xid *address xid*
	
	Syntax Description:
	
	• *address*—Address of the SDLC station associated with this interface.
	
	• *xid*—XID the Cisco IOS software will use to respond to XID requests the router receives. This value must be 4 bytes (8 digits) in length and is specified with hexadecimal digits.
	
	Example:
	
	The following example specifies an XID value of 01720002 at address C2:
	
	`interface serial 0`
	`  sdlc xid c2 01720002`

	Step 4 Make sure that the XID information on the hosts is properly defined. If a 317X device is a channel-attached gateway, the XID must be 0000000 for IDBLK and IDNUM.
Host problem	Check for activation, application problems, VTAM and NCP misconfigurations, configuration mismatches, and other problems on the IBM host.

[1] FEP = front-end processor
[2] XID = exchange of identification

Virtual Token Ring Addresses and SDLLC

The **sdllc traddr** command specifies a virtual Token Ring MAC address for an SDLC-attached device (the device you are spoofing to look like a Token Ring device). The last two hexadecimal digits of the virtual MAC address *must* be 00. The router then reserves any virtual ring address that falls into the range xxxx.xxxx.xx00 to xxxx.xxxx.xxff for the SDLLC serial interface.

As a result, other IBM devices on an internetwork might have an LAA that falls in the same range. This can cause problems if you are using local acknowledgment because routers examine only the first 10 digits of the LAA address of a packet (not the last two, which are considered wildcards).

If the router sees an address that matches an assigned SDLLC LAA address, it automatically forwards that packet to the SDLLC process. This can result in packets being incorrectly forwarded to the SDLLC process and sessions never being established.

NOTES

To avoid assigning conflicting addresses, be certain you know the LAA naming convention used in the internetwork before assigning a virtual ring address for any SDLLC implementation.

SDLC: Sessions Fail over Router Running STUN

Symptom: SDLC sessions between two nodes fail when they are attempted over a router that is running serial tunnel (STUN).

NOTES

This section discusses troubleshooting procedures for STUN without local acknowledgment (LACK). For STUN with LACK, the procedures are essentially the same, but remember that there are two sessions, one from the primary to the router, and one from the secondary to the router.

Table 10–12 outlines the problems that might cause this symptom and describes solutions to those problems.

Table 10–12   *SDLC: Sessions Fail over Router Running STUN*

Possible Problem	Solution	
Peers are not open	Step 1	Use the **show stun** exec command to see whether the peers are open. If the peers are open, one of the other problems in this table is probably the cause.
		The following is sample output from the **show stun** command:

		<pre>Router# show stun
		This peer: 131.108.10.1
		Serial0 -- 3174 Controller for test lab (group 1 [sdlc])
		                       state rx-pkts tx-pkts drops poll
		   7[1] IF Serial1 open 20334 86440 5 8P
		  10[1] TCP 131.108.8.1 open 6771 7331 0
		 all[1] TCP 131.108.8.1 open 612301 2338550 1005</pre>

		In this display, the first entry reports that proxy polling is enabled for address 7 and serial 0 is running with modulus 8 on the primary side of the link. The link has received 20,334 packets, transmitted 86,440 packets, and dropped 5 packets.
	Step 2	If the peers are not open, use the **debug stun** command on the core router to see whether the peers are trying to open. Peers do not open if there is no traffic on the link.
		Caution: Do not enable **debug** commands on a heavily loaded router. Doing so can cause performance and connectivity problems. Use a protocol analyzer or **show** commands instead.
	Step 3	If you do not see the peers trying to open, use the **show interface** exec command to make sure the interface and line protocol are both up. If they are not both up, there could be a link problem. Proceed to the problem "SDLC physical or link-layer problem" later in this table.
	Step 4	If the peers are trying to open, use the **show running-config** privileged exec command to make sure that the **stun route** and other STUN configuration commands are configured correctly. Reconfigure the router if necessary.
	Step 5	Use the **debug stun packet** privileged exec command on the core router. Look for SNRMs or XIDs being sent.
	Step 6	If you do not see SNRMs or XIDs, there is probably a basic link problem. See the problem "SDLC physical or link-layer problem" later in this table.
	Step 7	Check to make sure that there are not other network problems occurring, such as interface drops, buffer misses, overloaded Frame Relay switches, and IP routing problems.

Table 10–12   *SDLC: Sessions Fail over Router Running STUN, Continued*

Possible Problem	Solution	
SNRMs or XIDs not sent	**Step 1**	Use the **show stun** command to see whether the peers are open. If the peers are not open, see the preceding problem in this table.
	Step 2	If the peers are open, use the **debug stun packet** privileged exec command on the remote end. Check for SNRMS or XIDs from the primary arriving as NDI packets.
	Step 3	If SNRMs or XIDs are arriving, proceed to the next problem in this table.
	Step 4	If SNRMS or XIDs are not arriving, use the **debug stun packet** command on the core router to see whether SNRMs or XIDs are being sent.
	Step 5	If the core router is not sending SNRMs or XIDs, make sure that the physical and link layers are operating properly. See the problem "SDLC physical or link-layer problem" later in this table.
	Step 6	If the core router is sending SNRMs or XIDs, use the **show running-config** privileged exec command to make sure the **stun route** command is properly configured on the router.
	Step 7	Check to make sure that there are not other network problems occurring, such as interface drops, buffer misses, overloaded Frame Relay switches, and IP routing problems.
No reply to SNRMs or XIDs	**Step 1**	Use the **show stun** command to see whether the peers are open. If the peers are not open, see the first problem in this table.
	Step 2	If the peers are open, use the **debug stun packet** privileged exec command on the remote end. Check for SNRMS or XIDs from the primary arriving as NDI packets.
	Step 3	If SNRMs or XIDs are not arriving, refer to the preceding problem in this table.
	Step 4	If SNRMs or XIDs are arriving, make sure that the core router is sending UA or XID responses as SDI packets.
	Step 5	If the router is not sending responses, there might be a link problem. Refer to the problem "SDLC physical or link-layer problem" later in this table.

Table 10–12 *SDLC: Sessions Fail over Router Running STUN, Continued*

Possible Problem	Solution
No reply to SNRMs or XIDs (*Continued*)	**Step 6** If the router is sending responses, use the **debug stun packet** command to see whether the UA or XID responses are getting back to the primary as SDI packets.
	Step 7 If the responses are not getting back to the primary, use the **show running-config** privileged exec command to make sure that the **stun route** and other STUN configuration commands are properly configured on the remote router. The following is the syntax for the **stun route** command:
	stun route address *address-number* **tcp** *ip-address* [*local-ack*] [*priority*] [*tcp-queue-max*]
	Syntax Description:
	• *address-number*—Number that conforms to TCP addressing conventions.
	• *ip-address*—IP address by which this STUN peer is known to other STUN peers that are using the TCP as the STUN encapsulation.
	• *local-ack*—(Optional) Enables local acknowledgment for STUN.
	• *priority*—(Optional) Establishes the four levels used in priority queuing: low, medium, normal, and high.
	• *tcp-queue-max*—(Optional) Sets the maximum size of the outbound TCP queue for the SDLC link.
	Example:
	In the following example, a frame with a source-route address of 10 is propagated using TCP encapsulation to a device with an IP address of 131.108.8.1:
| | ```
stun route address 10 tcp 131.108.8.1
``` |
| | **Step 8** Check to make sure that there are not other network problems occurring, such as interface drops, buffer misses, overloaded Frame Relay switches, and IP routing problems. |
| | **Step 9** If packets are passed end-to-end in both directions, check end station configurations, duplex settings, configurations, and so forth. |
```

Table 10–12 *SDLC: Sessions Fail over Router Running STUN, Continued*

Possible Problem	Solution
SDLC physical or link-layer problem	**Step 1** Use the **show interfaces** exec command on the link connecting to the primary device. Make sure that the interface and line protocol are both up.
	Step 2 If the interface or line protocol is not up, make sure the devices are powered up and connected correctly. Check the line to make sure it is active. Check for clocking, address misconfigurations, correct NRZ or NRZI specifications, and so forth.
	Step 3 Try slowing the clock rate of the connection. Use the **clock rate** interface configuration command to configure the clock rate for the hardware connections on serial interfaces such as NIMs and interface processors to an acceptable bit rate.
	The following is the syntax of the **clock rate** command:
	clock rate *bps*
	Syntax Description:
	• *bps*—Desired clock rate in bits per second: 1200, 2400, 4800, 9600, 19200, 38400, 56000, 64000, 72000, 125000, 148000, 250000, 500000, 800000, 1000000, 1300000, 2000000, 4000000, or 8000000.
	Example:
	The following example sets the clock rate on the first serial interface to 64000 bits per second:
| | ```
interface serial 0
  clock rate 64000
``` |
| | For more information about troubleshooting SDLC physical and link-layer problems, see the section "SDLC: Router Cannot Communicate with SDLC Device" earlier in this chapter. |
```

CIP: CLAW Connection Does Not Come Up

Symptom: Common Link Access for Workstations (CLAW) connections do not come up properly over a Channel Interface Processor (CIP). The output of the **show extended channel** *slot/port* **statistics** exec command shows N for CLAW connections, indicating that they are down.

Table 10–13 outlines the problems that might cause this symptom and describes solutions to those problems.

Table 10–13   *CIP: CLAW Connection Does Not Come Up*

Possible Problem	Solution	
TCP/IP not running on host	**Step 1**	Check whether TCP/IP is running on the host.
	Step 2	If TCP/IP is not running, start it.
CIP devices not online to host	**Step 1**	Check the mainframe to see whether the CIP devices are online to the host.
	Step 2	If the CIP devices are not online, vary them online. If devices do not come online, see the section "CIP: CIP Will Not Come Online to Host" later in this chapter.
	Step 3	Check whether the TCP/IP device has been started.
	Step 4	If the device has not been started, start it.
		Note: It might be necessary to stop and start the TCP/IP application to start the device. If you are using obey files, this might not be necessary.
	Step 5	Check the configuration for the CIP in the TCP/IP profile on the host, and check the router configuration for the CIP device.
	Step 6	Use the **moretrace claw** command on the host, either from an obey file or in the TCP/IP profile. This command traces the establishment of CLAW connections and can provide information that is useful for determining causes of connection problems.

CIP: No Enabled LED On

Symptom: The Enabled LED on the CIP card does not come on.

Table 10–14 outlines the problems that might cause this symptom and describes solutions to those problems.

Table 10–14   *CIP: No Enabled LED On*

Possible Problem	Solution	
Hardware problem	**Step 1**	Check to make sure that the router is plugged in and turned on.
	Step 2	Use the **show version** exec command and see whether the CIP card appears in the output.
	Step 3	If the CIP card appears in the output, the Enabled LED might be faulty.
	Step 4	If the CIP card does not appear in the output, reseat the CIP card, reboot the router, and check the output of the **show version** command again.
Old Cisco IOS release	**Step 1**	Use the **show version** exec command to find out what version of the Cisco IOS software you are running.
	Step 2	If you are using Cisco IOS software prior to Release 10.2(6), you should upgrade to a more recent version.

CIP: CIP Will Not Come Online to Host

Symptom: The CIP card will not come online to the host.

Table 10–15 outlines the problem that might cause this symptom and describes solutions to that problem.

Table 10–15   *CIP: CIP Will Not Come Online to Host*

Possible Problem	Solution	
CHPID[1] not online to host	**Step 1**	Make sure the Enabled LED on the CIP card is on. If it is not on, refer to the section "CIP: No Enabled LED On" earlier in this chapter.
	Step 2	Use the **show extended channel** *slot/port* **subchannel** command and check for the SIGNAL flag in the output.
	Step 3	If the SIGNAL flag is not present, check whether the CHPID is online to the host. If it is not, configure it to come online.
		Note: On a bus and tag channel, the SIGNAL flag is turned on by OP_OUT being high from the host. On an ESCON channel, the SIGNAL flag is turned on by the presence of light on the channel.
	Step 4	If the CHPID does not come online to the host, check the physical cabling.
	Step 5	If the CIP still does not come online, check the IOCP[2] definitions for the CIP device, and check the router configuration.

[1] CHPID = channel path identifier
[2] IOCP = input/output control program

CIP: Router Cannot ping Host or Host Cannot ping Router

Symptom: Attempts to **ping** are unsuccessful, either from the CIP card in a router to a host or from a host to the CIP card in a router.

Table 10–16 outlines the problem that might cause this symptom and describes solutions to that problem.

Table 10–16 *CIP: Router Cannot **ping** Host or Host Cannot **ping** Router*

Possible Problem	Solution	
Addressing problem between CIP and host	**Step 1**	Verify that the CLAW connection is up by checking the output of the **show extended channel** *slot/port* **statistics** exec command on the router.
	Step 2	If the output shows that CLAW connections are not up (indicated by a N), refer to the section "CIP: CLAW Connection Does Not Come Up" earlier in this chapter.
	Step 3	If the CLAW connections are up (indicated by a Y), issue the **clear counters** privileged exec command. Then attempt a basic **ping** to the host from the router or to the router from the host.
	Step 4	When the ping is completed, use the **show extended channel** *slot/port* **statistics** exec command on the router.
		If you issued the **ping** from the router to the host, the host should have read five 100-byte ICMP echos from the router. The Total Blocks field in the **show** command output should indicate five blocks read. If the host replied, the output should indicate five blocks written.
		If you issued the **ping** from the host to the router, the host should have sent one 276-byte ICMP echo to the router. The Write field should indicate one block written. If the router replied, the output should indicate one block in the Read field.
	Step 5	If this is not the case, there could be an addressing problem between the CIP and the host. Check all IP addresses on the router and in the host TCP/IP profile and make sure they are correct.

CIP: Host Cannot Reach Remote Networks

Symptom: Mainframe host cannot access networks across a router.

Table 10–17 outlines the problem that might cause this symptom and describes solutions to that problem.

Table 10–17   *CIP: Host Cannot Reach Remote Networks*

Possible Problem	Solution	
Missing or misconfigured IP routes	**Step 1**	If the mainframe host is unable to communicate with networks on the other side of the router, try to **ping** the remote network from the router.
		If the **ping** succeeds, proceed to Step 4.
	Step 2	If the **ping** fails, use the **show ip route** privileged exec command to verify that the network is accessible by the router.
	Step 3	If there is no route to the network, check the network and router configuration for problems.
	Step 4	Verify that the host connection is active by **ping**ing the host IP address from the router. If the **ping** is unsuccessful, see the section "CIP: Router Cannot **ping** Host or Host Cannot **ping** Router" earlier in this chapter.
	Step 5	Issue the **netstat gate** command on the host and check for a route to the network.
	Step 6	If a route does not exist, make sure the host is using the address of the CIP in the router as the default route. If it is not, add a GATEWAY statement in the TCP/IP profile that points to the network, or set the CIP in the router as the default route using a DEFAULTNET statement in the TCP/IP profile.

CIP: Host Running Routed Has No Routes

Symptom: A host running routed has no routes to remote networks.

Table 10–18 outlines the problems that might cause this symptom and describes solutions to those problems.

Table 10–18 *CIP: Host Running Routed Has No Routes*

Possible Problem	Solution
RIP not properly configured on the router	**Step 1** Use the **show running-config** privileged exec command to view the router configuration. Make sure RIP is configured on the router. If RIP is not configured, configure it.
	Step 2 Check the configuration to see whether there are **network** statements for each of the networks that should be advertised in RIP updates. If they are missing, add them to the configuration.
	Step 3 Make sure the **passive-interface** command is not configured on the channel interface.
	Step 4 If the command is present, remove it using the **no passive-interface** router configuration command.
	Step 5 Make sure there are no **distribute-list** statements filtering RIP routing updates.
	Step 6 Check the router configuration to be sure the **broadcast** keyword has been specified in the **claw** interface configuration command. The following is the **claw** command syntax: **claw** *path device-address ip-address host-name device-name host-app device-app* [*broadcast*] **Example:** The following example shows how to enable IBM channel-attach routing on the CIP port 0, which is supporting a directly connected ESCON channel: ``` interface channel 3/0 ip address 198.92.0.1 255.255.255.0 claw 0100 00 198.92.0.21 CISCOVM EVAL TCPIP TCPIP ```
	Step 7 If there is no **broadcast** keyword specified, add it to the configuration.

Table 10–18   *CIP: Host Running Routed Has No Routes, Continued*

Possible Problem	Solution
Host misconfiguration	**Step 1** Use the **netstat gate** command on the host. Check whether there are routes learned from RIP updates.
	Step 2 If you do not see RIP routes, verify that the host connection is active by **ping**ing the host IP address from the router.
	Step 3 If the **ping** is unsuccessful, see the section "CIP: Router Cannot **ping** Host or Host Cannot **ping** Router" earlier in this chapter.
	Step 4 Verify that the *routed* daemon is running on the host.
	Step 5 Use the **show extended channel** *slot/port* **stat** exec command to see whether RIP routing updates are incrementing the counters.
	Step 6 Check the TCP/IP profile on the host to be sure that there are BSDROUTINGPARMS instead of GATEWAY statements.

CHAPTER 11

Troubleshooting DECnet

Digital Equipment Corporation (Digital) developed the DECnet protocol family to provide a well-thought-out way for its computers to communicate with one another. The first version of DECnet, released in 1975, allowed two directly attached PDP-11 minicomputers to communicate. In more recent years, Digital has included support for nonproprietary protocols, but DECnet remains the most important of Digital's network product offerings.

DECnet is currently in its fifth major product release (sometimes called *Phase V* and referred to as DECnet/OSI in Digital literature). DECnet Phase V is a superset of the OSI protocol suite and supports all OSI protocols as well as several other proprietary and standard protocols that were supported in previous versions of DECnet. As with past changes to the protocol, DECnet Phase V is compatible with the previous release (Phase IV, in this case).

DIGITAL NETWORK ARCHITECTURE

Contrary to popular belief, DECnet is not a network architecture at all but is, rather, a series of products conforming to Digital's Digital Network Architecture (DNA). Like most comprehensive network architectures from large systems vendors, DNA supports a large set of both proprietary and standard protocols. The list of DNA-supported technologies grows constantly as Digital implements new protocols. Figure 11–1 illustrates an incomplete snapshot of DNA and the relationship of some of its components to the OSI reference model.

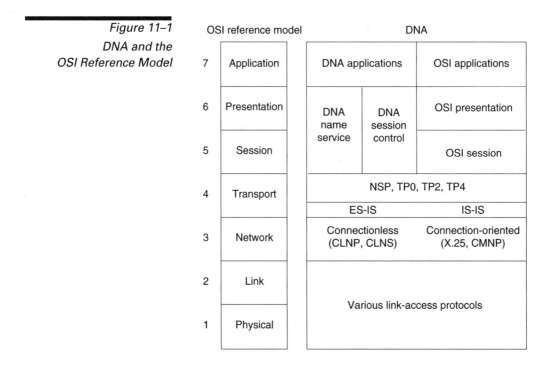

Figure 11–1

DNA and the
OSI Reference Model

As Figure 11–1 shows, DNA supports a variety of media and link implementations. Among these are well-known standards such as Ethernet, Token Ring, Fiber Distributed Data Interface (FDDI), IEEE 802.2, and X.25. DNA also offers a traditional point-to-point link-layer protocol called *Digital Data Communications Message Protocol* (DDCMP) and a 70-Mbps bus used in the VAX cluster called the *computer-room interconnect bus* (CI bus).

THE NETWORK LAYER

DECnet supports both connectionless and connection-oriented network layers. Both network layers are implemented by OSI protocols. The connectionless implementation uses the Connectionless Network Protocol (CLNP) and the Connectionless Network Service (CLNS). The connection-oriented network layer uses the X.25 Packet-Level Protocol (PLP), which is also known as X.25 Level 3, and the Connection-Mode Network Protocol (CMNP).

Although most of DNA was brought into OSI conformance with DECnet Phase V, DECnet Phase IV routing was already very similar to OSI routing. Phase V DNA routing consists of OSI routing (ES-IS and IS-IS), plus continued support for the DECnet Phase IV routing protocol.

DECnet Phase IV Routing Frame Format

The DECnet Phase IV routing protocol differs from IS-IS in several ways. One difference is in the protocol header. The DNA Phase IV routing layer header is shown in Figure 11–2; IS-IS packet formats are shown in Chapter 12, "Troubleshooting ISO CLNS."

Field length,
in bytes   1   2   2   1

Routing flags	Destination node	Source node	Nodes traversed

Figure 11–2

A DNA Phase IV Routing Layer Header

The first field in a DNA Phase IV routing header is the routing flags field, which includes:

- A return-to-sender bit that, if set, indicates that the packet is returning to the source.
- A return-to-sender-request bit that, if set, indicates that request packets should be returned to the source if they cannot be delivered to the destination.
- An intraLAN bit, which is on by default. If the router detects that the two communicating end systems are not on the same subnetwork, it turns the bit off.
- Other bits that indicate header format, whether padding is being used, and other functions.

The destination node and source node fields identify the network addresses of the destination nodes and the source node.

The nodes traversed field shows the number of nodes the packet has traversed on its way to the destination. This field allows implementation of a maximum hop count so that obsolete packets can be removed from the network.

DECnet identifies two types of nodes: end nodes and routing nodes. Both end nodes and routing nodes can send and receive network information, but only routing nodes can provide routing services for other DECnet nodes.

DECnet routing decisions are based on cost, an arbitrary measure assigned by network administrators to be used in comparing various paths through an internetwork environment. Costs are typically based on hop count, media bandwidth, or other measures. The lower the cost, the better the path. When network faults occur, the DECnet Phase IV routing protocol uses cost values to recalculate the best paths to each destination. Figure 11–3 illustrates the calculation of costs in a DECnet Phase IV routing environment.

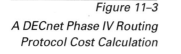

Figure 11–3

A DECnet Phase IV Routing Protocol Cost Calculation

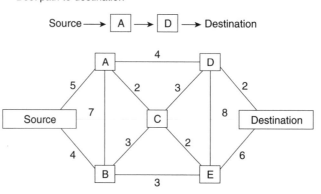

Addressing

DECnet addresses are not associated with the physical networks to which the nodes are connected. Instead, DECnet locates hosts using area/node address pairs. An area's value ranges from 1 to 63, inclusive. A node address can be between 1 and 1,023, inclusive. Therefore, each area can have 1,023 nodes, and approximately 65,000 nodes can be addressed in a DECnet network. Areas can span many routers, and a single cable can support many areas. Therefore, if a node has several network interfaces, it uses the same area/node address for each interface. Figure 11–4 shows a sample DECnet network with several addressable entities.

Figure 11–4

Examples of DECnet Addresses

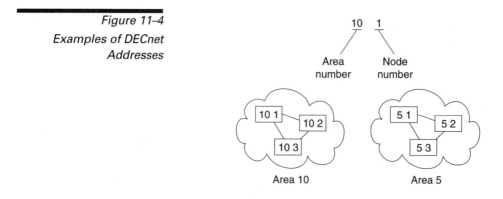

DECnet hosts do not use manufacturer-assigned Media Access Control (MAC)-layer addresses. Instead, network-level addresses are embedded in the MAC-layer address according to an algorithm that multiplies the area number by 1,024 and adds the node number to the product. The resulting 16-bit decimal address is converted to a hexadecimal number and appended to the address AA00.0400 in byte-swapped order, with the least significant byte first. For example, DECnet address 12.75 becomes 12363 (base 10), which equals 304B (base 16). After this byte-swapped address is appended to the standard DECnet MAC address prefix, the resulting address is AA00.0400.4B30.

Routing Levels

DECnet routing nodes are referred to as either Level 1 or Level 2 routers. A Level 1 router communicates with end nodes and with other Level 1 routers in a particular area. Level 2 routers communicate with Level 1 routers in the same area and with Level 2 routers in different areas. Together, Level 1 and Level 2 routers form a hierarchical routing scheme. This relationship is illustrated in Figure 11–5.

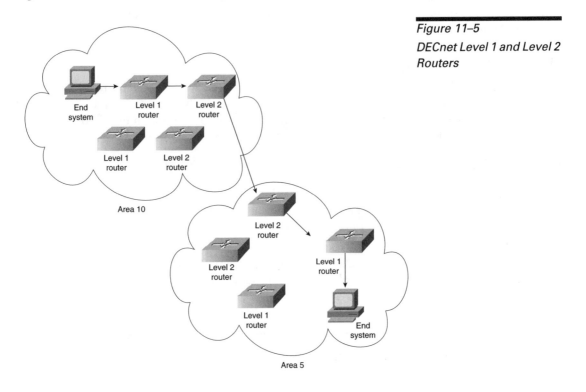

Figure 11–5
DECnet Level 1 and Level 2 Routers

End systems send routing requests to a designated Level 1 router. The Level 1 router with the highest priority is elected to be the designated router. If two routers have the same priority, the one with the larger node number becomes the designated router. A router's priority can be manually configured to force it to become the designated router.

As shown in Figure 11–5, multiple Level 2 routers can exist in any area. When a Level 1 router wishes to send a packet outside its area, it forwards the packet to a Level 2 router in the same area. In some cases, the Level 2 router may not have the optimal path to the destination, but the mesh network configuration offers a degree of fault tolerance not provided by the simple assignment of one Level 2 router per area.

THE TRANSPORT LAYER

The DNA transport layer is implemented by a variety of transports, both proprietary and standard. OSI transports TP0, TP2, and TP4 are supported.

Digital's own Network Services Protocol (NSP) is functionally similar to TP4 in that it offers connection-oriented, flow-controlled service with message fragmentation and reassembly. Two subchannels are supported—one for normal data and one for expedited data and flow control information. Two flow control types are supported—a simple start/stop mechanism where the receiver tells the sender when to terminate and resume data transmission and a more complex flow control technique, where the receiver tells the sender how many messages it can accept. NSP can also respond to congestion notifications from the network layer by reducing the number of outstanding messages it will tolerate.

UPPER-LAYER PROTOCOLS

Above the transport layer, DECnet supports its own proprietary upper-layer protocols as well as standard OSI upper-layer protocols. DECnet application protocols use the DNA session control protocol and the DNA name service. OSI application protocols are supported by OSI presentation- and session-layer implementations.

TROUBLESHOOTING DECNET

This section presents protocol-related troubleshooting information for DECnet Phase IV connectivity and performance problems. The procedures outlined apply only to environments in which DECnet routing is enabled on the router, not to environments in which DECnet is being bridged (that is, bridging is enabled on the router interfaces and EtherType 6003 is being passed).

This chapter does not discuss other Digital protocols, such as Maintenance Operation Protocol (MOP), local-area transport (LAT), local-area VAX cluster (LAVC), and local-area systems technology (LAST).

NOTES

For information about troubleshooting ISO CLNS (DECnet Phase V) problems, refer to Chapter 12, "Troubleshooting ISO CLNS."

The section "Using DECnet in a Multiprotocol Environment" discusses possible problems when using DECnet in an internetwork running other protocols as well. The remaining sections describe specific DECnet symptoms, the problems that are likely to cause each symptom, and the solutions to those problems.

The following sections outline the most common network issues in DECnet networks:

- DECnet: Connections to DEC Hosts Fail over Router (End Node Problem)
- DECnet: Connections to DEC Hosts Fail over Router (Router Problem)

- DECnet: End Nodes Cannot Find Designated Router
- DECnet: Router or End Node Sees Incorrect Designated Router
- DECnet: Routers Not Establishing Adjacencies
- DECnet: Routing Node Adjacencies Toggle Up and Down
- DECnet: No Phase IV Connectivity over Phase V Backbone
- DECnet: Poor Performance

NOTES

In some of the symptom discussions that follow, Operator Communication Manager (OPCOM) messages are used to illustrate certain errors. These examples assume that OPCOM is running and event logging is enabled. For more information about event logging, see the section "Configuring a DECnet Node to Log DECnet Events" later in this chapter.

Using DECnet in a Multiprotocol Environment

It is important to remember that DECnet changes the MAC addresses of router interfaces. This behavior can cause problems for other protocols that are already enabled on the router.

If after enabling DECnet on a router interface other protocols (such as Novell IPX or XNS) experience connectivity loss due to address resolution problems, the problem is probably a result of DECnet changing the MAC address of the router interface.

As a rule, enable DECnet on router interfaces first, and then enable other protocols. Otherwise, use the **copy running-config startup-config** command to save the router configuration and then reload the router.

DECnet: Connections to DEC Hosts Fail over Router (End Node Problem)

Symptom: DECnet nodes cannot communicate when attempting to make connections over routers.

NOTES

This section focuses on problems in end nodes. For router-related problems and solutions, see the section "DECnet: Connections to DEC Hosts Fail over Router (Router Problem)" later in this chapter.

Table 11–1 outlines the problems that might cause this symptom and describes solutions to those problems.

Table 11–1 *DECnet: Connections to DEC Hosts Fail over Router (End Node Problem)*

Possible Problem	Solution
Misconfigured end node	**Step 1** Check the end node configuration using the **show executor characteristics** NCP[1] command.
	Step 2 Make sure that the end node type (nonrouting Phase IV, routing Phase IV, area), node address, node name, and routing and link parameters are correctly specified.
	Step 3 Check the circuit characteristics using the **show known circuit characteristics** NCP command.
	Step 4 Make sure that the designated router, hello timer, router priority (if the node is a routing node), and other circuit characteristics are properly configured.
	The following **decnet** commands are used to set the designated router, hello timers, and router priority on a Cisco router:
	decnet hello-timer *seconds*
	• *seconds*—Interval at which the Cisco IOS software sends hello messages. It can be a decimal number in the range 1 to 8191 seconds. The default is 15 seconds.
	decnet router-priority *value*
	To elect a designated router to which packets will be sent when no destination is specified, use the **decnet router-priority** interface configuration command.
	• *value*—Priority of the router. This can be a number in the range 0 through 127. The larger the number, the higher the priority. The default priority is 64.
	Step 5 Reconfigure the end node if any of the end node or circuit characteristics are misconfigured. For information on configuring end nodes, refer to the vendor documentation.

Table 11–1 *DECnet: Connections to DEC Hosts Fail over Router (End Node Problem), Continued*

Possible Problem	Solution
Host access control rejects connection	With this problem, users see the message "connect failed, access control rejected." This is typically a session-layer problem.
	Step 1 Make sure that the following requirements are satisfied:
	• User-supplied access control information is correct
	• Proxy access is set up correctly
	• Proxy database and proxy account are correct
	Step 2 Make sure that the user's security access matches the access specifications for the user on the remote systems.
	Step 3 If there are problems in any of these areas, make changes as necessary.
Unrecognized object	With this problem, users see the message "connect failed, unrecognized object."
	Step 1 Use the **tell** NCP command to determine whether the object is defined on the target node. The syntax of the **tell** command is as follows:
	tell *target-node-name* **show known** *objects*
	Step 2 If the object is not defined, log in as superuser and run NCP to define the object with the **set object** NCP command, as follows:
	set object *object-id*
	Step 3 After the object is defined, use the **tell** NCP command to determine whether the object has a file specified, as follows:
	tell *target-node-name* **show object** *object-id* **character**
	Step 4 Exit NCP and determine whether the file specified for the object exists.
	Step 5 If the file for the requested object does not exist, create the file.
	Step 6 Make sure the permissions for the specified file are correct.

Table 11–1   *DECnet: Connections to DEC Hosts Fail over Router (End Node Problem), Continued*

Possible Problem	Solution

Insufficient resource error	With an insufficient resource error, VMS[2] users see the following message:
	
	`% system-E-REMRSC, insufficient system resource at remote node`
	
	Note: This error message might not indicate a problem. These parameter values can be set intentionally to prevent network connections beyond a certain number.
	
	Try tuning the following DEC target system parameters:
	• SYSGEN parameters:
	  — MAXPROCESSCNT
	• NCP parameters:
	  — MAXIMUM LINKS
	  — ALIAS MAXIMUM LINKS
	• AUTHORIZE parameters:
	  — MAXJOBS
	  — MAXACCTJOBS

[1] NCP = Network Control Program
[2] VMS = Virtual Memory System

Configuring a DECnet Node to Log DECnet Events

In addition to the diagnostic tools available on your router, DECnet environments provide a wealth of diagnostic information. DECnet nodes can use the DECnet Event Logging Facility (EVL) to track DECnet events. EVL allows you to monitor significant network events, such as lost packets and circuit failures.

The following steps outline the basic tasks required to enable event logging on a VMS system:

Step 1   Determine whether the OPCOM process is running:

```
$ show system
```

Step 2   If OPCOM does not appear in the list of running processes, enter the following command to start it:

```
$ @sys$system:STARTUP.com OPCOM
```

Step 3   Use the NCP to enable event logging:

```
$ MCR NCP
NCP> SET logging MONITOR KNOWN Events
NCP> DEFINE logging MONITOR KNOWN Events
NCP> SET logging MONITOR STATE ON
NCP> DEFINE logging MONITOR STATE ON
```

Step 4 Exit NCP:

```
NCP> Exit
```

Step 5 To monitor network events from a console terminal, enter the following command at the VMS system prompt:

```
$ REPLY/ENABLE = NETWORK
```

(This command is equivalent to the **terminal monitor** privileged exec command.)

DECnet: Connections to DEC Hosts Fail over Router (Router Problem)

Symptom: DECnet nodes cannot communicate when attempting to make connections over routers.

NOTES

This section focuses on problems in the router. For end node–related problems and solutions, see the section "DECnet: Connections to DEC Hosts Fail over Router (End Node Problem)" earlier in this chapter.

Table 11–2 outlines the problems that might cause this symptom and describes solutions to those problems.

Table 11–2 *DECnet: Connections to DEC Hosts Fail over Router (Router Problem)*

Possible Problem	Solution
DECnet is not enabled on router	**Step 1** Use the **show decnet interface** privileged exec command to see on which interfaces, if any, DECnet is enabled.
	Step 2 If the output shows that DECnet is not enabled, use the **show running-config** privileged exec command to view the router configuration. Determine whether DECnet global and interface command specifications are configured on the router.
	Step 3 Enable DECnet routing on the appropriate routers and interfaces. For detailed information on configuring DECnet, refer to the Cisco IOS *Network Protocols Configuration Guide, Part 2*.
Missing **decnet cost** command	**Step 1** Make sure that there is a cost configured on DECnet interfaces. Check the configuration for a **decnet cost** *cost-value* interface configuration command entry.
	Step 2 If the command is not present, add the **decnet cost** command for each interface on which DECnet is enabled.

Table 11–2 *DECnet: Connections to DEC Hosts Fail over Router (Router Problem), Continued*

Possible Problem	Solution
End nodes and router area number mismatch	**Step 1** Check the configuration of end nodes and routers on the network segment. Check the area address specified on end nodes and routers.
	Step 2 If an end node is not in the same area as a router on the segment, you must either change the address of the end node to be the same as a router on the segment, or you must reconfigure a router on the segment with the same area number as the end node.
Actual cost to the destination area is more than the configured cost	**Step 1** Use the **show decnet interface** exec command to determine the configured maximum cost to the destination area.
	Step 2 Use the **show decnet route** exec command to determine the actual cost to the destination area.
	Step 3 If the actual cost is more than the configured maximum cost, increase the maximum cost configured on the router.
	On Level 1 routers, use the **decnet max-cost** global configuration command to increase the area maximum cost.
	On Level 2 routers, use the **decnet area-max-cost** global configuration command to increase the area maximum cost.
Actual number of hops to the destination is more than the configured maximum number of hops	**Step 1** Use the **show decnet interface** command to determine the maximum number of hops allowed for intra-area routing.
	Step 2 Use the **show decnet route** exec command to determine the actual number of hops to the destination as shown in the DECnet routing table.
	Step 3 If the actual number of hops is more than the configured maximum allowed hops, increase the maximum hops configured on the router.
	On Level 1 routers, use the **decnet max-hops** global configuration command to increase the maximum hops.
	On Level 2 routers, use the **decnet area-max-hops** global configuration command to increase the maximum number of hops.

Table 11–2 *DECnet: Connections to DEC Hosts Fail over Router (Router Problem), Continued*

Possible Problem	Solution
Access list is misconfigured	**Step 1** Use the **show decnet access-list** privileged exec command to determine whether there are DECnet access lists configured on the router.
	Step 2 If there are access lists applied to router interfaces, use the **debug decnet connects** privileged exec command to determine whether important packets are being forwarded properly.
	Caution: Because debugging output is assigned high priority in the CPU process, it can render the system unusable. For this reason, use **debug** commands only to troubleshoot specific problems or during troubleshooting sessions with Cisco technical support staff. Moreover, it is best to use **debug** commands during periods of lower network traffic and fewer users. Debugging during these periods decreases the likelihood that increased **debug** command processing overhead will affect system use.
	Step 3 If packets are being dropped, disable all access lists on the router using the **no decnet access-group** interface configuration command.
	Step 4 Determine whether connections to hosts are now possible. If connections are made successfully, a misconfigured access list is probably the problem.
	Step 5 Enable access lists on the router using the **decnet access-group** interface configuration command. Enable the lists one at a time until connectivity is lost, at which point you have found the problem access list.
	Step 6 Modify the access list as necessary. Make sure to include explicit **permit** statements for traffic that you want to be forwarded normally.
	Step 7 If problems persist, continue the process until you have isolated all problem access lists.

Table 11–2 *DECnet: Connections to DEC Hosts Fail over Router (Router Problem), Continued*

Possible Problem	Solution
Node address out of range	**Step 1** Use the **show running-config** privileged exec command to view router configurations. Check to see whether the **decnet max-address** global configuration command has been configured. This command sets the highest DECnet node number allowed in the area. **Note:** The **decnet max-address** command specifies the highest node number allowed in an area, *not* the maximum number of node addresses allowed in an area. For example, if you configure the command **decnet max-address 1000** on a router and you configure a node with a node address of 1001, the address is out of range. **Step 2** The default maximum address is 1023. However, if another value is configured, the node address might be more than the configured value. If this is the case, increase the maximum address value using the **decnet max-address** command.
Partitioned area	Make sure the network topology has no discontiguous areas. If any discontiguous areas exist, reconfigure the topology by changing area addresses or by creating a path (with a router) to create a contiguous network.
Media problem	For information on troubleshooting serial lines, refer to Chapter 15, "Troubleshooting Serial Line Problems." For information on troubleshooting LAN media, refer to the media troubleshooting chapter that covers the media type used in your network.

DECnet: End Nodes Cannot Find Designated Router

Symptom: End nodes cannot find a designated router. End nodes cannot access nodes that are on different LANs, but other nodes connected to the same LAN are accessible.

Table 11–3 outlines the problems that might cause this symptom and describes solutions to those problems.

Table 11–3   *DECnet: End Nodes Cannot Find Designated Router*

Possible Problem	Solution	
DECnet not enabled on router	Step 1	Use the **show running-config** privileged exec command to view the router configuration. Determine whether DECnet global configuration and interface command specifications are configured on the router.
	Step 2	Enable DECnet routing on the appropriate routers and interfaces. For detailed information on configuring DECnet, refer to the *Cisco IOS Network Protocols Configuration Guide, Part 2*.
End nodes and router area number mismatch	Step 1	Check the configuration of end nodes and routers on the network segment. Check the area address specified on end nodes and routers. Use the **show running-config** privileged exec command to view the router configuration.
	Step 2	If an end node is not in the same area as a router on the segment, you must either change the address of the end node to be the same as that of a router on the segment, or you must reconfigure a router on the segment with the same area number as the end node.
Hello packets are not being exchanged	Step 1	Use the **debug decnet adj** privileged exec command to determine whether the router is sending hello packets and whether hellos are being received.
	Step 2	**Caution:** Because debugging output is assigned high priority in the CPU process, it can render the system unusable. For this reason, use **debug** commands only to troubleshoot specific problems or during troubleshooting sessions with Cisco technical support staff. Moreover, it is best to use **debug** commands during periods of lower network traffic and fewer users. Debugging during these periods decreases the likelihood that increased **debug** command processing overhead will affect system use.
	Step 3	If no exchange is occurring, use the **show interfaces** exec command to determine whether the interface input and output queues are full. A full input queue is indicated by a value of 75/75, and a full output queue is indicated by a value of 40/40.
	Step 4	If the queues are full and no hello packets are being exchanged, contact your technical support representative.
	Step 5	If routers are sending hello packets, check end nodes to determine why end nodes are rejecting hello packets.

Table 11–3   *DECnet: End Nodes Cannot Find Designated Router, Continued*

Possible Problem	Solution
Media problem	For information on troubleshooting serial lines, refer to Chapter 15, "Troubleshooting Serial Line Problems." For information on troubleshooting LAN media, refer to the media troubleshooting chapter that covers the media type used in your network.

DECnet: Router or End Node Sees Incorrect Designated Router

Symptom: Routers and end nodes see an incorrect or an unexpected designated router. If your network requires a specific router to be elected the designated router, allowing another router to become a designated router can cause unpredictable network behavior and can block connectivity in and out of the area.

Table 11–4 outlines the problems that might cause this symptom and describes solutions to those problems.

Table 11–4   *DECnet: Router or End Node Sees Incorrect Designated Router*

Possible Problem	Solution
Priority of the expected designated router is not configured correctly	**Step 1** Use the **show decnet interface** exec command to determine which router is the designated router. Note the priority of the router that is shown in the command output. **Step 2** If the designated router identified in the output is not the correct router, use the **show decnet interface** command on the expected designated router and the actual designated router. **Step 3** Compare the priority of the actual designated router with that of the expected designated router. The router that you want to be the designated router should have the highest priority. Syntax: **Step 4** If necessary, use the **decnet router-priority** interface configuration command to give a higher priority to a router so that it will be elected the designated router. The following is the syntax for the **decnet router-priority** command: **decnet router-priority** *value* To elect a designated router to which packets will be sent when no destination is specified, use the **decnet router-priority** interface configuration command. Syntax: • *value*—Priority of the router. This can be a number in the range 0 through 127. The larger the number, the higher the priority. The default priority is 64.

Table 11–4 *DECnet: Router or End Node Sees Incorrect Designated Router, Continued*

Possible Problem	Solution
Multiple routers have the same router priority	**Step 1** Use the **show decnet interface** command to determine which router is the designated router. Note the priority of the router that is shown in the command output. **Step 2** Use the **show decnet interface** command on the expected designated router and compare the priorities of the actual and the expected designated routers. **Step 3** If the routers have the same priority, use the **decnet router-priority** interface configuration command to configure a higher priority on the router that should be elected the designated router. **Syntax:** The following is the syntax for the **decnet router-priority** command: **decnet router-priority** *value* To elect a designated router to which packets will be sent when no destination is specified, use the **decnet router-priority** interface configuration command. **Syntax:** • *value*—Priority of the router. This can be a number in the range 0 through 127. The larger the number, the higher the priority. The default priority is 64. **Note:** If two routers are configured with the same priority, the router with the higher node number will become the designated router.
Adjacency between nodes is not bidirectional	**Step 1** Use the **show decnet route** exec command to see whether the adjacency with the expected designated router is in a "down" or "initializing" state. **Step 2** Use the **debug decnet adj privileged** exec command to determine whether hello packets are being exchanged. **Caution:** Because debugging output is assigned high priority in the CPU process, it can render the system unusable. For this reason, use **debug** commands only to troubleshoot specific problems or during troubleshooting sessions with Cisco technical support staff. Moreover, it is best to use **debug** commands during periods of lower network traffic and fewer users. Debugging during these periods decreases the likelihood that increased **debug** command processing overhead will affect system use. **Step 3** If a router is not sending hello packets, use the **show interfaces** command to determine whether the interface input and output queues are full. A full input queue is indicated by a value of 75/75, and a full output queue is indicated by a value of 40/40. **Step 4** If the queues are full, and no hello packets are being exchanged, contact your router technical support representative.

Table 11–4   *DECnet: Router or End Node Sees Incorrect Designated Router, Continued*

Possible Problem	Solution
Adjacency between nodes is not bidirectional *(Continued)*	**Step 5** If routers are sending hello packets, contact end-node administrators to determine why end nodes are rejecting hello packets.

DECnet: Routers Not Establishing Adjacencies

Symptom: Routers do not establish adjacencies with other routers on the same LAN.

Table 11–5 outlines the problems that might cause this symptom and describes solutions to those problems.

Table 11–5   *DECnet: Router Not Establishing Adjacencies*

Possible Problem	Solution
More than 32 routers on the network	DECnet limits the number of adjacencies that can be established by a router to 32. **Step 1** Enable the **debug decnet events** privileged exec command to determine whether the adjacency is being rejected. Enable this command on one router at a time. **Caution:** Because debugging output is assigned high priority in the CPU process, it can render the system unusable. For this reason, use **debug** commands only to troubleshoot specific problems or during troubleshooting sessions with Cisco technical support staff. Moreover, it is best to use **debug** commands during periods of lower network traffic and fewer users. Debugging during these periods decreases the likelihood that increased **debug** command processing overhead will affect system use. **Step 2** If the adjacency is being rejected, reduce the number of adjacent routers or increase the priority of a router that you want to be adjacent so that it has a higher priority than one of the other neighboring routers. An adjacency will be established with the router you want instead of with a router assigned a lower priority. **Syntax:** The following is the syntax to adjust the priority of a router: **decnet router-priority** *value* To elect a designated router to which packets will be sent when no destination is specified, use the **decnet router-priority** interface configuration command. **Syntax Description:** • *value*—Priority of the router. This can be a number in the range 0 through 127. The larger the number, the higher the priority. The default priority is 64.

Table 11-5 *DECnet: Router Not Establishing Adjacencies, Continued*

Possible Problem	Solution
Node address out of range	**Step 1** Use the **show running-config** privileged exec command to view router configurations. Check to see whether the **decnet max-address** global configuration command has been configured. This command sets the highest DECnet node number allowed in the area. Note: The **decnet max-address** command specifies the highest node number allowed in an area, *not* the maximum number of node addresses allowed in an area. For example, if you configure the command **decnet max-address 1000** on a router and you configure a node with a node address of 1001, the address is out of range. **Step 2** The default maximum address is 1023. However, if another value is configured, the node address might be more than the configured value. If this is the case, increase the maximum address value using the **decnet max-address** command.
Router area number is higher than configured **decnet max-area**	If the area number of a DECnet node (such as a router) is higher than the configured **decnet max-area** value, the adjacency will be reset. **Step 1** Use the **show running-config** privileged exec command to view the router configuration. Look for **decnet max-area** global configuration command entries. This command sets the DECnet maximum area number for the router. Note: The **decnet max-area** command specifies the highest area value allowed in the network, *not* the maximum number of areas configurable. For example, if you configure the command **decnet max-area 60** and you configure a node with area number 61, the node's area address is out of range. **Step 2** Use the **show running-config** privileged exec command to find the area number configured on other DECnet routers. Compare the value configured by the **decnet max-area** command to the area numbers of other routers. **Step 3** If a router's area number is higher than the value configured by the **decnet max-area** global configuration command, reconfigure the **decnet max-area** command so that the DECnet maximum area is higher than the area number of all routers.

Table 11–5   *DECnet: Router Not Establishing Adjacencies, Continued*

Possible Problem	Solution
Adjacency between routers is not bidirectional	**Step 1** Use the **show decnet route** exec command to see if the adjacency with the expected designated router is in a "down" or "initializing" state.
	Step 2 If you are troubleshooting a nonbroadcast multiaccess network (such as Frame Relay or X.25), make sure that **map** statements are properly configured.
	To establish an address translation for selected nodes, use the **decnet map** global configuration command:
	Syntax:
	decnet *first-network* **map** *virtual-address second-network real-address*
	• *first-network*—DECnet network numbers in the range 0 to 3.
	• *virtual-address*—Numeric DECnet address (10.5, for example).
	• *second-network*—DECnet network number you map to; DECnet numbers range 0 to 3.
	Syntax Description:
	• *real-address*—Numeric DECnet address (10.5, for example).
	Step 3 Use the **debug decnet adj** privileged exec command to determine whether hello packets are being exchanged.
	Step 4 If a router is not sending hello packets, use the **show interfaces** command to determine whether the interface input and output queues are full. A full input queue is indicated by a value of 75/75, and a full output queue is indicated by a value of 40/40.
	Step 5 If the queues are full, and no hello packets are being exchanged, contact your router technical support representative.

DECnet: Routing Node Adjacencies Toggle Up and Down

Symptom: Routing adjacencies toggle up and down. Output such as the following appears repeatedly on the DEC system console:

```
%%%%%%%%%% OPCOM 30-JUN-1993 1:25:07.45 %%%%%%%%%%
Message from user DECNET on The Bay
DECnet event 4.16, adjacency rejected
From NODE 12.1 (The Bay), 30-JUN-1993 1:25:07.45
Circuit UNA-0, Adjacent node = 1.101 (Vax1)

%%%%%%%%%% OPCOM 30-JUN-1993 1:25:07.46 %%%%%%%%%%
Message from user DECNET on The Bay
DECnet event 4.15, adjacency up
From NODE 12.1 (The Bay), 30-JUN-1993 1:25:07.46
Circuit UNA-0, Adjacent node = 1.12 (Vax2)
```

This output indicates that routers are constantly being added to and removed from the routing table. The OPCOM messages specify DECnet events 4.16 (adjacency rejected) and 4.15 (adjacency up) for specific routing nodes.

Table 11–6 outlines the problems that might cause this symptom and describes solutions to those problems.

Table 11–6 *DECnet: Routing Node Adjacencies Toggle Up and Down*

Possible Problem	Solution
Total number of routing nodes on network segment is more than 32	DECnet limits the number of adjacencies that can be established by a router to 32.
	Step 1 Enable the **debug decnet events** privileged exec command to determine whether the adjacency is being rejected. Enable this command on one router at a time.
	Step 2 If the adjacency is being rejected, reduce the number of adjacent routers on the segment.
Hardware problem	Check the error message output to identify the routing node or nodes that are causing the adjacency to toggle.
	Follow the procedures outlined in Chapter 3, "Troubleshooting Hardware and Booting Problems."

DECnet: No Phase IV Connectivity over Phase V Backbone

Symptom: Communication between DECnet Phase IV areas separated by an ISO CLNS (Phase V) backbone fails. Phase IV nodes cannot communicate with other Phase IV nodes across a Phase V cloud. However, nodes can communicate with one another within the same Phase IV cloud.

NOTES

For more information about troubleshooting DECnet /OSI internetworks, see Chapter 12, "Troubleshooting ISO CLNS."

Table 11–7 outlines the problems that might cause this symptom and describes solutions to those problems.

Table 11–7   *DECnet: No DECnet Phase IV Connectivity over Phase V Backbone*

Possible Problem	Solution
Misconfigured addresses	**Step 1** Use the **show interfaces** command to confirm that CLNS and DECnet Phase IV are both configured on ISO CLNS backbone routers.
	Step 2 Make sure that the **decnet conversion** global configuration command is configured on backbone routers to allow DECnet Phase IV–to–ISO CLNS conversion.
	Step 3 Use the **show running-config** privileged exec command on backbone routers to verify that DECnet addresses agree with CLNS addresses.
	Two kinds of addresses are easily misconfigured: DECnet addresses, which should be specified in decimal, and CLNS Network Service Access Point addresses, which should be specified in hexadecimal.
	For more information, refer to the section "DECnet Phase IV and ISO CLNS Addresses" later in this chapter.
	Step 4 If the area addresses do not agree, confirm the address specifications and reconfigure the DECnet and CLNS addresses on the router.
	For detailed information on configuring DECnet Phase IV, CLNS, and conversion, refer to the *Cisco IOS Network Protocol Configuration Guide, Part 2*.

Table 11–7 *DECnet: No DECnet Phase IV Connectivity over Phase V Backbone, Continued*

Possible Problem	Solution
ISO CLNS or DECnet not enabled on appropriate interfaces	**Step 1** On Phase IV routers bordering the backbone, use the **show clns interface** and **show decnet interface** commands to see which interfaces are running which protocols.
	Verify that DECnet and ISO CLNS are enabled on backbone router interfaces where conversion will occur.
	Step 2 If DECnet is not configured on the correct interfaces, enable it. Make sure you specify the **decnet cost** interface configuration command to assign a cost to the interface. If ISO CLNS routing is not configured on the correct interfaces, use the **clns router** interface configuration command. The full syntax for this command is
	clns *routing*
	Use the **no clns** *routing* command to disable CLNS routing:
	no clns *routing*
	For detailed information on configuring DECnet Phase IV and ISO CLNS, refer to the Cisco IOS *Network Protocol Configuration Guide, Part 2.*

DECnet Phase IV and ISO CLNS Addresses

Address conversion between DECnet Phase IV and ISO CLNS (Phase V) requires that NSAP addresses be Phase IV compatible. If an address can be converted to a valid Phase IV address, it is Phase IV compatible.

To be compatible, the OSI area number must be between 1 and 63 (when converted to decimal) and the OSI station ID must be in the format AA00.0400.*xxxx*. In addition, the OSI area and the DECnet area (calculated from the OSI station ID) must match. This allows the DECnet Phase IV address to be extracted properly from the NSAP.

Table 11–8 shows addresses and their equivalent DECnet Phase IV addresses, and indicates whether the NSAP address is Phase IV compatible and why.

Table 11–8   *OSI NSAP–to–DECnet Phase IV Address Conversion*

OSI NSAP Address (Hex)	OSI Area	DECnet Address (Decimal)	Phase-IV Compatible
49.1111.0012.AA00.0400.0149.20	18	18.257	Yes
49.1111.0009.AA00.0400.BC04.20	9	1.188	No—OSI area does not match the DECnet area
49.1111.0041.AA00.0400.FFFF.20	65	63.1023	No—OSI area is greater than 63
49.1111.000E.AA00.0400.0000.20	14	0.0	No—DECnet address in NSAP station ID is invalid
49.1111.0009.0800.2B05.8297.20	9	—	No—NSAP station ID is not in the proper format (AA00.0400.*xxxx*)

DECnet: Poor Performance

Symptom: Performance in a DECnet network is slow or unreliable. Connections to hosts over one or more routers are periodically inaccessible or drop unexpectedly.

Table 11–9 outlines the problems that might cause this symptom and describes solutions to those problems.

Table 11–9   *DECnet: Poor Performance*

Possible Problem	Solution	
DECnet traffic problem	**Step 1**	Use the **show decnet traffic** exec command and check the Received and Forwarded fields in the output. In most cases, the values in these fields should match.
	Step 2	If the values do not match, check the Returned, Converted, Access Control Failed, No Route, and Encapsulation Failed fields to see what is causing the performance problem.
	Step 3	If the problem cannot be isolated or solved, contact your technical support representative for assistance.

Table 11–9 *DECnet: Poor Performance, Continued*

Possible Problem	Solution	
Timer mismatch	**Step 1**	Use the **show decnet interface** exec command on all routers in the network. Verify that the values configured for hello timers and routing update timers are consistent among all routers in the network.
		The following is example output from the **show decnet interface** command:
| | | ```
C4500#show decnet interface
[...]
Ethernet0 is up, line protocol is up, encapsulation is ARPA
  Interface cost is 50, priority is 64, DECnet network: 0
  We are the designated router
  Sending HELLOs every 15 seconds, routing updates 40 seconds
[...]
``` |
	Step 2	If timer values are inconsistent, bring routers into conformance using the **decnet hello-timer** and the **decnet routing-timer** interface configuration commands. The hello timer can be restored to its default, 15 seconds, by using the **no** form of the command.
Media problem	**Step 1**	Use the **show interfaces** exec command and look for CRCs[1] in the output.
	Step 2	If there are CRCs, there is probably a media problem. Refer to the media troubleshooting chapter that covers the media type used in your network.
Input and Output queue drops	**Step 1**	Use the **show interfaces** exec command to check the input and output queues. Look for drops. Each number is followed by a slash, the maximum size of the queue, and the number of packets dropped because the queue is full.
	Step 2	If drops are occurring, contact your technical support representative for assistance.

[1] CRC = cyclic redundancy checks
```

CHAPTER 12

Troubleshooting ISO CLNS

This chapter presents protocol-related troubleshooting information for International Organization for Standardization (ISO) Connectionless Network Service (CLNS) protocol connectivity and performance problems. ISO CLNS is a network layer standard that is part of the Open System Interconnection (OSI) protocol suite.

The Cisco IOS software supports packet forwarding and routing for ISO CLNS on networks using a variety of data link layers: Ethernet, Token Ring, Fiber Distributed Data Interface (FDDI), and serial. You can use CLNS routing on serial interfaces with High-Level Data Link Control (HDLC), Point-to-Point Protocol (PPP), Link Access Procedure, Balanced (LAPB), X.25, Switched Multimegabit Data Service (SMDS), or Frame Relay encapsulation. To use HDLC encapsulation, you must have a router at both ends of the link. If you use X.25 encapsulation, you must manually enter the network service access point (NSAP)-to-X.121 mapping. The LAPB, X.25, Frame Relay, and SMDS encapsulations interoperate with other vendors.

Cisco's CLNS implementation is also compliant with the Government Open Systems Interconnection Profile (GOSIP) Version 2. As part of its CLNS support, Cisco routers fully support the following ISO and American National Standards Institute (ANSI) standards:

- ISO 9542—Documents the End System-to-Intermediate System (ES-IS) routing exchange protocol.

- ISO 8473—Documents the ISO Connectionless Network Protocol (CLNP).

- ISO 8348/Ad2—Documents NSAP addresses.

- ISO 10589—Documents Intermediate System-to-Intermediate System (IS-IS) Intra-domain Routing Exchange Protocol.

Both the ISO-developed IS-IS routing protocol and Cisco's ISO Interior Gateway Routing Protocol (IGRP) are supported for dynamic routing of ISO CLNS. In addition, static routing for ISO CLNS is supported.

ISO CLNS TECHNOLOGY BASICS

The world of OSI networking has a unique terminology:

- *End system* (ES) refers to any nonrouting network device.
- *Intermediate system* (IS) refers to a router.
- *Area* is a group of contiguous networks and attached hosts that are specified by a network administrator or manager to be an area.
- *Domain* is a collection of connected areas. Routing domains provide full connectivity to all end systems within them.

ISO CLNS Addressing

Addresses in the ISO network architecture are referred to as NSAP addresses and network entity titles (NETs). Each node in an OSI network has one or more NETs. In addition, each node has many NSAP addresses. Each NSAP address differs from one of the NETs for that node in only the last byte (see Figure 12–1). This byte is called the *n-selector*. Its function is similar to the port number in other protocol suites.

Cisco's implementation supports all NSAP address formats that are defined by ISO 8348/Ad2; however, Cisco provides dynamic routing (ISO-IGRP or IS-IS routing) only for NSAP addresses that conform to the address constraints defined in the ISO standard for IS-IS (ISO 10589).

An NSAP address consists of two major fields:

- The initial domain part (IDP) is made up of 1-byte AFI and a variable-length initial domain identifier (IDI). The length of the IDI and the encoding format for the domain-specific part (DSP) are based on the value of the authority and format identifier (AFI).
- The DSP is made up of a high-order DSP, an area ID, a system ID, and a 1-byte n-selector.

The key difference between the ISO-IGRP and IS-IS NSAP addressing schemes is in the definition of area addresses. Both use the system ID for Level 1 routing. However, they differ in the way addresses are specified for area routing. An ISO-IGRP NSAP address includes three separate levels for routing: the domain, area, and system ID. An IS-IS address includes two fields: a single continuous area field comprising the domain and area fields defined for ISO-IGRP and the system ID.

Figure 12–1 illustrates the ISO-IGRP NSAP addressing structure.

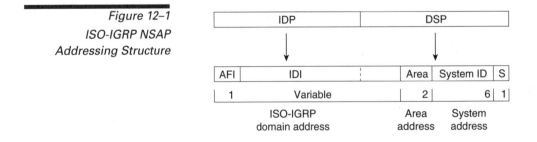

Figure 12–1
ISO-IGRP NSAP
Addressing Structure

The ISO-IGRP NSAP address is divided into three parts: a domain part, an area address, and a system ID. Domain routing is performed on the domain part of the address. Area routing for a given domain uses the area address. System ID routing for a given area uses the system ID part. The NSAP address is laid out as follows:

- The domain part is of variable length and comes before the area address.
- The area address is the 2 bytes before the system ID.
- The system ID is the 6 bytes before the n-selector.
- The n-selector (S) is the last byte of the NSAP address.

Our ISO-IGRP routing implementation interprets the bytes from the AFI up to (but not including) the area field in the DSP as a domain identifier. The area field specifies the area, and the system ID specifies the system.

Figure 12–2 illustrates the IS-IS NSAP addressing structure.

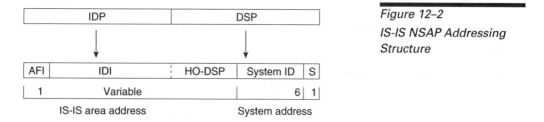

Figure 12–2

IS-IS NSAP Addressing Structure

An IS-IS NSAP address is divided into two parts: an area address (AA) and a system ID. Level 2 routing uses the AA. Level 1 routing uses the system ID address. The NSAP address is laid out as follows:

- The n-selector (S) is the last byte of the NSAP address.
- The system ID is found between the area address and the n-selector byte.
- The area address is the NSAP address, not including the system ID and n-selector.

The IS-IS routing protocol interprets the bytes from the AFI up to (but not including) the system ID field in the DSP as an area identifier. The system ID specifies the system.

Addressing Rules

All NSAP addresses must obey the following constraints:

- No two nodes can have addresses with the same NET; that is, addresses can match all but the n-selector (S) field in the DSP.
- ISO-IGRP requires at least 10 bytes of length; 1 for domain, 2 for area, 6 for system ID, and 1 for n-selector.

- Cisco's implementation of IS-IS requires at least 8 bytes; 1 for area, 6 for system ID, and 1 for n-selector.

- No two nodes residing within the same area can have addresses in which the system ID fields are the same.

The following are examples of OSI network and GOSIP NSAP addresses using the ISO-IGRP implementation. The second example is the OSI network NSAP address format:

```
47.0004.004D.0003.0000.0C00.62E6.00
| Domain| Area| System ID| S|
```

Entering Routes

Routes are entered by specifying pairs (NSAP prefix and next-hop NET). NETs are similar in function to NSAP addresses. In the routing table, the best match means the longest NSAP prefix entry that matches the beginning of the destination NSAP address. In Table 12-1, which is an example of a static routing table, the next-hop NETs are listed for completeness but are not necessary to understand the routing algorithm. Table 12-2 offers examples of how the longest matching NSAP prefix can be matched with routing table entries in Table 12-1.

Table 12–1   *Sample Routing Table Entries*

Entry	NSAP Address Prefix	Next-Hop NET
1	47.0005.000c.0001	47.0005.000c.0001.0000.1234.00
2	47.0004	47.0005.000c.0002.0000.0231.00
3	47.0005.0003	47.0005.000c.0001.0000.1234.00
4	47.0005.000c	47.0005.000c.0004.0000.0011.00
5	47.0005	47.0005.000c.0002.0000.0231.00

Table 12–2   *Hierarchical Routing Examples*

Datagram Destination NSAP Address	Table Entry Number Used
47.0005.000c.0001.0000.3456.01	1
47.0005.000c.0001.6789.2345.01	1
47.0004.1234.1234.1234.1234.01	2
47.0005.0003.4321.4321.4321.01	3
47.0005.000c.0004.5678.5678.01	4
47.0005.0001.0005.3456.3456.01	5

Octet boundaries must be used for the internal boundaries of NSAP addresses and NETs.

TROUBLESHOOTING ISO CLNS

This section presents protocol-related troubleshooting information for ISO CLNS protocol connectivity and performance problems. It describes specific ISO CLNS symptoms, the problems that are likely to cause each symptom, and the solutions to those problems.

NOTES

Discussions of host configuration problems in this chapter assume that the host is a UNIX system. Equivalent actions might also be applicable to non-UNIX hosts, but the discussions do not specifically address non-UNIX end-station problems.

The following sections cover the most common network issues in ISO CLNS networks:

- ISO CLNS: Host Cannot Access Hosts on Local or Remote Network
- ISO CLNS: Host Cannot Access Hosts in Same Area
- ISO CLNS: Host Cannot Access Hosts in Different Area
- ISO CLNS: Connections Fail Using Certain Protocols
- ISO CLNS: Users Cannot Make Connections over Parallel Path
- ISO CLNS: Redistribution Causes Routing Problems
- ISO CLNS: Poor Performance

ISO CLNS: Host Cannot Access Hosts on Local or Remote Network

Symptom: Hosts cannot communicate with other hosts. Hosts might be located on the local or a remote network. Connections to some hosts on a network might be possible, whereas connections to other hosts on the same network fail.

Table 12–3 outlines the problems that might cause this symptom and describes solutions to those problems.

Table 12–3   *ISO CLNS: Host Cannot Access Hosts on Local or Remote Network*

Possible Problem	Solution	
Missing or mis-configured default gateway specification	Step 1	Determine whether a default gateway is specified in the adjacency table of the host attempting to make a connection. Use the following UNIX command: `host% netstat -rn` Check the output of this command for a default gateway specification. **Syntax Description:** • netstat—Displays protocol statistics and current TCP/IP[1] network connections • r—Displays the contents of the routing table • n—Displays addresses and port numbers in numeric form
	Step 2	If the default gateway specification is incorrect, or if it is not present at all, you can change or add a default gateway using the following UNIX command at the local host: `host% route add default address 1` where *address* is the IP address of the default gateway (the router local to the host). The value 1 indicates that the specified gateway is one hop away.
	Step 3	It is recommended that you specify a default gateway as part of the boot process. Specify the ISO CLNS address of the gateway in the following UNIX host file: `/etc/defaultrouter` This filename might be different on your UNIX system.
End system has no Level 1 router	Step 1	Use the **show clns neighbors detail** privileged exec command to show all ESs[2] and ISs[3] to which the router is directly connected.
	Step 2	Make sure there is at least one Level 1 router on the same network as the end system.
Level 1 router or ES has bad address	Step 1	Verify that the Level 1 router has the same address as the ES.
	Step 2	Verify that all bytes of the NSAP[4] address, up to but not including the system ID, are the same on both the router and the ES. The domain and area addresses must match, and the station IDs must be unique. (The value of the n-selector byte has no impact in this case.)

Table 12–3 *ISO CLNS: Host Cannot Access Hosts on Local or Remote Network, Continued*

Possible Problem	Solution

ES host is not running ES-IS[5] protocol	**Step 1** Use the appropriate host commands to verify that an ES-IS process is running. If necessary, initiate the ES-IS process on the host.
	
	Step 2 Check the adjacency database on the host and verify that it has an entry for its directly connected router.
	
	Step 3 Use the **debug clns packet** privileged exec command on the Level 1 router to verify that it sees and forwards packets from the ES.
	
	Caution: Because debugging output is assigned high priority in the CPU process, it can render the system unusable. For this reason, use **debug** commands only to troubleshoot specific problems or during troubleshooting sessions with Cisco technical support staff. Moreover, it is best to use **debug** commands during periods of lower network traffic and fewer users. Debugging during these periods decreases the likelihood that increased **debug** command processing overhead will affect system use.
	
	Step 4 If necessary, statically configure the router to recognize the ES by using the **clns es-neighbor** interface configuration command. The following is the syntax for the **clns es-neighbor** command:
	
	clns es-neighbor *nsap snpa*
	
	Syntax Description:
	
	• *nsap*—Specific NSAP to map to a specific MAC[6] address.
	
	• *snpa*—Data link (MAC) address.
	
	Example:
	
	The following example defines an ES neighbor on Ethernet interface 0:
	
	`interface ethernet 0`
	`  clns es-neighbor 47.0004.004D.0055.0000.0C00.A45B.00`
	`0000.0C00.A45B`
	
	In this case, the end systems with the following NSAP, or NET[7], are configured with an Ethernet MAC address of 0000.0C00.A45B:
	
	• `47.0004.004D.0055.0000.0C00.A45B.00`

Table 12–3   *ISO CLNS: Host Cannot Access Hosts on Local or Remote Network, Continued*

Possible Problem	Solution

Router between hosts is down	**Step 1** Use the **trace** exec command to check connectivity between routers and the source ES.
	
	Step 2 If the **trace** fails at a router, use the **show clns neighbors** exec command to see which neighboring routers and ESs are recognized.
	
	Sample Display:
	
	The following is sample output from the **show clns neighbors** command. This display is a composite of the **show clns es-neighbor** and **show clns is-neighbor** commands:
	
	<pre>router# show clns neighbors
	System Id SNPA Interface State Holdtime Type Protocol
	0000.0000.0007 aa00.0400.6408 Ethernet0 Init 277 IS ES-IS
	0000.0C00.0C35 0000.0c00.0c36 Ethernet1 Up 91 L1 IS-IS
	0800.2B16.24EA aa00.0400.2d05 Ethernet0 Up 29 L1L2 IS-IS
	0800.2B14.060E aa00.0400.9205 Ethernet0 Up 1698 ES ES-IS
	0000.0C00.3E51 *HDLC* Serial1 Up 28 L2 IS-IS
	0000.0C00.62E6 0000.0c00.62e7 Ethernet1 Up 22 L1 IS-IS
	0A00.0400.2D05 aa00.0400.2d05 Ethernet0 Init 24 IS ES-IS</pre>
	Step 3 If neighboring routers and end systems are up, perform one of the following procedures:
	
	• For ISO-IGRP[8], check the routing table and see whether the routes are being learned. Use the **show clns route** exec command to display the routing tables.
	
	• For IS-IS[9], check the LSP[10] database to see whether the links are being reported in link state advertisements. Check the IS-IS routing table to see whether the routes are being installed in the routing table. Use the **show isis database detail** exec command to display the routing tables.

Route redistribution problem	Misconfigured route redistribution can cause connectivity problems. For specific troubleshooting information, see the section "ISO CLNS: Redistribution Causes Routing Problems" later in this chapter.

[1] TCP/IP = Transmission Control Protocol/Internet Protocol
[2] ES = end system
[3] IS = intermediate system
[4] NSAP = Network service access point
[5] ES-IS = End System-to-Intermediate System
[6] MAC = Media Access Control
[7] NET = network entity title
[8] IGRP = Interior Gateway Routing Protocol
[9] IS-IS = Intermediate System-to-Intermediate System
[10] LSP = Link State Protocol

ISO CLNS: Host Cannot Access Hosts in Same Area

Symptom: Hosts cannot access other hosts in the same area. The hosts might be on the same network or they might be in a different network in the same area.

Table 12–4 outlines the problems that might cause this symptom and describes solutions to those problems.

Table 12–4 *ISO CLNS: Host Cannot Access Hosts in Same Area*

Possible Problem	Solution	
Area address is configured incorrectly on the host	Step 1	Check all Level 1 routing tables and link-state databases.
	Step 2	Verify that the hosts are in the same area.
	Step 3	Check that the NSAP address is entered correctly on the hosts.
Different area addresses are merged into a single area, but the router is configured incorrectly	Step 1	Use the **show running-config** privileged exec command to see router configurations. Check whether multiple area addresses are configured.
	Step 2	If multiple network addresses are configured, verify that the router is configured to support a multihomed area (a single area that has more than one area address; see Figure 12–3).
	Step 3	To communicate, routers must establish a Level 1 adjacency. Therefore, area addresses in a multihomed area must overlap across routers.
		For example, in the multihomed area shown in Figure 12–3, to configure Area 1 and Area 2 as a multihomed area, both Router A and Router B must be configured to be in both areas. IS-IS routing supports the assignment of multiple area addresses on the same router. This concept is referred to as *multihoming*. Multihoming provides a mechanism for smoothly migrating network addresses, as follows:
		• Splitting up an area—Nodes within a given area can accumulate until they are difficult to manage, cause excessive traffic, or threaten to exceed the usable address space for an area. Multiple area addresses can be assigned so that you can smoothly partition a network into separate areas without disrupting service.

Table 12–4 *ISO CLNS: Host Cannot Access Hosts in Same Area, Continued*

Possible Problem	Solution
Different area addresses are merged into a single area, but the router is configured incorrectly (*Continued*)	• Merging areas—Use transitional area addresses to merge as many as three separate areas that have a common area address into a single area. • Transition to a different address—You may need to change an area address for a particular group of nodes. Use multiple area addresses to allow incoming traffic intended for an old area address to continue being routed to associated nodes. You must statically assign the multiple area addresses on the router. Cisco currently supports assignment of up to three area addresses on a router. The number of areas allowed in a domain is unlimited. All the addresses must have the same system ID. For example, you can assign one address (area1 plus system ID) and two additional addresses in different areas (area2 plus system ID and area3 plus system ID) where the system ID is the same. **Step 4** Alternatively, one router can be configured in both areas, while the other router remains configured for a single area. Provided that the area numbers on routers overlap, the routers will establish a Level 1 adjacency, allowing them to communicate.
ES host is not running ES-IS protocol	**Step 1** Use the appropriate host commands to verify that an ES-IS process is running. If necessary, initiate the ES-IS process on the host. **Step 2** Check the adjacency database on the host and verify that it has an entry for its directly connected router. **Step 3** Use the **debug clns packet** privileged exec command on the Level 1 router to verify that it sees and forwards packets from the ES.

Table 12–4 *ISO CLNS: Host Cannot Access Hosts in Same Area, Continued*

Possible Problem	Solution
ES host is not running ES-IS protocol (*Continued*)	**Caution:** Because debugging output is assigned high priority in the CPU process, it can render the system unusable. For this reason, use **debug** commands only to troubleshoot specific problems or during troubleshooting sessions with Cisco technical support staff. Moreover, it is best to use **debug** commands during periods of lower network traffic and fewer users. Debugging during these periods decreases the likelihood that increased **debug** command processing overhead will affect system use.
	Step 4 If necessary, statically configure the router to recognize the ES by using the **clns es-neighbor** interface configuration command. The following is the syntax for the **clns es-neighbor** command:
	clns es-neighbor *nsap snpa*
	Syntax Description:
	• *nsap*—Specific NSAP to map to a specific MAC address.
	• *snpa*—Data link (MAC) address.
	Example:
	The following example defines an ES neighbor on Ethernet interface 0:
| | ```
interface ethernet 0
 clns es-neighbor 47.0004.004D.0055.0000.0C00.A45B.00
0000.0C00.A45B
``` |
| Route redistribution problem | Misconfigured route redistribution can cause connectivity problems. For specific troubleshooting information, see the section "ISO CLNS: Redistribution Causes Routing Problems" later in this chapter. |
```

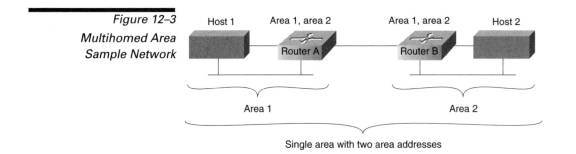

Figure 12–3
Multihomed Area
Sample Network

Area 1

Area 2

Single area with two area addresses

ISO CLNS: Host Cannot Access Hosts in Different Area

Symptom: Host cannot access hosts in a different area. Hosts in the same area are accessible.

Table 12–5 outlines the problems that might cause this symptom and describes solutions to those problems.

Table 12–5   *ISO CLNS: Host Cannot Access Hosts in Different Area*

Possible Problem	Solution
Level 2 routers are not routing packets to the correct area	**Step 1** Use the **trace** command to verify that Level 1 routers are routing packets to the nearest Level 2 router. **Sample Display:** The following display shows an example of ISO CLNS **trace** output: ``` router# trace Protocol [ip]: clns Target CLNS address: thoth Timeout in seconds [3]: Probe count [3]: Minimum Time to Live [1]: Maximum Time to Live [30]: Type escape sequence to abort. Tracing the route to THOTH (55.0006.0100.0000.0000.0001.8888.1112.1314.1516) HORUS(55.0006.0100.0000.0000.0001.6666.3132.3334.3536) 32 msec ! 28 msec 28 msec ! 2 ISIS(55.0006.0100.0000.0000.0001.7777.2122.2324.2526) 56 msec ! 80 msec 56 msec ! 3 THOTH(55.0006.0100.0000.0000.0001.8888.1112.1314.1516) 80 msec ! 80 msec ! 8 ```

Table 12–5 *ISO CLNS: Host Cannot Access Hosts in Different Area, Continued*

Possible Problem	Solution
	Step 2 Use the **trace** exec command to verify that Level 2 routers are routing packets to the correct destination area.
	Step 3 If packets are not being routed to the correct area, check the Level 2 routing tables (ISO-IGRP[1]) or the Level 2 link state databases (IS-IS) to see whether the packets are being forwarded to another area.
	Step 4 If necessary, reconfigure routers with the correct area addresses and Level 2 (IS-IS) routing information.
ES host is not running ES-IS protocol	**Step 1** Use the appropriate host commands to verify that an ES-IS process is running. If necessary, initiate the ES-IS process on the host.
	Step 2 Check the adjacency database on the host and verify that it has an entry for its directly connected router.
	Step 3 Use the **debug clns packet** privileged exec command on the Level 1 router to verify that it sees and forwards packets from the ES.
	Caution: Because debugging output is assigned high priority in the CPU process, it can render the system unusable. For this reason, use **debug** commands only to troubleshoot specific problems or during troubleshooting sessions with Cisco technical support staff. Moreover, it is best to use **debug** commands during periods of lower network traffic and fewer users. Debugging during these periods decreases the likelihood that increased **debug** command processing overhead will affect system use.
	Step 4 If necessary, statically configure the router to recognize the ES by using the **clns es-neighbor** interface configuration command.
Route redistribution problem	Misconfigured route redistribution can cause connectivity problems. For specific troubleshooting information, see the section "ISO CLNS: Redistribution Causes Routing Problems" later in this chapter.

Table 12–5   *ISO CLNS: Host Cannot Access Hosts in Different Area, Continued*

Possible Problem	Solution
| Router between hosts is down | **Step 1**  Use the **trace** exec command to check connectivity between routers and the source ES.<br><br>**Sample Display:**<br><br>The following display shows an example of ISO CLNS **trace** output:<br><br>```
router# trace
Protocol [ip]: clns
Target CLNS address: thoth
Timeout in seconds [3]:
Probe count [3]:
Minimum Time to Live [1]:
Maximum Time to Live [30]:
Type escape sequence to abort.
Tracing the route to THOTH
(55.0006.0100.0000.0000.0001.8888.1112.1314.1516)
   HORUS(55.0006.0100.0000.0000.0001.6666.3132.3334.3536)
32 msec ! 28 msec
28 msec !
 2 ISIS(55.0006.0100.0000.0000.0001.7777.2122.2324.2526)
56 msec ! 80 msec
56 msec !
 3 THOTH(55.0006.0100.0000.0000.0001.8888.1112.1314.1516)
80 msec ! 80 msec ! 8
```<br><br>**Step 2**  If the **trace** fails at a router, use the **show clns neighbors** exec command to see which neighboring routers and ESs are recognized.<br><br>**Step 3**  If neighboring routers and end systems are up, perform one of the following procedures:<br><br>• For ISO-IGRP, check the routing table and see whether the routes are being learned. Use the **show clns route** exec command to display the routing tables.<br><br>• For IS-IS, check the LSP[2] database to see whether the links are being reported in link state advertisements. Check the IS-IS routing table to see whether the routes are being installed in the routing table. Use the **show isis database detail** exec command to display the routing tables. |

[1] IGRP = Interior Gateway Routing Protocol
[2] LSP = Link State Protocol
```

ISO CLNS: Connections Fail Using Certain Protocols

Symptom: Host connections fail using certain protocols. Hosts might be able to connect to other hosts using some protocols but are unable to connect using others.

Table 12–6 outlines the problems that might cause this symptom and describes solutions to those problems.

Table 12–6 *ISO CLNS: Connections Fail Using Certain Protocols*

Possible Problem	Solution
Host is not configured to support the service	Verify that the needed protocols are correctly installed and configured on the host system. Consult your vendor's documentation for information on configuring hosts.
Misconfigured access list	**Step 1** Use the **trace** exec command to determine the path taken to reach remote hosts.
	Step 2 If you discover a router that is stopping traffic, use the **show access-lists** privileged exec command to see whether any access lists are configured on the router.
	Step 3 Disable all access lists on the router using **no access-group** interface configuration commands on the appropriate interfaces.
	Step 4 Determine whether hosts can now use the protocol in question. If traffic can get through, it is likely that an access list is blocking protocol traffic.
	Step 5 Make sure the access list does not filter traffic from ports that are used by the protocol in question. Configure explicit **permit** statements for traffic that you want the router to forward normally.
	Step 6 Enable the access list and verify that the protocol still functions correctly. If problems persist, continue isolating and analyzing access lists on all routers in the path from source to destination.

ISO CLNS: Users Cannot Make Connections over Parallel Path

Symptom: In environments with multiple paths between networks, when one link goes down, connections across a parallel link are not possible.

NOTES

IS-IS has equal-cost load balancing for both Level 1 and Level 2 routes. If there are parallel paths in an IS-IS network and one goes down, the other should serve as a backup that is ready to be used immediately.

Table 12–7 outlines the problems that might cause this symptom and describes solutions to those problems.

Table 12–7 *ISO CLNS: Users Cannot Make Connections over Parallel Path*

Possible Problem	Solution
Routing has not converged	**Step 1** Use the **show clns route** privileged exec command to view the CLNS routing table. Examine the table for routes listed as "possibly down." This indicates that the routing protocol has not converged.
	Step 2 Wait for the routing protocol to converge. Use the **show clns route** command again to see whether the routes are now up.
	Note: ISO-IGRP does load balancing only for domain prefix routes. If you are doing Level 1 or Level 2 routing in ISO-IGRP, only a single path is maintained. If that path goes down, you must wait for the network to converge before the alternate path is available.
Misconfigured access list	**Step 1** Use the **trace** exec command to determine the path taken to reach remote hosts.
	Step 2 If you discover a router that is stopping traffic, use the **show access-lists** privileged exec command to see whether any access lists are configured on the router.
	Step 3 Disable all access lists on the router using **no access-group** interface configuration commands on the appropriate interfaces.
	Step 4 Determine whether hosts can now use the protocol in question. If traffic can get through, it is likely that an access list is blocking protocol traffic.
	Step 5 Make sure the access list does not filter traffic from ports that are used by the protocol in question. Configure explicit **permit** statements for traffic that you want the router to forward normally.
	Step 6 Enable the access list and verify that the protocol still functions correctly. If problems persist, continue isolating and analyzing access lists on all routers in the path from source to destination.
Hardware or media problem	For information on troubleshooting hardware problems, see Chapter 3. "Troubleshooting Hardware and Booting Problems." For information on troubleshooting media problems, refer to the media troubleshooting chapter that covers the media type used in your network.

ISO CLNS: Redistribution Causes Routing Problems

Symptom: Route redistribution does not work properly and causes routing problems. Traffic does not get through a router that is redistributing routes between two different routing areas or domains—typically IS-IS and ISO-IGRP. Observed symptoms range from poor performance to no communication at all.

Table 12–8 outlines the problems that might cause this symptom and describes solutions to those problems.

Table 12–8 *ISO CLNS: Redistribution Causes Routing Problems*

Possible Problem	Solution
Misordered sequence numbers	The sequence numbers used in **route-map** router configuration commands determine the order in which conditions are tested. Misordered sequence numbers can cause redistribution problems.
	Step 1 Use the **show running-config** privileged exec command to display the router configuration. Look for **route-map** router configuration command entries.
	Step 2 If **route-map** commands are configured, look at the sequence numbers that are assigned. Lower sequence numbers are tested before higher sequence numbers, regardless of the order in which they are listed in the configuration.
	Step 3 If conditions are not being tested in the order you want, you must modify the sequence numbers to change the testing order. The syntax for the route-map command to adjust the sequence number is as follows:
	route-map *map-tag* {**permit** | **deny**} *sequence-number*
	Syntax Description:
	• *map-tag*—Meaningful name for the route map. The redistribute command uses this name to reference this route map. Multiple route maps can share the same map tag name. Can either be an expression or a filter set.
	• **permit**—If the match criteria are met for this route map and **permit** is specified, the route is redistributed as controlled by the set actions. If the match criteria are not met, and permit is specified, the next route map with the same map tag is tested. If a route passes none of the match criteria for the set of route maps sharing the same name, it is not redistributed by that set.

Table 12–8   *ISO CLNS: Redistribution Causes Routing Problems, Continued*

Possible Problem	Solution
Misordered sequence numbers (*Continued*)	• **deny**—If the match criteria are met for the route map and **deny** is specified, the route is not redistributed and no further route maps sharing the same map tag name will be examined. • *sequence-number*—Number that indicates the position a new route map is to have in the list of route maps already configured with the same name. If given with the no form of this command, it specifies the position of the route map that should be deleted.
Missing or misconfigured **default-metric** command	**Step 1** Use the **show running-config** exec command to view the router configuration. Look for a **default-metric** router configuration command entry. **Step 2** If the **default-metric** router configuration command or the **distance** router configuration command is missing, add the appropriate version of the missing command. **Syntax:** The following is the syntax for the **default-metric** command: **default-metric** *number* **Syntax Description:** • *number*—Default metric value appropriate for the specified routing protocol. **Syntax:** The following is the syntax for the **distance** command: **distance** *value* [**clns**] **Syntax Description:** • *value*—Administrative distance, indicating the trustworthiness of a routing information source. This argument has a numeric value between 0 and 255. A higher relative value indicates a lower trustworthiness rating. Preference is given to routes with smaller values. The default, if unspecified, is 110. • **clns**—(Optional) CLNS-derived routes for IS-IS. Refer to the *Cisco IOS Network Protocols Configuration Guide, Part 2 and Network Protocols Command Reference, Part 2* for information about adjusting ISO CLNS default metrics.

Table 12–8 *ISO CLNS: Redistribution Causes Routing Problems, Continued*

Possible Problem	Solution
Missing or misconfigured **distance** command	**Step 1** Use the **show running-config** exec command to view the router configuration. Look for a **distance** router configuration command entry.
	Step 2 If the **distance** command is missing, configure a distance specification on the router. Use the **distance** router configuration command to configure the administrative distance for CLNS routes learned.
	Syntax:
	The following is the syntax for the **distance** command:
	distance *value* [**clns**]
	Syntax Description:
	• *value*—Administrative distance, indicating the trustworthiness of a routing information source. This argument has a numeric value between 0 and 255. A higher relative value indicates a lower trustworthiness rating. Preference is given to routes with smaller values. The default, if unspecified, is 110.
	• **clns**—(Optional) CLNS-derived routes for IS-IS.
	Example:
	In the following example, the **distance** value for CLNS routes learned is 90. Preference is given to these CLNS routes rather than routes with the default administrative **distance** value of 110:
| | ```
router isis
 distance 90 clns
``` |
```

Table 12–8   *ISO CLNS: Redistribution Causes Routing Problems, Continued*

Possible Problem	Solution

Redistribution feedback loop exists	Redistribution between an IS-IS cloud and an ISO-IGRP cloud should be performed only at a single point. If it is not, routing information can be advertised back into one of the clouds, causing routing feedback loops.
	
	Examples:
	
	The following example illustrates redistribution of ISO-IGRP routes of Michigan and ISO-IGRP routes of Ohio into the IS-IS area tagged USA:
	
	``
	router isis USA
	  redistribute iso-igrp Michigan
	  redistribute iso-igrp Ohio
	``
	
	The following example illustrates redistribution of IS-IS routes of France and ISO-IGRP routes of Germany into the ISO-IGRP area tagged **Backbone:**
	
	``
	router iso-igrp Backbone
	  redistribute isis France
	  redistribute iso-igrp Germany
	``
	
	If you must redistribute at another point, use default metrics to perform the redistribution in one direction only.
	
	Refer to the Cisco IOS *Network Protocols Configuration Guide, Part 2* and *Network Protocols Command Reference, Part 2* for information about adjusting ISO CLNS default metrics.

ISO CLNS: Poor Performance

Symptom: Users experience poor performance or sudden loss of connections. One or more routers might be receiving duplicate routing updates and might see routers and ESs on multiple interfaces.

Table 12–9 outlines the problems that might cause this symptom and describes solutions to those problems.

Table 12–9 *ISO CLNS: Poor Performance*

Possible Problem	Solution
Multiple ISO-IGRP processes are configured on a single interface	**Step 1** Use the **show clns interface** exec command to view the interface configuration. Look for multiple ISO-IGRP processes that are configured on a single interface.
	Step 2 If multiple ISO-IGRP processes are configured on a single interface, different Level 2 updates are being sent out through the same interface.
	Multiple Level 2 updates on the same interface can cause congestion problems, especially if the network is large and links are flapping outside the damping intervals. Flapping is a routing problem where an advertised route between two nodes alternates (flaps) back and forth between two paths due to a network problem that causes intermittent interface failures.
	Step 3 Remove one of the ISO-IGRP processes from the interface configuration using the appropriate **no clns router iso-igrp** interface configuration command.
Bridge or repeater in parallel with router	A bridge or repeater in parallel with a router can cause updates and traffic to be seen from both sides of an interface.
	Step 1 Use the **show clns is-neighbors detail** and the **show clns neighbors detail** exec commands to see through which routers and protocols the router's adjacencies were learned.

Table 12–9   *ISO CLNS: Poor Performance, Continued*

Possible Problem	Solution

Bridge or repeater in parallel with router (*Continued*)	The following is sample output from the **show clns neighbors detail** command:
	
	`router# `**`show clns neighbors detail`**
	`System Id       SNPA            Interface  State Holdtime Type Protocol`
	`000.0000.0007  aa00.0400.6408  Ethernet0  Init  291      IS   ES-IS`
	`  Area Address(es): 47.0005.80FF.F500.0000.0003.0020`
	`0000.0C00.0C35  0000.0c00.0c36  Ethernet1  Up    94       L1   IS-IS`
	`  Area Address(es): 47.0004.004D.0001 39.0001`
	`0800.2B16.24EA  aa00.0400.2d05  Ethernet0  Up    9        L1L2 IS-IS`
	`  Area Address(es): 47.0004.004D.0001`
	`0800.2B14.060E  aa00.0400.9205  Ethernet0  Up    1651     ES   ES-IS`
	`  Area Address(es): 49.0040`
	`0000.0C00.3E51  *HDLC*          Serial1    Up    27       L2   IS-IS`
	`  Area Address(es): 39.0004`
	`0000.0C00.62E6  0000.0c00.62e7  Ethernet1  Up    26       L1   IS-IS`
	`  Area Address(es): 47.0004.004D.0001`
	`oA00.0400.2D05  aa00.0400.2d05  Ethernet0  Init  29       IS   ES-IS`
	`    Area Address(es): 47.0004.004D.0001`
	
	Look for routers that are known to be on a remote network. A router listed in the adjacency table but that is not on a directly connected network indicates a problem.
	
	You can also look for paths to networks (or areas) on multiple interfaces.
	
	Step 2 If you determine that there is a parallel bridge or repeater, remove the device or configure filters that block routing updates from being learned from the device.

Route redistribution problem	Misconfigured route redistribution can cause performance problems. For specific troubleshooting information, see the section "ISO CLNS: Redistribution Causes Routing Problems" earlier in this chapter.

## CHAPTER 13

Troubleshooting Banyan VINES

Banyan Virtual Integrated Network Service (VINES) implements a distributed network operating system based on a proprietary protocol family derived from Xerox Corporation's Xerox Network Systems (XNS) protocols (see Chapter 14, "Troubleshooting XNS"). VINES uses a client/server architecture in which clients request certain services, such as file and printer access, from servers. Along with Novell's NetWare, IBM's LAN Server, and Microsoft's LAN Manager, VINES is one of the best-known distributed system environments for microcomputer-based networks.

VINES TECHNOLOGY BASICS

The VINES protocol stack is shown in Figure 13–1.

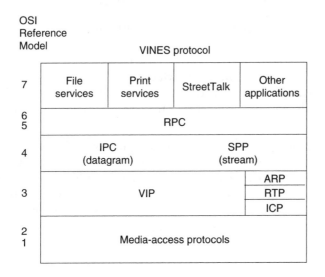

Figure 13–1

The VINES Protocol Stack

VINES MEDIA ACCESS

The two lower layers of the VINES stack are implemented with a variety of well-known media-access mechanisms, including High-Level Data Link Control (HDLC), Synchronous Data Link Control (SDLC) and derivatives, X.25, Ethernet, and Token Ring.

THE NETWORK LAYER

VINES uses the VINES Internetwork Protocol (VIP) to perform Layer 3 activities (including internetwork routing). VINES also supports its own Address Resolution Protocol (ARP), its own version of the Routing Information Protocol (RIP) called the Routing Table Protocol (RTP), and the Internet Control Protocol (ICP), which provides exception handling and special routing cost information. ARP, ICP, and RTP packets are encapsulated in a VIP header.

VIP

VINES network-layer addresses are 48-bit entities subdivided into network (32 bits) and subnetwork (16 bits) portions. The network number is better described as a server number because it is derived directly from the server's key (a hardware module that identifies a unique number and the software options for that server). The subnetwork portion of a VINES address is better described as a host number because it is used to identify hosts on VINES networks. Figure 13–2 illustrates the VINES address format.

Figure 13–2
The VINES Address Format

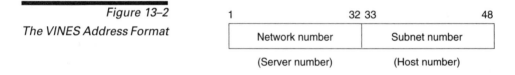

The network number identifies a VINES logical network, which is represented as a two-level tree with the root at a service node. Service nodes, which are usually servers, provide address resolution and routing services to clients, which represent the leaves of the tree. The service node assigns VIP addresses to clients.

When a client is powered on, it broadcasts a request for servers. All servers that hear the request respond. The client chooses the first response and requests a subnetwork (host) address from that server. The server responds with an address consisting of its own network address (derived from its key), concatenated with a subnetwork (host) address of its own choosing. Client subnetwork addresses are typically assigned sequentially, starting with 8001H. Server subnetwork addresses are always 1. The VINES address selection process is shown in Figure 13–3.

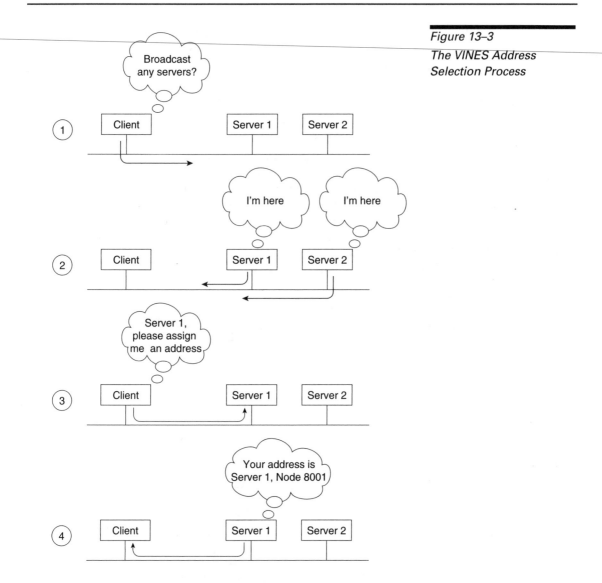

Figure 13–3
The VINES Address
Selection Process

Dynamic address assignment is not unique in the industry (AppleTalk also uses this process), but it is certainly not as common as static address assignment. Because addresses are chosen exclusively by a particular server (whose address is unique as a result of the uniqueness of the hardware key), there is very little chance of a duplicate address (a potentially devastating problem on Internet Protocol [IP] and other networks).

In the VINES network scheme, all servers with multiple interfaces are essentially routers. A client always chooses its own server as a first-hop router, even if another server on the same cable provides a better route to the ultimate destination. A client can learn about other routers by receiving redirect messages from its own server. Because clients rely on their servers for first-hop routing, VINES servers maintain routing tables to help them find remote nodes.

VINES routing tables consist of host/cost pairs, where host corresponds to a network node that can be reached and cost corresponds to a delay, expressed in milliseconds, to get to that node. RTP helps VINES servers find neighboring clients, servers, and routers.

Periodically, all clients advertise both their network-layer and their Media Access Control (MAC)–layer addresses with the equivalent of a hello packet. Hello packets indicate that the client is still operating and network ready. The servers themselves send routing updates to other servers periodically. Routing updates alert other routers to changes in node addresses and network topology.

When a VINES server receives a packet, it checks whether the packet is destined for another server or if it's a broadcast. If the current server is the destination, the server handles the request appropriately. If another server is the destination, the current server either forwards the packet directly (if the server is a neighbor) or routes it to the next server in line. If the packet is a broadcast, the current server checks whether the packet came from the least-cost path. If it did not, the packet is discarded. If it did, the packet is forwarded on all interfaces except the one on which it was received. This approach helps diminish the number of broadcast storms, a common problem in other network environments. The VINES routing algorithm is shown in Figure 13–4.

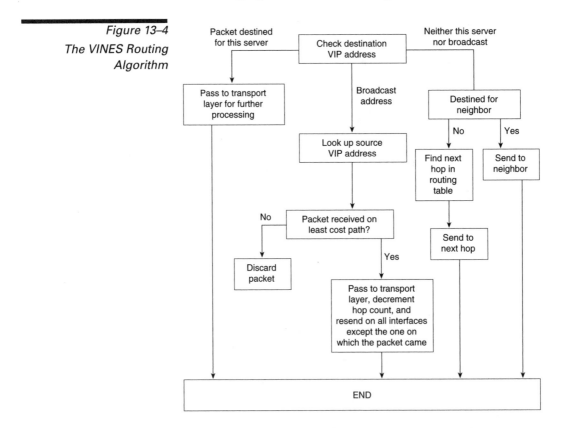

Figure 13–4
The VINES Routing
Algorithm

The VIP packet format is shown in Figure 13–5.

Field length, in bytes	2	2	1	1	4	2	4	2	Variable
	Check-sum	Packet length	Trans-port control	Protocol type	Destination network number	Destination subnetwork number	Source network number	Source subnetwork number	Data

Figure 13–5

The VIP Packet Format

The fields of a VIP packet are as follows:

- Checksum—Used to detect packet corruption.

- Packet length—Indicates the length of the entire VIP packet.

- Transport control—Consists of several subfields. If the packet is a broadcast packet, two subfields are provided: class (bits 1 through 3) and hop-count (bits 4 through 7). If the packet is not a broadcast packet, four subfields are provided: error, metric, redirect, and hop count. The class subfield specifies the type of node that should receive the broadcast. For this purpose, nodes are broken into various categories having to do with the type of node and the type of link the node is on. By specifying the type of nodes to receive broadcasts, the class subfield reduces the disruption caused by broadcasts. The hop count subfield represents the number of hops (router traversals) the packet has been through. The error subfield specifies whether the ICP protocol should send an exception notification packet to the packet's source if a packet turns out to be unroutable. The metric subfield is set to 1 by a transport entity when it needs to learn the routing cost of moving packets between a service node and a neighbor. The redirect subfield specifies whether the router should generate a redirect (when appropriate).

- Protocol type—Indicates the network- or transport-layer protocol for which the metric or exception notification packet is destined.

- Destination network number, destination subnetwork number, source network number, and source subnetwork number—Provide VIP address information.

RTP

RTP distributes network topology information. Routing update packets are broadcast periodically by both client and service nodes. These packets inform neighbors of a node's existence and indicate whether the node is a client or a service node. Service nodes also include, in each routing update packet, a list of all known networks and the cost factors associated with reaching those networks.

Two routing tables are maintained: a table of all known networks and a table of neighbors. For service nodes, the table of all known networks contains an entry for each known network except the service node's own network. Each entry contains a network number, a routing metric, and a pointer to the entry for the next hop to the network in the table of neighbors. The table of neighbors contains an entry for each neighbor service node and client node. Entries include a network number, a subnetwork number, the media-access protocol (for example, Ethernet) used to reach that node, a local-area network (LAN) address (if the medium connecting the neighbor is a LAN), and a neighbor metric.

RTP specifies four packet types:

- Routing update—Issued periodically to notify neighbors of an entity's existence.
- Routing request—Exchanged by entities when they need to learn the network's topology quickly.
- Routing response—Contains topological information and is used by service nodes to respond to routing request packets.
- Routing redirect—Provides better path information to nodes using inefficient paths.

Each RTP packet has a 4-byte header consisting of the following 1-byte fields:

- Operation type—Indicates the packet type.
- Node type—Indicates whether the packet came from a service node or a nonservice node.
- Controller type—Indicates whether the controller in the node transmitting the RTP packet has a multibuffer controller.
- Machine type—Indicates whether the processor in the RTP sender is fast or slow.

Both the controller type and the machine type fields are used for pacing.

ARP

ARP entities are classified as either address resolution clients or address resolution services. Address resolution clients are usually implemented in client nodes, whereas address resolution services are typically provided by service nodes.

An ARP packet has an 8-byte header consisting of a 2-byte packet type, a 4-byte network number, and a 2-byte subnetwork number. There are four packet types: a query request, which is a request for an ARP service; a service response, which is a response to a query request; an assignment request, which is sent to an ARP service to request a VINES internetwork address; and an assignment response, which is sent by the ARP service as a response to the assignment request. The network number and subnet number fields have meaning only in an assignment response packet.

ARP clients and services implement the following algorithm when a client starts up. First, the client broadcasts query request packets. Then, each service that is a neighbor of the client responds with a service response packet. The client then issues an assignment request packet to the first service that responded to its query request packet. The service responds with an assignment response packet containing the assigned internetwork address.

ICP

ICP defines exception notification and metric notification packets. Exception notification packets provide information about network-layer exceptions; metric notification packets contain information about the final transmission used to reach a client node.

Exception notifications are sent when a VIP packet cannot be routed properly, and the error sub-field in the VIP header's transport control field is enabled. These packets also contain a field identifying the particular exception by its error code.

ICP entities in service nodes generate metric notification messages when the metric subfield in the VIP header's transport control field is enabled, and the destination address in the service node's packet specifies one of the service node's neighbors.

THE TRANSPORT LAYER

VINES provides three transport-layer services:

- Unreliable datagram service—Sends packets that are routed on a best-effort basis but not acknowledged at the destination.

- Reliable message service—A virtual-circuit service that provides reliable sequenced and acknowledged delivery of messages between network nodes. A reliable message can be transmitted in a maximum of four VIP packets.

- Data stream service—Supports the controlled flow of data between two processes. The data stream service is an acknowledged virtual circuit service that supports the transmission of messages of unlimited size.

Upper-Layer Protocols

As a distributed network, VINES uses the remote-procedure call (RPC) model for communication between clients and servers. RPC is the foundation of distributed service environments. The NetRPC protocol (Layers 5 and 6) provides a high-level programming language that allows access to remote services in a manner transparent to both the user and the application.

At Layer 7, VINES offers file-service and print-service applications, as well as StreetTalk, which provides a globally consistent name service for an entire internetwork.

VINES also provides an integrated applications development environment under several operating systems, including DOS and UNIX. This development environment allows third parties to develop both clients and services that run in the VINES environment.

TROUBLESHOOTING BANYAN VINES

This section presents protocol-related troubleshooting information for connectivity problems related to Banyan VINES. It describes specific VINES symptoms, the problems that are likely to cause each symptom, and the solutions to those problems.

The following sections describe the most common errors experienced in Banyan VINES networks:

- VINES: Clients Cannot Communicate with Servers over Router
- VINES: Client Cannot Connect to Server over PSN
- VINES: Client on Serverless Network Cannot Connect to Server over PSN

VINES: Clients Cannot Communicate with Servers over Router

Symptom: Clients cannot connect to VINES servers over one or more routers. Clients might or might not be able to connect to servers on their directly connected networks.

Table 13–1 outlines the problems that might cause this symptom and describes solutions to those problems.

Table 13–1 *VINES: Clients Cannot Communicate with Servers over Router*

Possible Problem	Solution
Router interface is down	**Step 1** Use the **show interfaces** exec command to check the status of the router interfaces.
	Step 2 If the status line indicates that an interface that should be up is "administratively down," use the **no shutdown** interface configuration command on the interface.
	Refer to the troubleshooting chapter that covers the media type used in your network.
Hardware or media problem	For information on troubleshooting hardware problems, refer to the troubleshooting chapter that covers the media type used in your network.
Addressing problem	**Step 1** On a serverless segment, use the **show vines route** exec command to make sure the router is seeing server network layer addresses.
	Step 2 If the router is not seeing server addresses, make sure that the server and router addresses are correct. To change the address, use the following syntax:
	vines routing [*address* | *recompute*]
	Syntax Description:
	• *address* (Optional)—Network address of the router. You should specify an address on a router that does not have any Ethernet or FDDI[1] interfaces. You can also specify an address in the unlikely event that two routers map themselves to the same address.
	• *recompute* (Optional)—Dynamically redetermines the router's network address.

Table 13–1 *VINES: Clients Cannot Communicate with Servers over Router, Continued*

Possible Problem	Solution
VINES metric value is not specified	**Step 1** Use the **show vines** interface exec command to check the status of VINES interfaces on the router. Make sure all VINES interfaces have the **vines metric** interface configuration command configured. The **metric** command enables VINES processing on the interface.
	Step 2 If the **vines-metric** interface configuration command is not configured on the interface, specify the command for the interface.
	Configure the **vines metric** based on whether the interface is LAN or WAN connected. Suggested metrics for LAN and WAN connections follow:
	• Ethernet and 16-Mbps Token Ring: **vines-metric 2**
	• 4-Mbps Token Ring: **vines-metric 4**
	• T1 line: **vines-metric 35**
	• Other WAN link: **vines-metric 45**
Missing **vines serverless** or **vines arp-enable** commands	A network that does not have an attached server must be configured with the **vines serverless broadcast** and **vines arp-enable** router configuration commands.
	Note: These commands are enabled by default in Cisco IOS Release 10.3 and later.
	Step 1 Use the **show running-config** privileged exec command on routers attached to networks with no VINES servers attached. Look for **vines serverless** and **vines arp-enable** router configuration commands entries.
	Step 2 If both the **vines serverless** and the **vines arp-enable** commands are not present, specify the commands for router interfaces in serverless networks.
	Syntax:
	The following syntax is required to enable **vines serverless**:
	vines serverless [*dynamic*	*broadcast*]

Table 13–1   *VINES: Clients Cannot Communicate with Servers over Router, Continued*

Possible Problem	Solution
Missing **vines serverless** or **vines arp-enable** commands (*Continued*)	**Syntax Description:** • *dynamic* (Optional)—Forward broadcasts toward one server only if there are no servers present on this interface. • *broadcast* (Optional)—Always flood broadcasts out all other router interfaces to reach all servers. **Syntax:** The following syntax is required to enable **vines arp-enable**: **vines arp-enable** [*dynamic*] **Syntax Description:** • *dynamic* (Optional)—Responds to ARP[2] and SARP[3] requests on this interface only if there are no other VINES servers present.
Misconfigured access list	**Step 1** Use the **show vines access-list** privileged exec command on routers in the path from source to destination. This command shows whether there are access lists configured on the router. **Step 2** Disable all access lists configured on the router using **no vines access-group** commands. **Step 3** Test the connection from the client to the server to see whether connections are now possible. If the connection is successful, an access list is blocking traffic. **Step 4** To isolate the problem access list, apply one access list statement at a time until you can no longer create connections. **Step 5** When the problem list is identified, alter it so that necessary traffic is allowed to pass. On a serverless segment, make sure that well-known ports 0x06 (VINES file service) and 0x0F (StreetTalk) are not filtered. Configure explicit **permit** statements for traffic you want the router to forward. **Step 6** If problems persist, continue testing for problem access lists on all routers in the path from source to destination.

[1] FDDI = Fiber Distributed Data Interface
[2] ARP = Address Resolution Protocol
[3] SARP = Sequence Address Resolution Protocol

VINES: Client Cannot Connect to Server over PSN

Symptom: Clients cannot connect to VINES servers across a packet-switched network (PSN). Clients can connect to local VINES servers.

Table 13–2 outlines the problems that might cause this symptom and describes solutions to those problems.

Table 13–2   *VINES: Client Cannot Connect to Server over PSN*

Possible Problem	Solution	
Address mapping error	**Step 1**	Use the **show running-config** privileged exec command to view the configuration of the router.
	Step 2	For X.25 environments, make sure that LAN protocol-to-X.121 address mapping specified in **x25 map vines** interface configuration command entries use the VINES addresses and X.121 addresses of the destination routers. Confirm that the destination addresses used in the command entries are correct.
	Step 3	For Frame Relay environments, make sure that the LAN protocol-to-DLCI[1] address mapping specified in **frame-relay map** command entries use the VINES address of the destination router and the DLCI of the local interface. Confirm that the destination address and the local DLCI used in the command entries are correct.
PVC[2] is not set up	**Step 1**	Use the **show running-config** privileged exec command to view the configuration of the local and remote routers. Make sure there is an **x25 pvc n vines address** interface configuration command specified on the local and remote routers. This command sets up a PVC between the two routers.
	Step 2	If the command is not present, add it to the router configuration.

[1] DLCI = Data Link Connection Identifier
[2] PVC = permanent virtual circuit

VINES: Client on Serverless Network Cannot Connect to Server over PSN

Symptom: Clients on a serverless network (that is, a network segment that has no attached VINES servers) cannot open a connection to a VINES server over a PSN.

Table 13–3 outlines the problems that might cause this symptom and describes solutions to those problems.

Table 13–3   *VINES: Client on Serverless Network Cannot Connect to Server over PSN*

Possible Problem	Solution
Address mapping error	**Step 1** Use the **show running-config** privileged exec command to view the configuration of the router.
	Step 2 For X.25 environments, make sure that LAN protocol-to-X.121 address mapping specified in the **x25 map vines** interface configuration command entries use the VINES addresses and X.121 addresses of the destination routers. Confirm that the destination addresses used in the command entries are correct.
	Syntax:
	x25 map *protocol address* [*protocol2 address2*[...[*protocol9 address9*]]] *x121-address* [*option*] **no x25 map** *protocol address x121-address*
	Syntax:
	• *protocol*—Protocol type, entered by keyword. As many as nine *protocol* and *address* pairs can be specified in one command line.
	• *address*—Protocol address.
	• *x121-address*—X.121 address of the remote host.
	• *option*—(Optional) Additional functionality that can be specified for originated calls.
	Step 3 For Frame Relay environments, make sure the LAN protocol-to-DLCI[1] address mapping specified in **frame-relay map** command entries use the VINES address of the destination router and the DLCI of the local interface. Confirm that the destination address and the local DLCI used in the command entries are correct.
	Syntax:
	frame-relay map *protocol protocol-address dlci* [*broadcast*] [*ietf* | *cisco*] [*payload-compress* {*packet-by-packet* | *frf9 stac* [*hardware-options*]}] **no frame-relay map** *protocol protocol-address*

Table 13-3 *VINES: Client on Serverless Network Cannot Connect to Server over PSN, Continued*

Possible Problem	Solution
Address mapping error (*Continued*)	**Syntax Description:** • *protocol*—Supported protocol, bridging, or logical link control keywords: **appletalk, decnet, dlsw, ip, ipx, llc2, rsrb, vines,** and **xns.** • *protocol-address*—Destination protocol address. • *dlci*—DLCI number used to connect to the specified protocol address on the interface. • *broadcast*—(Optional) IETF[2] form of Frame Relay encapsulation. Used when the router or access server is connected to another vendor's equipment across a Frame Relay network. • *cisco*—(Optional) Cisco encapsulation method. • *payload-compress packet-by-packet*—(Optional) Enables FRF.9 compression using the **Stacker** method. • *compress frf9 stac*—If the CSA is not available, compression is performed in the software installed on the VIP2 (distributed compression). If the router contains a CSA[3], compression is performed in the CSA hardware (hardware compression). If the VIP2 is not available, compression is performed in the router's main processor (software compression). • *hardware-options*—(Optional) One of the following keywords: **distributed, software,** or **csa.**
PVC[4] is not set up	**Step 1** Use the **show running-config** privileged exec command to view the configuration of the router. Make sure a PVC is set up between the routers on each side of the PSN using the **x25 pvc n vines address** interface configuration command. **Step 2** If the command is not present, add it to the configuration.

Table 13–3   *VINES: Client on Serverless Network Cannot Connect to Server over PSN, Continued*

Possible Problem	Solution
VINES broadcasts are not forwarded across the PSN	**Step 1** Use the **show running-config** command to examine the configuration of the router. Make sure the **vines propagate** interface configuration command is configured on the serial interface of the router that provides the serverless packet-switched node service. **Step 2** If the command is not present, add it to the configuration.
VINES broadcasts not forwarded to all router interfaces	**Step 1** Use the **show running-config** privileged exec command to view the router configuration. Check whether the **vines serverless broadcast** interface configuration command is configured on the router. **Step 2** If the command is not present, configure the router using the **vines serverless broadcast** command. This command configures the router to always flood VINES broadcasts on all interfaces. **Note:** The **vines serverless broadcast** command is enabled by default in Cisco IOS Release 10.3 and later.

[1] DLCI = Data Link Connection Identifier
[2] IETF = Internet Engineering Task Force
[3] CSA = compression service adapter
[4] PVC = permanent virtual circuit

## CHAPTER 14

Troubleshooting XNS

The Xerox Network Systems (XNS) protocols were created by Xerox Corporation in the late 1970s and early 1980s. They were designed to be used across a variety of communication media, processors, and office applications. Several XNS protocols resemble the Internet Protocol (IP) and Transmission Control Protocol (TCP), developed by the Defense Advanced Research Projects Agency (DARPA) for the U.S. Department of Defense (DoD).

Because of its availability and early entry into the market, XNS was adopted by most of the early LAN companies, including Novell, Inc., Ungermann-Bass, Inc. (now a part of Tandem Computers), and 3Com Corporation. Each of these companies has since made various changes to the XNS protocols. Novell added the Service Advertising Protocol (SAP) to permit resource advertisement and modified the OSI Layer 3 protocols (which Novell renamed IPX, for Internetwork Packet Exchange) to run on IEEE 802.3 rather than Ethernet networks. Ungermann-Bass modified Routing Information Protocol (RIP) to support delay as well as hop count and made other small changes. Over time, the XNS implementations for PC networking have become more popular than XNS as it was designed by Xerox.

Although XNS documentation mentions X.25, Ethernet, and High-Level Data Link Control (HDLC), XNS does not expressly define what it refers to as a Level 0 protocol. Like many other protocol suites, XNS leaves media access an open issue, implicitly allowing any such protocol to host the transport of XNS packets over a physical medium.

THE NETWORK LAYER

The XNS network-layer protocol is called the Internet Datagram Protocol (IDP). IDP performs standard Layer 3 functions, including logical addressing and end-to-end datagram delivery across an internetwork. The format of an IDP packet is shown in Figure 14–1.

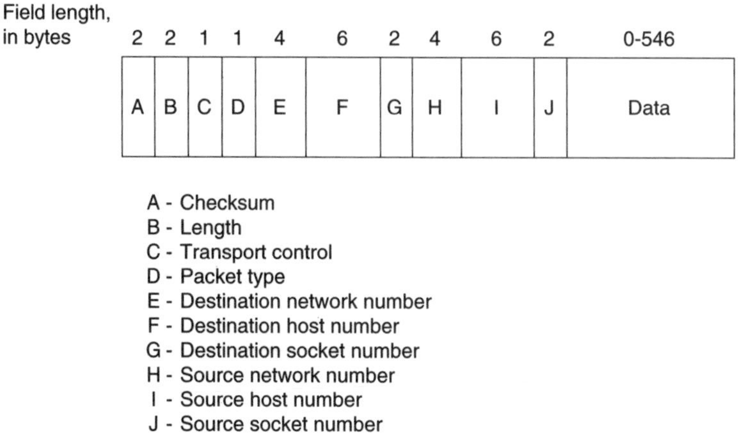

Figure 14–1 Field length,
The IDP Packet Format in bytes

2	2	1	1	4	6	2	4	6	2	0-546
A	B	C	D	E	F	G	H	I	J	Data

A - Checksum
B - Length
C - Transport control
D - Packet type
E - Destination network number
F - Destination host number
G - Destination socket number
H - Source network number
I - Source host number
J - Source socket number

The fields of the IDP packet are as follows:

- Checksum—A 16-bit field that helps gauge the integrity of the packet after it traverses the internetwork.

- Length—A 16-bit field that carries the complete length (including checksum) of the current datagram.

- Transport control—An 8-bit field that contains hop count and maximum packet lifetime (MPL) subfields. The hop count subfield is initialized to zero by the source and incremented by one as the datagram passes through a router. When the hop count field reaches 16, the datagram is discarded on the assumption that a routing loop is occurring. The MPL subfield provides the maximum amount of time, in seconds, that a packet can remain on the internetwork.

- Packet type—An 8-bit field that specifies the format of the data field.

- Destination network number—A 32-bit field that uniquely identifies the destination network in an internetwork.

- Destination host number—A 48-bit field that uniquely identifies the destination host.

- Destination socket number—A 16-bit field that uniquely identifies a socket (process) within the destination host.

- Source network number—A 32-bit field that uniquely identifies the source network in an internetwork.

- Source host number—A 48-bit field that uniquely identifies the source host.

- Source socket number—A 16-bit field that uniquely identifies a socket (process) within the source host.

IEEE 802 addresses are equivalent to host numbers, so a host that is connected to more than one IEEE 802 network has the same address on each segment. This makes network numbers redundant, but nevertheless useful for routing. Certain socket numbers are well known, meaning that the service performed by the software using them is statically defined. All other socket numbers are reusable.

XNS supports Ethernet Version 2.0 encapsulation for Ethernet and three types of encapsulation for Token Ring: 3Com, Subnet Access Protocol (SNAP), and Ungermann-Bass.

XNS supports unicast (point-to-point), multicast, and broadcast packets. Multicast and broadcast addresses are further divided into directed and global types. Directed multicasts deliver packets to members of the multicast group on the network specified in the destination multicast network address. Directed broadcasts deliver packets to all members of a specified network. Global multicasts deliver packets to all members of the group within the entire internetwork, whereas global broadcasts deliver packets to all internetwork addresses. One bit in the host number indicates a single versus a multicast address. All ones in the host field indicate a broadcast address.

To route packets in an internetwork, XNS uses the dynamic routing scheme RIP. Today, RIP is still in use, but has largely been replaced by more scalable protocols, such as Open Shortest Path First (OSPF) and Border Gateway Protocol (BGP).

THE TRANSPORT LAYER

OSI transport-layer functions are implemented by several protocols. Each of the following protocols is described in the XNS specification as a Layer 2 protocol.

The Sequenced Packet Protocol (SPP) provides reliable, connection-based, flow-controlled packet transmission on behalf of client processes. It is similar in function to the Internet Protocol suite's TCP and the OSI protocol suite's Transport Protocol 4 (TP4).

Each SPP packet includes a sequence number, which is used to order packets and to determine whether any have been duplicated or missed. SPP packets also contain two 16-bit connection identifiers. One connection identifier is specified by each end of the connection. Together, the two connection identifiers uniquely identify a logical connection between client processes.

SPP packets cannot be longer than 576 bytes. Client processes can negotiate use of a different packet size during connection establishment, but SPP does not define the nature of this negotiation.

The Packet Exchange Protocol (PEP) is a request-response protocol designed to have greater reliability than simple datagram service (as provided by IDP, for example), but less reliability than SPP. PEP is functionally similar to the Internet Protocol suite's User Datagram Protocol (UDP). PEP is single-packet based, providing retransmissions but no duplicate packet detection. As such, it is useful in applications where request-response transactions can be repeated without damaging data, or where reliable transfer is executed at another layer.

The Error Protocol (EP) can be used by any client process to notify another client process that a network error has occurred. This protocol is used, for example, in situations where an SPP implementation has identified a duplicate packet.

UPPER-LAYER PROTOCOLS

XNS offers several upper-layer protocols. The Printing Protocol provides print services. The Filing Protocol provides file-access services. The Clearinghouse Protocol provides name services. Each of these three protocols runs on top of the Courier Protocol, which provides conventions for data structuring and process interaction.

XNS also defines Level 4 protocols. These are application protocols but, because they have little to do with actual communication functions, the XNS specification does not include any pertinent definitions for them.

The Level 2 Echo Protocol is used to test the reachability of XNS network nodes and to support functions such as that provided by the **ping** command found in UNIX and other environments.

TROUBLESHOOTING XNS

This section presents protocol-related troubleshooting information for XNS connectivity problems. It describes specific XNS symptoms, the problems that are likely to cause each symptom, and the solutions to those problems.

This section covers the most common network issues in XNS environments:

- XNS: Clients Cannot Connect to Servers over Router
- XNS: XNS Broadcast Packets Not Forwarded by Router
- XNS: Clients Cannot Connect to Server over PSN

XNS: Clients Cannot Connect to Servers over Router

Symptom: Clients cannot make connections to XNS servers across a router. Clients might be able to connect to servers on their directly connected networks.

Table 14–1 outlines the problems that might cause this symptom and describes solutions to those problems.

Table 14–1 *XNS: Clients Cannot Connect to Servers over Router*

Possible Problem	Solution	
Router interface is down	**Step 1**	Use the **show interfaces** exec command to check the status of the router interfaces.
	Step 2	If the status line indicates that an interface that should be up is "administratively down," use the **no shutdown** interface configuration command on the interface.
	Step 3	If the status line indicates that the interface or line protocol is in any other state, refer to the chapter that discusses your media type.

Table 14–1 *XNS: Clients Cannot Connect to Servers over Router, Continued*

Possible Problem	Solution
Hardware or media problem	For information on troubleshooting hardware problems, see the chapter that discusses your media type. For information on troubleshooting media problems, see Chapter 15, "Troubleshooting Serial Line Problems."
| XNS routing is not enabled on router | **Step 1** Use the **show running-config** privileged exec command to view the router configuration. Check whether XNS routing is enabled on the router.<br><br>**Step 2** If XNS routing is not enabled, add the **xns routing** router configuration command and related commands as necessary.<br><br>**Example:**<br><br>This example starts XNS routing and assigns XNS network numbers to the physical networks connected to two of the router's Ethernet interfaces:<br><br>```
xns routing
interface ethernet 0
xns network 20
interface ethernet 1
xns network 21
```<br><br>For more information on configuring XNS routing, see the *Network Protocols Configuration Guide, Part 2.* |
| Mismatched router network number | If the network number specified on the router is different from that configured on XNS servers, RIP[1] is not able to forward traffic correctly.

Step 1 Check the network numbers of network servers. The local XNS server administrator provides the server network numbers.

Step 2 Use the **show xns interface** exec command to obtain the network number specified on the server side of the router. |
```

Table 14–1   *XNS: Clients Cannot Connect to Servers over Router, Continued*

Possible Problem	Solution

Mismatched router network number (*Continued*)	**Step 3** Compare the network numbers. If they do not match, reconfigure the router or the server, as appropriate, with the correct network number. To reconfigure the router, use the following command:
	
	xns network *number*
	
	The argument *number* is the network number, in decimal format. Every XNS interface in a system must have a unique XNS network number.
	
	Example:
	
	This example starts XNS routing and assigns XNS network numbers to the physical networks connected to two of the router's Ethernet interfaces:
	
	`xns routing`
	`interface ethernet 0`
	`xns network 20`
	`interface ethernet 1`
	`xns network 21`
	
	Step 4 If the network numbers match, check the router interface on the client side and make sure that the assigned network number is unique with respect to all network numbers in the XNS internetwork.

Misconfigured access list	**Step 1** Use the **show xns access-list** privileged exec command on routers in the path from source to destination. This command shows whether there are access lists configured on the router. **Step 2** Disable all access lists that are configured on the router using the **no xns access-group** command. **Step 3** Test the connection from the client to the server to see whether connections are now possible. If the connection is successful, an access list is blocking traffic. **Step 4** To isolate the problem access list, apply one access list statement at a time until you can no longer create connections. **Step 5** When the problem list is identified, alter it so that necessary traffic is allowed to pass. Configure explicit **permit** statements for traffic that you want to be forwarded by the router. **Step 6** If problems persist, continue testing for problem access lists on all routers in the path from source to destination.

Table 14–1 *XNS: Clients Cannot Connect to Servers over Router, Continued*

Possible Problem	Solution
Backdoor bridge between segments	**Step 1** Use the **show xns traffic** exec command to determine whether the bad hop count field is incrementing. The XNS network updates by default occur every 30 seconds: ``` C4000#show xns traffic Rec: 3968 total, 0 format errors, 0 checksum errors, 0 bad hop count, 3968 local destination, 0 multicast [...] ``` **Step 2** If this counter is increasing, use a network analyzer to look for packet loops on suspect segments. Look for routing updates. If a backdoor bridge exists, you will probably see hop counts that increment up to 15, at which point the route disappears. The route reappears unpredictably. **Step 3** Use a network analyzer to examine the traffic on each segment. Look for known remote network numbers that appear on the local network. That is, look for packets from a remote network whose source address is not the source address of the router. The backdoor is located on the segment on which a packet from a remote network appears whose source address is not the source address of a local router. To prevent XNS routing updates from being learned from the interface connected to the same segment as the backdoor bridge, you can use the **xns input-network-filter** command. **Example:** In the following example, access list 476 controls which networks are added to the routing table when RIP packets are received on Ethernet interface 1. Network 16 is the only network whose information will be added to the routing table. Routing updates for all other networks are implicitly denied and are not added to the routing table: ``` access-list 476 permit 16 interface ethernet 1 xns input-network-filter 476 ```

[1] RIP = Routing Information Protocol

XNS: XNS Broadcast Packets Not Forwarded by Router

Symptom: XNS servers do not respond to broadcast requests from clients.

Table 14–2 outlines the problems that might cause this symptom and describes solutions to those problems.

Table 14–2   *XNS: XNS Broadcast Packets Not Forwarded by Router*

Possible Problem	Solution
Missing or misconfigured **xns helper-address** command	**Caution:** Because debugging output is assigned high priority in the CPU process, it can render the system unusable. For this reason, use **debug** commands only to troubleshoot specific problems or during troubleshooting sessions with Cisco technical support staff. Moreover, it is best to use **debug** commands during periods of lower network traffic and fewer users. Debugging during these periods decreases the likelihood that increased **debug** command processing overhead will affect system use.
	Step 1 Enable the **debug xns packet** privileged exec command and check the output for XNS packets that have an unknown type *xx* specification.
	Step 2 Use the **show running-config** privileged exec command to view the router configuration. Check the configuration of the client-side interface to see whether an **xns helper-address** interface configuration command entry is present.
	Step 3 If the **xns helper-address** command is not present, add it to the client-side interface.
	Syntax:
	xns helper-address *network.host*
	Syntax Description:
	• *network*—Network on which the target XNS server resides. This is a 32-bit decimal number.
	• *host*—Host number of the target XNS server. This is a 48-bit hexadecimal value represented as a dotted triplet of four-digit hexadecimal numbers (xxxx.xxxx.xxxx). The host must be directly connected to one of the router's directly attached networks. The number FFFF.FFFF.FFFF indicates all hosts on the specified network.

Table 14–2 *XNS: XNS Broadcast Packets Not Forwarded by Router, Continued*

Possible Problem	Solution	
Missing or misconfigured **xns helper-address** command (*Continued*)	**Example:** In the following example, the server at address 0000.0c00.23fe receives all broadcasts on network 51: `xns helper-address 51.0000.0c00.23fe`	

	Step 4	If the command is present, make sure the MAC address specified in this command is a type of broadcast.
		
		Following is an example of an all-nets broadcast:
		
		`interface ethernet 0`
		`xns helper-address -1.ffff.ffff.ffff`
		
		Following is an example of a directed broadcast:
		
		`interface ethernet 1`
		`xns helper-address 40.ffff.ffff.ffff`
		
		The helper address specification differs depending on the network configuration. For more information, refer to the Cisco IOS *Network Protocols Configuration Guide, Part 2* and *Network Protocols Command Reference, Part 2*.

Missing **xns forward-protocol** router configuration command	**Caution:** Because debugging output is assigned high priority in the CPU process, it can render the system unusable. For this reason, use **debug** commands only to troubleshoot specific problems or during troubleshooting sessions with Cisco technical support staff. Moreover, it is best to use **debug** commands during periods of lower network traffic and fewer users. Debugging during these periods decreases the likelihood that increased **debug** command processing overhead will affect system use.	
	Step 1	Enable the **debug xns packet** privileged exec command and check the output for XNS packets that have an unknown type *xx* specification.

Table 14–2   *XNS: XNS Broadcast Packets Not Forwarded by Router, Continued*

Possible Problem	Solution	
Missing **xns forward-protocol** router configuration command (*Continued*)	**Step 2**	Use the **show running-config** privileged exec command to view the router configuration. Look for an **xns forward-protocol** global configuration command entry.
	Step 3	If the **xns forward-protocol** command is not present, add it as appropriate. **Syntax:** xns *forward-protocol* **protocol** **Syntax Description:** • **protocol**—Number of an XNS protocol, in decimal. See the documentation accompanying your host's XNS implementation for a list of protocol numbers.
Misconfigured access list	**Step 1**	Use the **show access-lists** command to check whether there are access lists configured on the router.
	Step 2	Disable any access lists that are enabled on the router.
	Step 3	Test the connection to see whether connections are now possible. If the connection is successful, an access list is blocking traffic.
	Step 4	Enable access lists one at a time until connections are no longer possible.
	Step 5	Alter the problem list so traffic can pass. Configure explicit **permit** statements for traffic that you want to be forwarded by the router.
	Step 6	If problems persist, continue testing for problem access lists on all routers in the path from source to destination.

XNS: Clients Cannot Connect to Server over PSN

Symptom: Clients cannot connect to servers across a PSN. Clients can communicate with servers located on the local network.

Table 14–3 outlines the problems that might cause this symptom and describes solutions to those problems.

Table 14–3 *XNS: Clients Cannot Connect to Server over PSN*

Possible Problem	Solution
Address mapping error	**Step 1** Use the **show running-config** privileged exec command to view the configuration of the router.
	Step 2 If you are running X.25, make sure **x25 map xns** interface configuration commands are properly configured. Make sure MAC addresses and X.121 addresses are correctly specified.
	Step 3 If you are running Frame Relay, make sure **frame-relay map xns** interface configuration commands are properly configured. Make sure MAC addresses and DLCIs[1] are correctly specified.
Mismatched router network number	**Step 1** Check the network numbers of network servers. This information will be provided by the local XNS server administration staff.
	Step 2 Check the network number specified on the server side of the router.
	Step 3 Compare the network numbers. If they do not match, reconfigure the router or servers as appropriate, with the correct network number.
	Step 4 If the network numbers match, check the router interface on the client side and make sure the assigned network number is unique with respect to all network numbers in the XNS internetwork.
Encapsulation mismatch	**Step 1** Use the **show interfaces** exec command to determine the encapsulation type being used (such as **encapsulation x25**).
	Step 2 If an encapsulation command is not present, the default is HDLC[2] encapsulation. For PSN interconnection, you must explicitly specify an encapsulation type. To set the encapsulation method used by the interface, use the **encapsulation** interface configuration command.

Table 14–3   *XNS: Clients Cannot Connect to Server over PSN, Continued*

Possible Problem	Solution
Encapsulation mismatch (*Continued*)	**Syntax:** encapsulation *encapsulation-type* **Syntax Description:** *encapsulation-type*—One of the following keywords: • **atm-dxi**—Asynchronous Transfer Mode-Data Exchange Interface. • **bstun**—Block Serial Tunnel. • **frame-relay**—Frame Relay (for serial interface). • **hdlc**—HDLC protocol for serial interface. This encapsulation method provides the synchronous framing and error detection functions of HDLC without windowing or retransmission. • **lapb**—X.25 LAPB DTE operation (for serial interface). • **ppp**—PPP[3] (for serial interface). • **sdlc**—IBM serial SNA[4]. • **sdlc-primary**—IBM serial SNA (for primary serial interface). • **sdlc-secondary**—IBM serial SNA (for secondary serial interface). • **smds**—SMDS[5] (for serial interface).

[1] DLCI = data link connection identifiers
[2] HDLC = High-Level Data Link Control
[3] PPP = Point-to-Point Protocol
[4] SNA = Systems Network Architecture
[5] SMDS = Switched Multimegabit Data Services

PART 4

Troubleshooting Serial Lines and WAN Connections

Troubleshooting Serial Line Problems

This chapter presents general troubleshooting information and a discussion of tools and techniques for troubleshooting serial connections. The chapter consists of the following sections:

- Troubleshooting Using the **show interfaces serial** Command
- Using the **show controllers** Command
- Using **debug** Commands
- Using Extended **ping** Tests
- Troubleshooting Clocking Problems
- Adjusting Buffers
- Special Serial Line Tests
- Detailed Information on the **show interfaces serial** Command

TROUBLESHOOTING USING THE SHOW INTERFACES SERIAL COMMAND

The output of the **show interfaces serial** exec command displays information specific to serial interfaces. Figure 15–1 shows the output of the **show interfaces serial** exec command for a High-Level Data Link Control (HDLC) serial interface.

This section describes how to use the **show interfaces serial** command to diagnose serial line connectivity problems in a wide-area network (WAN) environment. The following sections describe some of the important fields of the command output.

Other fields shown in the display are described in detail in the section "Detailed Information on the **show interfaces serial** Command" later in this chapter.

Serial Lines: show interfaces serial Status Line Conditions

You can identify five possible problem states in the interface status line of the **show interfaces serial** display (see Figure 15–1):

- Serial x is down, line protocol is down
- Serial x is up, line protocol is down
- Serial x is up, line protocol is up (looped)
- Serial x is up, line protocol is down (disabled)
- Serial x is administratively down, line protocol is down

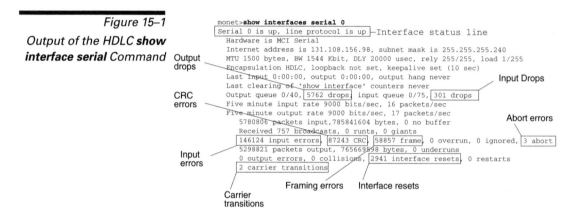

Figure 15–1

*Output of the HDLC **show interface serial** Command*

Table 15–1 shows the interface status conditions, possible problems associated with the conditions, and solutions to those problems.

Table 15–1   *Serial Lines: **show interfaces serial** Status Line Conditions*

Status Line Condition	Possible Problem	Solution
Serial x is up, line protocol is up	—	This is the proper status line condition. No action required.
Serial x is down, line protocol is down (DTE[1] mode)	Typically indicates that the router is not sensing a CD[2] signal (that is, CD is not active). • Telephone company problem—Line is down or line is not connected to CSU[3]/DSU[4] • Faulty or incorrect cabling • Hardware failure (CSU/DSU)	**Step 1** Check the LEDs on the CSU/DSU to see whether CD is active, or insert a breakout box on the line to check for the CD signal. **Step 2** Verify that you are using the proper cable and interface (see your hardware installation documentation). **Step 3** Insert a breakout box and check all control leads. **Step 4** Contact your leased-line or other carrier service to see whether there is a problem. **Step 5** Swap faulty parts. **Step 6** If you suspect faulty router hardware, change the serial line to another port. If the connection comes up, the previously connected interface has a problem.

Table 15–1 *Serial Lines:* ***show interfaces serial*** *Status Line Conditions, Continued*

Status Line Condition	Possible Problem	Solution
Serial *x* is up, line protocol is down (DTE mode)	• Local or remote router is misconfigured • Keepalives are not being sent by remote router • Leased-line or other carrier service problem—noisy line, or misconfigured or failed switch • Timing problem on cable (SCTE[5] not set on CSU/DSU) • Failed local or remote CSU/DSU • Router hardware failure (local or remote)	**Step 1** Put the modem, CSU, or DSU in local loopback mode and use the **show interfaces serial** command to determine whether the line protocol comes up. If the line protocol comes up, a telephone company problem or a failed remote router is the likely problem. **Step 2** If the problem appears to be on the remote end, repeat Step 1 on the remote modem, CSU, or DSU. **Step 3** Verify all cabling. Make certain that the cable is attached to the correct interface, the correct CSU/DSU, and the correct telephone company network termination point. Use the **show controllers** exec command to determine which cable is attached to which interface. **Step 4** Enable the **debug serial interface** exec command. **Caution:** Because debugging output is assigned high priority in the CPU process, it can render the system unusable. For this reason, use **debug** commands only to troubleshoot specific problems or during troubleshooting sessions with Cisco technical support staff. Moreover, it is best to use **debug** commands during periods of lower network traffic and fewer users. Debugging during these periods decreases the likelihood that increased **debug** command processing overhead will affect system use.

Table 15-1 *Serial Lines: **show interfaces serial** Status Line Conditions, Continued*

Status Line Condition	Possible Problem	Solution
Serial *x* is up, line protocol is down (DTE mode) (*Continued*)		**Step 5** If the line protocol does not come up in local loopback mode and if the output of the **debug serial interface** exec command shows that the keepalive counter is not incrementing, a router hardware problem is likely. Swap router interface hardware.
		Step 6 If the line protocol comes up and the keepalive counter increments, the problem is *not* in the local router. Troubleshoot the serial line as described in the sections "Troubleshooting Clocking Problems" and "CSU and DSU Loopback Tests" later in this chapter.
		Step 7 If you suspect faulty router hardware, change the serial line to an unused port. If the connection comes up, the previously connected interface has a problem.

Table 15–1   *Serial Lines:* **show interfaces serial** *Status Line Conditions, Continued*

Status Line Condition	Possible Problem	Solution
Serial *x* is up, line protocol is down (DCE[6] mode)	• Missing **clockrate** interface configuration command • DTE device does not support or is not set up for SCTE mode (terminal timing) • Failed remote CSU or DSU • Failed or incorrect cable • Router hardware failure	**Step 1** Add the **clockrate** interface configuration command on the serial interface. **Syntax:** **clock rate** *bps* **Syntax Description:** • *bps*—Desired clock rate in bits per second: 1200, 2400, 4800, 9600, 19200, 38400, 56000, 64000, 72000, 125000, 148000, 250000, 500000, 800000, 1000000, 1300000, 2000000, 4000000, or 8000000. **Step 2** Set the DTE device to SCTE mode if possible. If your CSU/DSU does not support SCTE, you might have to disable SCTE on the Cisco router interface. Refer to the section "Inverting the Transmit Clock" later in this chapter. **Step 3** Verify that the correct cable is being used. **Step 4** If the line protocol is still down, there is a possible hardware failure or cabling problem. Insert a breakout box and observe leads. **Step 5** Replace faulty parts as necessary.

Table 15-1 *Serial Lines:* ***show interfaces serial*** *Status Line Conditions, Continued*

Status Line Condition	Possible Problem	Solution	
Serial *x* is up, line protocol is up (looped)	Loop exists in circuit. The sequence number in the keepalive packet changes to a random number when a loop is initially detected. If the same random number is returned over the link, a loop exists.	Step 1	Use the **show running-config** privileged exec command to look for any **loopback** interface configuration command entries.
		Step 2	If you find a **loopback** interface configuration command entry, use the **no loopback** interface configuration command to remove the loop.
		Step 3	If you do not find the **loopback** interface configuration command, examine the CSU/DSU to determine whether they are configured in manual loopback mode. If they are, disable manual loopback.
		Step 4	Reset the CSU or DSU and inspect the line status. If the line protocol comes up, no other action is needed.
		Step 5	If the CSU or DSU is not configured in manual loopback mode, contact the leased-line or other carrier service for line troubleshooting assistance.
Serial *x* is up, line protocol is down (disabled)	• High error rate due to telephone company service problem • CSU or DSU hardware problem • Bad router hardware (interface)	Step 1	Troubleshoot the line with a serial analyzer and breakout box. Look for toggling CTS[7] and DSR[8] signals.
		Step 2	Loop CSU/DSU (DTE loop). If the problem continues, it is likely that there is a hardware problem. If the problem does not continue, it is likely that there is a telephone company problem.
		Step 3	Swap out bad hardware as required (CSU, DSU, switch, local or remote router).

Table 15–1   *Serial Lines: **show interfaces serial** Status Line Conditions, Continued*

Status Line Condition	Possible Problem	Solution
Serial *x* is administratively down, line protocol is down	• Router configuration includes the **shutdown** interface configuration command • Duplicate IP address	**Step 1** Check the router configuration for the **shutdown** command. **Step 2** Use the **no shutdown** interface configuration command to remove the **shutdown** command. **Step 3** Verify that there are no identical IP addresses using the **show running-config** privileged exec command or the **show interfaces** exec command. **Step 4** If there are duplicate addresses, resolve the conflict by changing one of the IP addresses.

[1] DTE = data terminal equipment
[2] CD = Carrier Detect
[3] CSU = channel service unit
[4] DSU = digital service unit
[5] SCTE = serial clock transmit external
[6] DCE = data circuit-terminating equipment
[7] CTS = clear-to-send
[8] DSR = data-set ready

Serial Lines: Increasing Output Drops on Serial Link

Output drops appear in the output of the **show interfaces serial** command (refer to Figure 15–1) when the system is attempting to hand off a packet to a transmit buffer but no buffers are available.

Symptom: Increasing output drops on serial link.

Table 15–2 outlines the possible problem that might cause this symptom and describes solutions to that problem.

Table 15–2 *Serial Lines: Increasing Output Drops on Serial Link*

Possible Problem	Solution
Input rate to serial interface exceeds bandwidth available on serial link	**Step 1** Minimize periodic broadcast traffic such as routing and SAP[1] updates by using access lists or by other means. For example, to increase the delay between SAP updates, use the **ipx sap-interval** interface configuration command.
	Step 2 Increase the output hold queue size in small increments (for instance, 25 percent), using the **hold-queue out** interface configuration command.
	Step 3 On affected interfaces, turn off fast switching for heavily used protocols. For example, to turn off IP fast switching, enter the **no ip route-cache** interface configuration command. For the command syntax for other protocols, consult the Cisco IOS configuration guides and command references.
	Step 4 Implement priority queuing on slower serial links by configuring priority lists. For information on configuring priority lists, see the Cisco IOS configuration guides and command references.
	Note: Output drops are acceptable under certain conditions. For instance, if a link is known to be overused (with no way to remedy the situation), it is often considered preferable to drop packets than to hold them. This is true for protocols that support flow control and can retransmit data (such as TCP/IP and Novell IPX[2]). However, some protocols, such as DECnet and local-area transport are sensitive to dropped packets and accommodate retransmission poorly, if at all.

[1] SAP = Service Advertising Protocol
[2] IPX = Internetwork Packet Exchange

Serial Lines: Increasing Input Drops on Serial Link

Input drops appear in the output of the **show interfaces serial** exec command (refer to Figure 15–1) when too many packets from that interface are still being processed in the system.

Symptom: Increasing number of input drops on serial link.

Table 15–3 outlines the possible problem that might cause this symptom and describes solutions to that problem.

Table 15–3 *Serial Lines: Increasing Input Drops on Serial Link*

Possible Problem	Solution
Input rate exceeds the capacity of the router or input queues exceed the size of output queues	**Note:** Input drop problems are typically seen when traffic is being routed between faster interfaces (such as Ethernet, Token Ring, and FDDI[1]) and serial interfaces. When traffic is light, there is no problem. As traffic rates increase, backups start occurring. Routers drop packets during these congested periods.
	Step 1 Increase the output queue size on common destination interfaces for the interface that is dropping packets. Use the **hold-queue out** interface configuration command. Increase these queues by small increments (for instance, 25%) until you no longer see drops in the **show interfaces** output. The default output hold queue limit is 100 packets.
	Step 2 Reduce the input queue size, using the **hold-queue in** interface configuration command, to force input drops to become output drops. Output drops have less impact on the performance of the router than do input drops. The default input hold queue is 75 packets.

[1] FDDI = Fiber Distributed Data Interface

Serial Lines: Increasing Input Errors in Excess of 1% of Total Interface Traffic

If input errors appear in the **show interfaces serial** output (refer to Figure 15–1), there are several possible sources of those errors. The most likely sources are summarized in Table 15–4.

NOTES

Any input error value for cyclic redundancy check (CRC) errors, framing errors, or aborts above 1 percent of the total interface traffic suggests some kind of link problem that should be isolated and repaired.

Symptom: Increasing number of input errors in excess of 1 percent of total interface traffic.

Table 15–4   *Serial Lines: Increasing Input Errors in Excess of 1% of Total Interface Traffic*

Possible Problem	Solution
The following problems can result in this symptom: • Faulty telephone company equipment • Noisy serial line • Incorrect clocking configuration (SCTE not set) • Incorrect cable or cable too long • Bad cable or connection • Bad CSU or DSU • Bad router hardware • Data converter or other device being used between router and DSU	**Note:** Cisco strongly recommends against the use of data converters when you are connecting a router to a WAN or serial network. **Step 1** Use a serial analyzer to isolate the source of the input errors. If you detect errors, it is likely that there is a hardware problem or a clock mismatch in a device that is external to the router. **Step 2** Use the loopback and **ping** tests to isolate the specific problem source. For more information, see the sections "Using the **trace** Command" and "CSU and DSU Loopback Tests" later in this chapter. **Step 3** Look for patterns. For example, if errors occur at a consistent interval, they could be related to a periodic function such as the sending of routing updates.

Serial Lines: Troubleshooting Serial Line Input Errors

Table 15–5 describes the various types of input errors displayed by the **show interfaces serial** command (see Figure 15–1), possible problems that might be causing the errors, and solutions to those problems.

Table 15–5 *Serial Lines: Troubleshooting Serial Line Input Errors*

Input Error Type (Field Name)	Possible Problem	Solution
CRC errors (CRC)	CRC errors occur when the CRC calculation does not pass (indicating that data is corrupted) for one of the following reasons: • Noisy serial line • Serial cable is too long or cable from the CSU/DSU to the router is not shielded • SCTE mode is not enabled on DSU • CSU line clock is incorrectly configured • Ones density problem on T1 link (incorrect framing or coding specification)	**Step 1** Ensure that the line is clean enough for transmission requirements. Shield the cable if necessary. **Step 2** Make sure the cable is within the recommended length (no more than 50 feet [15.24 meters], or 25 feet [7.62 meters] for T1 link). **Step 3** Ensure that all devices are properly configured for a common line clock. Set SCTE on the local and remote DSU. If your CSU/DSU does not support SCTE, see the section "Inverting the Transmit Clock" later in this chapter. **Step 4** Make certain that the local and remote CSU/DSU are configured for the same framing and coding scheme as that used by the leased-line or other carrier service (for example, ESF/B8ZS). **Step 5** Contact your leased-line or other carrier service and have it perform integrity tests on the line.

Table 15–5   *Serial Lines: Troubleshooting Serial Line Input Errors, Continued*

Input Error Type (Field Name)	Possible Problem	Solution	
Framing errors (frame)	A framing error occurs when a packet does not end on an 8-bit byte boundary for one of the following reasons: • Noisy serial line • Improperly designed cable; serial cable is too long; the cable from the CSU or DSU to the router is not shielded • SCTE mode is not enabled on the DSU; the CSU line clock is incorrectly configured; one of the clocks is configured for local clocking • Ones density problem on T1 link (incorrect framing or coding specification)	**Step 1**	Ensure that the line is clean enough for transmission requirements. Shield the cable if necessary. Make certain you are using the correct cable.
		Step 2	Make sure the cable is within the recommended length (no more than 50 feet [15.24 meters], or 25 feet [7.62 meters] for T1 link)
		Step 3	Ensure that all devices are properly configured to use a common line clock. Set SCTE on the local and remote DSU. If your CSU/DSU does not support SCTE, see the section "Inverting the Transmit Clock" later in this chapter.
		Step 4	Make certain that the local and remote CSU/DSU is configured for the same framing and coding scheme as that used by the leased-line or other carrier service (for example, ESF[1]/B8ZS[2]).
		Step 5	Contact your leased-line or other carrier service and have it perform integrity tests on the line.

Table 15–5　*Serial Lines: Troubleshooting Serial Line Input Errors, Continued*

Input Error Type (Field Name)	Possible Problem	Solution
Aborted transmission (abort)	Aborts indicate an illegal sequence of one bits (more than seven in a row) The following are possible reasons for this to occur: • SCTE mode is not enabled on DSU • CSU line clock is incorrectly configured • Serial cable is too long or cable from the CSU or DSU to the router is not shielded • Ones density problem on T1 link (incorrect framing or coding specification) • Packet terminated in middle of transmission (typical cause is an interface reset or a framing error) • Hardware problem—bad circuit, bad CSU/DSU, or bad sending interface on remote router	**Step 1** Ensure that all devices are properly configured to use a common line clock. Set SCTE on the local and remote DSU. If your CSU/DSU does not support SCTE, see the section "Inverting the Transmit Clock" later in this chapter. **Step 2** Shield the cable if necessary. Make certain the cable is within the recommended length (no more than 50 feet [15.24 meters], or 25 feet [7.62 meters] for T1 link). Ensure that all connections are good. **Step 3** Check the hardware at both ends of the link. Swap faulty equipment as necessary. **Step 4** Lower data rates and determine whether aborts decrease. **Step 5** Use local and remote loopback tests to determine where aborts are occurring (see the section "Special Serial Line Tests" later in this chapter). **Step 6** Contact your leased-line or other carrier service and have it perform integrity tests on the line.

[1] ESF = Extended Superframe Format
[2] B8ZS = binary eight-zero substitution

Serial Lines: Increasing Interface Resets on Serial Link

Interface resets that appear in the output of the **show interfaces serial** exec command (see Figure 15–1) are the result of missed keepalive packets.

Symptom: Increasing interface resets on serial link.

Table 15–6 outlines the possible problems that might cause this symptom and describes solutions to those problems.

Table 15–6 *Serial Lines: Increasing Interface Resets on Serial Link*

Possible Problem	Solution
The following problems can result in this symptom: • Congestion on link (typically associated with output drops) • Bad line causing CD transitions • Possible hardware problem at the CSU, DSU, or switch	When interface resets are occurring, examine other fields of the **show interfaces serial** command output to determine the source of the problem. Assuming that an increase in interface resets is being recorded, examine the following fields: **Step 1** If there is a high number of output drops in the **show interfaces serial** output, see the section "Serial Lines: Increasing Output Drops on Serial Link" earlier in this chapter. **Step 2** Check the carrier transitions field in the **show interfaces serial** display. If carrier transitions are high while interface resets are being registered, the problem is likely to be a bad link or bad CSU or DSU. Contact your leased-line or carrier service and swap faulty equipment as necessary. **Step 3** Examine the input errors field in the **show interfaces serial** display. If input errors are high while interface resets are increasing, the problem is probably a bad link or bad CSU/DSU. Contact your leased-line or other carrier service and swap faulty equipment as necessary.

Serial Lines: Increasing Carrier Transitions Count on Serial Link

Carrier transitions appear in the output of the **show interfaces serial** exec command whenever there is an interruption in the carrier signal (such as an interface reset at the remote end of a link).

Symptom: Increasing carrier transitions count on serial link.

Table 15–7 outlines the possible problems that might cause this symptom and describes solutions to those problems.

Table 15-7 *Serial Lines: Increasing Carrier Transitions Count on Serial Link*

Possible Problem	Solution
The following problems can result in this symptom: • Line interruptions due to an external source (such as physical separation of cabling, red or yellow T1 alarms, or lightning striking somewhere along the network) • Faulty switch, DSU, or router hardware	**Step 1** Check hardware at both ends of the link (attach a breakout box or a serial analyzer and test to determine source of problems). **Step 2** If an analyzer or breakout box is unable to identify any external problems, check the router hardware. **Step 3** Swap faulty equipment as necessary.

USING THE SHOW CONTROLLERS COMMAND

The **show controllers** exec command is another important diagnostic tool when troubleshooting serial lines. The command syntax varies depending on platform:

- For serial interfaces on Cisco 7000 series routers, use the **show controllers cbus** exec command
- For Cisco access products, use the **show controllers** exec command
- For the AGS, CGS, and MGS, use the **show controllers mci** exec command

Figure 15–2 shows the output from the **show controllers cbus** exec command. This command is used on Cisco 7000 series routers with the Fast Serial Interface Processor (FSIP) card. Check the command output to make certain that the cable to the channel service unit/digital service unit (CSU/DSU) is attached to the proper interface. You can also check the microcode version to see whether it is current.

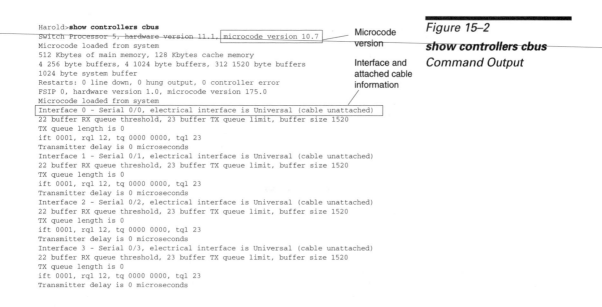

```
Harold>show controllers cbus
Switch Processor 5, hardware version 11.1, microcode version 10.7
Microcode loaded from system
512 Kbytes of main memory, 128 Kbytes cache memory
4 256 byte buffers, 4 1024 byte buffers, 312 1520 byte buffers
1024 byte system buffer
Restarts: 0 line down, 0 hung output, 0 controller error
FSIP 0, hardware version 1.0, microcode version 175.0
Microcode loaded from system
Interface 0 - Serial 0/0, electrical interface is Universal (cable unattached)
22 buffer RX queue threshold, 23 buffer TX queue limit, buffer size 1520
TX queue length is 0
ift 0001, rql 12, tq 0000 0000, tql 23
Transmitter delay is 0 microseconds
Interface 1 - Serial 0/1, electrical interface is Universal (cable unattached)
22 buffer RX queue threshold, 23 buffer TX queue limit, buffer size 1520
TX queue length is 0
ift 0001, rql 12, tq 0000 0000, tql 23
Transmitter delay is 0 microseconds
Interface 2 - Serial 0/2, electrical interface is Universal (cable unattached)
22 buffer RX queue threshold, 23 buffer TX queue limit, buffer size 1520
TX queue length is 0
ift 0001, rql 12, tq 0000 0000, tql 23
Transmitter delay is 0 microseconds
Interface 3 - Serial 0/3, electrical interface is Universal (cable unattached)
22 buffer RX queue threshold, 23 buffer TX queue limit, buffer size 1520
TX queue length is 0
ift 0001, rql 12, tq 0000 0000, tql 23
Transmitter delay is 0 microseconds
```

Microcode version

Interface and attached cable information

Figure 15–2

show controllers cbus
Command Output

On access products such as the Cisco 2000, Cisco 2500, Cisco 3000, and Cisco 4000 series access servers and routers, use the **show controllers** exec command. Figure 15–3 shows the **show controllers** command output from the Basic Rate Interface (BRI) and serial interfaces on a Cisco 2503 access server. (Note that some output is not shown.)

The **show controllers** output indicates the state of the interface channels and whether a cable is attached to the interface. In Figure 15–3, serial interface 0 has an RS-232 DTE cable attached. Serial interface 1 has no cable attached.

Figure 15–4 shows the output of the **show controllers mci** command. This command is used on AGS, CGS, and MGS routers only. If the electrical interface is displayed as UNKNOWN (instead of V.35, EIA/TIA-449, or some other electrical interface type), an improperly connected cable is the likely problem. Abad applique or a problem with the internal wiring of the card is also possible. If the electrical interface is unknown, the corresponding display for the **show interfaces serial** exec command will show that the interface and line protocol are down.

Figure 15–3

show controllers

Command Output

```
Maude>show controllers
BRI unit 0
D Chan Info:                                    D channel is
Layer 1 is DEACTIVATED                          deactivated

[. . .]
0 missed datagrams, 0 overruns, 0 bad frame addresses
0 bad datagram encapsulations, 0 memory errors
0 transmitter underruns

B1 Chan Info:                                   B channel 1 is
Layer 1 is DEACTIVATED                          deactivated

[. . .]
0 missed datagrams, 0 overruns, 0 bad frame addresses
0 bad datagram encapsulations, 0 memory errors
0 transmitter underruns

B2 Chan Info:

[. . .]
LANCE unit 0, idb 0x9515C, ds 0x96F00, regaddr = 0x2130000, reset_mask 0x2
IB at 0x40163F4: mode=0x0000, mcfilter 0000/0000/0000/0000
station address 0000.0c0a.28a7  default station address 0000.0c0a.28a7
buffer size 1524

[. . .]
0 missed datagrams, 0 overruns, 0 late collisions, 0 lost carrier events
0 transmitter underruns, 0 excessive collisions,  0 tdr, 0 babbles
0 memory errors, 0 spurious initialization done interrupts
0 no enp status, 0 buffer errors, 0 overflow errors
0 one_col, 0 more_col, 3 deferred, 0 tx_buff
0 throttled, 0 enabled
Lance csr0 = 0x73

HD unit 0, idb = 0x98D28, driver structure at 0x9AAD0    Attached cable on
buffer size 1524 HD unit 0, RS-232 DTE cable             serial interface 0

[. . .]
0 missed datagrams, 0 overruns, 0 bad frame addresses
0 bad datagram encapsulations, 0 memory errors
0 transmitter underruns

HD unit 1, idb = 0x9C1B8, driver structure at 0x9DF60    No attached cable on
buffer size 1524 HD unit 1, No DCE cable                 serial interface 1

[. . .]
0 missed datagrams, 0 overruns, 0 bad frame addresses
0 bad datagram encapsulations, 0 memory errors
0 transmitter underruns
```

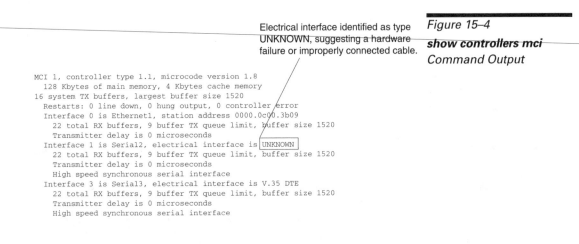

Electrical interface identified as type UNKNOWN, suggesting a hardware failure or improperly connected cable.

Figure 15–4
show controllers mci
Command Output

```
MCI 1, controller type 1.1, microcode version 1.8
  128 Kbytes of main memory, 4 Kbytes cache memory
16 system TX buffers, largest buffer size 1520
  Restarts: 0 line down, 0 hung output, 0 controller error
  Interface 0 is Ethernet1, station address 0000.0c00.3b09
    22 total RX buffers, 9 buffer TX queue limit, buffer size 1520
    Transmitter delay is 0 microseconds
  Interface 1 is Serial2, electrical interface is UNKNOWN
    22 total RX buffers, 9 buffer TX queue limit, buffer size 1520
    Transmitter delay is 0 microseconds
    High speed synchronous serial interface
  Interface 3 is Serial3, electrical interface is V.35 DTE
    22 total RX buffers, 9 buffer TX queue limit, buffer size 1520
    Transmitter delay is 0 microseconds
    High speed synchronous serial interface
```

USING DEBUG COMMANDS

The output of the various **debug** privileged exec commands provides diagnostic information relating to protocol status and network activity for many internetworking events.

CAUTION

Because debugging output is assigned high priority in the CPU process, it can render the system unusable. For this reason, use **debug** commands only to troubleshoot specific problems or during troubleshooting sessions with Cisco technical support staff. Moreover, it is best to use **debug** commands during periods of lower network traffic and fewer users. Debugging during these periods decreases the likelihood that increased **debug** command processing overhead will affect system use. When you finish using a **debug** command, remember to disable it with its specific **no debug** command or with the **no debug all** command.

Following are some **debug** commands that are useful when troubleshooting serial and WAN problems. More information about the function and output of each of these commands is provided in the *Debug Command Reference* publication:

- *debug serial interface*—Verifies whether HDLC keepalive packets are incrementing. If they are not, a possible timing problem exists on the interface card or in the network.

- *debug x25 events*—Detects X.25 events, such as the opening and closing of switched virtual circuits (SVCs). The resulting "cause and diagnostic" information is included with the event report.

- *debug lapb*—Outputs Link Access Procedure, Balanced (LAPB) or Level 2 X.25 information.

- *debug arp*—Indicates whether the router is sending information about or learning about routers (with ARP packets) on the other side of the WAN cloud. Use this command when some nodes on a TCP/IP network are responding but others are not.

- *debug frame-relay lmi*—Obtains Local Management Interface (LMI) information useful for determining whether a Frame Relay switch and a router are sending and receiving LMI packets.

- *debug frame-relay events*—Determines whether exchanges are occurring between a router and a Frame Relay switch.

- *debug ppp negotiation*—Shows Point-to-Point Protocol (PPP) packets transmitted during PPP startup, where PPP options are negotiated.

- *debug ppp packet*—Shows PPP packets being sent and received. This command displays low-level packet dumps.

- *debug ppp errors*—Shows PPP errors (such as illegal or malformed frames) associated with PPP connection negotiation and operation.

- *debug ppp chap*—Shows PPP Challenge Handshake Authentication Protocol (CHAP) and Password Authentication Protocol (PAP) packet exchanges.

- *debug serial packet*—Shows Switched Multimegabit Data Service (SMDS) packets being sent and received. This display also prints error messages to indicate why a packet was not sent or was received erroneously. For SMDS, the command dumps the entire SMDS header and some payload data when an SMDS packet is transmitted or received.

USING EXTENDED PING TESTS

The **ping** command is a useful test available on Cisco internetworking devices as well as on many host systems. In TCP/IP, this diagnostic tool is also known as an Internet Control Message Protocol (ICMP) Echo Request.

NOTES

The **ping** command is particularly useful when high levels of input errors are being registered in the **show interfaces serial** display. See Figure 15–1.

Cisco internetworking devices provide a mechanism to automate the sending of many **ping** packets in sequence. Figure 15–5 illustrates the menu used to specify extended **ping** options. This example specifies 20 successive **pings**. However, when testing the components on your serial line, you should specify a much larger number, such as 1000 **pings**.

```
Betelgeuse# ping
Protocol [ip]:
Target IP address: 129.44.12.7
Repeat count [5]: 20 ───────────── ping count
Datagram size [100]: 64                specification
Timeout in seconds [2]:
Extended commands [n]: yes ──────────── Extended commands
Source address:                          selected option
Type of service [0]:
Set DF bit in IP header? [no]:
Validate reply data? [no]:
Data pattern [0xABCD]: 0xffff ─────────── Data pattern
Loose, Strict, Record, Timestamp, Verbose[none]:   specification
Sweep range of sizes [n]:
Type escape sequence to abort.
Sending 20, 64-byte ICMP Echos to  129.44.12.7, timeout is 2 seconds:
Packet has data pattern 0xFFFF
!!!!!!!!!!!!!!!!!!!!!!
Success rate is 100 percent, round-trip min/avg/max = 1/3/4 ms
```

Figure 15–5

*Extended **ping** Specification Menu*

In general, perform serial line **ping** tests as follows:

Step 1   Put the CSU or DSU into local loopback mode.

Step 2   Configure the extended **ping** command to send different data patterns and packet sizes. Figure 15–6 and Figure 15–7 illustrate two useful **ping** tests, an all-zeros 1500-byte **ping** and an all-ones 1500-byte **ping**, respectively.

Step 3   Examine the **show interfaces serial** command output (see Figure 15–1) and determine whether input errors have increased. If input errors have not increased, the local hardware (DSU, cable, router interface card) is probably in good condition.

Assuming that this test sequence was prompted by the appearance of a large number of CRC and framing errors, a clocking problem is likely. Check the CSU or DSU for a timing problem. See the section "Troubleshooting Clocking Problems" later in this chapter.

Step 4   If you determine that the clocking configuration is correct and is operating properly, put the CSU or DSU into remote loopback mode.

Step 5   Repeat the **ping** test and look for changes in the input error statistics.

Step 6   If input errors increase, there is either a problem in the serial line or on the CSU/DSU. Contact the WAN service provider and swap the CSU or DSU. If problems persist, contact your technical support representative.

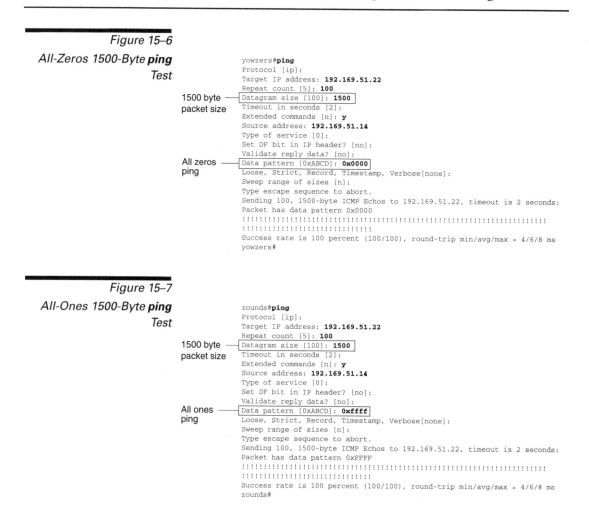

Figure 15–6

All-Zeros 1500-Byte **ping** Test

1500 byte packet size

All zeros ping

```
yowzers#ping
Protocol [ip]:
Target IP address: 192.169.51.22
Repeat count [5]: 100
Datagram size [100]: 1500
Timeout in seconds [2]:
Extended commands [n]: y
Source address: 192.169.51.14
Type of service [0]:
Set DF bit in IP header? [no]:
Validate reply data? [no]:
Data pattern [0xABCD]: 0x0000
Loose, Strict, Record, Timestamp, Verbose[none]:
Sweep range of sizes [n]:
Type escape sequence to abort.
Sending 100, 1500-byte ICMP Echos to 192.169.51.22, timeout is 2 seconds:
Packet has data pattern 0x0000
!!!!!!!!!!!!!!!!!!!!!!!!!!!!!!!!!!!!!!!!!!!!!!!!!!!!!!!!!!!!!!!!!!!!!!!
!!!!!!!!!!!!!!!!!!!!!!!!!!!!!!!!!!
Success rate is 100 percent (100/100), round-trip min/avg/max = 4/6/8 ms
yowzers#
```

Figure 15–7

All-Ones 1500-Byte **ping** Test

1500 byte packet size

All ones ping

```
zounds#ping
Protocol [ip]:
Target IP address: 192.169.51.22
Repeat count [5]: 100
Datagram size [100]: 1500
Timeout in seconds [2]:
Extended commands [n]: y
Source address: 192.169.51.14
Type of service [0]:
Set DF bit in IP header? [no]:
Validate reply data? [no]:
Data pattern [0xABCD]: 0xffff
Loose, Strict, Record, Timestamp, Verbose[none]:
Sweep range of sizes [n]:
Type escape sequence to abort.
Sending 100, 1500-byte ICMP Echos to 192.169.51.22, timeout is 2 seconds:
Packet has data pattern 0xFFFF
!!!!!!!!!!!!!!!!!!!!!!!!!!!!!!!!!!!!!!!!!!!!!!!!!!!!!!!!!!!!!!!!!!!!!!!
!!!!!!!!!!!!!!!!!!!!!!!!!!!!!!!!!
Success rate is 100 percent (100/100), round-trip min/avg/max = 4/6/8 ms
zounds#
```

TROUBLESHOOTING CLOCKING PROBLEMS

Clocking conflicts in serial connections can lead either to chronic loss of connection service or to degraded performance. This section discusses the important aspects of clocking problems: clocking problem causes, detecting clocking problems, isolating clocking problems, and clocking problem solutions.

Clocking Overview

The CSU/DSU derives the data clock from the data that passes through it. In order to recover the clock, the CSU/DSU hardware *must* receive at least one 1-bit value for every 8 bits of data that pass through it; this is known as *ones density*. Maintaining ones density allows the hardware to recover the data clock reliably.

Newer T1 implementations commonly use Extended Superframe Format (ESF) framing with binary eight-zero substitution (B8ZS) coding. B8ZS provides a scheme by which a special code is substituted whenever eight consecutive zeros are sent through the serial link. This code is then interpreted at the remote end of the connection. This technique guarantees ones density independent of the data stream.

Older T1 implementations use D4 (also known as Superframe Format [SF]) framing and Alternate Mark Inversion (AMI) coding. AMI does not utilize a coding scheme like B8ZS. This restricts the type of data that can be transmitted because ones density is not maintained independent of the data stream.

Another important element in serial communications is serial clock transmit external (SCTE) terminal timing. SCTE is the clock echoed back from the data terminal equipment (DTE) device (for example, a router) to the data communications equipment (DCE) device (for example, the CSU/DSU).

When the DCE device uses SCTE instead of its internal clock to sample data from the DTE, it is better able to sample the data without error even if there is a phase shift in the cable between the CSU/DSU and the router. Using SCTE is highly recommended for serial transmissions faster than 64 kbps. If your CSU/DSU does not support SCTE, see the section "Inverting the Transmit Clock" later in this chapter.

Clocking Problem Causes

In general, clocking problems in serial WAN interconnections can be attributed to one of the following causes:

- Incorrect DSU configuration
- Incorrect CSU configuration
- Cables out of specification (longer than 50 feet [15.24 meters] or unshielded)
- Noisy or poor patch panel connections
- Several cables connected together in a row

Detecting Clocking Problems

To detect clocking conflicts on a serial interface, look for input errors as follows:

Step 1   Use the **show interfaces serial** exec command on the routers at both ends of the link.

Step 2   Examine the command output for CRC, framing errors, and aborts.

Step 3   If either of these steps indicates errors exceeding an approximate range of 0.5% to 2.0% of traffic on the interface, clocking problems are likely to exist somewhere in the WAN.

Step 4   Isolate the source of the clocking conflicts as outlined in the following section, "Isolating Clocking Problems."

Step 5   Bypass or repair any faulty patch panels.

Isolating Clocking Problems

After you determine that clocking conflicts are the most likely cause of input errors, use the following procedure will help you isolate the source of those errors:

Step 1   Perform a series of **ping** tests and loopback tests (both local and remote), as described in the section "CSU and DSU Loopback Tests" earlier in this chapter.

Step 2   Determine which end of the connection is the source of the problem, or whether the problem is in the line. In local loopback mode, run different patterns and sizes in the **ping** tests (for example, use 1500-byte datagrams). Using a single pattern and packet size may not force errors to materialize, particularly when a serial cable to the router or CSU/DSU is the problem.

Step 3   Use the **show interfaces serial** exec command and determine whether input errors counts are increasing and where they are accumulating.

If input errors are accumulating on both ends of the connection, clocking of the CSU is the most likely problem.

If only one end is experiencing input errors, there is probably a DSU clocking or cabling problem.

Aborts on one end suggests that the other end is sending bad information or that there is a line problem.

NOTES

Always refer to the **show interfaces serial** command output (see Figure 15–1) and log any changes in error counts or note if the error count does not change.

Clocking Problem Solutions

Table 15–8 outlines suggested remedies for clocking problems, based on the source of the problem.

Table 15-8 *Serial Lines: Clocking Problems and Solutions*

Possible Problem	Solution
Incorrect CSU configuration	**Step 1** Determine whether the CSUs at both ends agree on the clock source (local or line).
	Step 2 If the CSUs do not agree, configure them so that they do (usually the line is the source).
	Step 3 Check the LBO[1] setting on the CSU to ensure that the impedance matches that of the physical line. For information on configuring your CSU, consult your CSU hardware documentation.
Incorrect DSU configuration	**Step 1** Determine whether the DSUs at both ends have SCTE mode enabled.
	Step 2 If SCTE is not enabled on both ends of the connection, enable it.
	(For any interface that is connected to a line of 128 kbps or faster, SCTE *must* be enabled. If your DSU does not support SCTE, see the section "Inverting the Transmit Clock" later in this chapter.)
	Step 3 Make sure that ones density is maintained. This requires that the DSU use the same framing and coding schemes (for example, ESF and B8ZS) used by the leased-line or other carrier service.
	Check with your leased-line provider for information on its framing and coding schemes.
	Step 4 If your carrier service uses AMI coding, either invert the transmit clock on both sides of the link or run the DSU in bit-stuff mode. For information on configuring your DSU, consult your DSU hardware documentation.
Cable to router out of specification	If the cable is longer than 50 feet (15.24 meters), use a shorter cable.
	If the cable is unshielded, replace it with shielded cable.

[1] LBO = Line Build Out

Inverting the Transmit Clock

If you are attempting serial connections at speeds greater than 64 kbps with a CSU/DSU that does not support SCTE, you might have to invert the transmit clock on the router. Inverting the transmit clock compensates for phase shifts between the data and clock signals.

The specific command used to invert the transmit clock varies between platforms. On a Cisco 7000 series router, enter the **invert-transmit-clock** interface configuration command. For Cisco 4000 series routers, use the **dte-invert-txc** interface configuration command.

To ensure that you are using the correct command syntax for your router, refer to the user guide for your router or access server and to the Cisco IOS configuration guides and command references.

NOTES

On older platforms, inverting the transmit clock might require that you move a physical jumper.

ADJUSTING BUFFERS

Excessively high bandwidth utilization over 70% results in reduced overall performance and can cause intermittent failures. For example, DECnet file transmissions might be failing due to packets being dropped somewhere in the network.

If the situation is bad enough, you *must* increase the bandwidth of the link. However, increasing the bandwidth might not be necessary or immediately practical. One way to resolve marginal serial line overutilization problems is to control how the router uses data buffers.

CAUTION

In general, do *not* adjust system buffers unless you are working closely with a Cisco technical support representative. You can severely affect the performance of your hardware and your network if you incorrectly adjust the system buffers on your router.

Use one of the following three options to control how buffers are used:

- Adjust parameters associated with system buffers
- Specify the number of packets held in input or output queues (hold queues)
- Prioritize how traffic is queued for transmission (priority output queuing)

The configuration commands associated with these options are described in the Cisco IOS configuration guides and command references.

The following section focuses on identifying situations in which these options are likely to apply and defining how you can use these options to help resolve connectivity and performance problems in serial/WAN interconnections.

Tuning System Buffers

There are two general buffer types on Cisco routers: *hardware buffers* and *system buffers*. Only the system buffers are directly configurable by system administrators. The hardware buffers are specifically used as the receive and transmit buffers associated with each interface and (in the absence of any special configuration) are dynamically managed by the system software itself.

The system buffers are associated with the main system memory and are allocated to different-size memory blocks. A useful command for determining the status of your system buffers is the **show buffers** exec command. Figure 15–8 shows the output from the **show buffers** command.

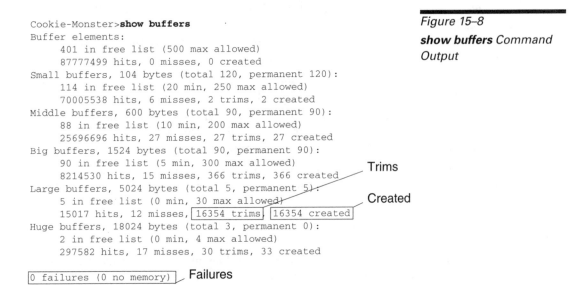

Figure 15–8

show buffers *Command Output*

```
Cookie-Monster>show buffers
Buffer elements:
     401 in free list (500 max allowed)
     87777499 hits, 0 misses, 0 created
Small buffers, 104 bytes (total 120, permanent 120):
     114 in free list (20 min, 250 max allowed)
     70005538 hits, 6 misses, 2 trims, 2 created
Middle buffers, 600 bytes (total 90, permanent 90):
     88 in free list (10 min, 200 max allowed)
     25696696 hits, 27 misses, 27 trims, 27 created
Big buffers, 1524 bytes (total 90, permanent 90):
     90 in free list (5 min, 300 max allowed)
     8214530 hits, 15 misses, 366 trims, 366 created    Trims
Large buffers, 5024 bytes (total 5, permanent 5):
     5 in free list (0 min, 30 max allowed)              Created
     15017 hits, 12 misses, 16354 trims  16354 created
Huge buffers, 18024 bytes (total 3, permanent 0):
     2 in free list (0 min, 4 max allowed)
     297582 hits, 17 misses, 30 trims, 33 created

0 failures (0 no memory)    Failures
```

In the **show buffers** output

- **total** identifies the total number of buffers in the pool, including used and unused buffers.
- **permanent** identifies the permanent number of allocated buffers in the pool. These buffers are always in the pool and cannot be trimmed away.
- **in free list** identifies the number of buffers currently in the pool that are available for use.
- **min** identifies the minimum number of buffers that the Route Processor (RP) should attempt to keep in the free list:
  - The **min** parameter is used to anticipate demand for buffers from the pool at any given time.
  - If the number of buffers in the free list falls below the **min** value, the RP attempts to create more buffers for that pool.

- **max allowed** identifies the maximum number of buffers allowed in the free list:
  - The **max allowed** parameter prevents a pool from monopolizing buffers that it doesn't need anymore, and frees this memory back to the system for further use.
  - If the number of buffers in the free list is greater than the **max allowed** value, the RP should attempt to trim buffers from the pool.
- **hits** identifies the number of buffers that have been requested from the pool. The hits counter provides a mechanism for determining which pool must meet the highest demand for buffers.
- **misses** identifies the number of times a buffer has been requested and the RP detected that additional buffers were required. (In other words, the number of buffers in the free list has dropped below **min**.) The misses counter represents the number of times the RP has been forced to create additional buffers.
- **trims** identifies the number of buffers that the RP has trimmed from the pool when the number of buffers in the free list exceeded the number of **max allowed** buffers.
- **created** identifies the number of buffers that have been created in the pool. The RP creates buffers when demand for buffers has increased until the number of buffers in the free list is less than **min** buffers and/or a miss occurs because of zero buffers in the free list.
- **failures** identifies the number of failures to grant a buffer to a requester even after attempting to create an additional buffer. The number of **failures** represents the number of packets that have been dropped due to buffer shortage.
- **no memory** identifies the number of failures caused by insufficient memory to create additional buffers.

The **show buffers** command output in Figure 15–8 indicates high numbers in the **trims** and **created** fields for large buffers. If you are receiving high numbers in these fields, you can increase your serial link performance by increasing the **max free** value configured for your system buffers. **trims** identifies the number of buffers that the RP has trimmed from the pool when the number of buffers in free list exceeded the number of **max allowed** buffers.

Use the **buffers max free** *number* global configuration command to increase the number of free system buffers. The value you configure should be approximately 150% of the figure indicated in the **total** field of the **show buffers** command output. Repeat this process until the **show buffers** output no longer indicates trims and created buffers.

If the **show buffers** command output shows a large number of failures in the (**no memory**) field (see the last line of output in Figure 15–8), you must reduce the usage of the system buffers or increase the amount of shared or main memory (physical RAM) on the router. Call your technical support representative for assistance.

Implementing Hold Queue Limits

Hold queues are buffers used by each router interface to store outgoing or incoming packets. Use the **hold-queue** interface configuration command to increase the number of data packets queued before the router will drop packets. Increase these queues by small increments (for instance, 25%) until you no longer see drops in the **show interfaces** output. The default output hold queue limit is 100 packets.

NOTES

The **hold-queue** command is used for process-switched packets and periodic updates generated by the router.

Use the **hold-queue** command to prevent packets from being dropped and to improve serial-link performance under the following conditions:

- You have an application that cannot tolerate drops and the protocol is able to tolerate longer delays. DECnet is an example of a protocol that meets both criteria. Local-area transport (LAT) does not because it does not tolerate delays.

- The interface is very slow (bandwidth is low or anticipated utilization is likely to sporadically exceed available bandwidth).

NOTES

When you increase the number specified for an output hold queue, you might need to increase the number of system buffers. The value used depends on the size of the packets associated with the traffic anticipated for the network.

Using Priority Queuing to Reduce Bottlenecks

Priority queuing is a list-based control mechanism that allows traffic to be prioritized on an interface-by-interface basis. Priority queuing involves two steps:

Step 1   Create a priority list by protocol type and level of priority.

Step 2   Assign the priority list to a specific interface.

Both of these steps use versions of the **priority-list** global configuration command. In addition, further traffic control can be applied by referencing **access-list** global configuration commands from **priority-list** specifications. For examples of defining priority lists and for details about command syntax associated with priority queuing, refer to the Cisco IOS configuration guides and command references.

NOTES

Priority queuing automatically creates four hold queues of varying size. This overrides any hold queue specification included in your configuration.

Use priority queuing to prevent packets from being dropped and to improve serial link performance under the following conditions:

- When the interface is slow, there are a variety of traffic types being transmitted, and you want to improve terminal traffic performance.

- If you have a serial link that is intermittently experiencing very heavy loads (such as file transfers occurring at specific times) and priority queuing will help select which types of traffic should be discarded at high traffic periods.

In general, start with the default number of queues when implementing priority queues. After enabling priority queuing, monitor output drops with the **show interfaces serial** exec command. If you notice that output drops are occurring in the traffic queue you have specified to be high priority, increase the number of packets that can be queued (using the **queue-limit** keyword option of the **priority-list** global configuration command). The default **queue-limit** arguments are 20 packets for the high-priority queue, 40 for medium, 60 for normal, and 80 for low.

NOTES

When bridging Digital Equipment Corporation (Digital) LAT traffic, the router must drop very few packets, or LAT sessions can terminate unexpectedly. A high-priority queue depth of about 100 (specified with the **queue-limit** keyword) is a typical working value when your router is dropping output packets and the serial lines are subjected to about 50% bandwidth utilization. If the router is dropping packets and is at 100% utilization, you need another line.

Another tool to relieve congestion when bridging Digital LAT is LAT compression. You can implement LAT compression with the interface configuration command **bridge-group** *group* **lat-compression**.

Special Serial Line Tests

In addition to the basic diagnostic capabilities available on routers, a variety of supplemental tools and techniques can be used to determine the conditions of cables, switching equipment, modems, hosts, and remote internetworking hardware. For more information, consult the documentation for your CSU, DSU, serial analyzer, or other equipment.

CSU and DSU Loopback Tests

If the output of the **show interfaces serial** exec command indicates that the serial line is up but the line protocol is down, use the CSU/DSU loopback tests to determine the source of the problem. Perform the local loop test first, and then the remote test. Figure 15–9 illustrates the basic topology of the CSU/DSU local and remote loopback tests.

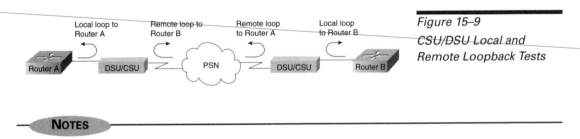

Figure 15–9
CSU/DSU Local and
Remote Loopback Tests

NOTES

These tests are generic in nature and assume attachment of the internetworking system to a CSU or DSU. However, the tests are essentially the same for attachment to a multiplexer with built-in CSU/DSU functionality. Because there is no concept of a loopback in X.25 or Frame Relay packet-switched network (PSN) environments, loopback tests do not apply to X.25 and Frame Relay networks.

CSU and DSU Local Loopback Tests for HDLC or PPP Links

Following is a general procedure for performing loopback tests in conjunction with built-in system diagnostic capabilities:

Step 1   Place the CSU/DSU in local loop mode (refer to your vendor documentation). In local loop mode, the use of the line clock (from the T1 service) is terminated, and the DSU is forced to use the local clock.

Step 2   Use the **show interfaces serial** exec command to determine whether the line status changes from "line protocol is down" to "line protocol is up (looped)," or if it remains down.

Step 3   If the line protocol comes up when the CSU or DSU is in local loopback mode, this suggests that the problem is occurring on the remote end of the serial connection. If the status line does not change state, there is a possible problem in the router, connecting cable, or CSU/DSU.

Step 4   If the problem appears to be local, use the **debug serial interface** privileged exec command.

Step 5   Take the CSU/DSU out of local loop mode. When the line protocol is down, the **debug serial interface** command output will indicate that keepalive counters are not incrementing.

Step 6   Place the CSU/DSU in local loop mode again. This should cause the keepalive packets to begin to increment. Specifically, the values for *mineseen* and *yourseen* keepalives will increment every 10 seconds. This information will appear in the **debug serial interface** output.

If the keepalives do not increment, there may be a timing problem on the interface card or on the network. For information on correcting timing problems, refer to the section "Troubleshooting Clocking Problems," earlier in this chapter.

Step 7   Check the local router and CSU/DSU hardware, and any attached cables. Make
certain the cables are within the recommended lengths (no more than 50 feet
[15.24 meters], or 25 feet [7.62 meters] for a T1 link). Make certain the cables are
attached to the proper ports. Swap faulty equipment as necessary.

Figure 15–10 shows the output from the **debug serial interface** command for an HDLC serial connection, with missed keepalives causing the line to go down and the interface to reset.

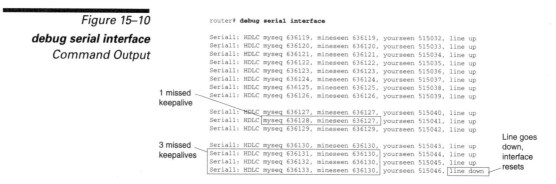

Figure 15–10

debug serial interface
Command Output

CSU and DSU Remote Loopback Tests for HDLC or PPP Links

If you determine that the local hardware is functioning properly but you still encounter problems
when attempting to establish connections over the serial link, try using the remote loopback test to
isolate the problem cause.

NOTES

This remote loopback test assumes that HDLC encapsulation is being used and that the preceding
local loop test was performed immediately before this test.

The following are the steps required to perform loopback testing:

Step 1   Put the remote CSU or DSU into remote loopback mode (refer to the vendor
documentation).

Step 2   Using the **show interfaces serial** exec command, determine whether the line
protocol remains up with the status line indicating "Serial x is up, line protocol is
up (looped)," or if it goes down with the status line indicating "line protocol is
down."

Step 3 If the line protocol remains up (looped), the problem is probably at the remote end of the serial connection (between the remote CSU/DSU and the remote router). Perform both local and remote tests at the remote end to isolate the problem source.

Step 4 If the line status changes to "line protocol is down" when remote loopback mode is activated, make certain that ones density is being properly maintained. The CSU/DSU must be configured to use the same framing and coding schemes used by the leased-line or other carrier service (for example, ESF and B8ZS).

Step 5 If problems persist, contact your WAN network manager or the WAN service organization.

DETAILED INFORMATION ON THE SHOW INTERFACES SERIAL COMMAND

This section covers the **show interfaces serial** command's parameters, syntax description, sample output display, and field descriptions.

show interfaces serial

To display information about a serial interface, use the **show interfaces serial** privileged exec command:

> **show interfaces serial** [*number*] [**accounting**]
> **show interfaces serial** [*number* [*:channel-group*] [**accounting**] (Cisco 4000 series)
> **show interfaces serial** [*slot* ¦ *port* [*:channel-group*]] [**accounting**] (Cisco 7500 series)
> **show interfaces serial** [*type slot* ¦ *port-adapter* ¦ *port*] [**serial**] (ports on VIP cards in the Cisco 7500 series)
> **show interfaces serial** [*type slot* ¦ *port-adapter* ¦ *port*] [*:t1-channel*] [**accounting** ¦ **crb**] (CT3IP in Cisco 7500 series)

Syntax Description

- *number*—(Optional) Port number.

- **accounting**—(Optional) Displays the number of packets of each protocol type that have been sent through the interface.

- *:channel-group*—(Optional) On the Cisco 4000 series with an NPM or a Cisco 7500 series with a MIP, specifies the T1 channel-group number in the range of 0 to 23, defined with the channel-group controller configuration command.

- *slot*—Refers to the appropriate hardware manual for slot information.

- *port*—Refers to the appropriate hardware manual for port information.

- *port-adapter*—Refers to the appropriate hardware manual for information about port adapter compatibility.

- *:t1-channel*—(Optional) For the CT3IP, the T1 channel is a number between 1 and 28.

T1 channels on the CT3IP are numbered 1 to 28 rather than the more traditional zero-based scheme (0 to 27) used with other Cisco products. This is to ensure consistency with telco numbering schemes for T1 channels within channelized T3 equipment.

- crb—(Optional) Shows interface routing and bridging information.

Command Mode

Privileged exec

Usage Guidelines

This command first appeared in Cisco IOS Release 10.0 for the Cisco 4000 series. It first appeared in Cisco IOS Release 11.0 for the Cisco 7000 series, and it was modified in Cisco IOS Release 11.3 to include the CT3IP.

Sample Displays

The following is sample output from the **show interfaces** command for a synchronous serial interface:

```
Router# show interfaces serial
Serial 0 is up, line protocol is up
    Hardware is MCI Serial
    Internet address is 150.136.190.203, subnet mask is 255.255.255.0
    MTU 1500 bytes, BW 1544 Kbit, DLY 20000 usec, rely 255/255, load 1/255
    Encapsulation HDLC, loopback not set, keepalive set (10 sec)
    Last input 0:00:07, output 0:00:00, output hang never
    Output queue 0/40, 0 drops; input queue 0/75, 0 drops
    Five minute input rate 0 bits/sec, 0 packets/sec
    Five minute output rate 0 bits/sec, 0 packets/sec
        16263 packets input, 1347238 bytes, 0 no buffer
        Received 13983 broadcasts, 0 runts, 0 giants
        2 input errors, 0 CRC, 0 frame, 0 overrun, 0 ignored, 2 abort
 1 carrier transitions
        22146 packets output, 2383680 bytes, 0 underruns
        0 output errors, 0 collisions, 2 interface resets, 0 restarts
```

Table 15–9 describes significant fields shown in the output.

Table 15–9 *Show Interfaces Serial Field Descriptions*

Field	Description
Serial...is {*up* | *down*} ...is administratively down	Indicates whether the interface hardware is currently active (whether carrier detect is present) or whether it has been taken down by an administrator.
line protocol is {*up* ¦ *down*}	Indicates whether the software processes that handle the line protocol consider the line usable (that is, whether keepalives are successful) or whether it has been taken down by an administrator.
Hardware is	Specifies the hardware type.

Table 15–9 *Show Interfaces Serial Field Descriptions, Continued*

Internet address is	Specifies the Internet address and subnet mask.
MTU	Maximum transmission unit of the interface.
BW	Indicates the value of the bandwidth parameter that has been configured for the interface (in kilobits per second). The bandwidth parameter is used to compute IGRP metrics only. If the interface is attached to a serial line with a line speed that does not match the default (1536 or 1544 for T1 and 56 for a standard synchronous serial line), use the **bandwidth** command to specify the correct line speed for this serial line.
DLY	Delay of the interface in microseconds.
rely	Reliability of the interface as a fraction of 255 (255/255 is 100% reliability), calculated as an exponential average over five minutes.
load	Load on the interface as a fraction of 255 (255/255 is completely saturated), calculated as an exponential average over five minutes.
Encapsulation	Encapsulation method assigned to the interface.
loopback	Indicates whether loopback is set.
keepalive	Indicates whether keepalives are set.
Last input	Number of hours, minutes, and seconds since the last packet was successfully received by an interface. Useful for knowing when a dead interface failed.
Last output	Number of hours, minutes, and seconds since the last packet was successfully transmitted by an interface.
output hang	Number of hours, minutes, and seconds (or never) since the interface was last reset because of a transmission that took too long. When the number of hours in any of the *last* fields exceeds 24, the number of days and hours is printed. If that field overflows, asterisks are printed.
Output queue, drops input queue, drops	Number of packets in output and input queues. Each number is followed by a slash, the maximum size of the queue, and the number of packets because the queue is full.

Table 15–9 *Show Interfaces Serial Field Descriptions, Continued*

5 minute input rate **5 minute output rate**	Average number of bits and packets transmitted per second in the past five minutes. The five-minute input and output rates should be used only as an approximation of traffic per second during a given five-minute period. These rates are exponentially weighted averages with a time constant of five minutes. A period of four time constants must pass before the average will be within 2% of the instantaneous rate of a uniform stream of traffic over that period.
packets input	Total number of error-free packets received by the system.
bytes	Total number of bytes, including data and MAC encapsulation, in the error-free packets received by the system.
no buffer	Number of received packets discarded because there was no buffer space in the main system. Compare with ignored count. Broadcast storms on Ethernet networks and bursts of noise on serial lines are often responsible for no input buffer events.
Received...broadcasts	Total number of broadcast or multicast packets received by the interface.
runts	Number of packets that are discarded because they are smaller than the medium's minimum packet size.
giants	Number of packets that are discarded because they exceed the medium's maximum packet size.
input errors	Total number of no buffer, runts, giants, CRCs, frame, overrun, ignored, and abort counts. Other input-related errors can also increment the count, so this sum might not balance with the other counts.
CRC	Cyclic redundancy check generated by the originating station or far-end device does not match the checksum calculated from the data received. On a serial link, CRCs usually indicate noise, gain hits, or other transmission problems on the data link.
frame	Number of packets received incorrectly having a CRC error and a noninteger number of octets. On a serial line, this is usually the result of noise or other transmission problems.
overrun	Number of times the serial receiver hardware was unable to hand received data to a hardware buffer because the input rate exceeded the receiver's ability to handle the data.

Table 15-9 *Show Interfaces Serial Field Descriptions, Continued*

ignored	Number of received packets ignored by the interface because the interface hardware ran low on internal buffers. Broadcast storms and bursts of noise can cause the ignored count to be increased.
abort	Illegal sequence of one bits on a serial interface. This usually indicates a clocking problem between the serial interface and the data link equipment.
carrier transitions	Number of times the carrier detect signal of a serial interface has changed state. For example, if data carrier detect (DCD) goes down and comes up, the carrier transition counter will increment two times. Indicates modem or line problems if the carrier detect line is changing state often.
packets output	Total number of messages transmitted by the system.
bytes output	Total number of bytes, including data and MAC encapsulation, transmitted by the system.
underruns	Number of times that the transmitter has been running faster than the router can handle. This might never be reported on some interfaces.
output errors	Sum of all errors that prevented the final transmission of datagrams out of the interface being examined. Note that this might not balance with the sum of the enumerated output errors because some datagrams can have more than one error, and others can have errors that do not fall into any of the specifically tabulated categories.
collisions	Number of messages retransmitted due to an Ethernet collision. This usually is the result of an overextended LAN (Ethernet or transceiver cable too long, more than two repeaters between stations, or too many cascaded multiport transceivers). Some collisions are normal. However, if your collision rate climbs to around 4% or 5%, you should consider verifying that there is no faulty equipment on the segment and/or moving some existing stations to a new segment. A packet that collides is counted only once in output packets.

Table 15–9   *Show Interfaces Serial Field Descriptions, Continued*

interface resets	Number of times an interface has been completely reset. This can happen if packets queued for transmission were not sent within several seconds' time. On a serial line, this can be caused by a malfunctioning modem that is not supplying the transmit clock signal, or by a cable problem. If the system notices that the carrier detect line of a serial interface is up but the line protocol is down, it periodically resets the interface in an effort to restart it. Interface resets can also occur when an interface is looped back or shut down.
restarts	Number of times the controller was restarted because of errors.
alarm indications, remote alarms, rx LOF, rx LOS	Number of CSU/DSU alarms, and number of occurrences of receive loss of frame and receive loss of signal.
BER inactive, NELR inactive, FELR inactive	Status of G.703-E1 counters for bit error rate (BER) alarm, near-end loop remote (NELR), and far-end loop remote (FELR). Note that you cannot set the NELR or FELR.

Troubleshooting Dialin Connections

This chapter describes procedures for troubleshooting dialin connections. The chapter begins with the following sections:

- Using the **modem autoconfigure** Command
- Establishing a Reverse Telnet Session to a Modem
- Interpreting **show line** Output

The remainder of the chapter presents symptoms, problems, and solutions for router-to-router and PC-to-router dialin connections:

- Dialin: No Connectivity Between Modem and Router
- Dialin: Modem Does Not Dial
- Dialin: Modem Does Not Answer
- Dialin: Modem Hangs Up Shortly After Connecting
- Dialin: Dialin Client Receives No exec Prompt
- Dialin: Dialin Session Sees "Garbage"
- Dialin: Dialin Session Ends Up in Existing Session
- Dialin: Modem Cannot Send or Receive Data
- Dialin: Modem Cannot Send or Receive IP Data
- Dialin: Modem Cannot Send or Receive IPX Data
- Dialin: Modem Does Not Disconnect Properly
- Dialin: Link Goes Down Too Soon
- Dialin: Link Does Not Go Down or Stays Up Too Long
- Dialin: Poor Performance

This chapter does not cover Apple Remote Access (ARA) dialin connections. For information on troubleshooting ARA connections, see Chapter 9, "Troubleshooting AppleTalk."

USING THE MODEM AUTOCONFIGURE COMMAND

If you are using Cisco Internetwork Operating System (Cisco IOS) Release 11.1 or later, you can configure your Cisco router to communicate with and configure your modem automatically.

Use the following procedure to configure a Cisco router to automatically attempt to discover what kind of modem is connected to the line and then to configure the modem:

Step 1   To discover the type of modem attached to your router, use the **modem autoconfigure discovery** line configuration command.

Step 2   When the modem is successfully discovered, configure the modem automatically using the **modem autoconfigure type** *modem-name* line configuration command.

If you want to display the list of modems for which the router has entries, use the **show modemcap** *modem-name*. If you want to change a modem value that was returned from the **show modemcap** command, use the **modemcap edit** *modem-name attribute value* line configuration command.

For complete information on the use of these commands, refer to the Cisco IOS *Access Services Configuration Guide* and *Access Services Command Reference*.

ESTABLISHING A REVERSE TELNET SESSION TO A MODEM

If you are running Cisco IOS Release 11.0 or earlier, you must establish a reverse Telnet session to configure a modem to communicate with a Cisco device. As long as you lock the data terminal equipment (DTE)–side speed of the modem (see Table 16–5 for information on locking the modem speed), the modem will always communicate with the access server or router at the desired speed. Be certain that the speed of the Cisco device is configured prior to issuing commands to the modem via a reverse Telnet session. (See Table 16–5 for information on configuring the speed of the access server or router.)

To initiate a reverse Telnet session to your modem, perform the following steps:

Step 1   From your terminal, use the command

telnet *ip-address* **20**yy

where *ip-address* is the IP address of any active, connected interface on the Cisco device, and *yy* is the line number to which the modem is connected. For example, the following command would connect you to the auxiliary port on a Cisco router with IP address 192.169.53.52:

```
telnet 192.169.53.52 2001
```

Generally, a Telnet command of this kind can be issued from anywhere on the network that can **ping** the IP address in question.

NOTES

On a Cisco router, port 01 is the auxiliary port. On a Cisco access server, the auxiliary port is another *last_tty+1*, so on a 16-port access server, the auxiliary port is port 17. Use the **show line** exec command to make certain you are working with the correct line.

Step 2   If the connection is refused, there may already be a user connected to that port. Use the **show users** exec command to determine whether the line is being used. If desired, the line can be cleared from the console using the **clear line** privileged exec command. When you are certain the line is not in use, attempt the Telnet connection again.

Step 3   If the connection is again refused, confirm that you have set modem control to **modem inout** for that line. See Table 16–2 for more information on configuring modem control on a line.

Step 4   If the connection is still refused, the modem might be asserting Carrier Detect (CD) all the time. Disconnect the modem from the line, establish a reverse Telnet session, and then connect the modem.

Step 5   After successfully making the Telnet connection, enter **AT** and make sure the modem replies with OK.

Figure 16–1 shows a typical Hayes-compatible modem command string. Be certain to check the documentation for your specific modem to verify the exact syntax of these commands.

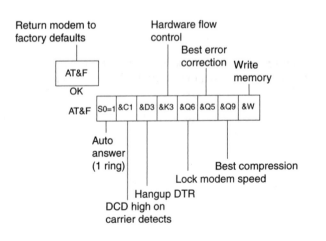

Figure 16–1

A Typical Hayes-Compatible Modem Command String

INTERPRETING SHOW LINE OUTPUT

The output from the **show line** *line-number* exec command is useful when troubleshooting a modem-to-access server or router connection. Figure 16–2 shows the output from the **show line** command.

Figure 16–2

show line *Command*

Output

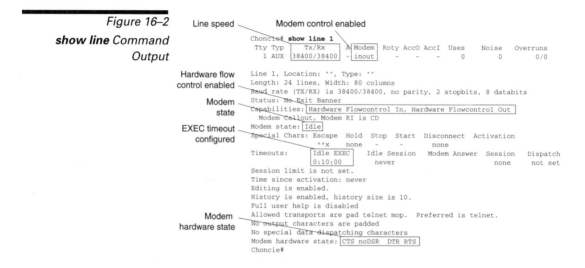

When connectivity problems occur, important output appears in the Modem state and the Modem hardware state fields.

NOTES

The Modem hardware state field does not appear in the **show line** output for every platform. In certain cases, the indications for signal states will be shown in the Modem state field instead.

Table 16–1 shows typical Modem state and Modem hardware state strings from the output of the **show line** command and explains the meaning of each state.

Table 16–1 *Modem and Modem Hardware States in* **show line** *Output*

Modem State	Modem Hardware State	Meaning
Idle	CTS noDSR DTR RTS	These are the proper modem states for connections between an access server or router and a modem (when there is no incoming call). Output of any other kind generally indicates a problem.

Ready	—	If the modem state is Ready instead of Idle, there are three possibilities:
		
		• Modem control is not configured on the access server or router. Configure the access server or router with the **modem inout** line configuration command.
		
		• A session exists on the line. Use the **show users** exec command and use the **clear line** privileged exec command to stop the session if desired.
		
		• DSR is high. There are two possible reasons for this:
		
		  ○ *Cabling problems*—If your connector uses DB-25 pin 6 and has no pin 8, you must move the pin from 6 to 8 or get the appropriate connector.
		
		  ○ *Modem configured for DCD always high*—The modem should be reconfigured to have DCD high only on CD.[1] This is usually done with the &C1 modem command (refer to Figure 16–1), but check your modem documentation for the exact syntax for your modem.
		
		If your software does not support modem control, you must configure the access server line to which the modem is connected with the **no exec** line configuration command. Clear the line with the **clear line** privileged exec command, initiate a reverse Telnet session with the modem, and reconfigure the modem so that DCD is high only on CD.
		
		End the Telnet session by entering **disconnect** and reconfigure the access server line with the **exec** line configuration command.

Table 16–1 *Modem and Modem Hardware States in* **show line** *Output, Continued*

Modem State	Modem Hardware State	Meaning
Ready	noCTS noDSR DTR RTS	There are four possibilities for the noCTS string appearing in the Modem hardware state field: • The modem is turned off. • The modem is not properly connected to the access server. Check the cabling connections from the modem to the access server. • Incorrect cabling (either rolled MDCE, or straight MDTE, but without the pins moved). See Table 16–2 for information on the recommended cabling configuration. • The modem is not configured for hardware flow control. Disable hardware flow control on the access server with the **no flowcontrol hardware** line configuration command and then enable hardware flow control on the modem via a reverse Telnet session. (Consult your modem documentation and see the section "Establishing a Reverse Telnet Session to a Modem" earlier in this chapter.) Reenable hardware flow control on the access server with the **flowcontrol hardware** line configuration command.

Table 16-1 *Modem and Modem Hardware States in **show line** Output, Continued*

Modem State	Modem Hardware State	Meaning
Ready	CTS DSR DTR RTS	There are two possibilities for the presence of the DSR string instead of the noDSR string in the Modem hardware state field: • Incorrect cabling (either rolled MDCE, or straight MDTE, but without the pins moved). See Table 16–2 for information on the recommended cabling configuration. • The modem is configured for DCD always high. Reconfigure the modem so that DCD is only high on CD. This is usually done with the **&C1** modem command (see Figure 16–1), but check your modem documentation for the exact syntax for your modem. Configure the access server line to which the modem is connected with the **no exec** line configuration command. Clear the line with the **clear line** privileged exec command, initiate a reverse Telnet session with the modem, and reconfigure the modem so that DCD is high only on CD. End the Telnet session by entering **disconnect**. Reconfigure the access server line with the **exec** line configuration command.
Ready	CTS* DSR* DTR RTS[2]	If this string appears in the Modem hardware state field, modem control is probably not enabled on the access server. Use the **modem inout** line configuration command to enable modem control on the line. See Table 16–2 for more information on configuring modem control on an access server or router line.

[1] CD = Carrier Detect
[2] A * next to a signal indicates one of two things: The signal has changed within the past few seconds or the signal is not being used by the modem control method selected.

TROUBLESHOOTING DIALIN CONNECTIONS

This section presents troubleshooting information for dialin connectivity problems. It describes specific dialin connections symptoms, the problems that are likely to cause each symptom, and the solutions to those problems.

Dialin: No Connectivity Between Modem and Router

Symptom: The connection between a modem and a Cisco access server or router does not work. Attempts to initiate a reverse Telnet session to the modem have no result, or the user receives a "connection refused by foreign host" message.

NOTES

More specific symptoms for dialin connection problems are covered later in this chapter.

Table 16–2 outlines the problems that might cause this symptom and describes solutions to those problems.

Table 16–2 *Dialin: No Connectivity Between Modem and Router*

Possible Causes	Suggested Actions	
Modem control is not enabled on the access server or router	Step 1	Use the **show line** exec command on the access server or router. The output for the auxiliary port should show **inout** or **RIisCD** in the Modem column. This indicates that modem control is enabled on the line of the access server or router.
		For an explanation of **show line** output, see the "Using **debug** Commands" section earlier in this chapter.
	Step 2	Configure the line for modem control using the **modem inout** line configuration command. Modem control is now enabled on the access server.
		Example:
		The following example illustrates how to configure a line for both incoming and outgoing calls:
| | | ```
line 5
modem inout
``` |
```

Table 16–2 Dialin: No Connectivity Between Modem and Router, Continued

Possible Causes	Suggested Actions
Modem control is not enabled on the access server or router (*Continued*)	**Note:** Be certain to use the **modem inout** command and not the **modem ri-is-cd** command while the connectivity of the modem is in question. The latter command allows the line to accept incoming calls only. Outgoing calls will be refused, making it impossible to establish a Telnet session with the modem to configure it. If you want to enable the **modem ri-is-cd** command, do so only after you are certain the modem is functioning correctly.
Incorrect cabling	**Step 1** Check the cabling between the modem and the access server or router. Confirm that the modem is connected to the auxiliary port on the access server or router with a rolled RJ-45 cable and an MMOD DB-25 adapter. This cabling configuration is recommended and supported by Cisco for RJ-45 ports. (These connectors are typically labelled "Modem.") **Step 2** Use the **show line** exec command to verify that the cabling is correct. See the explanation of the **show line** command output in the section "Using **debug** Commands" earlier in this chapter.
Hardware problem	**Step 1** Verify that you are using the correct cabling and that all connections are good. **Step 2** Check all hardware for damage, including cabling (broken wires), adapters (loose pins), access server ports, and modem. **Step 3** See Chapter 3, "Troubleshooting Hardware and Booting Problems," for more information on hardware troubleshooting.

Dialin: Modem Does Not Dial

Symptom: Dialin sessions cannot be established because the modem does not dial properly.

Table 16–3 outlines the problems that might cause this symptom and describes solutions to those problems.

Table 16–2   *Dialin: Modem Does Not Dial*

Possible Causes	Suggested Actions
Incorrect cabling	**Step 1** Check the cabling between the modem and the access server or router. Confirm that the modem is connected to the auxiliary port on the access server or router with a rolled RJ-45 cable and an MMOD DB-25 adapter. This cabling configuration is recommended and supported by Cisco for RJ-45 ports. (These connectors are typically labelled "Modem.")

Types of RJ-45 Cabling:

There are two types of RJ-45 cabling: straight and rolled. If you hold the two ends of an RJ-45 cable side-by-side, you'll see eight colored strips, or pins, at each end. If the order of the colored pins is the same at each end, then the cable is straight. If the order of the colors is reversed at each end, then the cable is rolled.

The rolled cable (CAB-500RJ) is standard with Cisco's 2500/CS500.

Note: CAB-OCTAL-ASYNC, the eight-port RJ-45 adapter that is used with the Cisco 2509, 2510, 2511, and 2512, is the same as a rolled cable.

RJ-45 Port Pinouts:

This chart shows the pinouts for RJ-45 console and AUX ports. The console port does not use RTS/CTS:

Console/Auxiliary Port (DTE[1])

Pin	Signal	Input/Output
1	RTS	Output
2	DTR	Output
3	TXD	Output
4	GND	—
5	GND	—
6	RXD	Input
7	DSR	Input
8	CTS	Input

Step 2 Use the **show line** exec command to verify that the cabling is correct. See the explanation of the **show line** command output in the section "Using **debug** Commands" earlier in this chapter.

Table 16–2 *Dialin: Modem Does Not Dial, Continued*

Possible Causes	Suggested Actions
Modem hardware problem	Check the modem's physical connection. Make sure the modem is on and is connected securely to the correct port. Make sure the transmit and receive indicator lights flash when the chat script is running.
No interesting packets defined	**Step 1** Use the **show running-config** privileged exec command to view the router configuration. Check the **dialer-list** interface configuration command entries to see which access lists, if any, are being used to define interesting traffic. **Step 2** Make sure the access lists referenced by the **dialer-list** commands specify all traffic that should bring up the link (interesting traffic). **Step 3** If necessary, modify the **access list** commands so that they define the proper traffic as interesting.
Missing chat script	**Step 1** Use the **debug chat** privileged exec command to check whether there is a chat script running. **Step 2** If there is no chat script running, use the **start-chat** privileged exec command or another appropriate command to start the chat script on the line. For detailed information about creating and configuring chat scripts, refer to the Cisco IOS *Access Services Configuration Guide* and *Access Services Command Reference*.
Bad chat script	**Step 1** Establish a reverse Telnet session to the modem and step through each step of the chat script. **Step 2** Verify that the command response to each chat script step is correct. **Step 3** Fix any inconsistencies you find in the chat script. For detailed information about creating and configuring chat scripts, refer to the Cisco IOS *Access Services Configuration Guide* and *Access Services Command Reference*.

[1] DTE = data terminal equipment

Dialin: Modem Does Not Answer

Symptom: When attempting to open a dialin connection to a modem, the modem does not answer the call.

Table 16–4 outlines the problems that might cause this symptom and describes solutions to those problems.

Table 16–4 *Dialin: Modem Does Not Answer*

Possible Causes	Suggested Actions	
Incorrect cabling	**Step 1**	Check the cabling between the modem and the access server or router. Confirm that the modem is connected to the auxiliary port on the access server or router with a rolled RJ-45 cable and an MMOD DB-25 adapter. This cabling configuration is recommended and supported by Cisco for RJ-45 ports. (These connectors are typically labeled "Modem.")
		There are two types of RJ-45 cabling: straight and rolled. If you hold the two ends of an RJ-45 cable side-by-side, you'll see eight colored strips, or pins, at each end. If the order of the colored pins is the same at each end, then the cable is straight. If the order of the colors is reversed at each end, then the cable is rolled.
		The rolled cable (CAB-500RJ) is standard with Cisco's 2500/CS500.
	Step 2	Use the **show line** exec command to verify that the cabling is correct. See the explanation of the **show line** command output in the section "Using **debug** Commands" earlier in this chapter.
Modem control not enabled on access server or router	**Step 1**	Observe the remote modem to see whether it is receiving a DTR signal from the router. Most modems have a DTR indicator light. Check the modem documentation to interpret the indicator lights.
	Step 2	If the DTR indicator light is on, the modem is seeing a DTR signal from the router. You can also enter the **show line** exec command to check for DTR. If the modem hardware state shows the string noDTR, then the router is configured to hold DTR low and the modem is not seeing a DTR signal.
	Step 3	Configure modem control using either the **modem inout** or the **modem ri-is-cd** line configuration command.

Table 16–4 *Dialin: Modem Does Not Answer, Continued*

Possible Causes	Suggested Actions
Misconfigured **dialer map** commands	**Step 1** Use the **show running-config** privileged exec command to view the router configuration. Check all **dialer map** statements to make sure they are configured correctly. **Step 2** Correct **dialer map** statements as necessary, making certain that all options are specified properly. For detailed information on configuring dialer maps, refer to the Cisco IOS *Wide-Area Networking Configuration Guide* and *Wide-Area Networking Command Reference*.
Remote modem not set to auto-answer	**Step 1** Check the remote modem to see whether it is set to auto-answer. Usually, an AA indicator light is on when auto-answer is set. **Step 2** Set the remote modem to auto-answer if it is not already set. To find out how to verify and change the modem's settings, refer to your modem documentation.
Wrong telephone line attached to remote modem	**Step 1** Make sure you are using the correct telephone line. Replace the remote modem with a telephone and call again. If the phone rings, you are using the correct telephone line. **Step 2** Contact the telephone company to make sure that the line is good.
Remote modem not attached to a router	**Step 1** Make sure the remote modem is attached to a router or other device that is asserting DTR. **Step 2** Most modems have an LED indicator for DTR. Check to make sure this indicator comes on.

Dialin: Modem Hangs Up Shortly After Connecting

Symptom: A dialin connection is successful but the modem hangs up after 30 to 90 seconds.

Table 16–5 outlines the problems that might cause this symptom and describes solutions to those problems.

Table 16–5   *Dialin: Modem Hangs Up Shortly After Connecting*

Possible Causes	Suggested Actions

Modem speed setting is not locked	**Step 1** Use the **show line** exec command on the access server or router. The output for the auxiliary port should indicate the currently configured Tx[1] and Rx[2] speeds.
	
	For an explanation of the output from the **show line** command, see the section "Using **debug** Commands" earlier in this chapter.
	
	Step 2 If the line is not configured to the correct speed, use the **speed** line configuration commands to set the line speed on the access server or router line. Set the value to the highest speed in common between the modem and the access server or router port.
	
	To set the terminal baud rate, use the **speed** line configuration command. This command sets both the transmit (to terminal) and receive (from terminal) speeds.
	
	Syntax:
	
	speed *bps*
	
	Syntax Description:
	
	• *bps*—Baud rate in bits per second (bps). The default is 9600 bps.
	
	Example:
	
	The following example sets lines 1 and 2 on a Cisco 2509 access server to 115200 bps:
	
	`line 1 2`
	` speed 115200`
	
	Note: If for some reason you cannot use flow control, limit the line speed to 9600 bps. Faster speeds are likely to result in lost data.
	
	Step 3 Use the **show line** exec command again and confirm that the line speed is set to the desired value.

Table 16–5 *Dialin: Modem Hangs Up Shortly After Connecting, Continued*

Possible Causes	Suggested Actions
Modem speed setting is not locked (*Continued*)	**Step 4** When you are certain the access server or router line is configured for the desired speed, initiate a reverse Telnet session to the modem on that line. For more information, see the section "Establishing a Reverse Telnet Session to a Modem" earlier in this chapter.
	Step 5 Use a modem command string that includes the **lock DTE** speed command for your modem. See your modem documentation for exact configuration command syntax.
	Note: The **lock DTE** speed command, which might also be referred to as *port rate adjust* or *buffered mode*, is often related to the way the modem handles error correction. This command varies widely from one modem to another.
	Locking the modem speed ensures that the modem always communicates with the Cisco access server or router at the speed configured on the Cisco auxiliary port. If this command is not used, the modem reverts to the speed of the data link (the telephone line) instead of communicating at the speed configured on the access server.
Modem control is not enabled on the access server or router	**Step 1** Use the **show line** exec command on the access server or router. The output for the auxiliary port should show **inout** or **RIisCD** in the Modem column. This indicates that modem control is enabled on the line of the access server or router.
	For an explanation of the **show line** output, see the "Using **debug** Commands" section earlier in this chapter.
	Step 2 Configure the line for modem control using the **modem inout** line configuration command. Modem control is now enabled on the access server.
	Example:
	The following example illustrates how to configure a line for both incoming and outgoing calls:
	``` line 5 modem inout ```

Table 16–5 *Dialin: Modem Hangs Up Shortly After Connecting, Continued*

Possible Causes	Suggested Actions	
Modem control is not enabled on the access server or router (*Continued*)		**Note:** Be certain to use the **modem inout** command instead of the **modem ri-is-cd** command while the connectivity of the modem is in question. The latter command allows the line to accept incoming calls only. Outgoing calls will be refused, making it impossible to establish a Telnet session with the modem to configure it. If you want to enable the **modem ri-is-cd** command, do so only after you are certain the modem is functioning correctly.
PPP authentication fails	**Step 1**	Use the **debug ppp chap** privileged exec command to see whether PPP authentication was successful. Check the output for the phrase "Passed authentication with remote." If you see this output, authentication was successful.
	Step 2	If PPP authentication was not successful, verify the username and password configured on the router. The username and password you enter must be identical to those configured on the router.
		Note: Usernames and passwords are case sensitive.
Local router not waiting long enough to connect	**Step 1**	Use the **show dialer** exec command to see the configured dialer timeout. A timeout value shorter than 120 seconds will not be long enough.
	Step 2	Configure the local router to wait longer for the connection. Use the **dialer wait-for-carrier-time** *seconds* **command** to modify the configuration. Make sure you specify at least a 120-second timeout.

Table 16–5 *Dialin: Modem Hangs Up Shortly After Connecting, Continued*

Possible Causes	Suggested Actions
Chat script problem	**Step 1** Enter the **debug chat** privileged exec command. If you see the output "Success" at the end of the chat script, the chat script completed successfully.
	Step 2 Make the timeout in the chat script longer at the point where it fails.
	Step 3 If the problem persists, verify that the command response to each chat script step is correct. Open a reverse Telnet session to the modem and step through the chat script.
	Step 4 Fix any inconsistencies you find in the chat script.
	For detailed information about creating and configuring chat scripts, refer to the Cisco IOS *Access Services Configuration Guide* and *Access Services Command Reference*.

[1] Tx = transmit
[2] Rx = receive

Dialin: Dialin Client Receives No exec Prompt

Symptom: A remote dialin client opens a session and appears to be connected, but the user does not receive an exec prompt (for example, a **Username** or **Router>** prompt).

Table 16–6 outlines the problems that might cause this symptom and describes solutions to those problems.

Table 16–6 *Dialin: Dialin Client Receives No exec Prompt*

Possible Causes	Suggested Actions	
Autoselect is enabled on the line	Attempt to access exec mode by issuing a carriage return.	
Line is configured with the **no exec** command	**Step 1**	Use the **show line** exec command to view the status of the appropriate line.
		Check the Capabilities field to see whether it says "exec suppressed." If this is the case, the **no exec** line configuration command is enabled.
	Step 2	Configure the **exec** line configuration command on the line to allow exec sessions to be initiated. This command has no arguments or keywords.
		Example:
		The following example turns on the exec on line 7:
		``` line 7 exec ```
Flow control is not enabled, is enabled only on one device (either DTE or DCE), or is misconfigured	**Step 1**	Use the **show line** *aux-line-number* exec command and look for the following in the Capabilities field (see Figure 16–2):
		``` Capabilities: Hardware Flowcontrol In, Hardware Flowcontrol Out ```
		If there is no mention of hardware flow control in this field, hardware flow control is not enabled on the line. Hardware flow control for access server-to-modem connections is recommended.
		For an explanation of the output from the **show line** command, see the "Using **debug** Commands" section earlier in this chapter.

Table 16–6 *Dialin: Dialin Client Receives No exec Prompt, Continued*

Possible Causes	Suggested Actions

Flow control is not enabled, is enabled only on one device (either DTE or DCE), or is misconfigured (*Continued*)	**Step 2** Configure hardware flow control on the line using the **flowcontrol hardware** line configuration command.
	
	 Example:
	
	 The following example sets hardware flow control on line 7:
	
	 ```line 7```
	``` flowcontrol hardware```
	
	 Note: If for some reason you cannot use flow control, limit the line speed to 9600 bps. Faster speeds are likely to result in lost data.
	
	 Step 3 After enabling hardware flow control on the access server or router line, initiate a reverse Telnet session to the modem via that line. For more information, see the section "Establishing a Reverse Telnet Session to a Modem" earlier in this chapter.
	
	 Step 4 Use a modem command string that includes the **RTS/CTS Flow** command for your modem. This command ensures that the modem is using the same method of flow control (that is, hardware flow control) as the Cisco access server or router. See your modem documentation for exact configuration command syntax. Figure 16–1 shows the hardware flow control command string for a Hayes-compatible modem.

Modem speed setting is not locked	**Step 1** Use the **show line** exec command on the access server or router. The output for the auxiliary port should indicate the currently configured Tx and Rx speeds. For an explanation of the output of the **show line** command, see the "Using **debug** Commands" section earlier in this chapter.

Table 16–6   *Dialin: Dialin Client Receives No exec Prompt, Continued*

Possible Causes	Suggested Actions

Modem speed setting is not locked (*Continued*)	**Step 2** If the line is not configured to the correct speed, use the **speed** line configuration command to set the line speed on the access server or router line. Set the value to the highest speed in common between the modem and the access server or router port.
	
	To set the terminal baud rate, use the **speed** line configuration command. This command sets both the transmit (to terminal) and receive (from terminal) speeds.
	
	Syntax:
	
	speed *bps*
	
	Syntax Description:
	
	• *bps*—Baud rate in bits per second (bps). The default is 9600 bps.
	
	Example:
	
	The following example sets lines 1 and 2 on a Cisco 2509 access server to 115200 bps:
	
	`line 1 2`
	` speed 115200`
	
	Note: If for some reason you cannot use flow control, limit the line speed to 9600 bps. Faster speeds are likely to result in lost data.
	
	Step 3 Use the **show line** exec command again and confirm that the line speed is set to the desired value.
	
	Step 4 When you are certain that the access server or router line is configured for the desired speed, initiate a reverse Telnet session to the modem via that line. For more information, see the section "Establishing a Reverse Telnet Session to a Modem" earlier in this chapter.

Table 16–6 *Dialin: Dialin Client Receives No exec Prompt, Continued*

Possible Causes	Suggested Actions
Modem speed setting is not locked (*Continued*)	**Step 5** Use a modem command string that includes the **lock** DTE speed command for your modem. See your modem documentation for exact configuration command syntax. **Note:** The **lock** DTE speed command, which might also be referred to as *port rate adjust* or *buffered mode*, is often related to the way in which the modem handles error correction. This command varies widely from one modem to another. Locking the modem speed ensures that the modem always communicates with the Cisco access server or router at the speed configured on the Cisco auxiliary port. If this command is not used, the modem reverts to the speed of the data link (the telephone line) instead of communicating at the speed configured on the access server.

Dialin: Dialin Session Sees "Garbage"

Symptom: Attempts to establish remote dialin sessions over a modem to a Cisco access server or router return "garbage" and ultimately result in no connection to the remote site. Users might see a "Connection Closed by Foreign Host" message.

Table 16–7 outlines the problems that might cause this symptom and describes solutions to those problems.

Table 16–7　*Dialin: Dialin Sessions Sees "Garbage"*

Possible Causes	Suggested Actions
Modem speed setting is not locked	**Step 1**　Use the **show line** exec command on the access server or router. The output for the auxiliary port should indicate the currently configured Tx and Rx speeds.
	For an explanation of the output of the **show line** command, see the "Using **debug** Commands" section earlier in this chapter.
	Step 2　If the line is not configured to the correct speed, use the **speed** line configuration command to set the line speed on the access server or router line. Set the value to the highest speed in common between the modem and the access server or router port.
	To set the terminal baud rate, use the **speed** line configuration command. This command sets both the transmit (to terminal) and receive (from terminal) speeds.
	Syntax:
	speed *bps*
	Syntax Description:
	• *bps*—Baud rate in bits per second (bps). The default is 9600 bps.
	Example:
	The following example sets lines 1 and 2 on a Cisco 2509 access server to 115200 bps:
	`line 1 2` `  speed 115200`
	Note: If for some reason you cannot use flow control, limit the line speed to 9600 bps. Faster speeds are likely to result in lost data.

Table 16-7 *Dialin: Dialin Sessions Sees "Garbage," Continued*

Possible Causes	Suggested Actions
Modem speed setting is not locked (*Continued*)	**Step 3** Use the **show line** exec command again and confirm that the line speed is set to the desired value.
	Step 4 When you are certain that the access server or router line is configured for the desired speed, initiate a reverse Telnet session to the modem via that line. For more information, see the section "Establishing a Reverse Telnet Session to a Modem."
	Step 5 Use a modem command string that includes the **lock** DTE speed command for your modem. See your modem documentation for exact configuration command syntax.
	Note: The **lock** DTE speed command, which might also be referred to as *port rate adjust* or *buffered mode*, is often related to the way in which the modem handles error correction. This command varies widely from one modem to another.
	Locking the modem speed ensures that the modem always communicates with the Cisco access server or router at the speed configured on the Cisco auxiliary port. If this command is not used, the modem reverts to the speed of the data link (the telephone line) instead of communicating at the speed configured on the access server.

Dialin: Dialin Session Ends Up in Existing Session

Symptom: Remote dialin session ends up in an already existing session initiated by another user. That is, instead of getting a login prompt, a dialin user sees a session established by another user (which might be a UNIX command prompt, a text editor session, and so forth).

Table 16-8 outlines the problems that might cause this symptom and describes solutions to those problems.

Table 16–8 *Dialin: Dialin Session Ends up in Existing Session*

Possible Causes	Suggested Actions
Modem configured for DCD always high	**Step 1** The modem should be reconfigured to have DCD high only on CD. This is usually done with the **&C1** modem command string (see Figure 16–1), but check your modem documentation for the exact syntax for your modem.
	Step 2 You might have to configure the access server line to which the modem is connected with the **no exec** line configuration command. Clear the line with the **clear line** privileged exec command, initiate a reverse Telnet session with the modem, and reconfigure the modem so that DCD is high only on CD.
	Step 3 End the Telnet session by entering **disconnect** and reconfigure the access server line with the **exec** line configuration command.
Modem control is not enabled on the access server or router	**Step 1** Use the **show line** exec command on the access server or router. The output for the auxiliary port should show **inout** or **RIisCD** in the Modem column. This indicates that modem control is enabled on the line of the access server or router.
	For an explanation of the **show line** output, see the "Using **debug** Commands" section earlier in this chapter.
	Step 2 Configure the line for modem control using the **modem inout** line configuration command. Modem control is now enabled on the access server.
	Note: Be certain to use the **modem inout** command instead of the **modem ri-is-cd** command while the connectivity of the modem is in question. The latter command allows the line to accept incoming calls only. Outgoing calls will be refused, making it impossible to establish a Telnet session with the modem to configure it. If you want to enable the **modem ri-is-cd** command, do so only after you are certain the modem is functioning correctly.

Table 16–8   *Dialin: Dialin Session Ends up in Existing Session, Continued*

Possible Causes	Suggested Actions	
Incorrect cabling	**Step 1**	Check the cabling between the modem and the access server or router. Confirm that the modem is connected to the auxiliary port on the access server or router with a rolled RJ-45 cable and an MMOD DB-25 adapter. This cabling configuration is recommended and supported by Cisco for RJ-45 ports. (These connectors are typically labelled "Modem.") There are two types of RJ-45 cabling: straight and rolled. If you hold the two ends of an RJ-45 cable side-by-side, you'll see eight colored strips, or pins, at each end. If the order of the colored pins is the same at each end, then the cable is straight. If the order of the colors is reversed at each end, then the cable is rolled. The rolled cable (CAB-500RJ) is standard with Cisco's 2500/CS500.
	Step 2	Use the **show line** exec command to verify that the cabling is correct. See the explanation of the **show line** command output in the section "Using **debug** Commands" earlier in this chapter.

Dialin: Modem Cannot Send or Receive Data

Symptom: After a dialin connection is established, a modem cannot send or receive data of any kind.

Table 16–9 outlines the problems that might cause this symptom and describes solutions to those problems.

Table 16–9   *Dialin: Modem Cannot Send or Receive Data*

Possible Causes	Suggested Actions

Modem speed setting is not locked	**Step 1** Use the **show line** exec command on the access server or router. The output for the auxiliary port should indicate the currently configured Tx and Rx speeds.
	
	For an explanation of the output of the **show line** command, see the "Using **debug** Commands" section earlier in this chapter.
	
	Step 2 If the line is not configured to the correct speed, use the **speed** line configuration command to set the line speed on the access server or router line. Set the value to the highest speed in common between the modem and the access server or router port.
	
	To set the terminal baud rate, use the **speed** line configuration command. This command sets both the transmit (to terminal) and receive (from terminal) speeds.
	
	Syntax:
	
	speed *bps*
	
	Syntax Description:
	
	• *bps*—Baud rate in bits per second (bps). The default is 9600 bps.
	
	Example:
	
	The following example sets lines 1 and 2 on a Cisco 2509 access server to 115200 bps:
	
	`line 1 2`
	` speed 115200`
	
	Note: If for some reason you cannot use flow control, limit the line speed to 9600 bps. Faster speeds are likely to result in lost data.

Table 16–9 *Dialin: Modem Cannot Send or Receive Data, Continued*

Possible Causes	Suggested Actions
Modem speed setting is not locked (*Continued*)	**Step 3** Use the **show line** exec command again and confirm that the line speed is set to the desired value.
	Step 4 When you are certain that the access server or router line is configured for the desired speed, initiate a reverse Telnet session to the modem via that line. For more information, see the section "Establishing a Reverse Telnet Session to a Modem" earlier in this chapter.
	Step 5 Use a modem command string that includes the **lock** DTE speed command for your modem. See your modem documentation for exact configuration command syntax.
	Note: The **lock** DTE speed command, which might also be referred to as *port rate adjust* or *buffered mode*, is often related to the way in which the modem handles error correction. This command varies widely from one modem to another.
	Locking the modem speed ensures that the modem always communicates with the Cisco access server or router at the speed configured on the Cisco auxiliary port. If this command is not used, the modem reverts to the speed of the data link (the telephone line) instead of communicating at the speed configured on the access server.
Hardware flow control not configured on local or remote modem or router	**Step 1** Use the **show line** *aux-line-number* exec command and look for the following in the Capabilities field (see Figure 16–2): `Capabilities: Hardware Flowcontrol In, Hardware Flowcontrol Out` If there is no mention of hardware flow control in this field, hardware flow control is not enabled on the line. Hardware flow control for access server-to-modem connections is recommended. For an explanation of the output of the **show line** command, see the section "Using **debug** Commands" earlier in this chapter.

Table 16–9   *Dialin: Modem Cannot Send or Receive Data, Continued*

Possible Causes	Suggested Actions
Hardware flow control not configured on local or remote modem or router (*Continued*)	**Step 2** Configure hardware flow control on the line using the **flowcontrol hardware** line configuration command.

To set the method of data flow control between the terminal or other serial device and the router, use the **flowcontrol** line configuration command. Use the **no** form of this command to disable flow control.

Syntax:

flowcontrol {none | software [lock] [in | out] | hardware [in | out]}

Syntax Description:

- **none**—Turns off flow control.

- **software**—Sets software flow control. An optional keyword specifies the direction: **in** causes the Cisco IOS software to listen to flow control from the attached device, and **out** causes the software to send flow control information to the attached device. If you do not specify a direction, both are assumed.

- **lock**—Makes it impossible to turn off flow control from the remote host when the connected device needs software flow control. This option applies to connections using the Telnet or rlogin protocols.

- **hardware**—Sets hardware flow control. An optional keyword specifies the direction: **in** causes the software to listen to flow control from the attached device, and **out** causes the software to send flow control information to the attached device. If you do not specify a direction, both are assumed. For more information about hardware flow control, see the hardware manual that was shipped with your router.

Example:

The following example sets hardware flow control on line 7:

```
line 7
  flowcontrol hardware
```

Note: If for some reason you cannot use flow control, limit the line speed to 9600 bps. Faster speeds are likely to result in lost data.

Table 16–9 *Dialin: Modem Cannot Send or Receive Data, Continued*

Possible Causes	Suggested Actions
Hardware flow control not configured on local or remote modem or router (*Continued*)	**Step 3** After enabling hardware flow control on the access server or router line, initiate a reverse Telnet session to the modem via that line. For more information, see the section "Establishing a Reverse Telnet Session to a Modem."
	Step 4 Use a modem command string that includes the **RTS/CTS Flow** command for your modem. This command ensures that the modem is using the same method of flow control (that is, hardware flow control) as the Cisco access server or router. See your modem documentation for exact configuration command syntax. Figure 16–1 shows the hardware flow control command string for a Hayes-compatible modem.
Misconfigured **dialer map** commands	**Step 1** Use the **show running-config** privileged exec command to view the router configuration. Check the **dialer map** command entries to see whether the **broadcast** keyword is specified.
	Step 2 If the keyword is missing, add it to the configuration. **Syntax:** **dialer map** *protocol next-hop-address* [**name** *hostname*] [**broadcast**] [*dial-string*] **Syntax Description:** • *protocol*—The protocol subject to mapping. Options include IP, IPX[1], bridge, and snapshot. • *next-hop-address*—The protocol address of the opposite site's async interface. • **name** *hostname*—A required parameter used in PPP authentication. It is the name of the remote site for which the dialer map is created. The name is case sensitive and must match the hostname of the remote router. • **broadcast**—An optional keyword that broadcast packets (e.g., IP RIP or IPX RIP/SAP updates) to be forwarded to the remote destination. In static routing sample configurations, routing updates are not desired and the **broadcast** keyword is omitted.

Table 16–9 *Dialin: Modem Cannot Send or Receive Data, Continued*

Possible Causes	Suggested Actions
Misconfigured **dialer map** commands (*Continued*)	• *dial-string*—The remote site's phone number. Any access codes (e.g., 9 to get out of an office, international dialing codes, area codes) must be included. **Step 3** Make sure that **dialer map** commands specify the correct next hop addresses. **Step 4** If the next hop address is incorrect, change it using the **dialer map** command. **Step 5** Make sure all other options in **dialer map** commands are correctly specified for the protocol you are using. For detailed information on configuring dialer maps, refer to the Cisco IOS *Wide-Area Networking Configuration Guide* and *Wide-Area Networking Command Reference*.
Old PC UART problem	This problem only applies to PC-to-router dialin connections. **Step 1** Use the **terminal download** command at the exec prompt before you Telnet. **Step 2** If the problem persists, use the DOS program MSD to see what PC UART is on your comm port. Older PC UARTs, such as the 8250, can't run at speeds over 19200 bps. **Step 3** If you have an older UART, try lowering your connection speed or get a faster serial card for your PC.
Problem with dialing modem	Make sure that the dialing modem is operational and is securely connected to the correct port. See whether another modem works when connected to the same port.

[1] IPX = Internetwork Packet Exchange

Dialin: Modem Cannot Send or Receive IP Data

Symptom: After a dialin connection is established, a modem cannot send or receive IP data.

NOTES

For general problems associated with a modem that cannot send or receive data, refer to the section "Dialin: Modem Cannot Send or Receive Data" earlier in this chapter.

For information on troubleshooting IP problems not specific to dialin connections, refer to Chapter 7, "Troubleshooting TCP/IP."

Table 16–10 outlines the problems that might cause this symptom and describes solutions to those problems.

Table 16–10 *Dialin: Modem Cannot Send or Receive IP Data*

Possible Causes	Suggested Actions	
IP routing not configured on local or remote router	Make sure that IP routing is enabled on the local and remote routers. For detailed information about configuring IP routing, refer to the Cisco IOS *Network Protocols Configuration Guide, Part 1.*	
No default gateway specified on PC	**Step 1**	Use the **show slip** exec command and make sure that the specified IP address is the same as the default gateway specification on the PC.
	Step 2	Check the specified default gateway address on the PC. If the IP address is not correct, specify the correct address. For instructions on verifying and changing the default gateway address on the workstation, refer to the vendor documentation.
Hardware flow control not configured on local or remote modem or router	**Step 1**	Use the **show line** *aux-line-number* exec command and look for the following in the Capabilities field (see Figure 16–2):
		`Capabilities: Hardware Flowcontrol In, Hardware Flowcontrol Out`
		If there is no mention of hardware flow control in this field, hardware flow control is not enabled on the line. Hardware flow control for access server-to-modem connections is recommended.
		For an explanation of the output of the **show line** command, see the "Using **debug** Commands" section earlier in this chapter.

Table 16–10   *Dialin: Modem Cannot Send or Receive IP Data, Continued*

Possible Causes	Suggested Actions

Hardware flow control not configured on local or remote modem or router (*Continued*)	**Step 2** Configure hardware flow control on the line using the **flowcontrol hardware** line configuration command.
	
	To set the method of data flow control between the terminal or other serial device and the router, use the **flowcontrol** line configuration command. Use the **no** form of this command to disable flow control.
	
	Syntax:
	
	flowcontrol {**none** | **software** [**lock**] [**in** | **out**] | **hardware** [**in** | **out**]}
	
	Syntax Description:
	
	• **none**—Turns off flow control.
	
	• **software**—Sets software flow control. An optional keyword specifies the direction: **in** causes the Cisco IOS software to listen to flow control from the attached device, and **out** causes the software to send flow control information to the attached device. If you do not specify a direction, both are assumed.
	
	• **lock**—Makes it impossible to turn off flow control from the remote host when the connected device needs software flow control. This option applies to connections using the Telnet or rlogin protocols.
	
	• **hardware**—Sets hardware flow control. An optional keyword specifies the direction: **in** causes the software to listen to flow control from the attached device, and **out** causes the software to send flow control information to the attached device. If you do not specify a direction, both are assumed. For more information about hardware flow control, see the hardware manual that was shipped with your router.
	
	Example:
	
	The following example sets hardware flow control on line 7:
	
	`line 7`
	`  flowcontrol hardware`
	
	Note: If for some reason you cannot use flow control, limit the line speed to 9600 bps. Faster speeds are likely to result in lost data.

Table 16–10 *Dialin: Modem Cannot Send or Receive IP Data, Continued*

Possible Causes	Suggested Actions
Hardware flow control not configured on local or remote modem or router (*Continued*)	**Step 3** After enabling hardware flow control on the access server or router line, initiate a reverse Telnet session to the modem via that line. For more information, see the section "Establishing a Reverse Telnet Session to a Modem." **Step 4** Use a modem command string that includes the **RTS/CTS Flow** command for your modem. This command ensures that the modem is using the same method of flow control (that is, hardware flow control) as the Cisco access server or router. See your modem documentation for exact configuration command syntax. Figure 16–1 shows the hardware flow control command string for a Hayes-compatible modem.
Misconfigured **dialer map** commands	**Step 1** Use the **show running-config** privileged exec command to view the router configuration. Check the **dialer map** command entries to see whether the **broadcast** keyword is specified. **Step 2** If the **broadcast** keyword is missing, add it to the configuration. For detailed information on configuring dialer maps, refer to the Cisco IOS *Wide-Area Networking Configuration Guide* and *Wide-Area Networking Command Reference*.

Table 16–10   *Dialin: Modem Cannot Send or Receive IP Data, Continued*

Possible Causes	Suggested Actions
Static routes not configured	**Step 1** Use the **show ip route** privileged exec command to see whether there is a static route to the remote network in the routing table.
	Step 2 If there is not a static route to the remote network, configure one using the **ip route** command. The static route should point to the remote network via the next hop in the dialer map.
	To establish static routes, use the **ip route** global configuration command. To remove static routes, use the **no** form of this command.
	Syntax:
	ip route *prefix mask* {*address*	*interface*} [*distance*] [**tag** *tag*] [**permanent**]
	Syntax Description:
	• *prefix*—IP route prefix for the destination.
	• *mask*—Prefix mask for the destination.
	• *address*—IP address of the next hop that can be used to reach that network.
	• *interface*—Network interface to use.
	• *distance*—(Optional) An administrative distance.
	• **tag** *tag*—(Optional) Tag value that can be used as a "match" value for controlling redistribution via route maps.
	• **permanent**—(Optional) Specifies that the route will not be removed, even if the interface shuts down.

Table 16–10 *Dialin: Modem Cannot Send or Receive IP Data, Continued*

Possible Causes	Suggested Actions
DNS[1] server not specified on router or workstation	**Step 1** Check to see whether the workstation and router both have DNS information specified. On the router, use the **show running-config** privileged exec command to see whether DNS is configured. For information on verifying the workstation configuration, refer to the vendor documentation.
	Step 2 If the router and workstation are not configured to use DNS, use the **ip domain-lookup**, **ip domain-name**, and **ip name-server** commands to configure the router.
	Example:
	The following example enables the IP DNS-based host name-to-address translation:
| | ```
ip domain-lookup
``` |
| | **Example:** |
| | The following example defines *cisco.com* as the default domain name: |
| | ```
ip domain-name cisco.com
``` |
| | **Example:** |
| | The following example specifies host 131.108.1.111 as the primary name server and host 131.108.1.2 as the secondary server: |
| | ```
ip name-server 131.108.1.111 131.108.1.2
``` |
| | This command is reflected in the configuration file as follows: |
| | ```
ip name-server 131.108.1.111
ip name-server 131.108.1.2
``` |
| | Configure a DNS server address in the TCP/IP software on the PC. For more information, refer to the vendor documentation. |

[1] DNS = Domain Name System

Dialin: Modem Cannot Send or Receive IPX Data

Symptom: After a dialin connection is established, a modem cannot send or receive Novell IPX data.

 NOTES

For general problems associated with a modem that cannot send or receive data, refer to the section "Dialin: Modem Cannot Send or Receive Data" earlier in this chapter.

For information on troubleshooting Novell IPX problems not specific to dialin connections, refer to Chapter 8, "Troubleshooting Novell IPX."

Table 16–11 outlines the problems that might cause this symptom and describes solutions to those problems.

Table 16–11 *Dialin: Modem Cannot Send or Receive IPX Data*

Possible Causes	Suggested Actions
IPX not enabled on the router	Make sure that IPX routing is enabled on the router. For detailed information on enabling IPX routing, refer to the Cisco IOS *Network Protocols Configuration Guide, Part 1*.
Incorrect Ethernet encapsulation	**Step 1** Enter the **show ipx servers** privileged exec command on your router. If the router is not in the listing, the Ethernet encapsulation might be incorrect.
	Step 2 Configure the correct Ethernet encapsulation on the router's Ethernet port using the **ipx network** *network* **encapsulation** *encapsulation-type* interface configuration command. The encapsulation must be the same as on your server.
IPX stack not installed correctly on PC	This problem applies only to PC-to-router dialin connections. Make sure that the IPX software is properly installed on the PC. For more information on installing the IPX stack, refer to the vendor documentation.

Dialin: Modem Does Not Disconnect Properly

Symptom: Modem does not disconnect properly. Connections to the modem do not terminate when the **quit** command is entered.

Table 16–12 outlines the problems that might cause this symptom and describes solutions to those problems.

Table 16–12   *Dialin: Modem Does Not Disconnect Properly*

Possible Causes	Suggested Actions
Modem is not sensing DTR	Enter the **Hangup DTR** modem command string. This command tells the modem to drop carrier when the DTR signal is no longer being received. On a Hayes-compatible modem the **&D3** string is commonly used to configure **Hangup DTR** on the modem, as shown in Figure 16–1. For the exact syntax of this command, see the documentation for your modem.
Modem control is not enabled on the router or access server	**Step 1** Use the **show line** exec command on the access server or router. The output for the auxiliary port should show **inout** or **RIisCD** in the Modem column. This indicates that modem control is enabled on the line of the access server or router. For an explanation of the **show line** output, see the "Using **debug** Commands" section earlier in this chapter. **Step 2** Configure the line for modem control using the **modem inout** line configuration command. Modem control is now enabled on the access server. **Note:** Be certain to use the **modem inout** command instead of the **modem ri-is-cd** command while the connectivity of the modem is in question. The latter command allows the line to accept incoming calls only. Outgoing calls will be refused, making it impossible to establish a Telnet session with the modem to configure it. If you want to enable the **modem ri-is-cd** command, do so only after you are certain the modem is functioning correctly.

Dialin: Link Goes Down Too Soon

Symptom: After a dialin connection is established, the link goes down again too quickly.

Table 16–13 outlines the problems that might cause this symptom and describes solutions to those problems.

Table 16–13 *Dialin: Link Goes Down Too Soon*

Possible Causes	Suggested Actions
Dialer timeout is too short	**Step 1** Use the **show running-config** privileged exec command to view the router configuration. Check the value configured with the **dialer idle-timeout** command. **Step 2** Increase the timeout value using the **dialer idle-timeout** *seconds* command. The default is 120 seconds.
Dialer lists are too restrictive	**Step 1** Use the **show running-config** privileged exec command to view the router configuration. Check the access lists referenced by **dialer list** commands. **Step 2** Make sure the access lists describe all the traffic that should keep the link active. Reconfigure the access lists to include additional traffic if necessary.

Dialin: Link Does Not Go Down or Stays Up Too Long

Symptom: After a dialin connection is established, the link stays up indefinitely or stays up for too long in an idle state.

Table 16–14 outlines the problems that might cause this symptom and describes solutions to those problems.

Table 16–14   *Dialin: Link Does Not Go Down or Stays Up Too Long*

Possible Causes	Suggested Actions
Dialer lists not restrictive enough	**Step 1** Use the **show running-config** privileged exec command to view the router configuration. Check the access lists referenced by **dialer list** commands. **Step 2** Make sure the access lists do not describe traffic that should not keep the link active. Reconfigure the access lists to exclude uninteresting traffic if necessary.
Modems misconfigured	Make sure the local and remote modems are properly configured. In particular, both modems should be configured to disconnect on loss of DTR (**Hangup DTR**). On a Hayes-compatible modem the **&D3** string is commonly used to configure **Hangup DTR** on the modem, as shown in Figure 16–1. For the exact syntax of this command, see the documentation for your modem.

Dialin: Poor Performance

Symptom: After a dialin connection is established, performance over the link is slow or unreliable, often due to a high rate of data loss.

Table 16–15 outlines the problems that might cause this symptom and describes solutions to those problems.

Table 16–15 *Dialin: Poor Performance*

Possible Causes	Suggested Actions
Error correction is not configured on the modem	Make certain the modem is configured for error correction. For the exact syntax of the command, see your modem documentation.
Flow control is not enabled, is enabled only on one device (either DTE or DCE), or is misconfigured	**Step 1** Use the **show line** *aux-line-number* exec command and look for the following in the Capabilities field (see Figure 16–2): `Capabilities: Hardware Flowcontrol In, Hardware Flowcontrol Out` If there is no mention of hardware flow control in this field, hardware flow control is not enabled on the line. Hardware flow control for access server-to-modem connections is recommended. For an explanation of the output of the **show line** command, see the "Using **debug** Commands" section earlier in this chapter. **Step 2** Configure hardware flow control on the line using the **flowcontrol hardware** line configuration command. To set the method of data flow control between the terminal or other serial device and the router, use the **flowcontrol** line configuration command. Use the **no** form of this command to disable flow control. **Syntax:** **flowcontrol {none	software [lock] [in	out]	hardware [in	out]}**

Table 16–15 *Dialin: Poor Performance, Continued*

Possible Causes	Suggested Actions

Flow control is not enabled, is enabled only on one device (either DTE or DCE), or is misconfigured (*Continued*)	**Syntax Description:**
	
	• **none**—Turns off flow control.
	
	• **software**—Sets software flow control. An optional keyword specifies the direction: **in** causes the Cisco IOS software to listen to flow control from the attached device, and **out** causes the software to send flow control information to the attached device. If you do not specify a direction, both are assumed.
	
	• **lock**—Makes it impossible to turn off flow control from the remote host when the connected device needs software flow control. This option applies to connections using the Telnet or rlogin protocols.
	
	• **hardware**—Sets hardware flow control. An optional keyword specifies the direction: **in** causes the software to listen to flow control from the attached device, and **out** causes the software to send flow control information to the attached device. If you do not specify a direction, both are assumed. For more information about hardware flow control, see the hardware manual that was shipped with your router.
	
	Example:
	
	The following example sets hardware flow control on line 7:
	
	`line 7`
	` flowcontrol hardware`
	
	Note: If for some reason you cannot use flow control, limit the line speed to 9600 bps. Faster speeds are likely to result in lost data.
	
	Step 3 After enabling hardware flow control on the access server or router line, initiate a reverse Telnet session to the modem via that line. For more information, see the section "Establishing a Reverse Telnet Session to a Modem."

Table 16–15 *Dialin: Poor Performance, Continued*

Possible Causes	Suggested Actions
Flow control is not enabled, is enabled only on one device (either DTE or DCE), or is misconfigured (*Continued*)	**Step 4** Use a modem command string that includes the **RTS/CTS Flow** command for your modem. This command ensures that the modem is using the same method of flow control (that is, hardware flow control) as the Cisco access server or router. See your modem documentation for exact configuration command syntax. Figure 16–1 shows the hardware flow control command string for a Hayes-compatible modem.
Congestion or line noise	**Step 1** If the network is congested, dial-up connections can freeze for a few seconds. The only solution is to reduce congestion on the network by increasing bandwidth or redesigning the network.
	Step 2 Line noise can also freeze up a dialup connection. For information on how to account for line noise on your modem, refer to the vendor documentation.
Old PC UART	This problem applies only to PC-to-router dialin connections.
	Step 1 Use the DOS program MSD to see what PC UART is on your comm port. Older PC UARTs, such as the 8250, cannot run at speeds over 19200 bps.
	Step 2 If you have an older UART, try lowering your connection speed or get a faster serial card for your PC.

## CHAPTER 17

Troubleshooting ISDN Connections

Integrated Services Digital Network (ISDN) refers to a set of digital services that are becoming available to end users. ISDN involves the digitization of the telephone network so that voice, data, text, graphics, music, video, and other source material can be provided to end users from a single end-user terminal over existing telephone wiring. Proponents of ISDN imagine a worldwide network much like the present telephone network, but with digital transmission and a variety of new services.

ISDN is an effort to standardize subscriber services, user/network interfaces, and network and internetwork capabilities. Standardizing subscriber services attempts to ensure a level of international compatibility. Standardizing the user/network interface stimulates development and marketing of these interfaces by third-party manufacturers. Standardizing network and internetwork capabilities helps achieve the goal of worldwide connectivity by ensuring that ISDN networks easily communicate with one another.

ISDN applications include high-speed image applications (such as Group IV facsimile), additional telephone lines in homes to serve the telecommuting industry, high-speed file transfer, and video conferencing. Voice, of course, will also be a popular application for ISDN.

Many carriers are beginning to offer ISDN under tariff. In North America, large local-exchange carriers (LECs) are beginning to provide ISDN service as an alternative to the T1 connections (digital carrier facilities provided by telephone companies) that currently carry bulk wide-area telephone service (WATS) services.

ISDN COMPONENTS

ISDN components include terminals, terminal adapters (TAs), network-termination devices, line-termination equipment, and exchange-termination equipment. ISDN terminals come in two types. Specialized ISDN terminals are referred to as *terminal equipment type 1* (TE1). Non-ISDN terminals such as DTE that predate the ISDN standards are referred to as *terminal equipment type*

2 (TE2). TE1s connect to the ISDN network through a four-wire, twisted-pair digital link. TE2s connect to the ISDN network through a terminal adapter. The ISDN TA can either be a standalone device or a board inside the TE2. If the TE2 is implemented as a standalone device, it connects to the TA via a standard physical-layer interface. Examples include EIA/TIA-232-C (formerly RS-232-C), V.24, and V.35.

Beyond the TE1 and TE2 devices, the next connection point in the ISDN network is the *network termination type 1* (NT1) or *network termination type 2* (NT2) device. These are network-termination devices that connect the four-wire subscriber wiring to the conventional two-wire local loop. In North America, the NT1 is a customer premises equipment (CPE) device. In most other parts of the world, the NT1 is part of the network provided by the carrier. The NT2 is a more complicated device, typically found in digital private branch exchanges (PBXs), that performs Layer 2 and 3 protocol functions and concentration services. An NT1/2 device also exists; it is a single device that combines the functions of an NT1 and an NT2.

A number of reference points are specified in ISDN. These reference points define logical interfaces between functional groupings such as TAs and NT1s. ISDN reference points include the following:

- R—The reference point between non-ISDN equipment and a TA.
- S—The reference point between user terminals and the NT2.
- T—The reference point between NT1 and NT2 devices.
- U—The reference point between NT1 devices and line-termination equipment in the carrier network. The U reference point is relevant only in North America, where the NT1 function is not provided by the carrier network.

A sample ISDN configuration is shown in Figure 17–1. This figure shows three devices attached to an ISDN switch at the central office. Two of these devices are ISDN compatible, so they can be attached through an S reference point to NT2 devices. The third device (a standard, non-ISDN telephone) attaches through the R reference point to a TA. Any of these devices could also attach to an NT1/2 device, which would replace both the NT1 and the NT2. And, although they are not shown, similar user stations are attached to the far right ISDN switch.

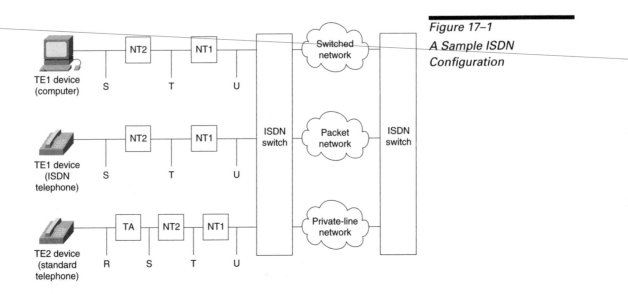

Figure 17–1
A Sample ISDN
Configuration

ISDN SERVICES

The ISDN Basic Rate Interface (BRI) service offers two B channels and one D channel (2B+D). BRI B-channel service operates at 64 kbps and is meant to carry user data; BRI D-channel service operates at 16 kbps and is meant to carry control and signaling information, although it can support user data transmission under certain circumstances. The D-channel signaling protocol comprises Layers 1 through 3 of the OSI reference model. BRI also provides for framing control and other overhead, bringing its total bit rate to 192 kbps. The BRI physical layer specification is International Telecommunication Union Telecommunication Standardization Sector (ITU-T; formerly the Consultative Committee for International Telegraph and Telephone [CCITT]) I.430.

ISDN Primary Rate Interface (PRI) service offers 23 B channels and one D channel in North America and Japan, yielding a total bit rate of 1.544 Mbps (the PRI D channel runs at 64 kbps). ISDN PRI in Europe, Australia, and other parts of the world provides 30 B plus one 64-kbps D channel and a total interface rate of 2.048 Mbps. The PRI physical layer specification is ITU-T I.431.

LAYER 1

ISDN physical layer (Layer 1) frame formats differ depending on whether the frame is outbound (from terminal to network) or inbound (from network to terminal). Both physical layer interfaces are shown in Figure 17–2.

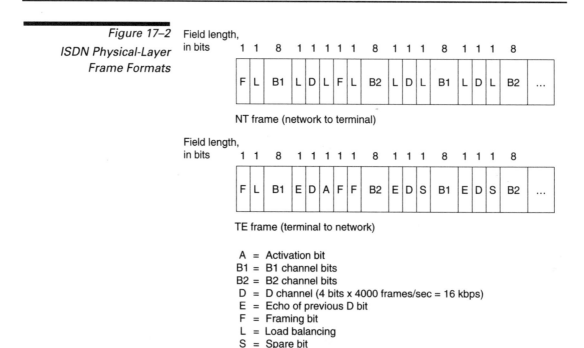

Figure 17–2
ISDN Physical-Layer
Frame Formats

NT frame (network to terminal)

TE frame (terminal to network)

A = Activation bit
B1 = B1 channel bits
B2 = B2 channel bits
D = D channel (4 bits x 4000 frames/sec = 16 kbps)
E = Echo of previous D bit
F = Framing bit
L = Load balancing
S = Spare bit

The frames are 48 bits long, of which 36 bits represent data. The bits of an ISDN physical layer frame are used as follows:

- F—Provides synchronization.
- L—Adjusts the average bit value.
- E—Used for contention resolution when several terminals on a passive bus contend for a channel.
- A—Activates devices.
- S—Unassigned.
- B1, B2, and D—For user data.

Multiple ISDN user devices can be physically attached to one circuit. In this configuration, collisions can result if two terminals transmit simultaneously. ISDN therefore provides features to determine link contention. When an NT receives a D bit from the TE, it echoes back the bit in the next E-bit position. The TE expects the next E bit to be the same as its last transmitted D bit.

Terminals cannot transmit into the D channel unless they first detect a specific number of ones (indicating "no signal") corresponding to a preestablished priority. If the TE detects a bit in the echo (E) channel that is different from its D bits, it must stop transmitting immediately. This simple technique ensures that only one terminal can transmit its D message at one time. After successful D message transmission, the terminal has its priority reduced by being required to detect more continuous ones before transmitting. Terminals cannot raise their priority until all other devices on the same line have had an opportunity to send a D message. Telephone connections have higher priority than all other services, and signaling information has a higher priority than nonsignaling information.

LAYER 2

Layer 2 of the ISDN signaling protocol is Link Access Procedure on the D channel, also known as LAPD. LAPD is similar to High-Level Data Link Control (HDLC) and Link Access Procedure, Balanced (LAPB). As the expansion of the LAPD abbreviation indicates, it is used across the D channel to ensure that control and signaling information flows and is received properly. The LAPD frame format (see Figure 17–3) is very similar to that of HDLC and, like HDLC, LAPD uses supervisory, information, and unnumbered frames. The LAPD protocol is formally specified in ITU-T Q.920 and ITU-T Q.921.

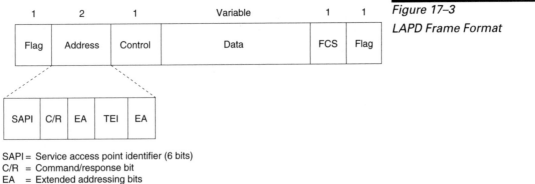

Figure 17–3
LAPD Frame Format

The LAPD Flag and Control fields are identical to those of HDLC. The LAPD Address field can be either 1 or 2 bytes long. If the extended address bit of the first byte is set, the address is 1 byte; if it is not set, the address is 2 bytes. The first address field byte contains the service access point identifier (SAPI), which identifies the portal at which LAPD services are provided to Layer 3. The C/R bit indicates whether the frame contains a command or a response. The terminal endpoint identifier (TEI) field identifies either a single terminal or multiple terminals. A TEI of all ones indicates a broadcast.

LAYER 3

Two Layer 3 specifications are used for ISDN signaling: ITU-T (formerly CCITT) I.450 (also known as ITU-T Q.930) and ITU-T I.451 (also known as ITU-T Q.931). Together, these protocols support user-to-user, circuit-switched, and packet-switched connections. A variety of call establishment, call termination, information, and miscellaneous messages are specified, including SETUP, CONNECT, RELEASE, USER INFORMATION, CANCEL, STATUS, and DISCONNECT.

These messages are functionally similar to those provided by the X.25 protocol (see Chapter 19, "Troubleshooting X.25 Connections," for more information). Figure 17–4, from ITU-T I.451, shows the typical stages of an ISDN circuit-switched call.

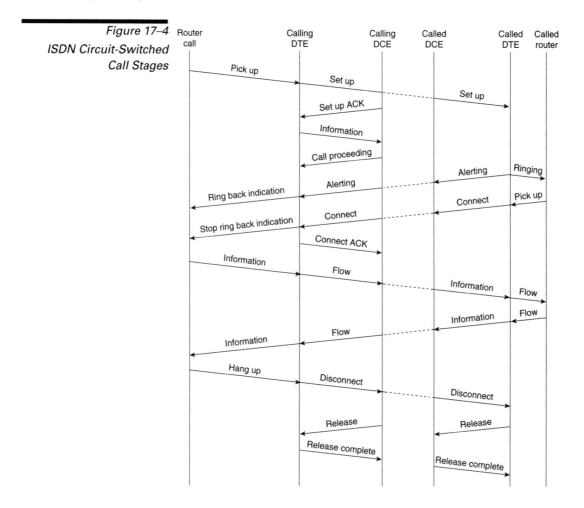

Figure 17–4
ISDN Circuit-Switched
Call Stages

TROUBLESHOOTING ISDN

This section presents troubleshooting information for ISDN connectivity and performance problems. It describes specific ISDN symptoms, the problems that are likely to cause each symptom, and the solutions to those problems.

The following sections describe the most common network issues when working with ISDN:

- ISDN: Router Does Not Dial
- ISDN: Dial Does Not Go Through BRI

- ISDN: Dial Does Not Go Through PRI
- ISDN: No Communication with Remote Router
- ISDN: No Communication End-to-End
- ISDN: Second B Channel Does Not Come Up
- ISDN: Second B Channel Comes Up Too Late
- ISDN: Second B Channel Comes Up Too Early
- ISDN: Slow Performance
- ISDN: Line Disconnects Too Slowly
- ISDN: Line Disconnects Too Quickly

ISDN: Router Does Not Dial

Symptom: Router configured for ISDN does not dial.

Table 17–1 outlines the problems that might cause this symptom and describes solutions to those problems.

Table 17–1 *ISDN: Router Does Not Dial*

Possible Problem	Solution	
Interface down	Step 1	Enter the **show interfaces** exec command to check the status of the ISDN interface.
	Step 2	If the output of the **show interfaces** command indicates that the interface is administratively down, bring the interface back up using the **no shutdown** interface configuration command.
	Step 3	If the interface or line protocol is down, check all cabling and connections. Troubleshoot the hardware and the media. For more information, refer to Chapter 3, "Troubleshooting Hardware and Booting Problems," and Chapter 15, "Troubleshooting Serial Line Problems."

Table 17-1 *ISDN: Router Does Not Dial, Continued*

Possible Problem	Solution
Missing or misconfigured **dialer map** commands	**Step 1** Use the **show running-config** privileged exec command to view the router configuration. Check whether there are **dialer map** interface configuration commands configured for the protocols you are using.
	Step 2 If there is not a dialer map configured for the protocol you are using, create a dialer map for each protocol.
	For example, if you want to configure a dialer map for IP, enter **dialer map** commands similar to the following on the interface:

	<pre>dialer map ip 172.16.20.2 name C4000 speed 56 broadcast 14155551234
	dialer map ip 172.16.20.2 name C4000 speed 56 broadcast 14155556789</pre>

	Step 3 If there are already **dialer map** commands present, make sure that the next hop address is in the same subnet as the local interface address.
	Step 4 If you want broadcast traffic to trigger the dialer, make sure that the **broadcast** keyword is specified in your dialer map statements.
	For detailed information on configuring dialer maps, refer to the Cisco IOS *Wide-Area Networking Configuration Guide* and *Wide-Area Networking Command Reference*.
No dialer group configured	**Step 1** Use the **show running-config** privileged exec command to view the router configuration. Check whether there are **dialer-group** interface configuration command entries present for the interface.
	Step 2 If the local interface does not belong to a dialer group, configure the interface as part of a dialer group by using the **dialer-group** *group-number* interface configuration command. This command associates an interface with a dialer group.
	Step 3 Make sure the *group-number* is the same number used in the associated **dialer-list** global configuration commands.

Table 17-1   *ISDN: Router Does Not Dial, Continued*

Possible Problem	Solution
Missing or misconfigured dialer lists	**Step 1** Use the **show running-config** privileged exec command to view the router configuration. Check whether there are **dialer-list** interface command entries present for the interface. **Step 2** If there are no dialer lists configured, enter the **dialer-list protocol** or the **dialer-list list** global configuration command to associate a dialer group with an access list. In the following example, dialer group 1 is associated with access list 101: ```dialer-list 1 list 101``` **Step 3** Make sure that **dialer-list** commands reference existing dialer groups and existing access lists, or create the appropriate dialer groups or access lists before attempting to dial.

Missing or misconfigured access lists	**Step 1** Use the **show running-config** privileged exec command to view the router configuration. Check whether the access list numbers specified in **dialer-list** commands refer to existing **access-list** command entries.
	
	Step 2 If the referenced access list is not defined, dialing does not occur. Configure access lists that define interesting traffic and make sure the lists are referenced correctly by **dialer-list** commands.
	
	In the following example, IGRP[1] routing updates are classified as uninteresting (they do not cause the router to dial), whereas all other IP packets are classified as interesting:
	
	```access-list 101 deny igrp 0.0.0.0 255.255.255.255 255.255.255.255 0.0.0.0```
	```access-list 101 permit ip 0.0.0.0 255.255.255.255 0.0.0.0 255.255.255.255```
	
	Step 3 If access lists are already present and they are referenced correctly by **dialer-list** commands, make sure that the traffic you want to trigger the dialer is defined as interesting by the access list.

Table 17-1 *ISDN: Router Does Not Dial, Continued*

Possible Problem	Solution
Missing **pri-group** command	On Cisco 7000 series routers, use the **pri-group** controller configuration command to specify ISDN PRI[2] on a channelized T1 card.
	Step 1 Use the **show running-config** privileged exec command to view the router configuration. Check whether there is a **pri-group** command entry.
	Step 2 If the command is not present, configure the controller with the **pri-group** command.
	Following is an example of a configuration for a Cisco 7000 series router with a channelized T1 card: ```controller t1 0 framing esf line code b8zs pri-group timeslots 1-24```

[1] IGRP = Interior Gateway Routing Protocol
[2] PRI = Primary Rate Interface

ISDN: Dial Does Not Go Through BRI

Symptom: ISDN router using a Basic Rate Interface (BRI) port successfully dials, but the call does not go through.

Table 17-2 outlines the problems that might cause this symptom and describes solutions to those problems.

Table 17–2   *ISDN: Dial Does Not Go Through BRI*

Possible Problem	Solution
Speed setting mismatch	**Step 1** Use the **show running-config** privileged exec command to view the router configuration. Check the **dialer map** interface configuration command entries in the local and remote router. These entries should look similar to the following: `dialer map ip 131.108.2.5 speed 56 name C4000` **Step 2** Compare the speed setting configured on the router interface to the speed of your ISDN service. The speeds must be the same. To set the speed on the router, use the **speed 56 | 64** keyword in the **dialer map** command. **Step 3** If you do not know the speed of your ISDN service, contact your ISDN provider. Long-distance calls are usually 56 kbps. For detailed information on configuring dialer maps, refer to the Cisco IOS *Wide-Area Networking Configuration Guide* and *Wide-Area Networking Command Reference*.
Misconfigured dialer map	**Step 1** Use the **show running-config** privileged exec command to view the router configuration. Look for **dialer map** interface configuration command entries. **Step 2** Make sure that each dialer map contains the phone number of the remote BRI. **Step 3** If the phone number of the remote BRI is properly specified in each dialer map statement but the dial does not go through, the first call failed and there are no numbers left to try. **Step 4** Make sure that a phone number is configured, and then clear the interface using the **clear interface** privileged exec command and try dialing again. For detailed information on configuring dialer maps, refer to the Cisco IOS *Wide-Area Networking Configuration Guide* and *Wide-Area Networking Command Reference*.

Table 17–2   *ISDN: Dial Does Not Go Through BRI, Continued*

Possible Problem	Solution
Number in use	**Step 1** Turn on ISDN debugging using the following privileged exec commands: ```C4000#debug isdn event\nISDN events debugging is on\nC4000#debug isdn q931\nISDN Q931 packets debugging is on``` **Caution:** Because debugging output is assigned high priority in the CPU process, it can render the system unusable. For this reason, use **debug** commands only to troubleshoot specific problems or during troubleshooting sessions with Cisco technical support staff. Moreover, it is best to use **debug** commands during periods of lower network traffic and fewer users. Debugging during these periods decreases the likelihood that increased **debug** command processing overhead will affect system use. **Step 2** If the **debug** output says "User busy," the remote ISDN number is probably in use.
Misconfigured SPIDs[1]	**Step 1** Use the **show running-config** privileged exec command to view the router configuration. Look for an **isdn spid1** *spid-number* interface configuration command entry. **Step 2** Verify that the SPID specified in the command is that assigned to you by your service provider. Use the *set spid* command to enter the correct spid: **set spid** set [*spid id*] *spid* [**spid** *number*] **Syntax Description:** • *spid id*—(Optional if there is only one SPID) Used as a convenient single-digit number to identify the actual long SPIDs allocated by service providers. • **spid** *number*—Number identifying the service to which you have subscribed. This value is assigned by the ISDN service provider and is usually a 10-digit telephone number with some extra digits. The SPID number can consist of 1 to 20 digits.

Table 17–2 *ISDN: Dial Does Not Go Through BRI, Continued*

Possible Problem	Solution

Misconfigured SPID (*Continued*)	**Examples:**
	
	The following example sets two SPIDs for the line:
	
	`Host> set 1 spid 0408555123401`
	`Host> set 2 spid 0405555123402`
	
	The following example deletes the first SPID:
	
	`Host> set 1 spid`

Incorrect cable	**Step 1** Make sure you use a straight-through RJ-45 cable. To check the cable, hold the RJ-45 cable ends side by side. If the pins are in the same order, the cable is straight-through. If the order of the pins is reversed, the cable is rolled. **Step 2** If you are using a rolled cable, replace it with a straight-through cable.
Port not attached to proper device or port	**Step 1** The ISDN BRI port of a router must be attached to an NT1[2] device. In ISDN, NT1 is a device that provides the interface between the customer premises equipment and central office switching equipment. If the router does not have an internal NT1, obtain and connect an NT1 to the BRI port. (The Cisco 1004 router has an internal NT1. An internal NT1 is optional in the Cisco 2524 and 2525 routers.) **Step 2** Make sure that the BRI or terminal adapter is attached to the S/T port of the NT1.

Table 17–2   *ISDN: Dial Does Not Go Through BRI, Continued*

Possible Problem	Solution
Layer 1 logic states hung	**Step 1** Check the status lights on the NT1. For information on interpreting the status lights, refer to the hardware documentation for the NT1.
	Step 2 If the NT1 status lights do not indicate a problem, check the NT1 for a switch to set the ohm termination. If the switch is present, set it to 100 ohms.
	Step 3 Power cycle the NT1.
	Step 4 Check the output of the **show isdn status** privileged exec command. The command output should say "Layer 1 active."
	Step 5 If the router still does not dial, clear the BRI interface using the **clear interface bri** privileged exec command.
	Step 6 Again check the output of the **show isdn status** command to see whether Layer 1 is active.
	Step 7 If Layer 1 is not active, contact your carrier to confirm the connection.
Media problem	For information on troubleshooting WAN media, refer to the appropriate chapter for your media and WAN implementation elsewhere in this book.
Hardware problem	**Step 1** Use the **show isdn status** privileged exec command. The output of this command should indicate "Layer 1 active."
	Step 2 If the output does not say "Layer 1 active," verify that the configured switch type is correct (check with your service provider to find out the correct switch type).
	Step 3 Check the cable connecting the BRI or terminal adapter to the telco jack or NT1. Replace the cable if it is damaged.
	Step 4 Make sure the NT1 is functioning correctly. If there is faulty or malfunctioning hardware, replace as necessary.
	Step 5 Make sure that the router is functioning correctly. If there is faulty or malfunctioning hardware, replace as necessary. For more information, refer to Chapter 3, "Troubleshooting Hardware and Booting Problems."

[1] SPID = service profile identifier
[2] NT1 = network termination type 1

ISDN: Dial Does Not Go Through PRI

Symptom: ISDN router using a PRI port successfully dials, but the call does not go through.

Table 17–3 outlines the problems that might cause this symptom and describes solutions to those problems.

Table 17–3   *ISDN: Dial Does Not Go Through PRI*

Possible Problem	Solution
Speed setting mismatch	**Step 1** Use the **show running-config** privileged exec command to view the router configuration. Check the **dialer map** interface configuration command entries in the local and remote router. These entries should look similar to the following: `dialer map ip 131.108.2.5 speed 56 name C4000` **Step 2** Compare the speed setting configured on the router interfaces to the speed of your ISDN service. The speeds must be the same. To set the speed on the router, use the **speed 56 | 64** keyword in the **dialer map** command. **Note:** If the speed is not explicitly specified, the **dialer map** defaults to 64 kbps. **Step 3** If you do not know the speed of your ISDN service, contact your ISDN provider. Long-distance calls are usually 56 kbps. For detailed information on configuring dialer maps, refer to the Cisco IOS *Wide-Area Networking Configuration Guide* and *Wide-Area Networking Command Reference*.

Table 17–3   *ISDN: Dial Does Not Go Through PRI, Continued*

Possible Problem	Solution
Misconfigured dialer map	**Step 1** Use the **show running-config** privileged exec command to view the router configuration. Look for **dialer map** interface configuration command entries.
	Step 2 Make sure that each dialer map contains the phone number of the remote PRI.
	Step 3 If the phone number of the remote PRI is properly specified in each dialer map statement but the dial does not go through, the first call failed and there are no numbers left to try.
	Step 4 Make sure a phone number is configured, and then clear the interface using the **clear interface** privileged exec command and try dialing again.
	For detailed information on configuring dialer maps, refer to the Cisco IOS *Wide-Area Networking Configuration Guide* and *Wide-Area Networking Command Reference*.
Number in use	**Step 1** Turn on ISDN debugging by using the **debug isdn events** privileged exec command.
	Step 2 If the debug output says "User busy," the remote ISDN number is probably in use.

Table 17–3 *ISDN: Dial Does Not Go Through PRI, Continued*

Possible Problem	Solution

Mismatched framing or linecoding	**Step 1** Use the **show controllers t1** privileged exec command to see the framing and linecoding types currently configured on the MIP[1] card.
	
	Step 2 Compare the configured framing and linecoding with those configured on the CSU[2]. (Refer to the vendor documentation for information on how to check the CSU configuration.) The framing and linecoding configured on the MIP card and the CSU must be the same.
	
	Step 3 Change the framing or linecoding types as necessary to make them the same on the MIP card and the CSU.
	
	On the router, use the following controller configuration commands to configure the framing and linecoding on the MIP card:
	
	`c7000(config)#controller t1 interface-number`
	`c7000(config-controller)#framing [esf¦sf]`
	`c7000(config-controller)#linecode [ami¦b8zs]`
	
	On the CSU, consult the vendor documentation for information on changing the configuration.

Incorrect cable	**Step 1** Make sure you using a straight-through DB-15 cable. **Step 2** If you are using any other cable, replace it with a straight-through DB-15 cable.
Port not attached to proper device or port	The ISDN PRI port of a router must be attached to a CSU device. If the port is not connected to a CSU, obtain a CSU and attach the PRI port to it.

Table 17–3   *ISDN: Dial Does Not Go Through PRI, Continued*

Possible Problem	Solution
Layer 1 logic states hung	**Step 1** Check the status lights of the CSU. For information on interpreting the status lights, refer to your vendor documentation.
	Step 2 If the CSU status lights do not indicate a problem, power cycle the CSU.
	Step 3 Check the output of the **show isdn status** privileged exec command. The command output should say "Layer 1 active."
	Step 4 If the router still does not dial, clear the PRI interface using the **clear interface serial** privileged exec command.
	Step 5 Again check the output of the **show isdn status** command to see whether Layer 1 is active.
	Step 6 If Layer 1 is not active, contact your carrier to confirm the connection.
Media problem	For information on troubleshooting WAN media, refer to the appropriate chapter for your media elsewhere in this book.
Hardware problem	**Step 1** Use the **show isdn status** privileged exec command. The output of this command should indicate "Layer 1 active."
	Step 2 If the output does not say "Layer 1 active," verify that the configured switch type is correct (check with your service provider to determine the switch type).
	Step 3 Check the cable connecting the PRI to the CSU. Replace the cable if it is damaged.
	Step 4 Make sure that the router is functioning correctly. If there is faulty or malfunctioning hardware, replace as necessary. For more information, refer to Chapter 3, "Troubleshooting Hardware and Booting Problems."

[1] MIP = MultiChannel Interface Processor
[2] CSU = channel service unit

ISDN: No Communication with Remote Router

Symptom: ISDN connection attempts are successful, but attempts to **ping** or otherwise communicate with the remote ISDN router interface fail.

Table 17–4 outlines the problems that might cause this symptom and describes solutions to those problems.

Table 17–4 *ISDN: No Communication with Remote Router*

Possible Problem	Solution
CHAP[1] misconfigured	**Step 1** Use the **debug ppp chap** privileged exec command.
	Step 2 Try to **ping** the remote router. Look for the message "Passed chap authentication."
	Step 3 If you do not see this message, use the **show running-config** privileged exec command to view the router configuration. Make sure that the **ppp authentication chap** interface configuration command is configured on both the local and remote routers.
	Syntax:
	ppp authentication {**chap** | **chap pap** | **pap chap** | **pap**} [**if-needed**] [*list-name* | **default**] [**callin**] [*one-time*]
	• **chap**—Enables CHAP on a serial interface.
	• **pap**—Enables PAP[2] on a serial interface.
	• **chap pap**—Enables both CHAP and PAP, and performs CHAP authentication before PAP.
	• **pap chap**—Enables both CHAP and PAP, and performs PAP authentication before CHAP.
	• **if-needed**—(Optional) Used with TACACS[3] and extended TACACS. Does not perform CHAP or PAP authentication if the user has already provided authentication. This option is available only on asynchronous interfaces.

Table 17–4 *ISDN: No Communication with Remote Router, Continued*

Possible Problem	Solution
CHAP misconfigured (*Continued*)	• *list-name*—(Optional) Used with AAA[4]. Specifies the name of a list of methods of authentication to use. If no list name is specified, the system uses the default. The list is created with the **aaa authentication ppp** command.
	• **default**—The name of the method list is created with the **aaa authentication ppp** command.
	• **callin**—Specifies authentication on incoming (received) calls only.
	• *one-time*—(Optional) Accepts the username and password in the username field.
	Step 4 Check **username** global configuration command entries. Make sure that username statements use the host name of the remote router. Make sure that the passwords on both the local and remote router are identical. Use the **username** command to add or alter username entries. For more information, refer to the Cisco IOS configuration guides and command references.
PPP[5] encapsulation not configured on interface	**Step 1** Use the **show running-config** privileged exec command to view the interface state. Check the output to see whether the **encapsulation ppp** interface configuration command is present.
	Step 2 If PPP encapsulation is not configured, configure the interface with the **encapsulation ppp** command.
	Step 3 Verify that PPP encapsulation is being used by checking the **show running-config** output again.

Table 17–4 *ISDN: No Communication with Remote Router, Continued*

Possible Problem	Solution
No route to remote network	**Step 1** Enter the **show route** privileged exec command for the particular protocol you are using. For example, if you are using IP, enter **show ip route** *ip-address*. If the output says "Network not in table," there is no route to the remote network. **Step 2** If there are no routes to remote networks, you need to add static routes using the appropriate command for the protocol you are running. For example, to configure static IP routes, use the **ip route** global configuration command. **Step 3** You also need to configure floating static routes so that there will be routes to the remote networks if the primary link goes down. For information on configuring floating static routes, refer to the Cisco IOS *Wide-Area Networking Configuration Guide* and *Wide-Area Networking Command Reference*.
Misconfigured **dialer map** command	**Step 1** Use the **show running-config** privileged exec command to view the router configuration. Look for **dialer map** interface configuration command entries. **Step 2** Make sure that the dialer maps point to the correct next hop address. Also ensure that the next hop address is in the same subnet as the local DDR[6] interface address. For detailed information on configuring dialer maps, refer to the Cisco IOS *Wide-Area Networking Configuration Guide* and *Wide-Area Networking Command Reference*.

Table 17–4 *ISDN: No Communication with Remote Router, Continued*

Possible Problem	Solution
Missing **dialer-group** command	**Step 1** A dialer group must be configured on the local and remote router interfaces. Use the **show running-config** privileged exec command to view the remote router configuration. Look for a **dialer-group** interface configuration command entry. **Step 2** If the remote router interface has no **dialer-group** command entry, you must configure a dialer group on the interface. Use the **dialer-group** *group-number* interface configuration command. Make sure the group number corresponds to the group number referenced in **dialer list** command entries. For more information, refer to the Cisco IOS *Wide-Area Networking Configuration Guide* and *Wide-Area Networking Command Reference.*

[1] CHAP = Challenge Handshake Authentication Protocol
[2] PAP = Password Authentication Protocol
[3] TACACS = Terminal Access Controller Access Control System
[4] AAA = authentication, authorization, and accounting
[5] PPP = Point-to-Point Protocol
[6] DDR = dial-on-demand routing

ISDN: No Communication End-to-End

Symptom: ISDN connection attempts are successful, but attempts to **ping** or otherwise communicate end-to-end over an ISDN connection are unsuccessful.

Table 17–5 outlines the problems that might cause this symptom and describes solutions to those problems.

Table 17–5 *ISDN: No Communication End-to-End*

Possible Problem	Solution
No default gateway configured on end systems	**Step 1** Check the configuration of local and remote end systems. Make certain that end systems are configured with a default-gateway specification.
	Step 2 If an end systems is not configured with a default gateway, you must configure one. For information on configuring your end system, refer to the vendor documentation.
	Step 3 If there is already a default gateway specification, make sure it points to the correct address. The default gateway should point to a local router LAN interface.
No route to remote network	**Step 1** Enter the **show route** privileged exec command for the particular protocol you are using. For example, if you are using IP, enter **show ip route** *ip-address*. If the output says "Network not in table," then there is no route to the remote network.
	Step 2 If there are no routes to remote networks, you need to add static routes using the appropriate command for the protocols you are running. For example, to configure static IP routes, use the **ip route** global configuration command.
	Step 3 You also need to configure floating static routes so there will be routes to the remote networks after the primary link goes down.
	For information on configuring floating static routes, refer to the Cisco IOS *Wide-Area Networking Configuration Guide* and *Wide-Area Networking Command Reference*.
LAN media problem	Make certain that your LAN media are functioning properly and that addressing and other configurations are correct. For more information on troubleshooting LAN problems, refer to the media troubleshooting chapter that covers the media type used in your network.
Hardware problem	**Step 1** Check all hardware on end systems (workstations and servers). Replace any damaged or malfunctioning hardware.
	Step 2 Check all router hardware. Replace any damaged or malfunctioning router hardware. For more information, refer to Chapter 3, "Troubleshooting Hardware and Booting Problems."

ISDN: Second B Channel Does Not Come Up

Symptom: When using a second B channel as a backup connection to a single destination, the second B channel does not come up.

Table 17–6 outlines the problems that might cause this symptom and describes solutions to those problems.

Table 17–6   *ISDN: Second B Channel Does Not Come Up*

Possible Problem	Solution	
Missing or misconfigured **dialer load-threshold** command	**Step 1**	Use the **show running-config** privileged exec command to view the router configuration. Check for a **dialer load-threshold** interface configuration command entry.
		The following is the syntax for the **dialer load-threshold** command:
		dialer load-threshold *load* [**outbound**	**inbound**	**either**]
		This command defines the load level that must be exceeded on the first ISDN B channel before the router attempts to bring up a second B channel for a multilink PPP connection. The load is a value between 1 and 255 and defines a fraction taken over 255. The load can be calculated based on outbound, inbound, or either inbound or outbound traffic on the interface. For instance, the sample configurations use "dialer load-threshold 200 either." If the combination of both inbound and outbound traffic levels reaches 200/255 (about 80%, or roughly 50 kbps) capacity of the first ISDN B channel, the router attempts to bring up a second B channel to assist with the traffic load. Thus, the second B channel is activated only when the traffic demands exceed the capacity of one B channel.
		Note: In scenarios where it is desired to have both B channels all the time, use the value 1. This causes both B channels to be brought up whenever the router dials.
	Step 2	If the command is not present, configure the router interface with the **dialer load-threshold** *load* command. This command specifies what the load on the first B channel must be before the second B channel is activated.
		Note: The range is 1 to 255.
	Step 3	If the command is already configured, make sure that the load value specified is not too high. Reduce the specified load in increments of 25 or 50 to see whether the second channel comes up.

Table 17–6 *ISDN: Second B Channel Does Not Come Up, Continued*

Possible Problem	Solution
No dialer map configured for second B channel	**Step 1** Use the **show running-config** privileged exec command to view the router configuration. Look for **dialer map** interface configuration command entries.
	Step 2 If there is not a dialer map configured for the second remote ISDN telephone number, configure one for the missing telephone number.
	In some topologies (PRIs, or a BRI with a 5ESS switch), one telephone number refers to both B channels. If this is the case, you will not be able to add a second **dialer map** statement.
	For detailed information on configuring dialer maps, refer to the Cisco IOS *Wide-Area Networking Configuration Guide* and *Wide-Area Networking Command Reference*.
No service profile handler (SPID) specified for second B channel (BRI only)	**Step 1** Use the **show running-config** privileged exec command to view the router configuration. Look for **isdn spid1** interface configuration command entries.
	Step 2 Make sure that there are **isdn spid1** command entries for each of the B channels. Make sure that the specified SPIDs are those assigned to you by your service provider.
No second B channel on remote router	The remote ISDN router must have at least two B channels for the local router to be able to use its second B channel. Contact your service provider to find out whether the remote ISDN router has at least two B channels.

ISDN: Second B Channel Comes Up Too Late

Symptom: When using a second B channel as a backup connection to a single destination, the load on the first B channel is higher than desired before the second B channel comes up.

Table 17–7 outlines the problem that might cause this symptom and describes solutions to that problem.

Table 17–7   *ISDN: Second B Channel Comes Up Too Late*

Possible Problem	Solution	
Misconfigured **dialer load-threshold** command	**Step 1**	Use the **show running-config** privileged exec command to view the router configuration. Check the **dialer load-threshold** interface configuration command entry.
		The following is the syntax for the **dialer load-threshold** command:
		dialer load-threshold *load* [outbound | inbound | either]
		This command defines the load level that must be exceeded on the first ISDN B channel before the router attempts to bring up a second B channel for a multilink PPP connection. The load is a value between 1 and 255 and defines a fraction taken over 255. The load can be calculated based on outbound, inbound, or either inbound or outbound traffic on the interface. For instance, the sample configurations use "dialer load-threshold 200 either." If the combination of both inbound and outbound traffic levels reaches 200/255 (about 80%, or roughly 50 kbps) capacity of the first ISDN B channel, the router attempts to bring up a second B channel to assist with the traffic load. Thus, the second B channel is activated only when the traffic demands exceed the capacity of one B channel.
		Note: In scenarios where it is desired to have both B channels all the time, use the value 1. This causes both B channels to be brought up whenever the router dials.
	Step 2	Make sure the value configured by this command is not too high. This command specifies what the load on the first B channel must be before the second B channel is activated.
		Note: The range is 1 to 255.
	Step 3	If the load value specified is too high, decrease the specified load in increments of 25 or 50 to allow the second B channel to dial earlier.

ISDN: Second B Channel Comes Up Too Early

Symptom: When using a second B channel as a backup connection to a single destination, the second B channel comes up before the load on the first B channel is high enough.

Table 17–8 outlines the problem that might cause this symptom and describes solutions to that problem.

Table 17–8 *ISDN: Second B Channel Comes Up Too Early*

Possible Problem	Solution	
Misconfigured **dialer load-threshold** command	**Step 1**	Use the **show running-config** privileged exec command to view the router configuration. Check the **dialer load-threshold** interface configuration command entry.
		The following is the syntax for the **dialer load-threshold** command:
		dialer load-threshold *load* [**outbound** | **inbound** | **either**]
		This command defines the load level that must be exceeded on the first ISDN B channel before the router attempts to bring up a second B channel for a multilink PPP connection. The load is a value between 1 and 255 and defines a fraction taken over 255. The load can be calculated based on outbound, inbound, or either inbound or outbound traffic on the interface. For instance, the sample configurations use "dialer load-threshold 200 either." If the combination of both inbound and outbound traffic levels reaches 200/255 (about 80%, or roughly 50 kbps) capacity of the first ISDN B channel, the router attempts to bring up a second B channel to assist with the traffic load. Thus, the second B channel is activated only when the traffic demands exceed the capacity of one B channel.
		Note: In scenarios where it is desired to have both B channels all the time, use the value 1. This causes both B channels to be brought up whenever the router dials.
	Step 2	Make sure that the value configured by this command is not too low. This command specifies what the load on the first B channel must be before the second B channel is activated.
		Note: The range is 1 to 255.
	Step 3	If the load value specified is too low, increase the specified load in increments of 25 or 50 to allow the load on the first B channel to reach a greater value before the second B channel dials.

ISDN: Slow Performance

Symptom: ISDN connections are successfully established and communication occurs, but performance across the link is slow.

Table 17–9 outlines the problems that might cause this symptom and describes solutions to those problems.

Table 17–9   *ISDN: Slow Performance*

Possible Problem	Solution
Hold queues too small	**Step 1** Check for input or output drops on the ISDN interface: • For a BRI interface, use the **show interfaces bri** *number* **1 2** privileged exec command • For a PRI interface, use the **show interfaces serial** *slot/port* privileged exec command • For a serial interface, use the **show interfaces serial** *number* privileged exec command Look for drops in the command output. The output line looks similar to the following: `output queue 0/40 0 drops; input queue 0/75 0 drops` **Step 2** If there are excessive drops on the interface, use the appropriate **clear counters** privileged exec command to clear the interface counters. Check for drops on the interface again. If the values are incrementing, you should increase the size of the input or output hold queues. **Step 3** Increase the hold queue for the interface that is dropping packets. Use the **hold-queue** *length* **out** or the **hold-queue** *length* **in** interface configuration command, depending on whether you are seeing output or input drops on the interface. Increase these queues by small increments (for instance, 25%) until you no longer see drops in the **show interfaces** output.

Table 17–9 *ISDN: Slow Performance, Continued*

Possible Problem	Solution

Poor line quality	**Step 1** Check for input or output errors on the ISDN interface.
	
	• For a BRI interface, use the **show interfaces bri number 1 2** privileged exec command
	
	• For a PRI interface, use the **show interfaces serial** *slot/port* privileged exec command
	
	• For a serial interface, use the **show interfaces serial** *number* privileged exec command.
	
	Look for errors in the command output. The output lines look similar to the following:
	
	`0 input errors, 0 CRC, 0 frame, 0 overrun, 0 ignored, 0 abort`
	`    0 packets output, 0 bytes, 0 underruns`
	`    0 output errors, 0 collisions, 2 interface resets`
	
	Step 2 If there are excessive errors on the interface, use the appropriate **clear counters** privileged exec command to clear the interface counters. Check for errors on the interface again. If the values are incrementing, it is probably the result of poor line quality.
	
	Step 3 Reduce the line speed to 56 kbps to see whether the error rate slows or stops.
	
	Step 4 Contact your carrier to see whether something can be done to improve the line quality. Make sure the DCE device is configured properly as well.

ISDN: Line Disconnects Too Slowly

Symptom: ISDN connections are successfully established but idle connections do not disconnect quickly enough.

Table 17–10 outlines the problems that might cause this symptom and describes solutions to those problems.

Table 17–10 *ISDN: Line Disconnects Too Slowly*

Possible Problem	Solution
No **dialer hold-queue** command configured	**Step 1** Use the **show running-config** privileged exec command to view the router configuration. Check for a **dialer hold-queue** interface configuration command entry.
	Step 2 Configure the **dialer hold-queue** *packets* command on the outgoing interface if it is not present already. This command allows interesting outgoing packets to be queued until a modem connection is established.
	The number of packets specified by this command should be less than 20.
Misconfigured **dialer idle-timeout** command	**Step 1** Use the **show running-config** privileged exec command to view the router configuration. Check for a **dialer idle-timeout** interface configuration command entry.
	Syntax:
	dialer idle-timeout *seconds*
	This command specifies the number of seconds before the router disconnects an ISDN call due to lack of interesting traffic as defined by the **dialer-list** command. Whenever an interesting packet is forwarded over the ISDN line, the **dial idle-timeout** counter resets to 0 and begins counting up again. When the counter reaches the specified value, the router terminates the call. For proper operation, both routers should have matching **idle-timeout** values. The default value is 120 seconds but can be configured to a value between 1 and 2,147,483 seconds.
	Step 2 Check the value specified by this command. If the ISDN line disconnects too slowly when idle, the value is probably set too high.
	Step 3 Decrease the value specified by the **dialer idle-timeout** command. This forces connections to disconnect more quickly when they are idle.

Table 17–10 *ISDN: Line Disconnects Too Slowly, Continued*

Possible Problem	Solution
dialer fast-idle time too high	**Step 1** Use the **show running-config** privileged exec command to view the router configuration. Check for a **dialer fast-idle** interface configuration command entry. This command does not appear in the configuration unless it has been changed from the default. **Syntax:** **dialer fast-idle** *seconds* The **fast-idle** timer is activated if there is contention for a line. In other words, if a line is in use and a packet for a different next hop address is received, and the busy line is required to send the competing packet, the **dialer fast-idle** timer is activated. **Step 2** Check the value specified by the dialer fast-idle command. If there is contention for an ISDN line but an idle connection does not disconnect quickly enough, the value is probably set too high. **Step 3** Decrease the value specified by the **dialer fast-idle** command. This forces idle connections to disconnect more quickly when there is contention for the line.

Table 17–10 *ISDN: Line Disconnects Too Slowly, Continued*

Possible Problem	Solution
Dialer list **access-list** commands not restrictive enough	**Step 1** Use the **show access-list** privileged exec command to see the access lists configured on the router. Access lists determine which packets cause dialing to occur and which packets reset the **idle-timer**, keeping the connection up.
	Step 2 Use the **show running-config** privileged exec command to view the router configuration. Check which access lists are applied to the interface with **dialer-list** commands.
	Syntax:
	dialer-list dialer-group protocol *protocol* {**permit** | **deny** | **list** *access-list-number*}
	This command creates a list that defines what traffic is interesting enough to initiate and sustain an ISDN call for an interface that belongs to the same **dialer-group** number.
	Step 3 Examine the specified access lists to make sure the line is not being kept up for uninteresting traffic. The access lists need to be more restrictive if the line never goes down.
	In particular, make sure that routing updates or SNMP[1] packets do not reset the idle timer or bring the line up.
	Step 4 If necessary, modify access lists to restrict uninteresting traffic.

[1] SNMP = Simple Network Management Protocol

ISDN: Line Disconnects Too Quickly

Symptom: ISDN connections are successfully established, but connections disconnect too quickly when idle.

Table 17–11 outlines the problems that might cause this symptom and describes solutions to those problems.

Table 17–11   *ISDN: Line Disconnects Too Quickly*

Possible Problem	Solution
Misconfigured **dialer idle-timeout** command	**Step 1** Use the **show running-config** privileged exec command to view the router configuration. Check for a **dialer idle-timeout** interface configuration command entry. If the command is not present on the interface, the interface uses the default of 120 seconds. **Step 2** Check the value specified by this command. If the ISDN line disconnects too quickly when idle, the value is probably set too low. **Step 3** Increase the value specified by the **dialer idle-timeout** command. This allows connections to stay idle longer before disconnecting.
dialer fast-idle time too high	**Step 1** Use the **show running-config** privileged exec command to view the router configuration. Check for a **dialer fast-idle** interface configuration command entry. The **fast-idle** timer is activated if there is contention for a line. In other words, if a line is in use and a packet for a different next hop address is received, and the busy line is required to send the competing packet, the **dialer fast-idle** timer is activated. This command does not appear in the configuration unless it has been changed from the default of 20 seconds. **Step 2** Check the value specified by this command. If there is contention for an ISDN line and the line disconnects too quickly, the value is probably set too low. **Step 3** Increase the value specified by the **dialer fast-idle** command. This allows idle connections to stay connected longer when there is contention for the line.

## CHAPTER 18

Troubleshooting Frame Relay Connections

Frame Relay was originally conceived as a protocol for use over ISDN interfaces. Initial proposals to this effect were submitted to the International Telecommunication Union Telecommunication Standardization Sector (ITU-T), formerly the Consultative Committee for International Telegraph and Telephone (CCITT), in 1984. Work on Frame Relay was also undertaken in the American National Standards Institute (ANSI)-accredited T1S1 standards committee in the United States.

There was a major development in Frame Relay's history in 1990 when Cisco Systems, StrataCom, Northern Telecom, and Digital Equipment Corporation formed a consortium to focus Frame Relay technology development and accelerate the introduction of interoperable Frame Relay products. This consortium developed a specification conforming to the basic Frame Relay protocol being discussed in T1S1 and ITU-T, but extended it with features that provide additional capabilities for complex internetworking environments. These Frame Relay extensions are referred to collectively as the Local Management Interface (LMI).

FRAME RELAY TECHNOLOGY BASICS

Frame Relay provides a packet-switching data communications capability that is used across the interface between user devices (for example, routers, bridges, host machines) and network equipment (for example, switching nodes). User devices are often referred to as data terminal equipment (DTE), whereas network equipment that interfaces to DTE is often referred to as data circuit-terminating equipment (DCE). The network providing the Frame Relay interface can be either a carrier-provided public network or a network of privately owned equipment serving a single enterprise.

As an interface to a network, Frame Relay is the same type of protocol as X.25 (see Chapter 19, "Troubleshooting X.25 Connections"). However, Frame Relay differs significantly from X.25 in its functionality and format. In particular, Frame Relay is a more streamlined protocol, facilitating higher performance and greater efficiency.

As an interface between user and network equipment, Frame Relay provides a means for statistically multiplexing many logical data conversations (referred to as *virtual circuits*) over a single physical transmission link. This contrasts with systems that use only time-division-multiplexing (TDM) techniques for supporting multiple data streams. Frame Relay's statistical multiplexing provides more flexible and efficient use of available bandwidth. It can be used without TDM techniques or on top of channels provided by TDM systems.

Another important characteristic of Frame Relay is that it exploits the recent advances in wide-area network (WAN) transmission technology. Earlier WAN protocols such as X.25 were developed when analog transmission systems and copper media were predominant. These links are much less reliable than the fiber media/digital transmission links available today. Over links such as these, link-layer protocols can forgo time-consuming error correction algorithms, leaving these to be performed at higher protocol layers. Greater performance and efficiency is therefore possible without sacrificing data integrity. Frame Relay is designed with this approach in mind. It includes a cyclic redundancy check (CRC) algorithm for detecting corrupted bits (so the data can be discarded), but it does not include any protocol mechanisms for correcting bad data (for example, by retransmitting it at this level of protocol).

Another difference between Frame Relay and X.25 is the absence of explicit, per-virtual-circuit flow control in Frame Relay. Now that many upper-layer protocols are effectively executing their own flow control algorithms, the need for this functionality at the link layer has diminished. Frame Relay, therefore, does not include explicit flow control procedures that duplicate those in higher layers. Instead, very simple congestion notification mechanisms are provided to allow a network to inform a user device that the network resources are close to a congested state. This notification can alert higher-layer protocols that flow control may be needed.

Current Frame Relay standards address permanent virtual circuits (PVCs) that are administratively configured and managed in a Frame Relay network. Another type, switched virtual circuits (SVCs), has also been proposed. The Integrated Services Digital Network (ISDN) signaling protocol is proposed as the means by which DTE and DCE can communicate to establish, terminate, and manage SVCs dynamically.

LMI Extensions

In addition to the basic Frame Relay protocol functions for transferring data, the consortium Frame Relay specification includes LMI extensions that make supporting large, complex internetworks easier. Some LMI extensions are referred to as "common" and are expected to be implemented by everyone who adopts the specification. Other LMI functions are referred to as "optional." A summary of the LMI extensions follows:

- Virtual circuit status messages (common)—Provides communication and synchronization between the network and the user device, periodically reporting the existence of new PVCs and the deletion of already existing PVCs, and generally provides information about PVC integrity. Virtual circuit status messages prevent the sending of data into black holes, that is, over PVCs that no longer exist.

- Multicasting (optional)—Allows a sender to transmit a single frame but have it delivered by the network to multiple recipients. Thus, multicasting supports the efficient conveyance of routing protocol messages and address resolution procedures that typically must be sent to many destinations simultaneously.

- Global addressing (optional)—Gives connection identifiers global rather than local significance, allowing them to be used to identify a specific interface to the Frame Relay network. Global addressing makes the Frame Relay network resemble a local-area network (LAN) in terms of addressing; address resolution protocols therefore perform over Frame Relay exactly as they do over a LAN.

- Simple flow control (optional)—Provides for an XON/XOFF flow control mechanism that applies to the entire Frame Relay interface. It is intended for devices whose higher layers cannot use the congestion notification bits and that need some level of flow control.

Frame Format

The Frame Relay frame is shown in Figure 18–1. The flags fields delimit the beginning and end of the frame. Following the leading Flags field are 2 bytes of address information. Ten bits of these 2 bytes make up the actual circuit ID (called the DLCI, for data link connection identifier).

Field length, in bytes	1	2	Variable	2	1
	Flags	Address	Data	FCS	Flags

Figure 18–1

The Frame Relay Frame

The 10-bit DLCI value is the heart of the Frame Relay header. It identifies the logical connection that is multiplexed into the physical channel. In the basic (not extended by the LMI) mode of addressing, DLCIs have local significance; that is, the end devices at two different ends of a connection may use a different DLCI to refer to that same connection. Figure 18–2 provides an example of the use of DLCIs in nonextended Frame Relay addressing.

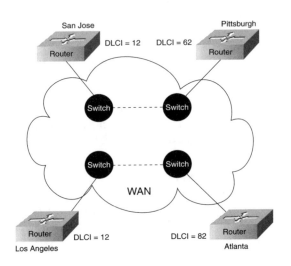

Figure 18–2

Frame Relay Addressing

In Figure 18–2, assume two PVCs, one between Atlanta and Los Angeles and one between San Jose and Pittsburgh. Los Angeles uses DLCI 12 to refer to its PVC with Atlanta, whereas Atlanta refers to the same PVC as DLCI 82. Similarly, San Jose uses DLCI 12 to refer to its PVC with Pittsburgh. The network uses internal proprietary mechanisms to keep the two locally significant PVC identifiers distinct.

At the end of each DLCI byte is an extended address (EA) bit. If this bit is 1, the current byte is the last DLCI byte. All implementations currently use a 2-byte DLCI, but the presence of the EA bits means that longer DLCIs may be agreed on and used in the future.

The bit marked *C/R* following the most significant DLCI byte is currently not used.

Finally, 3 bits in the 2-byte DLCI provide congestion control. The forward explicit congestion notification (FECN) bit is set by the Frame Relay network in a frame to tell the DTE receiving the frame that congestion was experienced in the path from source to destination. The backward explicit congestion notification (BECN) bit is set by the Frame Relay network in frames traveling in the opposite direction from frames encountering a congested path. The notion behind both of these bits is that the FECN or BECN indication can be promoted to a higher-level protocol that can take flow control action as appropriate. (FECN bits are useful to higher-layer protocols that use receiver-controlled flow control, whereas BECN bits are significant to those that depend on "emitter-controlled" flow control.)

The discard eligibility (DE) bit is set by the DTE to tell the Frame Relay network that a frame has lower importance than other frames and should be discarded before other frames if the network becomes short of resources. Thus, it represents a very simple priority mechanism. This bit is usually set only when the network is congested.

LMI Message Format

The previous section describes the basic Frame Relay protocol format for carrying user data frames. The consortium Frame Relay specification also includes the LMI procedures. LMI messages are sent in frames distinguished by an LMI-specific DLCI (defined in the consortium specification as DLCI = 1023). The LMI message format is shown in Figure 18–3.

Figure 18–3
The LMI Message Format

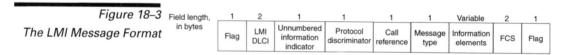

In LMI messages, the basic protocol header is the same as in normal data frames. The actual LMI message begins with 4 mandatory bytes, followed by a variable number of information elements (IEs). The format and encoding of LMI messages is based on the ANSI T1S1 standard.

The first of the mandatory bytes (*unnumbered information indicator*) has the same format as the Link Access Procedure, Balanced (LAPB) unnumbered information (UI) frame indicator with the poll/final bit set to 0. (For more information about LAPB, see Chapter 19, "Troubleshooting X.25 Connections.") The next byte is referred to as the *protocol discriminator*, which is set to a value that indicates LMI. The third mandatory byte (*call reference*) is always filled with zeros.

The final mandatory byte is the *Message type* field. Two message types have been defined. Status-enquiry messages allow the user device to inquire about network status. Status messages respond to status-enquiry messages. Keepalives (messages sent through a connection to ensure that both sides will continue to regard the connection as active) and PVC status messages are examples of these messages and are the common LMI features that are expected to be a part of every implementation that conforms to the consortium specification.

Together, status and status-enquiry messages help verify the integrity of logical and physical links. This information is critical in a routing environment because routing algorithms make decisions based on link integrity.

Following the message type field is some number of IEs. Each IE consists of a single-byte IE identifier, an IE length field, and 1 or more bytes containing actual data.

Global Addressing

In addition to the common LMI features, several optional LMI extensions are extremely useful in an internetworking environment. The first important optional LMI extension is global addressing. As noted previously, the basic (nonextended) Frame Relay specification supports only values of the DLCI field that identify PVCs with local significance. In this case, no addresses identify network interfaces or nodes attached to these interfaces. Because these addresses do not exist, they cannot be discovered by traditional address resolution and discovery techniques. This means that with normal Frame Relay addressing, static maps must be created to tell routers which DLCIs to use to find a remote device and its associated internetwork address.

The global addressing extension permits node identifiers. With this extension, the values inserted in the DLCI field of a frame are globally significant addresses of individual end-user devices (for example, routers). This is implemented as shown in Figure 18–4.

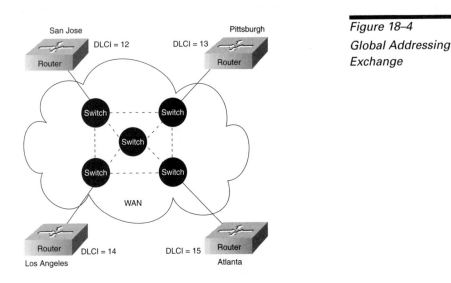

Figure 18–4

Global Addressing Exchange

In Figure 16–4, note that each interface has its own identifier. Suppose that Pittsburgh must send a frame to San Jose. The identifier for San Jose is 12, so Pittsburgh places the value 12 in the DLCI field and sends the frame into the Frame Relay network. At the exit point, the DLCI field contents are changed by the network to 13 to reflect the source node of the frame. Each router interface has a distinct value as its node identifier, so individual devices can be distinguished. This permits adaptive routing in complex environments.

Global addressing provides significant benefits in a large, complex internetwork. The Frame Relay network now appears to the routers on its periphery like any LAN. No changes to higher-layer protocols are needed to take full advantage of their capabilities.

Multicasting

Multicasting is another valuable optional LMI feature. Multicast groups are designated by a series of four reserved DLCI values (1,019 to 1,022). Frames sent by a device using one of these reserved DLCIs are replicated by the network and sent to all exit points in the designated set. The multicasting extension also defines LMI messages that notify user devices of the addition, deletion, and presence of multicast groups.

In networks that take advantage of dynamic routing, routing information must be exchanged among many routers. Routing messages can be sent efficiently by using frames with a multicast DLCI. This allows messages to be sent to specific groups of routers.

Network Implementation

Frame Relay can be used as an interface to either a publicly available carrier-provided service or to a network of privately owned equipment. A typical means of private network implementation is to equip traditional T1 multiplexers with Frame Relay interfaces for data devices, as well as non-Frame Relay interfaces for other applications such as voice and video-teleconferencing. Figure 18–5 shows this configuration.

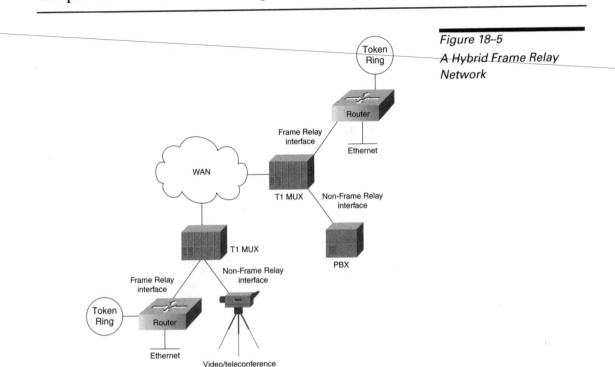

Figure 18–5
A Hybrid Frame Relay Network

A public Frame Relay service is deployed by putting Frame Relay switching equipment in the central offices of a telecommunications carrier. In this case, users can realize economic benefits from traffic-sensitive charging rates and are relieved from the work necessary to administer and maintain the network equipment and service.

In either type of network, the lines that connect user devices to the network equipment can operate at a speed selected from a broad range of data rates. Speeds between 56 kbps and 2 mbps are typical, although Frame Relay can support lower and higher speeds.

Whether in a public or private network, the support of Frame Relay interfaces to user devices does not necessarily dictate that the Frame Relay protocol is used between the network devices. No standards for interconnecting equipment inside a Frame Relay network currently exist. Thus, traditional circuit-switching, packet-switching, or a hybrid approach combining these technologies can be used.

TROUBLESHOOTING FRAME RELAY

This section discusses troubleshooting procedures for connectivity problems related to Frame Relay links. It describes specific Frame Relay symptoms, the problems that are likely to cause each symptom, and the solutions to those problems.

The following sections cover the most common network issues in Frame Relay networks:

- Frame Relay: Frame Relay Link Is Down
- Frame Relay: Cannot **ping** Remote Router
- Frame Relay: Cannot **ping** End-to-End

Frame Relay: Frame Relay Link Is Down

Symptom: Connections over a Frame Relay link fail. The output of the **show interfaces serial** exec command shows that the interface and line protocol are down or that the interface is up and the line protocol is down.

Table 18–1 outlines the problems that might cause this symptom and describes solutions to those problems.

Table 18–1   *Frame Relay: Frame Relay Link Is Down*

Possible Problem	Solution
Cabling, hardware, or carrier problem	Perform these steps for the local and remote router:
	Step 1 Use the **show interfaces serial** command to see whether the interface and line protocol are up.
	Step 2 If the interface and line protocol are down, check the cable to make sure it is a DTE[1] serial cable. Make sure cables are securely attached.
	Step 3 If the cable is correct, try moving it to a different port. If that port works, then the first port is defective. Replace either the card or the router.
	Step 4 If the cable doesn't work on the second port, try replacing the cable. If it still doesn't work, there might be a problem with the DCE[2]. Contact your carrier about the problem.
	For detailed information on troubleshooting serial lines, refer to Chapter 15, "Troubleshooting Serial Line Problems."
LMI[3] type mismatch	**Step 1** Use the **show interfaces serial** command to check the state of the interface.
	Step 2 If the output shows that the interface is up but the line protocol is down, use the **show frame-relay lmi** exec command to see which LMI type is configured on the Frame Relay interface.
	Step 3 Make sure that the LMI type is the same for all devices in the path from source to destination. Use the **frame-relay lmi-type {ansi	cisco	q933a}** interface configuration command to change the LMI type on the router.

Table 18–1 *Frame Relay: Frame Relay Link Is Down, Continued*

Possible Problem	Solution
Keepalives not being sent	**Step 1** Enter the **show interfaces** command to find out whether keepalives are configured. If you see a line that says "keepalives not set," keepalives are not configured. **Step 2** Use the **keepalive** *seconds* interface configuration command to configure keepalives. The default value for this command is 10 seconds.
Encapsulation mismatch	**Step 1** When connecting Cisco devices with non-Cisco devices, you must use IETF[4] encapsulation on both devices. Check the encapsulation type on the Cisco device with the **show frame-relay map** exec command. **Step 2** If the Cisco device is not using IETF encapsulation, use the **encapsulation frame-relay ietf** interface configuration command to configure IETF encapsulation on the Cisco Frame Relay interface. For information on viewing or changing the configuration of the non-Cisco device, refer to the vendor documentation.
DLCI[5] inactive or deleted	**Step 1** Use the **show frame-relay pvc** exec command to view the status of the interface's PVC. **Step 2** If the output shows that the PVC[6] is inactive or deleted, there is a problem along the path to the remote router. Check the remote router or contact your carrier to check the status of the PVC.

Table 18–1   *Frame Relay: Frame Relay Link Is Down, Continued*

Possible Problem	Solution
DLCI assigned to wrong subinterface	**Step 1** Use the **show frame-relay pvc** privileged exec command to check the assigned DLCIs. Make sure that the correct DLCIs are assigned to the correct subinterface. If the DLCI is incorrect, use the **no frame-relay map** command to delete the incorrect DLCI number entry under the interface. Use the **frame-relay map** interface configuration command to define the mapping between an address and the correct DLCI used to connect to the address. Syntax: **frame-relay map** *protocol protocol-address dlci* [*broadcast*] [*ietf* | *cisco*] Syntax Description: • *protocol*—Supported protocols: AppleTalk, DECnet, IP, XNS, IPX, and VINES. • *protocol-address*—Address for the protocol. • *dlci*—DLCI number for the interface. • *broadcast*—(Optional) Broadcasts should be forwarded to this address when multicast is not enabled. • *ietf*—(Optional) IETF form of Frame Relay encapsulation. Use when the communication server is connected to another vendor's equipment across a Frame Relay network. • *cisco*—(Optional) Cisco encapsulation method. Example: The following example maps IP address 131.108.123.1 to DLCI 100: ```\ninterface serial 0\nframe-relay map ip 131.108.123.1 100 broadcast\n``` **Step 2** If the DLCIs appear to be correct, shut down the main interface using the **shutdown** interface configuration command, and then bring the interface back up using the **no shutdown** command.

[1] DTE = data terminal equipment
[2] DCE = data circuit-terminating equipment
[3] LMI = Local Management Interface
[4] IETF = Internet Engineering Task Force
[5] DLCI = Data Link Connection Identifier
[6] PVC = permanent virtual circuit

Frame Relay: Cannot ping Remote Router

Symptom: Attempts to **ping** the remote router across a Frame Relay connection fail.

Table 18–2 outlines the problems that might cause this symptom and describes solutions to those problems.

Table 18–2 *Frame Relay: Cannot **ping** Remote Router*

Possible Problem	Solution	
Encapsulation mismatch	Step 1	When connecting Cisco devices with non-Cisco devices, you must use IETF encapsulation on both devices. Check the encapsulation type on the Cisco device with the **show frame-relay map** exec command.
	Step 2	If the Cisco device is not using IETF encapsulation, use the **encapsulation frame-relay ietf** interface configuration command to configure IETF encapsulation on the Cisco Frame Relay interface.
		For information on viewing or changing the configuration of the non-Cisco device, refer to the vendor documentation.
DLCI inactive or deleted	Step 1	Use the **show frame-relay pvc** exec command to view the status of the interface's PVC.
	Step 2	If the output shows that the PVC is inactive or deleted, there is a problem along the path to the remote router. Check the remote router or contact your carrier to check the status of the PVC.
DLCI assigned to wrong subinterface	Step 1	Use the **show frame-relay pvc** privileged exec command to check the assigned DLCIs. Make sure that the correct DLCIs are assigned to the correct subinterfaces.
	Step 2	If the DLCIs appear to be correct, shut down the main interface using the **shutdown** interface configuration command, and then bring the interface back up using the **no shutdown** command.

Table 18–2 *Frame Relay: Cannot **ping** Remote Router, Continued*

Possible Problem	Solution
Misconfigured access list	**Step 1** Use the **show access-list** privileged exec command to see whether there are access lists configured on the router.
	Step 2 If there are access lists configured, test connectivity by disabling access lists using the **no access-group** global configuration command. Check whether connectivity is restored.
	Step 3 If connections work, reenable access lists one at a time, checking connections after enabling each access list.
	Step 4 If enabling an access list blocks connections, make sure that the access list does not deny necessary traffic. Make sure to configure explicit **permit** statements for any traffic you want to pass.
	Step 5 Continue testing access lists until all access lists are restored and connections still work.
frame-relay map command missing	**Step 1** Use the **show frame-relay map** privileged exec command to see whether an address map is configured for the DLCI.
	Step 2 If you do not see an address map for the DLCI, enter the **clear frame-relay-inarp** privileged exec command and then use the **show frame-relay map** command again to see whether there is now a map to the DLCI.
	Step 3 If there is no map to the DLCI, add a static address map. Use the **frame-relay map** interface configuration command.
	Syntax:
	frame-relay map *protocol protocol-address dlci* [*broadcast*] [*ietf* | *cisco*]

Table 18–2   *Frame Relay: Cannot **ping** Remote Router, Continued*

Possible Problem	Solution

frame-relay map command missing (*Continued*)	**Syntax Description:**
	
	• *protocol*—Supported protocols: AppleTalk, DECnet, IP, XNS, IPX, and VINES.
	
	• *protocol-address*—Address for the protocol.
	
	• *dlci*—DLCI number for the interface.
	
	• *broadcast*—(Optional) Broadcasts should be forwarded to this address when multicast is not enabled.
	
	• *ietf*—(Optional) IETF form of Frame Relay encapsulation. Use when the communication server is connected to another vendor's equipment across a Frame Relay network.
	
	• *cisco*—(Optional) Cisco encapsulation method.
	
	Example:
	
	The following example maps IP address 131.108.123.1 to DLCI 100:
	
	`interface serial 0`
	`frame-relay map ip 131.108.123.1 100 broadcast`
	
	Step 4 Make sure that the DLCIs and next-hop addresses specified in **frame-relay map** commands are correct. The specified protocol address should be in the same network as your local Frame Relay interface.
	
	For complete information on configuring Frame Relay address maps, refer to the Cisco IOS *Wide-Area Networking Configuration Guide*.

Table 18–2   *Frame Relay: Cannot **ping** Remote Router, Continued*

Possible Problem	Solution
| No **broadcast** keyword in **frame-relay map** statements | **Step 1**  Use the **show running-config** privileged exec command on local and remote routers to view the router configuration. Check **frame-relay map** command entries to see whether the **broadcast** keyword is specified.<br><br>**Step 2**  If the keyword is not specified, add the **broadcast** keyword to all **frame-relay map** commands.<br><br>**Syntax:**<br><br>**frame-relay map** *protocol protocol-address dlci* [*broadcast*] [*ietf* \| *cisco*]<br><br>**Syntax Description:**<br><br>• *protocol*—Supported protocols: AppleTalk, DECnet, IP, XNS, IPX, and VINES.<br><br>• *protocol-address*—Address for the protocol.<br><br>• *dlci*—DLCI number for the interface.<br><br>• *broadcast*—(Optional) Broadcasts should be forwarded to this address when multicast is not enabled.<br><br>• *ietf*—(Optional) IETF form of Frame Relay encapsulation. Use when the communication server is connected to another vendor's equipment across a Frame Relay network.<br><br>• *cisco*—(Optional) Cisco encapsulation method.<br><br>**Example:**<br><br>The following example maps IP address 131.108.123.1 to DLCI 100:<br><br>```
interface serial 0
frame-relay map ip 131.108.123.1 100 broadcast
```<br><br>**Note:** By default, the **broadcast** keyword is added to dynamic maps learned via Inverse ARP[1]. |

[1] ARP = Address Resolution Protocol
```

Frame Relay: Cannot ping End-to-End

Symptom: Attempts to **ping** devices on a remote network across a Frame Relay connection fail.

Table 18–3 outlines the problems that might cause this symptom and describes solutions to those problems.

Table 18–3 *Frame Relay: Cannot* **ping** *End-to-End*

Possible Problem	Solution
Split horizon problem	In a hub-and-spoke Frame Relay environment, you must configure subinterfaces in order to avoid problems with split horizon. For detailed information on configuring subinterfaces, refer to the Cisco IOS *Wide-Area Networking Configuration Guide* and *Wide-Area Networking Command Reference*.
	Frame Relay subinterfaces provide a mechanism for supporting partially meshed Frame Relay networks. Most protocols assume transitivity on a logical network; that is, if station A can talk to station B, and station B can talk to station C, then station A should be able to talk to station C directly. Transitivity is true on LANs, but not on Frame Relay networks, unless A is directly connected to C.
	Additionally, certain protocols such as AppleTalk and transparent bridging cannot be supported on partially meshed networks because they require *split horizon*, in which a packet received on an interface cannot be transmitted out the same interface even if the packet is received and transmitted on different virtual circuits.
	Configuring Frame Relay subinterfaces ensures that a single physical interface is treated as multiple virtual interfaces. This capability allows us to overcome split horizon rules. Packets received on one virtual interface can now be forwarded out another virtual interface, even if they are configured on the same physical interface.
	Subinterfaces address the limitations of Frame Relay networks by providing a way to subdivide a partially meshed Frame Relay network into a number of smaller, fully meshed (or point-to-point) subnetworks. Each subnetwork is assigned its own network number and appears to the protocols as if it is reachable through a separate interface. (Note that point-to-point subinterfaces can be unnumbered for use with IP, reducing the addressing burden that might otherwise result.)

Table 18–3   *Frame Relay: Cannot **ping** End-to-End, Continued*

Possible Problem	Solution
No default gateway on workstation	**Step 1** From the local workstation or server, try to **ping** the remote workstation or server. Make several attempts to **ping** the remote device if the first **ping** is unsuccessful.
	Step 2 If all your attempts fail, check whether the local workstation or server can **ping** the local router's Frame Relay interface.
	Step 3 If you are unable to **ping** the local interface, check the local workstation or server to see whether it is configured with a default gateway specification.
	Step 4 If there is no default gateway specified, configure the device with a default gateway. The default gateway should be the address of the local router's LAN interface.
	For information on viewing or changing the workstation or server's default gateway specification, refer to the vendor documentation.

Troubleshooting X.25 Connections

In the 1970s, a set of protocols was needed to provide users with wide-area network (WAN) connectivity across public data networks (PDNs). PDNs such as Telnet and TYMNET had achieved remarkable success, but it was felt that protocol standardization would increase subscriptions to PDNs by providing improved equipment compatibility and lower cost. The result of the ensuing development effort was a group of protocols, the most popular of which is X.25.

X.25 was developed by the common carriers (telephone companies, essentially) rather than any single commercial enterprise. The specification is therefore designed to work well regardless of a user's system type or manufacturer. Users contract with the common carriers to use their packet-switched networks (PSNs) and are charged based on PSN use. Services offered (and charges levied) are regulated by the Federal Communications Commission (FCC).

One of X.25's unique attributes is its international nature. X.25 and related protocols are administered by an agency of the United Nations called the International Telecommunications Union (ITU). The ITU Telecommunication Standardization Sector (ITU-T; formerly CCITT, Consultative Committee for International Telegraph and Telephone) is the ITU committee responsible for voice and data communications. ITU-T members include the FCC, the European Postal Telephone and Telegraph organizations, the common carriers, and many computer and data communications companies. As a result, X.25 is truly a global standard.

X.25 TECHNOLOGY BASICS

X.25 defines a telephone network for data communications. To begin communication, one computer calls another to request a communication session. The called computer can accept or refuse the connection. If the call is accepted, the two systems can begin full-duplex information transfer. Either side can terminate the connection at any time.

The X.25 specification defines a point-to-point interaction between data terminal equipment (DTE) and data circuit-terminating equipment (DCE). DTEs (terminals and hosts in the user's facilities) connect to DCEs (modems, packet switches, and other ports into the PDN, generally located in the carrier's facilities), which connect to packet switching exchanges (PSEs, or switches) and other DCEs inside a PSN and, ultimately, to another DTE. The relationship between the entities in an X.25 network is shown in Figure 19–1.

Figure 19–1

The X.25 Model

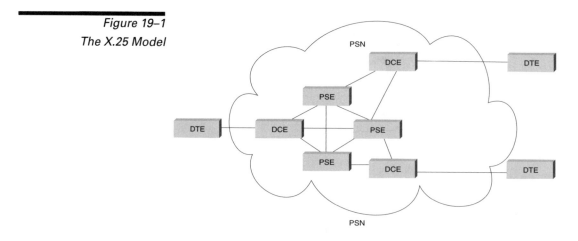

A DTE can be a terminal that does not implement the complete X.25 functionality. A DTE is connected to a DCE through a translation device called a packet assembler/disassembler (PAD). The operation of the terminal-to-PAD interface, the services offered by the PAD, and the interaction between the PAD and the host are defined by ITU-T Recommendations X.28, X.3, and X.29, respectively.

The X.25 specification maps to Layers 1 through 3 of the OSI reference model. Layer 3 X.25 describes packet formats and packet exchange procedures between peer Layer 3 entities. Layer 2 X.25 is implemented by Link Access Procedure, Balanced (LAPB). LAPB defines packet framing for the DTE/DCE link. Layer 1 X.25 defines the electrical and mechanical procedures for activating and deactivating the physical medium connecting the DTE and the DCE. This relationship is shown in Figure 19–2. Note that Layers 2 and 3 are also referred to as the ISO standards ISO 7776 (LAPB) and ISO 8208 (X.25 packet layer).

Figure 19–2

X.25 and the OSI Reference Model

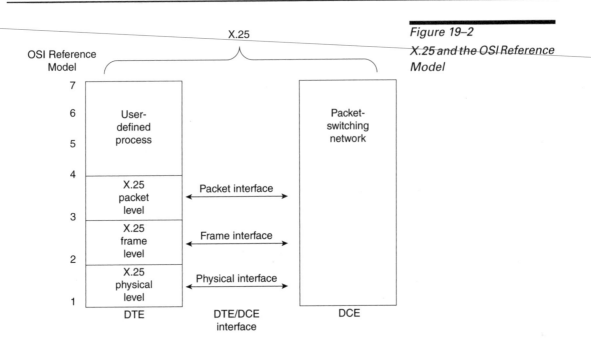

End-to-end communication between DTEs is accomplished through a bidirectional association called a *virtual circuit*. Virtual circuits permit communication between distinct network elements through any number of intermediate nodes without the dedication of portions of the physical medium that characterizes physical circuits. Virtual circuits can be either permanent or switched (temporary). Permanent virtual circuits (PVCs) are typically used for the most often used data transfers, whereas switched virtual circuits (SVCs) are used for sporadic data transfers. Layer 3 X.25 is concerned with end-to-end communication involving both PVCs and SVCs.

When a virtual circuit is established, the DTE sends a packet to the other end of the connection by sending it to the DCE using the proper virtual circuit. The DCE looks at the virtual circuit number to determine how to route the packet through the X.25 network. The Layer 3 X.25 protocol multiplexes between all the DTEs served by the DCE on the destination side of the network, and the packet is delivered to the destination DTE.

X.25 FRAME FORMAT

An X.25 frame is composed of a series of fields, as shown in Figure 19–3. Layer 3 X.25 fields make up an X.25 packet and include a header and user data. Layer 2 X.25 (LAPB) fields include frame-level control and addressing fields, the embedded Layer 3 packet, and a frame check sequence (FCS).

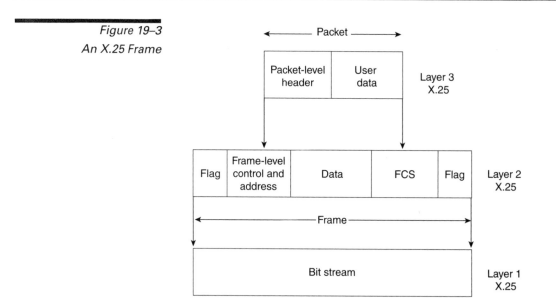

Figure 19–3
An X.25 Frame

Layer 3

The Layer 3 X.25 header is made up of a general format identifier (GFI), a logical channel identifier (LCI), and a packet type identifier (PTI). The GFI is a 4-bit field that indicates the general format of the packet header. The LCI is a 12-bit field that identifies the virtual circuit. The LCI is locally significant at the DTE/DCE interface. In other words, the PDN connects two logical channels, each with an independent LCI, on two DTE/DCE interfaces to establish a virtual circuit. The PTI field identifies 1 of X.25's 17 packet types.

Addressing fields in call setup packets provide source and destination DTE addresses. These are used to establish the virtual circuits that constitute X.25 communication. ITU-T Recommendation X.121 specifies the source and destination address formats. X.121 addresses (also referred to as *international data numbers*, or IDNs) vary in length and can be up to 14 decimal digits long. Byte four in the call setup packet specifies the source DTE and destination DTE address lengths. The first four digits of an IDN are called the *data network identification code* (DNIC). The DNIC is divided into two parts, the first three digits specifying the country and the last digit specifying the PSN itself. The remaining digits are called the national terminal number (NTN) and are used to identify the specific DTE on the PSN. The X.121 address format is shown in Figure 19–4.

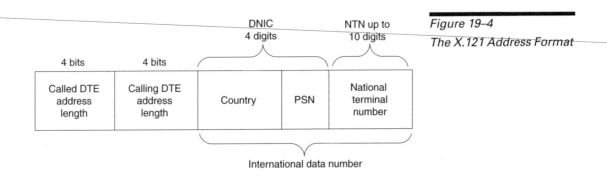

Figure 19–4
The X.121 Address Format

The addressing fields that make up the X.121 address are necessary only when an SVC is used, and then only during call setup. After the call is established, the PSN uses the LCI field of the data packet header to specify the particular virtual circuit to the remote DTE.

Layer 3 X.25 uses three virtual circuit operational procedures: call setup, data transfer, and call clearing. Execution of these procedures depends on the virtual circuit type being used. For a PVC, Layer 3 X.25 is always in data transfer mode because the circuit has been permanently established. If an SVC is used, all three procedures are used.

Packets are used to transfer data. Layer 3 X.25 segments and reassembles user messages if they are too long for the maximum packet size of the circuit. Each data packet is given a sequence number, so error and flow control can occur across the DTE/DCE interface.

Layer 2

Layer 2 X.25 is implemented by LAPB, which allows each side (the DTE and the DCE) to initiate communication with the other. During information transfer, LAPB checks that the frames arrive at the receiver in the correct sequence and free of errors.

As with similar link-layer protocols, LAPB uses three frame format types:

- Information (I) frames—These frames carry upper-layer information and some control information (necessary for full-duplex operations). Send and receive sequence numbers and the poll final (P/F) bit perform flow control and error recovery. The send sequence number refers to the number of the current frame. The receive sequence number records the number of the frame to be received next. In full-duplex conversation, both the sender and the receiver keep send and receive sequence numbers. The poll bit is used to force a final bit message in response; this is used for error detection and recovery.

- Supervisory (S) frames—These frames provide control information. They request and suspend transmission, report on status, and acknowledge the receipt of I frames. They do not have an information field.

- Unnumbered (U) frames—These frames, as the name suggests, are not sequenced. They are used for control purposes. For example, they can initiate a connection using standard or extended windowing (modulo 8 versus 128), disconnect the link, report a protocol error, or carry out similar functions.

The LAPB frame is shown in Figure 19–5.

Figure 19–5 Field length,
The LAPB Frame in bytes

The fields of an LAPB frame are as follows:

- Flag—Delimits the LAPB frame. Bit stuffing is used to ensure that the flag pattern does not occur within the body of the frame.
- Address—Indicates whether the frame carries a command or a response.
- Control—Provides further qualifications of command and response frames, and also indicates the frame format (I, S, or U), frame function (for example, receiver ready or disconnect), and the send/receive sequence number.
- Data—Carries upper-layer data. Its size and format vary, depending on the Layer 3 packet type. The maximum length of this field is set by agreement between a PSN administrator and the subscriber at subscription time.
- FCS—Ensures the integrity of the transmitted data.

Layer 1

Layer 1 X.25 uses the X.21 bis physical-layer protocol, which is roughly equivalent to EIA/TIA-232-C (formerly RS-232-C). X.21 bis was derived from ITU-T Recommendations V.24 and V.28, which identify the interchange circuits and electrical characteristics, respectively, of a DTE-to-DCE interface. X.21 bis supports point-to-point connections, speeds up to 19.2 kbps, and synchronous, full-duplex transmission over four-wire media. The maximum distance between DTE and DCE is 15 meters.

TROUBLESHOOTING X.25

This section presents troubleshooting information relating to X.25 connectivity. The "Using the **show interfaces serial** Command," section discusses the use of the **show interfaces serial** command in an X.25 environment and describes some of the key fields of the command output.

The remaining sections describe specific X.25 symptoms, the problems that are likely to cause each symptom, and the solutions to those problems.

Using the show interfaces serial Command

This section describes the information provided by the **show interfaces serial** exec command in an X.25 environment. For additional information about the output of the **show interfaces serial** exec command, refer to Chapter 15, "Troubleshooting Serial Line Problems," and the Cisco IOS *Configuration Fundamentals Command Reference*.

The show interfaces serial command provides important information useful for identifying problems in X.25 internetworks. The following fields provide especially important information:

- REJs—Number of rejects
- SABMs—Number of Set Asynchronous Balance Mode requests
- RNRs—Number of Receiver Not Ready events
- FRMRs—Number of protocol frame errors
- RESTARTs—Number of restarts
- DISCs—Number of disconnects

All but the RESTARTs count are LAPB events. Because X.25 requires a stable data link, LAPB problems commonly cause an X.25 restart event that implicitly clears all virtual connections. If unexplained X.25 restarts occur, examine the underlying LAPB connection for problems. Use the **debug lapb** exec command to display all traffic for interfaces using LAPB encapsulation. The **no** form of this command disables debugging output:

[no] debug lapb

The [no] debug lapb command displays information on the X.25 Layer 2 protocol. It is useful to users who are familiar with LAPB. You can use the **debug lapb** command to determine why X.25 interfaces or LAPB connections are going up and down. It is also useful for identifying link problems, as evidenced when the **show interfaces** command displays a large number of rejects or frame errors over the X.25 link.

CAUTION

Exercise care when using **debug** commands. Many **debug** commands are processor intensive and can cause serious network problems (such as degraded performance or loss of connectivity) if they are enabled on an already heavily loaded router. When you finish using a **debug** command, remember to disable it with its specific **no debug** command (or use the **no debug all** command to turn off all debugging).

Figure 19–6 shows the output of the X.25 version of the **show interfaces serial** exec command and indicates the important fields.

Figure 19–6

*Output from the X.25 Version of the **show interfaces serial** Command*

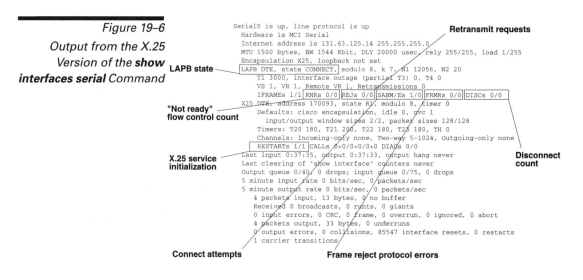

LAPB state

"Not ready" flow control count

X.25 service initialization

Connect attempts

Retransmit requests

Disconnect count

Frame reject protocol errors

X.25: No Connections over X.25 Link

Symptom: Connections over an X.25 link fail.

Table 19–1 outlines the problems that might cause this symptom and describes solutions to those problems.

Table 19–1   *X.25: No Connections over X.25 Link*

Possible Problem	Solution
Link is down	Use the **show interfaces serial** exec command to determine whether the link is down. If the link is down, refer to Chapter 15, "Troubleshooting Serial Line Problems."

Table 19–1 *X.25: No Connections over X.25 Link, Continued*

Possible Problem	Solution	
Incorrect cabling or bad router hardware	Step 1	Use the **show interfaces serial** exec command to determine the status of the interface.
	Step 2	If the interface is down, refer to Chapter 15, "Troubleshooting Serial Line Problems." If the interface is up but the line protocol is down, check the LAPB[1] state in the output of the **show interfaces serial** command.
	Step 3	If the LAPB state is not CONNECT, use the **debug lapb** privileged exec command (or attach a serial analyzer) to look for SABMs being sent, and for UA[2] packets being sent in reply to SABMs[3]. If UAs are not being sent, one of the other possible problems described in this table is the likely cause.
		Caution: Exercise care when using **debug** commands. Many **debug** commands are processor intensive and can cause serious network problems (such as degraded performance or loss of connectivity) if they are enabled on an already heavily loaded router. When you finish using a **debug** command, remember to disable it with its specific **no debug** command (or use the **no debug all** command to turn off all debugging).
		Use **debug** commands to isolate problems, not to monitor normal network operation. Because the high processor overhead of **debug** commands can disrupt router operation, you should use **debug** commands only when you are looking for specific types of traffic or problems and have narrowed your problems to a likely subset of causes.
	Step 4	If the **show interfaces serial** exec command indicates that the interface and line protocol are up but no connections can be made, there is probably a router or switch misconfiguration. Refer to the other possible problems outlined in this table.
	Step 5	Check all cabling and hardware for damage or wear. Replace cabling or hardware as required. For more information, refer to Chapter 3, "Troubleshooting Hardware and Booting Problems."

Table 19–1 *X.25: No Connections over X.25 Link, Continued*

Possible Problem	Solution
Misconfigured protocol parameters	**Step 1** Enable the **debug lapb** privileged exec command and look for SABMs being sent. If no SABMs are being sent, disable the **debug lapb** command and enable the **debug x25 events** privileged exec command.
	Step 2 Look for RESTART messages (for PVCs[4]) or CLEAR REQUESTS with nonzero cause codes (for SVCs[5]).
	To interpret X.25 cause and diagnostic codes provided in the **debug x25 events** output, refer to the *Debug Command Reference*.
	Step 3 Verify that all critical LAPB parameters (modulo, T1, N1, N2, and k) and the critical X.25 parameters (modulo, X.121 addresses, SVC ranges, PVC definitions, and default window and packet sizes) match the parameters required by the service provider.
Misconfigured **x25 map** command	**Step 1** Use the **show running-config** privileged exec command to view the router configuration. Look for **x25 map** interface configuration command entries.
	Step 2 Make sure that **x25 map** commands specify the correct address mappings.
	To retract a prior mapping, use the **no** form of the **x25 map** command with the appropriate network protocol(s) and X.121 address argument:
	no x25 map *protocol address x121-address*
	To set up the LAN protocols-to-remote host mapping, use the **x25 map** interface configuration command:
	x25 map *protocol address [protocol2 address2[...[protocol9 address9]]] x121-address [option]*

Table 19–1 *X.25: No Connections over X.25 Link, Continued*

Possible Problem	Solution
Misconfigured **x25 map** command (*Continued*)	**Syntax Description:** • *protocol*—Protocol type, entered by keyword. Supported protocols are entered by keyword. As many as nine protocol and address pairs can be specified in one command line. • *address*—Protocol address. • *x121-address*—X.121 address of the remote host. • *option*—(Optional) Additional functionality that can be specified for originated calls. **Step 3** Ensure that all router X.25 configuration options match the settings of attached switches. Reconfigure the router or switch as necessary. **Step 4** Enable the **debug x25 events** command and look for RESTART messages (for PVCs) or CLEAR REQUESTs with nonzero cause codes (for SVCs). To interpret X.25 cause and diagnostic codes provided in the **debug x25 events** output, refer to the *Debug Command Reference*.

[1] LAPB = Link Access Procedure, Balanced
[2] UA = Unnumbered Ack
[3] SAMB = Set Asynchronous Balance Mode
[4] PVC = permanent virtual circuit
[5] SVC = switched virtual circuit

X.25: Excess Serial Errors on X.25 Link

Symptom: The output of the **show interfaces serial** command shows REJs, RNRs, FRMRs, RESTARTs, or DISCs in excess of 0.5% of information frames (IFRAMEs).

— **NOTES** ——————————————————————————

If any of these fields are increasing and represent more than 0.5% of the number of IFRAMEs, there is probably a problem somewhere in the X.25 network. There should always be at least one SABM. However, if there are more than 10, the packet switch probably is not responding.

————————————————————————————————

Table 19–2 outlines the problem that might cause this symptom and describes solutions to that problem.

Table 19–2   *X.25: Excess Serial Errors on X.25 Link*

Possible Problem	Solution
Incorrect cabling or bad router hardware	**Step 1** Use the **show interfaces serial** exec command to determine the status of the interface.
	Step 2 If the interface is down, refer to Chapter 15, "Troubleshooting Serial Line Problems." If the interface is up but the line protocol is down, check the LAPB state in the output of the **show interfaces serial** command.
	Step 3 If the LAPB state is not CONNECT, use the **debug lapb** privileged exec command (or attach a serial analyzer) to look for SABMs being sent, and for UA packets being sent in reply to SABMs.
	Step 4 If the **show interfaces serial** exec command indicates that the interface and line protocol are up but no connections can be made, there is probably a router or switch misconfiguration.
	Step 5 Check all cabling and hardware for damage or wear. Replace cabling or hardware as required. For more information, refer to Chapter 3, "Troubleshooting Hardware and Booting Problems."

PART 5

Troubleshooting Bridging and Switching Environments

Troubleshooting Transparent Bridging Environments

Transparent bridges were first developed at Digital Equipment Corporation (Digital) in the early 1980s. Digital submitted its work to the Institute of Electrical and Electronic Engineers (IEEE), which incorporated the work into the IEEE 802.1 standard. Transparent bridges are very popular in Ethernet/IEEE 802.3 networks

TRANSPARENT BRIDGING TECHNOLOGY BASICS

Transparent bridges are so named because their presence and operation are transparent to network hosts. When transparent bridges are powered on, they learn the network's topology by analyzing the source address of incoming frames from all attached networks. If, for example, a bridge sees a frame arrive on line 1 from Host A, the bridge concludes that Host A can be reached through the network connected to line 1. Through this process, transparent bridges build a table such as the one in Figure 20–1.

Host address	Network number
15	1
17	1
12	2
13	2
18	1
9	1
14	3

Figure 20–1

A Transparent Bridging Table

553

The bridge uses its table as the basis for traffic forwarding. When a frame is received on one of the bridge's interfaces, the bridge looks up the frame's destination address in its internal table. If the table contains an association between the destination address and any of the bridge's ports aside from the one on which the frame was received, the frame is forwarded out the indicated port. If no association is found, the frame is flooded to all ports except the inbound port. Broadcasts and multicasts are also flooded in this way.

Transparent bridges successfully isolate intrasegment traffic, thereby reducing the traffic seen on each individual segment. This usually improves network response times as seen by the user. The extent to which traffic is reduced and response times are improved depends on the volume of intersegment traffic relative to the total traffic as well as the volume of broadcast and multicast traffic.

Bridging Loops

Without a bridge-to-bridge protocol, the transparent bridge algorithm fails when there are multiple paths of bridges and local-area networks (LANs) between any two LANs in the internetwork. Figure 20–2 illustrates such a bridging loop.

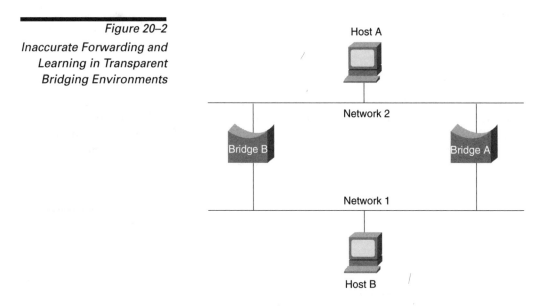

Figure 20–2

Inaccurate Forwarding and Learning in Transparent Bridging Environments

Suppose Host A sends a frame to Host B. Both bridges receive the frame and correctly conclude that Host A is on Network 2. Unfortunately, after Host B receives two copies of Host A's frame, both bridges again receive the frame on their Network 1 interfaces because all hosts receive all messages on broadcast LANs. In some cases, the bridges will then change their internal tables to indicate that Host A is on Network 1. If this is the case, when Host B replies to Host A's frame, both bridges receive and subsequently drop the replies because their tables indicate that the destination (Host A) is on the same network segment as the frame's source.

In addition to basic connectivity problems such as the one just described, the proliferation of broadcast messages in networks with loops represents a potentially serious network problem. Referring again to Figure 20–2, assume that Host A's initial frame is a broadcast. Both bridges will forward the frames endlessly, using all available network bandwidth and blocking the transmission of other packets on both segments.

A topology with loops such as that shown in Figure 20–2 can be useful as well as potentially harmful. A loop implies the existence of multiple paths through the internetwork. A network with multiple paths from source to destination can increase overall network fault tolerance through improved topological flexibility.

The Spanning-Tree Algorithm

The spanning-tree algorithm (STA) was developed by Digital, a key Ethernet vendor, to preserve the benefits of loops while eliminating their problems. Digital's algorithm was subsequently revised by the IEEE 802 committee and published in the IEEE 802.1d specification. The Digital algorithm and the IEEE 802.1d algorithm are not the same, nor are they compatible.

The STA designates a loop-free subset of the network's topology by placing those bridge ports that, if active, would create loops into a standby (blocking) condition. Blocking bridge ports can be activated in the event of primary link failure, providing a new path through the internetwork.

The STA uses a conclusion from graph theory as a basis for constructing a loop-free subset of the network's topology. Graph theory states the following: "For any connected graph consisting of nodes and edges connecting pairs of nodes, there is a spanning tree of edges that maintains the connectivity of the graph but contains no loops."

Figure 20–3 illustrates how the STA eliminates loops. The STA calls for each bridge to be assigned a unique identifier. Typically, this identifier is one of the bridge's Media Access Control (MAC) addresses plus a priority. Each port in every bridge is also assigned a unique (within that bridge) identifier (typically, its own MAC address). Finally, each bridge port is associated with a path cost. The path cost represents the cost of transmitting a frame onto a LAN through that port. In Figure 20–3, path costs are noted on the lines emanating from each bridge. Path costs are usually default values, but they can be assigned manually by network administrators.

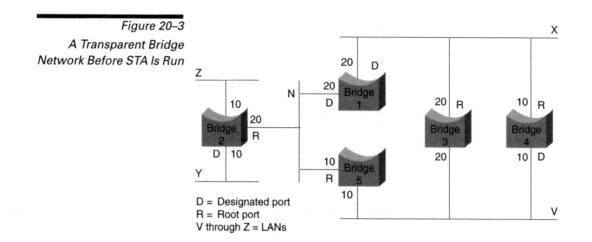

Figure 20–3

*A Transparent Bridge
Network Before STA Is Run*

The first activity in spanning-tree computation is the selection of the root bridge, which is the bridge with the lowest-value bridge identifier. In Figure 20–3, the root bridge is Bridge 1. Next, the root port on all other bridges is determined. A bridge's root port is the port through which the root bridge can be reached with the least aggregate path cost. The value of the least aggregate path cost to the root is called the *root path cost*.

Finally, designated bridges and their designated ports are determined. A designated bridge is the bridge on each LAN that provides the minimum root path cost. A LAN's designated bridge is the only bridge allowed to forward frames to and from the LAN for which it is the designated bridge. A LAN's designated port is the port that connects it to the designated bridge.

In some cases, two or more bridges can have the same root path cost. For example, in Figure 20–3, Bridges 4 and 5 can both reach Bridge 1 (the root bridge) with a path cost of 10. In this case, the bridge identifiers are used again, this time to determine the designated bridges. Bridge 4's LAN V port is selected over Bridge 5's LAN V port.

Using this process, all but one of the bridges directly connected to each LAN are eliminated, thereby removing all two-LAN loops. The STA also eliminates loops involving more than two LANs, while still preserving connectivity. Figure 20–4 shows the results of applying the STA to the network shown in Figure 20–3. Figure 20–4 shows the tree topology more clearly. Comparing this figure to the pre-spanning-tree figure shows that the STA has placed both Bridge 3's and Bridge 5's ports to LAN V in standby mode.

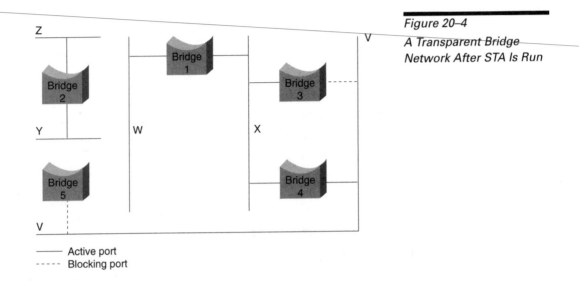

Figure 20–4

A Transparent Bridge Network After STA Is Run

—— Active port
----- Blocking port

The spanning-tree calculation occurs when the bridge is powered up and whenever a topology change is detected. The calculation requires communication between the spanning-tree bridges, which is accomplished through configuration messages (sometimes called *bridge protocol data units,* or BPDUs). Configuration messages contain information identifying the bridge that is presumed to be the root (root identifier) and the distance from the sending bridge to the root bridge (root path cost). Configuration messages also contain the bridge and port identifier of the sending bridge and the age of information contained in the configuration message.

Bridges exchange configuration messages at regular intervals (typically one to four seconds). If a bridge fails (causing a topology change), neighboring bridges soon detect the lack of configuration messages and initiate a spanning-tree recalculation.

All transparent bridge topology decisions are made locally. Configuration messages are exchanged between neighboring bridges. There is no central authority on network topology or administration.

Frame Format

Transparent bridges exchange configuration messages and topology change messages. Configuration messages are sent between bridges to establish a network topology. Topology change messages are sent after a topology change has been detected to indicate that the STA should be rerun.

The IEEE 802.1d configuration message format is shown in Figure 20–5.

Figure 20–5
The Transparent Bridge
Configuration
Message Format

The fields of the transparent bridge configuration message are as follows:

- Protocol identifier—Contains the value 0.
- Version—Contains the value 0.
- Message type—Contains the value 0.
- Flag—A one-byte field, of which only the first 2 bits are used. The topology change (TC) bit signals a topology change. The topology change acknowledgment (TCA) bit is set to acknowledge receipt of a configuration message with the TC bit set.
- Root ID—Identifies the root bridge by listing its 2-byte priority followed by its 6-byte ID.
- Root path cost—Contains the cost of the path from the bridge sending the configuration message to the root bridge.
- Bridge ID—Identifies the priority and ID of the bridge sending the message.
- Port ID—Identifies the port from which the configuration message was sent. This field allows loops created by multiply attached bridges to be detected and dealt with.
- Message age—Specifies the amount of time since the root sent the configuration message on which the current configuration message is based.
- Maximum age—Indicates when the current configuration message should be deleted.
- Hello time—Provides the time period between root bridge configuration messages.
- Forward delay—Provides the length of time bridges should wait before transitioning to a new state after a topology change. If a bridge transitions too soon, not all network links may be ready to change their state, and loops can result.

Topological change messages consist of only 4 bytes. They include a protocol identifier field, which contains the value 0; a version field, which contains the value 0; and a message type field, which contains the value 128.

TROUBLESHOOTING TRANSPARENT BRIDGING

This section presents troubleshooting information for connectivity problems in transparent bridging internetworks. It describes specific transparent bridging symptoms, the problems that are likely to cause each symptom, and the solutions to those problems.

NOTES

Problems associated with source-route bridging (SRB), translational bridging, and source-route transparent (SRT) bridging are addressed in Chapter 10, "Troubleshooting IBM."

The following sections describe the most common network problems in transparent bridged networks:

- Transparent Bridging: No Connectivity
- Transparent Bridging: Sessions Terminate Unexpectedly
- Transparent Bridging: Looping and Broadcast Storms Occur

Transparent Bridging: No Connectivity

Symptom: Client cannot connect to hosts across a transparently bridged network.

Table 20–1 outlines the problems that might cause this symptom and describes solutions to those problems.

Table 20–1 *Transparent Bridging: No Connectivity*

Possible Causes	Suggested Actions	
Hardware or media problem	**Step 1**	Use the **show bridge** exec command to see whether there is a connectivity problem. If there is, the output will not show any MAC[1] addresses in the bridging table.
	Step 2	Use the **show interfaces** exec command to determine whether the interface and line protocol are up.
	Step 3	If the interface is down, troubleshoot the hardware or the media. Refer to Chapter 3, "Troubleshooting Hardware and Booting Problems."
	Step 4	If the line protocol is down, check the physical connection between the interface and the network. Make sure that the connection is secure and that cables are not damaged.
		If the line protocol is up but input and output packet counters are not incrementing, check the media and host connectivity. Refer to the media troubleshooting chapter that covers the media type used in your network.

Table 20–1   *Transparent Bridging: No Connectivity, Continued*

Possible Causes	Suggested Actions	
Hellos not being exchanged	**Step 1**	Check whether bridges are communicating with one another. Use a network analyzer or the **debug spanning-tree** privileged exec command to see whether spanning-tree hello frames are being exchanged.
		Caution: Exercise caution when using the **debug spanning-tree** command. Because debugging output is assigned high priority in the CPU process, it can render the system unusable. For this reason, use **debug** commands only to troubleshoot specific problems or during troubleshooting sessions with Cisco technical support staff. Moreover, it is best to use **debug** commands during periods of lower network traffic and fewer users. Debugging during these periods decreases the likelihood that increased **debug** command processing overhead will affect system use.
	Step 2	If hellos are not being exchanged, check the physical connections and software configuration on bridges.
Misconfigured bridging filters	**Step 1**	Use the **show running-config** privileged exec command to determine whether bridge filters are configured.
	Step 2	Disable bridge filters on suspect interfaces and determine whether connectivity returns.
	Step 3	If connectivity does not return, the filter is not the problem. If connectivity is restored after removing filters, one or more bad filters are causing the connectivity problem.
	Step 4	If multiple filters or filters using access lists with multiple statements exist, apply each filter individually to identify the problem filter. Check the configuration for input and output LSAP[2] and TYPE filters, which can be used simultaneously to block different protocols. For example, LSAP (F0F0) can be used to block NetBIOS and **TYPE** (6004) can be used to block local-area transport.
	Step 5	Modify any filters or access lists that are blocking traffic. Continue testing filters until all filters are enabled and connections still work.

Table 20–1 *Transparent Bridging: No Connectivity, Continued*

Possible Causes	Suggested Actions
Input and output queues full	Excessive multicast or broadcast traffic can cause input and output queues to overflow, resulting in dropped packets. **Step 1** Use the **show interfaces** command to look for input and output drops. Drops suggest excessive traffic over the media. If the current number of packets on the input queue is consistently at or greater than 80% of the current size of the input queue, the size of the input queue may require tuning to accommodate the incoming packet rate. Even if the current number of packets on the input queue never seems to approach the size of the input queue, bursts of packets may still be overflowing the queue. **Step 2** Reduce broadcast and multicast traffic on attached networks by implementing bridging filters, or segment the network using more internetworking devices. **Step 3** If the connection is a serial link, increase bandwidth, apply priority queuing, increase the hold queue size, or modify the system buffer size. For more information, refer to Chapter 15, "Troubleshooting Serial Line Problems."
Host is down	**Step 1** Use the **show bridge** exec command on bridges to make sure that the bridging table includes the MAC addresses of attached end nodes. The bridging table comprises the source and destination MAC addresses of hosts and is populated when packets from a source or destination pass through the bridge. **Step 2** If any expected end nodes are missing, check the status of the nodes to verify that they are connected and properly configured. **Step 3** Reinitialize or reconfigure end nodes as necessary and reexamine the bridging table using the **show bridge** command.

[1] MAC = Media Access Control
[2] LSAP = Link Service Access Point

Transparent Bridging: Sessions Terminate Unexpectedly

Symptom: Connections in a transparently bridged environment are successfully established, but sessions sometimes terminate abruptly.

Table 20–2 outlines the problems that might cause this symptom and describes solutions to those problems.

Table 20–2 *Transparent Bridging: Sessions Terminate Unexpectedly*

Possible Causes	Suggested Actions
Excessive retransmissions	**Step 1** Use a network analyzer to look for host retransmissions.
	Step 2 If you see retransmissions on slow serial lines, increase the transmission timers on the host. For information on configuring your hosts, refer to the vendor documentation. For information on troubleshooting serial lines, refer to Chapter 15, "Troubleshooting Serial Line Problems."
	If you see retransmissions on high-speed LAN media, check for packets sent and received in order, or dropped by any intermediate device such as a bridge or switch. Troubleshoot the LAN media as appropriate. For more information, refer to the media troubleshooting chapter that covers the media type used in your network.
	Step 3 Use a network analyzer to determine whether the number of retransmissions subsides.
Excessive delay over serial link	Increase bandwidth, apply priority queuing, increase the hold queue size, or modify the system buffer size. For more information, refer to Chapter 15, "Troubleshooting Serial Line Problems."

Table 20-2 *Transparent Bridging: Sessions Terminate Unexpectedly, Continued*

Possible Causes	Suggested Actions
Multiple root bridges	If there are multiple root bridges in the network, the root of the spanning tree can periodically change, causing connections to drop.
	Step 1 Use a network analyzer to find out whether there are multiple root bridges. You can also use the **show span** exec command on each bridge to see whether a bridge is a root bridge.
	Step 2 If there are multiple root bridges in the network, eliminate the extraneous root bridges. Use the **bridge** *group* **priority** *number* command on root bridges to force the desired bridge to become the root. The lower the priority, the more likely the bridge is to become the root.

Transparent Bridging: Looping and Broadcast Storms Occur

Symptom: Packet looping and broadcast storms occur in transparent bridging environments. End stations are forced into excessive retransmission, causing sessions to time out or drop.

NOTES

Packet loops are typically caused by network design problems.

Table 20-3 outlines the problems that might cause this symptom and describes solutions to those problems.

Table 20–3   *Transparent Bridging: Looping and Broadcast Storms Occur*

Possible Causes	Suggested Actions	
No spanning tree implemented	**Step 1**	Examine a topology map of your internetwork to check for possible loops.
	Step 2	Eliminate any loops that exist or make sure that the appropriate links are in backup mode.
	Step 3	If broadcast storms and packet loops persist, use the **show interfaces** exec command to obtain input and output packet count statistics. If these counters increment at an abnormally high rate (with respect to your normal traffic loads), a loop is probably still present in the network.
	Step 4	Implement a spanning-tree algorithm to prevent loops.
Spanning-tree algorithm mismatch	**Step 1**	Use the **show span** exec command on each bridge to determine which spanning-tree algorithm is being used.
	Step 2	Make sure that all bridges are running the same spanning-tree algorithm (either DEC or IEEE)[1]. If both DEC and IEEE algorithms are being used, reconfigure bridges as appropriate so that all bridges use the same spanning-tree algorithm.
		Note: The DEC and IEEE spanning-tree algorithms are incompatible.
Multiple bridging domains incorrectly configured	**Step 1**	Use the **show span** exec command on bridges to ensure that all domain group numbers match for given bridging domains.
	Step 2	If multiple domain groups are configured for the bridge, ensure that all domain specifications are assigned correctly. Use the **bridge** *group* **domain** *domain-number* global configuration command to make any necessary changes.
	Step 3	Make sure that no loops exist between bridging domains. An interdomain bridging environment does not provide loop prevention based on spanning tree. Each domain has its own spanning tree, which is independent of the spanning tree in another domain.

[1] IEEE = Institute of Electrical and Electronic Engineers

Troubleshooting ATM Switching Environments

This chapter describes the Asynchronous Transfer Mode (ATM) technology on which the Light-Stream 2020 multiservice ATM switch (LS2020 switch) is based. ATM is a communications standard based on cell relay techniques. The next sections discuss cell relay and ATM technology. They also contrast ATM techniques with time-division multiplexing (TDM) and other packet-handling technologies.

CELL RELAY PACKET HANDLING

Cell relay is a flexible and responsive method for multiplexing all forms of digital traffic (data, voice, image, and video). Cell relay can handle rapid changes in the quantity and pattern of the traffic in the network. All traffic is placed in fixed-length packets of information (cells) and switched at high speeds. Cell relay is generally acknowledged as the best multiplexing technology for modern communication applications because it combines the strengths of TDM and conventional packet switching. Using cell relay packet-handling techniques, a mixture of bursty and delay-sensitive traffic can be processed simultaneously, while at the same time providing the services required by each traffic type.

Also, because cell relay processing is based on the use of small packets, the process technology is adaptable and cost-effective for a wide range of interface speeds.

TECHNOLOGIES COMPARED

ATM technology first appeared in the Broadband Integrated Services Digital Network (BISDN). However, ATM is now recognized as a useful technology in and of itself and is based on the specifications and standards being developed by ITU-T (International Telecommunications Union Telecommunication Standardization Sector), ANSI (American National Standards Institute), and the ATM Forum.

NOTES

ITU-T carries out the functions of the former Consultative Committee for International Telegraph and Telephone (CCITT).

Each ATM cell contains a header and the data to be transferred. Cells are switched in the network based on routing information contained in the cell headers. ATM transports all types of traffic (data, voice, image, and video) using the same cell format.

ATM contrasts with TDM in the way it allocates communications channels. In TDM, communications channels are divided into fixed periods of time called *frames*. The frames are divided into a fixed number of time slots of equal duration (see Figure 21–1). Each user is assigned certain time slots within each frame. As Figure 21–1 indicates, a user can be given more than one time slot in a frame.

Figure 21–1
User Assignments on
Communications Channel
Using TDM

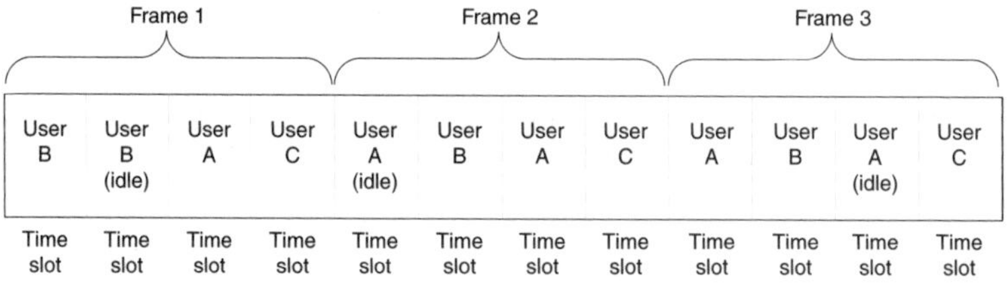

The time slots allocated for each user occur at precisely the same time in every frame. Because the time slots are synchronous, TDM is sometimes referred to as synchronous transfer mode (STM).

Users can access the communications channel only when a time slot that has been allocated to them is available. For example, User A can send messages over the communications channel only during the time slot(s) designated for User A. If no traffic is ready to send when the designated time slot occurs, that time slot is unused. If a user has a burst of traffic that exceeds the capacity of the designated time slots, additional slots cannot be used, even if they are idle. As a result, a long delay could result before the burst of traffic is transferred over the TDM network.

In ATM, access to the communications channel is more flexible. Any user needing the communications channel can use it whenever it is available. In contrast to TDM, ATM imposes no regular pattern on the way users are given access to the communications channel. ATM is also described as providing bandwidth on demand.

In other packet-handling technologies, such as High-Level Data Link Control (HDLC), any user can gain access to the communications channel, but a user who has a long message to send can prevent other users from gaining access to the channel until the entire message has been passed. However, with ATM, every message is divided into small, fixed-length cells. Thus, no single user can monopolize access to the communications channel while other users have messages to send (see Figure 21–2).

User A	User C	User D	User C	(idle)	User B	User A	User C	User C	User C	User B	User D
Cell	Cell	Cell	Cell	Cell	Cell	Cell	Cell	Cell	Cell	Cell	Cell

Figure 21–2

User Assignments on ATM Communications Channel

Fitting ATM into the OSI Model

ATM standards define protocols that operate at Layer 2 (the data link layer) of the International Organization for Standardization (ISO) seven-layer Open Systems Interconnection (OSI) reference model. Figure 21–3 shows the layered architecture of the OSI model.

Layer 6: Presentation layer	Layer 6: Presentation layer
Layer 5: Session layer	Layer 5: Session layer
Layer 4: Transport layer	Layer 4: Transport layer
Layer 3: Network layer	Layer 3: Network layer
Layer 2: Data link layer	Layer 2: Data link layer
Layer 1: Physical layer	Layer 1: Physical layer

Physical media

Figure 21–3

The OSI Reference Model

The data link layer is concerned with data transmission between two network switches. This layer is not concerned with the transmission of an entire message between a source and a destination switch—this responsibility belongs to Layer 3 (the network layer). Rather, the data link layer transports portions of messages (cells, in the case of ATM) between two points in the network. These points may be the source and the destination of the message, or they may be only intermediate hops between the source and the destination.

The data link layer may divide higher-level data into smaller units (cells, in this case), whose sizes are compatible with overall network requirements. Layer 2 data units contain a cell header, an information field, and some method of checking for transmission errors.

Placing User Data into ATM Cells

Before frames can be transported across an ATM network, they must be divided into ATM cells. The processes that divide the frames into cells occur at Layer 2. Layer 2 is divided into two parts: the ATM adaptation layer (AAL) and the ATM layer. After frames are divided into ATM cells, the cells can be transferred to Layer 1 (see Figure 21–4).

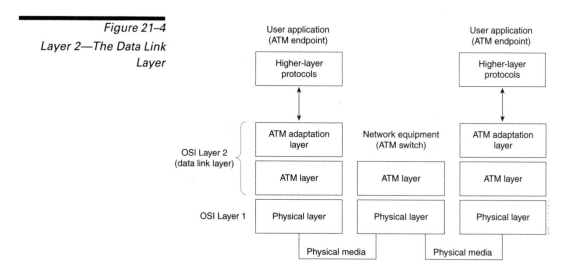

Figure 21–4
Layer 2—The Data Link
Layer

ATM LABEL SWITCHING

ATM uses label switching, a technique in which a simple label is placed in the header of each cell. The label provides information used in transporting the cell across the next hop in the network. Networks that do not use label switching usually require each packet (or cell) to contain the explicit address of the final destination. ATM uses label switching because it is simpler, thereby making faster switching possible.

Here is how label switching works:

1. A switching unit reads an incoming cell from a particular port. The incoming cell has a routing label.

2. The switching unit uses the combination of the input port on which the cell was received and the information in the label to determine where the cell should go next. It does this by referring to a routing table that correlates the incoming port and label with an outgoing port and label.

3. The switch replaces the incoming label with a new outgoing label and sends the cell through the outgoing port, which is connected to another switching device. (The new outgoing label is taken from the routing table.)

4. This process is repeated until the cell reaches its final destination in the ATM network.

For example, suppose your network includes a switching unit called Boston. A number of data paths go through the Boston switch. When those data paths are created, a routing table is set up within the Boston switch. The table in the Boston switch has one entry for each data path that goes through the switch. The entries in the table map the incoming port and label to an outgoing port and label for each data path, as shown in Table 21–1.

Table 21-1 A Sample Routing Table for a Boston Switch

Port In	Label In	Port Out	Label Out
1	L	6	Z
1	M	7	X
2	N	7	Y

When the Boston switch receives an incoming cell on port 1 with label M, it consults the routing table and finds that label M should be replaced with label X and that the cell should be passed out of the Boston switch on port 7. The cell is then transported to the switch in the network that is connected to port 7 of the Boston switch, as shown in Figure 21–5.

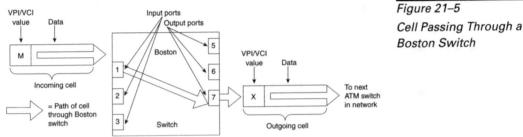

Figure 21-5

Cell Passing Through a Boston Switch

In all cases, transporting cells through the use of label switching requires a connection. Information about the connections is provided in the routing tables (sometimes called *lookup tables*) of switching and multiplexing units. ATM uses virtual channel connections and virtual paths to accomplish routing functions.

Virtual Channel Connections and Virtual Paths

A virtual channel connection (VCC) is a series of virtual channel links (VCLs) between two ATM points. A VCL is a means of bidirectional transport of ATM cells between a point where a virtual channel identifier (VCI) value is assigned and the point where the same value is either reassigned or terminated. The VCI identifies the VCL to which a cell belongs and determines where the cell should go next. Figure 21–6 shows the relationship between VCLs and VCCs in an ATM network.

Figure 21–6

The Relationship Between
VCLs and VCCs
in an ATM Network

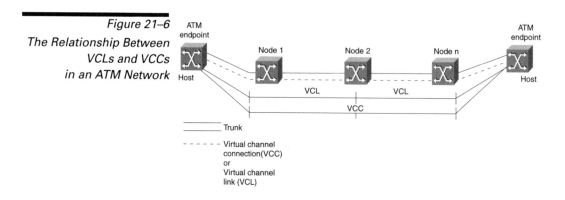

VCCs are sometimes transported within virtual paths (VPs). A VP is identified by its virtual path identifier (VPI). VPs provide a convenient way of bundling traffic directed to the same destination or traffic requiring the same Quality of Service (QoS) in the network (see Figure 21–7).

Figure 21–7

VCCs Transported
Within VPs

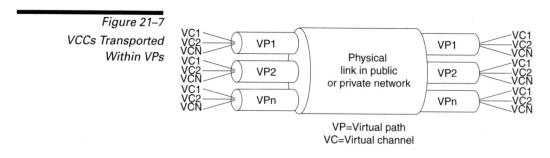

THE ATM CELL

The ATM cell is the fixed-length transmission unit defined by the ATM standard. An ATM cell contains two major types of information: the payload and the header. The payload is the information to be transferred through an ATM network. It can include data, voice, image, or video. The header is the information used to route the cell through the network and to ensure that the cell is forwarded to its destination.

Every ATM cell is 53 bytes long. The first 5 bytes contain header information, and the remaining 48 bytes contain the payload (see Figure 21–8).

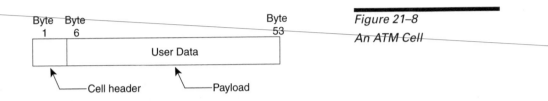

Figure 21–8

An ATM Cell

The 5-byte header (see Figure 21–9) contains several different fields (see Table 21–2). The 48 bytes following the header (the payload) contain user data.

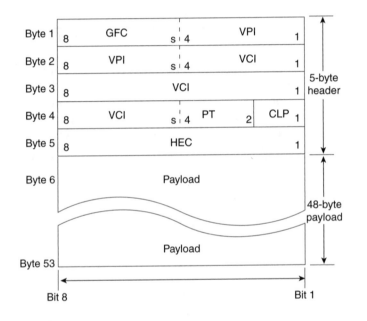

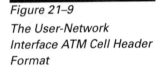

Figure 21–9

The User-Network Interface ATM Cell Header Format

Table 21–2 *Fields in an ATM Cell Header*

Header Field Name	Location in Header	Description
GFC[1]	First 4 bits of Byte 1	Controls the flow of traffic across the user network interface and thus into the ATM network.
VPI[2]	Second 4 bits of Byte 1 and the first 4 bits of Byte 2	Identifies a particular VPC[3]. A VPC is a group of virtual connections carried between two points and may involve several ATM links. VPIs provide a way to bundle traffic heading to the same destination.
VCI[4]	Second 4 bits of Byte 2, Byte 3, and the first 4 bits of Byte 4	Identifies a particular VCC[5]. A VCC is a connection between two active, communicating ATM entities. The VCI consists of a concatenation of several ATM links.

Table 21–2 *Fields in an ATM Cell Header, Continued*

PT[6]	The fifth, sixth, and seventh bits of Byte 4	Indicates the type of information in the payload field. ATM cells carry different types of information that may require different handling by the network or terminating equipment.
CLP[7]	The eighth bit of Byte 4	Indicates the cell loss priority set by the user. This bit indicates the eligibility of the cell for discard by the network under congested conditions. If the bit is set to 1, the cell may be discarded by the network if congestion occurs.
HEC[8]	Byte 5	Contains an error-correcting code calculated across the previous four bytes of the header. The HEC detects multiple-bit header errors and can be used to correct single-bit errors. The HEC provides protection against incorrect delivery of messages caused by address errors. The HEC does not provide any protection for the payload field itself.

[1] GFC = generic flow control. For a network-to-node (NNN) interface, there is no GFC field. These 4 bits are part of the VPI field.
[2] VPI = virtual path identifier
[3] VPC = virtual path connection
[4] VCI = virtual channel identifier
[5] VCC = virtual channel connection
[6] PT = payload type
[7] CLP = cell loss priority
[8] HEC = header error control

THE ATM ADAPTATION LAYER

The AAL accepts frames from higher OSI layers and adapts them to the 48-byte segments that are placed into the Payload field of ATM cells. The ATM layer accepts the 48-byte segments, adds the 5-byte header, and produces ATM cells to be transferred to the physical layer, as illustrated in Figure 21–10.

Figure 21–10
ATM Adaptation
Layer Functions

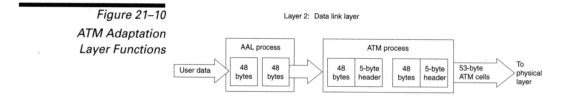

When ATM cells are transferred through a network, each cell is processed in isolation from all other cells. All processing decisions are made based on the cell header; no processing of the data in the payload field occurs.

Figure 21–11 shows some examples of AAL processing.

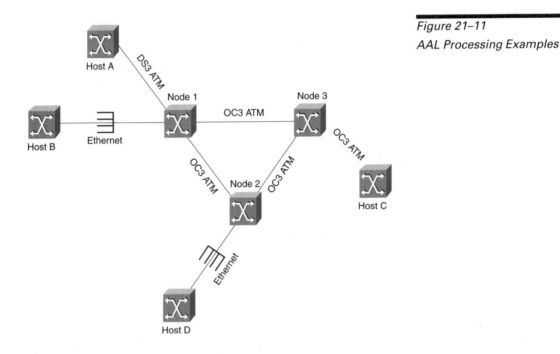

Figure 21–11
AAL Processing Examples

Hosts A and C are connected to the network through ATM interfaces, so they do all their AAL processing internally. The network does not do any processing for hosts A and C. Hosts B and D are connected to native Ethernet interfaces on Nodes 1 and 2. Therefore, Node 2 does all the AAL processing for Host D. Node 3 does no AAL processing.

Depending on the type of traffic entering the ATM network, the AAL uses one of four different AAL types to divide the traffic into small segments. These types are classified according to the timing relationship between the source and destination, the constant or variable bit rate, and the mode (connection-oriented or connectionless). The AAL types defined in the ATM standard are listed in Table 21–3.

Table 21–3 *AAL Types*

AAL Type	Examples of Traffic Type
1	Circuit emulation, constant bit rate video
2	Variable bit rate video and audio
3/4	Connection-oriented or connectionless data transfer (AAL 3/4 has cell-by-cell error checking and multiplexing)
5	Connectionless data transfer (AAL 5 has lower overhead than AAL 3/4)

The AAL is divided into two sublayers: the convergence sublayer (CS) and the segmentation and reassembly sublayer (SAR; see Figure 21–12).

Figure 21–12

Information Flow

Through AAL

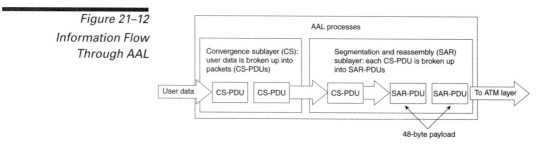

The convergence sublayer (CS) accepts higher-layer traffic for transmission across the network. Depending on the AAL type, header and/or trailer fields are added to the packet. The packet is then segmented by the SAR sublayer to form 48-byte payloads (also known collectively as SAR-PDUs).

Upon receipt of cell payloads, the AAL removes any AAL-specific information from each payload and reassembles the entire packet before passing it to a higher layer (see Figure 21–14).

Figure 21–13

The SAR Portion of the

AAL Process

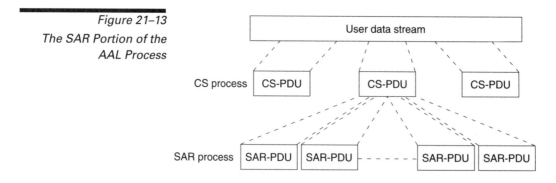

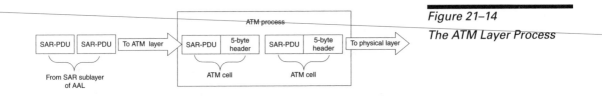

Figure 21–14
The ATM Layer Process

THE ATM LAYER

The ATM layer accepts the 48-byte SAR-PDUs from the SAR process, adds a 5-byte header to each, and produces ATM cells for transfer to the physical layer (see Figure 21–14).

PLACING CELLS ON A PHYSICAL TRANSPORT MEDIUM

After the data is packaged into 53-byte ATM cells, the cells are transferred to the physical layer, where they are placed on a physical transport medium, such as fiber optic cable or coaxial cable. The process of placing cells on the physical medium takes place in two sublayers: the physical medium dependent (PMD) sublayer and the transmission convergence (TC) sublayer.

Each PMD is specific to a particular physical medium and includes definitions of proper cabling as well as bit timing. The TC sublayer generates and receives transmission frames and performs all overhead functions associated with the transmission frame. The TC sublayer performs a convergence function by receiving a bit stream from the PMD and extracting cells.

Although PMD operation depends on the physical medium, the following TC functions remain common to all physical layers:

- Cell delineation—Extraction of cells from the bit stream received from the PMD

- Cell rate decoupling—Adaptation of the speed of the ATM layer cell stream to the rate of the physical interface

- Header error control (HEC) generation and checking—Performed when the TC sublayer checks where each received cell starts and ends by calculating the HEC for that cell

- Various operation and maintenance (OAM) functions—ATM Forum specification for cells used to monitor virtual circuits. OAM cells provide a virtual circuit-level loopback in which a router responds to the cells, demonstrating that the circuit is up and the router is operational.

TROUBLESHOOTING ATM SWITCHING ENVIRONMENTS

This section presents troubleshooting information for connectivity and performance problems in ATM switching environments. The chapter begins with general information about checking ports, performing loopback tests, and using the **ping** command on a LightStream 2020 ATM switch.

The remaining sections describe specific ATM switching symptoms, the problems that are likely to cause each symptom, and the solutions to those problems.

- ATM Switching: Trunk Does Not Come Up
- ATM Switching: Frame Relay Port Does Not Come Up
- ATM Switching: Virtual Circuit Fails to Be Created
- ATM Switching: Partial Data Delivered over Virtual Circuit

Basic Port Checks

The following steps outline the procedure for performing basic port checks. It is important to perform basic port checks to verify that a LightStream 2020 port is enabled and functioning correctly:

Step 1   Use the **show port** *port-number* **all** command to display information about a port.

Step 2   Check the Admin Status field to make sure that the port is up.

Step 3   Check for excessive line errors, packet drops, or a lack of receive data. If there is no receive data or if the error rate on the receive data is excessive, check the hardware, cabling, and other physical layer components.

           For more information on troubleshooting hardware, refer to Chapter 3, "Troubleshooting Hardware and Booting Problems."

Step 4   If the port is directly connected to a host, ensure that one side of the connection is configured as data communications equipment (DCE) and the other side is configured as data circuit-terminating equipment (DTE).

           If two ports are connected through a channel service unit (CSU), ensure that the ports on both sides of the connection are configured as DTE.

Step 5   If you are working with a low-speed line card (LSC) port, check the bit rate. Refer to the section "Checking Bit Rates" later in this chapter.

Step 6   If you are working with a medium-speed line card (MSC) port, check for mismatches in port configuration attributes such as cell payload scrambling, line type, and cable length.

Checking Bit Rates

This procedure outlines the steps for determining whether the bit rate for a port is correctly configured. This procedure applies only to low-speed line cards:

Step 1   Use the **show port** *port-number* **all** command to display information about a port.

Step 2   Check the Measured Bit Rate field to ensure that the specified bit rate is legal. If the bit rate is not legal, use the **set port** *c.p* **characteristics dce-bitrate-***bps* or **set port** *c.p* **characteristics dte-bitrate-***bps* command, as appropriate, to configure a legal bit rate for the port. The following is the syntax for the **set port** command:

characteristics {dce-bitrate *Kbits* ¦ **dte-bitrate** *bits*}

Set the DCE or DTE bit rate for the specified port, depending on the **dce-dte-type** value described below. The value of *Kbits* for the DCE bit rate may be 56, 64, 128, 192, 256, 384, 448, 512, 768, 896, 1344, 1536, 1792, 2688, 3584, 4000, or 5376. The value of *bits* for the DTE bit rate is unrestricted in the range of decimal integers 9,000—6,000,000.

Step 3   Compare the Measured Bit Rate with the Admin DCE Rcv Bit Rate field. If the value shown in the Measured Bit Rate field is significantly different from that shown in the Admin DCE Rcv Bit Rate field, a problem exists.

Step 4   If the port is DCE, it provides the clocking function. Make sure that the cabling is correct and that the configured bit rate is valid. If an attempt is made to activate the port when an invalid bit rate is configured, problems will occur. The value of *Kbits* for the DCE bit rate may be 56, 64, 128, 192, 256, 384, 448, 512, 768, 896, 1344, 1536, 1792, 2688, 3584, 4000, or 5376.

Step 5   If the port is DTE, it uses the clock supplied by the attached device (such as a CSU/DSU or a router). If the correct clock is not being detected, make sure that the correct cable type is used to connect the port to the attached device and that the attached device is providing a clock function.

Performing Loopback Tests

Loopback tests can help you pinpoint faults by looping a signal at various points in the network. The LightStream 2020 ATM switch provides the following two types of loopback tests:

- Remote loopback test—The remote loopback test loops data from an external device through the I/O module and back. This test verifies that the data sent from the remote end can cross the telephone company line or cable, pass through the I/O module, and return to the remote end.

- Internal loopback test—The internal loopback test loops data from the line card to the line chip or to the physical layer protocol processor (PLPP) I/O module to see whether the I/O module is able to receive data intact.

    If the test is successful, data is reaching the I/O module properly. However, a successful test does not verify whether the I/O module correctly encodes the data that will be sent onto the line.

NOTES

You can loop any port. However, only trunk ports and Frame Relay ports have active port management protocols that automatically verify the port's ability to process data.

Looping Trunk Ports

This procedure outlines the steps for looping data through a trunk, the physical and logical connections between two LightStream 2020 trunk ports. If you know that data is not passing on a trunk between two trunk ports, follow these steps to set up a remote loop on one of the trunk ports:

Step 1   Enter the **set port** *port-number* **loop remote** command. The port is set to testing mode and the loopback test begins automatically.

Step 2   If the remote loop succeeds, the trunk port comes up at the remote end. If the local port displays an operational status of down during the loopback test, there is probably a problem with the local port. Proceed to Step 3.

If the remote loop fails and the trunk does not come up, then a problem exists somewhere between the local access card and the remote system.

Step 3   To run an internal loop on the port, enter the **set port** *port-number* **loop internal** command. The port is set to testing mode and the loopback test begins automatically.

Step 4   If the internal loop succeeds and the local trunk comes up, the problem is the local access card.

Step 5   To stop the loopback test, enter the **set port** *port-number* **unloop** command.

Looping Edge Ports

This procedure outlines the steps for looping data through an edge port. The line from the port connects a LightStream 2020 ATM switch to a third-party external device. If you suspect that data is not passing between the LightStream 2020 edge port and the host, or that the line is unreliable, use this looping procedure to isolate the problem:

Step 1   If the port is a Frame Relay User-Network Interface (UNI) port, enter the **set port** *port-number* **framerelay netinterfacetype nni** command to set the **netinterfacetype** attribute to Network-to-Network Interface (NNI).

Internal loopback tests do not work on Frame Relay ports with the Local Management Interface (LMI) type set to UNI.

Step 2   Run a remote loop on the LightStream 2020 edge port by entering the **set port** *port-number* **loop remote** command. The port is set to testing mode and the loopback test begins automatically.

Step 3   If the internal loop fails and the line does not come up, the problem is in the line or access card.

Step 4 To stop the loopback test, enter the **set port** *port-number* **unloop** command.

Step 5 If you changed a Frame Relay UNI port to NNI for the loopback test, reset the port to the UNI network interface type by entering the **set port** *port-number* **framerelay netinterfacetype uni** command.

Using the ping Command

The **ping** command is useful for determining whether communication is possible over a particular Internet Protocol (IP) connection. The **ping** command sends an Internet Control Message Protocol (ICMP) echo packet to the specified IP address. If communication with that address is possible, the host replies with an ICMP-echo-reply message.

The following steps describe how to perform a **ping** test from a LightStream 2020 ATM switch:

Step 1 Log in as root on the LightStream 2020 switch from which you want to send ICMP echo packets.

Step 2 Enter the **ping** [*packet-size*] *hostname* command (where *packet-size* is the size of the packets to send and *hostname* is the name or IP address of the host). The packet size argument is optional. The default packet size is 64 bytes.

Step 3 To stop the **ping** and display a summary of the results, press ^C.

ATM Switching: Trunk Does Not Come Up

Symptom: An ATM trunk does not come up properly and connections cannot be made.

Table 21–4 outlines the problems that might cause this symptom and describes solutions to those problems.

Table 21–4 *ATM Switching: Trunk Does Not Come Up*

Possible Problem	Solution	
Card not configured as a trunk card	**Step 1**	Check the port at each end of the trunk with the **show port** *port-number* **statistics** command. Make sure that both ports are periodically sending cells.
	Step 2	Check the Octets Sent field to verify that it is incrementing.
	Step 3	If one port never sends trunk-up-down messages, make sure the card is correctly configured as a trunk card.
	Step 4	Make sure that a trunk is configured on port 0. The trunk can be configured as inactive if desired.
	Step 5	If both sides of the trunk show that they are sending cells, find out which side is not receiving cells. Perform a basic port check as described in the section "Basic Port Checks" earlier in this chapter.

Table 21–4   *ATM Switching: Trunk Does Not Come Up, Continued*

Possible Problem	Solution
Incorrect line type	Make sure that the line type parameter (**dsx3Linetype**) is correctly configured. Check with your carrier for the correct line type for your connection. Use the **show port** *physical* command to display the line type as well as the following information: • Port type • Operational and administrative CSU type • Operational and administrative DCE receive bit rate • Operational transmit bit rate • Measured bit rate • Link transmit utilization rate (data plus control) • Administrative expected **dte** rate and operational and administrative net interface type (**dte/dce**; these are for low-speed line cards only) • Operational and administrative protocol • LC auto enable state and debug level • Data cell capacity and available capacity • Call setup retry and backoff times • Operational maximum frame size • Modem status (DCD, DSR)
Framing type mismatch	**Step 1** Check to see whether both ends of the trunk are configured to use the same framing type (PLCP, HEC, or G.804). Enter the **show port** command. If there is a mismatch, the display for both ports will indicate "DS3 other failure." **Step 2** Change the framing type on one of the ports, as appropriate, using the **set port** *c.p* **characteristics framing type** {**plcp** | **t3-hec** | **q-804**} command.

Table 21–4 *ATM Switching: Trunk Does Not Come Up, Continued*

Possible Problem	Solution
Cell payload scrambling mismatch	If there is a cell payload scrambling mismatch, the trunk-up-down (TUD) protocol will fail because the payload of the cells is scrambled at one end and not unscrambled at the other end. The trunks will never come up. However, packets will appear to be received and transmitted without error in the port statistics display.
	Step 1 Check to see whether one end of a trunk has cell payload scrambling enabled and the other end has cell payload scrambling disabled. Use the **show port** *c.p* **physical** command to verify the status of the payload scrambling.
	Step 2 Reconfigure the trunk ports using the **set port** *c.p* **characteristics cell-scrambling {enable	disable}** command so that cell payload scrambling is either enabled or disabled on both ends of the trunk.
Telephone company network problem	Isolate the problem by running the loopback tests described in the section "Performing Loopback Tests" earlier in this chapter. If you determine that the problem is occurring in the telephone company network, contact your carrier to solve the problem.
Hardware or cabling problem	**Step 1** Check all cabling and connections to make sure there are no worn cables or loose connections.
	Step 2 Make sure that cable lengths are within specification and that the cable length port attribute is properly configured. Use the **set port** *c.p* **characteristics cable len** *length* command to change the cable length attribute.
	Step 3 Check all hardware for problems. For more information on troubleshooting hardware, refer to Chapter 3, "Troubleshooting Hardware and Booting Problems."

ATM Switching: Frame Relay Port Does Not Come Up

Symptom: A Frame Relay port on a LightStream 2020 ATM switch does not come up properly. Data cannot be transmitted out the port.

Table 21–5 outlines the problems that might cause this symptom and describes solutions to those problems.

Table 21-5 *ATM Switching: Frame Relay Port Does Not Come Up*

Possible Problem	Solution
LMI[1] type mismatch [1] LMI = Local Management Interface [2] DLCI = Data Link Connection Identifier [3] UNI = User-Network Interface	**Step 1** Use the **show port** *port-number* **all** command to see whether the Normal Packets Received counter is incrementing. A packet should be received every 10 seconds from the Frame Relay host. **Step 2** If the counter is not incrementing, check the Discarded Received Packets statistic. If the Discarded Received Packets entry is incrementing, the packets are coming in but on a different DLCI[2]. This occurs when there is an LMI type mismatch. **Step 3** Make sure that both the Frame Relay port and the Frame Relay host are configured to use the same LMI protocol (FRIF, ANSI T1 617D, or Q933A). Use the **show port** *c.p* **framerelay** command to check the LightStream 2020 port. For information on checking and configuring the LMI type on the Frame Relay host, refer to the vendor documentation. **Step 4** Change the LMI type on the port using the **set port** *c.p* **framerelay lmiconfig {none | frif | ansi_t1_617d | q933a}** command and see whether the port becomes active. If the LMI does not come up, make sure that packets are being received on the LMI DLCI. The FRIF LMI uses DLCI 1023. The ANSI and Q933A LMIs use DLCI 0.
Port protocol incorrect	**Step 1** Use the **show port** *c.p* **framerelay** command to make sure that the LightStream 2020 port is correctly configured as a UNI[3] port or an NNI[4] port. In general, ports should be configured to use the UNI protocol. The NNI protocol is designed for network device–to–network device connection and is rarely used. **Step 2** If the port protocol is incorrect, use the **set port** *port-number* **framerelay netinterfacetype {nni | uni}** command to reconfigure it.

Table 21–5 *ATM Switching: Frame Relay Port Does Not Come Up, Continued*

Possible Problem	Solution
DLCI is not activated	**Step 1** Use the **show port** *c.p* **listdlci** command to see whether the Frame Relay DLCI is deactivated. The output will show an uppercase *I* in front of the DLCI entry if it has been manually deactivated. **Step 2** If the DLCI is deactivated, use the **set port** *port-number* **dlci** *dlci-number* **activate** command to activate the DLCI.

ⁱ NNI = Network-to-Network Interface

ATM Switching: Virtual Circuit Fails to Be Created

Symptom: A Frame Relay, frame forwarding, UNI, or constant bit rate (CBR) virtual circuit fails to be created.

Table 21–6 outlines the problems that might cause this symptom and describes solutions to those problems.

Table 21–6 *ATM Switching: Virtual Circuit Fails to Be Created*

Possible Problem	Solution
Virtual circuit not configured on both endpoints	**Step 1** Use the **show port** command to verify that the virtual circuit is configured on both endpoints. The virtual circuit must be configured on both endpoints for the circuit to be created. **Step 2** If one endpoint does not have the virtual circuit configured, reconfigure the endpoint. For each virtual circuit you must specify the node, card, and port at each end and the required bandwidth. For detailed information on configuring virtual circuits, refer to the *LightStream 2020 Configuration Guide*.
Port in inactive mode	**Step 1** Check to see whether the virtual circuit is configured on an inactive port. Use the **show port** command to check the status of the port. **Step 2** If the port is in inactive or testing mode, bring the port up using the **set port** *port-number* **active** command.
cardMaxVCs attribute set too low	If the **cardMaxVCs** attribute is set too low on a line card, there might be insufficient resources available for creating a virtual circuit. Increase the value of this attribute and reboot the line card. The following switchwide attribute may be configured only in expert mode in the configuration tool: • Max VCs for this card—**setsnmp cardMaxVCs.card# nnn**

Table 21–6   *ATM Switching: Virtual Circuit Fails to Be Created, Continued*

Possible Problem	Solution
Bandwidth or other circuit attributes misconfigured	If the virtual circuit has illegal attributes set, the circuit will not be created. Review the bandwidth values in particular. Use the following commands to review the settings:

• Use the **show port c.p vci VCI#** command to display, for the specified ATM UNI port, the following attributes of the PVC[1] with the specified VCI[2]:

  ○ Source node, port, and VCI

  ○ Source insured rate, insured burst, maximum rate, and maximum burst (operational and administrative)

  ○ Destination operational node, port, VCI, insured rate, insured burst, maximum rate, and maximum burst

  ○ To-net and from-net circuit ID and circuit state, last error reported by ATM management, and cells required

  ○ Counts of cells to the switch with CLP= 0 or 1, a count of cells to the switch with CLP = 0 upon arrival at the port, but forwarded with CLP = 1, and a count of discarded cells

A virtual circuit cannot have a **MaxRate** larger than the port. Also, certain combinations of parameters are illegal. If a virtual circuit uses guaranteed bandwidth, it cannot have any excess bandwidth. The insured rate must equal the max rate.

• Use the **set port c.p vci vci# insured-rate cells/sec** command to set the insured rate to cells/sec for the specified ATM UNI PVC. The insured rate is the upper bound on the non-sharable bandwidth that the connection may use in a sustained way. The range is 0–100,000,000 bits per second. The default for ATM UNI circuits is 0 cells per second.

• Use the **set port c.p vci vci# max-rate cells/sec** command to set the maximum rate to cells/sec for the specified ATM UNI PVC. The maximum rate is the upper bound on the rate of all traffic (insured and noninsured) allowed to enter the LightStream 2020 network, congestion permitting. The default rate is the line rate for all cards except the CLC[3], for which the default rate is 218 cells/sec.

Refer to the *LightStream 2020 Configuration Guide* for more information.

Table 21–6 *ATM Switching: Virtual Circuit Fails to Be Created, Continued*

Possible Problem	Solution
Not enough bandwidth	**Step 1** If there is not enough bandwidth available to support the virtual circuit, the circuit cannot be created. Check the **cells available** attribute to determine how much bandwidth is available (that is, how much has not been allocated to other virtual circuits). Use the **show port c.p all** command to display all port attributes (**name, status, statistics, physical, frameforward, framerelay, DLCI, VCI, PVC, VPI**). This is the default, with **show port c.p** followed by no arguments.
	Step 2 Check the **cells required** attribute to see how many cells of bandwidth are needed to carry the virtual circuit over a trunk. Use the **show port c.p vci VCI#** command to display, for the specified ATM UNI port, the following attributes of the PVC with the specified VCI:
	• Source node, port, and VCI
	• Source insured rate, insured burst, maximum rate, and maximum burst (operational and administrative)
	• Destination operational node, port, VCI, insured rate, insured burst, maximum rate, and maximum burst
	• To-net and from-net circuit ID and circuit state, last error reported by ATM management, and cells required
	• Counts of cells to the switch with CLP= 0 or 1, a count of cells to the switch with CLP = 0 upon arrival at the port, but forwarded with CLP = 1, and a count of discarded cells
Trunk down	Make sure that any trunks in the path between the endpoints are active. For more information, see the section "ATM Switching: Trunk Does Not Come Up" earlier in this chapter.

[1] PVC = permanent virtual circuit
[2] VCI = virtual channel identifier
[3] CLC = cell line card

ATM Switching: Partial Data Delivered over Virtual Circuit

Symptom: Partial data is delivered over a Frame Relay, frame forwarding, UNI, or CBR virtual circuit.

Table 21–7 outlines the problems that might cause this symptom and describes solutions to those problems.

Table 21–7   *ATM Switching: Partial Data Delivered over Virtual Circuit*

Possible Problem	Solution
Network congestion	Check whether the network is congested. Check your traffic management configuration and make adjustments as appropriate. Use the **show chassis congestion** command to display the maximum and minimum intervals between permit limit updates and the minimum interval between CA updates.
	For detailed information, refer to the *LightStream 2020 System Overview*.
Target depth and maximum depth parameters misconfigured (CBR[1] only)	Use the **set port c.p cbrpvc PVC# {targetdepth | maxdepth}** bytes command to control the reassembly buffer at the point where input cells are converted back into a CBR stream. An adaptive control loop maintains data in the buffer close to the level specified by **targetdepth** bytes. Data in excess of **maxdepth** bytes is discarded.
	The default values of the **targetdepth** and **maxdepth** attributes are usually best left unchanged. If the target depth is set too high or if the maximum depth is set too far above the target, end-to-end delay for the entire circuit increases. With voice traffic, such delay can cause annoying echo. If the target depth is set too low or if the maximum depth is set too close to the target depth, random CDV[2] may cause the circuit to overflow or underflow sporadically, causing data errors and reframe events for equipment downstream. For certain applications, such as video and phone, where some discarding of overflow data is an acceptable cost of maintaining a constant bit rate, it may be preferable to set these two parameters closer together.

[1] CBR = constant bit rate
[2] CDV = cell delay variation

Troubleshooting LAN Switching Environments

This chapter presents troubleshooting information for connectivity and performance problems in LAN switching environments.

TROUBLESHOOTING LAN SWITCHING ENVIRONMENTS

The sections in this chapter describe specific LAN switching symptoms, the problems that are likely to cause each symptom, and the solutions to those problems.

The following sections cover the most common network issues in switched network environments:

- LAN Switching: No Connectivity to the Directly Connected LAN
- LAN Switching: No Connectivity to LAN or WAN
- LAN Switching: Cannot Access Out-of-Band Management
- LAN Switching: Catalyst 1600 Token Ring Port Fails to Open
- LAN Switching: Catalyst 1600 Does Not Forward Source-Routed Frames
- LAN Switching: Catalyst 1600 Does Not Forward Source-Route Broadcast Frames
- LAN Switching: Poor Performance

LAN Switching: No Connectivity to the Directly Connected LAN

Symptom: A LAN switch cannot connect to devices on its directly connected LAN.

Table 22–1 outlines the problems that might cause this symptom and describes solutions to those problems.

Table 22–1 *LAN Switching: No Connectivity to the Directly Connected LAN*

Possible Problem	Solution	
Incorrect or faulty cabling	**Step 1**	Check whether the Connected LED on the LAN switch port is on.
	Step 2	If the LED is not on, check to make sure you are using the correct cable and that it is properly and securely attached. For example, make sure that you are not using a rolled cable where a straight-through cable is required, or vice versa.
	Step 3	Make sure the cable is correctly wired. Refer to the user guide for your LAN switch for information on cable pinouts.
	Step 4	Use a TDR[1] or other cable-checking device to verify that the cable has no opens, shorts, or other problems.
	Step 5	Swap the cable with another of the same kind to see whether the cable is bad. If connections are now possible, the cable is faulty.
	Step 6	Replace or fix the faulty cable as necessary.
Power supply problem	**Step 1**	Check the Power LED. If it is not on, make sure the LAN switch is plugged in and is powered on.
	Step 2	Check for a blown fuse. If the fuse is blown, refer to the user guide for your LAN switch for information on replacing the fuse.
Hardware problem	**Step 1**	Check whether the Connected LED on the port is on.
	Step 2	If the LED is not on and the cabling is intact, there might be a bad switch port or other hardware problem.
	Step 3	Check whether the Module Enabled LED is on for FDDI and Fast Ethernet modules.
	Step 4	If the LED is not on, remove and reseat the module.
	Step 5	Check the switch hardware and replace any faulty components.

[1] TDR = Time Domain Reflectometer

LAN Switching: No Connectivity to LAN or WAN

Symptom: A LAN switch cannot connect to devices on another LAN or across a WAN. Attempts to **ping** the switch from remote devices or to **ping** from the switch to remote devices fail.

Table 22–2 outlines the problems that might cause this symptom and describes solutions to those problems.

Table 22–2   *LAN Switching: No Connectivity to LAN or WAN*

Possible Problem	Solution
IP address misconfigured or not specified	**Step 1** Check whether there is an IP address configured on the LAN switch. Check to make sure there is an IP address on the device from which you are **ping**ing the switch. **Step 2** If the IP address is misconfigured or is not specified on either device, change or add the IP address as appropriate. Refer to the user guide for your LAN switch for information on how to check and configure the IP address on the switch. Refer to the vendor documentation for the other device for information on how to check and configure the IP address on that device.
Subnet mask configuration error	**Step 1** Check to see whether you can **ping** the switch from a device in the same subnet. **Step 2** Check the subnet mask on the device from which you are **ping**ing. Check the subnet mask on the LAN switch. **Step 3** Determine whether the subnet mask on either device is incorrectly specified. If it is, reconfigure the switch or the device, as appropriate, with the correct subnet mask. Refer to the user guide for your LAN switch for information on how to check and configure the subnet mask on the switch. Refer to the vendor documentation for the other device for information on how to check and configure the subnet mask on that device.
No default gateway specified on switch or server	**Step 1** Check whether there is a default gateway configured on the LAN switch. Check to make sure that all servers and other end systems on the LAN have a default gateway specification. **Step 2** If any of these devices does not have a default gateway specified, configure a default gateway using the IP address of a router interface on the directly connected LAN. Refer to the user guide for your LAN switch for information on how to configure a default gateway on the switch. Refer to the vendor documentation for the other devices for information on how to configure a default gateway on those devices.

Table 22–2   *LAN Switching: No Connectivity to LAN or WAN, Continued*

Possible Problem	Solution	
VLAN[1] misconfiguration	Step 1	Make sure that all nodes that should communicate are attached to ports on the same VLAN. If ports are assigned to different VLANs, the attached devices cannot communicate.
	Step 2	If a port belongs to two or more VLANs, make sure that the VLANs are connected only by the overlapping port. If there are other connections, an unstable network topology can be created.
	Step 3	Eliminate any extraneous connections between the two VLANs.
Wrong port 25 connector option	If a switch port has two possible connectors, make sure that the physical connection matches the one configured in the Management Console.	

[1] VLAN = virtual LAN

LAN Switching: Cannot Access Out-of-Band Management

Symptom: The out-of-band Management Console on the LAN switch is inaccessible.

Table 22–3 outlines the problems that might cause this symptom and describes solutions to those problems.

Table 22–3   *LAN Switching: Cannot Access Out-of-Band Management*

Possible Problem	Solution	
Baud rate misconfigured	Step 1	Make sure that the LAN switch and the attached terminal or modem are configured to use the same baud rate and character format.
		The autobaud feature on most switches can match the baud rate for incoming calls, but the switch will not change from its configured rate when it is dialing out. Also, the autobaud feature will only match a rate lower than its configured rate. When it completes a call and disconnects, the switch returns to the last configured baud rate.
	Step 2	Test the connection using different baud rates. Refer to the user guide for your LAN switch for more information on how to attach a terminal or modem.
Incorrect cabling	A null-modem cable is needed when attaching a LAN switch directly to terminals or other stations. A straight-through cable is needed when attaching the switch to a modem. Figure 22-1 illustrates the pin connections to use when you connect the Catalyst 1600 to a terminal using a null-modem EIA/TIA-232 cable, or to a modem using a straight-through EIA/TIA-232 cable.	

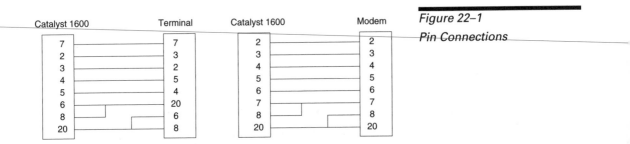

Figure 22–1

Pin Connections

LAN Switching: Catalyst 1600 Token Ring Port Fails to Open

Symptom: Connections to a Token Ring fail because a Catalyst 1600 Token Ring switch port fails to open correctly.

Table 22–4 outlines the problems that might cause this symptom and describes solutions to those problems.

Table 22–4   *LAN Switching: Catalyst 1600 Token Ring Port Fails to Open*

Possible Problem	Solution
Incorrect connector	Check to make sure that the Token Ring switch port is connected to the correct connector on the attached device. For detailed information on connector types, refer to the *Catalyst 1600 Token Ring Switch User Guide*.
Interface mode incorrect	**Step 1** Make sure that the interface mode of the Token Ring switch port is appropriate for the attached device. The options are node mode and concentrator mode. **Step 2** Check the port interface mode by reading the port LEDs or LCD panel. **Step 3** You can change the port interface mode using the TrueView Catalyst 1600 Manager or by connecting a terminal to the serial interface and using the **set port ifmode** command. **Command: set port ifmode** *port mode* **Description:** Sets the port interface to node or concentrator mode. **Parameters: port** *Port number* **mode** *Port interface* (node or concentrator) For detailed information on interface modes, refer to the *Catalyst 1600 Token Ring Switch User Guide*.

Table 22–4   *LAN Switching: Catalyst 1600 Token Ring Port Fails to Open, Continued*

Possible Problem	Solution
Port ring speed incorrect	**Step 1** Make sure the port ring speed is correct for the ring connected to the port. The options are 4 Mbps and 16 Mbps. **Step 2** Check the ring speed by reading the port LEDs or LCD panel. **Step 3** You can change the ring speed using the TrueView Catalyst 1600 Manager or by connecting a terminal to the serial interface and using the **set port ifspeed** command. **Command: set port ifspeed** *port speed* **Description:** Sets the ring speed for the port to 4 or 16 Mbps. **Parameters: port** *Port number* **speed** *Ring speed* (4 or 16) For more information on setting the port ring speed, refer to the *Catalyst 1600 Token Ring Switch User Guide*.

LAN Switching: Catalyst 1600 Does Not Forward Source-Routed Frames

Symptom: A Catalyst 1600 Token Ring switch fails to forward source-routed frames correctly.

Table 22–5 outlines the problems that might cause this symptom and describes solutions to those problems.

Table 22–5   *LAN Switching: Catalyst 1600 Does Not Forward Source-Routed Frames*

Possible Problem	Solution
Source routing not enabled	**Step 1** Check whether source routing is enabled on the Catalyst 1600 and on the appropriate port. Check the status of source routing by reading the LCD panel. **Step 2** You can enable source routing on the Catalyst 1600 and on each port using the TrueView Catalyst 1600 Manager or by connecting a terminal to the serial interface and using the **enable port srb** command. **Command: enable port srb** *port* **Description:** Enables the forwarding of source-routed frames by the port. **Parameters: port** *Port number*

Table 22-5 *LAN Switching: Catalyst 1600 Does Not Forward Source-Routed Frames, Continued*

Possible Problem	Solution
Bridge number misconfigured	**Step 1** Check whether the bridge number of the Catalyst 1600 is a hexadecimal number in the range 0 through F and that there are no other devices with the same bridge number connecting the same rings. Check the bridge number by reading the LCD panel.

	Step 2 You can view the bridge number by using the TrueView Catalyst 1600 Manager or by connecting a terminal to the serial interface and using the **show bridge characteristics** command.
	
	Example:
	<pre>show bridge characteristics
	Bridge Name: switch B
	Bridge Number: 2
	IP Address: 194.32.220.119
	IP Subnet Mask: 255.255.255.0
	Spanning Tree Root Priority: 40000</pre>

Ring number misconfigured	**Step 1** Check the ring number of each Token Ring switch port and make sure each port has a different ring number. Check the ring number by reading the LCD panel.
	Step 2 If two Catalyst 1600 devices are connected by their Token Ring switch ports, make sure the ring number is identical for both Token Ring ports.
	Step 3 You can set the ring number using the TrueView Catalyst 1600 Manager, or by connecting a terminal to the serial interface and using the **set port segment** command. **Command: set port segment** *port segment* **Description:** Sets the ring number. **Parameters: port** *Port number segment Ring number* (001-FFF hexadecimal)

LAN Switching: Catalyst 1600 Does Not Forward Source-Route Broadcast Frames

Symptom: A Catalyst 1600 Token Ring switch fails to forward source-route broadcast frames correctly.

Table 22–6 outlines the problems that might cause this symptom and describes solutions to those problems.

Table 22–6   *LAN Switching: Catalyst 1600 Does Not Forward Source-Route Broadcast Frames*

Possible Problem	Solution
VLAN misconfigured	**Step 1** Make sure that VLANs are configured correctly and that each Catalyst 1600 has an up-to-date record of VLANs. To check the VLAN configuration, use the TrueView Catalyst 1600 Manager.
	Step 2 Before creating new VLANs, make sure you delete the existing VLANs that are causing problems with forwarding source-route broadcast frames.
	For detailed information on configuring VLANs, refer to the *Catalyst 1600 Token Ring Switch User Guide*.
Station type incorrect	**Step 1** Check to make sure that the type of station connected to each Token Ring switch port is defined correctly. The options are Workstations and Anything.
	On Novell IPX and NetBIOS networks, the Catalyst 1600 uses the station type to block broadcast frames originating on workstation-only rings from being forwarded on other workstation-only rings.
	Step 2 To configure the station type for each Token Ring switch port, use the TrueView Catalyst 1600 Manager.

LAN Switching: Poor Performance

Symptom: Connections across a LAN switch are slow or unreliable.

Table 22–7 outlines the problems that might cause this symptom and describes solutions to those problems.

Table 22–7 *LAN Switching: Poor Performance*

Possible Problem	Solution
Full- or half-duplex settings incorrect	**Step 1** Check the switch port statistics. The following steps can be performed with the use of the Cisco TrueView Catalyst 1600 Manager application. The TrueView Catalyst 1600 Manager enables you to • Find the status of a port • Set the ring speed of a Token Ring port • Select the port interface mode to be node or concentrator • Select the port type to be classic or full duplex • Assign a locally administered address to a Token Ring port or reset the hard-wired address • Configure source routing and spanning-tree parameters for a Token Ring port • View source-routing counters for a Token Ring port • Set the type of station that is connected to the Token Ring port, to enable the Catalyst 1600 to block IPX and NetBIOS all-routes broadcast and single-route broadcast frames originating on workstation-only rings and destined for other workstation-only rings **Step 2** If there are FCS[1] and alignment errors on the port, check whether the port is configured for full duplex. **Step 3** If the port is full duplex, check whether the other device is a repeater or half-duplex device. If it is half duplex, configure the switch port for half duplex. **Step 4** If there are late collisions, check whether the port is configured for half duplex. **Step 5** If the port is half duplex, check whether the other device is full duplex. If it is, configure the switch port for full duplex.
Cabling distance exceeded	**Step 1** Check the switch port statistics. If you see excessive FCS, late-collision, or alignment errors, the maximum cabling distance might be exceeded. **Step 2** Check the cable distance using a cable tester or TDR[2]. Verify that the VLAN segment lengths attached to the switch meet Ethernet/IEEE 802.3 specifications. **Step 3** If the distance is out of specification, reduce the length of the cable run.

Table 22–7   *LAN Switching: Poor Performance, Continued*

Possible Problem	Solution
Bad adapter in attached device	Check the switch port statistics. If excessive errors are found, run the adapter card diagnostic utility to determine the problem. Refer to the user guide for your LAN switch for more information. The following example of the **show port counters** command displays the type of information that can be collected for each port on the switch: ``` show port counters 2 Bytes Transmitted: 19,339,380 Bytes Received: 455,390 Non-broadcast Frames Transmitted: 1,029 Non-broadcast Frames Received: 2,747 All Routes Explorer Frames Received: 0 All Routes Explorer Frames Transmitted: 4,289 Spanning Tree Explorer Frames Received: 259 Spanning Tree Explorer Frames Transmitted:28,065 Receiving Segment Mismatch Discards: 0 Duplicate Segment Mismatch Discards: 0 ARE Hop Count Exceeded Discards: 0 ```

[1] FCS = frame check sequence
[2] TDR = Time Domain Reflectometer

PART 6

Troubleshooting Other Internetwork Problems

Troubleshooting CiscoWorks Problems

This chapter presents troubleshooting information for problems commonly encountered when using CiscoWorks. This chapter first provides basic procedures for checking your CiscoWorks installation. It then describes specific CiscoWorks symptoms, the problems that are likely to cause each symptom, and the solutions to those problems.

Symptoms, problems, and solutions are not provided for every CiscoWorks application. For information about applications not covered in this chapter, refer to the *CiscoWorks Administration and Installation Guide* and the *CiscoWorks User Guide*.

TESTING BASIC CONNECTIVITY AND SETUP

The following steps describe how to test the basic connectivity and setup of a CiscoWorks installation. Perform these steps first when presented with a CiscoWorks-related problem:

Step 1 Begin by testing IP connectivity. From the UNIX workstation, try to **ping** the router's IP address. If the **ping** is unsuccessful, make sure that IP routing is properly enabled and is functioning normally. For detailed information about troubleshooting IP routing problems, see Chapter 7, "Troubleshooting TCP/IP."

Step 2 Try to **ping** the device by its name as well as by its IP address. If you can **ping** the device by its IP address but not by its resolved name, there is a name resolution problem. Consult your system administrator for assistance in resolving the problem.

Step 3 Open a Telnet session to the router. Enter the **show running-config** privileged exec command to view the router configuration. Check whether there is an **snmp-server community** *string* **rw** command entry in the configuration.

If the command is not present, configure the router with the **snmp-server community** command. If the command is present, make sure that the **rw** (read-write) keyword, not the **ro** (read only) keyword, is specified.

For complete information on the use of the **snmp-server community** command, refer to the Cisco IOS *Configuration Fundamentals Configuration Guide* and *Configuration Fundamentals Command Reference*.

Step 4   On the management station, check for the proper **community** *string* command on the base platform (CiscoWorks obtains **community** *string* information from the base platform). On Netview/6000 and HP OpenView, choose Options, SNMP Configuration, and check community for the device. On SunNetManager, choose Properties and check community for the device. The community name configured on the router (with the **snmp-server community** command) and that configured on the management station should be the same.

Step 5   Try a Management Information Base (MIB) browse of the device from the base platform. On Netview/6000, choose Tools, MIB-Browser, SNMP. On HP OpenView, choose Monitor, MIB Values, Browse MIB: SNMP. On SunNetManager, choose the device and then select a Quick Dump of SNMP.

If MIB values are not returned for the device, check the documentation for your base platform and re-check the **snmp-server** information in the router.

Testing Basic TFTP Connectivity

The following steps describes the procedure to follow to test the connectivity of your Trivial File Transfer Protocol (TFTP) server:

Step 1   Check whether the inetd daemon is running on the UNIX workstation. On AIX, HPUX, or Solaris, enter **ps -ef | grep inetd**. On Sun, enter **ps -aux | grep inetd**. If the inetd daemon is not running, start it. For information on starting the inetd daemon, refer to your operating system manual.

Step 2   Use the **netstat -a | grep tftp** command to see whether the TFTP daemon is running on the UNIX workstation. If the TFTP daemon is not running, start it. For instructions on starting the TFTP daemon, refer to the *CiscoWorks Installation and Reference Guide*.

Step 3   Test TFTP functionality from the router to the UNIX workstation. On the UNIX workstation, enter the command **cd /tftpboot** and then the command **ls -l** *filename* to check for the presence of a scratch configuration file for the router (the default is *router_name*-**confg**).

If there is not a configuration file for the router, create one by entering the command **touch** *filename* and then the command **chmod 777** *filename*.

Step 4   Open a Telnet session to the router, enter privileged mode (to enter privileged exec mode, use the **enable** exec command), and enter the **copy running-config tftp** command. Specify the TFTP server and the file you just created (*filename*) to overwrite the file on the TFTP server. If the file transfer fails, check connectivity between the router and the host and refer to your operating system manual to troubleshoot TFTP server problems.

CiscoWorks Environment Variables

Frequently, misconfigured environment variables cause problems in the operation of CiscoWorks. The following sections describe the default values, descriptions, and locations of CiscoWorks environment variables for each platform.

Default Variable Values

The following sections provide the default values assigned to the CiscoWorks environment variables for each platform.

SunOS and HP-UX Installations

On SunOS and HP-UX installations, the values assigned to the CiscoWorks environment variables should be similar to the following, provided that you chose the defaults during installation of the software:

- NMSROOT—*/usr/nms*
- SYBASE—*/usr/nms/sybase*
- PATH—*$NMSROOT/bin, /$NMSROOT/etc, $SYBASE/bin*
- DSQUERY—*CW_SYBASE*

If you did not load your software in the default directories, your values should point to the locations you chose.

Use the **printenv** UNIX command to see the current environment variable settings.

For descriptions of these variables, see the section "Descriptions of Environment Variables" later in this chapter.

AIX Installations

On AIX installations, the values assigned to the CiscoWorks environment variables should be similar to the following, provided that you chose the defaults during installation of the software:

- NMSROOT—*/usr/nms*
- SYBASE—*/usr/nms/sybase10*
- PATH—*/usr/OV/bin, $NMSROOT/bin, /$NMSROOT/etc, $SYBASE/bin*
- DSQUERY—*CW_SYBASE*

If you did not load your software in the default directories, your values should point to the locations you chose.

Use the **printenv** UNIX command to see the current environment variable settings.

For descriptions of these variables, see the section "Descriptions of Environment Variables" later in this chapter.

Solaris Installations

On Solaris installations, the values assigned to the CiscoWorks environment variables should be similar to the following, provided that you chose the defaults during installation of the software:

- NMSROOT—/opt/CSCOcw
- SYBASE—/opt/CSCOcw/sybase
- PATH—$NMSROOT/bin, /$NMSROOT/etc, $SYBASE/bin
- DSQUERY—CW_SYBASE

If you did not load your software in the default directories, your values should point to the locations you chose.

Use the **printenv** UNIX command to see the current environment variable settings.

For descriptions of these variables, see the section "Descriptions of Environment Variables" later in this chapter.

Descriptions of Environment Variables

The following are descriptions of the CiscoWorks environment variables:

- NMSROOT—Default directory for CiscoWorks installation. If the software was installed in a different directory, substitute the appropriate directory path to ensure the correct definition of the NMSROOT environment variable.

- SYBASE—Default directory for Sybase installation. If the software was installed in a different directory, substitute the appropriate directory path to ensure the correct definition of the SYBASE environment variable. The SYBASE variable refers to the NMSROOT variable and the Sybase directory following it.

- PATH—Directory path for your NMS software and various CiscoWorks directories (including $NMSROOT/bin, $NMSROOT/etc, and $SYBASE/bin). The path should be specified to include SunNetManager, HP OpenView, or Netview; CiscoWorks; and Sybase.

- DSQUERY—Sybase server name. The default is CW_SYBASE.

Environment Variable Locations

The location of environment variable definitions differs depending on the UNIX shell you are using. This will typically be the Korn shell (ksh), the C shell (csh), or the Bourne shell (sh). The default UNIX shell for a user ID is set up in the /etc/passwd file. Use the **set** command to find out which shell you are using.

The following section provides information on files that are reviewed by the C shell and the Korn shell during login:

- C shell—At login, the system reads the .cshrc file in the user's home directory. CiscoWorks creates an install.cshrc file, which is found in $NMSROOT/etc under HPUX, Solaris, and SunOS, and in $NMSROOT/install under AIX. The variables in this file can be cut and pasted into the *.cshrc* file in the user's home directory. An example of variable definition in the *.cshrc* file is

```
setenv NMSROOT /usr/nms
```

- Korn shell—At login, the system reads the *.kshrc* file in the user's home directory. Cisco-Works creates an *install.kshrc* file, which is found in *$NMSROOT/etc* under HPUX, Solaris, and SunOS, and in *$NMSROOT/install* under AIX. The variables in this file can be cut and pasted into the *.kshrc* file in the user's home directory. An example of variable definition in the *.kshrc* file is

```
export NMSROOT=/usr/nms
```

TROUBLESHOOTING CISCOWORKS

This section discusses troubleshooting procedures for connectivity problems related to CiscoWorks. It describes specific CiscoWorks symptoms, the problems that are likely to cause each symptom, and the solutions to those problems.

CiscoWorks: No Devices in Application Window

Symptom: No devices appear in the windows of CiscoWorks applications (such as Configuration Management or Configuration Snap-In Manager).

Table 23–1 outlines the problem that might cause this symptom and describes the solution to that problem.

Table 23–1 *CiscoWorks: No Devices in Application Window*

Possible Problem	Solution
Sync with Sybase has not been run	You must run Sync with Sybase to populate the CiscoWorks application windows. With Netview/6000 and HP OpenView, choose a Sync entry under Misc. On SunNetManager, choose a Sync entry under Tools. For more information on running Sync with Sybase, refer to the *CiscoWorks User Guide*.

CiscoWorks: Sync with Sybase Fails

Symptom: Attempts to run Sync with Sybase in CiscoWorks fail.

Table 23–2 outlines the problems that might cause this symptom and describes solutions to those problems.

Table 23–2 *CiscoWorks: Sync with Sybase Fails*

Possible Problem	Solution
Basic connectivity or setup problem	Follow the steps outlined in the section "Testing Basic Connectivity and Setup" earlier in this chapter.
Community string, name resolution, or timeout problem	Run **nmadd** from the command line to determine whether the problem is related to community string, name resolution, or timing out. The **nmadd** syntax is **nmadd** [**-n** *device*] [**-r** *commstring*] [**-w** *rw_commstring*] [**-t** *timeout*] Use a process of elimination to isolate the specific problem.

CiscoWorks: Sybase Login Fails

Symptom: When attempting to use CiscoWorks applications that involve the use of Sybase, you receive a "Sybase login failed" error message.

Table 23–3 outlines the problems that might cause this symptom and describes solutions to those problems.

Table 23–3 *CiscoWorks: Sybase Login Fails*

Possible Problem	Solution
Misconfigured environment	**Step 1** Check the environment settings for your CiscoWorks installation using the **printenv** command. Make sure the settings shown point to the directories where you installed CiscoWorks. **Step 2** If any of these variables point at the wrong location, Sybase logins fail. Set any incorrect variables to the proper value and attempt to use the CiscoWorks application again. For more information about the default values, descriptions, or locations of the CiscoWorks environment variables, see the section "CiscoWorks Environment Variables" earlier in this chapter.
Dataserver is not running	Check whether the dataserver is running. On HP-UX, Solaris, and AIX use the command **ps -ef	grep** *dataserver.* On SunOS, use the command **ps -auxww	grep** *dataserver.* On any of these systems, executing *$NMSROOT/etc/isalive* also returns status.

Table 23–3 *CiscoWorks: Sybase Login Fails, Continued*

Possible Problem	Solution

nscpwd file is corrupted	**Step 1** Check to see whether the *nscpwd* file is corrupted. Enter the command **ls -al $NMSROOT/etc/ncspwd** and check the output for the following:
	
	`4 (date) (year) (time) ncspwd`
	
	Step 2 If the output begins with anything other than 4, run the following command, answering the prompts as shown:
	
	`$NMSROOT/bin/nmsanms`
	`Name: `**`sa`**
	`Password: `**`sybasesa`**
	`Key: `**`beta`**

$SYBASE interfaces file has been modified	**Step 1** Check to make sure that the *$SYBASE* **interfaces** file is present in the *$SYBASE* directory and that *$SYBASE* and the path to *$SYBASE* are defined in the environment variables. If you are using Solaris and the IP address of the management station has changed, you must recalculate the decimal-to-hexadecimal IP address specification. See the section "The *$SYBASE* Interfaces File Format" later in this chapter. **Step 2** Make sure the DSQUERY environment variable correctly specifies the Sybase server name indicated in the *$SYBASE* interfaces file (the default is *CW_SYBASE*). For more information, see the section "CiscoWorks Environment Variables" earlier in this chapter. To find out the proper format for the *$SYBASE* interfaces file on your platform, see the section "The *$SYBASE* Interfaces File Format" later in this chapter.

The $SYBASE Interfaces File Format

If the *$SYBASE* interfaces file has been modified, Sybase logins can fail. The *$SYBASE* **interfaces** file should always be found in the *$SYBASE* directory. This section describes the format for the **interfaces** file for different platforms.

On AIX, HP-UX, and SunOS, the *$SYBASE* interfaces file should resemble the following:

```
## CW_BACKUP_SERVER on oak
##    Services:
##        query    tcp  (3001)
##        master   tcp  (3001)

CW_BACKUP_SERVER 5 5
    query tcp ether oak 3001
    master tcp ether oak 3001

## CW_SYBASE on oak
##    Services:
##        query    tcp  (10000)
##        master   tcp  (10000)

CW_SYBASE 0 0
    query tcp ether oak 10000
    master tcp ether oak 10000
```

On the AIX, HP-UX, and SunOS platforms, the entries in the *$SYBASE* interfaces file take the following generic format:

```
CW_BACKUP_SERVER # #
    query tcp interface machine port
    master tcp interface machine port

CW_SYBASE # #
    query tcp interface machine port
    master tcp interface machine port
```

On Solaris, the *$SYBASE* interfaces file should resemble the following:

```
## CW_BACKUP_SERVER on Bamboo
##    Services:
##        query    tcp  (3000)
##        master   tcp  (3000)

CW_BACKUP_SERVER 5 5
    query tli tcp /dev/tcp \x00020bb8ab44766a0000000000000000
    master tli tcp /dev/tcp \x00020bb8ab44766a0000000000000000

## CW_SYBASE on Bamboo
##    Services:
##        query    tcp  (2002)
##        master   tcp  (2002)

CW_SYBASE 0 0
    query tli tcp /dev/tcp \x000207d2ab44766a0000000000000000
    master tli tcp /dev/tcp \x000207d2ab44766a0000000000000000
```

On the Solaris platform, the entries in the *$SYBASE* interfaces file take the following generic format, where *P* is the 5-digit port address converted to hex and the *I* is the IP address converted to hex on an octet-by-octet basis:

```
CW_BACKUP_SERVER 5 5
        query tli tcp /dev/tcp \x00020PPPPPIIIIIIII0000000000000000
        master tli tcp /dev/tcp \x00020PPPPPIIIIIIII0000000000000000

CW_SYBASE 0 0
        query tli tcp /dev/tcp \x00020PPPPPIIIIIIII0000000000000000
        master tli tcp /dev/tcp \x00020PPPPPIIIIIIII0000000000000000
```

If you are using Solaris and the IP address of the management station has changed, you must recalculate the decimal-to-hexadecimal IP address specification, as shown in the following example:

```
CW_SYBASE 0 0
        query tli tcp /dev/tcp \x000207d0ab44766a0000000000000000
        master tli tcp /dev/tcp \x000207d0ab44766a0000000000000000
##                             7d0 = 2000 port number
##                                  ab = 171
##                                    44 = 68
##                                      76 = 118
##                                        6a = 106
##                     IP address = 171.68.118.106
```

CiscoWorks: Locked Out of Security Manager

Symptom: When you try to use the Administer, a CW-Security menu selection, regardless of the name and password you enter on the User Identification screen, you receive a "Sybase login failed" error. When you try entering the sa user ID and password, the message returned is "Sorry, the username [sa] is reserved to the CiscoWorks system."

Table 23–4 outlines the problem that might cause this symptom and describes solutions to that problem.

Table 23–4 *CiscoWorks: Locked Out of Security Manager*

Possible Problem	Solution

Security Manager on without an enabled group	If Security Manager is on without having a group enabled to use it, all users can be locked out of Security Manager.
	
	Step 1 Temporarily disable Security Manager to allow security administration. Enter the following commands from the command line:
	
	`$SYBASE/bin/isql -Usa -Psybasesa`
	
	`1> use nms`
	`2> go`
	`1> setuser "SAnms"`
	`2> go`
	`1> update applications set authority_ck = 0`
	`2> where app_name = "nmadmin"`
	`3> go`
	`1> quit`
	
	Step 2 All security is now removed from the CiscoWorks application. You must reconfigure Security Manager with a group enabled to use it.
	
	For information on configuring Security Manager, refer to the *CiscoWorks User Guide*.

Configuration Management: Device-to-Database or Database-to-Device Does Not Run

Symptom: The device-to-database or the database-to-device operation in the Configuration Management application does not work.

Table 23–5 outlines the problems that might cause this symptom and describes solutions to those problems.

Table 23–5 *Configuration Management: Device-to-Database or Database-to-Device Does Not Run*

Possible Problem	Solution
Basic connectivity or setup problem	Perform the steps outlined in the section "Testing Basic Connectivity and Setup" earlier in this chapter.
TFTP problem	Perform the steps outlined in the section "Testing Basic TFTP Connectivity" earlier in this chapter.

Configuration Snap-In Manager: Cannot Modify DoItNow

Symptom: The DoItNow operation in the Configuration Snap-In Manager application does not work.

Table 23–6 outlines the problems that might cause this symptom and describes solutions to those problems.

Table 23–6 *Configuration Snap-In Manager: Cannot Modify DoItNow*

Possible Problem	Solution
Basic connectivity or setup problem	Perform the steps outlined in the section "Testing Basic Connectivity and Setup" earlier in this chapter.
TFTP problem	Perform the steps outlined in the section "Testing Basic TFTP Connectivity" earlier in this chapter.

CiscoView: Timeout Error Messages

Symptom: When attempting to use the CiscoView application, you receive timeout messages and cannot view a device.

Table 23–7 outlines the problems that might cause this symptom and describes solutions to those problems.

Table 23–7 *CiscoView: Timeout Error Messages*

Possible Problem	Solution
Basic connectivity or setup problem	Perform the steps outlined in the section "Testing Basic Connectivity and Setup" earlier in this chapter.
Polling interval too low	Try increasing the polling interval. To increase the polling interval, select Options, then Properties, and increase the value in the Timeout (secs): field. If the polling interval is too low, CiscoView will time out.
Community string, name resolution, or timeout problem	If CiscoView still fails, try running **nmcview** from the command line to determine whether the problem is related to community string, name resolution, or timing out. The **nmcview** command syntax is **nmcview** [-h *host*] [-c | -rd *read community*] [-C | -rw *write community*] [-t *timeout*] [-r *retries*] [-P *poll frequency*] Use a process of elimination to isolate the specific problem.

Troubleshooting Security Implementations

This chapter outlines troubleshooting information relating to security implementations. The first part of the chapter describes problems commonly encountered in Terminal Access Controller Access Control System (TACACS+) and XTACACS security implementations. The section "Recovering a Lost Password" describes password-recovery procedures for common Cisco router platforms.

TROUBLESHOOTING TACACS+ AND XTACACS

This section presents troubleshooting information for TACACS+ and XTACACS security implementations. It describes specific TACACS+ and XTACACS security implementation issues, the problems that are likely to cause each symptom, and the solutions to those problems.

The sections on troubleshooting TACACS+ include the following:

- TACACS+: Errors Unarchiving Source File
- TACACS+: Cannot Compile Daemon
- TACACS+: Daemon Not Up and Running
- TACACS+: Daemon Does Not Run
- TACACS+: Users Cannot Log In Using TACACS+

The sections on troubleshooting XTACACS include the following:

- XTACACS: Errors Decompressing File
- XTACACS: Cannot Compile Daemon
- XTACACS: Daemon Not Up and Running
- XTACACS: Slow Response from Daemon
- XTACACS: Users Cannot Connect Using XTACACS

If you want detailed information about configuring and using TACACS+ and XTACACS, refer to the Cisco IOS *Configuration Fundamentals Configuration Guide* and *Configuration Fundamentals Command Reference*. In addition, for TACACS+, download the TACACS+ User Guide from the TACACS+ Software Images page on Cisco Connection Online (CCO). For more information about XTACACS, refer to the README file that you downloaded with your XTACACS source file.

TACACS+: Errors Unarchiving Source File

Symptom: Errors are generated when the TACACS+ archive file (*tac_plus.2.1.tar*) is being unarchived.

Table 24–1 outlines the problems that might cause this symptom and describes solutions to those problems.

Table 24–1 *TACACS+: Errors Unarchiving Source File*

Possible Problem	Solution
Archive file was not transferred using FTP binary (image) mode	The TACACS+ archive file must be transferred using FTP binary (image) mode. FTP the *tac_plus.2.1.tar* file again, using binary transfer mode. From the FTP command line, enter the **image** command to set the image mode. For other FTP software, refer to your documentation for instructions on setting the image mode.
Insufficient disk space	Make sure there is sufficient disk space for the expanded *tac_plus.2.1.tar* file. If there is not enough space on your UNIX system, free up enough disk space to accommodate decompression of the file. TACACS+ requires about 900 KB.

TACACS+: Cannot Compile Daemon

Symptom: Attempts to compile the TACACS+ daemon result in errors.

Table 24–2 outlines the problems that might cause this symptom and describes solutions to those problems.

Table 24–2 *TACACS+: Cannot Compile Daemon*

Possible Problem	Solution	
make is not in $PATH or is not installed on the UNIX machine	**Step 1**	Enter the command **which make** at the UNIX prompt. If the output says "No **make** in $PATH...," **make** is not in the specified path or is not installed.
	Step 2	If **make** is already installed, modify the $PATH variable to include the directory in which **make** is located.
		If **make** is not installed, see your system administrator for help installing it.
	Step 3	Compile the TACACS+ daemon again.

Table 24–2 *TACACS+: Cannot Compile Daemon, Continued*

Possible Problem	Solution
gcc not in $PATH or not installed correctly	**Step 1** Enter the command **which gcc** at the UNIX prompt. If the output says "No gcc in $PATH...," **gcc** is not in the specified path or is not installed.
	Step 2 If **gcc** is already installed, modify the $PATH variable to include the directory in which **gcc** is located.
	If **gcc** is not installed, ask your system administrator to install it.
	Step 3 Compile the TACACS+ daemon again.
UNIX platform commented out or not in makefile	Your UNIX platform must be listed and uncommented in the makefile for **make** to compile the TACACS+ source code properly. The makefile is located in the *tac_plus.2.1* directory.
	Step 1 Make sure that your UNIX platform is not commented out in the makefile.
	Step 2 If your platform is not listed at all, see your system administrator for help compiling the source code. The only supported platforms are those listed in the makefile.
	Step 3 Compile the TACACS+ daemon again.

TACACS+: Daemon Not Up and Running

Symptom: The TACACS+ daemon is not running.

Table 24–3 outlines the problems that might cause this symptom and describes solutions to those problems.

Table 24–3 *TACACS+: Daemon Not Up and Running*

Possible Problem	Solution
TACACS+ has not been launched	Launch TACACS+ with the command **tac_plus -C** *configuration filename*.
TACACS+ not specified in */etc/services* file	**Step 1** Check the */etc/services* file for the following line: `tacacs 49/tcp`
	Step 2 This line must be included in the file. If the line is not present, add the line to the file.

Table 24–3   *TACACS+: Daemon Not Up and Running, Continued*

Possible Problem	Solution
tac_plus executable does not exist	The TACACS+ daemon cannot run if the **tac_plus** executable does not exist.
	Step 1 Check the directory where you installed *tac_plus.2.1* to see whether the *tac_plus* file exists.
	Step 2 If the file does not exist, use the **make tac_plus** command to compile *tac_plus*.

TACACS+: Daemon Does Not Run

Symptom: The TACACS+ daemon does not run when invoked.

Table 24–4 outlines the problem that might cause this symptom and describes solutions to that problem.

Table 24–4   *TACACS+: Daemon Does Not Run*

Possible Problem	Solution
TACACS+ configuration file not present	**Step 1** Check the directory in which you installed TACACS+ for a configuration file in the TACACS+ format.
	Step 2 If there is no TACACS+ configuration file present and you are upgrading from XTACACS, convert your password file into a configuration file by issuing the following command:
| | ```
unix_host% convert.pl /etc/passwd > configuration-file
``` |
| | **Step 3** If there is no TACACS+ configuration file present, create one using a text editor. At a minimum, the configuration file must contain the following text: |
| | ```
user = userid {
login = cleartext "passwd"
}
``` |
| | The configuration file can have any name you want. |
| | For more information, refer to the user guide located in the *tac_plus.2.1* directory. |

TACACS+: Users Cannot Log In Using TACACS+

Symptom: Users cannot log in using TACACS+. Either users cannot get the "Username" prompt or they get the prompt but authentication or authorization fails.

Table 24–5 outlines the problems that might cause this symptom and describes solutions to those problems.

Table 24–5 *TACACS+: Users Cannot Log In Using TACACS+*

Possible Problem	Solution	

Router missing minimum configuration	**Step 1**	Use the **show running-config** privileged exec command to view the local router configuration. Look for the following commands:
		
		`aaa new-model`
		`aaa authentication login default tacacs+ enable`
		`[...]`
		`tacacs-server host name`
		`tacacs-server key key`
		
		where *name* is the IP address or DNS[1] hostname of the TACACS+ server and *key* is the authentication and encryption key.

	Step 2	If all these commands are not present, add the missing commands to the configuration. If there is no key configured on the TACACS+ daemon, the **tacacs-server key** command is not necessary.
aaa authorization command present	**Step 1**	Use the **show running-config** privileged exec command to view the local router configuration. Look for an **aaa authorization exec tacacs+** global configuration command entry.
	Step 2	If the command is present, remove it from the configuration using the **no** version of the command.

Table 24–5   *TACACS+: Users Cannot Log In Using TACACS+, Continued*

Possible Problem	Solution
PPP[2] not functioning correctly	If PPP is not functioning properly, problems will occur when using TACACS+. Use the **debug ppp negotiation** privileged exec command to see whether both sides are communicating.
	Caution: Because debugging output is assigned high priority in the CPU process, it can render the system unusable. For this reason, use **debug** commands only to troubleshoot specific problems or during troubleshooting sessions with Cisco technical support staff. Moreover, it is best to use **debug** commands during periods of lower network traffic and fewer users. Debugging during these periods decreases the likelihood that increased **debug** command processing overhead will affect system use.
	For information on configuring PPP, refer to the Cisco IOS *Configuration Fundamentals Configuration Guide* and *Configuration Fundamentals Command Reference*.
PAP[3] is misconfigured	**Step 1** Use the **show running-config** privileged exec command to make sure your configuration includes the following global configuration command:
	`aaa authentication ppp default if-needed tacacs+`
	Step 2 If the command is not present, add it to the configuration.
	Step 3 In addition, check the configuration of the async interface being used. Use the **show running-config** privileged exec command. The interface must have the following commands configured:
	`encapsulation ppp` `ppp authentication pap`
	Step 4 If these commands are not present, add them to the interface configuration.

Table 24–5 *TACACS+: Users Cannot Log In Using TACACS+, Continued*

Possible Problem	Solution	
CHAP[4] is misconfigured	**Step 1**	Use the **show running-config** privileged exec command to make sure your configuration includes the following global configuration command: `aaa authentication ppp default if-needed tacacs+`
	Step 2	If the command is not present, add it to the configuration.

	Step 3	In addition, check the configuration of the async interface being used. Use the **show running-config** privileged exec command. The interface must have the following commands configured:
		
		`encapsulation ppp`
		`ppp authentication chap`

	Step 4	If these commands are not present, add them to the interface configuration.

	Step 5	Make sure your daemon configuration file, located in the *tac_plus.2.1* directory, includes one of the following lines, as appropriate:
		
		`chap = cleartext password`
		
		or
		
		`global = cleartext password`

Username and password not in */etc/passwd*	**Step 1**	Check to make sure that the appropriate username and password pairs are contained in the */etc/passwd* file.
	Step 2	If the appropriate users are not specified, generate a new user with the correct username and password using the **add user** command.
No TCP[5] connection to TACACS+ daemon	**Step 1**	From the router, try to Telnet to port 49 on the TACACS+ daemon.
	Step 2	If the Telnet is unsuccessful, make sure the daemon is running. For more information, refer to the section "TACACS+: Daemon Not Up and Running" earlier in this chapter.
	Step 3	If the daemon is running but the Telnet times out, check IP connectivity. For more information, see Chapter 7, "Troubleshooting TCP/IP."

[1] DNS = Domain Name System
[2] PPP = Point-to-Point Protocol
[3] PAP = Password Authentication Protocol
[4] CHAP = Challenge Handshake Authentication Protocol
[5] TCP = Transmission Control Protocol

XTACACS: Errors Decompressing File

Symptom: Error messages are generated when unarchiving the XTACACS archive file (either *xtacacsd.tar.z* or *xtacacsd.tar*).

Table 24–6 outlines the problems that might cause this symptom and describes solutions to those problems.

Table 24–6 *XTACACS: Errors Decompressing File*

Possible Problem	Solution
File was not transferred using FTP binary (image) mode	The XTACACS archive file must be transferred using FTP binary (image) mode.
	Step 1 FTP the *xtacacsd.tar.z* or the *xtacacsd.tar* file again using binary transfer mode.
	Step 2 From the FTP command line, enter the **image** command to set the image mode.
	For other FTP software, refer to your documentation for instructions on setting the image mode.
Insufficient disk space	Make sure there is sufficient disk space for the expanded *xtacacsd.tar.z* or *xtacacsd.tar* file. If there is not enough space on your UNIX system, free up enough disk space to accommodate decompression of the file. XTACACS requires about 350 KB.

XTACACS: Cannot Compile Daemon

Symptom: Attempts to compile the XTACACS daemon result in errors.

Table 24–7 outlines the problems that might cause this symptom and describes solutions to those problems.

Table 24–7 *XTACACS: Cannot Compile Daemon*

Possible Problem	Solution
make is not in $PATH or is not installed on the UNIX machine	**Step 1** Enter the command **which make** at the UNIX prompt. If the output says "No **make** in $PATH...," **make** is not in the specified path or is not installed.
	Step 2 If **make** is already installed, modify the $PATH variable to include the directory in which **make** is located.
	If **make** is not installed, see your system administrator for help installing it.
	Step 3 Compile the XTACACS daemon again.

Table 24–7 *XTACACS: Cannot Compile Daemon, Continued*

Possible Problem	Solution
gcc not in $PATH or not installed correctly	**Step 1** Enter the command **which gcc** at the UNIX prompt. If the output says "No **gcc** in $PATH...," **gcc** is not in the specified path or is not installed.
	Step 2 If **gcc** is already installed, modify the $PATH variable to include the directory in which **gcc** is located.
	If **gcc** is not installed, see your system administrator for help installing it.
	Step 3 Compile the TACACS+ daemon again.
UNIX platform commented out or not in makefile	Your UNIX platform must be listed and uncommented in the makefile for **make** to compile the XTACACS source code properly. The makefile is located in the directory where you installed XTACACS.
	Step 1 Make sure that your UNIX platform is not commented out in the makefile.
	Step 2 If your platform is not listed at all, see your system administrator for help compiling the source code. The only supported platforms are those listed in the makefile.
	Step 3 Compile the XTACACS daemon again.

XTACACS: Daemon Not Up and Running

Symptom: The XTACACS daemon is not up and running.

Table 24–8 outlines the problems that might cause this symptom and describes solutions to those problems.

Table 24–8 *XTACACS: Daemon Not Up and Running*

Possible Problem	Solution
XTACACS has not been launched	Launch the XTACACS daemon with the command **xtacacsd -s -l**.
XTACACS not specified in */etc/services* file	**Step 1** Check the */etc/services* file for the following line: `tacacs 49/udp`
	Step 2 This line must be included in the file. If the line is not present, add the line to the file.
xtacacsd executable does not exist	Check the directory where you installed *xtacacsd* for the *xtacacsd* file. If the executable is not present, use the **make** command to compile *xtacacsd*.

XTACACS: Slow Response from Daemon

Symptom: The response time from the XTACACS daemon is slow. Users have to wait a long time before being prompted for their username and password.

Table 24–9 outlines the problems that might cause this symptom and describes solutions to those problems.

Table 24–9   *XTACACS: Slow Response from Daemon*

Possible Problem	Solution
DNS is misconfigured	In order for XTACACS to function correctly, you must properly configure DNS.
	Consult your DNS software documentation or your system administrator for information on how to properly configure DNS.
DNS is not set up for reverse lookups	If the DNS server is not configured to perform reverse lookups, XTACACS can suffer excessive delays.
	Consult your DNS software documentation or your system administrator for information on how to properly configure the DNS for reverse lookups.

XTACACS: Users Cannot Connect Using XTACACS

Symptom: Users cannot log in using XTACACS. Either users cannot get the "Username" prompt or they get the prompt but authentication or authorization fails.

Table 24–10 outlines the problems that might cause this symptom and describes solutions to those problems.

Table 24–10   *XTACACS: Users Cannot Connect Using XTACACS*

Possible Problem	Solution	
Missing **login tacacs** command	**Step 1**	Use the **show running-config** privileged exec command on the router to see whether the **login tacacs** line configuration command is present.
	Step 2	If the command is not present, add the command on each line that should use XTACACS. For example, to configure line 2 to use XTACACS, enter the following commands:
		`C2500(config)#`**`line 2`** `C2500(config-line)#`**`login tacacs`**
		For detailed information on configuring XTACACS, refer to the Cisco IOS *Configuration Fundamentals Configuration Guide* and *Configuration Fundamentals Command Reference*.

Table 24–10 *XTACACS: Users Cannot Connect Using XTACACS, Continued*

Possible Problem	Solution

Router does not have minimum XTACACS configuration	**Step 1** Use the **show running-config** privileged exec command to view the local router configuration. Look for the following commands:
	
	```tacacs-server host hostname```
	```tacacs-server extended```
	
	where *name* is the DNS hostname or IP address of the XTACACS server.
	
	Step 2 If these commands are not present, add them to the configuration.
	
	Examples:
	
	The following example enables Extended TACACS mode:
	
	```tacacs-server extended```
	
	The following example specifies a TACACS host named Sea_Change:
	
	```tacacs-server host Sea_Change```

PPP not functioning correctly	If PPP is not functioning properly, problems will occur when using XTACACS. Use the **debug ppp negotiation** privileged exec command to see whether both sides are communicating. **Caution:** Because debugging output is assigned high priority in the CPU process, it can render the system unusable. For this reason, use **debug** commands only to troubleshoot specific problems or during troubleshooting sessions with Cisco technical support staff. Moreover, it is best to use **debug** commands during periods of lower network traffic and fewer users. Debugging during these periods decreases the likelihood that increased **debug** command processing overhead will affect system use. For information on configuring PPP, refer to the Cisco IOS *Configuration Fundamentals Configuration Guide* and *Configuration Fundamentals Command Reference*.

Table 24–10   *XTACACS: Users Cannot Connect Using XTACACS, Continued*

Possible Problem	Solution	
PAP is misconfigured	**Step 1**	Use the **show running-config** privileged exec command to make sure the router is configured for PAP authentication. The router configuration should include the following interface configuration commands for each async interface that should use PAP authentication: ```ppp authentication pap ppp use-tacacs```
	Step 2	If the commands are not present, add them to the configuration. In the following example, asynchronous interface 1 is configured to use TACACS for PAP authentication: ```interface async 1 ppp authentication pap ppp use-tacacs```
CHAP is misconfigured	**Step 1**	Use the **show running-config** privileged exec command to make sure the router is configured for CHAP authentication. The router configuration should include the following interface configuration commands for each async interface that should use CHAP authentication: ```encapsulation ppp ppp authentication chap ppp use-tacacs```
	Step 2	If the commands are not present, add them to the configuration. In the following example, asynchronous interface 1 is configured to use TACACS for CHAP authentication: ```interface async 1 encapsulation ppp ppp authentication chap ppp use-tacacs```

Table 24–10 *XTACACS: Users Cannot Connect Using XTACACS, Continued*

Possible Problem	Solution

No CHAP supplementary file defined on XTACACS server	**Step 1** Check to see whether there is a CHAP supplementary file defined on the XTACACS server. This file should be located in the *xtacacsd* directory.
	
	Step 2 If there is not a CHAP supplementary file, create one. The file should contain a list of usernames and cleartext CHAP passwords in the following format:
	
	`user:#:#:ARAP password:CHAP password`
	
	Note: You cannot use */etc/passwd* with CHAP.
	
	Step 3 After the supplementary file is created, restart the XTACACS daemon with the following command:
	
	`xtacacsd -s -l -f supplementary-filename`

Username and password not in */etc/passwd*	**Step 1** Make sure that the appropriate username and password pairs are contained in the */etc/passwd* file. **Step 2** If the appropriate users are not specified, generate a new user with the correct username and password using the **add user** command.
IP connectivity problem	For information on troubleshooting IP connectivity, see Chapter 7, "Troubleshooting TCP/IP."

RECOVERING A LOST PASSWORD

This section describes the procedures required to recover a lost login or enable password. The procedures differs depending on the platform and the software used, but in all cases, password recovery requires that the router be taken out of operation and powered down.

If you need to perform one of the following procedures, make certain that secondary systems can temporarily serve the functions of the router undergoing the procedure. If this is not possible, advise all potential users and, if possible, perform the procedure during low-use hours.

NOTES

Make a note of your password and store it in a secure place.

All the procedures for recovering lost passwords depend on changing the configuration register of the router. Depending on the platform and software you are using, this will be done by reconfiguring the router software or by physically moving a jumper or DIP switch on the router.

Table 24–11 shows which platforms have configuration registers in software and which require that you change the jumper or DIP switch position to change the configuration register.

Table 24–11 *Configuration Registers for Specific Cisco Platforms and Software*

Platform (and Software, if Applicable)	Software Configuration Register	Hardware Configuration Register (Jumper)	Hardware Configuration Register (DIP Switch)
Cisco 2000 series	Yes	—	—
Cisco 2500 series	Yes	—	—
Cisco 3000 series	Yes	—	—
Cisco 4000 series	Yes	—	—
Cisco 7000 series running Software Release 9.17(4) or later (Flash/netboot) or Cisco IOS Release 10.0 or later (ROM)	Yes	—	—
Cisco 7000 running Software Release 9.21 or earlier from ROM	—	Yes	—
Cisco 7200	Yes	—	—
Cisco 7500	Yes	—	—
Cisco IGS running Software Release 9.1 or later	Yes	—	—
Cisco IGS running software prior to Software Release 9.1	—	—	Yes
Cisco CGS	—	Yes	—
Cisco MGS	—	Yes	—
Cisco AGS	—	Yes	—
Cisco AGS+	—	Yes	—

Password-Recovery Procedure: Platforms Running Current Cisco IOS Releases

More recent Cisco platforms run from Flash memory or are netbooted and can ignore the contents of nonvolatile RAM (NVRAM) upon booting. (Cisco 7000 series routers that boot from Flash memory or netboot have this capability as well; a Cisco 7000 that boots from ROM has this capability if it is running Cisco IOS Release 10.0 or later.) Ignoring the contents of NVRAM permits you to bypass the configuration file (which contains the passwords) and gain complete access to the router. You can then recover the lost password or configure a new one.

If your password is encrypted, you cannot recover it. You must configure a new password.

Figure 24–1 shows a flowchart describing the password-recovery procedure for the following platforms:

- Cisco 2000, Cisco 2500, Cisco 3000, and Cisco 4000 series access servers and routers
- Cisco 7000 series routers running Software Release 9.17(4) and later from Flash/netboot *or* Cisco IOS Release 10.0 or later from ROM
- Cisco IGS routers running Software Release 9.1 or later
- Cisco CGS, MGS, AGS, and AGS+ routers running Software Release 9.1(7) or later
- Cisco 7000 series routers running Software Release 9.17(4) through 9.21 from ROM

Some of these platforms are configurable in software. Others require that you physically change the position of the configuration register jumper on the processor card. Figure 24–1 shows diverging paths, when necessary, to take you through the steps required for the platform and software with which you are working.

Refer to Table 24–11 to determine whether the platform with which you are working is configurable in software, or if it requires you to physically move the jumper.

The next procedure describes the password-recovery process for the following platforms *only*:

- Cisco 2000, Cisco 2500, Cisco 3000, and Cisco 4000 series routers
- Cisco 7000 series routers running Software Release 9.17(4) or later (Flash memory or netboot) or Cisco IOS Release 10.0 or later from ROM
- Cisco IGS Running Software Release 9.1 or later

For the platforms listed, be certain to follow the path labeled "Cisco 2000, 2500, 3000, 4000 series; Cisco 7000 series running Software Release 9.17(4) or later (Flash/netboot) or Cisco IOS Release 10.0 or later (ROM); IGS running Software Release 9.1 or later" in the flowchart (see Figure 24–1).

For the step-by-step password recovery sequence for other platforms, see one of the following sections:

- Password-Recovery Procedure: Platforms Running Recent Software Releases
- Password-Recovery Procedure: Platforms Running Earlier Software Releases
- Password-Recovery Procedure: IGS Running Software Prior to Software Release 9.1
- Password-Recovery Procedure: Cisco 500-CS Communication Server

NOTES

To complete this procedure, you must have a terminal or a personal computer (running terminal emulation software) connected to the console port of the router. In addition, make sure you know the **break** command key sequence.

Following is the password-recovery procedure for Cisco platforms running current Cisco IOS software:

Step 1   Power cycle the router.

Step 2   Use the **break** key sequence for your terminal or terminal emulation software within 60 seconds of turning on the power.

The ROM monitor (>) prompt will appear.

Step 3   Enter the command **e/s 2000002**. (For Cisco 7000 series routers, enter **e/s XXXXXXXX**.) This command examines the short (16-bit) memory location for the software configuration register.

Record the output resulting from this command. This is the software configuration register value.

Step 4   Enter **q** (quit) to return to the ROM monitor (>) prompt.

Step 5   Enter the **o/r 0x42** command. The value 42 sets the software configuration register bit to position 6, which allows the router to ignore the contents of NVRAM when booting. (Be sure to enter **0x** followed by the configuration register value.)

Step 6   Enter **i** (initialize) at the ROM monitor (>) prompt. The router will reboot.

Step 7   Answer **no** to all the setup questions.

Step 8   Enter the **enable** exec command at the Router> prompt.

Step 9   Enter the **show startup-config** or **show configuration** privileged exec command to see whether your password is cleartext (is not encrypted) or if it is encrypted.

Step 10   If your password is cleartext, proceed to Step 14.

or

If your password is encrypted, continue with Step 11.

Step 11   If your password is encrypted, enter the **configure memory** privileged exec command. This transfers the stored configuration into running memory.

Step 12   Enter the **configure terminal** privileged exec command to enter router configuration mode.

Step 13   If you lost the enable password, use the **enable password** global configuration command to configure a new password and press **^Z** to exit configuration mode. The following is the command syntax for the **enable password** command:

enable password [level *level*] {*password* | *encryption-type encrypted-password*}

Syntax Description:

- **level** *level*—(Optional) Level for which the password applies. You can specify up to 16 privilege levels, using numbers 0 through 15. Level 1 is normal exec-mode user privileges. If this argument is not specified in the command or the **no** form of the command, the privilege level defaults to 15 (traditional enable privileges).

- *password*—Password users type to enter enable mode.

- *encryption-type*—(Optional) Cisco-proprietary algorithm used to encrypt the password. Currently the only encryption type available is 7. If you specify *encryption-type*, the next argument you supply must be an encrypted password (a password already encrypted by a Cisco router).

- *encrypted-password*—Encrypted password you enter, copied from another router configuration.

Example:

In the following example, the password **pswd2** is enabled for privilege level 2:

```
enable password level 2 pswd2
```

If you lost the login password, configure the console line using the **login** and **password** line configuration commands. Enter ^Z to exit configuration mode and proceed to Step 15.

Syntax:

To enable password checking at login, use the **login** line configuration command:

login [*local* | *tacacs*]

Syntax Description:

- *local*—(Optional) Selects local password checking. Authentication is based on the username specified with the username global configuration command.

- *tacacs*—(Optional) Selects the TACACS-style user ID and password-checking mechanism.

Examples:

The following example sets the password **letmein** on virtual terminal line 4:

```
line vty 4
password letmein
login
```

Syntax:

To specify a password on a line, use the **password** line configuration command:

password *password*

Syntax Description:

- *password*—Character string that specifies the line password. The first character cannot be a number. The string can contain any alphanumeric characters, including spaces, up to 80 characters. You cannot specify *password* in the format *number-space-anything*. The space after the number causes problems. For example, *hello 21* is a legal password, but *21 hello* is not. The password checking is case sensitive. For example, the password *Secret* is different from the password *secret*.

  When an exec process is started on a line with password protection, the exec prompts for the password. If the user enters the correct password, the exec prints its normal privileged prompt. The user can try three times to enter a password before the exec exits and returns the terminal to the idle state.

Example:

The following example removes the password from virtual terminal lines 1 to 4:

```
line vty 1 4
 no password
```

Step 14   If you lost the enable password, locate the **enable-password** global configuration command entry in the configuration and record the password.

   If you lost the login password, find the configuration entries for the console line and record the password indicated by the **password** line configuration command.

Step 15   Use the **copy running-config startup-config** or **write memory** privileged exec command to write the configuration into NVRAM.

CAUTION

Issuing the **copy running-config startup-config** or **write memory** command at this point on a Cisco 2500, Cisco 3000, or Cisco 4000 will overwrite the configuration. Make certain you have a backup of your configuration file.

Step 16   The router is now fully functional, and you can use your recovered or reconfigured passwords as usual.

NOTES

Restore the software configuration register to its original value as soon as possible. If it is not returned to the value you noted in Step 3, the router will always ignore the contents of NVRAM and enter the Setup routine upon booting. Continue with Step 17 to return the software configuration register to its original value.

Step 17 In privileged exec mode, enter router configuration mode using the **configure terminal** privileged exec command.

Step 18 Change the software configuration register to its original value by using the **config-register** global configuration command. You must enter **0x** and then the software configuration register value that you recorded in Step 3. Using the sample value 2102, the command would be **config-register 0x2102**.

Syntax:

The following is the syntax for **config-register** command:

config-register *value*

Syntax Description:

- *value*—Hexadecimal or decimal value that represents the 16-bit configuration register value that you want to use the next time the router is restarted. The value range is from 0x0 to 0xFFFF (0 to 65535 in decimal).

Step 19 Exit router configuration mode by entering ^Z.

The next time the router is power cycled or restarted with the **reload** privileged exec command, the bootup process will proceed as normal. Use your new or recovered password to gain access to the router after it reboots.

Figure 24–1

Password Recovery: Platforms Running Current Cisco IOS Releases and Recent Software Releases

Password-Recovery Procedure: Platforms Running Recent Software Releases

The Cisco CGS, MGS, AGS, and AGS+ platforms, and Cisco 7000 series routers running software prior to Cisco IOS Release 10.0 from ROM, all have their configuration registers in hardware, so you must physically change the position of the configuration register jumper during the password-recovery process.

It might be necessary to remove the processor card from the router chassis in order to access the hardware configuration register jumper. Consult your hardware documentation for detailed instructions on removing and inserting the processor card from the router chassis if necessary.

Moving the hardware configuration register jumper to bit position 6 allows the router to ignore the contents of NVRAM while booting. This permits you to bypass the configuration file (and therefore the passwords) and gain complete access to the router. You can then recover the lost password or configure a new one.

NOTES

If your password is encrypted, you cannot recover it. You must configure a new password.

Figure 24–1 shows a flowchart describing the password-recovery procedure for the following platforms:

- Cisco 2000, Cisco 2500, Cisco 3000, and Cisco 4000 series access servers and routers
- Cisco 7000 series routers running Software Release 9.17(4) and later from Flash memory/netboot

  or

  Cisco 7000 series routers running Cisco IOS Release 10.0 or later from ROM
- Cisco IGS routers running Software Release 9.1 or later
- Cisco CGS, MGS, AGS, and AGS+ routers running Software Release 9.1(7) or later
- Cisco 7000 series routers running Software Release 9.17(4) through 9.21 from ROM

Some of these platforms are configurable in software and do not require a hardware change. Others require that you physically change the position of the configuration register jumper on the processor card. takes you through the steps required for the platform and software with which you are working, and shows diverging paths when necessary to account for platform-specific requirements.

Refer to Table 24–11 to determine whether the platform on which you are working is configurable in the software, or whether it requires you to physically move the jumper.

The following procedure describes the password-recovery process for the following platforms *only*:

- Cisco CGS, MGS, AGS, and AGS+ routers running Software Release 9.1(7) and later
- Cisco 7000 series routers running Software Release 9.17(4) through 9.21 from ROM

For these platforms, follow the path labeled "Cisco CGS, MGS, AGS, AGS+ running Software Release 9.1(7) or later; Cisco 7000 series running Software Release 9.17(4) through 9.21 from ROM" in the flowchart (see Figure 24–1).

For the step-by-step password recovery sequence for other platforms, see one of the following sections:

- Password-Recovery Procedure: Platforms Running Current Cisco IOS Releases
- Password-Recovery Procedure: Platforms Running Earlier Software Releases
- Password-Recovery Procedure: IGS Running Software Prior to Software Release 9.1
- Password-Recovery Procedure: Cisco 500-CS Communication Server

---

NOTES

To complete this procedure, you must have a terminal or a personal computer (running terminal emulation software) connected to the console port of the router.

Following is the password-recovery procedure for Cisco platforms running recent software releases:

Step 1   Power down the router.

Step 2   Change the hardware configuration register by moving the jumper from bit position 0 or 1 to bit position 6. This will force the router to ignore the contents of NVRAM, and therefore the configuration file, after it loads the operating system. Note the original position of the jumper.

NOTES

To move the hardware configuration register jumper, you might need to remove the processor card from the router chassis. This is the case with the Route Processor (RP) card in Cisco 7000 series routers. Refer to your hardware documentation for complete instructions on removing and inserting the processor card. If you had to remove the processor card, reinsert it before continuing.

Step 3   Power up the router.

The router will boot but will ignore the contents of NVRAM and enter the Setup routine.

Step 4   Answer **no** to all the setup questions.

The Router> prompt appears.

Step 5   Enter the **enable** exec command.

Step 6   Enter the **show configuration** privileged exec command to see whether the password is cleartext (is not encrypted) or if it is encrypted.

If the password is cleartext, go to Step 10. If the password is encrypted, continue with Step 7.

Step 7   If the password is encrypted, enter the **configure memory** privileged exec command. This writes the stored configuration into running memory.

Step 8   Enter the **configure terminal** privileged exec command to enter router configuration mode.

Step 9   If you have lost the enable password, use the **enable-password** global configuration command to configure a new password.

If you have lost the login password, configure the console line with a new login password using the **login** and **password** line configuration commands. Press ^Z to exit configuration mode. Proceed to Step 11.

Syntax:

To enable password checking at login, use the **login** line configuration command:

login [*local* | *tacacs*]

Syntax Description:

- *local*—(Optional) Selects local password checking. Authentication is based on the username specified with the username global configuration command.

- *tacacs*—(Optional) Selects the TACACS-style user ID and password-checking mechanism.

Examples:

The following example sets the password **letmein** on virtual terminal line 4:

```
line vty 4
password letmein
login
```

Syntax:

To specify a password on a line, use the **password** line configuration command:

password *password*

Syntax Description:

- *password*—Character string that specifies the line password. The first character cannot be a number. The string can contain any alphanumeric characters, including spaces, up to 80 characters. You cannot specify *password* in the format *number-space-anything*. The space after the number causes problems. For example, *hello 21* is a legal password, but *21 hello* is not. The password checking is case sensitive. For example, the password *Secret* is different from the password *secret*.

  When an exec process is started on a line with password protection, the exec prompts for the password. If the user enters the correct password, the exec prints its normal privileged prompt. The user can try three times to enter a password before the exec exits and returns the terminal to the idle state.

Example:

The following example removes the password from virtual terminal lines 1 to 4:

```
line vty 1 4
no password
```

Step 10   If you have lost the enable password, locate the **enable-password** global
               configuration command entry and record the password.

               If you have lost the login password, find the configuration entries for the console
               line and record the password indicated by the **password** line configuration
               command.

Step 11   Use the **write memory** privileged exec command to write the configuration into
               running memory.

Step 12   The router is now fully functional and you can use your recovered or reconfigured
               passwords as usual.

NOTES ──

Return the hardware configuration register jumper to its original position as soon as possible. If the
jumper is not returned to the bit position you noted in Step 2, the router will always ignore the contents of NVRAM and enter the Setup routine upon booting. Continue with Step 13 to return the
jumper to its original position.

Step 13   Power down the router.

Step 14   Move the hardware configuration register jumper from bit position 6 to its
               original position (the position you noted in Step 2).

               It might be necessary to remove the processor card to gain access to the jumper.
               Consult your hardware documentation for complete instructions on removing and
               inserting the processor card if necessary. If you had to remove the processor card,
               reinsert it before continuing.

Step 15   Power up the router. Use your new or recovered password to gain access to the
               router.

Password-Recovery Procedure: Platforms Running Earlier Software Releases

Cisco CGS, MGS, AGS, and AGS+ platforms, and Cisco 7000 series routers running software prior
to Cisco IOS Release 10.0 from ROM, all have their configuration registers in the hardware, so you
must physically change the position of the configuration register jumper during the
password-recovery process.

It might be necessary to remove the processor card from the router chassis in order to access the
hardware configuration register jumper. Consult your hardware documentation for detailed
instructions on removing and inserting the processor card from the router chassis if necessary.

If your password is encrypted, you cannot recover it. You must configure a new password.

Figure 24–2 shows a flowchart that describes the password-recovery procedure for the following platforms:

- CGS, MGS, AGS, and AGS+ routers running Software Release 9.1(6) and earlier
- Cisco 7000 series routers running Software Release 9.17(3) and earlier from ROM

The step-by-step procedure that follows and the password recovery flowchart shown in Figure 24–2 apply only to the indicated platforms running the indicated software. There is another procedure for recovering a password on these platforms if they are running more recent software. See the previous section, "Password-Recovery Procedure: Platforms Running Recent Software Releases."

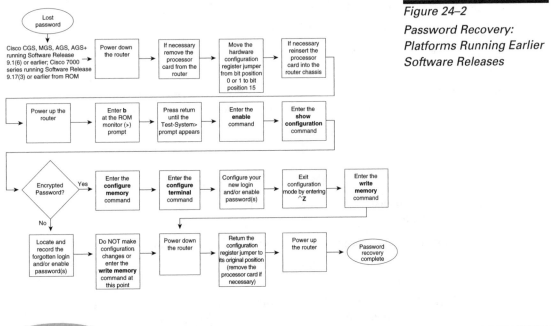

Figure 24–2

Password Recovery: Platforms Running Earlier Software Releases

To complete this procedure, you must have a terminal or a personal computer (running terminal emulation software) connected to the console port of the router.

Following is the password-recovery procedure for Cisco platforms running earlier software releases:

Step 1   Power down the router.

Step 2   Change the hardware configuration register by moving the jumper from bit position 0 or 1 to bit position 15.

    Note the original position of the jumper.

NOTES

To move the hardware configuration register jumper, you might need to remove the processor card from the router chassis. This is the case with the RP card in Cisco 7000 series routers. Consult your hardware documentation for complete instructions on removing and inserting the processor card. If you had to remove the processor card, reinsert it before continuing.

Step 3   Power up the router. The ROM monitor (>) prompt appears.

Step 4   Enter **b** (bootstrap) at the (>) prompt.

Step 5   Press the Return key until the Test-System> prompt appears.

Step 6   Enter privileged mode by issuing the **enable** exec command.

Step 7   Enter the **show configuration** privileged exec command to see whether the password is cleartext (is not encrypted) or if it is encrypted.

    If the password is cleartext, go to Step 12.

    or

    If the password is encrypted, continue with Step 8.

Step 8   If the password is encrypted, enter the **configure memory** privileged exec command.

    This writes the stored configuration into running memory.

Step 9   Enter the **configure terminal** privileged exec command to enter router configuration mode.

Step 10   If you have lost the enable password, use the **enable-password** global configuration command to configure a new password and press ^Z to exit configuration mode.

    If you have lost the login password, configure the console line with a new password using the **login** and **password** line configuration commands. Press ^Z to exit configuration mode.

Syntax:

To enable password checking at login, use the **login** line configuration command:

login [*local* | *tacacs*]

Syntax Description:

- *local*—(Optional) Selects local password checking. Authentication is based on the username specified with the username global configuration command.
- *tacacs*—(Optional) Selects the TACACS-style user ID and password-checking mechanism.

Examples:

The following example sets the password **letmein** on virtual terminal line 4:

```
line vty 4
password letmein
login
```

Syntax:

To specify a password on a line, use the **password** line configuration command:

password *password*

Syntax Description:

- *password*—Character string that specifies the line password. The first character cannot be a number. The string can contain any alphanumeric characters, including spaces, up to 80 characters. You cannot specify *password* in the format *number-space-anything*. The space after the number causes problems. For example, *hello 21* is a legal password, but *21 hello* is not. The password checking is case sensitive. For example, the password *Secret* is different from the password *secret*.

  When an exec process is started on a line with password protection, the exec prompts for the password. If the user enters the correct password, the exec prints its normal privileged prompt. The user can try three times to enter a password before the exec exits and returns the terminal to the idle state.

Example:

The following example removes the password from virtual terminal lines 1 to 4:

```
line vty 1 4
no password
```

Step 11   Use the **write memory** privileged exec command to write the configuration into running memory. Proceed to Step 13.

Step 12 If you have lost the enable password, locate the **enable-password** global configuration command entry in the configuration and record the password.

If you have lost the login password, find the configuration entries for the console line and record the password indicated by the **password** line configuration command. Do *not* make configuration changes or use the **write memory** command at this time.

Step 13 Power down the router.

Step 14 Remove the processor card and move the hardware configuration register jumper from bit position 15 to its original position (the position you noted in Step 2).

Step 15 Power up the router. Use your new or recovered password to gain access to the router.

Password-Recovery Procedure: IGS Running Software Prior to Software Release 9.1

Cisco IGS routers have a bank of DIP switches located on the rear panel. These DIP switches are used to set the hardware configuration register and must be used in the password-recovery process if the router is running system software prior to Software Release 9.1.

NOTES
_____

If your password is encrypted, you cannot recover it. You must configure a new password.

Figure 24–3 shows the password-recovery procedure for the Cisco IGS running software prior to Software Release 9.1. There is another procedure for the IGS platform if it is running Software Release 9.1 or later. See the section "Password-Recovery Procedure: Platforms Running Current Cisco IOS Releases."

NOTES
_____

To complete this procedure, you must have a terminal or a personal computer (running terminal emulation software) connected to the console port of the router.

Following is the password-recovery procedure for IGS routers running software prior to Software Release 9.1:

Step 1 Power down the router.

Step 2 Record the settings of the DIP switches located on the rear panel of the router. You will need to return these switches to their original positions after you have recovered your password.

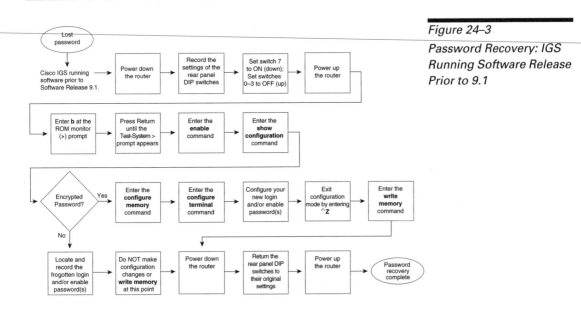

Figure 24–3

Password Recovery: IGS Running Software Release Prior to 9.1

Step 3   Set switch number 7 to the ON position (down).

Step 4   Set switches 0–3 to the OFF position (up).

Step 5   Power up the router.

The router will boot up, and the terminal will display the ROM monitor (>) prompt.

Step 6   Enter **b** (bootstrap) at the (>) prompt.

Step 7   Press the Return key until the Test-System> prompt appears.

Step 8   Enter the **enable** privileged exec command at the Test-System> prompt.

Step 9   If the password is cleartext (is not encrypted), go to Step 14.

If the password is encrypted, continue with Step 10.

Step 10   If the password is encrypted, enter the **configure memory** privileged exec command. This writes the stored configuration into running memory.

Step 11   Enter the **configure terminal** privileged exec command to enter router configuration mode.

Step 12   If you have lost the enable password, use the **enable-password** global configuration command to configure a new password and press ^Z to exit configuration mode.

If you have lost the login password, configure a new password on the console line using the **login** and **password** line configuration commands. Press ^Z to exit configuration mode.

Syntax:

To enable password checking at login, use the **login** line configuration command:

login [*local* | *tacacs*]

Syntax Description:

- *local*—(Optional) Selects local password checking. Authentication is based on the username specified with the username global configuration command.

- *tacacs*—(Optional) Selects the TACACS-style user ID and password-checking mechanism.

Examples:

The following example sets the password **letmein** on virtual terminal line 4:

```
line vty 4
password letmein
login
```

Syntax:

To specify a password on a line, use the **password** line configuration command:

password *password*

Syntax Description:

- *password*—Character string that specifies the line password. The first character cannot be a number. The string can contain any alphanumeric characters, including spaces, up to 80 characters. You cannot specify *password* in the format *number-space-anything*. The space after the number causes problems. For example, *hello 21* is a legal password, but *21 hello* is not. The password checking is case sensitive. For example, the password *Secret* is different from the password *secret*.

  When an exec process is started on a line with password protection, the exec prompts for the password. If the user enters the correct password, the exec prints its normal privileged prompt. The user can try three times to enter a password before the exec exits and returns the terminal to the idle state.

Example:

The following example removes the password from virtual terminal lines 1 to 4:

```
line vty 1 4
 no password
```

Step 13 Enter the **write memory** privileged exec command to write the configuration changes into stored memory. Proceed to Step 16.

Step 14 If your password is cleartext (is not encrypted), enter the **show configuration** privileged exec command.

Step 15 If you have lost the enable password, locate the **enable-password** global configuration command entry in the configuration and record the password.

If you have lost the login password, find the configuration entries for the console line and record the password indicated by the **password** line configuration command. Do *not* make configuration changes or use the **write memory** command at this time.

Step 16 Power down the router.

Step 17 Return the hardware configuration register DIP switches located on the back panel of the router to their original settings (the settings you noted in Step 2).

Step 18 Power up the router. Use your new or recovered password to gain access to the router.

Password-Recovery Procedure: Cisco 500-CS Communication Server

Lost passwords cannot be recovered from Cisco 500-CS communication servers. The only way to recover from a lost password is to return the communication server to its factory default configuration using the reset button located on the top of the case.

The following procedure describes how to restore the Cisco 500-CS to its default configuration.

CAUTION

When you perform this procedure, your configuration *will* be lost.

Step 1 Power down the communication server.

Step 2 Press and hold down the reset button on the top of the case while turning on the power to the communication server.

Step 3 The 500-CS is returned to its factory default configuration.

You must reconfigure the communication server.

PART 7

Appendixes

Creating Core Dumps

When a router crashes, it is sometimes useful to obtain a full copy of the memory image (called a *core dump*) to identify the cause of the crash. Core dumps are generally useful only to your technical support representative.

CAUTION

Use the commands discussed in this appendix only under the direction of a technical support representative. Creating a core dump while the router is functioning in a network can disrupt network operation. The resulting binary file, which is very large, must be transferred to a Trivial File Transfer Protocol (TFTP), File Transfer Protocol (FTP), or Remote Copy Protocol (RCP) server and subsequently interpreted by technical personnel who have access to source code and detailed memory maps.

This appendix describes the **exception, write core,** and **show** commands.

EXCEPTION COMMANDS

Use the **exception** class of configuration commands only after consulting with a technical support representative. These commands are useful for debugging purposes, but they can result in unexpected behavior.

Creating a Core Dump

To obtain a core dump when a router crashes, use the **exception dump** *ip-address* router configuration command (where *ip-address* is the address of your TFTP server).

Including this command in your configuration causes the router to attempt to make a core dump when it crashes. The core dump is written to a file named hostname-core on your TFTP server, where *hostname* is the name of the router. You can change the name of the core file by configuring the **exception core-file** *filename* command. This procedure can fail for certain types of system crashes. However, if it is successful, the core dump file will be the size of the memory available on the processor (for example, 16 MB for a CSC/4).

If you use TFTP to dump the core file to a server, the router will only dump the first 16 MB of the core file. If the router's memory is larger than 16 MB, the whole core file will not be copied to the server. Therefore, use RCP or FTP to dump the core file.

A Core Dump Creation Example

The following example configures a router to use FTP to dump a core file to the FTP server at 172.17.92.2 when it crashes:

```
ip ftp username red
ip ftp password blue
exception protocol ftp
exception dump 172.17.92.2
```

Creating an Exception Memory Core Dump

During the debugging process, you can cause the router to create a core dump and reboot when certain memory size parameters are violated. The **exception memory** commands define a minimum contiguous block of memory in the free pool and a minimum size for the free memory pool. The following is the syntax for the **exception memory fragment** and **exception memory minimum** commands:

```
[no] exception memory fragment size
[no] exception memory minimum size
```

The value of *size* is in bytes and is checked every 60 seconds. If you enter a size that is greater than the free memory and the **exception dump** command has been configured, a core dump and router reload is generated after 60 seconds. If the **exception dump** command is not configured, the router reloads without generating a core dump.

The following example configures the router to monitor the free memory. If it falls below 250000 bytes, it dumps the core and reloads:

```
exception dump 131.108.92.2
exception core-file memory.overrun
exception memory minimum 250000
```

THE WRITE CORE COMMAND

You can test core dumps by using the **write core** privileged exec command. This command causes the router to generate a core dump without reloading and is useful if the router is malfunctioning but has not crashed.

Depending on your TFTP server, you might need to create an empty target file to which the router can write the core.

SHOW COMMANDS

When a router fails with an unexpected reload and you report the problem to a technical support representative, always include a copy of the output from the **show stacks** and **show version** exec commands. Output from these commands provides the support representative with important information about the state of your router when it failed.

The show stacks Command

The **show stacks** command displays data saved by the ROM monitor, which includes a failure type, an operand address, and a failure program counter. This data is overwritten when the system is reloaded, so check your configuration register settings and decide how you want to recover from system crashes.

Appendix B, "Memory Maps," provides an example of **show stacks** output and memory map information that can help you determine whether a system crash was caused by a software or hardware problem.

The show version Command

The **show version** command displays the image type, version number, and function sets that identify the exact software that is running on your router. Also displayed is the current configuration register setting. The following example displays sample output from the **show version** command:

```
milou>show version
Cisco Internetwork Operating System Software
IOS (tm) GS Software (GS7-K-M), Version 11.0(9), RELEASE SOFTWARE (fc1)
Copyright (c) 1986-1996 by cisco Systems, Inc.
Compiled Tue 11-Jun-96 03:52 by tstevens
Image text-base: 0x00001000, data-base: 0x007614F0

ROM: System Bootstrap, Version 5.2(2), RELEASE SOFTWARE
ROM: GS Software (GS7), Version 10.2(2), RELEASE SOFTWARE (fc1)

milou uptime is 2 days, 20 hours, 26 minutes
System restarted by error - Software forced crash, PC 0x1CF82C at 20:25:38 PDT M
on Aug 5 1996
System image file is "images/gs7-k-mz.110-9", booted via flash

cisco RP1 (68040) processor (revision B0) with 16384K bytes of memory.
Processor board ID 00130334
G.703/E1 software, Version 1.0.
Bridging software.
X.25 software, Version 2.0, NET2, BFE and GOSIP compliant.
Primary Rate ISDN software, Version 1.0.
1 Silicon Switch Processor.
1 EIP controller (6 Ethernet).
1 FEIP controller (2 FastEthernet).
1 FIP controller (1 FDDI).
1 MIP controller (2 T1)
6 Ethernet/IEEE 802.3 interfaces.
```

```
2 FastEthernet/IEEE 802.3 interfaces.
48 Serial network interfaces.
1 FDDI network interface.
2 Channelized T1/PRI ports.
128K bytes of non-volatile configuration memory.
4096K bytes of flash memory sized on embedded flash.

Configuration register is 0x102
milou>
```

Version Numbering

Cisco uses a numbering scheme that uniquely identifies each release of the Cisco IOS software. Understanding this scheme will help you distinguish between the different types of releases that are available.

The following formula is used to identify releases of the Cisco IOS software:

```
A.a (x.y)
```

Major releases are indicated by the numbers outside the parentheses (*A* and *a*). Examples of major release numbers are 9.21, 10.0, 10.2, 11.1, and so on. The initial release available for customers is indicated by a 1 in parentheses following the major release number, for example, 9.21(1), 10.0(1), 10.2(1), and 11.1(1).

Maintenance releases are indicated by a whole number (*x*) within the parentheses. Each periodic maintenance release number is incremented sequentially—for example, 10.2(2), 10.2(3), 10.2(4), 10.2(5), and so on. Maintenance releases are periodic revisions of major releases. These are fully regression tested releases incorporating the most recent bug fixes.

Be extremely cautious with any release that has a number following the maintenance release number inside the parentheses (*y*)—for example, the .5 in parentheses in the version number 10.2(3.5). These numbers indicate that this version of software is an interim build. Interim builds are unit tested, but have *not* been fully regression tested and should be used only for short-term, urgent point-fix situations until the next maintenance release is available.

APPENDIX B

Memory Maps

This appendix presents memory maps for selected product platforms, processors, and interface cards. Memory map information is useful for technically qualified users who understand concepts of low-level operating systems, bus structures, and address mapping in computer systems.

When using this appendix, be aware of the distinct difference between program counter values and operand addresses. The addresses that appear in this appendix are operand values and should not be confused with program counter values.

NOTES

All memory addresses are in hexadecimal, unless otherwise noted.

MEMORY MAPS AND TROUBLESHOOTING

Memory map information can be useful when you are determining whether a problem exists in the software or in the hardware. The system software can provide information about the reasons for a system crash. This information appears in the form of error messages issued by the ROM monitor when an exception is encountered.

Failure Types

When a system crashes, the ROM monitor reports a failure type. The failure type is important both in its own right and as a guide to interpreting the other information the system provides. Failure types are usually one of the following:

- Bus error
- Address error
- Watchdog timeout
- Parity error
- Emulator trap

Bus Error

The system encounters a bus error when the processor tries to use a device or a memory location that either does not exist or does not respond properly. Bus errors typically indicate either a software bug or a hardware problem. The address the processor was trying to access when the system crashed provides a key as to whether the failure is due to software or hardware.

If the operand address is valid, the problem is probably in the hardware. The memory maps listed later in this appendix list addresses for selected hardware platforms.

Bus errors on an address not in the map usually indicate a software bug.

Address Error

Address errors occur when the software tries to access data on incorrectly aligned boundaries. For example, 2- and 4-byte accesses are allowed only on even addresses. An address error usually indicates a software bug.

Watchdog Timeout

Cisco processors have timers that guard against certain types of system hangs. The CPU periodically resets a watchdog timer. If the timer is not reset, a trap will occur. Failure to service the watchdog timer indicates either a hardware or a software bug.

Parity Error

Parity errors indicate that internal hardware error checks have failed. A parity failure is almost always due to a hardware problem. Use the memory maps listed later in this chapter to identify the affected hardware.

Emulator Trap

Emulator traps indicate that the processor has executed an illegal instruction. Emulator traps can be caused either by software taking illegal branches or by hardware failures, notably ROM failures.

Error Addresses

By observing the operand address, you can locate the general area of the router where the error occurred. Hardware problems can be inferred only from a bus error on a legal address, not from an emulator trap or illegal instruction trap. When looking at the bus error, the operand address—not the program counter address—provides the memory map location of the error.

show stacks Command

You can use the **show stacks** exec command to display data saved by the ROM monitor, which includes a failure type, an operand address, and a failure program counter. This data is overwritten when the system is reloaded, so you might want to check your configuration register settings and decide how you want to recover from system crashes. Stack traces can be used by qualified technical support representatives who have access to symbol tables, object files, and source code.

Figure B–1 shows an example of the **show stacks** output from a software failure. The message "Software forced crash" indicates that the software detected a condition it did not expect and from which it could not recover. A technical support representative can use the listed program counter as a trace to the code responsible for the failure.

```
ROUTER> show stacks

Minimum process stacks:
Free/Size  Name
 972/1000  env delay init
 866/1000  Router Init
 556/1000  Init
 638/1000  RSRB Connector
1230/2000  Virtual Exec

Interrupt level stacks:
Level    Called Free/Size  Name
  1      306611  952/1000  env-flash
  3    22294573  496/1000  Multiport Communications Interfaces
  5        2986  968/1000  Console UART

System was restarted by error - Software forced crash, PC 0x4854E
GS Software (GS3-K), Version 9.1(4) [fc1], SOFTWARE
Compiled Thu 25-Mar-93 09:49 by daveu
Stack trace from system failure:
FP: 0x2B0424, RA: 0x3B04
FP: 0x2B0458, RA: 0xF39C2
FP: 0x2B046C, RA: 0xF4566
FP: 0X2B0490, RA: 0x112F0
FP: 0x2B04B0, RA: 0x2560
```

program counter address

Figure B–1

show stacks *Command Output Showing the Software Program Counter Address*

Figure B–2 shows output from a hardware error and includes an example of a hardware operand address that can be used with the memory maps in this appendix. The operand address points to the register space for MCI unit 0 and indicates a hardware or microcode problem with that unit.

```
Minimum process stacks:
Free/Size  Name
 970/1000  env delay init
 866/1000  Router Init
 554/1000  Init
1500/2000  Exec

Interrupt level stacks:
Level    Called Free/Size  Name
  1       16803  956/1000  env-flash
  3     4827380  772/1000  cBus Interfaces
  5        5627  968/1000  Console UART

System was restarted by bus error at PC 0x71EAE, address 0x210C008
GS Software (GS3-K), Version 9.1(5), RELEASE SOFTWARE
Compiled Wed 19-May-93 18:35 by daveu
Stack trace from system failure:
FP: 0x2B6BA0, RA: 0xF496
FP: 0x2B6BCC, RA: 0xABDFA
FP: 0x2B6C2C, RA: 0xABA2C
FP: 0x2B6C40, RA: 0xAB338
FP: 0x2B6C68, RA: 0x258C
```

Hardware address
in the bus controller
address space

MEMORY MAPS

The following tables summarize memory map information for the various Cisco platforms:

- Table B–1 describes the Cisco 1000 memory map.
- Table B–2 describes the Cisco 2000 memory map.
- Table B–3 describes the Cisco 2500 memory map.
- Table B–4 describes the Cisco 3000 memory map.
- Table B–5 describes the memory map for the Cisco 3104 and Cisco 3204; Table B–6 describes the Cisco 3104 and Cisco 3204 memory map of onboard registers and chips.
- Table B–7 describes the Cisco 4000 memory map; Table B–8 describes the Cisco 4000 memory map of onboard resources.
- Table B–9 describes the Cisco 4500 memory map; Table B–10 describes the Cisco 4500 memory map of onboard resources.
- Table B–11 describes the Cisco 7000 memory map.
- Table B–12 describes the Cisco 7200 series (NPE-150) memory map for hardware.
- Table B–13 describes the Cisco 7200 series (NPE-150) memory map for software.
- Table B–14 describes the Cisco 500-CS memory map.

- Table B–15 describes the RP/Cisco 7000 series memory map.
- Table B–16 describes the Cisco RSP memory map.
- Table B–17 describes Multibus memory space assignment; Table B–18 describes Multibus I/O space assignment.
- Table B–19 describes the Cisco CSC/3 memory map.
- Table B–20 describes the Cisco CSC/4 memory map.
- Table B–21 describes the processor memory map for the Cisco CSC/2, CSC/3, CSC/4 cards, including the IGS and Cisco 3000.

Table B–1   *Cisco 1000 Memory Map*

Address	Size	Chip Select	Description
0000000–00FFFFF	1 MB	CS0	ROM
2000000–2FFFFFF	16 MB	CS1,2	DRAM up to 16 MB
6000000–600FFFF	64 Kb	CS6	PCMCIA I/O space
8000000–800FFFF	16 MB	CS5	PCMCIA/PC card attribute memory
8010000–8FFFFFF	16 MB	CS5	PCMCIA/PC card common memory
C0003E0–C0003E1	64 Kb	CS4	PCMCIA controller index and data register
E000000–E007FFF	32 Kb	CS7	NVRAM
FF00000–FF00FFF	1 MB	360DPR	68360 dual port memory (top 1 MB)
CPU Space:			
003ff00–003ff03	4 bytes		MBAR for 68360

Table B–2   *Cisco 2000 Memory Map*

Address	Description	Comments
00000000–0017FFFF	CPU and packet memory (DRAM)	1.5 MB
01000000–011FFFFF	ROM monitor and system image code space (EPROM)	2 MB
02000000–02007FFF	Configuration RAM	32 KB
02100000–0213FFFF	Control registers and I/O devices	Details follow
02110000	Control register 1	—
02110002	Control register 2	—
02110040	PROM cookie	—

Table B–2   *Cisco 2000 Memory Map, Continued*

Address	Description	Comments
02110100	Status register	—
02120040	Timer control register	—
02130000–02130003	Ethernet controller	—
02130000–0213000F	Token Ring controller	—
02130040–02130043	Serial controller	—
02130080	Serial control register 1	—
02130081	Serial control register 2	—

Table B–3   *Cisco 2500 Memory Map*

Address	Bit Width	Description	Comments
00000000–00FFFFFF	32	DRAM	2, 4, 8, or 16 MB
00000000–001FFFFF	32	DRAM 2 MB	—
00000000–003FFFFF	32	DRAM 4 MB	—
00000000–007FFFFF	32	DRAM 8 MB	—
00000000–00FFFFFF	32	DRAM 16 MB	—
00000000–001FFFFF	8/16	Boot Flash memory	1 or 2 MB, when Flash memory PCMCIA card is not installed
00000000–001FFFFF	16	Flash memory PCMCIA card	Boot mode
01000000–011FFFFF	16	Boot EPROMs for ROM monitor and RXBOOT images	1 or 2 MB ROM; 2 MB Flash memory
01000000–011FFFFF	16	Flash memory PCMCIA card	When installed
02000000–0201FFFF	8	Configuration NVRAM	32 or 128 KB
02000000–02007FFF	8	Configuration NVRAM (32 KB)	—
02000000–0201FFFF	8	Configuration NVRAM (128 KB)	—
02100000–0213FFFF	8/16	Onboard I/O registers and chips	—
03000000–03FFFFFF	32	Flash memory RAM (SIMMs)	4, 8, or 16 MB

Table B–3 *Cisco 2500 Memory Map, Continued*

Address	Bit Width	Description	Comments
03000000–033FFFFF	32	Flash memory RAM (4 MB)	—
03000000–037FFFFF	32	Flash memory RAM (8 MB)	—
03000000–03FFFFFF	32	Flash memory RAM (16 MB)	—
08000000–081FFFFF	8/16	Onboard boot EPROMs (remapped)	1 or 2 MB, when PCMCIA Flash memory card is installed

Table B–4 *Cisco 3000 Memory Map*

Address	Description	Comments
00000000–00FFFFFF	Main memory DRAM	—
01000000–011FFFFF	Secondary DRAM	—
02000000–0201FFFF	NVRAM	—
02100000–02100FFF	Channel B: 68302 registers	—
02101000–02101FFF	Channel B: 63802 RAM	—
02110000	System control register 1	—
02110002	System control register 2	—
02110100	System status register	—
02110040–0211005F	Cookie	—
02120000–02120003	Counter/timer (CNTR)	—
02120040	Counter control register (CCTL)	—
02120100–0212013F	Console ports	—
02130000–02130003	Channel A: LANCE chip	—
02130040–02130043	Channel B: LANCE/serial chip	—
02130080–02130083	Channel B: serial DTR register	—
03000000–03FFFFFF	Flash memory	—
04000000–042FFFFF	Secondary RAM	When main memory = 16 MB

Table B–5   *Cisco 3104 and Cisco 3204 Memory Map*

Address	Description	Comments
00000000–00FFFFFF	Main DRAM	1-, 4-, 8-, and 16-MB sizes
01000000–010FFFFF	Boot EPROMs for ROM monitor and bootstrap image	—
01000000–011FFFFF	Boot Flash memory for ROM monitor and bootstrap image	Onboard Flash memory or PCMCIA Flash memory card, 2 MB
02000000–0201FFFF	Configuration NVRAM	32 or 128 KB size
02100000–0213FFFF	Onboard registers and chips	—
03000000–03FFFFFF	Flash memory SIMM	Up to 16 MB
04000000–041FFFFF	I/O memory (packet memory)	512 KB or 2 MB sizes
08000000–081FFFFF	Remapped onboard boot Flash memory	Remapped when PCMCIA Flash memory card is installed

Table B–6   *Cisco 3104 and Cisco 3204 Memory Map of Onboard Registers and Chips*

Address	Description	Comments
021000F2–021000F3	Base address register for 68302	—
021000F4–021000F7	System control register for 68302	—
02101000–021013FF	System RAM for 68302	—
02101400–021017FF	Parameter RAM for 68302	—
02101800–02101FFF	Internal registers for 68302	—
02110000	System control register 1	—
02110002	System control register 2	—
02110004	System control register 3	—
02110006	System interrupt register	—
02110060	Serial NVRAM control register	—
02120000–02120003	Timer counter	—
02120040	Counter control register	—
02120100–0212013F	Console interfaces	—

Table B–6 *Cisco 3104 and Cisco 3204 Memory Map of Onboard Registers and Chips, Continued*

Address	Description	Comments
02130000–0213003	Ethernet controller	—
02131000–0213100F	Token Ring controller	—
02131010–02131011	Hardware map register 0	—
02131012–02131013	Hardware map register 1	—
02132000–021320FF	Serial controller	—
02132100–02132101	Serial 0 device register	—
02132102–02132103	Serial 1 device register	—

Table B–7 *Cisco 4000 Memory Map*

Address	Bit Width	Description	Comments
00000000–0003FFFF	32	System SRAM	256 KB, fixed; 0 wait read, 1 wait write
00040000–00FFFFFF	32	System DRAM memory (SIMMs)	8-, 16-, 32-bit unaligned access supported; 4, 8, 16, or 32[1] MB
00040000–003FFFFF		4 MB	—
00040000–00FFFFFF		16 MB	—
01000000–01FFFFFF	16	Boot EPROM	2 MB, fixed
01000000–010FFFFF		1 MB	—
01000000–011FFFFF		2 MB	—
01000000–013FFFFF		4 MB	—
01000000–017FFFFF		8 MB	—
02000000–02FFFFFF	8 or 32	Onboard resources	—
02020000		System I/O	—
03000000–03FFFFFF	32	Flash memory EPROM or EPROM	32-bit read/write access
03000000–031FFFFF		2 MB	—
03000000–033FFFFF		4 MB	—
03000000–037FFFFF		8 MB[2]	—

Table B–7   *Cisco 4000 Memory Map, Continued*

Address	Bit Width	Description	Comments
05000000		System DRAM	Upper 16 MB of 32-MB configuration
06000000–06FFFFFF	32	Shared (I/O) memory	8-, 16-, 32-bit unaligned access supported; 1–16 MB
06000000–060FFFFF		1 MB	—
06000000–063FFFFF		4 MB	—
06000000–067FFFFF		8 MB	—
04000000–05FFFFFF		Undefined	—
07000000–07FFFFFF		Undefined	—
08000000–08FFFFFF	32	I/O expansion	NIM slots
08000000–080FFFFF	16	NIM at I/O expansion slot 1	16-bit aligned access only
08100000–081FFFFF	16	NIM at I/O expansion slot 2	16-bit aligned access only
08200000–082FFFFF	16	NIM at I/O expansion slot 3	16-bit aligned access only

[1] Only the Cisco 4000-M supports 32-MB DRAM. The 32-MB configuration is split into two discontiguous pieces, with the upper 16 MB mapped to begin at location 05000000.
[2] Only the Cisco 4000-M supports 8-MB Flash memory.

Table B–8 *Cisco 4000 Memory Map of Onboard Resources*

Address	Bit Width	Description	Comments
02000000–0201FFFF	8	NVRAM battery backed up CMOS SRAM	128 KB, fixed; also accommodates 32 KBx8 and 8 KBx8
02110000	32	System status and control registers	—
02110002		Hardware revision	—
02110040–0211005F	8	System ID PROM cookie	24 bytes
02110100	32	Shared memory control register	—
02120000	8	Counter timer	—
02120040	8	Counter interrupt control register	—
02120100–0212013F	8	Control serial I/O	—

Table B–9 *Cisco 4500 Memory Map*

Address	Bit Width	Description	Comments
60000000–61FFFFFF	64	System DRAM	Capable of 8- to 64-bit access, cached
60000000–607FFFFF		8 MB	—
60000000–60FFFFFF		16 MB	—
60000000–61FFFFFF		32 MB	—
BFC00000–BFC7FFFF	8	Boot EPROM	—
BFC00000–BFC1FFFF		128 KB	—
BFC00000–BFC7FFFF		512 KB	—
3E000000–3EFFFFFF	8	Onboard resources	—
30000000–30FFFFFF	32	System Flash memory EPROM	—
30000000–303FFFFF		4 MB	—
30000000–307FFFFF		8 MB	—
30000000–30FFFFFF		16 MB	—

Table B–9 *Cisco 4500 Memory Map, Continued*

Address	Bit Width	Description	Comments
38000000–387FFFFF	32	Boot Flash memory EPROM	—
38000000–383FFFFF		4 MB	—
38000000–387FFFFF		8 MB	—
40000000–40FFFFFF	32	Shared memory	8-, 16-, 32-bit access
40000000–403FFFFF		4 MB	—
40000000–40FFFFFF		16 MB	—

Table B–10 *Cisco 4500 Memory Map of Onboard Resources*

Address	Bit Width	Description	Comments
3E000000–3E07FFFF	8	NVRAM	Battery backed up SRAM
3E000000–3E01FFFF	8	128 KB	—
3E000000–3E07FFFF	8	512 KB	—
3E000000	8	Time of day clock	—
3E800400	8	System ID PROM cookie	—

Table B–11 *Cisco 7000 Memory Map*

Address	Description	Comments
11110100	System status register	—
11110400	Flash memory card status	—
11110C00	I/O address base	SwitchBus address space. Each unit occupies 64 bytes (0x40).
11120040	Timer control register	—
11120200	Environmental monitor control	16 bits
11120300	Environmental monitor status	32 bits
11130000	Diagnostic bus	—
11131000	ID PROM	—
11140000	NVRAM	—

Table B-11   *Cisco 7000 Memory Map, Continued*

Address	Description	Comments
1115FC00	Environmental monitor NVRAM base address	—
1115FFFF	Real time calendar bit	—
11200000–11FFFFFF	Reserved	14 MB reserved
12000000	Onboard Flash memory	—
14000000	External Flash memory	—

Table B-12   *Cisco 7200 Series (NPE-150) Memory Map–Hardware*

Memory Base	Memory Limit	Size	Device
0x0 0000 0000	0x0 07FF FFFF	128 MB	System DRAM
0x0 0800 0000	0x0 0FFF FFFF	128 MB	System DRAM (reserved)
0x0 1000 0000	0x0 13FF FFFF	62 MB	Reserved
0x0 1400 0000	0x0 141F FFFF	2 MB	GT-64010 registers
0x0 1420 0000	0x0 19FF FFFF	94 MB	Reserved
0x0 1A00 0000	0x0 1A3F FFFF	4 MB	Internal Flash SIMM
0x0 1A40 0000	0x0 1BFF FFFF	28 MB	Larger Flash SIMM (reserved)
0x0 1C00 0000	0x0 1DFF FFFF	32 MB	Reserved
0x0 1E00 0000	0x0 1E1F FFFF	2 MB	NVRAM (TOD)
0x0 1E20 0000	0x0 1E7F FFFF	6 MB	Reserved
0x0 1E80 0000	0x0 1E9F FFFF	2 MB	I/O Registers
0x0 1EA0 0000	0x0 1EFF FFFF	6 MB	Reserved
0x0 1F00 0000	0x0 1FBF FFFF	12 MB	Read/write null
0x0 1FC0 0000	0x0 1FDF FFFF	2 MB	Boot EPROM
0x0 1FE0 0000	0x0 3FFF FFFF	x MB	Reserved
0x0 4000 0000	0x0 43FF FFFF	64 MB	PCI-to-PCMCIA interface (top slot)
0x0 4400 0000	0x0 47FF FFFF	64 MB	PCI-to-PCMCIA interface (bottom slot)
0x0 4800 0000	0x0 487F FFFF	8 MB	Fast Ethernet—memory-mapped I/O

Table B–12 *Cisco 7200 Series (NPE-150) Memory Map–Hardware, Continued*

Memory Base	Memory Limit	Size	Device
0x0 4880 0000	0x0 48FF FFFF	8 MB	PA1—memory-mapped I/O
0x0 4900 0000	0x0 497F FFFF	8 MB	PA3—memory-mapped I/O
0x0 4980 0000	0x0 49FF FFFF	8 MB	PA5—memory-mapped I/O
0x0 4A00 0000	0x0 4A7F FFFF	8 MB	PA7—memory-mapped I/O (reserved)
0x0 4A80 0000	0x0 4AFF FFFF	8 MB	PA9—memory-mapped I/O (reserved
0x0 4B00 0000	0x0 4B0F FFFF	1 MB	PCI PM, first 1M, no byte swap
0x0 4B10 0000	0x0 4B7F FFFF	7 MB	PCI PM, larger PM, no swap (reserved)
0x0 4B80 0000	0x0 4B8F FFFF	1 MB	PCI PM, first 1M, byte swap
0x0 4B90 0000	0x0 4BFF FFFF	7 MB	PCI PM, larger PM, byte swap (reserved)
0x0 4C00 0000	0x0 4C0F FFFF	1 MB	PCI Alias PM, first 1M, no byte swap
0x0 4C10 0000	0x0 4C7F FFFF	7 MB	PCI Alias PM, larger PM, no swap (reserved)
0x0 4C80 0000	0x0 4C8F FFFF	1 MB	PCI Alias PM, first 1M, byte swap
0x0 4C90 0000	0x0 4CFF FFFF	7 MB	PCI Alias PM, larger PM, byte swap (reserved)
0x0 4D00 0000	0x0 4D7F FFFF	8 MB	PA2—memory-mapped I/O
0x0 4D80 0000	0x0 4DFF FFFF	8 MB	PA4—memory-mapped I/O
0x0 4E00 0000	0x0 4E7F FFFF	8 MB	PA6—memory-mapped I/O
0x0 4E80 0000	0x0 4EFF FFFF	8 MB	PA8—memory-mapped I/O (reserved)
0x0 4F00 0000	0x0 4F7F FFFF	8 MB	PA10—memory-mapped I/O (reserved)
0x0 4F80 0000	0x0 4FFF FFFF	8 MB	I/O—memory-mapped I/O (reserved)
0x0 5000 0000	0x0 FFFF FFFF	x MB	Reserved
0x1 0000 0000	0x0 001F FFFF	2 MB	PCI I/O address space
0x1 0020 0000	0x1 4B7F FFFF	~1 GB	Reserved
0x1 4B00 0000	0x1 4B0F FFFF	1 MB	CPU PM, first 1M, no byte swap
0x1 4B10 0000	0x1 4B7F FFFF	7 MB	CPU PM, larger PM, no swap (reserved)
0x1 4B80 0000	0x1 FFFF FFFF	~0 GB	Reserved
0x2 0000 0000	0x3 FFFF FFFF	8 GB	L2 cache is disabled (alias) for low 8 GB
0x4 0000 0000	0x7 FFFF FFFF	16 GB	Cache Controller Tag Op 0
0x8 0000 0000	0xF FFFF FFFF	32 GB	Cache Controller Tag Op 1

Table B–13 *Cisco 7200 Series (NPE-150) Memory Map–Software*

Memory	CPU Physical	CPU Virtual	Attributes
Non-packet DRAM	0x00000000–0x015fffff	0x60000000–0x615fffff	Cached, write back, L2 cached
I/O DRAM (packet)	0x01600000–0x01ffffff	0x01600000–0x01ffffff	Uncached
		0x61600000–0x61ffffff	Cached, write back, L2 cached
	0x2,01600000–0x2, 01ffffff	0x31600000–0x31ffffff	Cached, write through, no L2 cache
I/O SRAM (packet), direct access by CPU	0x4b000000–0x4b0fffff	0x4b000000–0x4b0fffff	Uncached
	0x2,4b000000–0x2, 4b0fffff	0x7b000000–0x7b0fffff	Cached, write through, no L2 cache

Table B–14 *Cisco 500-CS Memory Map*

Address	Description	Comments
000000–3FFFFF	ROM	4 MB or less
400000–407FFF	EEPROM (NVRAM)	32 KB
420000–427FFF	LCD registers (not used)	—
428000–42FFFF	Future hardware	—
430000–440000	Reserved	—
460000–460004	LANCE registers	Ethernet controller registers
500000–50007F	Octal UART 0	—
500400–50047F	Octal UART 1	—
600000–7FFFFF	Onboard RAM	—
800000–BFFFFF	2-MB SIMM expansion	—
800000–FFFFFF	8-MB SIMM expansion	—

Table B-15   *RP/Cisco 7000 Series Memory Map*

Address	Bit Width	Description	Comments
00000000–0FFFFFFF		DRAM	—
10000000–100FFFFF		ROML	—
10400000–104FFFFF		ROMU	—
11000000–110FFFFF		Multibus memory	—
11100000–1110FFFF		Multibus I/O	—
11110000–1112FFFF		Local I/O	—
11130000–11130FFF		Diagnostic bus	—
11131000–111314FF		ID PROM	—
11140000–1115FFFF		NVRAM	—
12000000–13FFFFFF		Internal Flash memory	—
14000000–15FFFFFF		External Flash memory card	—
11110000	16	System control	—
11110100	32	System status register	—
11110400		Flash memory card status	—
11110C00		I/O address base	SwitchBus address space. Each unit occupies 64 bytes (0x40).
11120000	8	Counter timer	—
11120040	8	Counter control register	—
11120100–1112013F	8	Serial I/O ports	—
11120200		Environmental monitor control	16 bits
11120300		Environmental monitor status	32 bits
11130000		Diagnostic bus	—
11131000		ID PROM	—
11140000		NVRAM	—

Table B–15 *RP/Cisco 7000 Series Memory Map, Continued*

Address	Bit Width	Description	Comments
1115FC00		Environmental monitor NVRAM base address	—
1115FFFF	1	Real time calendar bit	1 bit (bit 0)
11200000–11FFFFFF		Reserved	14 MB reserved
12000000		Onboard Flash memory	—
14000000		External Flash memory	—

Table B–16 *RSP Memory Map*

Address	Bit Width	Description
80000000–FFFFFFFF		Available for expansion
60000000–77FFFFFF		Main memory Common
40000000–5FFFFFFF		Packet memory canonical address bit ordering Bits in byte-swapped packet memory Common
38000000–3FFFFFFF		Boot EPROM and I/O space
30000000–37FFFFFF		System Flash memory
20000000–2FFFFFFF		Reserved platform specific address space
18000000–1FFFFFFF		Boot EPROM and I/O space
10000000–17FFFFFF		System Flash memory
08000000–0FFFFFFF		Packet memory
00000000–07FFFFFF		Main memory
Individual Addresses:		
11110000	16	System control
11110100	32	System status
11120000	8	Counter timer
11120040	8	Counter control register
11120100–1112013F	8	Serial I/O ports

Table B–16   *RSP Memory Map, Continued*

Address	Bit Width	Description
11120200	16	Environmental monitor control
11120300	32	Environmental monitor status
1115FFFF	1	Calendar (1 bit "bit 0")
111104000	8	Flash card status
Virtual Address:		
E00000		Slot 0
E20000		Slot 1
E40000		Slot 2
E60000		Slot 3
E80000		Slot 4
EA0000		Slot 5
EC0000		Slot 6
EE0000		Slot 7
F00000		Slot 8
F20000		Slot 9
F40000		Slot 10
F60000		Slot 11
F80000		Slot 12

Table B–17   *Multibus Memory Space Assignment*

Address	Description	Comments
20000000–2000FFFF	Memory card	64 KB
20010000–2002FFFF	CSC-R16 card	Unit 0 address, 128 KB
20030000–2004FFFF	CSC-R16 card	Unit 1 address, 128 KB
20050000–2006FFFF	CSC-R16 card	Unit 2 address, 128 KB
20070000–2008FFFF	CSC-R16 card	Unit 3 address, 128 KB
20090000–200AFFFF	CSC-R16 card	Unit 4 address, 128 KB

Table B–17 *Multibus Memory Space Assignment, Continued*

Address	Description	Comments
200B0000–200BFFFF	NVRAM	64 KB
200C0000–200DFFFF	CSC-R16 card	Unit 5 address, 128 KB
200E0000–200FFFFF	CSC-R16 card	Unit 6 address, 128 KB (shared)

Table B–18 *Multibus I/O Space Assignment*

Address	Description	Size (in Hex)	Comments
20100000	ENVM card	2	Environmental monitor
20100002–2010008F	Unused		
20100090		2	CSC-R16M Ethernet mailbox, Unit 0
20100092		2	CSC-R16M Ethernet mailbox, Unit 1
20100098	CSC-R16 card	2	Unit 0
2010009A	CSC-R16 card	2	Unit 1
201000A0	CSC-R card	4	Unit 0
201000A4	CSC-R card	4	Unit 1
201000A8	CSC-R card	4	Unit 2
201000AC	CSC-R card	4	Unit 3
201000B0	CSC-R16M card	2	Unit 0
201000B2	CSC-R16M card	2	Unit 1
201000B4	CSC-R16M card	2	Unit 2
201000B6	CSC-R16M card	2	Unit 3
201000B8	CSC-R16M card	2	Unit 4
201000BA	CSC-R16M card	2	Unit 5
201000BC	CSC-R16M card	2	Unit 6
201000BE	CSC-R16M card	2	Unit 7
201000C0	MLP	20	Unit 0
201000E0	MLP	20	Unit 1
20100100	3 MB	100	Unit 0

Table B–18   *Multibus I/O Space Assignment, Continued*

Address	Description	Size (in Hex)	Comments
20100200	3 MB	100	Unit 1
20100300	3 MB	100	Unit 2
20100400	3 MB	100	Unit 3
20100500	Interlan	10	Unit 0
20100510	Interlan	10	Unit 1
20100520	Interlan	10	Unit 2
20100530	Interlan	10	Unit 3
20100540	Interlan	10	Unit 4
20100550	Interlan	10	Unit 5
20100560	Interlan	10	Unit 6
20100570–201005FF	Unused		
20100600	ACC	100	Unit 0
20100700	ACC	100	Unit 1
20100800	ACC	100	Unit 2
20100900	ACC	100	Unit 3
20100A00	HUB	100	Unit 0
20100B00	HUB	100	Unit 1
20100C00–20101FFF	Unused		
20102000	3COM	2000	Unit 0
20104000	3COM	2000	Unit 1
20106000	3COM	2000	Unit 2
20108000	3COM	2000	Unit 3
2010A000	3COM	2000	Unit 4
2010C000	CSC-MCI card	40	Unit 0
2010C040	CSC-MCI card	40	Unit 1
2010C080	CSC-MCI card	40	Unit 2
2010C0C0	CSC-MCI card	40	Unit 3

Table B-18 *Multibus I/O Space Assignment, Continued*

Address	Description	Size (in Hex)	Comments
2010C100	CSC-MCI card	40	Unit 4
2010C140	CSC-MCI card	40	Unit 5
2010C180	CSC-MCI card	40	Unit 6
2010D000–2010 FFFF	Unused	—	—

Table B-19 *CSC/3 Memory Map*

Address	Bit Width	Description	Comments
00000000–003FFFFF		RAM	—
01000000–0107FFFF		ROML	—
0108FFFF–010FFFFF		ROMH	—
02000000–020FFFFF		Multibus memory	—
02100000–0210FFFF		Multibus I/O	—
02110000–02110001	16	System control register	—
02110100–02110103	32	System status register	—
02120000	8	Counter timer	—
02120040	8	Counter control register	—
02120100–0212013F		Serial ports	—
020B0000–020B7FFF		NVRAM	Over Multibus

Table B-20 *CSC/4 Memory Map*

Address	Bit Width	Description	Comments
00000000–00FFFFFF		RAM	—
01000000–013FFFFF		ROML	—
01400000–017FFFFF		ROMH	—
02000000–020FFFFF		Multibus memory	—
02100000–0210FFFF		Multibus I/O	—

Table B–20 *CSC/4 Memory Map, Continued*

Address	Bit Width	Description	Comments
02110000–02110001	16	System control register	—
02110100–02110103	32	System status register	—
02120000	8	Counter timer	—
02120040	8	Counter control register	—
02120100–0212013F		Serial ports	—
020B0000–020B7FFF		NVRAM	Over Multibus

Table B–21 *Processor Memory Map for CSC/2, CSC/3, and CSC/4 Cards, Including IGS and Cisco 3000*

Address	Description	Comments
D0D0D0D	"Poisoned free" address	Used by the "poisoned free" code to make sure the system is not accessing freed memory. An error at or near this location usually indicates a software bug.
2100000–21FFFFF	Multibus I/O space	Not all I/O space is occupied by interface cards. Bus errors that do not correspond to a real interface card are probably software bugs.
210C000–210C200	MCI and ciscoBus controllers (CSC-CCTL and CSC-CCTL2)	Common failures result from attempts to access the command and argument registers that occupy the first 4 bytes of the address space of each board.
21000A0–21000AF	Netrionix 4-Mbps Token Ring card	Each card occupies 4 bytes.
21000B0–21000BD	CSC-C2CTR card	Each card occupies 2 bytes.
2100000–2100003	Control register for the ENVM	Environmental monitor card.
2000000–20FFFFF	Multibus memory space	Used by interface cards and by shared Multibus memory.
20C0000–20FFFFF	Shared memory on CSC-R16 cards	Token Ring units 5 and 6. Each card has 0x20000 bytes of memory.

Table B–21 *Processor Memory Map for CSC/2, CSC/3, and CSC/4 Cards, Including IGS and Cisco 3000, Continued*

Address	Description	Comments
20B0000–20BFFFF	Multibus NVRAM (CSC/2, CSC/3, CSC/4 cards)	Cards with 32 KB RAM only go through 0x20B7FFF.
2040000–20405FF	CSC-16 card asynchronous lines (CSC/2, CSC/3, CSC/4 cards)	Each UART[1] is 0x20 bytes; there are two lines per UART.
2010000–20AFFFF	Shared memory on CSC-R16 cards	Units 0–4. Each card has 0x20000 bytes of memory.
2000000–2007FFF	Shared Multibus memory primarily used by CSC-R Token Ring cards	Each card has a system control area within this memory, but the address of each area is decided at runtime and is difficult to predict.
—	System ROM address space	The ROM monitor starts at the bottom of ROM and is followed by the system image. The location of the system image is not always known and is important only for images that are run from ROM. A bus error in valid ROM space might indicate bad ROMs, a bad processor card, or in the case of run-from-ROM images, a software bug in which the software tries to write into ROM.
1000000–107FFFF	System ROM address space	512-KB system ROMs on the CSC/2, CSC/3, and CSC/4 cards, IGS, CS-3000. Run from ROM, system images exist only on the CSC/2 card.
1000000–10FFFFF	System ROM address space	1-MB system ROMs on the CSC/2, CSC/3, and CSC/4 cards, IGS, CS-3000. Run from ROM, system images exist only on the CSC/2 card.
1000000–11FFFFF	System ROM address space	2-MB system ROMs on the CSC/2, CSC/3, and CSC/4 cards and the IGS. Run from ROM, system images exist only on the CSC/2 card.

Table B–21 *Processor Memory Map for CSC/2, CSC/3, and CSC/4 Cards, Including IGS and Cisco 3000, Continued*

Address	Description	Comments
—	Main processor RAM	Bus errors here are usually caused by a hardware failure on the processor card.
0000–0FFFFF	Main processor RAM	CSC/2 card and IGS with 1 MB. On the IGS, the top 0.5 MB is shared packet memory.
0000–17FFFF	Main processor RAM	IGS with 1.5 MB. The top 0.5 MB is shared packet memory.
0000–3FFFFF	Main processor RAM	CSC/3 card
0000–FFFFFF	Main processor RAM	CSC/4 card
0000–47FFFF	Main processor RAM	IGS with 4.5 MB. The top 0.5 MB is shared packet memory.
0000–0FFF	System page	The system page contains several processor and ROM monitor data structures, primarily the trap and interrupt vectors. If the low page gets corrupted, the system might hang rather than crash.

[1] UART = Universal Asynchronous Receiver/Transmitter

Technical Support Information

When you have a problem that you cannot resolve, the resource of last resort is your Cisco Systems technical support representative. To analyze a problem, your technical support representative will need certain information about the situation and the symptoms you are experiencing. To speed the problem isolation and resolution process, present this data when you contact your representative.

This appendix describes how to collect relevant information about your internetwork and how to present that information to your technical support representative. In addition, some sections describe Cisco Connection Online, Cisco's primary, real-time support channel on the World Wide Web (WWW), and Cisco Connection Documentation, Cisco's library of product information on CD-ROM.

GATHERING INFORMATION ABOUT YOUR INTERNETWORK

Before gathering any specific data, compile a list of all symptoms that users have reported on the internetwork (such as connections dropping or slow host response).

The next step is to gather specific information. Typical information needed to troubleshoot internetworking problems falls into two general categories: information required for any situation and information specific to the topology, technology, protocol, or problem.

Information that is always required by technical support engineers includes the following:

- Configuration listing of all routers involved
- Complete specifications of all routers involved
- Version numbers of software (obtained with the **show version** command) and firmware (obtained with the **show controllers** command) on all relevant routers
- Network topology map

- List of hosts and servers (host and server type, number on network, description of host operating systems implemented)
- List of network layer protocols, versions, and vendors

To assist you in gathering this required data, the **show tech-support** exec command has been added in Cisco IOS Release 11.1(4) and later. This command provides general information about the router that you can provide to your technical support representative when you are reporting a problem.

The **show tech-support** command outputs the equivalent of the **show version, show running-config, show controllers, show stacks, show interfaces, show buffers, show process memory,** and **show process cpu** exec commands.

Specific requirements that vary depending on the situation include the following:

- Output from general **show** commands:

  show interfaces

  show controllers

  show processes {cpu | mem}

  show buffer

  show mem summary

- Output from protocol-specific **show** commands:

  show *protocol* **route**

  show *protocol* **traffic**

  show *protocol* **interfaces**

  show *protocol* **arp**

  show appletalk globals (AppleTalk only)

  show ipx servers (Novell IPX only)

- Output from relevant **debug** privileged exec commands
- Output from protocol-specific **ping** and **trace** diagnostic tests, as appropriate
- Network analyzer traces, as appropriate
- Core dumps obtained using the **exception dump** router configuration command, or using the **write core** router configuration command if the system is operational, as appropriate

Getting the Data from Your Router

You must tailor the way you obtain information from the router to the system you are using to retrieve the information. Following are some hints for different platforms:

- *PC and Macintosh*—Connect a PC or Macintosh to the console port of the router and log all output to a disk file (using a terminal emulation program). The exact procedure varies depending on the communication package used with the system.

- *Terminal connected to console port or remote terminal*—The only way to get information with a terminal connected to the console port or with a remote terminal is to attach a printer to the auxiliary port on the terminal (if one exists) and force all screen output to go to the printer. Using a terminal is undesirable because in that situation there is no way to capture the data to a file.

- *UNIX workstation*—At the UNIX prompt, enter the command **script** *filename*, and then Telnet to the router. The UNIX **script** command captures all screen output to the specified filename. To stop capturing output and close the file, enter the end-of-file character (typically ^D) for your UNIX system.

NOTES

To get your system to automatically log specific error messages or operational information to a UNIX syslog server, use the **logging** *internet-address* router configuration command. For more information about using the **logging** command and setting up a syslog server, refer to the Cisco IOS configuration guides and command references.

Remote Console Port and Auxiliary Port Access

You can access a router from a remote location without a router being connected to a network by dialing directly to the console or auxiliary port on a router. In general, the console port is recommended because it displays router startup messages, whereas the auxiliary port does not provide this information. In addition, if a router is hung in the read-only memory monitor, you can reboot the system if you are connected using the console port. However, if you have a local terminal connected to your console, you might have no other choice than to connect to the auxiliary port. The following discussions provide the general requirements for connecting to a Cisco router remotely via the console or auxiliary ports.

Console Port Connected Modem

To connect remotely to the console port on a Cisco router, you need the following:

- Null modem cable
- PC or equivalent with suitable communications software
- 14.4 kbps–capable modem

When you have your communications software installed, set your PC's comm port (or equivalent) to 9600 baud (a software setting).

The modem attached to your router's console port must be configured as follows:

- Lock the DTE speed to 9600
- Set no flow control
- Set auto-answer
- Set no echo
- Set no result

NOTES ───

Refer to your modem documentation to determine the commands required to set these options on your modem. Refer to your modem and router hardware documentation for specific cabling requirements.

Auxiliary Port Connected Modem

To connect remotely to the console port on a Cisco router, you need the following:

- Straight through serial cable
- PC or equivalent with suitable communications software
- 14.4 kbps–capable modem

NOTES ───

Refer to your modem documentation to determine the commands required to set these options on your modem. Refer to your modem and router hardware documentation for specific cabling requirements.

In order to use the router's auxiliary port for remote access, you must include several configuration commands. The required commands are as follows:

```
line aux 0
modem inout
```

If you are using software prior to Cisco IOS 11.1, set the modem options as specified for the console port.

If you are using Cisco IOS 11.1 or later, you do not need to set the modem configuration manually, but you must include the **modem autoconfigure discovery** line configuration subcommand.

NOTES ───

You can also refer to Chapter 16, "Troubleshooting Dialin Connections," for additional related information.

PROVIDING DATA TO YOUR TECHNICAL SUPPORT REPRESENTATIVE

If you need technical assistance with a Cisco product that is under warranty or covered by a maintenance contract, contact Cisco's Technical Assistance Center (TAC) to open a case. Contact the TAC with a phone call or an e-mail message:

- North America: 800-553-2447, e-mail: `tac@cisco.com`
- Europe: 32 2 778 4242, e-mail: `euro-tac@cisco.com`
- Asia-Pacific: 61 2 9935 4107, e-mail: `asiapac-tac@cisco.com`

When submitting information to your technical support representative, electronic data is preferred. Electronic data significantly eases the transfer of information between technical support personnel and development staff. Common electronic formats include data sent via electronic mail and files sent using FTP.

If you are submitting data to your technical support representative, use the following list to determine the preferred method for submission:

- The preferred method of information submission is via File Transfer Protocol (FTP) service over the Internet. If your environment supports FTP, you can place your file in the *incoming* directory on the host *cco.cisco.com*.

- The next best method is to send data by e-mail. Before using this method, be sure to contact your technical support representative, especially when transferring binary core dumps or other large files.

- If you use e-mail, do not use encoding methods such as binhex or zip. Only MIME-compliant mail should be used.

- Transfer via a PC-based communications protocol, such as Kermit, to upload files to Cisco Connection Online (CCO). Again, be sure to contact your technical support representative before attempting any transfer.

- Transfer by disk or tape.

- The least favorable method is hardcopy transfer by fax or physical mail.

CCO

CCO, formerly Cisco Information Online (CIO), is Cisco Systems' primary, real-time support channel. Maintenance customers and partners can self-register on CCO to obtain additional content and services.

Available 24 hours a day, seven days a week, CCO provides a wealth of standard and value-added services to Cisco's customers and business partners. CCO services include product information, software updates, release notes, technical tips, the Bug Navigator, the Troubleshooting Engine, configuration notes, brochures, descriptions of service offerings, and download access to public and authorized files.

CCO serves a wide variety of users through two interfaces that are updated and enhanced simultaneously—a character-based version and a multimedia version that resides on the WWW. The character-based CCO supports Zmodem, Kermit, Xmodem, FTP, Internet e-mail, and fax download options, and is excellent for quick access to information over lower bandwidths. The WWW version of CCO provides richly formatted documents with photographs, figures, graphics, and video, as well as hyperlinks to related information.

You can access CCO in the following ways:

- WWW: http://www.cisco.com.
- Telnet: cco.cisco.com.

- Modem: From North America, 408-526-8070; from Europe, 33 1 64 46 40 82. Use the following terminal settings: VT100 emulation; databits: 8; stop bits: 1; parity: none; baud rate: up to 14.4 kbps.

For a copy of CCO's Frequently Asked Questions (FAQ), send e-mail to `cco-help@cisco.com`. For additional information, send e-mail to `cco-team@cisco.com`.

CCO Troubleshooting Services

Registered CCO users can take advantage of a number of WWW-based support services offered by Cisco's Customer Support Engineering organization. These services are offered to help you diagnose and resolve problems in your network. WWW-based troubleshooting services include the following:

- Open Forum—An interactive tool that provides database searches for quick answers to technical questions. For more difficult questions, you receive access to experts to help solve your problem.

- Automated TAC Case Management—Problem cases can be opened and monitored through CCO's Case tools.

- Troubleshooting Engine—Resolve a variety of common internetworking problems using an intuitive Web interface. Supports a variety of technologies and protocols.

All CCO users, registered users and guests alike, can obtain answers to frequently asked questions, implementation case studies, technical tips, implementation procedures, sample configurations, and more at CCO's public site (`http://www.cisco.com/public/Support_root.shtml`).

You can sign up as a registered CCO user at `http://www.cisco.com/public/registration.shtml`.

APPENDIX D

References and Recommended Reading

This appendix lists technical publications that you might find useful when troubleshooting your internetwork.

CISCO PRESS REFERENCES AND RECOMMENDED READING

Cisco CCIE Fundamentals: Network Design & Case Studies. Indianapolis, Indiana: Cisco Press; 1998.

Cisco IOS Bridging and IBM Network Solutions. San Jose, California: Cisco Systems; 1997.

Cisco IOS Configuration Fundamentals. Indianapolis, Indiana: Cisco Press; 1997.

Cisco IOS Network Security. Indianapolis, Indiana: Cisco Press; 1998.

Cisco IOS Solutions for Network Protocols, IP. San Jose, California: Cisco Systems; 1998.

Cisco IOS Solutions for Network Protocols, IPX, APP. San Jose, California: Cisco Systems; 1998.

Cisco IOS Switching Services. Indianapolis, Indiana: Cisco Press; 1998.

Cisco IOS Dial Solutions. Indianapolis, Indiana: Cisco Press; 1998.

Cisco IOS Wide-Area Networking Solutions. Indianapolis, Indiana: Cisco Press; 1998.

OTHER REFERENCES AND RECOMMENDED READING

Apple Computer, Inc. *Planning and Managing AppleTalk Networks.* Reading, Massachusetts: Addison-Wesley; 1991.

Breyer, B. and S. Riley. *Switched and Fast Ethernet: How It Works and How to Use It.* Emeryville, California: Ziff-Davis Press; 1995.

Chappell, L. *Novell's Guide to NetWare LAN Analysis.* San Jose, California: Novell Press; 1993.

Comer, D. E. *Internetworking with TCP/IP: Principles, Protocols, and Architecture*, Vol. 1, 3rd ed. Englewood Cliffs, New Jersey: Prentice Hall; 1995.

Held, G. *Data Communications Testing and Troubleshooting.* 2nd Ed. New York, New York: Van Nostrand Reinhold; 1992.

IBM. *Token-Ring Problem Determination Guide.* SX27-3710-04; 1990.

Jones, N. E. H., and D. Kosiur. *Macworld Networking Handbook.* Foster City, California: IDG Books Worldwide, Inc.; 1992.

Malamud, C. *Analyzing DECnet/OSI Phase V.* New York, New York: Van Nostrand Reinhold; 1991.

Malamud, C. *Analyzing Sun Networks.* New York, New York: Van Nostrand Reinhold; 1992.

Miller, M. A. *Internetworking: A Guide to Network Communications LAN to LAN; LAN to WAN,* 2nd ed. San Mateo, California: M&T Books; 1995.

Miller, M. A. *LAN Protocol Handbook.* San Mateo, California: M&T Publishing; 1990.

Miller, M. A. *LAN Troubleshooting Handbook.* San Mateo, California: M&T Publishing; 1989.

Miller, M. A. *Troubleshooting Internetworks.* San Mateo, California: M&T Publishing; 1991.

Miller, M. A. *Troubleshooting TCP/IP.* San Mateo, California: M&T Books; 1992.

Perlman, R. *Interconnections: Bridges and Routers.* Reading, Massachusetts: Addison-Wesley; 1992.

Sidhu, G. S., R. F. Andrews, and A. B. Oppenheimer. *Inside AppleTalk,* 2nd ed. Reading, Massachusetts: Addison-Wesley; 1990.

Stevens, W. R. *TCP/IP Illustrated,* Vol 1. Reading, Massachusetts: Addison-Wesley; 1994.

Troubleshooting Worksheets

To isolate problems in your internetwork, you must first compile all the relevant facts and then methodically address each suspect problem. The following troubleshooting worksheets can help you in this process. Use these worksheets as *guidelines* to assist you in developing your own worksheets—worksheets tailored to your own internetworking environment.

1 Symptoms reported:

_____

_____

_____

_____

_____

_____

_____

_____

2 Network topology map—attach separate sheet(s)

3 Network protocols implemented:

_____

_____

_____

_____

_____

_____

_____

_____

4 Protocols routed:

_____

_____

_____

_____

_____

_____

_____

5 Protocols bridged:

_____

_____

_____

_____

_____

_____

_____

6 Points of contact to external networks:

_____

_____

_____

_____

_____

_____

_____

7 Internetwork equipment (including network address, vendor, model, and function):

_____

_____

_____

_____

_____

_____

_____

8 Suspect end system and internetwork nodes (including network address, vendor, model, and function):

_____

_____

_____

_____

_____

_____

9 Applications being used on the network (FTP, sendmail, NFS, NetWare, and so forth):

_____

_____

_____

_____

_____

_____

10 Symptoms and possible problems:

Symptom	Possible Problems

11 Action plan for each problem:

Problem	Action Plan

12 Action outcomes:

Problem	Action	Result/Outcome

Index

A

AAL (ATM adaption layer), 567, 572–573
    processing, 573–574
    sublayers, 574
AARP (AppleTalk Address Resolution Protocol), address
    assignment, 231
access lists
    AppleTalk, 246
    blocking applications, 140
    IPX RIP, configuring, 199–200
    ISDN, 497
    ISO CLNS, configuring, 373
    OSPF, 156
    TCP/IP, 140–142
accessing
    AppleTalk services, 244–248
    CCO (Cisco Connection Online), 677–678
    communications channel (ATM), 566
    LAN switches, out-of-band Management Console, 590
Acknowledgment number field (TCP packets), 125
acquiring system data (Cisco routers), 674–675
active mode
    AppleTalk EIGRP routers, 271–272
    EIGRP routers, 215
    IPX EIGRP routers, 213–215
address errors, 650
Address Resolution Protocol, *see* ARP

addressing
    AppleTalk
        assigning addresses, 231–232
        components, 233
    ATM label switching, 568–569
    Banyan VINES, VIP (Vines Internetwork Protocol),
        383–385
    DECnet, 336–337, 355–356
    duplicate addresses, 109
    Ethernet, 77
    Frame Relay
        DLCIs, 526
        global, 527–528
    IP (Internet Protocol), 120
        IGMP (Internet Group Membership Protocol), 128
        multicast, 126
        subnet broadcast, 128
        UDP flooding, 127
    ISO CLNS (Connectionless Network Service), 360–362
    MAC, duplicate, 109
    subnet masks, troubleshooting mismatches, 152
    VIP (VINES Internetwork Protocol), 382–383
    virtual Token Ring, SDLC devices, 320–321
    XNS (Xerox Network Service), 397
    X.121, 542–543

689

Z